Rolf Schwartmann
Marek Steffen Jansen
Moritz Köhler [eds.]

Casebook European Data Law

Ten Years of the GDPR – A Milestone in EU Data Regulation

HART

Nomos

Onlineversion
Nomos eLibrary

The Deutsche Nationalbibliothek lists this publication in the Deutsche Nationalbibliografie; detailed bibliographic data are available on the Internet at http://dnb.d-nb.de

ISBN (Print) 978-3-7560-4175-6 (Nomos Verlagsgesellschaft mbH & Co. KG, Baden-Baden)
ISBN (ePDF) 978-3-7489-7129-0 (Nomos Verlagsgesellschaft mbH & Co. KG, Baden-Baden)
ISBN (Print) 978-1-048-00110-5 (Hart Publishing)

1st Edition 2026

Preface

A decade is a long time in data policy. As the European Union becomes ever more deeply immersed in digitalisation, the challenge of maintaining an appropriate balance between the protection of personal data and the free flow of data has grown correspondingly. In the ten years since the GDPR entered into force, the EU legislator has not fundamentally revised the core legal framework for the harmonisation of privacy protection. However, it has significantly expanded and reshaped the broader regulatory landscape through the adoption of new legislation – such as the Data Act, the Data Governance Act, the Digital Markets Act, the Digital Services Act and the AI Act – which interacts with data protection law. As the GDPR enters its second decade, the European Commission has now initiated a legislative process to amend it.

Since its entry into force in May 2016, the case law of the Court of Justice of the European Union as well as the work of European data protection authorities have shaped the GDPR. On the occasion of its 10th anniversary, we have taken the opportunity to invite contributors from academia, practice, civil society and regulatory institutions to reflect on this development through commentaries on selected court decisions or supervisory authority guidance. As editors, we have structured these contributions thematically and provided a common analytical framework. The result is an impressive journey through ten years of European data regulation. The contributions reflect a wide range of perspectives and starting points, mirroring the diversity and complexity of the underlying case law. Appreciation does not necessarily imply agreement. Some decisions are celebrated, others are criticised. What all the contributions have in common is a respect for the legislature and its judicial interpretation by the courts.

We would like to express our sincere gratitude to all contributors for their insightful analyses, and the four key figures who played the central role in bringing the GDPR into being for their forewords to this volume. From within the ranks of the European Commission, this includes Viviane Reding; from within the European Parliament, the rapporteur Jan Philipp Albrecht and the shadow rapporteur Axel Voss. They took the opportunity to write a joint statement. We were also able to secure the participation of former State Secretary Ole Schröder from within the ranks of the Council of the European Union.

We live in an age of artificial intelligence. In light of this development, we have decided to permit the use of AI on a limited basis, to assist in the drafting of case summaries, while the commentary remains the sole responsibility of the respective authors. To the best of our knowledge, the use of AI in this volume has remained within the scope defined by the editorial policy.

Finally, we would like to thank Nomos Verlag, in particular Marco Ganzhorn and his team, for making this project—which is both fascinating in terms of its content and ambitious in terms of its timeline—possible.

No milestone birthday should go without a celebration. We look forward to presenting the book on 20 May 2026 at the Second Symposium of the Journal of European Data and Information Law (Zeitschrift für Europäisches Daten- und Informationsrecht, EuDIR) as a symbolic gesture and celebrating the 10th anniversary of the GDPR with contemporary witnesses. The event is being held in collaboration with the Cologne Research Centre for Media Law at the Cologne University of Applied Sciences, where, in the spirit of Gottfried Wilhelm Leibniz, scholarship is approached from a practical perspective. This is precisely the approach taken in our Casebook on European Data Law, captured in its guiding motto: 'Understanding Data Law from Practice — case by case'.

Cologne and Mainz in April 2026

Prof. Dr. Rolf Schwartmann

Dr. Marek Steffen Jansen

Dr. Moritz Köhler

Table of Contents

Eurpean Parliament 15

European Commission 17

Council of the European Union 19

Table of legal acts of the European Union and Germany 23

Chapter 1:
Foundations and Application of EU Data Protection Law

Sebastian Dienst
European data protection case law in numbers 31

Robert Spano/Miles Lynn
Privacy as a Fundamental Right: Digital Rights Ireland 35

Marek Steffen Jansen
Purpose of the regulation 45

Axel Spies
Applicability of the GDPR (Material and Territorial Scope) 53

Bernd Grzeszick
Applicability of the GDPR to national parliaments 59

Chapter 2:
Core Concepts of the GDPR

Per Meyerdierks
The Identifiability of the Data Subject 67

Peter Craddock
Personal data, pseudonymisation and the scope of data protection law 75

Sophie Sohm/Steffen Sundermann
The Scope of 'Processing' under Art. 4 no. 2 GDPR 85

Dominik Roderburg
Right to one's own image and data protection 93

Indra Spiecker gen. Döhmann/Loïc Reissner
Joint controllers 103

Florian Thoma
Processing on behalf of a controller 123

Chapter 3:
Principles of Data Processing

Pilar Arzuaga
Purpose limitation and further processing 133

María González Gordon/Antonio Negueruela Maldonado
Testing the limits: ECJ on purpose and storage limitation 139

Natallia Karniyevich/Beyza Ermis
The principle of data minimisation – 10 years of GDPR: Aspiration, reality, and future prospects 147

Thoralf Knuth
Basic Principles: Confidentiality and Integrity 157

Ulrich Baumgartner
Principles relating to the processing of personal data: accountability 165

Chapter 4: Lawfulness of Data Processing

Jonathan Dunne
An analysis of the Evolution of Consent under overlapping regulatory regimes since the ECJ's ruling in Meta Platforms Inc. v Bundeskartellamt (Case C-252/21) 173

Lilly Taranto
Contractual Necessity 179

Natascha Gerlach
The broad notion of 'legitimate interests' in Art. 6(1)(f) GDPR 185

Dimitrios Linardatos
Data processing to protect vital interests 195

Gero Ziegenhorn
Personal data of representatives of legal persons, interpretation of Art. 6(2) and (3) GDPR, public access 201

Arne Nordmeyer
Processing of special categories of personal data, and compensation for non-material damage 207

Christiane Wendehorst
Special categories of personal data 213

Wioletta Kulińska
Children's Data Protection 221

Chapter 5: Data Subject Rights

Carolin Loy
Transparency obligations and dark patterns 235

Rebekka Weiß
Credit Rating Score and Right to an Explanation 241

Yvette Reif
Rectification of Gender Data in Public Registers and Means of Proof 253

Frederick Richter
Principle of accuracy – Right to rectification 261

Daniel Pauly
Concerning the Scope of the Data Subject's Right of Access 267

Christoph Werkmeister/Katharina-Isabelle Prenzel
Limits of the right of access 275

Desara Dushi
Right to Erasure and Right to Object 281

Katelyn Ringrose
The Right to Erasure/The 'Right to be Forgotten' 287

Stefan Brink
On the deletion of personal data from government registers 295

Moritz Köhler
Strongly Drawing on Automated Decision-Making Preparations 301

Chapter 6:
Governance, Compliance and Accountability

Dieter Kugelmann
Record of Processing Activities 309

Christian Jaksch/Klaus Alpmann
Data protection management system (DPMS) in accordance with the GDPR in connection with the implementation of the AI Act 315

Marit Hansen
Technical and organisational measures 327

Tobias Keber/Peter Nägele
Navigating between GDPR and AI Act: FRIA and DPIA – Two Interplay Use Cases 335

Andreas Jaspers
Stricter national rules on the dismissal of data protection officers are compatible with the GDPR 345

Isabelle Stroot
Data breach notification requirements and supervisory discretion under Art. 33 and 34 of the GDPR 353

Gabriela Mercuri
Codes of Conduct under the GDPR 361

Chapter 7:
International Data Transfers, Enforcement and Institutional Architecture

Helen Dixon
Transfers of Personal Data (to the US) 373

Tim Wybitul
No *'Strict Liability'*: The ECJ on Corporate Liability under Fines and the Principle of Fault in Data Sanction Law 383

Boris P. Paal
Compensation for non-material damage under Art. 82(1) GDPR 389

Ruben Plum-Schneider
Compensation for non-material damages 399

Carolin Gäthke
Representative action for transparency breaches under Art. 80(2) GDPR 407

Henry Ogunrinde
One-Stop-Shop 417

Thomas Fuchs
Cooperation between Data Protection Authorities and Competition Authorities 423

Chapter 8:
The GDPR in the Context of Emerging Technologies

Kai Zenner
The Challenge of Defining Artificial Intelligence in EU Law 431

Eduardo Ustaran
Personal Data in AI Development and Use 439

Rolf Schwartmann
Sensitive data in AI development 455

Stepanka Havlikova
Licensing Datasets for Generative AI Training 463

Christian-Henner Hentsch
Gema ruling on AI training – transferability of copyright limitations to data law? 473

Isabel Hahn
The Emergence of Literacy Expectations in GDPR Enforcement 481

Simone Vogel
Data protection in connected vehicles 495

Chapter 9:
The GDPR within the EU Digital Regulatory Framework

Michael Dose
The tension between data protection and data use in EU digital law 509

Boris Rigod
The Google Android case: redefining the intersection of competition law and data governance 515

Chapter 10:
Opening Clauses

Rafaela Nicolazzi Corrêa da Silva
Artistic creativity and the GDPR: assessing the impact of Art. 85 GDPR in the European Union 527

Lorenz Fander
Art. 88 GDPR: National discretion or European constraint? 545

Overview 553

Author profiles 559

Eurpean Parliament

The GDPR entered into force on 24 May 2016. This year, it celebrates its first major milestone anniversary. For both of us, European Union data protection law is now almost 15 years old. That is how long ago the work of the EU institutions began. The Treaty of Lisbon, which entered into force at that time, finally introduced through the Charter of Fundamental Rights a binding and explicit fundamental right to data protection and, through Article 16 TFEU, conferred upon the EU legislator a comprehensive competence to legislate for its protection and for the free movement of data within the European market. The General Data Protection Regulation, which emerged from this framework, has been applicable since 25 May 2018. For an EU legislative act, it has not only become an exceptionally well-known and widely applied set of rules governing social and economic life on this continent; it has also become a regulatory export success of the European Union – its standards are now globally recognised and influential.

Yet we all know: this has not come without burdens and many people still groan when confronted with the data protection law "made in Brussels." The relationship remains ambivalent. However, on the occasion of its tenth anniversary, there may also be room for a degree of pride in a legal instrument that has placed the relationship between law, individuals, and a data-driven world on a new footing. The harmonised EU-wide framework has indeed contributed to trust and legal certainty among individuals; many of the dire predictions regarding its effects have not materialised. At the same time, however, it has not significantly facilitated data use. Those who argue that Germany overregulates in the field of data protection and point to countries such as Estonia, Denmark, or the Netherlands cannot meaningfully attribute their critique to the GDPR, as it applies equally and directly in all those jurisdictions.

At the same time, it is also evident: instead of treating the GDPR as the central guiding framework for data protection and interpreting it uniformly across Europe, a considerable number of special rules continue to exist across the 27 EU Member States and, within Germany, across the 16 federal states. Moreover, the rules are sometimes applied in markedly divergent and ambitious ways. Greater consistency and clarity must therefore become the guiding principle for the future. Economic actors who complain about the GDPR might also benefit from focusing more on the many possibilities it creates for data processing – not least where anonymous information is concerned. Such data, as is well known, falls entirely outside the scope of the GDPR. In truth, the GDPR is far better than its reputation suggests; however, its impact in achieving a genuinely unified data market within the European Union still falls short of expectations.

In the tenth year following its entry into force, the GDPR is no longer the sole instrument of European data law. It now forms part of an emerging ensemble of legal acts that address both data protection and the data economy. To prevent their interaction from descending into a cacophony, the application of EU legislation must be carefully orchestrated. The close interconnection between the digital economy, artificial intelligence, and data law is evident, and the legislator must act accordingly.

In a democracy, laws are not set in stone. Timed to coincide with its tenth anniversary, amendments to the GDPR are already being planned. The European Commission has identified a need for reform in data protection law and, in November 2025, launched a legislative proposal. The so-called "GDPR Digital Omnibus" is intended to liberalise data protection law in light of the needs of the digital economy. The GDPR is to be adjusted in order to streamline the legal framework and make it more accessible.

The Court of Justice of the European Union has significantly advanced the detailed interpretation of the GDPR and has, at the same time, shaped the European Union's transatlantic data policy with considerable determination. For this reason, it is only fitting to congratulate the GDPR through the lens of this case law. One may hope that the Court will receive both approval and constructive criticism from academia and practice, as reflected in this volume.

This book, published on the occasion of the GDPR's tenth anniversary and presented at the 2nd EuDIR Symposium in May, is a fitting birthday tribute. We, too, congratulate this legislative instrument and wish it continued success in guiding data protection in a fair manner for both individuals and businesses in the European Union into the next decade.

Jan-Philipp Albrecht

Axel Voss

European Commission

Since the beginning of the European construction, the ECJ was instrumental for turning abstract legal concepts into practical applied rules. Europewide. Also concerning the GDPR. That is why your publication, systematically reviewing case-law, is an interesting anniversary-gift for 10 years of GDPR. Thank you! It all began in 2009, when the Treaty of Lisbon and the Charter of Fundamental Rights entered into force, becoming a point of reference for rules-based policy-making. Art.8 of the Charter ("Everyone has the right to the protection of personal data") led the Commission to present a masterplan for data-protection in the digital age (4.11.2010).

The European Parliament, always keen to protect citizens rights, followed with the report by Axel Voss (06.07.2011). This endorsement accelerated the preparatory work, and on to 25. January 2012 I was ready to present the legal proposal for GDPR. Helped by the negotiation-skills of the EP-rapporteur Phillipp Albrecht and the good-will of several Council Presidencies, the text was agreed on 27.April 2016, to be applied on 25.May 2018. The long and complicated negotiation-period (strongly influenced by the Snowden-revelations) is explained in a brilliant way by David Bernet in his film "Democracy, im Rausch der Daten" a "food for thought" art work!

GDPR was a milestone- step from a mostly economic union to a union of citizens and fundamental rights. It was drafted at a time, when the influence of digitalisation on individuals and on the economy had only started. Nevertheless, its extraterritorial impact led it to become a world-standard rapidly. An important tool for facing "ubiquitous computing" and AI-centred revolutions. The digital changes in today's society are massive and ultra-rapid. It seems evident that an adaptation of GDPR to this evolving reality is a must. Preserving the personal rights and the industrial development possibilities in parallel is a challenge. May the impact of scholars, jurists and politicians be a valuable guide for the next decade...

Viviane Reding

Council of the European Union

Ten years after the GDPR was enacted, it is appropriate to assess its influence and at the same time to look ahead.

The surrounding conditions of data processing have developed very dynamically over the last ten years. On the one hand, we are experiencing exponentially increased surveillance and data analysis capacities, which are a potential threat to civil liberties.
On the other hand, data processing has become even more of a prerequisite for the exercise of central fundamental rights. Freedom of expression, for example, is nowadays largely be realized via digital communication platforms. Economic participation and social prosperity also depend inseparably on the ability to process data in a data-driven economy. This ambivalence has been further intensified by big data analyses and AI-supported systems. Today, more than ever, data protection law operates in a tension between the threat to fundamental rights by data processing and the availability of data that enables innovation and fundamental freedoms. Whether we have succeeded in balancing this tension without undermining the practical applicability and practical enforceability of the law is the central question that arises with new urgency after ten years of the GDPR.

The present volume, which systematically reviews the case law of the ECJ on the GDPR, makes an important contribution to this. After all, it is not least the ECJ that, through its interpretation, decisively decides how the abstractly formulated data protection law is applied in practice.

In my role as Parliamentary State Secretary to the Federal Minister of the Interior, I was directly involved in these negotiations. Many of the challenges we are discussing today were already present at the beginning of the of the legislative process. It was clear that the traditional data protection concepts of the GDPR were only of limited suitability for the digital environment and required substantial modernization. The regulatory approach of the GDPR is still rooted in an analogue world. It is based on a model of data processing that is subject to purpose limitation, controllable, and organized within clearly defined structures of responsibility. At the same time, developments such as Big Data, cloud computing, the Internet of Things, and interconnected systems were already central during the negotiations. In particular, the question of how to allow for further processing for new purposes was highly controversial in the light of these technologies. The so-called compatibility test was intended to provide a solution—an approach that was already recognized at the time as legally fragile and difficult to apply in practice.

With the rapid development of data-driven technologies, these challenges have been further intensified: Artificial intelligence, machine learning, large language models, and self-optimizing systems are fundamentally based on the idea that insights are generated only through the processing of large volumes of data. In such contexts, a precise specification of purpose in advance is structurally impossible. Against this background, core principles of the GDPR, such as purpose limitation, data minimization, and transparency, appear increasingly detached from reality: purpose limitation turns into a fiction, data minimization into a mere formality, and transparency into an illusion, while the specification of purpose is drafted so broadly as to become effectively meaningless

The fundamental approach of a system of prohibition subject to authorization also reaches its limits in this context. It seeks to prevent any unlawful data processing through ex ante regulation. However, the reality of large-scale, globally distributed data processing, particularly in the context of AI-driven applications, demonstrates that this approach is neither effectively enforceable nor capable of providing meaningful protection for individuals. Despite considerable bureaucratic effort, a structural enforcement deficit is evident, while individuals are often left largely exposed to actual data processing practices.

In addition, there is a considerable degree of legal uncertainty. The GDPR works with numerous indeterminate legal terms, the specification of which is largely left to the ECJ. In its case-law, the court focuses very much on the practical effectiveness (effet utile) of data protection and thus primarily strengthens the standard of protection, while taking less account of conflicting fundamental rights. In conjunction with the broad interpretation of Art. 82 GDPR, this creates a significant, hardly calculable liability risk for companies.

The GDPR was designed to be supplemented by national law. Its numerous opening clauses were intended to enable necessary specification at Member State level and thereby enhance legal certainty. The current lack of legal certainty is therefore also linked to the absence of such national rules. It is noteworthy that the ECJ itself refers to national law when interpreting the Regulation, for example in the interpretation of legitimate interests.

A look at the political objectives and their implementation is ambivalent. There is no doubt that a stronger and more binding enforcement of data protection law has been achieved. The marketplace principle has also been further strengthened, enabling the European Union to apply its regulatory standards beyond the internal market.

Nevertheless, the global impact of the GDPR remains limited. It is true that in parts it has developed into an international reference model and has influenced numerous legal systems. However, a strictly preventive prohibition model comparable to the GDPR has not prevailed internationally. Instead, other jurisdictions predominantly pursue more flexible, risk-based approaches that focus more on controlling specific threats than on the upstream control of data processing.

However, there are considerable missed targets. The "one-size-fits-all" approach places a particular burden on small and medium-sized enterprises, while large global platforms can take advantage of structural advantages, especially when it comes to obtaining consent. The intended openness to technology has been proven to be limited too.

For the future, the central question is whether the existing approach to data protection law is still suitable for meeting the challenges of a data-driven society. There are strong arguments for shifting the focus more from the formal control of data processing to the protection of specific legal interests and risks. A more risk-based, innovation-friendly and at the same time effective protection approach could help to better balance the existing tension.

This volume provides a valuable foundation for this discussion. It not only demonstrates how the CJEU interprets the current legal framework, but also opens the door to a necessary debate on its further development.

Ole Schröder

Table of legal acts of the European Union and Germany

I. Legal acts of the European Union

Charter of Fundamental Rights of the European Union, OJ C 326, 26.10.2012, p. 391, ELI: http://data.europa.eu/eli/treaty/char_2012/oj, hereinafter ‚CFR'

Commission Directive 2008/63/EC of 20 June 2008 on competition in the markets in telecommunications terminal equipment, OJ L 162, 21.6.2008, p. 20, ELI: http://data.europa.eu/eli/dir/2008/63/oj, hereinafter ‚Commission Directive on competition in the markets in telecommunications terminal equipment'

Commission Implementing Regulation (EU) 2024/2690 of 17 October 2024 laying down rules for the application of Directive (EU) 2022/2555 as regards technical and methodological requirements of cybersecurity risk-management measures and further specification of the cases in which an incident is considered to be significant with regard to DNS service providers, TLD name registries, cloud computing service providers, data centre service providers, content delivery network providers, managed service providers, managed security service providers, providers of online market places, of online search engines and of social networking services platforms, and trust service providers, OJ L, 2024/2690, 18.10.2024, ELI: http://data.europa.eu/eli/reg_impl/2024/2690/oj, hereinafter ‚Commission Implementing Regulation (EU) 2024/2690'

Consolidated version of the Treaty on European Union, OJ C 202, 7.6.2016, p. 1, hereinafter 'TEU'

Consolidated version of the Treaty on the Functioning of the European Union, OJ C 202, 7.6.2016, p. 1, hereinafter ‚TFEU'

Convention for the Protection of Human Rights and Fundamental Freedoms as amended by Protocol No. 15, UNTS 213. (1955), p. 22, hereinafter ‚ECHR'

Directive (EU) 2016/680 of the European Parliament and of the Council of 27 April 2016 on the protection of natural persons with regard to the processing of personal data by competent authorities for the purposes of the prevention, investigation, detection or prosecution of criminal offences or the execution of criminal penalties, and on the free movement of such data, and repealing Council Framework Decision 2008/977/JHA, OJ L 119, 4.5.2016, p. 89, ELI: http://data.europa.eu/eli/dir/2016/680/oj, hereinafter ‚LED'

Directive (EU) 2016/681 of the European Parliament and of the Council of 27 April 2016 on the use of passenger name record (PNR) data for the prevention, detection, investigation and prosecution of terrorist offences and serious crime, OJ L 119, 4.5.2016, p. 132, ELI: http://data.europa.eu/eli/dir/2016/681/oj, hereinafter ‚PNR Directive'

Directive (EU) 2019/1024 of the European Parliament and of the Council of 20 June 2019 on open data and the re-use of public sector information, OJ L 172, 26.6.2019, p. 56, ELI: http://data.europa.eu/eli/dir/2019/1024/oj, hereinafter ‚Open Data Directive'

Directive (EU) 2019/790 of the European Parliament and of the Council of 17 April 2019 on copyright and related rights in the Digital Single Market and amending Directives 96/9/EC and 2001/29/EC, OJ L 130, 17.5.2019, p. 92, ELI: http://data.euro pa.eu/eli/dir/2019/790/oj, hereinafter ‚DSM Directive'

Directive (EU) 2020/1828 of the European Parliament and of the Council of 25 November 2020 on representative actions for the protection of the collective interests of consumers and repealing Directive 2009/22/EC, OJ L 409, 4.12.2020, p. 1, ELI: http://data.europa.eu/eli/dir/2020/1828/oj, hereinafter ‚Representative Actions Directive'

Directive (EU) 2022/2555 of the European Parliament and of the Council of 14 December 2022 on measures for a high common level of cybersecurity across the Union, amending Regulation (EU) No 910/2014 and Directive (EU) 2018/1972, and repealing Directive (EU) 2016/1148 (NIS 2 Directive), OJ L 333, 27.12.2022, p. 80, ELI: http://data.europa.eu/eli/dir/2022/2555/oj, hereinafter ‚NIS2 Directive'

Directive (EU) 2023/2225 of the European Parliament and of the Council of 18 October 2023 on credit agreements for consumers and repealing Directive 2008/48/EC, OJ L, 2023/2225, 30.10.2023, ELI: http://data.europa.eu/eli/dir/2023/2225/oj, hereinafter ‚Consumer Credit Directive'

Directive 2002/58/EC of the European Parliament and of the Council of 12 July 2002 concerning the processing of personal data and the protection of privacy in the electronic communications sector (Directive on privacy and electronic communications), OJ L 201, 31.7.2002, p. 37, ELI: http://data.europa.eu/eli/dir/2002/58/oj, hereinfater ‚ePrivacy Directive'

Directive 2006/24/EC of the European Parliament and of the Council of 15 March 2006 on the retention of data generated or processed in connection with the provision of publicly available electronic communications services or of public communications networks and amending Directive 2002/58/EC, OJ L 105, 13.4.2006, p. 54, ELI: http://data.europa.eu/eli/dir/2006/24/oj, hereinafter ‚DRD'

Directive 2009/136/EC of the European Parliament and of the Council of 25 November 2009 amending Directive 2002/22/EC on universal service and users' rights relating to electronic communications networks and services, Directive 2002/58/EC concerning the processing of personal data and the protection of privacy in the electronic communications sector and Regulation (EC) No 2006/2004 on cooperation between national authorities responsible for the enforcement of consumer protection laws, OJ L 337, 18.12.2009, p. 11, ELI: http://data.europa.eu/eli/dir/2009/136/oj, hereinafter ‚Citizens' Rights Directive'

Directive 95/46/EC of the European Parliament and of the Council of 24 October 1995 on the protection of individuals with regard to the processing of personal data and on the free movement of such data, OJ L 281, 23.11.1995, p. 31, http://data.europa.eu/e li/dir/1995/46/oj, hereinafter ‚DPD'

Regulation (EU) 2016/679 of the European Parliament and of the Council of 27 April 2016 on the protection of natural persons with regard to the processing of personal data and on the free movement of such data, and repealing Directive 95/46/EC (General Data Protection Regulation), OJ L 119, 4.5.2016, p. 1, ELI: http://data.europ a.eu/eli/reg/2016/679/oj, hereninfater ‚GDPR'

Regulation (EU) 2018/1725 of the European Parliament and of the Council of 23 October 2018 on the protection of natural persons with regard to the processing of personal data by the Union institutions, bodies, offices and agencies and on the free movement of such data, and repealing Regulation (EC) No 45/2001 and Decision No 1247/2002/EC, OJ L 295, 21.11.2018, p. 39, ELI: http://data.europa.eu/eli/reg/2018/172 5/oj, hereinafter ‚EUDPR'

Regulation (EU) 2018/1807 of the European Parliament and of the Council of 14 November 2018 on a framework for the free flow of non-personal data in the European Union, OJ L 303, 28.11.2018, p. 59, ELI: http://data.europa.eu/eli/reg/2018/1807 /oj, hereinafter ‚Regulation on the free flow of non-personal data'

Regulation (EU) 2022/1925 of the European Parliament and of the Council of 14 September 2022 on contestable and fair markets in the digital sector and amending Directives (EU) 2019/1937 and (EU) 2020/1828 (Digital Markets Act), OJ L 265, 12.10.2022, p. 1, ELI: http://data.europa.eu/eli/reg/2022/1925/oj, hereinafter ‚DMA'

Regulation (EU) 2022/2065 of the European Parliament and of the Council of 19 October 2022 on a Single Market For Digital Services and amending Directive 2000/31/EC (Digital Services Act), OJ L 277, 27.10.2022, p. 1, ELI: http://data.eur opa.eu/eli/reg/2022/2065/oj, hereinafter ‚DSA'

Regulation (EU) 2023/2854 of the European Parliament and of the Council of 13 December 2023 on harmonised rules on fair access to and use of data and amending Regulation (EU) 2017/2394 and Directive (EU) 2020/1828 (Data Act), OJ L, 2023/2854, 22.12.2023, ELI: http://data.europa.eu/eli/reg/2023/2854/oj, hereinafter ‚DA'

Regulation (EU) 2024/1689 of the European Parliament and of the Council of 13 June 2024 laying down harmonised rules on artificial intelligence and amending Regulations (EC) No 300/2008, (EU) No 167/2013, (EU) No 168/2013, (EU) 2018/858, (EU) 2018/1139 and (EU) 2019/2144 and Directives 2014/90/EU, (EU) 2016/797 and (EU) 2020/1828 (Artificial Intelligence Act), OJ L, 2024/1689, 12.7.2024, ELI: http://d ata.europa.eu/eli/reg/2024/1689/oj, hereinafter ‚AI Act'

Regulation (EU) 2024/2847 of the European Parliament and of the Council of 23 October 2024 on horizontal cybersecurity requirements for products with digital elements and amending Regulations (EU) No 168/2013 and (EU) 2019/1020 and Directive (EU) 2020/1828 (Cyber Resilience Act), OJ L, 2024/2847, 20.11.2024, ELI: http://data.europa.eu/eli/reg/2024/2847/oj, hereinafter ‚CRA'

Regulation (EU) 2022/868 of the European Parliament and of the Council of 30 May 2022 on European data governance and amending Regulation (EU) 2018/1724 (Data Governance Act), OJ L 152, 3.6.2022, p. 1, ELI: http://data.europa.eu/eli/reg/2022/86 8/oj, hereinafter ‚DGA'

II. Legal acts of Germany

Betriebsverfassungsgesetz in der Fassung der Bekanntmachung vom 25. September 2001 (BGBl. I S. 2518), das zuletzt durch Artikel 1 des Gesetzes vom 19. Juli 2024 (BGBl. 2024 I Nr. 248) geändert worden ist, hereinafter ‚BetrVG'

Bundesdatenschutzgesetz vom 30. Juni 2017 (BGBl. I S. 2097), das zuletzt durch Artikel 7 des Gesetzes vom 6. Mai 2024 (BGBl. 2024 I Nr. 149) geändert worden ist, hereinafter ‚BDSG'

Bürgerliches Gesetzbuch in der Fassung der Bekanntmachung vom 2. Januar 2002 (BGBl. I S. 42, 2909; 2003 I S. 738), das zuletzt durch Artikel 1 des Gesetzes vom 3. Februar 2026 (BGBl. 2026 I Nr. 28) geändert worden ist, hereinafter ‚BGB'

Das Erste Buch Sozialgesetzbuch – Allgemeiner Teil – (Artikel I des Gesetzes vom 11. Dezember 1975, BGBl. I S. 3015), das zuletzt durch Artikel 62 Absatz 3 des Gesetzes vom 4. Februar 2026 (BGBl. 2026 I Nr. 33) geändert worden ist, hereinafter ‚SGB I'

Das Fünfte Buch Sozialgesetzbuch – Gesetzliche Krankenversicherung – (Artikel 1 des Gesetzes vom 20. Dezember 1988, BGBl. I S. 2477, 2482), das zuletzt durch Artikel 28 des Gesetzes vom 3. Februar 2026 (BGBl. 2026 I Nr. 28) geändert worden ist, hereinafter ‚SGB V'

Das Zehnte Buch Sozialgesetzbuch – Sozialverwaltungsverfahren und Sozialdatenschutz – in der Fassung der Bekanntmachung vom 18. Januar 2001 (BGBl. I S. 130), das zuletzt durch Artikel 14 des Gesetzes vom 16. Januar 2026 (BGBl. 2026 I Nr. 14) geändert worden ist, hereinafter ‚SGB X'

Gesetz betreffend das Urheberrecht an Werken der bildenden Künste und der Photographie in der im Bundesgesetzblatt Teil III, Gliederungsnummer 440-3, veröffentlichten bereinigten Fassung, das zuletzt durch Artikel 3 § 31 des Gesetzes vom 16. Februar 2001 (BGBl. I S. 266) geändert worden ist, hereinafter ‚KUG'

Gesetz betreffend die Gesellschaften mit beschränkter Haftung in der im Bundesgesetzblatt Teil III, Gliederungsnummer 4123-1, veröffentlichten bereinigten Fassung, das zuletzt durch Artikel 21 des Gesetzes vom 23. Oktober 2024 (BGBl. 2024 I Nr. 323) geändert worden ist, hereinafter ‚GmbHG'

Gesetz gegen Wettbewerbsbeschränkungen in der Fassung der Bekanntmachung vom 26. Juni 2013 (BGBl. I S. 1750, 3245), das zuletzt durch Artikel 3 des Gesetzes vom 10. Februar 2026 (BGBl. 2026 I Nr. 40) geändert worden ist, hereinafter ‚GWB'

Gesetz über Ordnungswidrigkeiten in der Fassung der Bekanntmachung vom 19. Februar 1987 (BGBl. I S. 602), das zuletzt durch Artikel 21 des Gesetzes vom 22. Dezember 2025 (BGBl. 2025 I Nr. 349) geändert worden ist, hereinafter ‚OWiG'

Grundgesetz für die Bundesrepublik Deutschland in der im Bundesgesetzblatt Teil III, Gliederungsnummer 100-1, veröffentlichten bereinigten Fassung, das zuletzt durch Artikel 1 des Gesetzes vom 22. März 2025 (BGBl. 2025 I Nr. 94) geändert worden ist, hereinafter ‚GG'

Handelsgesetzbuch in der im Bundesgesetzblatt Teil III, Gliederungsnummer 4100-1, veröffentlichten bereinigten Fassung, das zuletzt durch Artikel 4 des Gesetzes vom 4. Februar 2026 (BGBl. 2026 I Nr. 33) geändert worden ist, hereinafter ‚HGB'

Hessisches Datenschutz- und Informationsfreiheitsgesetz (HDSIG) vom 3. Mai 2018 (GVBl. 2018, 82), zuletzt geändert durch Art. 39 Erstes BürokratieabbauG vom 16.12.2025 (GVBl. Nr. 110), hereinafter ‚HDSIG'

Urheberrechtsgesetz vom 9. September 1965 (BGBl. I S. 1273), das zuletzt durch Artikel 28 des Gesetzes vom 23. Oktober 2024 (BGBl. 2024 I Nr. 323) geändert worden ist, hereinafter ‚UrhG'

Verwaltungsverfahrensgesetz in der Fassung der Bekanntmachung vom 23. Januar 2003 (BGBl. I S. 102), das zuletzt durch Artikel 2 des Gesetzes vom 15. Juli 2024 (BGBl. 2024 I Nr. 236) geändert worden ist, hereinafter ‚VwVfG'

Zivilprozessordnung in der Fassung der Bekanntmachung vom 5. Dezember 2005 (BGBl. I S. 3202; 2006 I S. 431; 2007 I S. 1781), die zuletzt durch Artikel 2 des Gesetzes vom 22. Dezember 2025 (BGBl. 2025 I Nr. 349) geändert worden ist, hereinafter ‚ZPO'

Chapter 1:
Foundations and Application of EU Data Protection Law

European data protection case law in numbers

Sebastian Dienst

With the GDPR of 2016, the EU significantly expanded its regulatory framework for data protection initially laid down by the DPD of 1995. For nearly 30 years, case law of the ECJ has been continuously shaping and sharpening European data protection law.

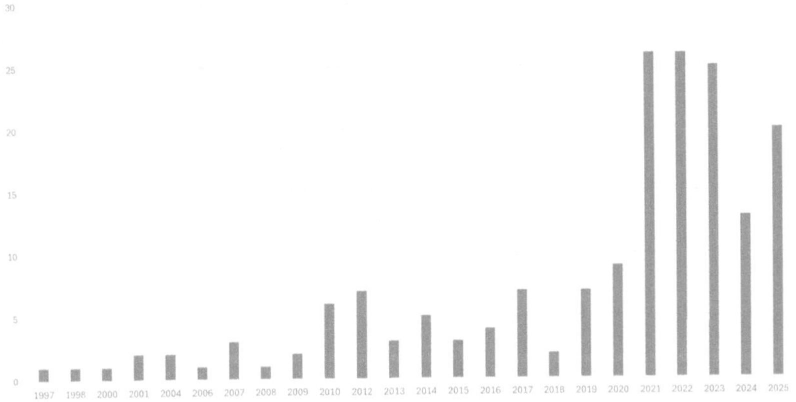

Figure 1: Numbers of new ECJ proceedings on DPD and GDPR by year

After the DPD came into force in 1995 (which still needed to be transformed into EU member state law), it took some time for the number of data protection law cases before the ECJ to increase. Since the GDPR came into force in 2016 (directly applying in all EU member states since 2018), we have seen a significant rise in the number of referrals on data protection law to the ECJ.

The first proceeding on the DPD at the ECJ was initiated on 2.6.1997 (C-209/97). This proceeding also led to the first judgment of the ECJ regarding the DPD on 18.11.1999.[1] The ECJ handed down its last judgment

1 ECJ 18.11.1999 – case C-209/97, ECLI:EU:C:1999:559.

regarding the DPD on 4.10.2024.[2] In total, 51 proceedings relating to the DPD were initiated at the ECJ. The first proceeding dealing with the GDPR was initiated on 17.8.2017 (C-496/17). In this proceeding, the ECJ also handed down its first judgment regarding the GDPR on 16.1.2019.[3] Until the end of 2025, 127 proceedings regarding the GDPR have been initiated at the ECJ. In less than 10 years, the GDPR has led to more than twice as many ECJ proceedings as the DPD since 1995.

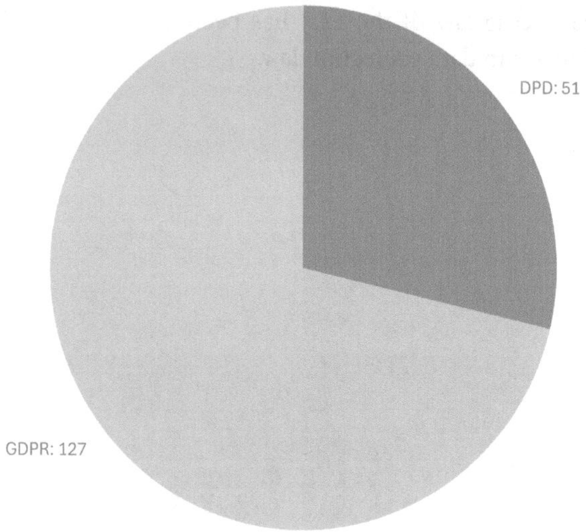

Figure 2: Total numbers of DPD and GDPR cases (until December 2025)

Looking at GDPR cases, by far most proceedings deal with general provisions and principles, with most cases on Art. 6 GDPR (Lawfulness of processing) (41 cases), followed by cases on Art. 4 GDPR (Definitions) (26 cases) and Art. 5 GDPR (Principles relating to processing of personal data) (23 cases). It is certainly not surprising that a significant number of cases also deal with Art. 82 GDPR (Right to compensation and liability) (20 cases) and Art. 15 GDPR (Right of access by the data subject) (16 cases), emphasizing both the practical relevance and need for clarification of these provisions.

2 ECJ 4.10.2024 – case C-21/23, ECLI:EU:C:2024:846.
3 ECJ 16.1.2019 – case C-496/17, ECLI:EU:C:2019:26.

Figure 3: GDPR cases by Article of the GDPR (until December 2025)

Most of the referrals to the ECJ on data protection law come from German (56) and Austrian (20) courts, followed by Bulgarian (12) and Belgian (11) courts.

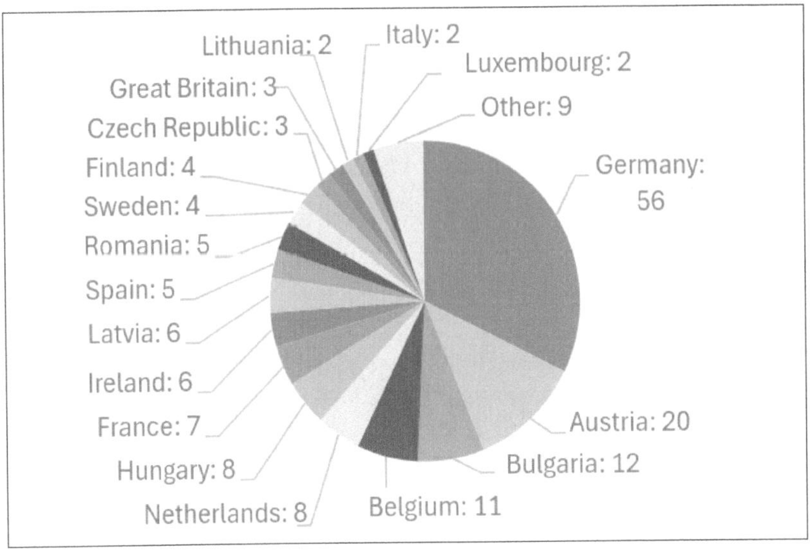

Figure 4: GDPR cases by country of origin (until December 2025)

2021 and 2022 both marked a record high of new data protection law proceedings at the ECJ (26 each), closely followed by 2023 (25). In 2024, for the first time since 2018, fewer proceedings were initiated (13) than the year before. 2025 again brought a rising number of new proceedings (20). Looking at the number of pending data protection cases in the beginning of 2026 (29), it is likely that we will continue to see a constant flow of data protection rulings over the next years.

Privacy as a Fundamental Right: Digital Rights Ireland

Robert Spano/Miles Lynn

ECJ 8.4.2014 – Joined Cases C-293/12 and C-594/12, ECLI:EU:C:2014:238 – Digital Rights Ireland Ltd v Minister for Communications, Marine and Natural Resources and Others and Kärntner Landesregierung and Others

I. Case summary

In Joined Cases C-293/12 and C-594/12 ('*Digital Rights Ireland*'),[1] decided on 8 April 2014, the Court of Justice of the European Union (Grand Chamber) declared the DRD invalid. The DRD had required providers of publicly available electronic communications services to retain traffic and location data for between six and twenty-four months to facilitate the investigation of serious crime. The Court held that the DRD violated Art. 7 and 8 of the CFR (rights to respect for private life and data protection). While acknowledging that the retained data could assist criminal investigations, the Court found the interference with fundamental rights was neither limited to what was strictly necessary nor accompanied by sufficient safeguards. The DRD applied indiscriminately to vast swathes of the European population without differentiation or exception. It lacked objective criteria limiting access to retained data, required no prior judicial or independent administrative review before access, and failed to specify retention periods based on objective criteria. Additionally, the DRD provided insufficient data security safeguards and did not mandate that data be retained within the European Union under supervisory authority control. The Court concluded that the European Union legislature exceeded the limits of proportionality under Art. 52(1) CFR.

1 ECJ 8.4.2014 – Joined Cases C-293/12 and C-594/12, ECLI:EU:C:2014:238 – Digital Rights Ireland Ltd v Minister for Communications, Marine and Natural Resources and Others and Kärntner Landesregierung and Others.

II. Key legal findings

The Court of Justice (Grand Chamber) declared the DRD invalid in its entirety, holding that the EU legislature exceeded the proportionality limits in Art. 52(1) CFR in light of Art. 7 (respect for private life and communications) and 8 (protection of personal data) CFR. It treated the retention obligation itself and subsequent access by competent authorities as distinct interferences with Art. 7 CFR[2] and held that the mandatory processing of retained data engaged Art. 8 CFR.[3] Given the scale and sensitivity of traffic and location data, the Court characterised the interferences as 'wide-ranging and particularly serious' and liable to generate a feeling of constant surveillance.[4] Although the measure did not, in the Court's view, adversely affect the essence of Art. 7 CFR because it excluded content (Art. 1(2) DRD),[5] nor the essence of Art. 8 CFR because it contained certain data protection and data security principles,[6] it nonetheless failed the proportionality assessment under Art. 52(1) CFR.[7]

Critically, the Court found that the DRD failed to lay down clear and precise rules governing the scope and application of the measure and imposing minimum safeguards to protect personal data against abuse and unlawful access.[8] The judgment identified multiple fatal deficiencies. First, the DRD applied indiscriminately to 'all persons and all means of electronic communication' without any differentiation, affecting 'practically the entire European population' despite the absence of any link to serious crime.[9] It

2 ECJ 8.4.2014 – Joined Cases C-293/12 and C-594/12, ECLI:EU:C:2014:238 para. 34 et seq. – Digital Rights Ireland.

3 ECJ 8.4.2014 – Joined Cases C-293/12 and C-594/12, ECLI:EU:C:2014:238 para. 36 – Digital Rights Ireland.

4 ECJ 8.4.2014 – Joined Cases C-293/12 and C-594/12, ECLI:EU:C:2014:238 para. 37 – Digital Rights Ireland.

5 ECJ 8.4.2014 – Joined Cases C-293/12 and C-594/12, ECLI:EU:C:2014:238 para. 39 – Digital Rights Ireland.

6 ECJ 8.4.2014 – Joined Cases C-293/12 and C-594/12, ECLI:EU:C:2014:238 para. 40 – Digital Rights Ireland.

7 ECJ 8.4.2014 – Joined Cases C-293/12 and C-594/12, ECLI:EU:C:2014:238 para. 69 – Digital Rights Ireland.

8 ECJ 8.4.2014 – Joined Cases C-293/12 and C-594/12, ECLI:EU:C:2014:238 para. 54 – Digital Rights Ireland.

9 ECJ 8.4.2014 – Joined Cases C-293/12 and C-594/12, ECLI:EU:C:2014:238 para. 56–59 – Digital Rights Ireland.

offered no exception for professional secrecy, capturing communications of lawyers, doctors, and journalists subject to confidentiality obligations.[10]

Second, the DRD lacked objective criteria concerning access to and use of retained data by competent national authorities.[11] It merely referred 'in a general manner to serious crime, as defined by each Member State' without defining this threshold.[12] Crucially, it imposed no requirement for prior review by a court or independent administrative body before authorities accessed data, a procedural safeguard deemed essential.[13] Nor did it limit access by reference to objective criteria governing the number of persons authorised.[14]

Third, retention periods of six to twenty-four months lacked differentiation based on data categories or objective justification related to their utility for combating crime.[15]

Fourth, the Court criticised inadequate data security provisions and the absence of an EU retention requirement. The DRD did not ensure a 'particularly high level' of protection, allowed providers to take economic considerations into account when determining security levels, and did not ensure irreversible destruction at the end of the retention period.[16] It also did not require that data be retained within the European Union, undermining effective independent control as required by Art. 8(3) CFR.[17]

The Court linked the intensity of review to the subject matter concerned, the nature of the Charter right, the nature and seriousness of the interference, and the objective pursued.[18] By establishing that serious interferences

10 ECJ 8.4.2014 – Joined Cases C-293/12 and C-594/12, ECLI:EU:C:2014:238 para. 58 – Digital Rights Ireland.

11 ECJ 8.4.2014 – Joined Cases C-293/12 and C-594/12, ECLI:EU:C:2014:238 para. 60–62 – Digital Rights Ireland.

12 ECJ 8.4.2014 – Joined Cases C-293/12 and C-594/12, ECLI:EU:C:2014:238 para. 60 – Digital Rights Ireland.

13 ECJ 8.4.2014 – Joined Cases C-293/12 and C-594/12, ECLI:EU:C:2014:238 para. 62 – Digital Rights Ireland.

14 ECJ 8.4.2014 – Joined Cases C-293/12 and C-594/12, ECLI:EU:C:2014:238 para. 62 – Digital Rights Ireland.

15 ECJ 8.4.2014 – Joined Cases C-293/12 and C-594/12, ECLI:EU:C:2014:238 para. 63–65 – Digital Rights Ireland.

16 ECJ 8.4.2014 – Joined Cases C-293/12 and C-594/12, ECLI:EU:C:2014:238 para. 66 et seq. – Digital Rights Ireland.

17 ECJ 8.4.2014 – Joined Cases C-293/12 and C-594/12, ECLI:EU:C:2014:238 para. 68 – Digital Rights Ireland.

18 ECJ 8.4.2014 – Joined Cases C-293/12 and C-594/12, ECLI:EU:C:2014:238 para. 47 – Digital Rights Ireland.

with fundamental rights trigger reduced legislative discretion subject to strict judicial review,[19] the Court imposed a substantive responsibility upon the EU legislature to adopt effective fundamental rights safeguards, rather than delegating this entirely to Member States. Having found invalidity on the basis of Art. 7 and 8, it did not examine Art. 11 (freedom of expression) CFR.[20]

III. Systematic context and legal classification

ePrivacy Directive, as amended by the Citizens' Rights Directive, establishes a sectoral principle of confidentiality of electronic communications and, as a rule, erasure of traffic data when no longer needed for transmission (Art. 5(1), 6(1) ePrivacy Directive). Art. 15(1) ePrivacy Directive permits Member State derogations only where they are 'necessary, appropriate and proportionate within a democratic society' to safeguard national security, defence, public security, or the prevention, investigation, detection, and prosecution of criminal offences.[21] The DRD inverted this architecture by transforming a permissive national derogation into a mandatory EU-wide obligation. Art. 11 DRD inserted Art. 15(1a) into the ePrivacy Directive and compelled providers to retain specified traffic and location data for six to twenty-four months. Adopted under internal market competence (ex Art. 95 EC) in the aftermath of the Madrid (2004) and London (2005) terrorist attacks, the DRD reflected a security-driven move towards preventive investigative capacity.

The case reached the Court via Art. 267 TFEU preliminary references from Irish and Austrian courts, following successful constitutional challenges to national implementing measures in several Member States[22] and Ireland's earlier failed legal basis challenge in C-301/06. The preliminary

19 ECJ 8.4.2014 – Joined Cases C-293/12 and C-594/12, ECLI:EU:C:2014:238 para. 48 – Digital Rights Ireland.

20 ECJ 8.4.2014 – Joined Cases C-293/12 and C-594/12, ECLI:EU:C:2014:238 para. 69–71 – Digital Rights Ireland.

21 Art. 15(1) ePrivacy Directive, as amended by the Citizens' Rights Directive.

22 See, e.g., Romanian Constitutional Court decision No. 1258/2009; BVerfG 2.3.2010 – 1 BvR 256/08, 1 BvR 263/08, 1 BvR 586/08, NJW 2010, 833; Czech Constitutional Court, decision (judgment) of 22 March 2011, case no. Pl. ÚS 24/10, published under No. 94/2011 Sb; Cyprus Supreme Court (Civil applications 65/2009, 78/2009, 82/2009 and 15/2010–22/2010).

references attracted extensive participation from Member States and Union institutions, and the Advocate General (Cruz Villalón) highlighted the Directive's 'functional duality' as both an internal market measure and a security instrument, arguing that the EU legislature could not rely on national implementation choices to supply missing safeguards.[23]

The Court grounded its insistence on 'clear and precise rules' and 'minimum safeguards'[24] by analogy with European Court of Human Rights ('ECtHR') case law on surveillance and retention.[25] The judgment also consolidated a prevailing legal concern visible in domestic constitutional case law: that generalised retention, detached from any objective link to serious crime and coupled with weak access governance, cannot be normalised within a rights-based communications framework.

IV. Author's analysis and commentary

Doctrinally, *Digital Rights Ireland* constitutes a rejection of general and indiscriminate retention as a normalised security paradigm, while stopping short of treating retention as *per se* incompatible with fundamental rights. The Court accepted that retention can be 'appropriate' and a 'valuable tool' for criminal investigations but insisted that the importance of combating serious crime and terrorism does not, 'in itself', establish necessity.[26] The decisive move is therefore not categorical prohibition but the constitutionalisation of a demanding 'strict necessity' standard in the design of retention regimes.[27]

The judgment's insistence that retention and access are separate interferences has practical consequences. It frames retention as an end-to-end governance problem: even where retention parameters are narrowed, deficient access safeguards can independently render a regime disproportionate

23 AG Cruz Villalón 12.12.2013 – Joined Cases C-293/12, ECLI:EU:C:2013:845 – Digital Rights Ireland.

24 ECJ 8.4.2014 – Joined Cases C-293/12 and C-594/12, ECLI:EU:C:2014:238 para. 54 – Digital Rights Ireland.

25 Liberty and Others v. the United Kingdom, 1 July 2008, no. 58243/00, § 62 and 63; *Rotaru v. Romania*, § 57 to 59, and *S. and Marper v. the United Kingdom*, § 99).

26 ECJ 8.4.2014 – Joined Cases C-293/12 and C-594/12, ECLI:EU:C:2014:238 para. 49–51 – Digital Rights Ireland.

27 ECJ 8.4.2014 – Joined Cases C-293/12 and C-594/12, ECLI:EU:C:2014:238 para. 52 – Digital Rights Ireland.

because access and use constitute a distinct interference requiring independent justification.[28] This bifurcation matters for both legislators and litigants. It ensures that access thresholds, prior authorisation, and oversight cannot be treated as secondary implementation detail once retention infrastructure is mandated at Union level.

Digital Rights Ireland also destabilises the orthodox content/metadata distinction. The Court held that traffic and location data permit 'very precise conclusions' about private life, including patterns of residence, movement, activity, social relationships, and the environments frequented.[29] Yet it treated the exclusion of content as decisive to its finding that the essence of Art. 7 CFR was not adversely affected,[30] and found the essence of Art. 8 CFR unaffected because the DRD contained certain data protection and security principles.[31] This internal tension continues to shape subsequent debates: the Court elevates metadata's constitutional importance while maintaining an 'essence' analysis that appears to privilege content.

The strictness of review announced in paras 47–48 operates as a constitutional constraint on the expansion of security measures through internal market harmonisation. Where protection of personal data plays an 'important role' and interference is extensive, legislative discretion is reduced and judicial review is strict.[32] This shifts responsibility upstream: EU framework legislation must embed safeguards at adoption, rather than relying on Member States to 'complete' rights compliance. In that sense, the judgment resonates, by analogy, with the Court's rule of law line in *Kadi* into ordinary legislative processes: legislative form and harmonisation competence do not insulate security measures from rights-based scrutiny.[33] By contrast in review methodology, the ECtHR in Big Brother Watch does not operationalise a Charter-style 'strict necessity' requirement as an ex

---

28 ECJ 8.4.2014 – Joined Cases C-293/12 and C-594/12, ECLI:EU:C:2014:238 para. 34 et seq., 60–62 – Digital Rights Ireland.

29 ECJ 8.4.2014 – Joined Cases C-293/12 and C-594/12, ECLI:EU:C:2014:238 para. 27 – Digital Rights Ireland.

30 ECJ 8.4.2014 – Joined Cases C-293/12 and C-594/12, ECLI:EU:C:2014:238 para. 39 – Digital Rights Ireland.

31 ECJ 8.4.2014 – Joined Cases C-293/12 and C-594/12, ECLI:EU:C:2014:238 para. 40 – Digital Rights Ireland.

32 ECJ 8.4.2014 – Joined Cases C-293/12 and C-594/12, ECLI:EU:C:2014:238 para. 48 – Digital Rights Ireland.

33 ECJ 3.9.2008 – Joined Cases C-402/05 P and C-415/05 P, ECLI:EU:C:2008:461 – Yassin Abdullah Kadi and Al Barakaat International Foundation v Council of the European Union and Commission of the European Communities.

ante constraint on legislative design; Strasbourg applies Art. 8(2) ECHR's 'necessary in a democratic society' test within a (wide but not unlimited) national security margin of appreciation, and assesses Convention compliance through a 'global assessment' of whether the domestic framework contains 'end-to-end safeguards', including independent authorisation at the outset.[34]

In *Digital Rights Ireland*, the Court's insistence on differentiation concerns the need for targeted and objectively delimited retention, rather than general and indiscriminate retention. The DRD failed because it applied to 'all persons' and all means of communication without any relationship to serious crime[35] and because it lacked objective criteria limiting retention by time periods, geographic zones, persons, or categories of data.[36] Subsequent jurisprudence operationalised and reiterated this logic (confirmed in Case C-746/18 ('*H.K. v. Prokuratuur*'),[37] Case C-140/20 ('*G.D. v Commissioner*'),[38] and Joined Cases C-793/19 and C-794/19 ('*SpaceNet/Telekom Deutschland*'),[39] and refined for civil identity and IP address access in Case C-470/21 ('*La Quadrature du Net II*')).[40] Joined Cases C-203/15 and C-698/15 ('*Tele2 Sverige/Watson*') precluded general and indiscriminate retention while permitting targeted retention linked to objective criteria and backed by minimum safeguards.[41] *La Quadrature du Net I* refined permissible categories, including time-limited general retention during a serious national security threat that is genuine and present or foreseeable, targeted retention using objective and non-discriminatory factors, expedited retention orders, and certain real-time retention or automated analysis

34 ECtHR 25.05.2021 – Big Brother Watch and Others v. the United Kingdom GC, nos. 58170/13, 62322/14 and 24960/15.

35 ECJ 8.4.2014 – Joined Cases C-293/12 and C-594/12, ECLI:EU:C:2014:238 para. 57–59 – Digital Rights Ireland.

36 ECJ 8.4.2014 – Joined Cases C-293/12 and C-594/12, ECLI:EU:C:2014:238 para. 59 et seq. – Digital Rights Ireland.

37 ECJ 2.3.2021 – case C-746/18, ECLI:EU:C:2021:152 – H.K. v Prokuratuur.

38 ECJ 5.4.2022 – case C-140/20, ECLI:EU:C:2022:258 – G.D. v Commissioner.

39 ECJ 20.10.2022 – Joined Cases C-793/19 and C-794/19, ECLI:EU:C:2022:702 – SpaceNet AG and Telekom Deutschland GmbH.

40 ECJ 30.4.2024 – case C-470/21, ECLI:EU:C:2020:791 – La Quadrature du Net and Others.

41 ECJ 21.12.2016 – Joined Cases C-203/15 and C-698/15, ECLI:EU:C:2016:970 – Tele2 Sverige AB v Post-och telestyrelsen and Secretary of State for the Home Department v Tom Watson.

under strict conditions.[42] That line also clarified that national security measures fall within EU law's scope where they impose obligations on providers governed by the ePrivacy Directive.

Implementation has, however, proven markedly fragmentary. The DRD's immediate invalidation removed the EU-wide framework yet left Member States uncertain whether transposition measures fell automatically or required case-by-case disapplication, producing divergent domestic pathways. After *La Quadrature du Net I*, Belgian review largely tracked Luxembourg's prohibition on generalised retention, whereas the French Conseil d'État sustained the core regime by invoking constant and genuine terrorist threats and adding national monitoring. A further pattern is tolerated non-compliance: Italy extended metadata retention to 72 months and treated public prosecutor authorisation as sufficient, while the Commission has largely adopted a wait-and-see posture.

The post-*Digital Rights Ireland* settlement remains contested in practice. Law enforcement authorities maintain that targeted retention cannot reliably detect emerging threats without access to comprehensive datasets, invoking a 'needle in a haystack' logic that treats general retention as a precondition for later differentiation. The Court's approach rejects that premise as sufficient justification: investigative usefulness cannot displace ex ante limitation, prior authorisation, and enforceable safeguards. In some senses, the ensuing case law is quasi-legislative, in that it develops an increasingly detailed taxonomy of permissible retention modalities and accompanying conditions—an architecture that may complicate legislative reset efforts and encourage selective national adaptation rather than harmonisation and uniform compliance.

V. Recommended further reading

Academic Articles

Lynskey Common Market Law Review (2014) 51(6), 1789–1812.
Guild/Carrera CEPS Papers in Liberty and Security in Europe No. 65, May 2014.
Granger/Irion European Law Review (2014) 39(6), 835–850.

42 ECJ 6.10.2020 – Joined Cases C-511/18, C-512/18 and C-520/18, ECLI:EU:C:2020:791 – La Quadrature du Net and Others.

Follow-Up ECJ Decisions

ECJ 21.12.2016 – Joined Cases C-203/15 and C-698/15, ECLI:EU:C:2016:970 – Tele2 Sverige AB v Post-och telestyrelsen and Secretary of State for the Home Department v Tom Watson.

ECJ 2.3.2021 – case C-746/18, ECLI:EU:C:2021:152 – H.K. v Prokuratuur.

ECJ 6.10.2020 – Joined Cases C-511/18, C-512/18 and C-520/18, ECLI:EU:C:2020:791 – La Quadrature du Net and Others.

Purpose of the regulation

Marek Steffen Jansen

ECJ 6.11.2003 – case C-101/01, ECLI:EU:C:2003:596 – Lindqvist

I. Case summary

In 2003, the ECJ delivered its judgment in Case C-101/01 (Lindqvist)[1] concerning the interpretation of the DPD. The case arose in criminal proceedings pending before a Swedish court against Ms *Lindqvist*, who had published personal information on her private website concerning eighteen fellow volunteers in a parish of the Church of Sweden. The website, intended to provide information for confirmation candidates, included names, details about family circumstances and telephone numbers, and humorous descriptions of colleagues' activities. In one instance, she mentioned that a colleague was on sick leave due to a foot injury.

Ms *Lindqvist* neither notified the Swedish Data Protection Authority nor informed the individuals concerned. After objections were raised, she removed the website. Nevertheless, criminal proceedings were initiated, and she was fined for having infringed the Swedish Personal Data Act implementing the DPD. She appealed, arguing that she had not committed a criminal offence. Since the court of first instance had doubts as to the interpretation of the applicable Community law it stayed the proceedings and referred several questions to the ECJ for a preliminary ruling.

II. Key legal findings

The ECJ interpreted the DPD broadly, emphasising its objective of ensuring both a high level of protection of fundamental rights and the free movement of personal data.

1 ECJ 6.11.2003 – case C-101/01 – ECLI:EU:C:2003:596 – Lindqvist.

Hence, it held that placing personal information on a website constitutes 'processing of personal data' within the meaning of Art. 2 and 3(1) DPD.[2] Uploading data to a server and making it accessible online necessarily involves at least partly automated processing.

Also, the ECJ rejected the applicability of the exemptions in Art. 3(2) DPD.[3] Publishing personal data on a publicly accessible website does not qualify as a purely personal or household activity. The household exemption must be interpreted narrowly and does not extend to disclosures directed at an indefinite number of persons.[4]

Furthermore, the ECJ construed 'data concerning health' under Art. 8(1) DPD broadly. Information that a person had injured her foot and was partially on sick leave constituted sensitive data, reflecting the Directive's protective rationale.[5]

The ECJ also clarified that making personal data accessible online does not amount to a 'transfer to a third country' within the meaning of Art. 25 DPD. A transfer requires an active transmission of data to a recipient in a third country; mere internet accessibility is insufficient.[6]

Finally, the ECJ held that the Directive does not infringe freedom of expression (Art. 10 ECHR).[7] Rather, it establishes a framework requiring national authorities and courts to ensure a fair balance between data protection and other fundamental rights, guided by proportionality and the Directive's overarching objective of reconciling privacy protection with the functioning of the internal market.[8]

III. Systematic context and legal classification

The decision is particularly relevant for the interpretation of the abovementioned aspects of the case. However, in its broader systematic context,

2 The ECJ states in his first headnote that ‚*the act of referring, on an internet page, to various persons and identifying them by name or by other means, for instance by giving their telephone number or information regarding their working conditions and hobbies, constitutes 'the processing of personal data*‘, ECJ 6.11.2003 – case C-101/01 – ECLI:EU:C:2003:596 para.48 – Lindqvist, I.

3 ECJ 6.11.2003 – case C-101/01 – ECLI:EU:C:2003:596 2nd headnote – Lindqvist.

4 ECJ 6.11.2003 – case C-101/01 – ECLI:EU:C:2003:596 para. 44 – Lindqvist, I.

5 ECJ 6.11.2003 – case C-101/01 – ECLI:EU:C:2003:596 3rd headnote – Lindqvist.

6 ECJ 6.11.2003 – case C-101/01 – ECLI:EU:C:2003:596 4th headnote, para. 71 – Lindqvist.

7 ECJ 6.11.2003 – case C-101/01 – ECLI:EU:C:2003:596 para. 90 – Lindqvist.

8 See Duller/Gritsch CR 7/2021, 465.

Lindqvist marks an early and significant step in the development of European data protection law.

Although decided under the DPD, the judgment articulates a structural understanding of data protection that can be seen as an anticipation of the logic later codified in Art. 1 GDPR.[9] The fundamental principle addressed is the structural orientation of EU data protection toward safeguarding individuals in conditions of expanding digital communication.[10] By interpreting 'processing'[11] broadly and the household exemption narrowly, the ECJ confirmed that the applicability of data protection law is triggered by an objective fact (here: processing) irrespective of (commercial) intent or technological complexity. It reflects a preventive regulatory orientation, where data protection law is triggered by the structural potential of processing operations to affect individual autonomy.[12] This anticipates the GDPR's risk-based architecture: data protection regulates the conditions under which risks arising from processing become controllable through technical and organisational safeguards.[13]

At the same time, the judgment rejects an absolutist conception of data protection. The DPD is compatible with the freedom of expression and requires contextual balancing. Significantly, the ECJ did not itself perform that balancing, but emphasised that national authorities and courts must ensure a fair balance, which reflects the pre-Charter constitutional setting of the DPD.

9 Kühling/Buchner DS-GVO BDSG/Buchner, 4th edn. 2024, DS-GVO Art. 1 mn. 2 stating that, with respect to its subject matter and objectives, the DPD was seamlessly carried forward by the GDPR, both in its commitment to safeguarding the protection of natural persons in the processing of personal data and in its prohibition of obstacles to the free movement of such data within the Union.

10 See also the term ‚*digital vulnerability*', Kroschwald ZfDR 2023, 1.

11 For the doctrinal analysis of data processing as a fundamental rights interference, see Roßnager NJW 2019, 1.

12 Paal/Pauly DS-GVO BDSG/Ernst, 4th edn. 2026, DS-GVO Art. 1 mn. 9; Sydow/Marsch DS-GVO – BDSG/Sydow, 3rd edn. 2022, DS-GVO Art. 1 mn. 11 stating that ‚The right to privacy is, to a considerable extent, replaced by the right to the protection of personal data.'; on the differing traditions of data protection and privacy in Europe and the United States, see Whitman The Yale Law Journal 2004, 1151.

13 On obligatory preventive measures aimed at avoiding data protection infringements including the implementation of appropriate technical and organisational measures, as well as data protection by design and by default see Schwartmann/Benedikt/Reif Datenschutz im Internet/Hansen/Felber, 2025, Chapter 17 mn. 104, 105.

Since the entry into force of the Treaty of Lisbon[14], the constitutional framework has changed.[15] Art. 16 TFEU establishes an explicit Union competence for data protection and Art. 8 CFR recognises it as a distinct fundamental right.[16] Under the GDPR and subsequent Charter-based jurisprudence, the ECJ has a central role in defining the parameters of proportionality. The reconciliation of Art. 7 and 8 CFR with competing rights is now structured within a Union-level constitutional framework grounded in Art. 52(1) CFR.[17]

The transition from Directive to Regulation reflects the shift to full harmonisation. Art. 1 GDPR therefore operates not merely as a descriptive purpose clause but as a system-directing provision anchoring the Regulation in primary Union law.[18] The guarantee of free movement of data under Art. 1(3) GDPR aims to prevent fragmentation by precluding divergent national standards.[19] Substantively, the case lasting significance lies in prefiguring the structural elements later codified in Art. 1(1)-(3) GDPR: broad applicability as an expression of rights protection, contextual balancing as a non-absolutist constraint, and sensitivity to market integration through harmonised standards.

---

14 Treaty of Lisbon amending the Treaty on European Union and the Treaty establishing the European Community, signed at Lisbon, 13 December 2007, OJ C 306, 17.12.2007, p. 1, ELI: http://data.europa.eu/eli/treaty/lis/sign.

15 Gola/Heckmann DS-GVO – BDSG/Pötters, 3rd edn. 2022, DS-GVO Art. 1 mn. 3.

16 Paal/Pauly/Ernst DS-GVO Art. 1 mn. 6.

17 Among the fundamental rights that may come into conflict with the right to data protection are, in particular, the freedom of expression and information reflected in Art. 85 GDPR (Art. 11 CFR), the freedom of scientific research (Article 13 CFR), and the freedom to conduct a business (Art. 16 CFR), see Kühling/Buchner/Buchner DS-GVO Art. 1 mn. 15, 16.

18 See Simitis/Hornung/Spiecker gen. Döhmann Datenschutzrecht/Hornung/Spiecker gen. Döhmann, 2nd edn. 2025, DS-GVO Art. 1 mn. 1; in the view of the European legislator, the objective of the DPD is i.a. to remove obstacles to the free movement of data by establishing an equivalent level of data protection had not been achieved which from their point of view led to the need for a regulation which is, pursuant to Article 288(2) TFEU, binding in its entirety and directly applicable in all Member States of the EU, see Kühling/Buchner/Buchner DS-GVO Art. 1 mn. 4.

19 Kühling/Buchner/Buchner DS-GVO Art. 1 mn. 1.

IV. Author's analysis and commentary

From today's perspective, the case is significant because it marked one of the ECJ's first attempts to define the scope of EU data protection law in a new digital environment. As the Internet once required a clarification of the DPD's normative application, emerging technologies with AI-driven and data-intensive processing now raise new structural questions concerning the constitutional purpose expressed in Art. 1 GDPR,[20] namely the balance between fundamental rights protection and the conditions of technological and societal development.[21]

Art. 1 GDPR defines the subject matter and objectives of the regulation as laying down rules on the protection of natural persons with regard to the processing of personal data and on the free movement of such data within the Union[22] – as a constitutional purpose clause and guiding norm.[23] It articulates the regulation's purpose as a dual commitment: the protection of the right to data protection as a fundamental right, and the safeguarding of the free movement of personal data within the Union.[24] These objectives are not antagonistic.[25] Uniform protection is presented as the structural precondition for unobstructed data flows.[26] Art. 1 GDPR reflects a dignity-based autonomy rationale: data protection safeguards the institutional conditions under which individuals can participate in social

---

20 Reichert/Radtke/Eske ZD 2024, 483.

21 See Hoffmann-Riem JuS 2023, 617 regarding the legal implication of the ‚*digital transformation*'; Wybitul/Brink NJW 2025, 2953; on the consolidation of information per se as an economic good and its legal conceptualisation, see Jansen, Der Nachrichtenmarkt in der Industriellen Revolution, 2022, 1.

22 Schantz NJW 2016, 1841 (1842), pointing out that the establishment of a uniform data protection regime was designed to create a level playing field for all market participants within the European internal market.

23 Kühling/Buchner/Buchner Art. 1 mn. 1. referring to Rec. 6 and 7 GDPR, it is recognised that rapid technological progress and globalisation are accompanied by expanding data flows, which in turn reshape both society and the economy.

24 See Streinz/Michl EuZW 2011, 384 (387).

25 Spindler/Schuster/Kaesling Recht der elektronischen Medien/Dalby, 5th edn. 2026, DS-GVO Art. 1 mn. 1; Kühling/Buchner/Buchner Art. 1 mn. 1; some voices argue that there is a priority relationship in favour of the protection of natural persons in the processing of personal data, see Sánchez-Bordona GRUR-RS 2022, 26562 Fn. 34.

26 Whether the GDPR had, in comparison to the DPD, generated a higher level of harmonisation in European data protection law is subject to debate, i.a. because of the GDPR's numerous opening clauses, see Kühling/Martini EuZW 2016, 448 (449); Roßnagel DuD 2017, 290 (291).

and economic life without being subjected to uncontrolled or opaque data processing.

This human-centred orientation is increasingly tested by emerging technologies and data-driven environments.[27] Lindqvist reflects a publication model of informational power based on visibility and dissemination: identifiable individuals are made accessible to an indefinite audience on the internet. With contemporary AI systems the regulatory focus shifts from governing communicative exposure to addressing probabilistic assessment and lifecycle-based accountability.[28]

The question, therefore, is how the constitutional function of Art. 1 GDPR evolves within an increasingly layered system of European digital governance. Data protection has become a central reference framework in this landscape, yet perceived tensions with innovation stem from the operationalisation of its open-textured principles.[29] The GDPR's risk-based and principle-oriented architecture provides considerable flexibility;[30] difficulties arise where uncertainty is treated as prohibition rather than as a space for responsible risk governance.[31]

At the same time, the GDPR operates alongside a growing body of parallel Union data legislation,[32] such as the AI Act and the DA,[33] reflecting distinct regulatory rationalities centred around risk management, interoperability and data access.[34] Governance actors must operationalise a constitutional purpose clause in environments that reward rapid technological deployment and data maximisation.[35] Each data regulation regime operates

27 Spindler/Schuster/Kaesling Recht der elektronischen Medien/Dalby, 5th edn. 2026, DS-GVO Art. 1 mn. 3.

28 Schwartmann EuDIR 2026, 3.

29 Simitis/Hornung/Spiecker gen. Döhmann/Hornung/Spiecker gen. Döhmann DS-GVO Art. 1 mn. 7 stating that the aspiration to establish a comprehensive data protection framework goes too far since the aim of regulating all processing operations relating to personal data can only be realised through a differentiated regulatory response oriented towards the particular nature of the processing in question.

30 See Veil ZD 2025, 347.

31 See Engeler NJW 2022, 3398.

32 Spindler/Schuster/Kaesling Recht der elektronischen Medien/Dalby DS-GVO Art. 1 mn. 3 naming i.a. the EU DA, DSA, the DMA and the DGA; Pfeiffer/Helmke MMR 2025, 561.

33 Dose, MMR 2025, 591.

34 Baumgartner/Paal NJW 2016, 1; Schröder, Datenschutzrecht für die Praxis, 6th edn. 2026, 267; Ehmann/Selmayr Datenschutz-Grundverordnung/Zerdick, 3rd edn. 2024, DS-GVO Art. 1 mn. 8.

35 Hüger/Radtke KIR 2025, 154.

with distinct trigger concepts yet in practice they converge on the same technological infrastructures.[36] The operationalisation of Art. 1 GDPR's dual objective in combination with the principles laid out in Art. 5 GDPR must therefore occur within a layered governance environment in which rights protection, risk regulation and market design intersect.[37]

Lindqvist may be understood as an early articulation of a value structure that later finds explicit codification in Art. 1 GDPR. The emergence of innovation-oriented, risk-based and access-driven regulatory instruments does not displace this constitutional framework, but reshapes the conditions under which it operates. Fundamental rights protection, innovation enablement, and market integration objectives coexist within the same regulatory ecosystem.[38] The challenge is the preventive and autonomy-protective logic of Art. 1 GDPR that must be translated into governance structures capable of integrating system-based risk regulation with processing-based rights protection.The enduring task for courts, legislators and governance actors is to ensure that the structured concordance between fundamental rights protection and data circulation articulated in Art. 1 GDPR remains effective in an era of rapid technological development with growing and systemic AI deployment.[39]

V. Recommended further reading

Laue/Nink/Kremer, European Data Protection Law in Practice, 2025.

Lynskey, The Foundations of EU Data Protection Law, 2016.

Rössler, Der Wert des Privaten, 2021.

Schiedermair, Der Schutz des Privaten als internationales Grundrecht, 2012.

Solove, Understanding Privacy, 2010.

v. Lewinski, Die Matrix des Datenschutzes, 2014.

Zech, Information als Schutzgegenstand, 2012.

---

36 Kindshofer ZD 2024, 673.

37 Given the systematic understanding of data protection law as technology law, assessments under uncertainty must be informed by a precaution-oriented reading of potential future developments, see Simitis/Hornung/Spiecker gen. Döhmann/Hornung/Spiecker gen. Döhmann DS-GVO Art. 1 mn. 2.

38 von Grafenstein/Schmitz ZD 2025, 607.

39 See Heberlein DVBl 2020, 1225; Specht-Riemenschneider ZEuP 2023, 638; Wunner ZUM 2025, 834.

Applicability of the GDPR (Material and Territorial Scope)

Axel Spies

ECJ 24.9.2019 – case C-507/17, ECLI:EU:C:2019:772 – Google LLC, successor in law to Google Inc. v. Commission nationale de l'informatique et des libertés (CNIL)

I. Case summary

The ECJ's judgment of 24 September 2019 in Case C-507/17 constitutes a milestone in defining the scope of European data protection law. It addresses the territorial reach of the so-called 'right to be forgotten,' which had previously been developed in the Google Spain judgment (C-131/12).[1] The case arose from a dispute between the French data protection supervisory authority, the CNIL, and Google LLC. The CNIL had ordered the company, in relation to certain search results containing personal data, to remove the relevant links on a worldwide basis.

The company refused to carry out a global deletion and instead limited the removal to the European domain versions of the search engine. In addition, it implemented geo-blocking measures designed to make access from within the EU to delisted search results via non-EU domains more difficult. On the ground that these measures were insufficient, the CNIL imposed a fine of EUR 100,000. The company challenged that decision before the courts, whereupon the French Conseil d'État referred to the ECJ the decisive question of whether EU law gives rise to an obligation to carry out worldwide de-referencing.[2]

At the centre of the ECJ's decision in Case C-507/17[3] was Art. 3 GDPR, which defines the territorial scope of application of the GDPR. Pursuant to Art. 3(1) GDPR, the GDPR applies to all processing of personal data

1 ECJ 13.5.2014 – C-131/12, ECLI:EU:C:2014:317 – Google Spain SL und Google Inc.

2 Conseil d'État, 10ème – 9ème chambres réunies, 19/07/2017, 399922.

3 ECJ 24.9.2019 – case C-507/17, ECLI:EU:C:2019:772 para. 64 et seqq.– Google LLC, successor in law to Google Inc. v. Commission nationale de l'informatique et des libertés (CNIL).

carried out in the context of the activities of an establishment in the EU. Under Art. 3(2) GDPR, it also applies to controllers outside the EU insofar as they process data of individuals in the EU in order to offer them goods or services or to monitor their behaviour. This provision forms the basis for the territorial reach of European data protection law beyond the borders of the EU.

II. Key legal findings

In its judgment, the ECJ first clarified that the GDPR does not give rise to an obligation of worldwide de-referencing.[4] While the global removal of personal data would be technically feasible and, from a data protection perspective, desirable, EU law requires a balancing exercise with the freedom of expression and information (Art. 11 CFR) as well as with the sovereignty of other states.[4] The GDPR pursues the objective of ensuring a high level of data protection within the Union, but not of establishing a worldwide data protection standard.[5]

The ECJ therefore held that search engine operators are required to limit de-referencing to the EU versions of their search engine.[6] At the same time, they must adopt technical measures to ensure that users within the Union are 'reliably prevented'[7] from accessing the delisted results via non-EU versions. Such measures may, for example, consist of geo-blocking or IP-based filtering.

The ECJ further emphasised that data protection as a fundamental right is not absolute, but must be interpreted in the light of the principle of proportionality and balanced against other fundamental rights.[8] The right

4 ECJ 24.9.2019 – case C-507/17, ECLI:EU:C:2019:772 para. 66 et seq.– Google LLC, successor in law to Google Inc. v. Commission nationale de l'informatique et des libertés (CNIL).

5 ECJ 24.9.2019 – case C-507/17, ECLI:EU:C:2019:772 para. 60, 68 et seq.– Google LLC, successor in law to Google Inc. v. Commission nationale de l'informatique et des libertés (CNIL).

6 ECJ 24.9.2019 – case C-507/17, ECLI:EU:C:2019:772 para. 64 et seq.– Google LLC, successor in law to Google Inc. v. Commission nationale de l'informatique et des libertés (CNIL).

7 ECJ 24.9.2019 – case C-507/17, ECLI:EU:C:2019:772 para. 70 – Google LLC, successor in law to Google Inc. v. Commission nationale de l'informatique et des libertés (CNIL).

8 ECJ 24.9.2019 – case C-507/17, ECLI:EU:C:2019:772 para. 72 – Google LLC, successor in law to Google Inc. v. Commission nationale de l'informatique et des libertés (CNIL).

to be forgotten must always be weighed against the public's interest in information, in particular where persons in public life are concerned.[9] That balancing exercise may be struck differently in other legal orders—such as those of the United States or Canada—so that EU law does not require a global obligation to delete.[10]

A further aspect of the judgment concerns cooperation between supervisory authorities. According to the ECJ, the cooperation and consistency mechanism enshrined in the GDPR (Articles 56 et seq. GDPR) ensures a coordinated application of the rules across the Union. Outside the Union, however, no comparable mechanisms exist. The ECJ therefore points out that, in exceptional cases, national supervisory authorities may order more far-reaching measures:

> Accordingly, a supervisory or judicial authority of a Member State remains competent to weigh up, in the light of national standards of protection of fundamental rights (...), a data subject's right to privacy and the protection of personal data concerning him or her, on the one hand, and the right to freedom of information, on the other, and, after weighing those rights against each other, to order, where appropriate, the operator of that search engine to carry out a de-referencing concerning all versions of that search engine.[11]

While EU law contains an autonomous obligation to de-list in the form of Art. 17(1) GDPR, it does not preclude more extensive de-listing obligations laid down in the law of a Member State beyond Art. 17 GDPR from being compatible with EU law.[12]

9 Ukrow, analysis of ECJ decision C-507/17 at ZD 2020, 35.

10 ECJ 24.9.2019 – case C-507/17, ECLI:EU:C:2019:772 paras. 60 and 73 – Google LLC, successor in law to Google Inc. v. Commission nationale de l'informatique et des libertés (CNIL).

11 ECJ 24.9.2019 – case C-507/17, ECLI:EU:C:2019:772 para. 72 – Google LLC, successor in law to Google Inc. v. Commission nationale de l'informatique et des libertés (CNIL).

12 Ukrow ZD 2020, 35.

III. Systematic context and legal classification

The judgment in Case C-507/17 had significant implications for data protection practice under EU law.[13] At the same time, the ECJ delivered its ruling in Case C-136/17 (GC and Others v CNIL), which concerned the handling of sensitive personal data. In that case as well, the Court confirmed the principle that the reach of European data protection law is linked to territorial jurisdiction.

The ECJ's judgment was also relied upon as a reference point in German case law. One example is the decision of the Federal Court of Justice (Bundesgerichtshof, BGH) concerning the conditions for a claim to de-listing against the controller of an internet search service under Art. 17 GDPR (VI ZR 405/18). In that judgment, the BGH specified and further concretised the EU-law standards developed in the ECJ's case law.[14] The fact that the search engine is operated by an undertaking established in a third country does not, in the BGH's view, mean that the processing of personal data carried out for the operation of the search engine in the context of the commercial and advertising activities of an establishment of the controller within the territory of a Member State is removed from the guarantees and obligations of the GDPR.[15]

The European Data Protection Board (EDPB) took up the core findings of the judgment in its (legally non-binding) Guidelines on Art. 17 GDPR ('Right to erasure').[16] The Guidelines set out the criteria for assessing requests for erasure under Art. 17 GDPR and require a balancing of the rights of the data subject against the public interest in access to the information. Accordingly, para. 10 of the Guidelines states:

> [...] search engine providers are not exempt in a general manner from the duty to fully erase. In some exceptional cases, they will need to carry out actual and full erasure in their indexes or caches. For example, in the event that search engine providers would stop respecting robots.txt requests implemented by the original publisher, they would actually have

13 ECJ 24.9.2019 – C-136/17, ECLI:EU:C:2019:773 – GC u. a. / CNIL.

14 BGH 27.7.2020 – VI ZR 405/18, NJW 2020, 3436.

15 BGH 27.7.2020 – VI ZR 405/18, NJW 2020, 3436 mn. 37.

16 EDPB, ‚Guidelines 5/2019 on the criteria of the Right to be Forgotten in the search engines cases under the GDPR (part 1)‘ version 2.0 (7.7.2020) <https://www.edpb.europa.eu/our-work-tools/our-documents/guidelines/guidelines-52019-criteria-right-be-forgotten-search-engines_en>.

a duty to fully erase the URL to the content, as opposed to delist which is mainly based on data subject's name.

IV. Author's analysis and commentary

For globally operating companies, the case law cited above implies that they must develop differentiated data protection strategies. The GDPR applies within the framework of Art. 3 GDPR and the so-called market location principle, whereas outside Europe other laws and judicial interpretations may apply. In the United States, this legal conflict is particularly difficult to resolve—especially as regards the compatibility of EU erasure obligations under Art. 17 GDPR with US principles of freedom of expression, notably 'commercial speech'.[17]

US courts have so far classified search engine results, including their ranking algorithms, as protected expression within the meaning of the First Amendment, in some instances even as a form of protected 'editorial judgment' rather than merely 'commercial speech'. This classification affords search engines a higher level of constitutional protection than typical commercial speech, which is subject only to intermediate scrutiny.

One illustration is the decision in e-ventures Worldwide, LLC v Google, Inc.[18] In 2017, the US court held that the results of an internet search engine constitute a form of expression protected by the First Amendment. Google's decision to remove the websites of e-ventures was likened by the judges to a newspaper editor's decision as to which content to publish:

> [T]he First Amendment protects as speech the results produced by an Internet search engine. (...). A search engine is akin to a publisher, whose judgments about what to publish and what not to publish are absolutely protected by the First Amendment.[19]

For practice, the ECJ's judgment entails far-reaching implications. Search engine operators must ensure that de-referencing is implemented across the Union and that access from within the EU to delisted content via non-EU

17 Spies ZD 2011, 12 with further references on the differing US and European approaches to privacy. In *Sorrell v. IMS Health*, Inc., 564 U.S. 552 (2011), the US Supreme Court held, for instance, that data mining for marketing purposes is a form of commercial speech protected by the First Amendment.

18 Case Nr. 2:14-cv-646, 2017 WL 2210029 (M.D. Fla., 8.2.2017).

19 Case Nr. 2:14-cv-646, 2017 WL 2210029 (M.D. Fla., 8.2.2017), p. 8.

versions is effectively prevented. This requires technical measures such as geo-blocking or the use of IP-based filters. They must closely integrate data protection compliance, technical implementation, and documentation obligations.

Practice shows that search engine operators increasingly rely on geo-blocking, IP filtering, and content segmentation to comply with obligations under EU law. For this purpose, companies must assess whether the technical measures adopted sufficiently restrict access from within the EU. These issues may also become relevant in contractual negotiations between companies and processors, or with customers of search engine operators.

From an EU perspective, the ECJ's decision in Case C-507/17 illustrates the balance between effective data protection and freedom of information. It limits the scope of the right to be forgotten to the territory of the European Union while at the same time strengthening the coherence of European data protection law. The Court deliberately opted for a restrained, territorially limited solution that respects the Charter of Fundamental Rights and avoids conflicts with third states.

At the same time, such measures do not prevent internet users from republishing the data online, which may result in new links appearing in search engine results that resemble those previously removed following a request for de-referencing. For this reason, a single request for the removal of links, even if granted at the European level and combined with geo-blocking measures, may not be sufficient to ensure effective protection of the data subject's right to privacy. How the tension between the US approach and the case law of the ECJ will affect AI algorithms and the deletion of information within AI systems remains to be seen.

Applicability of the GDPR to national parliaments

Bernd Grzeszick

ECJ 16.1.2024 – case C-33/22, ECLI:EU:C:2024:46 – Österreichische Datenschutzbehörde

I. Case summary

The Austrian National Council had set up a committee of inquiry tasked with shedding light on whether there was any political influence on the Federal Office for the Protection of the Constitution and for Counterterrorism. The committee heard an undercover investigator as a witness. Despite the investigator's request for anonymisation, the minutes of that hearing which contained his complete name were published. He lodged a complaint with the Austrian Data Protection Authority (Österreichische Datenschutzbehörde) in which he claimed that the publication infringed his right to the protection of personal data. The authority rejected the complaint arguing that the principle of the separation of powers precludes the legislator to be subject to scrutiny by the executive. The court hearing the appeal, however, held the GDPR for applicable to committees of inquiry. The Supreme Administrative Court (Verwaltungsgerichtshof), which was called upon by the data protection authority, referred the matter to the ECJ for a preliminary ruling.

II. Key legal findings

1. The GDPR applies in principle to national parliaments

In its judgement the ECJ held that the GDPR applies to national parliaments. Art. 2(1) GDPR in accordance with Art. 16(2) TFEU gives a very broad definition of the material scope of the GDPR. Neither the fact that the subject matter is the activity of a committee of inquiry set up by the parliament of a Member State in the exercise of its right to scrutinize the executive nor the fact that this committee can be directly attributed to the parliament, does preclude the applicability of the GDPR.

2. Exceptions must be interpreted strictly

According to the ECJ, the exception provided for in Art. 2(2)(a) GDPR must be interpreted strictly. It is designed solely to exclude the processing of personal data carried out by state authorities in the course of an activity which is intended to safeguard national security or of an activity which can be classified in the same category. The activity must be intended to protect essential state functions and the fundamental interests of society.

Indeed, the committee had the purpose of investigating whether there was any political influence over the Federal Office for the Protection of the Constitution and for Counterterrorism. However, in the opinion of the ECJ, this investigation alone, does not constitute an activity that safeguards the national security within the meaning of the exception. Rather, it must be examined whether the specific activity of the committee is excluded from the scope of the GDPR.

3. Legislator is able to establish more than one supervisory authority

Under the GDPR, every person has the right to lodge a complaint with a supervisory authority. In Austria, the Austrian Data Protection Authority is the only supervisory authority, which is therefore also competent for complaints from the parliamentary sphere. However, the Austrian legislator is able to establish more than one supervisory authority; the GDPR grants Member States a margin of discretion in this regard.

III. Systematic context and legal classification

With this ruling, the ECJ clarifies the question of whether national parliaments are subject to the GDPR. Opinions on this range from the full applicability of the GDPR[1] to the exclusion of the core areas of political and

1 Kosmider/Wolff ZG 2020, 190 et seqq.

parliamentary activity[2] to the complete inapplicability of the GDPR to the processing of personal data by members of parliament.[3]

The ECJ ruled on these issues for the first time in 2020 and considered the Petitions Committee of the Hessian State Parliament to be a controller within the meaning of Art. 4 no. 7 GDPR, against whom data subjects may assert their rights to information.[4] The decision was strongly criticized in the literature.[5]

Nevertheless, in its ruling on the Austrian Data Protection Authority, the ECJ confirms this decision and applies its principles to the Austrian parliament's committee of inquiry. In principle, the ECJ extends the scope of the GDPR to parliamentary activities. Political and parliamentary activities of members of parliament and parliamentary groups now fall within the scope of the GDPR.

IV. Author's analysis and commentary

1. Political and parliamentary activity falls within the competence of the Member States

The position of the ECJ does not convince. The GDPR does not apply to the core area of political and parliamentary activity, as this area falls within the competence of the Member States. According to the principle of conferred powers, the GDPR can only regulate activities that fall within the competence of the Union. Under Art. 2(2)(a) GDPR, the GDPR is therefore only applicable to activities which fall within the scope of Union law.[6] Accordingly, the GDPR only applies to parliamentary activities that are part of general commercial legal transactions. Data protection law in the core area of parliamentary and political activity, on the other hand, is subject

2 Grzeszick NVwZ 2018, 1505 (1508); Reimer, Verwaltungsdatenschutzrecht, 2019, mn. 45; Schwartmann/Grzeszick RDV 2020, 75 (76 et seq).

3 Schröder ZRP 2018, 129 (130); Auernhammer DSGVO/BDSG/v. Lewinski, 8. edition 2023, Art. 2 DSGVO mn. 18.

4 ECJ 9.7.2020 – case C-272/19, ECLI: EU:C:2020:535 – Land Hessen.

5 Grzeszick/Schwartmann/Mühlenbeck NVwZ 2020, 1491 et seqq.; Engelbrecht ZD 2020, 579; Hilbert NVwZ 2021, 1173.

6 Auernhammer/v. Lewinski DS-GVO Art. 2 mn. 3.

to national law and must be designed in accordance with constitutional requirements.[7]

The argument that the content of parliamentary legislation often must comply with Union law, and that therefore nothing else can apply to the procedure,[8] does not hold water. One must distinct between procedure and substantive obligations.[9] This distinction also shapes the distribution of competences between Member States and the Union. Union law must be observed and enforced by Member States within the framework of their competences and procedures. Enforcement by institutions of the Union must be expressly provided for in Union law, which requires a delegation of powers to the Union.

It is true that, together with the subject-matter competence, the regulation of the procedure can also be transferred to the competence of the Union. However, this has not been done for the organisation of the parliaments of the Member States. The primary law does not contain any specific provisions for the political and parliamentary activities of members of parliament.[10] Rather, in accordance with Art. 4(2) sent. 1 TEU, the Union respects the national identities of the Member States, inherent in their fundamental structures, political and constitutional.

2. Possible Reactions of the legislator

Since the ECJ has confirmed its contrary position with this ruling, the question arises how to deal with this case law in furtherance.[11]

On the one hand, the legislator could make data protection more restrictive in matters of national security. However, the exception to the scope of the GDPR for activities serving national security, as regulated in Art. 2(2)(a) GDPR, is interpreted strictly, which limits the options available to the legislator.

On the other hand, there is the option of a differentiated supervisory structure. The special characteristics of data protection in the parliamentary sphere can be addressed by establishing a sectoral supervisory authority

7 Schröder ZRP 2018, 129 (131); Schwartmann/Pabst LDSG NRW/Pabst, 2020, LDSG NRW § 5 mn. 35.

8 Kosmider/Wolff ZG 2020, 190 et seqq. with reference to the proceedings in 196, 200.

9 Schwartmann/Pabst/Pabst LDSG NRW § 5 mn. 32.

10 Grzeszick NVwZ 2018, 1505 (1508).

11 Grzeszick/Schwartmann NVwZ 2022, 122 et seqq.

specifically for this area. The processing of personal data in parliament can be subject to supervision by a commission composed of multiple members of parliament and operating independently. The specific constitutional characteristics of parliamentary operations can then be taken into account in the detailed design of data protection.

V. Recommended further reading

ECJ 9.7.2020 – case C-272/19, ECLI: EU:C:2020:535 – Land Hessen.
Kosmider/Wolff ZG 2020, 190 et seqq.
Grzeszick/Schwartmann NVwZ 2022, 122 et seqq.

Chapter 2:
Core Concepts of the GDPR

The Identifiability of the Data Subject

Per Meyerdierks

ECJ 6.12.2016 – case C-582/14, ECLI:EU:C:2016:779 – Patrick Breyer v Bundesrepublik Deutschland

I. Case summary

German digital activist Patrick Breyer challenged the Federal Republic of Germany regarding the retention of IP addresses following his visits to state-operated websites.

The litigation made its way through the German judicial system until it reached the Federal Court of Justice (BGH), which referred the following two questions to the ECJ for a preliminary ruling:[1]

1. Must Article 2(a) of [the DPD] be interpreted as meaning that an internet protocol address (IP address) stored by a service provider in connection with access to its website constitutes personal data for that service provider even if a third party (here: the access provider) possesses the additional knowledge required in order to identify the data subject?
2. Does Article 7(f) of the DPD preclude a provision of national law under which a service provider may collect and use a user's personal data without their consent only to the extent necessary in order to facilitate and bill for the specific use of the telemedium by the respective user, and under which the purpose of ensuring the general operability of the telemedium cannot justify use of the data beyond the end of the particular use of the telemedium?

1 BGH 28.10.2014 – VI ZR 135/13, MMR 2015, 131.

II. Key legal findings

While focussed on dynamic IP addresses, the ECJ's deliberations on the first question yielded three key findings possessing universal relevance for assessing identifiability under Art. 2(a) DPD:

1. Identifying information can be distributed: It is not required that all the information enabling the identification of the data subject resides in the hands of one party. It may be sufficient for identifiability if additional information required for identification is held by a third party.[2]
2. Identification risks can be negligible: If the risk of identifying a person is insignificant in reality, the person is not considered identifiable. This is the case, for example, if identification is prohibited by law or practically impossible because of a disproportionate effort in terms of time, cost and man-power.[3]
3. Legal means can give rise to identifiability: Identifiability is given in relation to a party if that party has legal means which enable it to obtain additional data required to identify the data subject which is held by a third party.[4]

The ECJ based the first finding on a straightforward reading of Rec. 26 of the DPD, which states that means used 'either by the controller or by any other person to identify the said person' must be taken into account, when examining identifiability.

However, the second key finding represented a genuine novelty by sharpening the contours to the concept of 'means reasonably likely to be used' in Rec. 26 DPD. The court clarified that the mere theoretical possibility of identifying the person is insufficient to assume identifiability. If the risk of identifiability is insignificant in reality, then according to the ECJ, the risk is negligible and there is no personal data. The court anchored this with two examples of negligible risk: where identification is legally prohibited or where the effort required is disproportionate.

The third finding – which is often cited as the judgement's core, as its essence is repeated in the operative part of the ruling as the answer to the

2 ECJ 6.12.2016 – case C-582/14, ECLI:EU:C:2016:779 para. 41 et seqq. – Patrick Breyer v Bundesrepublik Deutschland.

3 ECJ 6.12.2016 – case C-582/14, ECLI:EU:C:2016:779 para. 45 et seq. – Patrick Breyer v Bundesrepublik Deutschland.

4 ECJ 6.12.2016 – case C-582/14, ECLI:EU:C:2016:779 para. 49 – Patrick Breyer v Bundesrepublik Deutschland.

first referred question – is arrived at by the court based on an assumption, namely that legal channels exist enabling the website provider to contact a competent authority, so that the latter can take the steps necessary to obtain identifying information from the access provider. The court then goes on to say that these channels constitute means—specifically legal means—which may likely reasonably be used in order to identify the data subject and thereby give rise to identifiability in relation to the website provider.

Following from the three key findings, the ECJ's response to the first question was that a dynamic IP address constitutes personal data if the provider has the legal means to obtain data held by an internet service provider that enables linking that address to a specific individual.

Regarding the second question, the ECJ affirmed its previous case law[5]: Art. 7 DPD exhaustively regulates the lawfulness of processing, meaning Member States cannot introduce deviating or supplementary national rules.[6]

III. Systematic context and legal classification

While the answer to the second question largely reinforced existing precedents, the court's findings on the first question provided long-awaited clarity regarding the understanding of identifiability within the meaning of Art. 2(a) DPD.

Admittedly, there had already been court decisions on the question of whether certain data constitutes personal data. However, in these decisions the court merely made apodictic[7] or circular[8] seeming findings that contained no statements reaching beyond the specific types of data (fingerprints and a visual image of a person) considered.

The *Breyer* judgement was the first time the ECJ dissected the question of identifiability in any detail. The question of identifiability is a cardinal question of data protection law as it is at the same time the question of the presence of personal data and thereby determines whether the entire

5 ECJ 24.11.2011 – Joined cases C-468/10 and C-469/10, ECLI:EU:C:2011:777 – ASNEF und FECEMD.

6 ECJ 6.12.2016 – case C-582/14, ECLI:EU:C:2016:779 para. 57 et seqq. – Patrick Breyer v Bundesrepublik Deutschland.

7 ECJ 17.10.2013 – case C-291/12, ECLI:EU:C:2013:670 para. 27 – Michael Schwarz v Stadt Bochum.

8 ECJ 11.12.2014 – case C-212/13, ECLI:EU:C:2014:2428 para. 22 – František Ryneš v Úřad pro ochranu osobních údajů.

regulatory regime—along with its compliance burdens and liability risks —is triggered. Furthermore, the reach of the fundamental right to data protection under Art. 8 CFR hinges on this very term.

And *Breyer's* influence remains undiminished even under the GDPR. The ECJ continues to rely on *Breyer* without restrictions when examining whether data constitutes personal data within the meaning of the GDPR.[9] Notably, the court's emphasis on 'the cost of and the time required for identification'—a phrase that did not exist in the DPD —was directly integrated into Rec. 26 of the GDPR.

And with the regulatory efforts within the framework of the EUs Digital Agendas the *Breyer* legacy has further gained significance beyond core data protection law.

In the AI Act, the DA, the DSA, the DMA, the DGA, the Regulation on the free flow of non-personal data, and the Open Data Directive, the term 'personal data' appears a total of 333 times, often directly affecting the application of these legal acts and their provisions.

And with the introduction of the term 'non-personal data' (logically, defined as data that is not personal data) which can be found a total of 119 times in the DA, the DGA, and the Regulation on the free flow of non-personal data, the *Breyer* doctrine now goes beyond data protection law and serves as a critical boundary line for modern data governance more broadly.

IV. Author's analysis and commentary

The years preceding *Breyer* were marked by a fierce debate over the thresholds of identifiability. This debate brought about a wide spectrum of opinions, especially in Germany, between the so-called 'objective/absolute" and the 'relative" understanding of identifiability. The extreme variant of the objective/absolute understanding considered it sufficient for identifiability if identification was theoretically possible for anyone, even with the involvement of third parties. The extreme variant of the relative understanding, on the other hand, exclusively considered the specifically available means of the party processing the data in question and disregarded any knowledge and abilities of third parties in the examination.

9 I.a. ECJ 9.11.2023 – case C-319/22, ECLI:EU:C:2023:837 para. 45 – Gesamtverband Autoteile-Handel e. V. v Scania CV AB.

The judgment in the *Breyer* case has brought clarity by rejecting both extremes. On the one hand, according to *Breyer*, the theoretical possibility of identification alone is not sufficient to affirm the identifiability of the person. An existing identification risk can under certain circumstances be negligible. On the other hand, the examination of this risk cannot be limited to the means of the party processing the data in question but must take into account means of third parties that are available.

However, anyone who harbored the hope for a final, 'one-size-fits-all' answer was left wanting. Because *Breyer* left significant scope for argumentation.

Subsequent decisions of the ECJ have only marginally reduced this scope: The decision in the *Nowak* case[10] did refer to *Breyer*, but essentially addressed the question of when information relates to a person within the meaning of Art. 4 no. 1 GDPR and offered no new insights regarding the issue of identifiability. The decision in the case *Gesamtverband Autoteile-Handel*[11] merely confirmed that an alphanumeric code assigned by the manufacturer to a vehicle for the purpose of unambiguously identifying each vehicle can constitute personal data for anyone who, upon reasonable consideration, has the means to link it to a specific individual. Similarly, the ECJ's decision in the *IAB Europe* case[12] was essentially an application of the *Breyer* doctrine to a specific processing situation. And the decision in the case *OC/European Commission*[13] confirmed that, in the eyes of the ECJ, there can be negligible identification risks and added to the discussion an example in which the comparison of several characteristics of a person with publicly available data by a sufficiently motivated and knowledgeable third party led to an identification risk that was non-negligible.

Only the decision in the *SRB* case, although also based on the unchanged *Breyer* doctrine, seems noteworthy in this respect, since it enriched the

10 ECJ 20.12.2017 – case C-434/16, ECLI:EU:C:2017:994 – Peter Nowak v Data Protection Commissioner.

11 ECJ 9.11.2023 – case C-319/22, ECLI:EU:C:2023:837 para. 45 – Gesamtverband Autoteile-Handel e. V. v Scania CV AB.

12 ECJ 7.3.2024 – case C-604/22, ECLI:EU:C:2024:214 – IAB Europe v Gegevensbeschermingsautoriteit.

13 ECJ 7.3.2024 – case C-479/22 P, ECLI:EU:C:2024:215 – OC v European Commission.

examination of identifiability with aspects of the temporal and personal perspective from which it is to take place.[14]

The persistent uncertainty around identifiability is highlighted by a recent BGH referral from August 2025.[15] Almost 9 years after the *Breyer* decision, the BGH is still wondering about the identifiability of a person on the basis of a dynamic IP address, this time in the context of a transfer of that IP address. And the BGH also has a follow-up question regarding the third key statement of the ECJ in the *Breyer* decision: Must the legal means mentioned by the ECJ be concretely available, or is the abstract availability of such means sufficient to affirm identifiability and the presence of personal data?

And looking ahead, disputes focussed on identifiability are likely to intensify. Historically, practitioners often favoured an approach where they erred on the side of classifying data as personal data, for the purpose of risk minimization. But the emergence of rights and obligations regarding non-personal data increasingly makes this 'in dubio pro data protection" approach impossible. For example, Art. 17 DA now mandates the sharing of 'non-personal data', which creates a high-stakes dilemma: a provider must share non-personal data immediately or face penalties, but if they mistakenly share personal data, they violate the GDPR.

Situations like this are likely to occur more frequently in the future and will lead to even more situations giving rise to the question of identifiability, some of which will result in legal disputes, some of which will result in referrals to the ECJ.

Ultimately, while *Breyer* settled some important aspects of identifiability, it is now clear that it was only the first step on a longer journey towards a full understanding of this pivotal concept.

V. Recommended further reading

ECJ 9.11.2023 – case C-319/22, ECLI:EU:C:2023:837 para. 45 – Gesamtverband Autoteile-Handel e. V. v Scania CV AB.

ECJ 7.3.2024 – case C-604/22, ECLI:EU:C:2024:214 – IAB Europe v Gegevensbeschermingsautoriteit.

14 ECJ 4.9.2025 – case C-413/23 P, ECLI:EU:C:2025:645 – European Data Protection Supervisor v Single Resolution Board; see separate commentary by Peter Craddock, p. 75.

15 BGH 25.8.2025 – VI ZR 258/24, ZUM 2026, 33.

ECJ 7.3.2024 – case C-479/22 P, ECLI:EU:C:2024:215 – OC v European Commission.

ECJ 4.9.2025 – case C-413/23 P, ECLI:EU:C:2025:645 – European Data Protection Supervisor v Single Resolution Board.

Personal data, pseudonymisation and the scope of data protection law

Peter Craddock

ECJ 4.9.2025 – case C-413/23 P, ECLI:EU:C:2025:645 – EDPS v SRB

I. Case summary

On 4.9.2025, the ECJ ruled on a dispute regarding a decision of the European Data Protection Supervisory (EDPS) concerning the procedure followed by the Single Resolution Board (SRB) following the resolution of Banco Popular. Shareholders and creditors had been invited to share comments to the SRB in relation to that resolution, and the comments had been shared in pseudonymised form with a third party, Deloitte. The EDPS held that the SRB had breached its transparency obligations under EUDPR because it had not informed participants of the fact that Deloitte would receive such (pseudonymised) comments. The SRB then challenged this finding before the GC, whose judgment of 26.4.2023 (SRB v EDPS, T-557/20) was appealed before the ECJ.

The ECJ clarified three central issues under EUDPR: (1) those comments could be personal data, as personal opinions are intrinsically linked to their authors; (2) pseudonymisation can result in data not being 'personal data' for a recipient who lacks any reasonably likely (direct or indirect) means of (re-)identification; and (3) the controller's duty to identify recipients under Art. 15(1)(d) EUDPR must be assessed at the moment of collection from that controller's perspective.

II. Key legal findings

The notion of 'personal data' under EUDPR, also known as the EU Institutions GDPR or EUDPR, is identical to that under the GDPR and under the

DPD, as the ECJ stressed again in SRB.[1] References in SRB to Rec. 16, Art. 3 no. 1 and Art. 15 EUDPR can therefore also be read as references to Rec. 26, Art. 4 no. 1 and Art. 13 of the GDPR itself.

1. Personal data: opinions and subjective content

The ECJ confirmed that the comments submitted in the SRB's procedure can constitute 'personal data' under Art. 3 no. 1 EUDPR. Building on the Nowak[2], CRIF[3] and OLAF[4] cases, the ECJ reiterated that information relates to a person where, by reason of its content, purpose or effect, it is linked to that individual (paras 54 and 55). It held that personal opinions are 'an expression of a person's thinking' and therefore 'necessarily closely linked' to their author (para 58). The content of the comments was thus sufficient to make them capable of being personal data, without any need to examine the purpose or effects of the comments. This addresses only the relational element of the definition: subjective content inherently relates to a person, while identifiability remains a separate question.

2. Pseudonymised data and identifiability

The ECJ clarified that identifiability must be assessed in the context of pseudonymisation, and confirmed that the notion of 'personal data' is contextual: it depends on whether the individual is identifiable for the entity processing the data, on the basis of means reasonably likely to be used.

a) Anonymous and pseudonymised data

The ECJ recalled that 'anonymous information', i.e. information concerning a person who 'is not or is no longer identifiable', falls outside the scope of Rec. 16 EUDPR.[5]

1 ECJ 4.9.2025 – case C-413/23 P, ECLI:EU:C:2025:645 para. 52- EDPS v SRB.
2 ECJ 20.12.2017 – case C-434/16, ECLI:EU:C:2017:994 para. 34 et seq. – Nowak.
3 ECJ 4.5.2023 – case C-487/21, ECLI:EU:C:2023:369, para. 23 et seq. – Österreichische Datenschutzbehörde and CRIF.
4 ECJ 7.3.2024 – case C-479/22 P, ECLI:EU:C:2024:215 – OC v Commission (OLAF).
5 ECJ 4.9.2025 – case C-413/23 P, ECLI:EU:C:2025:645 para. 70 – EDPS v SRB.

On pseudonymisation, the ECJ emphasised that it 'presupposes the existence of information enabling the data subject to be identified'.[6] Pseudonymised data therefore cannot be equated with anonymous data in all circumstances. Its purpose is to ensure that identification cannot occur 'solely by means of the pseudonymised data',[7] provided that the additional information is stored separately and secured through appropriate technical and organisational measures, as required under Art. 3 no. 6 EUDPR.

Crucially, the ECJ held that where such measures effectively prevent attribution, 'the data subject is not or is no longer identifiable'.[8] In such cases, pseudonymised data may cease to be personal data from the perspective of a particular entity, even though it remains personal data for another entity that possesses the identifying information.

b) Nature of pseudonymised data for different entities

The ECJ's reasoning showed again that identifiability is inherently contextual, by highlighting that the legal question is whether a natural person can be identified by the entity processing the data, taking into account 'all the means reasonably likely to be used'.[9] These means include factors such as cost, time, available technology, and whether identification would be prohibited by law or impossible in practice.

In particular, the ECJ held that 'the existence of additional information enabling the data subject to be identified does not, in itself, mean that pseudonymised data must be regarded as constituting, in all cases and for every person, personal data'.[10] Identifiability thus depends on whether attribution is realistically possible for the entity in question, not on abstract or hypothetical possibilities.

The ECJ drew a clear distinction between the SRB and Deloitte, despite both entities processing the same dataset.

For the SRB, the comments in question constituted personal data. The SRB retained the 'additional information' – the key linking the alphanumeric identifiers to individual participants – and therefore had the means

6 ECJ 4.9.2025 – case C-413/23 P, ECLI:EU:C:2025:645 para. 73 – EDPS v SRB.
7 ECJ 4.9.2025 – case C-413/23 P, ECLI:EU:C:2025:645 para. 74 – EDPS v SRB.
8 ECJ 4.9.2025 – case C-413/23 P, ECLI:EU:C:2025:645 para. 75 – EDPS v SRB.
9 ECJ 4.9.2025 – case C-413/23 P, ECLI:EU:C:2025:645 para. 78 et seq., para. 82 et seqq – EDPS v SRB.
10 ECJ 4.9.2025 – case C-413/23 P, ECLI:EU:C:2025:645 para 82 – EDPS v SRB.

reasonably likely to be used for re-identification.[11] As a controller employing pseudonymisation, the SRB remained in a position to attribute the comments to specific individuals.

The assessment was fundamentally different for Deloitte, which did not possess the key and had no lawful or practical means of obtaining it. The ECJ held that the measures implemented by the SRB 'may have the effect' that, for Deloitte, the pseudonymised comments were not personal data.[12] This conclusion depends on two cumulative conditions:

- Deloitte must not be in a position to 'lift' or circumvent the technical and organisational measures; and
- Those measures must in fact prevent identification, including through potential cross-checking with other information.

Therefore, the same dataset containing pseudonymised information was personal data for the SRB, but it may not have been personal data for Deloitte.

c) Ties to prior case law

The ECJ based its analysis on a well-established line of jurisprudence. In OLAF[13], it held that the mere existence of identifying information elsewhere does not automatically render data personal for all actors.[14] In Breyer[15] and IAB Europe[16], data were considered personal because the controller could lawfully obtain additional information enabling identification.[17] Conversely, in Scania[18], the ECJ held that data initially non-personal may become personal when made available to an entity equipped with means reasonably likely to permit identification.[19] The ECJ added that 'in so far as it cannot be ruled out that those third parties have means reasonably allowing them to attribute pseudonymised data to the data subject, such as

11 ECJ 4.9.2025 – case C-413/23 P, ECLI:EU:C:2025:645 para. 76 – EDPS v SRB.
12 ECJ 4.9.2025 – case C-413/23 P, ECLI:EU:C:2025:645 para. 77 – EDPS v SRB.
13 ECJ 7.3.2024 – case C-479/22 P, ECLI:EU:C:2024:215 – OC v Commission (OLAF).
14 ECJ 4.9.2025 – case C-413/23 P, ECLI:EU:C:2025:645 para. 81 et seq. – EDPS v SRB.
15 ECJ 19.10.2016 – case C-582/14, ECLI:EU:C:2016:779 – Breyer.
16 ECJ 7.3.2024 – case C-604/22, ECLI:EU:C:2024:214 – IAB Europe.
17 ECJ 4.9.2025 – case C-413/23 P, ECLI:EU:C:2025:645 para. 83 – EDPS v SRB.
18 ECJ 9.11.2023 – case C-319/22, ECLI:EU:C:2023:837 – Gesamtverband Autoteile-Handel (Access to vehicle information).
19 ECJ 4.9.2025 – case C-413/23 P, ECLI:EU:C:2025:645 para. 84 et seq. – EDPS v SRB.

cross-checking with other data at their disposal, the data subject must be regarded as identifiable as regards both that transfer and any subsequent processing of those data by those third parties',[20] which suggests that the burden of proof may in some circumstances be reversed.

d) Safeguarding the level of protection

Finally, the ECJ emphasised that, although the concept of personal data is intentionally broad, it is not without boundaries. The data subject must still be identifiable.[21] Many legal obligations under EU data protection law presuppose that the entity processing the data can identify the individual concerned. Imposing such obligations on actors lacking any means of identification would be incompatible with the structure and logic of the regulatory framework.[22]

3. The controller's transparency obligations under Art. 15(1)(d) EUDPR

The ECJ ruled that, when personal data are collected, the obligation under Art. 15(1)(d) EUDPR to inform the data subject of the 'recipients or categories of recipients' must be assessed from the perspective of the controller. At that time, the SRB had all the information needed to identify the authors of the comments and was aware that, although the comments were pseudonymised, they would be transmitted to Deloitte. Therefore, Deloitte had to be indicated as a potential recipient.

The ECJ emphasised that the identifiable nature of the data subject must be assessed at the time of collection and from the controller's perspective.[23] Whether the data later cease to be personal for the recipient after pseudonymisation is irrelevant for the controller's obligation at the moment of collection.[24]

As the SRB failed to mention Deloitte in its privacy statement, it did not to comply with the transparency obligation under Art. 15(1)(d) EUDPR. As

---

20 ECJ 4.9.2025 – case C-413/23 P, ECLI:EU:C:2025:645 para. 85 – EDPS v SRB.
21 ECJ 4.9.2025 – case C-413/23 P, ECLI:EU:C:2025:645 para. 88 – EDPS v SRB.
22 ECJ 4.9.2025 – case C-413/23 P, ECLI:EU:C:2025:645 para. 88 et seq. – EDPS v SRB.
23 ECJ 4.9.2025 – case C-413/23 P, ECLI:EU:C:2025:645 para. 111 – EDPS v SRB.
24 ECJ 4.9.2025 – case C-413/23 P, ECLI:EU:C:2025:645 para. 102 et seqq. – EDPS v SRB.

the ECJ stated, the information had to be provided 'prior to the transfer of the data at issue and irrespective of whether or not those data were personal data from Deloitte's point of view after any potential pseudonymisation'.[25]

In other words, transparency obligations are to be assessed at the time of collection, and the classification of information as personal data or not depends on the controller's position and the means reasonably likely to be used for identification.

III. Systematic context and legal classification

This judgment provides the clearest confirmation so far of the relative or contextual nature of personal data.

The ECJ confirmed that identifiability must be assessed by reference to the means reasonably likely to be used by the specific entity processing the data.[26] Its many references to prior case law such as Breyer, Scania, IAB Europe and OLAF, as well as to Rec. 16 EUDPR (like its equivalent Rec. 26 GDPR), as well as the actual reasoning of the ECJ, may suggest that this was already clear, even if implicit.

Yet data protection authorities took the opposite view. Not only the EDPS but also the European Data Protection Board (which intervened in support of the EDPS) had claimed that pseudonymised data must 'in all cases and for every person' be treated as personal data,[27] i.e. an absolute approach to the concept of personal data.

The SRB judgment is therefore significant, as it rejects the argument of data protection authorities, in favour of a relative approach to the notion of personal data. That relative approach requires controllers but also supervisory authorities to make context-specific assessments rather than relying on broad classifications, making this approach complex but also better adapted to the actual risk.

It is not without its issues in relation to prior case law, though, as shown hereunder.

---

25 ECJ 4.9.2025 – case C-413/23 P, ECLI:EU:C:2025:645 para. 112 – EDPS v SRB.

26 ECJ 4.9.2025 – case C-413/23 P, ECLI:EU:C:2025:645 para. 74 et seqq., 87 – EDPS v SRB.

27 ECJ 4.9.2025 – case C-413/23 P, ECLI:EU:C:2025:645 para. 86 – EDPS v SRB.

IV. Author's analysis and commentary

While valuable due to the absence of prior explicit confirmation of the relative nature of personal data, the SRB judgment also leaves several operational questions unresolved.

1. Burden of proof

The interaction between paragraphs 84 and 85 of the SRB judgment appears awkward. Paragraph 84 states that, in line with the Scania judgment (and its paragraph 49), 'data which are in themselves impersonal may become 'personal' in nature where the controller puts them at the disposal of other persons who have means reasonably likely to enable the data subject to be identified'. The words 'who have' suggests proof of a positive is required, i.e. evidence that there are indeed means of identification. Paragraph 85 on the other hand states that 'in so far as it cannot be ruled out' that such other persons have means reasonably allowing identification, 'the data subject must be regarded as identifiable as regards both that transfer and any subsequent processing of those data by those third parties'. This suggests a refutable presumption of identifiability.

In this author's view, these paragraphs have to be read as requiring reasonable indications of identifiability (= 'who have means') before a reversal of the burden of proof can occur (= 'cannot be ruled out').

This approach is not conducive to higher risk in practice, as any entity that treats information as non-personal data without taking safeguards to prepare for compliance, should identification ever become possible, will likely be viewed by supervisory authorities as negligent. This in turn could form the basis for fines (in accordance with ECJ case law[28]) if the GDPR starts to apply.

This may instead lead to the idea of treating some information voluntarily as 'potentially personal data' and taking voluntary steps (due to the inapplicability of the GDPR until identification becomes possible) to limit the risk, such as contractual prohibitions on re-identification, monitoring vulnerabilities in pseudonymisation, escalation mechanisms, and avoiding transfers to actors with re-identification capabilities.

---

28 ECJ 5.12.2023 – case C-807/21, ECLI:EU:C:2023:950, para. 78 – Deutsche Wohnen; see also ECJ 5.12.2023 – case C-683/21, ECLI:EU:C:2023:949, para. 86 – Nacionalinis visuomenės sveikatos centras.

2. Processors vs controllers

The judgment does not determine whether its reasoning extends to processors. While one might assume Deloitte had acted as a processor, arguments about its role as processor were inadmissible (due to being raised too late in the proceedings), such that the judgment reads as though Deloitte acted as a controller.[29] Yet under the GDPR, processors act under the controller's authority just as a controller's own employees, and all processor obligations (and the very definition of a processor) presuppose the processing of personal data. Allowing a processor without access to identifying information to treat pseudonymised data as non-personal would, in this author's view, undermine the processor regime and create a risk of rogue processors and even rogue employees being able to avoid EUDPR and GDPR enforcement.

The more consistent interpretation is that the judgment's relational concept of identifiability applies only to independent controllers, not to processors operating under a controller's authority, and the Danish authority appears to consider this as well.[30]

3. Consequences of unlawfully obtained identification data

Some have held that SRB is compatible with the European Data Protection Board's Pseudonymisation Guidelines,[31] and that the assessment of whether information is personal data requires taking into account not only *lawful* means of identification but also *unlawful* means, i.e. cyberattacks[32] and the results thereof (e.g. credentials available online or on the dark web).

This author takes a different view, and considers that the SRB judgment does in fact exclude this, through confirming and compounding the Breyer (see separate commentary on Breyer by Per Meyerdierks) and OLAF judgments.

---

29 ECJ 4.9.2025 – case C-413/23 P, ECLI:EU:C:2025:645 para. 77, 97 et seqq. – EDPS v SRB.

30 Danish Data Protection Authority (Datatilsynet), 'Mere nyt om EU-Domstolens afgørelse om pseudonymiserede personoplysninger', [English: 'Further information on the ECJ judgment concerning pseudonymised personal data'], (22.10.2025) <https://www.datatilsynet.dk/internationalt/internationalt-nyt/2025/okt/mere-nyt-om-eu-domstolens-afgoerelse-om-pseudonymiserede-personoplysninger>.

31 EDPB, ‚Guidelines 01/2025 on Pseudonymisation' (16.1.2025) <https://www.edpb.europa.eu/system/files/2025-01/edpb_guidelines_202501_pseudonymisation_en.pdf>.

32 See e.g. Stalla-Bourdillon Privacy and Data Protection, 26(1), 6, in particular p. 9 et seq.

In SRB, the ECJ reaffirmed that information is not personal data notably if 'the identification of that data subject is prohibited by law'.[33] Yet cyberattacks are prohibited by law, notably through the Cybercrime Convention[34] and all national implementations thereof. In addition, the GDPR itself requires the processing of personal data to be lawful (Art. 5(1)(a) GDPR), rendering any processing of unlawfully obtained identification data unlawful in and of itself.

Pseudonymisation should therefore be assessed from a dual perspective:

- First, is pseudonymisation sufficiently effective to prevent a recipient of pseudonymised data from getting to identification (Rec. 26 and Art. 4 no. 1 GDPR)? If so, the recipient might be able to claim that it has no reasonable means at its disposal to (re)identify the data subject, with the consequence that the GDPR itself is inapplicable (at that time – see point IV.1 above).

Second, is pseudonymisation an appropriate measure for Art. 32 GDPR compliance? Here, the perspective of malicious actors can (and should) be taken into account, given that the real issue is not whether the malicious actor is subject to the GDPR but whether the malicious actor can use the data to cause harm.

4. Transparency and recipient naming

The judgment's approach to transparency[35] raises practical difficulties, as it means that even where a recipient receives only pseudonymised data and cannot identify individuals, that recipient may still need to be named. The reasoning is tied to the controller's duty to provide complete information at collection and, in this case, to reliance on consent as a legal ground. Where a recipient lack any means of (re)identification, though, the exercise of data subject rights may precisely trigger processing, leading to questions about

33 ECJ 4.9.2025 – case C-413/23 P, ECLI:EU:C:2025:645 para. 82 – EDPS v SRB.

34 United Nations Convention against Cybercrime, ‚Strengthening International Cooperation for Combating Certain Crimes Committed by Means of Information and Communications Technology Systems and for the Sharing of Evidence in Electronic Form of Serious Crimes', adopted by UN General Assembly Resolution 79/243 on 24.12.2024, UN Doc A/RES/79/243.

35 ECJ 4.9.2025 – case C-413/23 P, ECLI:EU:C:2025:645 para. 102 et seqq. – EDPS v SRB.

SRB's interaction with Art. 11 GDPR. It is also possible that with another legal ground (e.g. legitimate interest) the ECJ's conclusion would have been different.

This point further illustrates the fact that while SRB therefore significant, it leaves questions unanswered and does not appear to be the end of the saga when it comes to the most fundamental issue under data protection law: what constitutes personal data, and for whom?

V. Recommended further reading

NSA 16.10.2025 – III OSK 2595/22 <https://orzeczenia.nsa.gov.pl/doc/E1D0CC5377>.

NSA 15.10.2025 – III OSK 2357/22 <https://orzeczenia.nsa.gov.pl/doc/306B3BAAA9>.

Fortuna, 'A deep dive into the consequential SRB judgment(s): Between personal, impersonal, anonymous and pseudonymized data' (pdpEcho, 8.12.2025) <https://pdpecho.com/2025/12/08/a-deep-dive-into-the-consequential-srb-judgments-between-personal-impersonal-anonymous-and-pseudonymized-data/>.

The Scope of 'Processing' under Art. 4 no. 2 GDPR

Sophie Sohm/Steffen Sundermann

ECJ 7.3.2024 – case C-740/22, ECLI:EU:C:2024:216 – Endemol Shine Finland Oy

I. Introduction

The concept of 'processing' under Art. 4 no. 2 GDPR is one of the central elements of the European data protection regime. The recent judgment of the ECJ in Case C-740/22, delivered on 7.3.2024, provides clarification on the breadth of this concept, specifically addressing whether oral disclosure of personal data by a public authority constitutes 'processing' within the meaning of the GDPR. This commentary analyses the judgment, its doctrinal significance, and its practical implications for data controllers, public authorities, and data subjects.

II. Case summary

Endemol Shine Finland Oy, a commercial company, orally requested information from the District Court of South Savo, Finland, regarding the criminal record of a natural person participating in a competition. The purpose was to clarify whether the individual had any ongoing or completed criminal proceedings. The court refused the request, citing data protection concerns and the absence of a valid legal basis for processing criminal conviction data under Finnish law. Endemol Shine Finland Oy appealed, and the Court of Appeal of Eastern Finland, referred three questions to the ECJ, seeking clarification on whether oral disclosure of such information constitutes 'processing' under Art. 4 no. 2 GDPR (question one), and whether public access to official documents (Art. 86 GDPR) could justify such disclosure without restriction (questions two and three). The ECJ examined the scope of the GDPR, focusing on whether oral transmission of personal data from a court's register is covered by the regulation, and how the right to public access should be balanced against the protection of sensitive personal data, such as criminal convictions. The Court held that the GDPR applies to oral disclosures if the data is part of a filing system. Therefore the GDPR requirements such as a legitimate legal basis for the processing apply to such non-automated processing activities as well. The ECJ lastly held that public access to documents must be reconciled with the right to data protection, ruling that unrestricted oral disclosure of criminal conviction data is not permitted under EU law, regardless of whether the requester is a company or an individual.

III. Key legal findings

In the answer to the first question, the ECJ reiterates its previous case law, stating that the GDPR's definition of 'processing' in Art. 4 no. 2 GDPR is intentionally broad and technologically neutral in nature.[1] The term encompasses 'any operation or set of operations' performed on personal data, whether automated or manual, and includes activities such as collection, recording, storage, and notably, 'disclosure by transmission, dissemination or otherwise making available.' According to the ECJ, the list of operations is non-exhaustive, and the protection afforded by the GDPR should not depend on the technique or medium used. This means that oral disclosure of personal data constitutes 'processing' within the meaning of Art. 4 no. 2 GDPR.

The Court further reasoned that the GDPR applies to both automated and manual processing, provided the personal data forms part of a 'filing system' as defined in Art. 4 no. 6 GDPR as any structured set of personal data accessible according to specific criteria. The Court references previous case law, including C-25/17 Jehovan todistajat[2] and reinforces the broad interpretation of 'filing system,' noting that the structure or format of the specific data is less important than its general accessibility according to criteria.

In the answer to the second and third questions, the Court addressed the reconciliation of public access to official documents (Art. 86 GDPR) with data protection rights. The ECJ clarifies that all processing of personal data

1 ECJ 24.2.2022 – case C-25/17, ECLI:EU:C:2018:551 para. 35 – Valsts ieņēmumu dienests; ECJ 22.6.2023 – case C-579/21 ECLI:EU:C:2023:501 para. 46 – Pankki S.

2 ECJ 20.7.2018 – case C-25/17, ECLI:EU:C:2018:551 – Jehovan todistajat.

must comply with the principles set out in Art. 5 GDPR, including lawfulness, fairness, transparency, purpose limitation, data minimisation, accuracy, storage limitation, and integrity/confidentiality. For the oral disclosure in question to be legal, it must therefore satisfy one of the conditions of one of the legal bases in Art. 6 GDPR. In the context of public authorities, Art. 6(1)(e) GDPR permits the processing necessary for the performance of a task carried out in the public interest or in the exercise of official authority. For data on criminal convictions, Art. 10 GDPR imposes additional restrictions, requiring that processing be carried out only under the control of official authority or be specifically authorized by law with appropriate safeguards. Given the sensitivity of criminal conviction data pursuant to Art. 10 GDPR, the Court concluded that data protection interests generally prevail, and unrestricted oral disclosure is not permitted. The judgment thus affirms the need for a specific, legitimate interest and appropriate legal basis for any disclosure regardless of the requester's identity.

IV. Systematic context and legal classification

The ECJ's judgment in Case C-740/22 is situated at the intersection of several core principles of European data protection law, most notably the definition and scope of 'processing' under Art. 4 no. 2 GDPR and the reconciliation of data protection with other rights such as public access to official documents. By confirming that oral disclosure is 'processing', the Court reinforces the idea that data protection obligations apply regardless of the medium or method used, including informal or non-digital practices.

In terms of alignment with previous case law, the judgment builds on and is consistent with earlier decisions such as C-25/17 Jehovan todistajat[3] (definition of filing system), C-439/19 Latvijas Republikas Saeima[4] (balancing public access and data protection), and C-154/21 Österreichische Post[5] (scope of processing).

The judgment also contributes to the interpretation and development of the GDPR by clarifying the relationship between data protection and other public interests, such as transparency and access to official documents,

3 ECJ 20.7.2018 – case C-25/17, ECLI:EU:C:2018:551 – Jehovan todistajat.
4 ECJ 22.6.2021 – case C-439/19, ECLI:EU:C:2021:504 – Latvijas Republikas Saeima.
5 ECJ 21.1.2023 – case C-154/21, ECLI:EU:C:2023:3 – Österreichische Post.

a problem which is rarely discussed by the ECJ so far.[6] Art. 86 GDPR recognizes the importance of public access but requires that it be reconciled with the right to data protection. The Court's reasoning reflects its cautious approach to any exceptions that may lead to a lower level of data protection: while public access may serve legitimate interests, it cannot override the heightened protection required for sensitive data, such as criminal convictions.

V. Author's analysis and commentary

The ECJ's judgment in Case C-740/22 provides answers to fundamental questions regarding the meaning of 'processing' (Art. 4 no. 2 GDPR), the material scope of the GDPR (Art. 2(1) GDPR) and the limits of public access to information relating to criminal convictions (Art. 86 GDPR).

1. Oral processing and material scope of the GDPR

The ECJ confirms that the GDPR is technologically neutral, all forms of data handling, regardless of medium, are subject to the GDPR's definition of processing, including oral disclosure of personal data. The court thus reaffirms its approach to interpret the definitions of the GDPR in a way that ensures broad application of the GDPR. The ECJ's interpretation of the material scope of the GDPR for semi-automated processing in Art. 4 no. 2 GDPR also follows this. According to the ECJ, it is sufficient that the data in question are stored in any 'filing system' within the meaning of Art. 4 no. 6 GDPR. Thus, for the GDPR to apply, it is not necessary that the specific data set is itself structured in any particular form. The decision is insofar consistent with previous case law, such as Jehovan todistajat[7] and Latvijas Republikas Saeima[8], which have similarly emphasized the broad reach of the GDPR and the primacy of the protection of the rights of data subjects.

On the one hand, the ECJ's approach strengthens the effectiveness of the regulation by closing any potential blind spots, including for mostly

6 Even in cases where the matter was quite close, Art. 86 of the GDPR was not discussed, see for example ECJ 1.8.2022 – case C-184/20, ECLI:EU:C:2022:601 – Vyriausioji tarnybinės etikos komisija; see also: Gerhold/Lauenstein NVwZ 2024, 653 (657).

7 ECJ 20.7.2018 – case C-25/17, ECLI:EU:C:2018:551 – Jehovan todistajat.

8 ECJ 22.6.2021 – case C-439/19, ECLI:EU:C:2021:504 – Latvijas Republikas Saeima.

analog data processing (e.g. in person communication, by telephone or pen and paper) or for new forms of data use, which constantly emerge (e.g. AI). Insofar the ECJ's expansive interpretation aligns with the regulation's objective of providing a high and consistent level of protection for individuals across the EU, by applying the obligations of controllers and processors equally to oral, written, and electronic disclosures, preventing circumvention and ensuring comprehensive coverage.

On the other hand, the decision raises questions regarding the practicality of ever broader interpretations of the scope of the GDPR. While the ECJ's conclusion in the present case seems inevitable, given the very sensitive information at stake, there are other scenarios which include oral disclosure of personal data in which a broad interpretation of the scope of the GDPR may lead to overregulation of everyday activities. Since most data is ultimately stored in a filing system of some nature, most non-automated data processing can likely be linked to a filing system. This can lead to overbroad and complex compliance structures, increased administrative burdens, and the need for more detailed record-keeping and documentation of oral disclosures, which are by nature more difficult to keep track of than written disclosures. In most cases, such compliance measures can lead to unnecessary data processing which is not in the best interest of data subjects.

The difficulties and unintended consequences of applying the GDPR to analog and oral data processing became apparent during the Covid pandemic, when many supermarkets, restaurants or sports clubs struggled with questions relating to data protection compliance when trying to implement mandatory measures, such as asking for vaccination status or keep track of the number of customers in a store. Data protection authorities had to issue detailed guidance on the GDPR related implications, even for simple everyday activities such as entering a supermarket.[9] The now infamous 'Vienna doorbell sign debate' can be viewed as another example of unintended consequences of a broad interpretation of the material scope of the GDPR.[10] In every-day, low-risk constellations, the link between a processing activity and a 'filing system' should therefore be interpreted

9 E.g. Hamburg Data Protection Commissioner, 'Corona-FAQ' (27.3.2020) <https://datenschutz-hamburg.de/fileadmin/user_upload/HmbBfDI/Pressemitteilungen/2020/2020-03-27_Corona-FAQ.pdf>.

10 Noack, 'Europe's privacy laws are now so tough, they are taking names off doorbells in Vienna' (19.10.2018) <https://www.washingtonpost.com/world/2018/10/19/europes-privacy-laws-are-now-so-tough-they-are-taking-names-off-doorbells-vienna/>.

narrowly, for example by requiring a direct access to the data in the filing system by the person processing the data orally or manually. Otherwise, full GDPR applicability may be triggered for any subsequent oral disclosure and thereby considerably expanding compliance obligations.

The ECJ's decision comes at a time when the practicality of some far-reaching GDPR provisions is already under scrutiny.[11] This especially applies to the broad definition of data processing which not only includes oral disclosures but, according to data protection authorities, also processing activities like anonymisation.[12] In practice, this means that even if the end goal is to create anonymised data sets, for example for AI training, the anonymisation process itself must comply with GDPR obligations. For processors, this creates significant compliance challenges. Processors must ensure that all steps in the data pipeline comply with GDPR requirements, even though they are not interested in processing personal data for any purpose other than anonymization. This creates tension for innovation: while the GDPR aims to protect individuals, it can also make it extremely difficult to develop new technologies that rely on large-scale data analysis, such as AI and machine learning, even if the processing is carried out on the basis of anonymized data.

2. Public access to official documents on criminal convictions

As far as the decision concerns public access to official documents on criminal convictions pursuant to Art. 86 GDPR, the ECJ prioritizes the interests of the affected data subjects over the public's interest for access to information. In essence, even though the ECJ leaves the door open for national laws allowing for access to public documents, the court clearly states that unrestricted access to personal data on criminal convictions cannot be justified under Art. 86 GDPR.

---

11 As evidenced by the proposed changes in the EU Commission's Digital-/Data-Omnibus, <https://ec.europa.eu/commission/presscorner/detail/en/ip_25_2718>.

12 Article 29 Working Party, 'Opinion 05/2014 on data anonymization techniques' (WP216, 10.4.2014) <https://ec.europa.eu/justice/article-29/documentation/opinion-recommendation/files/2014/wp216_en.pdf>, p. 7; see also: Pohle/Hölzel, ‚Anonymisierung aus Sicht des Datenschutzes und des Datenschutzrechts' <https://www.bfdi.bund.de/SharedDocs/Downloads/DE/Konsultationsverfahren/1_Anonymisierung/Stellungnahmen/Alexander-von-Humboldt-Institut.pdf?__blob=publicationFile&v=5>.

3. Practical implications and outlook

In summary, the decision is in line with the ECJ's approach to a broad interpretation of the GDPR's material scope. DPOs, companies, and public authorities should be aware that the GDPR's requirements for lawfulness, transparency, and security apply regardless of the format of disclosure. In practice, controllers have to ensure that the information obligations under Art. 13 and 14 GDPR are met.

However, the ECJ may have to decide on the interpretation of these definitions again in the near future: The new 'Digital-/Data-Omnibus'[13], announced by the European Commission on 19.11.2025 intends to substantially amend numerous key GDPR provisions, and could become a central point of focus in upcoming legislative debates, potentially reshaping Europe's digital regulatory landscape and offering more flexible rules for innovation while preserving robust fundamental rights protections. While maintaining high standards of protection, European policymakers should clarify and streamline the general requirements for data processing. This would help avoid overregulation of everyday offline interactions and support innovation in new technologies. This could be achieved by providing more detailed guidance or safe harbours for certain processing situations. Comparative international law shows that other jurisdictions, such as the US, often take a more pragmatic approach, especially to everyday data use as well as for research and innovation. Europe must similarly find its own way to enable responsible data usage, including data-driven innovation, without undermining its core values.

VI. Recommended further reading

Relevant previous case law: ECJ's decisions in Jehovan todistajat[14], Latvijas Republikas Saeima[15] and Österreichische Post.[16]

---

13 European Commission, 'Simpler EU digital rules and new digital wallets to save billions for businesses and boost innovation' (19.11.2025) <https://ec.europa.eu/commission/presscorner/detail/en/ip_25_2718>.

14 ECJ 20.7.2018 – case C-25/17, ECLI:EU:C:2018:551 – Jehovan todistajat.

15 ECJ 22.6.2021 – case C-439/19, ECLI:EU:C:2021:504 – Latvijas Republikas Saeima.

16 ECJ 21.1.2023 – case C-154/21, ECLI:EU:C:2023:3 – Österreichische Post.

Regarding the anonmisation as processing see also: Article 29 Working Party, 'Opinion 05/2014 on data anonymization techniques' (WP216, 10.4.2014) <https://ec.europa.eu/justice/article-29/documentation/opinion-recommendation/files/2014/wp216_en.pdf>; Pohle/Hölzel, ‚Anonymisierung aus Sicht des Datenschutzes und des Datenschutzrechts' <https://www.bfdi.bund.de/SharedDocs/Downloads/DE/Konsultationsverfahren/1_Anonymisierung/Stellungnahmen/Alexander-von-Humboldt-Institut.pdf?__blob=publicationFile&v=5>.

European Commission, 'Simpler EU digital rules and new digital wallets to save billions for businesses and boost innovation' (19.11.2025) <https://ec.europa.eu/commission/presscorner/detail/en/ip_25_2718>.

Right to one's own image and data protection

Dominik Roderburg

ECJ 5.12.2023 – case C-683/21, ECLI:EU:C:2023:949 – Nacionalinis visuomenės sveikatos centras prie Sveikatos apsaugos ministerijos v Valstybinė duomenų apsaugos inspekcija

I. Case summary

In the judgment discussed here, the ECJ once again had to deal with open questions of interpretation of key terms in data protection law. Of fundamental importance was a question referred for a preliminary ruling on the conditions for the imposition of administrative fines under Art. 83 GDPR. The decision is of great practical relevance in this respect, particularly in connection with the further decision of the Court of Justice of 5 December 2023 in Case C-807/21.

The decision to be discussed can be found in the following summary of the facts of the case:[1]

During the COVID-19 pandemic, the Lithuanian Minister of Health instructed the director of the National Public Health Center under the Ministry of Health (hereinafter: NZÖG) to organize the immediate purchase of an IT system for recording and monitoring data on persons exposed to the virus.

The NZÖG then contacted the company 'IT sprendimai sėkmei' (hereinafter: ITSS) and informed it that it had been 'selected' to develop a corresponding app. Subsequently, emails were exchanged between the NZÖG and ITSS on various aspects of the application, in which the NZÖG gave instructions for the development of the application, which were followed by

1 ECJ 5.12.2023 – case C-683/21, ECLI:EU:C:2023:949 para. 12 et seq. – Nacionalinis visuomenės sveikatos centras prie Sveikatos apsaugos ministerijos v Valstybinė duomenų apsaugos inspekcija. A brief summary can be found, for example, in Schwartmann/Jaspers/Thüsing/Kugelmann Heidelberger Kommentar DS-GVO/BDSG/Kremer, 3rd edn. 2024, DS-GVO Art. 26 mn. 74.

ITSS. In particular, a privacy policy was drawn up in which ITSS and the NZÖG were named as data controllers.

After undergoing a test phase, during which (presumably) copies of personal data were used, the app was available in various app stores from April 2020 until May 26, 2020, and was used by approximately 4,000 people, each of whom transmitted numerous pieces of personal data to.

ITSS was not subsequently commissioned. Instead, NZÖG first requested ITSS not to mention it in the app 'in any way' and then announced that the procurement procedure had been terminated due to a lack of funds.

The Lithuanian supervisory authority investigated the events and, in 2021, imposed a fine on both the NZÖG and the ITSS as joint controllers for several violations of the GDPR on the basis of Art. 83 GDPR.

The NZÖG challenged the supervisory authority's decision before the Vilnius Regional Administrative Court, arguing that ITSS was solely responsible. IT SS, on the other hand, argued that it had processed the data on behalf of the NZÖG.

II. Key legal findings and legal classification

The court had to answer questions referred by the court of first instance on four clearly distinguishable, but partly interrelated aspects:[2]

1. Concept of ‚processing' in test operation (preliminary question 4)

In this context, the referring court asked the Court of Justice whether Art. 4 no. 2 GDPR also covers situations in which (copies of) personal data (e.g., employees' telephone numbers) are used for the sole purpose of testing a new app. The Court of Justice answered this question in the affirmative in a fairly clear manner. The Court pointed out that the purpose of the processing within the meaning of Art. 4 no. 2 GDPR was irrelevant and that it therefore did not matter whether personal data was used for IT testing or for another purpose. The only decisive factor in the case at hand was whether the data in question was personal data which is not affected by its

2 For details on the questions referred, see: ECJ 5.12.2023 – case C-683/21, ECLI:EU:C:2023:949 para. 26 – Nacionalinis visuomenės sveikatos centras prie Sveikatos apsaugos ministerijos v Valstybinė duomenų apsaugos inspekcija.

status as 'copies' and this was not the case with fictitious or anonymized data.[3] In this respect, the decision provides little new insight.[4]

2. Interpretation of the term ‚controller' (preliminary question 1 to 3)

With the above-mentioned questions referred, the court of first instance sought to clarify various questions of interpretation in connection with Art. 4 no. 7 GDPR.

The Court of Justice answered these questions on the concept of the controller jointly, stating that an institution that commissions a company to develop a mobile IT application and, in this context, has participated in the decision on the purposes and means of the processing of personal data carried out via the application, can be regarded as a controller within the meaning of this provision, even if it has not itself carried out any processing operations relating to personal data, has not given its explicit consent to the specific processing operations or to the provision of this mobile application to the public, and has not purchased the mobile application.

The Court of Justice refers to well-known aspects in this regard.[5] When interpreting the law, the objective of ensuring a high level of protection with regard to personal data must be taken into account.[6] In this regard, the Court of Justice had already[7] emphasized the criterion of 'own interest' in. The decisive factor is whether the determination of the purposes and means of processing was influenced by the entity´s own interests, in this

3 ECJ 5.12.2023 – case C-683/21, ECLI:EU:C:2023:949 para. 87 – Nacionalinis visuomenės sveikatos centras prie Sveikatos apsaugos ministerijos v Valstybinė duomenų apsaugos inspekcija.

4 Similarly, Schneider ZD 2024, 209 (215); Grosmann/Hansen K&R 2024, 102 (104); Marosi DSB 2024, 46 (48).

5 See, for example, the description by Schwartmann/Jaspers/Thüsing/Kugelmann/Kremer DS-GVO Art. 26 mn. 48; Heckmann/Paschke jurisPK-Internetrecht/Heckmann/Scheurer, 21.1.2026, Chapter 9, mn. 268 et seq.; Grosmann/Hansen K&R 2024, 102.

6 See, for example, ECJ 28.4.2022 — C-319/20, ECLI:EU:C:2022:322 — Meta Platforms Ireland Limited v Bundesverband der Verbraucherzentralen und Verbraucherverbände - Verbraucherzentrale Bundesverband eV.

7 ECJ 5.6.2018 — case C-210/16, ECLI:EU:C:2018:388 para. 67 et seq — Unabhängiges Landeszentrum für Datenschutz Schleswig-Holstein v Wirtschaftsakademie Schleswig-Holstein GmbH; cf. more recently: ECJ 2.12.2025 — case C-492/23, ECLI:EU:C:2025:935 para. 58 — X v Russmedia Digital SRL and Inform Media Press SRL.

case by initiating the development of the app[8]. Own processing is just as unnecessary[9] as it is for the purposes and means of processing to be decided by means of written instructions or directives from the potential controller[10] or for the latter to be formally designated as such.

In this respect, the decision is consistent with well-established case law. What is new, however, is which additional criteria the Court of Justice has deemed irrelevant to the question of responsibility.[11] This concerns, for example, the fact that the app was not acquired by NZÖG as a potentially responsible party[12] or that its distribution was not approved by NZÖG[13]. In this respect, however, the Court of Justice restricts that, in any case, no responsibility arising from the provision of the mobile application in question to the public can be assumed if the provision has been expressly objected to.

3. Joint responsibility (preliminary question 5)

With its fifth question, the referring court sought to clarify the conditions under which joint responsibility for data processing can be assumed in accordance with Art. 4 no. 7 and Art. 26(1) GDPR, in particular whether this exclusively covers 'deliberately coordinated actions with regard to the determination of the purpose of and means for data processing', or whether joint responsibility 'also covers situations where there is no clear 'agreement' on the purpose of and means for data processing' and/or 'the actions

8 See the description by Schwartmann/Jaspers/Thüsing/Kugelmann/Kremer DS-GVO Art. 26 mn. 48 et seq.

9 ECJ 5.6.2018 — case C-210/16, ECLI:EU:C:2018:388 para. 25 et seq — Unabhängiges Landeszentrum für Datenschutz Schleswig-Holstein v Wirtschaftsakademie Schleswig-Holstein GmbH.

10 See ECJ 5.12.2023 - case C-683/21, ECLI:EU:C:2023:949 para. 30 et seq. - Nacionalinis visuomenės sveikatos centras prie Sveikatos apsaugos ministerijos v Valstybinė duomenų apsaugos inspekcija; ECJ 5.6.2018 — case C-210/16, ECLI:EU:C:2018:388 para. 67 et seq — Unabhängiges Landeszentrum für Datenschutz Schleswig-Holstein v Wirtschaftsakademie Schleswig-Holstein GmbH.

11 Informative list in Schneider ZD 2024, 209 (214).

12 ECJ 5.12.2023 - case C-683/21, ECLI:EU:C:2023:949 para. 35 - Nacionalinis visuomenės sveikatos centras prie Sveikatos apsaugos ministerijos v Valstybinė duomenų apsaugos inspekcija.

13 ECJ 5.12.2023 - case C-683/21, ECLI:EU:C:2023:949 para. 35 - Nacionalinis visuomenės sveikatos centras prie Sveikatos apsaugos ministerijos v Valstybinė duomenų apsaugos inspekcija.

between the entities are not coordinated'. In its decision affirming this in the case at hand[14], the Court of Justice was able to refer to well-known principles[15], which it later confirmed again in its decision of December 2, 2025[16]. What is essentially new is the Court of Justice's statement that 'it is not necessary for there to be a formal agreement between these controllers on the purposes and means of processing'[17].

4. Conditions for the imposition of administrative fines (preliminary question 6)

With its sixth question, the referring court sought to clarify whether Art. 83(1) GDPR is to be understood as meaning that unlawful processing of personal data carried out by the processor is always automatically attributable to the controller, giving rise to liability, and whether Art. 83(1) GDPR is to be interpreted as also covering cases of strict liability of the controller.

In answering this question, which consists of two parts, the Court of Justice arrived at the central point of the decision, namely the conditions for the imposition of administrative fines under Art. 83 GDPR. In this respect, the Court followed the opinion of the Advocate General[18] and interpreted Art. 83 GDPR to mean that a fine requires at least a negligent

---

14 ECJ 5.12.2023 – case C-683/21, ECLI:EU:C:2023:949 para. 87 – Nacionalinis visuomenės sveikatos centras prie Sveikatos apsaugos ministerijos v Valstybinė duomenų apsaugos inspekcija.

15 ECJ 5.6.2018 — case C-210/16, ECLI:EU:C:2018:388 para. 25 et seq — Unabhängiges Landeszentrum für Datenschutz Schleswig-Holstein v Wirtschaftsakademie Schleswig-Holstein GmbH; ECJ 10.7.2018 – case C-25/17, ECLI:EU:C:2018:551; ECJ 29.7.2019 – case C-40/17, ECLI:EU:C:2019:629 – Fashion ID GmbH & Co.KG v Verbraucherzentrale NRW eV; Schwartmann/Jaspers/Thüsing/Kugelmann/Kremer DS-GVO Art. 26 mn. 56.

16 ECJ 2.12.2025 – case C-492/23, ECLI:EU:C:2025:935 para. 60 et seq. – X v Russmedia Digital SRL and Inform Media Press SRL.

17 ECJ 5.12.2023 – case C-683/21, ECLI:EU:C:2023:949 para. 87 – Nacionalinis visuomenės sveikatos centras prie Sveikatos apsaugos ministerijos v Valstybinė duomenų apsaugos inspekcija; cf. on this point: Schwartmann/Jaspers/Thüsing/Kugelmann/Kremer DS-GVO Art. 26 mn. 49, 78; Schlegel/Voelzke jurisPK-SGB V/Buchholtz, 1.4.2025, SGB V § 341 mn. 59.

18 AG Emiliou 4.5.2023 – case C-683/21, ECLI:EU:C:2023:376 – Nacionalinis visuomenės sveikatos centras prie Sveikatos apsaugos ministerijos v Valstybinė duomenų apsaugos inspekcija.

infringement within the meaning of Art. 83(4) to (6) GDPR.[19] The Court of Justice provided detailed and extensive reasoning,[20] which can only be briefly outlined here: The wording of Art. 83(1) to (6) GDPR contains no indication of strict liability or of any discretion on the part of the Member States to apply such liability.[21] The general structure and purpose of the GDPR confirm this interpretation.[22] In particular, the principle of ensuring a uniform and high level of protection for natural persons with regard to the processing of personal data does not require strict liability. The Court clarifies that, in the case of a legal person, the application of Art. 83 GDPR does not require any action or even knowledge on the part of the management body of that legal person.[23]

The Court then answers the question of attribution much more succinctly. Since a controller is responsible not only for any processing of personal data carried out by itself, but also for processing carried out on its behalf, which follows from Rec. 74 of the GDPR,[24] could be fined under Art. 83 of the GDPR if it had been aware of the processing carried out on its behalf and had not taken appropriate measures to prevent it. of the GDPR, a fine may be imposed on him under Art. 83 of the GDPR if personal data is processed unlawfully and the processing was not carried out by him but by a processor he has engaged on his behalf. However, an exception applies — and this is important — if the processor goes beyond the specifications of

19 ECJ 5.12.2023 – case C-683/21, ECLI:EU:C:2023:949 para. 87 – Nacionalinis visuomenės sveikatos centras prie Sveikatos apsaugos ministerijos v Valstybinė duomenų apsaugos inspekcija; see also Bergmann/Möhrle/Herb, Datenschutzrecht, 3. Normadressaten, Täterkreis und bußgeldrechtliche Besonderheiten, mn. 6.

20 ECJ 5.12.2023 – case C-683/21, ECLI:EU:C:2023:949 para. 61–81 – Nacionalinis visuomenės sveikatos centras prie Sveikatos apsaugos ministerijos v Valstybinė duomenų apsaugos inspekcija.

21 ECJ 5.12.2023 – case C-683/21, ECLI:EU:C:2023:949 para. 67 – Nacionalinis visuomenės sveikatos centras prie Sveikatos apsaugos ministerijos v Valstybinė duomenų apsaugos inspekcija.

22 ECJ 5.12.2023 – case C-683/21, ECLI:EU:C:2023:949 para. 74 – Nacionalinis visuomenės sveikatos centras prie Sveikatos apsaugos ministerijos v Valstybinė duomenų apsaugos inspekcija.

23 ECJ 5.12.2023 – case C-683/21, ECLI:EU:C:2023:949 para. 82 – Nacionalinis visuomenės sveikatos centras prie Sveikatos apsaugos ministerijos v Valstybinė duomenų apsaugos inspekcija, referring to earlier case law, see, for example, ECJ 16.2.2017 – case C-94/15 P, ECLI:EU:C:2017:124, para. 28 – Tudapetrol Mineralölerzeugnisse Nils Hansen KG v European Commission with further references.

24 ECJ 5.12.2023 – case C-683/21, ECLI:EU:C:2023:949 para. 84, 36 – Nacionalinis visuomenės sveikatos centras prie Sveikatos apsaugos ministerijos v Valstybinė duomenų apsaugos inspekcija.

the controller regarding the framework or modalities of the processing, or if the data processing is carried out in a manner that cannot reasonably be assumed to have been approved by the controller.[25] This corresponds to the provisions of Art. 28(10) GDPR.[26]

III. Author's analysis and commentary

The decision is of fundamental importance, particularly for the practice of supervisory authorities in imposing fines. Here, the Court of Justice provides significant new insights. The decision is also noteworthy with regard to questions of joint responsibility.

1. Conditions for the imposition of administrative fines

The decision´s primary contribution concerns the interpretation of Art. 83 GDPR. Here, the confirmation of the requirement of fault (and the rejection of strict liability, which may even vary from member state to member state) creates legal certainty on a very central issue and, at the same time, a necessary (moderate) restriction on the grounds for fines. However, this does not concluded the analysis,[27] nor does the decision constitute any form of 'free pass'. In the decision under discussion here, the ECJ (also) quickly resorts to the accusation of negligence, citing earlier case law: Sanctions may be imposed on a controller for conduct falling within the scope of the GDPR 'if the controller could not have been unaware of the unlawfulness of its conduct, regardless of whether it was aware that it violated the provisions of the GDPR'[28]. In practice, this results in considerable liability risks.[29] Furthermore, legal entities whose liability and applicable

25 ECJ 5.12.2023 – case C-683/21, ECLI:EU:C:2023:949 para. 87 – Nacionalinis visuomenės sveikatos centras prie Sveikatos apsaugos ministerijos v Valstybinė duomenų apsaugos inspekcija; cf. the discussion in Grosmann/Hansen K&R 2024, 102 (103): 'Excess of the processor.'

26 See Roßnagel/Rost ZD 2024, 183 (188).

27 Kamlah DSB 2024, 110.

28 ECJ 5.12.2023 – case C-683/21, ECLI:EU:C:2023:949 para. 81 – Nacionalinis visuomenės sveikatos centras prie Sveikatos apsaugos ministerijos v Valstybinė duomenų apsaugos inspekcija.

29 See on the standard of fault: Roßnagel/Rost ZD 2024, 183 (187 et seqq.); critical on this point: Kamlah DSB 2024, 110.

requirements have also been confirmed and clarified by the ECJ[30] must observe far-reaching rules of attribution[31].

According to these rules, it is not necessary to attribute an action to a specifically identified person within a company. This creates an independent concept of attribution within the GDPR and effectively nullifies §§ 30 and 130 of the OWiG[32]. Liability is further extended by the ECJ's[33] attribution of the actions of a processor, which was to be expected. In this respect, it will be necessary in practice to take into account the Court's restriction of liability to processing within the framework of party agreements by drafting processor contracts in as concrete a manner as possible.[34] Furthermore, recourse provisions will have to be considered and carefully examined with regard to their admissibility.[35]

2. Interpretation of the term 'controller' / joint responsibility

With regard to the question of responsibility, the Court of Justice has provided practical guidance, in particular by specifying the criteria to which it did not attach any significance. This can serve as a guide for future practice.

With regard to the term 'joint controller,' the Court of Justice has once again expanded the meaning of the term in another landmark decision by rejecting the requirement for a formal agreement on the purposes and means of processing[36]. The Court of Justice thus confirms its tendency

30 See Roßnagel/Rost ZD 2024, 183 (186).

31 See ECJ 5.12.2023 — case C-807/21, ECLI:EU:C:2023:950 — Deutsche Wohnen SE v Staatsanwaltschaft Berlin; see Ernst ZIP 2024, 990; Rost RDV 2024, 133; Wünschelbaum DSB 2024, 15 ff.

32 Roßnagel/Rost ZD 2024, 183 (185); Schneider ZD 2024, 209 (216); cf. comparative law with US law: Mertens DSB 2025, 266 (268).

33 ECJ 5.12.2023 – case C-683/21, ECLI:EU:C:2023:949 para. 83 et seq. – Nacionalinis vi suomenės sveikatos centras prie Sveikatos apsaugos ministerijos v Valstybinė duo menų apsaugos inspekcija.

34 Grosmann/Hansen 2024, 102 (103); Marosi DSB 2024, 46: 'Halfhearted commissioning means joint responsibility [...]'.

35 Moos, Datenschutz und Datennutzung, 4th edn. 2024, mn. 8.170 and 9.118.

36 ECJ 5.12.2023 – case C-683/21, ECLI:EU:C:2023:949 para. 87 – Nacionalinis visuomenės sveikatos centras prie Sveikatos apsaugos ministerijos v Valstybinė duomenų apsaugos inspekcija.

apparent in previous decisions[37]. A further expansion of the term is also to be expected in the future.[38]

37 ECJ 5.6.2018 — case C-210/16, ECLI:EU:C:2018:388 para. 25 et seq — Unabhängiges Landeszentrum für Datenschutz Schleswig-Holstein v Wirtschaftsakademie Schleswig-Holstein GmbH; ECJ 10.7.2018 - case C-25/17, ECLI:EU:C:2018:551; ECJ 29.7.2019 - case C-40/17, ECLI:EU:C:2019:629 - Fashion ID GmbH & Co.KG v Verbraucherzentrale NRW eV.

38 Schneider ZD 2024, 209 (215).

Joint controllers

Indra Spiecker gen. Döhmann/Loïc Reissner

ECJ 5.6.2018 – case C-210/16, ECLI:EU:C:2018:388 – Wirtschaftsakademie

ECJ 10.7.2018 – case C-25/17, ECLI:EU:C:2018:551 – Jehovan todistajat

ECJ 29.7.2019 – case C-40/17, ECLI:EU:C:2019:629 – FashionID

I. Case summaries

1. ECJ 5.6.2018 – case C-210/16, ECLI:EU:C:2018:388 – Wirtschaftsakademie

Wirtschaftsakademie Schleswig-Holstein GmbH, a German education provider, operated a so-called 'fan page', a professional website on the social media platform *Facebook* to promote its services. The *Unabhängiges Landeszentrum für Datenschutz Schleswig-Holstein (ULD)*, the relevant German data-protection authority, ordered *Wirtschaftsakademie* to deactivate the fan page because *Facebook* placed cookies and collected personal data from visitors without adequate notice or consent and without a valid legal ground. *Wirtschaftsakademie* challenged this, arguing it was not responsible for the data collected by *Facebook*. The German Federal Administrative Court (Bundesverwaltungsgericht) referred questions to the ECJ on the interpretation of the DPD, the predecessor of the GDPR, particularly whether the administrator of a fan page is a '(joint) controller' for personal data processing and whether national supervisory authorities can exercise their powers regarding establishments of companies with multiple Member State presences. The decision is still good law because of the comparability of the relevant provisions in the DPD and the GDPR.

2. ECJ 10.7.2018 – case C-25/17, ECLI:EU:C:2018:551 – Jehovan todistajat

The Tietosuojavaltuutettu (Finnish Data Protection Authority) challenged practices of the Jehovah's Witnesses religious community in Finland concerning collection and processing of personal data during door-to-door preaching and afterwards. Members of the community recorded visitors' names, addresses and other information without complying with Finnish data-protection law (implementing the DPD, the predecessor of the GDPR). The Supreme Administrative Court of Finland referred questions to the Court of Justice of the EU asking whether the data collected during preaching fell within the DPD's scope or was exempt as purely personal/household, whether such data constituted a structured 'filing system', and whether the religious community and its members were data controllers for these processing operations. The decision is still good law because of the comparability of the relevant provisions in the DPD and the GDPR.

3. ECJ 29.7.2019 – case C-40/17, ECLI:EU:C:2019:629 – FashionID

FashionID, a German online retailer, operated a website that embedded the social network Facebook's 'Like'-Button (a so-called 'social plugin'). When visitors accessed the site, their personal data (e.g., IP address and browser information) were automatically transmitted to *Facebook*, regardless of whether visitors used the plugin actively or had Facebook accounts. Verbraucherzentrale NRW, a German consumer-protection association, challenged this practice, arguing that *FashionID* collected and transferred personal data without legal ground, namely users' consent, and failed to provide required information under EU data-protection law (then DPD, the predecessor of the GDPR). It brought proceedings for an injunction to stop the practice before German courts. The Oberlandesgericht Düsseldorf referred questions to the ECJ under Art. 267 TFEU on (i) the definition of 'controller', (ii) the lawfulness of data processing (legitimate interests vs. consent), (iii) information obligations, and (iv) standing of consumer-protection associations to bring such claim. The case is still good law as most of the relevant provisions are in essence also in the GDPR and the GDPR was already in existence when the decision took place thus being obvious that the Court also decided in the light of the GDPR with the same concept in place.

II. Key legal findings

1. ECJ 5.6.2018 – case C-210/16, ECLI:EU:C:2018:388 – Wirtschaftsakademie

The ECJ decided that the concept of '(joint) controller' under Art. 2(d) DPD (now Art. 4 no. 7/Art. 26 GDPR) within the meaning of that provision encompasses the administrator of a fan page hosted on a social network together with this social network. For this, a joint responsibility does not require each of the controllers to have access to the (personal) data concerned.[1] Thus, a fan page administrator can be a controller although the audience statistics compiled by the platform are transmitted to the fan page administrator only in anonymised form. This is based on the consideration that those statistics derive from data that had previously been collected and further processed by means of cookies installed by *Facebook* on the computers or other devices of visitors to that page.[2] Using a platform provided by a third party in order to benefit from the associated services cannot exempt a fan page's administrator from compliance with its obligations concerning the protection of personal data.[3] Controllers may be involved at different stages of the processing and to different degrees.[4]

The other questions dealt with in the decision were specialities under the DPD not applicable to the GDPR today.

2. ECJ 10.7.2018 – case C-25/17, ECLI:EU:C:2018:551 – Jehovan todistajat

The decision is mostly of further importance because of the clarification of joint controllership (which has not changed under the GDPR) and the width of the household/purely personal exemption (also still in the GDPR). It also clarifies that the balancing between religious freedom and data protection has to occur within the EU data protection law and does not exclude religious activities from the obligation to adhere in principle to data protection.[5]

1 ECJ 5.6.2018 – case C-210/16, ECLI:EU:C:2018:388 para. 38 – Wirtschaftsakademie.
2 ECJ 5.6.2018 – case C-210/16, ECLI:EU:C:2018:388 para. 38 – Wirtschaftsakademie.
3 ECJ 5.6.2018 – case C-210/16, ECLI:EU:C:2018:388 para. 40 – Wirtschaftsakademie.
4 ECJ 5.6.2018 – case C-210/16, ECLI:EU:C:2018:388 para. 43 – Wirtschaftsakademie.
5 ECJ 10.7.2018 – case C-25/17, ECLI:EU:C:2018:551 para. 49 – Jehovan todistajat.

The Court regards a religious community as a (joint) controller together with its preaching members for the data processing carried out by the members in the context of door-to-door preaching when this is organised, coordinated and encouraged by that community. The Court clarifies that a controller need not determine purposes and means of the processing by written guidelines or instructions from the controller.[6] Furthermore, the Court once more finds that access to the personal data is not necessary in order to be joint controllers.[7] Also, the controllers can be involved at different stages of the processing and to different degrees.[8] It is sufficient to exert influence for own purposes as this results in the determination of the purposes and means of that processing.[9]

The ECJ finds organization and coordination of the preaching activities as sufficient determination of the means of the data processing under data protection law if the purposes are similar. In particular, the allocation of areas of activity to the various preaching members, their encouragement and the administration of lists of persons who do not wish to receive a visit, from those data which are transmitted to them by members who engage in preaching, is thus sufficient for a controllership. The Court does not regard the individual decisions of the preaching members as hindering joint controllership, even if they decide on the circumstances of a visit, which specific data are collected and subsequently processed, and as the data are collected as a memory aid for later use.[10] As the objective of the Community is to spread its faith, the Community and its preaching members pursue the same purpose.[11] The Court finds knowledge of the activities of the members together with the organization and coordination of the data collection activities sufficient.

The Court also – in two sentences – disagrees with the argument that religious freedom and organizational autonomy of religious communities, Art. 17 TFEU, would disagree with application of the data protection law.[12]

---

6 ECJ 10.7.2018 – case C-25/17, ECLI:EU:C:2018:551 para. 67 – Jehovan todistajat.
7 ECJ 10.7.2018 – case C-25/17, ECLI:EU:C:2018:551 para. 69 – Jehovan todistajat.
8 ECJ 10.7.2018 – case C-25/17, ECLI:EU:C:2018:551 para. 66 – Jehovan todistajat.
9 ECJ 10.7.2018 – case C-25/17, ECLI:EU:C:2018:551 para. 68 – Jehovan todistajat.
10 ECJ 10.7.2018 – case C-25/17, ECLI:EU:C:2018:551 para. 70 – Jehovan todistajat.
11 ECJ 10.7.2018 – case C-25/17, ECLI:EU:C:2018:551 para. 71 – Jehovan todistajat.
12 ECJ 10.7.2018 – case C-25/17, ECLI:EU:C:2018:551 para. 74 – Jehovan todistajat.

3. ECJ 29.7.2019 – case C-40/17, ECLI:EU:C:2019:629 – FashionID

The decision is mostly known to be the follow-up on *Wirtschaftsakademie* (C-210/16). As such, it strengthens the legal obligations of those enabling data processing of social networks, in this case through social plugins on their own websites. The decision clarifies the concept of joint controllership and enlarges it to consider the overall data processing procedure rather than individual steps and is still relevant under the GDPR.

The decision also deals with questions of the legitimation of data processing through social plugins. Here, the Court clearly states that both controllers need justification. Also, the decision makes clear that processing of data by a social network of persons who have no connection with that social network, i.e. an account, has to be considered to be of additional (detrimental) value.

Lastly, but under the GDPR of little relevance, the decision finds that the DPD did not block national legislation allowing consumer-protection associations legal proceedings against websites.

In regard to the core of the judgment, the joint controllership, the ECJ stresses first, again, that this concept has to be understood in a broad manner in order to protect those whose data is being processed.[13] Again, the concept requires no access to and no processing of the personal data concerned to be a controller.[14] Controllers may be involved at different stages of the processing and to different degrees.[15]

The operator of a website that embeds on that website a social plugin causing the browser of a visitor to that website to request content from the provider of that plugin and, to that end, to transmit to that provider personal data of the visitor is a (joint) controller under EU data protection law.[16]

In the judgement, the ECJ differentiates between the determination of the means and the purposes. *FashionID* made it possible for the social network to obtain personal data of visitors to its own website as soon as the visitor consults the website.[17] *FashionID* was fully aware of the fact that the like-button serves as a tool for the collection and disclosure by transmission

13 ECJ 29.7.2019 – case C-40/17, ECLI:EU:C:2019:629 para. 65 et seq. – FashionID.

14 ECJ 29.7.2019 – case C-40/17, ECLI:EU:C:2019:629 para. 69, 82 – FashionID.

15 ECJ 29.7.2019 – case C-40/17, ECLI:EU:C:2019:629 para. 70 – FashionID.

16 ECJ 29.7.2019 – case C-40/17, ECLI:EU:C:2019:629 para. 84 – FashionID.

17 ECJ 29.7.2019 – case C-40/17, ECLI:EU:C:2019:629 para. 75 – FashionID.

of the personal data of visitors to that website.[18] According to the ECJ, this indicates that *FashionID* exerts a decisive influence over the collection and transmission of the personal data. This is because the processing would not have occurred without that plugin.[19] Thus, knowledge is considered to be sufficient to create purpose. The Court makes clear that *FashionID* as the website had no interest in the results of the social networks' further data processing in order to enhance Facebook's business model and thus cannot be considered to be (joint) controller for those data processing.[20] In this regard, the fact of the case differs from the decision in *Wirtschaftsakademie* where the website (fan page) administrator shared the purposes of the social networks further data processing.

Having construed the purpose for joint controllership of both the website and the social network through the social plugin, the Court sees sufficient means. The activities in connection with the social plugin promise the website administrator more visibility and thus additional commercial advantages; this suffices as shared means.[21] The Court does not find different and separated commercial advantages of the social network and the website administrator to hinder joint controllership.[22]

This is sufficient for the ECJ to affirm a jointly determination of the purposes by *FashionID* and *Facebook* of the collection and disclosure by transmission of the data.

On the side, the Court also states that the responsibility of a website operator is even greater when the website is visited by those who do not have an account on the social network.[23] This is an important finding mostly relevant not for joint controllership but rather for the legal evaluation of interests of persons. Obviously, the Court sees a difference in data processing by a social network of those persons who already have an institutionalized relationship with it, in particular through being active users with an account on the social network, and the data processing by a social network of those persons not in such a relationship.

The further findings of the Court in regard to joint controllership are consequential: It finds that both parties of a joint controllership must fulfill

---

18 ECJ 29.7.2019 – case C-40/17, ECLI:EU:C:2019:629 para. 77 – FashionID.
19 ECJ 29.7.2019 – case C-40/17, ECLI:EU:C:2019:629 para. 78 – FashionID.
20 ECJ 29.7.2019 – case C-40/17, ECLI:EU:C:2019:629 para. 76 – FashionID.
21 ECJ 29.7.2019 – case C-40/17, ECLI:EU:C:2019:629 para. 80 – FashionID.
22 ECJ 29.7.2019 – case C-40/17, ECLI:EU:C:2019:629 para. 80 – FashionID.
23 ECJ 29.7.2019 – case C-40/17, ECLI:EU:C:2019:629 para. 83 – FashionID.

the requirements of a sufficient legal ground for the data processing.[24] Here, joint controllership does not lead to a privilege of the involved controllers: Legitimation of the one party may not count towards legitimation of the other party; rather, both are fully responsible for fulfilling the requirements of data protection law. Nevertheless, this legal obligation only covers any data processing still within the concept of joint controllership.[25] Consequently, the Court further finds that other obligations, here information obligations of the website administrator, also only need to address the data processing of which the website administrator is joint controller.

On more legal historical note, the Court also finds that Art. 22 to 24 DPD must be interpreted as not precluding national legislation which allows consumer-protection associations to bring or defend legal proceedings against a person allegedly responsible for an infringement of the protection of personal data.[26]

III. Systematic context and legal classification

Although all three cases were brought to the Court under the DPD, they still are fully effective under the GDPR (Art. 4 no. 7 GDPR) because the concept of joint controllership remains the same. Thus, they have a lasting effect under the GDPR until today.

Joint Controllership, Art. 4 no. 7 GDPR, is a core principle of the EU data protection law and establishes who is legally responsible. The norm defines 'controller' as the natural or legal person, public authority, agency or other body which, alone or jointly with others, determines the purposes and means of the processing of personal data. Art. 26 GDPR, on the basis of Art. 4 no. 7 GDPR, contains specific obligations for joint controllers in addition to the obligations for sole controllers which, however, are not mandatory to construe joint controllership. For this, the joint controllers have to determine the purposes and means of the processing of personal data. The means refer to the manner in which the objective is to be achieved, i.e. which means are to be used to achieve the objective whilst

24 ECJ 29.7.2019 – case C-40/17, ECLI:EU:C:2019:629 para. 87–97 – FashionID.
25 ECJ 29.7.2019 – case C-40/17, ECLI:EU:C:2019:629 para. 106 – FashionID.
26 ECJ 29.7.2019 – case C-40/17, ECLI:EU:C:2019:629 para. 43–63 – FashionID.

the purposes refers to the 'why' of the processing.[27] Thus, anyone who is a controller, has to comply with the requirements of the DPD/GDPR, e.g. the obligations of Art. 12 et. seq, 24 and 25 or 35 GDPR. Also, only a controller may be the addressee of fines and measures of the authorities or may have to pay damages.

Joint Controllership has to be distinguished from processors according to Art. 28, Art. 4 no. 8 GDPR as the other regulatory approach to a division of labor/tasks within data protection law. While a processor processes data *on behalf* of a controller, a controller has to determine means and purposes of the processing. Thus, there has to be a 'more' of cooperation and collaboration between the involved parties.[28]

Core elements are thus the determination of joint means and joint purposes.

1. ECJ 5.6.2018 – case C-210/16, ECLI:EU:C:2018:388 – Wirtschaftsakademie

The decision is the first major decision of the ECJ on joint controllership.

The Court holds that the objective of the broad definition of the concept of 'controller' is an effective and complete protection of the persons concerned.[29]

The ECJ bases its decision on the fact that the administrator of a fan page gives by choice the platform the opportunity to place cookies on the computer of a person visiting the fan page.[30] Thus, the decisive factor is the decision of the fan page administrator to use this particular means – that is the use of a fan page on a social network. Thus, the choice also includes the further data processing of the social network in order to increase visibility and reach users.

Only additionally, the following processing of the visitors' personal data is intended in particular to enable *Facebook* to improve its system of advertising. The processing also enables the fan page administrator to obtain

27 EDPB, 'Guidelines 07/2020 on the terms "controller" and "processor" in the GDPR', version 2.1 (7.7.2021), <https://www.edpb.europa.eu/system/files_en?file=2023-10/EDPB_guidelines_202007_controllerprocessor_final_en.pdf>, para. 33.

28 Spiecker gen. Döhmann GS Spindler, 707 (711).

29 ECJ 5.6.2018 – case C-210/16, ECLI:EU:C:2018:388 para. 28 – Wirtschaftsakademie.

30 ECJ 5.6.2018 – case C-210/16, ECLI:EU:C:2018:388 para. 25 – Wirtschaftsakademie.

statistics produced by *Facebook*.[31] The Court finds this connection to be sufficient to constitute that the fan page administrator has an influence on the processing of personal data of the platform in order to produce statistics on user behavior. In particular, he can define the criteria in accordance with which the statistics are to be drawn up. He can even designate the categories of persons whose personal data is to be made use of by the platform, including inter alia demographic data relating to its target audience like trends in terms of age, sex, relationship and occupation.[32] Thus, the Court assures that making use of a social network does not automatically turn a user to a (joint) controller.[33] But it is already clear in this first of many decisions that the court finds the professional use of a platform in order to target visitors of the website and enlarge one's audience sufficient grounds for common means and common purposes as joint controllers.

If data of persons not being registered members of the network is processed, the fan page administrator's responsibility for the processing of the personal data of those persons appears to be even greater, as the mere consultation of the website by visitors automatically starts the processing of their personal data for further purposes.[34]

The ECJ finds that access to personal data concerned is not required in order to be assumed to be a controller. By this, the ECJ lays down a fundamental element for all the following rulings on joint controllership until today. The Court has not revoked any of its finding in the case, but rather enlarged the concept of joint controllership ever since.

The Court clarifies and has stressed ever since in all further decisions, that joint responsibility means a shared responsibility in which the involved parties do not have to fulfill all requirements in full individually. Also, they need not each be involved equally and also not in all steps of a data processing. Rather, the division on labor which joint controllership is based on may also mean that one party can contribute significantly more than the other.

31 ECJ 5.6.2018 – case C-210/16, ECLI:EU:C:2018:388 para. 34 – Wirtschaftsakademie.

32 ECJ 5.6.2018 – case C-210/16, ECLI:EU:C:2018:388 para. 36 et seq. – Wirtschaftsakademie.

33 ECJ 5.6.2018 – case C-210/16, ECLI:EU:C:2018:388 para. 35 – Wirtschaftsakademie.

34 ECJ 5.6.2018 – case C-210/16, ECLI:EU:C:2018:388 para. 41 – Wirtschaftsakademie.

2. ECJ 10.7.2018 – case C-25/17, ECLI:EU:C:2018:551 – Jehovan todistajat

Jehovan todistajat was the second important decision of the ECJ on (joint) controllership and is best known for this.

The Court upholds, as in the decision *Wirtschaftsakademie* (C-210/16), that the concept of 'controller' has to be interpreted broadly in order to achieve an effective and complete protection of the persons concerned.[35] It also upholds that access to the personal data is not mandatory for (joint) controllership.[36] Again, the Court finds that knowledge of the activities of the other controller suffice to construe purpose, even if that knowledge is not precise on the exact data processing.[37]

The decision enlarges the concept of joint controllership in two regards: The Court finds that the determination of the means is already given if there is the exertion of (some, in this case very little) influence.[38] For this, the immediate controller who performs the actual data processing, may have full discretion and also act without any control by the joint controller in the background as the member who performed the preaching and collected and processed data chose freely whom to address and what to pass on to the community behind. The Court also sees the element of 'encouragement' together with a certain amount of organizational input as sufficient for determination of means in a joint manner.[39]

The judgment is kept relatively short in terms of joint controllership as it also examines the so called 'household-exemption' and whether the collected data constituted a structured 'filing system' and thus falls in the scope of the DPD. While the latter part of the decision is of little value under the GDPR, the findings on the household/personal exemption are still valid under the GDPR as this concept has not changed. Here, the Court determines that for EU data protection law not to apply, the purpose of the data processing has to be *purely* personal, meaning that any additional purpose excludes the exemption from being applicable and thus the GDPR applies.[40] Someone spreading faith to unknown addressees

35 ECJ 10.7.2018 – case C-25/17, ECLI:EU:C:2018:551 para. 66 – Jehovan todistajat.
36 ECJ 10.7.2018 – case C-25/17, ECLI:EU:C:2018:551 para. 69 – Jehovan todistajat.
37 ECJ 10.7.2018 – case C-25/17, ECLI:EU:C:2018:551 para. 71 – Jehovan todistajat.
38 ECJ 10.7.2018 – case C-25/17, ECLI:EU:C:2018:551 para. 68 – Jehovan todistajat.
39 ECJ 10.7.2018 – case C-25/17, ECLI:EU:C:2018:551 para. 73 – Jehovan todistajat.
40 Cf. ECJ 10.7.2018 – case C-25/17, ECLI:EU:C:2018:551 para. 40 et seq. – Jehovan todistajat.

by door-to-door-visitation does not fall under this privilege.[41] The Court finds the possibility of a accessibility by potentially unlimited number of persons to hinder the exception.[42] Also, only individuals may claim this exemption.[43]

Of interest is also the value the Court assigns to religious freedom in regard to the interpretation of the application of the GDPR: Although it acknowledges that the door-to-door-preaching as well as the data processing resulting from this is protected under freedom of religion, this does not exclude the applicability of EU data protection law as such.[44] A balancing of interests of data protection and freedom of religion thus has to be made within data protection law.

3. ECJ 29.7.2019 – case C-40/17, ECLI:EU:C:2019:629 – FashionID

FashionID is the follow-up decision on (joint) controllership and social networks. It upholds and enlarges the *Wirtschaftsakademie* decision: Where *Wirtschaftsakademie* held network and professional content provider within the network to be jointly responsible, *FashionID* clarifies that any outside website enabling a social network to use the website's users' data is also jointly responsible. Thus, an illegal data processing of the social network processing on the network also reflects on the website enabling this data processing. The *Wirtschaftsakademie* ruling remains the most relevant one; *FashionID* adds and clarifies some elements. In all: Joint controllership is far-reaching and hinders evasion of responsibility for data violations in today's attention economy driven profiling. Therefore, all that has been expressed in regard to the *Wirtschaftsakademie* decision, is still true under the *FashionID* verdict (and beyond this: The Court has never retracted from any of its joint controllership decisions, so far).

Beyond the holding in *Wirtschaftsakademie*, the Court dwells more on the share of each of the controllers in regard to means and purpose thus connecting its decision to the decision in *Jehovan todistajat* (C-25/17). In regard to means, the court refers to the manner in which the objective is

41 ECJ 10.7.2018 – case C-25/17, ECLI:EU:C:2018:551 para. 44 – Jehovan todistajat.

42 ECJ 10.7.2018 – case C-25/17, ECLI:EU:C:2018:551 para. 45 – Jehovan todistajat.

43 ECJ 10.7.2018 – case C-25/17, ECLI:EU:C:2018:551 para. 42 – Jehovan todistajat.

44 ECJ 10.7.2018 – case C-25/17, ECLI:EU:C:2018:551 para. 46 et. seq, in particular para. 49 – Jehovan todistajat.

to be achieved, i.e. which means are to be used to achieve the objective whilst the purposes refers to the 'why' of the processing.[45] As in *Wirtschaftsakademie* and *Jehovan todistajat*, the Court interprets the concept broadly in order to protect data and data subjects efficiently and finds that controllership does not require to have access to and actually process data.[46] Also following up on its earlier decisions, the Court does not require all controllers to be involved in all stages of the processing but rather division of labor may lead to involvement in different stages of the processing and to – even more importantly – different degrees. In regard to purpose, the Court also continues to require little: Whereas in *Jehovan todistajat* the purposes of the members of the church and the church itself were aligned, in *Wirtschaftsakademie* and in *FashionID* they were independent from each other. The Court finds diverse economic/commercial interests of both *FashionID* and the social network to be sufficient. Furthermore, the Court also lets increased visibility and publicity suffice as a purpose to be considered.[47]

The Court also clarifies what the consequences of a concept of joint controllership are: Each of the controllers has to fulfill the requirements of the GDPR such as legitimation, fulfillment of duties such as information of the data subject etc. Joint controllers may not rely on the other controller to oblige but have to take full responsibility for compliance, themselves.

IV. Author's analysis and commentary

1. ECJ 5.6.2018 – case C-210/16, ECLI:EU:C:2018:388 – Wirtschaftsakademie

The judgement is *the* fundamental decision laying down essential elements for the understanding of the concept of '(joint) controller' in regard to division of labor models in particular with platforms/social networks. It makes clear that the Court will – in regard to data protection – not allow professional administrators to hide behind operators of online platforms by pointing to a lesser degree of processing and/or no direct access to

45 EDPB, 'Guidelines 07/2020 on the terms "controller" and "processor" in the GDPR' (fn. 16), para. 33.

46 ECJ 29.7.2019 – case C-40/17, ECLI:EU:C:2019:629 para. 69 – FashionID.

47 Cf. ECJ 29.7.2019 – case C-40/17, ECLI:EU:C:2019:629 para. 80 – FashionID.

the processing. Rather, professional operators with content making use of platform infrastructures, functionalities and tools to enlarge audience as well as gain importance and visibility in typical digital platform business models also share the responsibility for any data protection violations of the platform. The decision and the following ones in line with it – often criticized as too far-reaching[48] – create the link between those providing the tools for analysis in the attention economy and those using these tools through the concept of joint control.

The decision provides the ground that professional users of fan pages have to accept responsibility for the violation of data protection law by the platform on which such pages are displayed under the DPD/GDPR's concept of joint responsibility. The decision is closely connected with the 2023 *Bundeskartellamt* decision (C-252/21), in which the Court found that only consent may constitute a valid legal ground for the data processing under *Facebook's* (and similar financed) platforms' business model. Under the condition of the broad interpretation of joint controllership that the Court favors, the result of *Wirtschaftsakademie* was not surprising as the co-determination of means and purposes by the fan page administrator was relatively obvious: The platform was the main data processor,[49] but the fan page administrator benefited directly from one element of the processing of the platform, i.e. the (anonymised) statistics of the visitors of the website, and the fan page administrator was able to influence his personal results of the processing directly be determining filters for the statistics. However, it is often not seen that the Court also pointed out in *Wirtschaftsakademie* and also in following decisions that the fan page administrator also profits from the distribution channels of the social network itself[50] and that the enabling of setting cookies and allowing the social network's business operations suffices[51]. So even if the statistics are not being used/available, these other elements remain to establish joint controllership.

The importance of the decision cannot be underestimated. Firstly, the ECJ makes clear that there is a broad concept of responsibility.[52] Consequently, in this and all further decisions, the Court has always confirmed joint controllership even if the degree of influence over means and pur-

48 Cf. Millard IDPL 9 (2019), 217; Wong IDPL 11 (2021), 375.

49 ECJ 5.6.2018 – case C-210/16, ECLI:EU:C:2018:388 para. 33 – Wirtschaftsakademie.

50 ECJ 5.6.2018 – case C-210/16, ECLI:EU:C:2018:388 para. 25 – Wirtschaftsakademie and ECJ 29.7.2019 - case C-40/17, ECLI:EU:C:2019:629 para. 80 - FashionID.

51 ECJ 5.6.2018 – case C-210/16, ECLI:EU:C:2018:388 para. 35 – Wirtschaftsakademie.

52 ECJ 5.6.2018 – case C-210/16, ECLI:EU:C:2018:388 para. 27 – Wirtschaftsakademie.

poses in these further decisions was always diminished in comparison to *Wirtschaftsakademie* and thus would have given easy ground to change the line of jurisprudence.

Secondly, the decision is based on a clear understanding of the functionalities and roles of social networks and those who professionally use social networks to reach out. The Court concentrates on the network structure with three groups of actors involved: Networks gain their value because of their ability to connect users and to distribute content of website administrators between these users. This naturally raises the question – and not only in data protection – how the legal responsibility of content providers/administrators and networks has to be construed. Way too often, networks are considered as mere infrastructure and thus relieved from further responsibilities – so under the notice-and-take-down-regime e.g. in intellectual property or the DSA. However, the ECJ does not fall into this trap. It clearly integrates the functionalities of networks into its ruling: Social networks like *Facebook* are professional operators. They use data processing of their users in order to increase their own revenue through advertisement and content-curation on the basis of profiles of their users. What the Court sees no need to mention and which might not be too well known at the time of the judgment (2018) is the fact that also the content distribution takes place according to the same mechanisms based on profiles of the users; the data processing is thus twice relevant for the design. Professional website administrators in networks with functionalities like *Facebook* – and that is e.g. YouTube, Instagram, TikTok and the like – profit from exactly this proceeding themselves and this is why they seek the professional cooperation: They are looking for ways how to increase the visibility of their content on the network and thus profit from the networks attribution of content and profiles.

In *Wirtschaftsakademie*, the ECJ bases its decision on the fact that the fan page administrator makes the processing of the personal data of its website visitors possible for *Facebook*.[53] It also relates to the fact that the fan page administrator may profit himself from the statistics which *Facebook* develops and provides. Even if social networks now sometimes offer an opt-out for website administrators to receive statistics, they nevertheless continue to provide the basis for the network's profiling on which the attribution of content is based. Thus, even in these circumstances, website

53 ECJ 5.6.2018 – case C-210/16, ECLI:EU:C:2018:388 para. 75 – Wirtschaftsakademie.

administrators profit from the reach the social networks provide on the basis of the users' data and have to be considered jointly responsible.

Accordingly, the purposes pursued do not have to be identical, and they do not have to be present in both of the cooperating parties.[54] Furthermore, it is not necessary for all parties involved to fully meet the criteria. The exact division of who determines the purposes and means is therefore flexible: a joint controller may have a greater influence on one element or the other; it may also be the case that only the purpose or only the means is determined, and even then only in part. Cooperation may be very close, for example if the joint purposes are completely identical, or it may be quite loose and only partial. The broad interpretation of the concept of responsibility includes all of this.

The decision is furthermore far reaching as it jointly discusses (and affirms) the responsibility of the fan page operator with regard to *all* processing operations. Contrary to the Advocate General,[55] the ECJ does not distinguish between the phase of collection and the phase of processing for the statistics.[56] Rather, it takes a holistic approach. Thus, controllership need not be present in all phases of the joint controllership activities.

For the question of joint controllership of a *Facebook* fan page administrator without the possibility to access statistics, the German Federal Data Protection Commissioner (BfDI) found a fan page entertained by the federal government to violate the GDPR because of joint controllership in line with the aforementioned decisions.[57] The decision has been challenged.[58]

There are a quite a few practical implications on social network/social media activities: Firstly, a professional website administrator aiming at range has to choose carefully on which social network he operates his website as data protection violations of the network will be attributed to him under the concept of joint controllership – with all measures, fines

54 EDPB, 'Guidelines 07/2020 on the terms "controller" and "processor" in the GDPR' (fn. 5) para. 60.

55 See AG Bot 24.10.2017- case C-210/16, ECLI:EU:C:2017:796 para. 42 – Wirtschaftsakademie.

56 ECJ 5.6.2018 – case C-210/16, ECLI:EU:C:2018:388 para. 25–44 – Wirtschaftsakademie.

57 BfDI, ‚BfDI untersagt Betrieb der Fanpage der Bundesregierung' (2023) <https://www.bfdi.bund.de/SharedDocs/Pressemitteilungen/DE/2023/06-Untersagung-Betrieb-Fanpage-BReg.html>.

58 BfDI, ‚Fan page proceedings go into the next round' (22.8.2025) <https://www.bfdi.bund.de/SharedDocs/Pressemitteilungen/EN/2025/12_Fanpage-appeals.html?nn=253682>.

and potential damages in tow because the network and the internal website (fan page) share the common purpose of range and controlled traffic with the means of data processing including profiling. Secondly, the fine line between joint controllership and processing on behalf of the controller may be quickly leading to full responsibility under joint controllership, considering that the ECJ does not require much alignment of purposes and/or means nor much parallel activities to construe joint controllership. Thirdly, the Court takes the concept of responsibility serious and obviously is not willing to let the complex structures and the various participants in today's social network operations lead to a diffusion of responsibility and legal uncertainty to the detriment of the data subject. And as a fourth point, the Court's decisions on joint controllership until today are all consistent and only clarify ideas of shared responsibility without ever restricting them – this should be a warning to anyone tempted to take joint controllership lightly.

2. ECJ 10.7.2018 – case C-25/17, ECLI:EU:C:2018:551 – Jehovan todistajat

As in all following decisions the court strengthens the concept of joint controllership effectively.

The decision is important because it sets further cornerstones in regard to several aspects of joint controllership. Other than the previous and the following judgments, in particular those in regard to social media and internet business models on the basis of data processing of user data (like *FashionID*, C-40/17, or *IAB*, C-604/22), the case has no strong digitization background. Nevertheless, the decision structures the relationship between means and purposes and whether joint controllers have to be fully part of both. Behind this is the question whether 'determination' in Art. 4 no. 7 GDPR may already consist of a relatively loose influence such as a very general organizational input like allocating areas for preaching activities in a non-binding way but without any further influence on the actual data processing and the type of data being processed.

In *Wirtschaftsakademie*, the Court already made clear that there need not be an equal share and that the shares can also be at different times and stages. In *Jehovan todistajat*, the Court stresses that the purposes and not the means are the key: It suffices that there is an influence over the processing of personal data in order to fulfill the criterium of 'determination of the purposes'. As the means are not influenced by the community – any member chose freely whether or not to collect data, when, how and where, which data and which to pass on –, it is obviously not necessary that both controllers control the means other than acknowledging the existence of some data processing activities to the common purpose. Determination of means thus becomes a very weak element, and there will be little possibility to avoid joint controllership on the basis of means.

This leads even further at close sight: The Court finds both in *Wirtschaftsakademie* and in *Jehovan todistajat* and also in the judgments to follow thereafter that the knowledge of one controller of the general – not the concise (!) – activities of data processing and its purposes is sufficient to embrace these means and their purposes. If knowledge is sufficient – and no intention necessary –, then knowledge results in 'determination' in the meaning of joint controllership of Art. 4 no. 7 GDPR, and that is true for both the means and the purpose. Thus, in the end, it suffices that the joint controllers share a common purpose and have a general idea of what data processing might take place. Therefore, joint controllership is established by the common purpose. And this, *Wirtschaftsakademie, Fashion ID, IAB* and other decisions have illustrated, is to the Court in a digitalized business model like social media, the common interest in reach, followers and publicity while in *Jehovan todistajat* a less profane common purpose – spreading a particular faith – bound the joint controllers together.

The history of decisions in regard to joint controllership has not seen the ECJ waver in any way. Rather, it has in all following cases kept up the guiding principle of a broad interpretation in order to protect data subjects in an effective manner. In more recent cases, the functionalities of the data processing in combination with the internet service models are in the center of the Court's decisions, e.g. *IAB*.

Thus, joint controllership links data processing to responsibility. Anyone relying on someone else's data processing, and that is the essence of *Jehovan todistajat* and *FashionID* – simply knowing about it and profiting from it even in a distant manner, falls within the scope of EU data protection law. In *ètat belge* (C-231/22), the Court even advanced this to a mandatory data processing without the possibility of influence.

3. ECJ 29.7.2019 – case C-40/17, ECLI:EU:C:2019:629 – FashionID

The judgement enlarges the concept of joint controllership in regard to purpose and means when a social network is included. It now suffices to enable data processing of visitors of an external website whereas in *Wirtschaftsakademie* data processing took place on an internal website of a social network. Although the website operator did not process data by himself, the ECJ affirms his status as (joint) controller. On this basis the EDPB states later: 'Different controllers may therefore define the means of the processing to a different extent, depending on who is effectively in a position to do so'.[59]

The difference between *Wirtschaftsakademie* and *FashionID* can be found in the responsibility for the further data processing of the social network: In *FashionID*, the ECJ underlines that the website operator is not responsible for further processing by *Facebook* after the collection and transfer of the data of visitors on *FashionID's* website. The reason for this is that the website does not profit from any of the further processing of data: The profiling activities of a social network beyond the original processing of visitors' data has no effect on *FashionID*. In *Wirtschaftsakademie*, this was different: The website administrator profited from the statistics – and the controlled traffic – on the basis of the further data processing of *Facebook*, because it entertained an internal website, a fan page. Thus, although the purpose must bind together the joint controllers, 'the most marginal influence over the means, such as enabling someone else's processing, suffices to be a controller'[60].

Thus, the case is another milestone for the application of the GDPR in the context of social media activities. As the Court has not so far retracted from any of its joint controllership decisions, DPOs and professional website administrators have to carefully assess their role within every specific data processing in order to fulfill the GDPR-requirements. If the social network is operating under violations of the GDPR – as does e.g. *Facebook*, according to *Bundeskartellamt* (C-252/21) –, one should refrain from professional use. The combination of the holdings in *Wirtschaftsakademie*, *FashionID* and *Bundeskartellamt* makes those enabling social networks and/or entertaining professional internal websites/profiles aiming at range

59 EDPB, 'Guidelines 07/2020 on the terms "controller" and "processor" in the GDPR' (fn. 16), para. 63.

60 Finck IDPL 11(2021), 333.

and making use of the curation and sorting procedures of the social network responsible under the GDPR which may then lead to measures and fines and also damages from data subjects.

The Court, less frequently noticed in the literature, also evaluates a data processing which takes place without the data subject knowing about this, to be an increase in the legal intensity of infringement. This may not be of extended importance in the assessment of joint controllership, but for any balancing of interest test this constitutes an important aspect.

V. Recommended further reading

See also the decisions

ECJ 11.1.2024 – case C-231/22, ECLI:EU:C:2024:7 – État belge.

ECJ 7.3.2024 – case C-604/22, ECLI:EU:C:2024:214 – IAB Europe.

ECJ 5.12.2023 – case C-683/21, ECLI:EU:C:2023:949 – Nacionalinis visuomenės sveikatos centras prie Sveikatos apsaugos ministerijos (NZÖG).

Compare also

EDPB, 'Guidelines 07/2020 on the terms "controller" and "processor" in the GDPR', version 2.1 (7.7.2021), <https://www.edpb.europa.eu/system/files_en?file=2023-10/EDPB_guidelines_202007_controllerprocessor_final_en.pdf>.

In the literature, of many

Ducuing/Schroers/Kindt EDPL 4 (2018), 547.

Blanc EDPL 4 (2018), 120.

Gellert EDPL 4 (2018), 391.

Gorkič EDPL 5 (2019), 579.

Spiecker gen. Döhmann GS Gerald Spindler, 2025, 709.

Spiecker gen. Döhmann/Papakonstantinou/Hornung/de Hert Data Protection Article-by-Article Commentary/Jori, 2023, GDPR Art. 4 no. 7 mn. 9 et. seq.

Kuner/Bygrave/Docksey The EU GDPR/Bygrave/Tosoni 2020, GDPR Art. 4 no. 7 C. 3 et. seq.

Processing on behalf of a controller

Florian Thoma

ECJ 5.12.2023 – case C-683/21, ECLI:EU:C:2023:949 – Nacionalinis visuomenės sveikatos centras prie Sveikatos apsaugos ministerijos v Valstybinė duomenų apsaugos inspekcija

I. Case summary

The judgment of the Court was made as a preliminary ruling[1] requested by the Regional Administrative Court in Vilnius, Lithuania. It is worth noting that the Court sat as a Grand Chamber of 15 judges, which is rather exceptional. A Grand Chamber usually decides if a case is particularly complex or important, or if so requested by a Member State or Union institution which is a party of the case.

According to the judgment of the Court and the opinion of the Advocate General, in March 2020 – i.e. in a relatively early stage of the Covid-19 pandemic – the Lithuanian Minister for Health instructed the National Public Health Centre ('NVSC') to organize the development and acquisition of a mobile application which could be used for tracing contact persons of infected individuals. Someone claiming to represent NVSC reached out to an IT company, ITSS, which started the development of the application. The NVSC representative and several NVSC employees provided direction to ITSS, particularly in relation to questions in the application. The application became publicly available for download in early April 2020 on the Google and Apple app stores. It identified both ITSS and NVSC as controllers.

Thereafter, the Minister for Health instructed NVSC to acquire the application, however the acquisition failed primarily due to a lack of funding. The application continued to be available for download.

On 15 May 2020, NVSC asked ITSS to remove links and references to NVSC in the application. On 18 May 2020, the Lithuanian supervisory

1 Art. 267 TFEU.

authority, VDAI, initiated an investigation concerning NVSC and ITSS. Following a request from VDAI, the application was suspended on 26 May 2020; approximately 3,800 users had used it and had provided personal data (including personal health data) through the app.

In February 2021, VDAI imposed administrative fines on NVSC and ITSS as joint controllers, for violations of GDPR. NVSC challenged VDAI's decision before the Regional Administrative Court, which stayed the proceedings to request a preliminary ruling of the ECJ.

II. Key legal findings

The Regional Administrative Court first asked[2] three specific questions regarding the interpretation of the concept of 'controller'[3], which reflect the peculiarities of the case. These questions focus on whether an entity can be regarded as a controller when the intended acquisition of and transfer of rights in the mobile app did not take place, and whether that interpretation might change due to the entity being designated, without its approval, as controller. In addition, the submitting court asked whether an entity can be considered a controller if it didn't perform any actual processing in the sense of Art. 4 no. 2 GDPR and has not permitted or consented to such activities.

The submitting court then asked[4] (question 4) whether 'processing'[5] includes the use of personal data for testing of an IT system, and (question 5) whether 'joint control'[6] requires deliberate coordination or can also exist if there is a mere lack of arrangements and coordination. Finally, the sixth question addressed administrative fines, in particular whether the potential controller should be held liable, even without fault, for improper processing by the processor.

2 ECJ 5.12.2023 – case C-683/21, ECLI:EU:C:2023:949 para. 26 – Nacionalinis visuomenės sveikatos centras prie Sveikatos apsaugos ministerijos v Valstybinė duomenų apsaugos inspekcija.

3 Art. 4 no. 7 GDPR.

4 ECJ 5.12.2023 – case C-683/21, ECLI:EU:C:2023:949 para. 26 – Nacionalinis visuomenės sveikatos centras prie Sveikatos apsaugos ministerijos v Valstybinė duomenų apsaugos inspekcija.

5 Art. 4 no. 2 GDPR.

6 Art. 26 GDPR.

The ECJ considers the first three questions together and reminds that the concept of 'controller' is defined broadly, given the aim to protect fundamental rights and freedoms effectively.[7] The ECJ refers back to previous jurisprudence that anyone who exerts influence, for their own purposes, and participates in the determination of purposes and means of processing may be regarded as a controller, and that this does not require a formal designation as controller nor the use of written guidelines or instructions.[8] The ECJ also points out that the mere reference to NVSC as a controller, the fact that NVSC did not itself process data, that there was no contract, that the intended acquisition failed and that the application was distributed without NVSC's authorization, would not hinder the classification of NVSC as a controller.[9] Consequently, the Court answers the first three questions finding that an entity that causes the development of an application and takes part in the determination of the purposes and means of processing can be regarded a controller.[10]

Answering question 5 next, the ECJ holds that joint controllership requires all entities to be controllers, while no equal responsibility is needed but the respective contributions can differ, and while no direct access to personal data is required.[11] The Court also holds that the classification of a joint controllers is based on their roles and acts, while the requirement of Art. 26(1) GDPR to enter into an arrangement governing the joint control is a consequence, not a prerequisite for being considered a joint controller.

Thereafter, the Court addresses question 4 and holds that 'processing' is to be construed broadly and the precise reasons for which an operation is performed cannot be considered; consequently, the use for 'IT system test-

7 ECJ 5.12.2023 – case C-683/21, ECLI:EU:C:2023:949 para. 28 et seq. – Nacionalinis visuomenės sveikatos centras prie Sveikatos apsaugos ministerijos v Valstybinė duomenų apsaugos inspekcija.

8 ECJ 5.12.2023 – case C-683/21, ECLI:EU:C:2023:949 para. 30 – Nacionalinis visuomenės sveikatos centras prie Sveikatos apsaugos ministerijos v Valstybinė duomenų apsaugos inspekcija.

9 ECJ 5.12.2023 – case C-683/21, ECLI:EU:C:2023:949 para. 34 et seq. – Nacionalinis visuomenės sveikatos centras prie Sveikatos apsaugos ministerijos v Valstybinė duomenų apsaugos inspekcija.

10 ECJ 5.12.2023 – case C-683/21, ECLI:EU:C:2023:949 para. 38 – Nacionalinis visuomenės sveikatos centras prie Sveikatos apsaugos ministerijos v Valstybinė duomenų apsaugos inspekcija.

11 ECJ 5.12.2023 – case C-683/21, ECLI:EU:C:2023:949 para. 42 – Nacionalinis visuomenės sveikatos centras prie Sveikatos apsaugos ministerijos v Valstybinė duomenų apsaugos inspekcija.

ing only' does not, in itself, suffice to disqualify an operation as processing in the sense of Art. 4 no. 2 GDPR, if the data involved is personal data.

In conclusion, the ECJ addresses question 6 which focuses on Art. 83 GDPR and requirements for administrative fines; for the purposes of this chapter, it may be sufficient to summarize that the ECJ concludes that only infringements committed intentionally or negligently by the controller may result in a fine under Art. 83(2) GDPR.[12] However, the ECJ also holds that the controller is responsible and liable for acts and omissions of the processor as long as the processor stays within the directions and arrangements set by the controller; the controller's responsibility ends if and to the extent the processor processes personal data for its own purposes or in a manner incompatible with the directions given by the controller.[13]

III. Systematic context and legal classification

Processing of personal data is a broad term, and the Court confirms this broad interpretation. In fact, all activities related to the lifecycle of personal data are considered processing, from the collection to the anonymization or deletion. In today's cooperative economic and IT environments, it is the norm rather than the exception that more than one party is involved in the processing, which requires a careful determination of the roles of each entity. Certain roles might be outside the scope of GDPR altogether, such as a software developer who does not use personal data. As soon as the processing of personal data of other individuals starts, however, at least one entity or person is the one 'in the driver seat', who bears accountability and responsibilities because they, through determining the purposes and means of processing, create a potential for risks for the rights and freedoms of the individuals. That is the most basic scenario – a controller collects and processes data with their own means and without reliance on other parties.

Quite frequently, though, controllers will involve others, such as to provide services and support requiring specific expertise or means, or to be able to concentrate on their 'core business' where supporting services

12 ECJ 5.12.2023 – case C-683/21, ECLI:EU:C:2023:949 para. 73 – Nacionalinis visuomenės sveikatos centras prie Sveikatos apsaugos ministerijos v Valstybinė duomenų apsaugos inspekcija.

13 ECJ 5.12.2023 – case C-683/21, ECLI:EU:C:2023:949 para. 84 et seq. – Nacionalinis visuomenės sveikatos centras prie Sveikatos apsaugos ministerijos v Valstybinė duomenų apsaugos inspekcija.

including IT are left to others. In these scenarios, the providers of such supportive services can normally be qualified as processors who are de facto a 'tool' of the controller, an extension of their operations. And sometimes, these other entities might have an own interest in determining how personal data is used and for which goals – that is where they determine to some extent the purposes and means of processing. In other words, this is where they start to contribute to the potential risk for individuals, and should accordingly bear a part of the responsibility and accountability.

Before GDPR, the DPD followed a relatively basic approach, defining in Art. 2(e) DPD a processor as anyone 'which processes personal data on behalf of the controller'; Art. 2(f) DPD clarified that a processor would not be considered a third party. Art. 16 and 17 DPD required the processor to only process data as instructed by the controller, and required certain contractual, technical and organizational measures.

Now, the concept of processing by a processor is well documented in GDPR. It starts with the definitions in Art. 4 GDPR – defining the controller and processor, and the activity of processing. This is complemented by Art. 26 GDPR regarding joint controllers. Then, Art. 28 GDPR defines the responsibilities of both the controller(s) and processor(s) for a processing on behalf of a controller. Finally, Art. 29 GDPR requires the processing to be governed by clear instructions of the controller, which the processor needs to respect.

In the case in question, quite some uncertainties came to light. The initial plans of NVSC to commission and acquire a mobile application, which ITSS should develop, ultimately failed. However, even before they failed, basic requirements were not implemented – apparently, there was no contract, no arrangements regarding each party's responsibilities, no clarity about each entity's roles and no process for the acceptance and publication of the application. This might partly be explained by the pressures of a novel pandemic event but of course led to an ex-post need for legal assessment and categorization.

IV. Author's analysis and commentary

Somewhat surprisingly, there is relatively little jurisprudence of the ECJ on the roles of controllers, joint controllers and processors post May 2018 when GDPR came into effect. This stands in contrast to the practical importance of identifying the precise role of those involved in processing activities. And while both 'processing' and 'processor' are terms defined in GDPR[14], they differ in scope and we lack (in English) a simple term for the 'processing on behalf of a controller'. Yet, processors play a vital role in today's data economy and might contribute significantly to the risk profile of personal data processing, mainly due to additional interfaces, sometimes unclear distribution of responsibilities and a decreasing intensity of oversight along a value chain that often doesn't consist of one controller and one processor but includes additional sub-processors.

The ECJ's finding that the main factor to determine the role of controller is the participation in the definition of purposes and means of processing, while no formal designation or own processing activities are required to be considered as a controller, is convincing and closely aligned to Art. 4 no. 7 GDPR. As the controller is the main person or entity responsible for the processing and should, as the term suggests, be 'in control', it is logical that the ECJ emphasizes the breadth of the definition, following its well-established line of thoughts that the ultimate goal is to ensure the effective protection of individuals' fundamental rights and freedoms in the context of the processing of their personal data. It also is not surprising that the ECJ did not consider formal arrangements or directions as a necessary element for being a controller – it is the substance of the role and the activities rather than the form that determines these roles.

Based on the questions submitted by the Regional Administrative Court, the ECJ had no need to clarify whether ITSS, on the other side, was to be considered a controller or a processor. Between the lines, we might be able to see a tendency that ITSS – given how they designated themselves and given their activities between early April and mid-May 2020 – would qualify as a controller, and thereby as a joint controller, but the final determination was left to the Lithuanian court (and might not even be required as ITSS apparently did not appeal the administrative fine).

Equally, the ECJ's finding that, in a joint controllership situation, no equal share of responsibilities in a joint controllership situation would be required, is convincing. The concept of Art. 26 GDPR is to provide flexibility to the arrangements between the controllers involved, as legislation cannot foresee and regulate ex ante every precise way of cooperative processing arrangements between various parties.

14 Art. 4 no. 4 and 8 GDPR.

Finally, while many would appreciate more differentiation when it comes to 'processing', the current definition is broad and comprehensive. It is therefore not surprising to see testing of IT systems being included – ultimately because personal data used for testing purposes is of course also potentially exposed to risks for the individuals concerned.

In summary, while the judgment presented an opportunity to the ECJ to formulate its interpretation of controllers, joint controllers, processors and their respective responsibilities, the essence of the judgment doesn't surprise but is well aligned to the legal text itself and builds on previous jurisprudence regarding the duties of controllers.

V. Recommended further reading

The European Data Protection Board has provided two main pieces addressing the responsibilities of controllers and processors.

EDPD, 'Guidelines 07/2020 on the concepts of controller and processor in the GDPR', version 2.1 (7.7.2021)[15] <https://www.edpb.europa.eu/system/files_en?file=2023-10/EDPB_guidelines_202007_controllerprocessor_final_en.pdf> address the definitions of controller, joint controller and processor as well as third parties/recipients in detail, followed by an in-depth discussion of the consequences of these concepts.

EDPB, 'Opinion 22/2024 on certain obligations following from the reliance on processor(s) and sub-processor(s)' (7.10.2024) <https://www.edpb.europa.eu/system/files/2024-10/edpb_opinion_202422_relianceonprocessors-sub-processors_en.pdf> clarifies the EDPB's expectations regarding the responsibilities of a controller, including oversight, in instances where one or many (sub-)processors are processing personal data on behalf of the controller. In principle, a controller's obligations are comprehensive and extend to sub-processors no matter how far away they might be in the value chain, however, while some obligations are always applicable, some are dependent on risk considerations.

15 In v. 2.1 of 20 september 2022 which includes minor corrections; the v. of 6 September 2020 is obsolete.

Chapter 3:
Principles of Data Processing

Purpose limitation and further processing

Pilar Arzuaga

EDPB, 'Guidelines 3/2019 on processing of personal data through video devices' version 2.0 (29.1.2020) <https://www.edpb.europa.eu/sites/default/files/files/file1/edpb_guidelines_201903_video_devices_en_0.pdf>

I. Guidance summary

Purpose limitation, as set out in Art. 5(1)(b) GDPR, is one of the core principles underpinning EU data protection law. It reflects a fundamental concern that personal data, once collected, should not be repurposed in ways that are incompatible with the expectations of the data subject or that undermine the balance between legitimate data use and the protection of fundamental rights.

Against this backdrop, the *European Data Protection Board (EDPB)* adopted Guidelines 03/2019 (Guidelines) to clarify the application of the GDPR to the processing of personal data through video devices.[1] Although the Guidelines are sector-specific in form, they address broader interpretative questions concerning purpose limitation and further processing that arise well beyond the context of video surveillance. Video devices involve continuous and often indiscriminate data collection, creating heightened risks of secondary use and function creep, and therefore provide a particularly illustrative setting in which to examine the boundaries of permissible further processing under the GDPR.

Taken together, the Guidelines reposition purpose limitation as a dynamic and ongoing governance obligation rather than a static drafting requirement, with particular significance for data-intensive and analytics-driven processing environments.

---

1 European Data Protection Board, 'Guidelines 3/2019 on processing of personal data through video devices' version 2.0 (29.1.2020) <https://www.edpb.europa.eu/sites/default/files/files/file1/edpb_guidelines_201903_video_devices_en_0.pdf>.

II. Key legal findings

The Guidelines provide insight on the interpretation and practical application of purpose limitation under the GDPR.

1. Purpose specification as a prerequisite for lawful processing

The Guidelines reaffirm that purpose limitation is not a peripheral compliance requirement, but a foundational condition for lawful processing. Controllers must determine and document the purposes of processing prior to collection, and define them with sufficient precision to ensure transparency and accountability. Vague, open-ended or overly abstract purposes are incompatible with Art. 5(1)(b) GDPR and undermine the ability of data subjects to understand how their data will be used and to exercise their rights effectively.[2]

2. Further processing and compatibility under Art. 6(4) GDPR

The EDPB confirms that further processing for a new purpose is not prohibited per se.[3] However, where such processing is not grounded in a new legal basis, it must satisfy the compatibility test set out in Art. 6(4) GDPR.[4] Compatibility must be assessed on a case-by-case basis, and no single factor is decisive.[5] Particular importance is attached to the reasonable expectations of data subjects at the time of collection based on their relationship with the controller, especially in contexts involving systematic observation (a research method to record specific behaviours) or processing in public or semi-public spaces.[6]

2 European Data Protection Board, 'Guidelines 3/2019 on processing of personal data through video devices' (fn. 1), p. 9.

3 European Data Protection Board, 'Guidelines 3/2019 on processing of personal data through video devices' (fn. 1), p. 7.

4 European Data Protection Board, 'Guidelines 3/2019 on processing of personal data through video devices' (fn. 1), p. 15.

5 European Data Protection Board, 'Guidelines 3/2019 on processing of personal data through video devices' (fn. 1), p. 12.

6 European Data Protection Board, 'Guidelines 3/2019 on processing of personal data through video devices' (fn. 1), p. 13.

3. Limits of safeguards and governance measures

While technical and organisational safeguards, such as access controls, logging and retention limits, are relevant to the compatibility assessment, the safeguards cannot in themselves render incompatible processing lawful. Where a new purpose departs materially from the original purpose, the controller must either refrain from further processing or identify a new legal basis in accordance with the GDPR.[7]

III. Systematic context and legal classification

The Guidelines must be situated within the broader architecture of the GDPR, in which purpose limitation performs a structural and normative function. Art. 5(1)(b) operates as a constraint on the accumulation and reuse of personal data, ensuring that processing remains anchored to clearly defined objectives. Rosemary Jay's commentary on this subject makes clear that the principle is designed to prevent function creep by constraining the gradual expansion of data use over time in ways that undermine individual autonomy and erode trust in data processing systems'.[8] Purpose limitation is not new, but it is increasingly difficult to apply in a world of continuous monitoring, repeated reuse of data, growing dependence on analytics, and deployment of generative artificial intelligence (AI).

The Guidelines align with the case law of the ECJ, which has consistently treated purpose specification as a safeguard against excessive or unforeseeable processing. In particular, the Guidelines emphasise the importance of the data subject's reasonable expectations, an approach reinforced by the Court in *Valsts ieņēmumu dienests*.[9] In that case, the Court highlighted (i) the relevance of factors such as the nature of the data; and (ii) the need to assess the purpose and proportionality of any proposed further processing.

This focus on reasonable expectations shows that purpose limitation is applied in a contextual, data subject-centred way. It ties the principle to fairness and transparency in practice, rather than treating it as a purely formal exercise based only on how purposes are written down. Purpose

---

7 European Data Protection Board, 'Guidelines 3/2019 on processing of personal data through video devices' (fn. 1), p. 21.

8 Jay, Data Protection Law and Practice, 5th Ed 2020, para. 6–89.

9 ECJ 24.02.2022 – case C-175/20, ECLI:EU:C:2022:124 para. 50 – 'SS' SIA v Valsts ieņēmumu dienests.

limitation is also closely entwined with other GDPR principles, in particular data minimisation and storage limitation. A clearly articulated purpose determines both the scope of data that may be processed and the duration for which it may be retained. In this sense, the EDPB's interpretation reinforces a restrictive and rights-protective reading of Art. 5(1)(b) GDPR, consistent with the Regulation's grounding in Art. 7 and 8 of the CFR.

IV. Author's analysis and commentary

The significance of the Guidelines lies not merely in their sector-specific application to video surveillance, but in their role as the most comprehensive and operational articulation of purpose limitation under the GDPR to date. Unlike many ECJ judgments, which address purpose limitation indirectly or in highly specific factual contexts, the Guidelines systematically integrate Art. 5(1)(b) GDPR with the compatibility framework under Art. 6(4) GDPR, translating abstract principles into a structured analytical methodology capable of being applied across sectors. Indeed, purpose limitation must be operationalised through technical design and organisational governance, requiring controllers to embed Art. 5(1)(b) GDPR into system architecture, internal policies, and the full lifecycle of processing.[10]

In this sense, the Guidelines play a governance role within the GDPR framework. They explain how controllers should move from defining purposes at the point of data collection to carrying out a legally robust assessment of any further processing. Importantly, the Guidelines make clear that compatibility is neither automatic nor a matter of managerial choice.

Further processing must be assessed by reference to what is foreseeable and trustworthy from the data subject's perspective, rather than being justified solely through ex post risk mitigation measures. This approach is illustrated through examples involving potentially sensitive data environments.

From a governance perspective, purpose limitation is a continuous compliance discipline, requiring ongoing assessment as technologies, datasets and use cases evolve. This has particular significance in environments characterised by analytics-driven reuse and generative AI, where the economic value of data often lies precisely in its potential for secondary

10 European Data Protection Board, 'Guidelines 3/2019 on processing of personal data through video devices' (fn. 1), p. 30.

exploitation. The EDPB's approach makes clear that such reuse cannot be justified through abstract purpose statements or technical safeguards alone, but must be grounded in a demonstrable link to the original purpose or grounded in a new legal basis.

Jay's analysis underscores this point by situating purpose limitation within the broader rationale behind EU data protection law. By constraining the evolution of data use, the principle mitigates structural power asymmetries between controllers and data subjects and ensures that processing remains foreseeable and contestable.

From a comparative standpoint, the Guidelines further highlight the distinctiveness of the EU approach. While the UK GDPR continues to mirror Art. 5(1)(b) GDPR, many non-EU regimes rely on broader notions of permissible use, often enforced ex post through unfairness or deception standards. By contrast, the EDPB's framework requires controllers to justify secondary uses ex ante through a structured compatibility analysis. For multinational organisations, this reinforces the position of EU law as the de facto global benchmark for purpose limitation, particularly in light of the GDPR's extraterritorial reach.

Looking ahead, the doctrinal importance of the Guidelines is likely to increase as courts and supervisory authorities grapple with the reuse of personal data for advanced analytics, machine learning and AI-driven decision-making and origination. We may also see a future revision of the Guidelines to reflect a specific focus on AI, particularly in light of emerging national approaches, such as the Information Commissioner's Office analysis on purpose limitation in the generative AI lifecycle.[11]

In the absence of a single landmark judicial ruling on purpose limitation, Guidelines provide a stable and authoritative reference point for interpreting one of the GDPR's most contested principles.

V. Recommended further reading

European Data Protection Board, 'Guidelines 2/2019 on the processing of personal data under Article 6(1)(b) GDPR' version 2.0 (16.9.2019) <https://www.edpb.europa.eu/sites/default/files/files/file1/edpb_guidelines-art_6-1-b-adopted_after_public_consultation_en.pdf>.

---

11 Information Commissioner's Office, 'Generative AI second call for evidence: Purpose limitation in the generative AI lifecycle' (8.4.2024) <https://ico.org.uk/about-the-ico/what-we-do/our-work-on-artificial-intelligence/generative-ai-second-call-for-evidence/>.

ECJ 24.2.2022 – case C-175/20, ECLI:EU:C:2022:124 – 'SS' SIA v Valsts ieņēmumu dienests.

Jay, Data Protection Law and Practice, 5th Ed, Mytholmroyd 2020.

Testing the limits: ECJ on purpose and storage limitation

María González Gordon/Antonio Negueruela Maldonado

ECJ 20.10.2022 – case C-77/21, ECLI:EU:C:2022:805 – Digi Távközlési és Szolgáltató Kft. v Nemzeti Adatvédelmi és Információszabadság Hatóság

I. Case summary

This ECJ Decision (Case C-77/21) takes place in relation to a dispute between *Digi Távközlési és Szolgáltató Kft* (hereinafter 'Digi'), one of the leading internet service and television providers in Hungary and *Nemzeti Adatvédelmi és Információszabadság Hatóság*, the Data Protection Authority in Hungary (hereinafter the 'Hungarian DPA').

Digi created a test database in April 2018 by copying personal data from its production environment to conduct tests and correct errors following a server failure. Around one third of private customers' data was copied. In September 2019, an ethical hacker accessed the test database, prompting Digi to fix the fault, delete the test database, and notify the Hungarian DPA, which imposed a fine to Digi for breaching the purpose limitation principle of Art. 5(1)(b) GDPR and the storage limitation principle of Art. 5(1)(e) GDPR. It should be noted that the initial data processing activity and database was carried out for the initial purpose of conclusion and performance of subscription contracts and that the lawfulness of the initial collection of the personal data was not called into question by the Hungarian DPA.

In essence, the Budapest High Court (*Fővárosi Törvényszék*) referred to the Court the following questions:

- Whether Art. 5(1)(b) of Regulation 2016/679 must be interpreted as meaning that the principle of 'purpose limitation', laid down in that provision, precludes the recording and storage by the controller, in a database created for the purposes of carrying out tests and correcting errors, of personal data previously collected and stored in another database; and

- Whether the storage by Digi, in the test database, of personal data of its customers, complies with the principle of 'storage limitation', appearing in Art. 5(1)(e) of Regulation 2016/679.

The Court held that recording and storing personal data in a test database constitutes further processing that may be compatible with the original purpose (and therefore, compliant with the purpose limitation principle) if assessed against Art. 6(4) GDPR criteria. However, the storage limitation principle precludes retaining test data longer than necessary for testing and error correction; controllers must demonstrate necessity under accountability.

II. Key legal findings

1. Purpose limitation principle

In relation to the first question raised by the Budapest High Court, the Court frames the dispute by juxtaposing Digi's claim that copying subscriber data into a parallel database merely preserved access for contract performance, thus sharing the 'same and identical' purpose as the initial processing (i.e. celebrating and executing subscription contracts with their clients), against the Hungarian DPA's view that the further purpose was different from the initial processing; namely testing and error correction.

The Court first clarifies that copying and storing personal data in a newly created database constitutes a 'processing' within the GDPR's broad definition[1], and that any operation subsequent to the initial collection is a 'further' processing irrespective of its aim. This anchors the analysis in the compatibility test for further processing.

Confirming that copying and storing personal data in a newly created database constitutes a 'further processing' with a different purpose from the initial purpose of concluding and performing subscription contracts, the legally significant question is whether that further processing is compatible with the initial purposes. To that end, and aligning with the Advocate

1 Art. 4 no. 2 GDPR: 'processing' means any operation or set of operations which is performed on personal data or on sets of personal data, whether or not by automated means, such as collection, recording, organisation, structuring, storage, adaptation or alteration, retrieval, consultation, use, disclosure by transmission, dissemination or otherwise making available, alignment or combination, restriction, erasure or destruction.

General, the Court expressly invokes Art. 6(4) GDPR, which includes a non-exhaustive list of criteria for assessing compatibility: links between purposes, collection context/relationship between data controller and data subject, data nature, possible consequences for data subjects, and the existence of appropriate safeguards. The fulfilment of even one criterion may be sufficient to comply with the principle of purpose limitation.

The Court, in order to apply these criteria, breaks down the analysis to these two anchor requirements: (i) the need for a specific, logical and sufficiently close link between the purposes for which the personal data were initially collected and the further processing of those data, and (ii) ensure that such further processing does not deviate from the legitimate expectations of data subjects (subscribers, in the case at stake) as to the subsequent use of their personal data.

Applying these guideposts, the Court points out a concrete link between testing/error correction affecting the subscriber database and performance of subscription contracts, and indicates such use typically aligns with subscribers' expectations (i.e. this processing does not deviate from the legitimate expectations of these data subject in relation to the further use of their personal data).

2. Storage limitation principle

In relation to the second question raised by the Budapest High Court, the Court restates storage limitation principle: personal data cannot be kept longer than necessary for the purposes for which they were collected or, as relevant, for compatible further purposes; accountability requires the controller to demonstrate necessity.

III. Systematic context and legal classification

1. Fundamental principles addressed in this ECJ Decision

This judgment interprets some of the GDPR's core principles, i.e. purpose limitation under Art. 5(1)(b) and storage limitation under Art. 5(1)(e).

Under the purpose limitation principle, personal data be collected for 'specified, explicit and legitimate' purposes and not further processed in ways incompatible with those original purposes.

Under the storage limitation principle, personal data should not be retained for longer than is necessary for the purposes for which the personal data are processed.

The Court reaffirms that 'further processing' must remain compatible with the original purposes, assessed against Art. 6(4) compatibility criteria and Rec. 50 of the GDPR, thereby balancing flexibility for controllers with data subject's legitimate expectations. In parallel, the storage limitation principle requires demonstrable necessity over time; initially lawful processing can become unlawful should retention outlives the purpose served. In sum, duplicating customer data from a live environment within a separate testing database constitutes 'further processing' in the sense of Art. 5(1)(b), given the definition of 'processing' under Art. 4(2) and the temporal 'further' character beyond initial collection. That further processing is not per se incompatible with the initial purpose when (i) its purpose maintains a specific and close link to the original purpose (in the case at stake, the execution of subscription contracts), (ii) remains within legitimate expectations, and (iii) certain criteria is met following Art. 6(4). On the contrary, retention within the test environment beyond the period objectively necessary to run tests and correct errors, violates storage limitation principle.

2. Consequences of the ECJ Decision at a national level (Hungary)

For the sake of completion, a short reference should be made to the proceeding followed in Hungary before the Budapest High Court after this ECJ Decision.

The Budapest High Court considered that: (i) the processing consisting on creating a parallel database for the purpose of ensuring access and correcting errors is clearly necessary to allow Digi to access and use subscriber data for the conclusion and performance of subscription contracts, and therefore this processing is in accordance with the principle of purpose limitation and compatible with the original purpose of the processing, and (ii) said processing was carried out for a longer period than strictly necessary, and therefore was not compatible with the principle of storage limitation. As a consequence, the Budapest Hight Court annulled the first decision regarding the infringement of the principle of purpose limitation, the amount of the fine imposed and instructed the Hungarian DPA to conduct a new proceeding (which resulted in another sanction for Digi).

3. Related previous guidelines/decisions

Beyond interpreting Art. 5(1)(b) GDPR (purpose limitation) and Art. 5(1)(e) GDPR (storage limitation), this ECJ Decision is noteworthy since it relates to prior soft-law guidance from the EDPB and, before that, the Article 29 Working Party, effectively interpreting these principles for further processing and retention.

Does this decision follow the interpretative line pursued so far? At first glance, yes, in substance (insofar as it does not depart from the GDPR), but it introduces nuanced clarifications and surfaces grey areas (in certain topics) that are particularly interesting, as set out below:

- This ECJ Decision is particularly interesting considering *Guidelines 06/2020 on the interplay of the Second Payment Services Directive and the GDPR*. Under these Guidelines and in relation to 'further processing', the EDPB states that:
- > Where the processing for a purpose other than that for which the personal data have been collected is not based on the data subject's consent or on a Union or Member State law, the restrictions laid down in Article 66(3)(g) and Article 67(2)(f) of the PSD2 make clear that any other purpose is not compatible with the purpose for which the personal data are initially collected. The compatibility test of Article 6(4) GDPR cannot result in a legal basis for processing.
-
- This raises several questions when analysing these Guidelines together with the ECJ Decision: does this statement mean that payment initiation service providers cannot create a parallel database for correcting errors? In light of PSD2, how would the interpretative criteria included in this ECJ Decision apply? Subject to a careful assessment of the PSD2 framework and its specific obligations, and only as a matter of applying the ECJ Decision, it could be concluded that the creation of a parallel database for testing and error correction—even in the PSD2 context—should be admissible provided that the controller carries out and documents the Art. 6(4) GDPR compatibility analysis, showing a specific, logical, and sufficiently close link to the original purposes and alignment with data subjects' legitimate expectations, and independently complies with storage-limitation by retaining such test data no longer than strictly necessary to run tests and correct errors.

- On the other hand, the Court stated that the compatibility of processing subsequent to data collection only arises where the further purposes were not identical to initial purposes of personal data processing. Although this could be inferred from Art. 5(1)(b), it might crush with Article 29 Working Party's Opinion 3/2013 on Purpose Limitation where it stated that 'any processing following collection, whether for the purposes initially specified or for any additional purposes, must be considered 'further processing' and must thus meet the requirement of compatibility'. However, given that this Opinion was issued under the former DPD, it makes sense that the ECJ Decision overrides this statement.

IV. Author's analysis and commentary

This ECJ Decision shows a lawful pathway for internal reuse: controllers may repurpose personal data for testing and correcting errors where Art. 6(4) of GDPR is met, grounded in (i) a specific link to the initial purpose and (ii) in the data subject's reasonable expectations.

However, controllers must implement granular retention governance for test datasets—retention to the duration strictly necessary for tests and fixes and triggering deletion thereafter—to satisfy storage limitation and accountability. The emphasis on cumulative compliance underscores that even compatible further processing will fail if retention is not independently justified throughout the processing lifecycle.

1. Practical significance

On a general basis, this ECJ Decision insist on the criteria that controllers must apply when considering whether personal data collected for an initial purpose may be further processed for a different purpose, in order to comply with the purpose limitation principle of Art. 5(1)(b) GDPR.

Specifically, the Court differentiate two operative benchmarks from Art. 6(4) GDPR and Rec. 50 GDPR: (i) the need for a specific, logical, and sufficiently close link between the purposes for which the personal data were initially collected and the further processing of those data, and (ii) ensuring that such further processing does not deviate from the legitimate expectations of subscribers as to the subsequent use of their data.

These two criteria translate the non-exhaustive list of requisites in Art. 6(4) GDPR —which refers, inter alia, to the links between purposes, contextual relationship, data nature, consequences, and safeguards—into a more practical, decision-ready test for compatibility assessments. Crucially, because Art. 6(4) GDPR's list is expressly non-exhaustive, a data controller may consider additional circumstances tailored to the processing purpose at stake; however, any such additional factor must ultimately be evaluated through, and be consistent with, the two core criteria above, which anchor the analysis in proximity of purposes and the data subject's reasonable expectations, ensuring predictability, lawful flexibility, and a consistently high level of protection.

2. Practical recommendations and implications

Considering this ECJ Decision and to ensure compliance with purpose limitation and data storage principles, data controllers and DPOs should operationalise further-processing assessments through a structured, documented compatibility test, under the suggested following steps:

- **First**, begin with a precise mapping of the original purposes and the contemplated new purpose.
- **Second**, to evaluate whether there is a specific, logical, and sufficiently close link between those purposes identified in the first step and whether the further use stays within data subjects' reasonable expectations. In doing so, Art. 6(4) GDPR's non-exhaustive requirements should be translated into concrete checkpoints-links between purposes, the collection context and controller-data subject relationship, the nature and sensitivity of the data, potential consequences for individuals, and the presence of safeguards such as segregation, access controls, encryption, or pseudonymisation-ensuring the analysis is recorded contemporaneously under the accountability principle. When considering any additional, context-specific factor not listed in Art. 6(4) GDPR, use the Court's two core benchmarks: proximity of purposes and data subject's legitimate expectations.
- **Third**, to maintain a living retention schedule that distinguishes operational and test environments and enforce automated deletion triggers.
- **Fourth**, ensure transparency updates where appropriate, align DPIAs and records of processing with the above controls, and prepare to evidence the cumulative compliance of purpose limitation, storage limitation, data minimisation, and lawfulness throughout the lifecycle of both operational and test processing.

In addition to these recommendations, organisations should review their records of processing activities (RoPA) to clearly distinguish processing operations from their purposes; given the broad definition of 'processing' in Art. 4 no. 2 GDPR, multiple operations grouped under a single stated purpose may in fact involve distinct purposes that must be separately articulated and assessed for compatibility and lawfulness. Data controllers should also revisit retention policies and implement them at the level of each specific purpose, since only by anchoring retention to the concrete purpose can controllers ensure data are not kept longer than necessary and can demonstrate compliance with storage limitation and accountability throughout the lifecycle of the processing.

Considering the current simplification process that the European Commission is considering of various legislation, including GDPR, it will be welcome that the outcome of this ECJ Decision will be materialized in the coming wording of Art. 6(4) GDPR in the sense that the anchor requirements for further processing included in this ECJ Decision are included (i.e. (i) the need for a specific, logical and sufficiently close link between the purposes for which the personal data were initially collected and the further processing of those data, and (ii) ensure that such further processing does not deviate from the legitimate expectations of data subjects as to the subsequent use of their personal data).

V. Recommended further reading

ECJ 4.10.2024 – case C-446/21, ECLI:EU:C:2024:834 – Maximilian Schrems v Meta Platforms Ireland Limited.

EDPB, 'Guidelines 06/2020 on the interplay of the Second Payment Services Directive and the GDPR' (15.12.2020) <https://www.edpb.europa.eu/sites/default/files/files/file1/edpb_guidelines_202006_psd2_afterpublicconsultation_en.pdf>.

EDPB, 'Guidelines 01/2025 on Pseudonymisation' (16.1.2025) <https://www.edpb.europa.eu/system/files/2025-01/edpb_guidelines_202501_pseudonymisation_en.pdf>.

EDPB, 'Opinion 28/2024 on certain data protection aspects related to the processing of personal data in the context of AI models' (17.12.2024) <https://www.edpb.europa.eu/system/files/2024-12/edpb_opinion_202428_ai-models_en.pdf>

Article 29 Data Protection Working Party, 'Opinion 03/2013 on purpose limitation' (WP203, 2.4.2013) <https://ec.europa.eu/justice/article-29/documentation/opinion-recommendation/files/2013/wp203_en.pdf>.

The principle of data minimisation – 10 years of GDPR: Aspiration, reality, and future prospects

Natallia Karniyevich/Beyza Ermis

ECJ 9.1.2025 – case C-394/23, ECLI:EU:C:2025:2 para. 64 – Mousse v Commission nationale de l'informatique et des libertés (CNIL), SNCF Connect

I. Introduction

With the entry into force of the General Data Protection Regulation (GDPR) 10 years ago, European data protection law underwent a paradigm shift. The Regulation not only established a harmonised legal framework but also elevated fundamental principles of data processing to central instruments of regulatory governance. Among these principles, data minimisation occupies a special position: It acts as a functional counterpart to a data economy shaped by digitalisation, big data analytics, and artificial intelligence models, which is inherently dependent on the availability of extensive datasets. This tension renders data minimisation more relevant today than ever before.

This article examines the doctrinal contours of the principle, its practical implementation, and the challenges it currently faces in the context of modern technologies. At the same time, it explores the extent to which data minimisation may assume a renewed role within future regulatory frameworks, such as the DA or the AI Act.

II. Doctrinal basis of data minimisation

The principle of data minimisation pursuant to Art. 5(1)(c) GDPR obliges controllers to process personal data in a manner that is adequate, relevant, and limited to what is necessary in relation to the purposes for which the data is processed. It is not merely a recommendation of conduct, but establishes a substantive legal standard that defines the limits of lawful data processing.[1] Its objective is to reduce risks for data subjects by structurally limiting the scope and depth of data collection, thereby confining interferences with fundamental rights to what is strictly necessary.[2] Pursuant to Art. 5(2) GDPR, the controller is responsible for and must be able to demonstrate compliance with the requirement of necessity under the accountability principle.

1. Relationship with other data protection principles

The principle of data minimisation does not operate in isolation, but is systematically embedded in the framework of the data protection principles set out in Art. 5(1) GDPR.[3] Its scope and practical significance become apparent only in conjunction with the other principles, which together structure the legal framework for lawful data processing.[4] Data minimisation functions less as an autonomous regulatory instrument than as a concretising and limiting corrective within the system of principles.[5]

Data minimisation and purpose limitation (Art. 5(1)(b) GDPR) are closely interrelated.[6] The principle of purpose limitation requires that personal data be collected and processed only for specified, explicit, and legitimate purposes. Only a clearly defined purpose determines which data is necessary as means to achieve it.[7] Data minimisation concretises purpose limitation by strictly limiting the scope of permissible data processing and preventing arbitrary expansion.[8] Data minimisation also complements the principle of storage limitation (Art. 5(1)(e) GDPR),[9] which requires personal data to be kept in identifiable form only for as long as is necessary for the purposes for which the data is processed. This confines data processing

1 Paal/Pauly DS-GVO BDSG/Frenzel, 4th edn. 2026, DSGVO Art. 5 mn. 1.
2 Simitis/Hornung/Spiecker gen. Döhmann Datenschutzrecht/Roßnagel, 2nd edn. 2025, DSGVO Art. 5 mn. 125.
3 Kühling/Buchner DS-GVO BDSG/Herbst, 4th edn. 2024, DSGVO Art. 5 mn. 1; Ehmann/Selmayr Datenschutz-Grundverordnung/Heberlein, 3rd edn. 2024, DSGVO Art. 5 mn. 2.
4 Sydow/Marsch DS-GVO – BDSG/Reimer, 3rd edn. 2022, DSGVO Art. 5 mn. 11.
5 Ehmann/Selmayr/Heberlein DSGVO Art. 5 mn. 2.
6 Gola/Heckmann DS-GVO – BDSG/Pötters, 3rd edn. 2022, DSGVO Art. 5 mn. 16.
7 Gola/Heckmann/Pötters DSGVO Art. 5 mn. 16.
8 Kühling/Buchner/Herbst DSGVO Art. 5 mn. 21, 56.
9 Leeb/Liebhaber JuS 2018, 534 (537).

to what is temporally necessary.[10] The principle of accuracy (Art. 5(1)(d) GDPR) obliges controllers to keep personal data accurate and up to date and to take appropriate measures to ensure that inaccurate or no longer relevant data is rectified or erased without delay. From a systematic perspective, this principle may partially counterbalance data minimisation, as a reduction in the volume of data must not result in the remaining data being incomplete or substantively inaccurate.[11] At the same time, there is a functional overlap between the two principles, since the prompt erasure or rectification of outdated or erroneous data not only serves accuracy but also limits the amount of personal data processed to what is necessary.[12]

2. Specification through case law

The Court of Justice of the European Union has expressly relied on the principle of data minimisation in several decisions, and generally considers it together with the principles of purpose limitation and lawfulness under the GDPR. For example, in *Schrems/Meta*[13] the Court held that Art. 5(1)(c) GDPR must be interpreted as meaning that the principle of data minimisation provided for therein precludes all of the personal data obtained by a controller, such as the operator of an online social network platform, from the data subject or third parties and collected either on or outside that platform, from being aggregated, analysed and processed for the purposes of targeted advertising without restriction as to time and without distinction as to type of data.

Similarly, in *Mousse/CNIL*[14], the Court examined the collection and processing of customers' titles, reflecting their gender identity, for the purpose of personalising commercial communications. Interpreting Art. 6(1) subpara. 1(b) and (f) GDPR in conjunction with Art. 5(1)(c) GDPR, the Court held that such processing is not objectively indispensable or essential for the performance of a transport contract and therefore cannot be

10 Ehmann/Selmayr/Heberlein DSGVO Art. 5 mn. 31, 34.

11 Paal/Pauly/Frenzel DSGVO Art. 5 mn. 41.

12 EDPB, 'Guidelines 4/2019 on Article 25' version 2.0 (20.10.2020), <https://www.edpb.europa.eu/sites/default/files/files/file1/edpb_guidelines_201904_dataprotection_by_design_and_by_default_v2.0_en.pdf>, p. 78.

13 ECJ 4.10.2024 – case C-446/21, ECLI:EU:C:2024:834 para. 65 – Maximilian Schrems v Meta Platforms Ireland Ltd.

14 ECJ 9.1.2025 – case C-394/23, ECLI:EU:C:2025:2 para. 64 – Mousse v Commission nationale de l'informatique et des libertés (CNIL), SNCF Connect.

regarded as necessary under Art. 6(1) subpara. 1(b) GDPR. Nor can it be justified under Art. 6(1) subpara. 1(f) GDPR, where customers were not informed of the legitimate interest pursued when that data was collected, or where the processing is not strictly necessary for the attainment of that interest, or where, in light of all relevant circumstances, the fundamental rights and freedoms of those customers – particularly in view of the risk of discrimination on grounds of gender identity – override that interest.

Taken together, these judgments illustrate that the Court gives concrete effect to the principle of data minimisation by requiring that the categories, scope, and duration of personal data processed be limited to what is objectively necessary for the specific purpose pursued, and by applying a strict necessity test when assessing the lawfulness of processing under Art. 6 GDPR.

In parallel, the European Data Protection Board has emphasised in several guidelines – particularly in the context of Art. 25 GDPR[15] – that data minimisation is to be understood as a proactive technical and organisational design principle that must be taken into account when determining the measures of a specific processing operation.[16] Its normative force is underscored by the GDPR's sanctions regime, under which infringements of Art. 5 GDPR may be sanctioned under Art. 83(5)(a) GDPR by administrative fines of up to EUR 20 million or 4 % of a company's total worldwide annual turnover of the preceding financial year, whichever is higher.

3. Substantive legal requirements

The specific scope of the principle of data minimisation can only be determined from the interpretation of the individual requirements set out in Art. 5(1)(c) GDPR.[17] Accordingly, all data processing must be adequate, relevant, and limited to what is necessary for the purposes of the processing. The provision brings together three concepts under a single regulatory approach, each addressing a different aspect of purpose-related data processing, yet overlapping in their doctrinal contours:[18]

15 EDPB, 'Guidelines 4/2019 on Article 25' (fn. 12).

16 EDPB, 'Guidelines 4/2019 on Article 25' (fn. 12), p. 61, 74, 76.

17 Sydow/Marsch/Reimer DSGVO Art. 5 mn. 32.

18 Kühling/Buchner/Herbst DSGVO Art. 5 mn. 57.

- **Adequacy** marks an initial, qualitative threshold: Data must be objectively related to the specified purpose on the basis of an evaluative assignment.[19] The term excludes purely precautionary data collection without any specific purpose.[20]
- **Relevance** reinforces this requirement by demanding that the data contribute to the achievement of the purpose.[21] Some authors argue for a higher threshold, requiring more than marginal utility.[22]
- **Necessity** is the central assessment criterion and is understood strictly: Only data without which the purpose could not be achieved, or could only be achieved with disproportionate difficulty, may be lawfully processed.[23] Considerations of convenience or efficiency on the part of the controller do not justify an expansion of processing.[24] Necessity is regarded as an expression of the principle of proportionality.[25]

For special categories of data, such as health or biometric data (Art. 9 GDPR), the necessity threshold is further heightened: Necessity must generally be demonstrated compellingly, and less intrusive alternatives must always be preferred.[26]

III. Data minimisation throughout the processing lifecycle

Data minimisation is a continuous obligation, not a one-off requirement at the outset of processing. Controllers must assess, not only before processing begins but also throughout its entire duration, whether the data being processed is still appropriate, relevant, and necessary.[27] This may require data to be erased or anonymised at a later stage.[28] The principle requires

19 AK Technik of the Conference of Independent Data Protection Authorities of the Federal Government and the Länder, 'The Standard Data Protection Model (SDM)' (26.2.2025), p. 16.
20 BeckOK Datenschutzrecht/Schantz, 54th edn. 2025, DSGVO Art. 5 mn. 26.
21 BeckOK Datenschutzrecht/Schantz DSGVO Art. 5 mn. 24.
22 Simitis/Hornung/Spiecker gen. Döhmann/Roßnagel DSGVO Art. 5 mn. 120.
23 Rec. 39 GDPR.
24 Simitis/Hornung/Spiecker gen. Döhmann/Roßnagel DSGVO Art. 5 mn. 121.
25 Gola/Heckmann/Pötters DSGVO Art. 5 mn. 16, 22.
26 Ehmann/Selmayr/Heberlein DSGVO Art. 9 mn. 57.
27 EDPB, 'Guidelines 4/2019 on Article 25' (fn. 12), p. 73 et seq.
28 AK Technik of the Conference of Independent Data Protection Authorities of the Federal Government and the Länder, 'The Standard Data Protection Model (SDM)', p. 16.

not only a reduction in the amount of data processed, but also in the frequency of use and in the number of authorised users and data subjects concerned.[29]

Accordingly, technical systems should be designed so that data collection and use are restricted or, where possible, avoided altogether.[30] Key design- and default-based data minimisation measures include, inter alia, data avoidance where the purpose can be achieved without personal data, limitation of the amount of personal data collected to what is necessary for the purpose, access restriction to a minimum number of authorised persons, the use of aggregated data where feasible, efficient data flows that prevent unnecessary duplication, and the application of state-of-the-art technologies. Where (identifiable) data is no longer required, timely pseudonymisation, anonymisation, or deletion must be ensured.[31]

Art. 25 GDPR specifies these requirements in the context of 'privacy by design' and 'privacy by default'. Further specifications can be found in Art. 32 and Art. 89(1) GDPR, which give data minimisation additional enforceability.[32]

IV. Data minimisation in the context of modern technologies

The principle of data minimisation faces practical limitations in the context of modern systems, particularly self-learning ones. These technologies rely on the continuous use and analysis of data, which makes it considerably more difficult to strictly limit processing to what is necessary.[33] This creates a structural tension between data protection requirements and the technical demands of modern data processing.

Modern AI systems, particularly deep-learning models, rely on large, diverse datasets. It is therefore essential to precisely specify the processing purpose to assess whether and to what extent personal data is necessary.[34] Vague purposes, such as 'model development', significantly impede this

29 EDPB, 'Guidelines 4/2019 on Article 25' (fn. 12), p. 76.
30 Gola/Heckmann/Pötters DSGVO Art. 5 mn. 23, 24.
31 EDPB, 'Guidelines 4/2019 on Article 25' (fn. 12), p. 76.
32 Paal/Pauly/Frenzel DSGVO Art. 5 mn. 34.
33 Simitis/Hornung/Spiecker gen. Döhmann/Roßnagel DSGVO Art. 5 mn. 133–135.
34 EDPB, 'Opinion 28/2024 on certain data protection aspects related to the processing of personal data in the context of AI models' (17.12.2024) < https://www.edpb.europa.eu/system/files/2024-12/edpb_opinion_202428_ai-models_en.pdf>, p. 64, 73.

assessment. Controllers must demonstrate the measures they have taken to minimise the use of personal data and explain why less-intrusive alternatives are insufficient.[35] If the purpose of the AI model has not yet been definitively determined at an early stage of development, the controller must at least disclose the essential parameters, such as the intended field of application (internal, research, or commercial) or an intended sale to third parties.[36]

The inherent data hunger of machine-learning systems raises the question of whether the mere improvement of a model constitutes a legitimate purpose. Some authors call for a proportional interpretation that permits the use of larger datasets where the associated risks are low.[37] Nevertheless, controllers should always select the model that requires the least amount of personal data.[38] Technical alternatives, such as synthetic data or federated learning, demonstrate that data-protective approaches are possible without stifling innovation.[39]

Big data processing typically follows the paradigm of comprehensive data collection in order to unlock future analytical and usage potential. While some regard this as a fundamental contradiction,[40] others argue that big data analytics are not per se unlawful, provided the purpose of processing is clearly defined and processing remains limited to that purpose.[41] Precautionary data collection without a concrete purpose – such as unstructured data lakes – is impermissible. Additional risks arise in the context of online services where broadly framed contractual clauses can undermine purpose limitation and data minimisation.[42]

---

35 EDPB, 'Opinion 28/2024 on certain data protection aspects related to the processing of personal data in the context of AI models' (fn. 34), p. 51, 58.

36 EDPB, 'Opinion 28/2024 on certain data protection aspects related to the processing of personal data in the context of AI models' (fn. 34), p. 64.

37 Niemann/Kevekordes CR 2020, 17 (22).

38 Niemann/Kevekordes CR 2020, 17 (23).

39 Kaulartz/Huth DSB 2019, 276 (277).

40 Deutscher Ethikrat, 'Big Data und Gesundheit – Datensouveränität als informationelle Freiheitsgestaltung' (30.11.2017) < https://www.ethikrat.org/fileadmin/Publikationen/Stellungnahmen/deutsch/stellungnahme-big-data-und-gesundheit.pdf>, p. 23.

41 Kühling/Buchner/Herbst DSGVO Art. 5 mn. 56.

42 EDPB, 'Guidelines 2/2019 on the processing of personal data under Article 6(1)(b) GDPR in the context of the provision of online services to data subjects' version 2.0 (8.10.2019) < https://www.edpb.europa.eu/sites/default/files/files/file1/edpb_guidelines-art_6-1-b-adopted_after_public_consultation_en.pdf>, p. 16.

V. European regulatory initiatives

New European legislative acts are shifting the normative framework towards greater promotion of data use and availability without abolishing the principle of data minimisation. Rather, data minimisation continues to operate as a cross-cutting protective principle that limits the use of data-driven innovation to what is necessary in each case. This approach is reflected, inter alia, in the following instruments:

- The DA explicitly emphasises that the design obligations in the DA are also without prejudice to the data minimisation principle and should not be understood as imposing an obligation to design connected products and related services in such a way that they store or otherwise process any personal data other than the personal data necessary in relation to the purposes for which the data is processed.[43]
- The CRA embeds data minimisation as part of essential cybersecurity requirements relating to the properties of products with digital elements: As reflected in Annex I, Part I point (2)(g) CRA, it requires that, on the basis of the cybersecurity risk assessment and where applicable, products with digital elements shall, inter alia, '*process only data, personal or other, that are adequate, relevant and limited to what is necessary in relation to the intended purpose of the product with digital elements*'.
- The ePrivacy Directive specifies the minimisation requirement in the field of electronic communications, in particular for traffic and location data, pursuant to Art. 6(1) and Art. 9(1) ePrivacy Directive.
- The DSA functionally safeguards data minimisation by ensuring that measures for the protection of minors do not incentivise providers of online platforms to collect or process more personal data than they already hold.[44]
- The AI Act emphasises that data minimisation in AI systems must be ensured throughout their entire lifecycle through. Measures taken by providers to ensure compliance with that principle may include not only anonymisation and encryption, but also the use of technology that permits algorithms to be brought to the data and allows training of AI systems without the transmission between parties, or copying of the raw

43 Rec. 20 DA.
44 Rec. 71 DSA.

> or structured data itself.[45] In addition, the European Data Protection Board clarifies that in line with the data minimisation principle, the development and deployment of AI models may involve processing personal data only insofar as it is adequate, relevant, and necessary for the defined purpose, including where such processing is required to mitigate biases or errors and cannot be effectively achieved through alternative means such as anonymised or synthetic data.[46]

In similar vein, the NIS2 Directive promotes the use of innovative technologies, including artificial intelligence, to improve the detection and prevention of cyberattacks, while expressly conditioning such use on full compliance with Union data protection law. In particular, the application of AI-driven and automated cybersecurity tools must respect data minimisation and be implemented through data protection by design and by default, ensuring that any data shared or processed for training or operational purposes is limited to what is necessary and secured by state-of-the-art technical measures.[47]

VI. Data minimisation as a future-oriented principle

Ten years after the GDPR came into force, it has become clear that data minimisation is not to be understood as an innovation-inhibiting prohibition, but rather as a principle of responsible design. In a data-driven society, it is increasingly a marker of high-quality, accountable technology development. In the ongoing tension between data availability and data protection, data minimisation therefore remains an indispensable element of European data protection law.

VII. Recommended further reading

EDPB, 'Guidelines 4/2019 on Article 25' version 2.0 (20.10.2020), <https://www.edpb.europa.eu/sites/default/files/files/file1/edpb_guidelines_201904_dataprotection_by_design_and_by_default_v2.0_en.pdf>.

45 Rec. 69 AI Act.

46 EDPB, 'Opinion 28/2024 on certain data protection aspects related to the processing of personal data in the context of AI models' (fn. 34), p. 64.

47 Rec. 51 NIS2 Directive.

EDPB, 'Opinion 28/2024 on certain data protection aspects related to the processing of personal data in the context of AI models' (17.12.2024) < https://www.edpb.europa.eu/system/files/2024-12/edpb_opinion_202428_ai-models_en.pdf>.

Basic Principles: Confidentiality and Integrity

Thoralf Knuth

ECJ 14.12.2023 – case C-340/21, ECLI:EU:C:2023:986 – VB v Natsionalna agentsia za prihodite

I. Case summary

The Bulgarian National Revenue Agency ('*Natsionalna agentsia za prihodite*', NRA) administers taxes such as income and corporate taxes and mandatory social security contributions like health and pension insurance contributions.

Media revealed in July 2019, that the NRA had suffered a cyber-attack. Unauthorised access to its IT systems had taken place and personal data of millions of individuals had been published on the internet.

One of the individuals affected by the cyber-attack sought non-material damages from the NRA for fear of misuse of her personal data.

The individual claimed that the NRA had failed to fulfil its obligations under the GDPR to process personal data in a manner that ensures appropriate security and that it had failed to implement appropriate technical and organisational measures. The individual claimed that this failure had resulted in a breach of security and thus in a personal data breach.

The respective supervisory authority had sanctioned the NRA with a significant fine and additional measures.

II. Key legal findings

1. A cyber-attack does not automatically mean insufficient technical organisational measures, but the controller bears the burden of proof for appropriateness

The ECJ held that the obligation set out in Art. 4 no. 1 and Art. 32(1) GDPR to implement appropriate technical and organisational measures is not to be understood in a way that all risks of personal data breaches are to be eliminated. The measures need to be appropriate which indicates that a risk management approach is required. This also means that a risk could materialize despite a proper risk management. The obligation and option of the controller to demonstrate appropriateness shows, too, that the measures do not need to eliminate all risks. Consequently, the court held that from the mere fact that unauthorised access took place it cannot be derived that the implemented measures were insufficient.

On the other hand, the controller is not exempt per Art. 82(3) GDPR from its obligation to compensate only because the personal data breach is a result of actions of a third party not under control of the controller. The controller must prove that it is in no way responsible.

The controller bears the burden of proof that the measures implemented were appropriate. This follows from the accountability principle set out in Art. 5(2) GDPR and is in line with a number of decisions by the ECJ.[1]

The ECJ also held, national courts need to analyse nature and content of the measures implemented by the controller in a concrete manner and in a two-step approach. They shall first review the risks associated with the processing and then assess whether the measures implemented are appropriate to mitigate these risks. In essence, national courts have to assess a risk management approach.

The referring court had asked the ECJ if an expert's report could be regarded as 'sufficient and necessary' means of proof by the controller. The ECJ denied this assessment and ruled that requiring such a report as necessary or automatically deeming it sufficient would violate the principle of effectiveness and, thus, the right to an effective judicial remedy as provided for by Art. 79(1) GDPR. An individual examination of the 'substance' of the measures is required for the assessment of the appropriateness.

2. Fear of possible misuse can be non-material damage, but the data subject needs to demonstrate actual damage

The mere fear by a data subject of a possible misuse of their personal data may in itself constitute non-material damage under Art. 82(1) GDPR. The

1 ECJ 4.7.2023 – case C-252/21, ECLI:EU:C:2023:537 para. 95 – Meta Platforms Inc and Others v Bundeskartellamt; ECJ 4.5.2023 – case C-60/22, ECLI:EU:C:2023:373 para. 53 – UZ v Bundesrepublik Deutschland; ECJ 24.2.2022 – case C-175/20, ECLI: EU:C:2022:124 para. 77 et seq., 81 – SIA 'SS' v Valsts ieņēmumu dienests.

court continues its line of argument from C-300/21 *Österreichische Post*, that the concept of damage should be interpreted broadly. However, the individual needs to demonstrate such non-material damage and national courts have to verify that the fear is well founded in the specific case.

III. Systematic context and legal classification

The ECJ clarifies a very fundamental concept in the GDPR in this decision. Protecting confidentiality and integrity is no absolute obligation, but is to be done with a risk assessment.

1. Confidentiality and integrity

The core principles in Art. 5 GDPR provide requirements and guidance for any processing of personal data. Most of them already were 'principles relating to data quality' under the former Data Protection Directive. The obligation in Art. 5(1)(f) GDPR to 'ensure appropriate security [...] using appropriate technical and organisational measures' was newly added with the GDPR and is summarised as 'integrity and confidentiality'. It does not aim at 'data quality' but at ensuring the other core principles.[2] The EDPB goes even one step further and requires the measures to be 'designed to prevent and manage data breach incidents' and to 'guarantee [...] compliance with the other principles'.[3]

This obligation to implement measures to ensure appropriate security is set out in a number of provisions of the GDPR. Art. 32(1)(b) GDPR further specifies the obligation to ensure confidentiality, integrity, availability and resilience of the processing systems. These all aim not at 'whether' personal data may be processed, but 'how'.[4] The GDPR does not provide a clear definition of these terms, but describes the expected outcome of the measures. The 'security' of personal data shall include protection against

2 Simitis/Hornung/Spiecker gen. Doehmann Datenschutzrecht/Roßnagel, 2nd edn. 2025, DSGVO Art. 5 mn. 168.

3 EDPB, 'Guidelines 4/2019 on Article 25', version 2.0 (20.10.2020) <https://www.edpb.europa.eu/sites/default/files/files/file1/edpb_guidelines_201904_dataprotection_by_design_and_by_default_v2.0_en.pdf>, mn. 83.

4 Gola/Heckmann DS-GVO – BDSG/Poetters, 3rd edn. 2022, DSGVO Art. 5 mn. 29.

unauthorised or unlawful processing, accidental loss, destruction or damage,[5] applying this also to the equipment used.[6]

These are the main protection targets of information security.[7] Typical definitions in information security should be applied. Confidentiality means protection against unauthorised (including accidental) disclosure, integrity against unauthorised (or unexpected) changes to information, and availability means being readily accessible when needed.[8]

2. Risk-appropriate

The measures required by the GDPR need to be appropriate, provide appropriate security (Art. 5(1)(f) GDPR), taking into account the risks (Art. 24(1)(1) GDPR), and result in measures appropriate to the risk (Art. 32(1) GDPR).

In its decision, the court now re-emphasises that the GDPR with these numerous mentions of 'appropriate' does not expect perfection from the measures, but a structured approach also when defining and reviewing measures addressing risks, i.e. a risk management system[9].

The first step always has to be to assess the data processing, specifically its nature, scope, context and purposes.[10] Based on this assessment, the risks to the rights of individuals arising from the processing need to be identified such as disclosure, loss or change of data. It does not matter, whether these risks materialize on purpose or by accident.[11] The GDPR provides a number of factors to assess the risks, including the standard risk management aspects likelihood and severity. While there is no specific definition of risk in the GDPR, the common combination of likelihood and damage or impact is a good way to define risks.[12] This is a standard risk-based approach[13]. Consequently, the GDPR provides in Art. 32(1) GDPR for

5 Art. 5(1)(b) GDPR.
6 Rec. 39 sent. 12 GDPR.
7 Simitis/Hornung/Spiecker gen. Doehmann/Hansen DSGVO Art. 32 mn. 44.
8 Forgó/Helfrich/Schneider Betriebl. Datenschutz/Schmitz/v. Dall'Armi, 3rd edn. 2019, Part XII, Ch. 1, mn. 33.
9 ECJ 14.12.2023 – case C-340/21, ECLI:EU:C:2023:986 para. 29 – VB v Natsionalna agentsia za prihodite.
10 Rec. 76 sent. 2, Art. 24 (1), Art. 32(1) GDPR.
11 BeckOK Datenschutzrecht/Paulus, 54th edn., Art. 32 mn. 10.
12 Taeger/Gabel DSGVO BDSG/Lang, 5th edn. 2026, DSGVO Art. 24 mn. 38.
13 Gola/Heckmann/Piltz, DSGVO Art. 32 mn. 22.

factors to be 'taken into account' when assessing the risks. They are to be considered, but do not automatically mean a specific risk or measure.[14]

Finally, the measures need to be appropriate to the risks and not absolutely eliminating all risks.[15]

3. Proof

Regarding the burden of proof, this decision brings nothing new but further strengthens the accountability principle in Art. 5(2) GDPR. The controller needs to be able to demonstrate the effectiveness of the measures (Art. 24(1) sent. 1 GDPR). Having to demonstrate the appropriateness of measures the ECJ deems to encourage controllers 'to do everything in their power' to prevent non-compliant data processing. The court also argues that the right to compensation would lose much of its effectiveness if the burden of proof were on the data subjects.

4. Fear as non-material damage

Regarding the damages for personal data breaches this decision continues the case C-300/21 *Österreichische Post*. With the broad interpretation of damages under the GDPR, the court finds that Art. 81(1) GDPR does not distinguish between damage linked to a misuse that has already occurred and the fear such misuse may occur in the future. It consequently held that such fear may constitute non-material damage without actual misuse.

Being aware of the impact of such a broad interpretation, the court stipulates clearly that the data subject must demonstrate that the claimed consequences constitute damage and that national courts have to verify this.

IV. Author's analysis and commentary

Two key points in this decision are relevant for data protection management practice. The core obligations to protect the 'security' of personal data

14 Gola/Heckmann/Piltz, DSGVO Art. 32 mn. 14.

15 ECJ 14.12.2023 – case C-340/21, ECLI:EU:C:2023:986 para. 29 – VB v Natsionalna agentsia za prihodite; Paal/Pauly DS-GVO BDSG/Martini, 4th edn. 2026, DSGVO Art. 32 mn. 26; Gola/Heckmann/Piltz DSGVO Art. 32 mn. 11.

follows similar considerations like the general protection of information in long-standing information security standards. Documenting transparently how the controller manages the measures is key.

1. Standard risk management also for technical and organisational measures

Data protection management can be integrated into compliance and security processes very systematically. A standardised risk approach can be used that is not limited to GDPR aspects or risks to personal data. Such a structured risk management approach always contains the same steps: identify risks, evaluate them, decide which level of risk is acceptable (or permissible) and then define appropriate measures to mitigate the risks down to the desired level. A regular iteration or review is required to react to changes in risks, risk appetite or requirements. These steps comprise a so-called PDCA-Cycle (plan, do, check, act).

The ECJ very clearly applies these considerations to the expectations controllers have to fulfil. That should encourage data controllers to make use of synergies in the implementation of data protection management with cyber or information security management. It is also very helpful that the court clearly states that the GDPR 'establishes a risk management system and that it in no way purports to eliminate the risks of personal data breaches.'[16] The ECJ has meanwhile repeated this assessment.[17]

In practice, this means existing risk management approaches, often quite developed in larger corporations, may be used also for addressing privacy-related risks. The GDPR requires the measures (addressing the risks) to be both, decided and assessed in a concrete manner. Doing so in a structured process not only provides more efficiency and speed. It also supports that similar risks are assessed and treated similarly, preventing the level of protection for data subjects from being undermined by inconsistent measures. On the other hand, such a structured approach helps to avoid inappropriate measures be implemented in the wrong expectation that each and every potential risk in data protection needs to be eliminated at any cost.

16 ECJ 14.12.2023 – case C-340/21, ECLI:EU:C:2023:986 para. 29 – VB gegen Natsionalna agentsia za prihodite.

17 ECJ 25.1.2024 – case C-687/21, ECLI:EU:C:2024:72 para. 38 – BL v MediaMarktSaturn Hagen-Iserlohn GmbH.

Recent legislation around cyber and information security follows a very similar approach. For example, the NIS2 Directive requires 'appropriate and proportionate technical, operational and organisational measures to manage the risks'[18], the European Commission requires 'a level of security of network and information systems appropriate to the risks' for the implementation.[19]

Making use of an existing Information Security Management System (ISMS) can help tremendously. Assessments, measures and procedures to protect confidential information are often established and familiar to many employees. These can and should be reused to a large extent to protect personal data with appropriate measures, making it easier for the employees who actually perform the risk assessments and implement the measures. Typical protection measures like limitations of access, protection of IT equipment used or regular review are exactly the same measures like those to be considered under Art. 32 GDPR. In the everlasting debate whether data protection hinders innovation, such an approach makes transparent what the real risks are and that typically high risks in data protection tend to have similarly high impact in other fields, too.

2. Documentation is key

Another aspect, which is not new, is strengthened even further by this decision. The burden of proof for compliance with most of the requirements of the GDPR is with the responsible entity, i.e. the controller. That is already evident from Art. 5(2) GDPR, but the court matches the flexibility, the risk management approach provides, with the obligation to demonstrate compliance with the regulation.

It raises the bar further by requiring the national courts to concretely review the measures for appropriateness. Controllers not only have to document their measures and how they came to the conclusion that these are appropriate, i.e. sufficient. Controllers also have to do so in a way, that this can convince a court. A standard challenge from compliance investigations will have to be considered here, too: the so-called hindsight bias. This simply means, that the court will review the measures only when they are challenged or an incident happened. So the review will very often take

18 Art. 21(1) NIS 2 Directive.

19 Art. 2(2) Commission Implementing Regulation (EU) 2024/2690.

place in a situation where the measures already failed. The controller will then have to demonstrate that the measures were appropriate and the incident happened anyhow. Any documentation should already aim to show that measures were already chosen with this in mind.

One point will potentially be misunderstood. The court decided that an expert's report cannot be considered always necessary or always sufficient. For a concrete review necessary proof depends on the case. The court in no way decided that such report cannot suffice or be required for proof.

V. Recommended further reading

ECJ 25.1.2024 – case C-687/21, ECLI:EU:C:2024:72 para. 38 – BL v MediaMarktSaturn Hagen-Iserlohn GmbH: Continuing this decision, reiterating that an incident is no automatic proof of insufficient measures, but that the controller needs to prove appropriateness.

ISO/IEC 27001:2022 with amendments and ISO/IEC 27701:2025: Both setting out requirements and guidance for information security and privacy management systems ('information security, cybersecurity and privacy protection')

ECJ 4.5.2023 – case C-300/21, ECLI:EU:C:2023:37 – UI v Österreichische Post AG: Setting out the base principles for damages and non-material damages under the GDPR.

Principles relating to the processing of personal data: accountability

Ulrich Baumgartner

ECJ 4.5.2023 – case C-60/22, ECLI:EU:C:2023:373 – UZ v Federal Republic of Germany

I. Case summary

In Case C-60/22,[1] an individual (a third-country national), challenged the rejection of his application for international protection by the *German Federal Office for Migration and Refugees ('**FOMR**')* before the domestic administrative courts. The *FOMR* had compiled an electronic file on the applicant which contained personal data concerning the applicant, otherwise known as a 'MARIS' file. It then transmitted the MARIS file to the Administrative Court of Wiesbaden, which was deciding on the applicant's administrative action against the rejection of his application, using an electronic court and administration mailbox. The Administrative Court of Wiesbaden then referred several questions to the ECJ, as it doubted whether the FOMR in its compilation of the MARIS file, and both the *FOMR* and the body operating the mailbox in their transmission of the MARIS file to the Administrative Court of Wiesbaden had complied with the requirements of the GDPR, especially the principle of accountability under Art. 5(2) GDPR due to the lack of a complete record of processing activities pursuant to Art. 30 GDPR or the lack of an arrangement between joint controllers under Art. 26 GDPR. It asked whether these failures regarding accountability rendered the processing 'unlawful', thereby triggering the right of the applicant to demand erasure or restriction of his personal data under Art. 17(1)(d) and Art. 18(1)(b) GDPR and whether the court could still rely on the transmitted file, with or without the data subject's consent. The ECJ held that breaches of Art. 26 and Art. 30 GDPR

1 ECJ 4.5.2023 – case C-60/22, ECLI:EU:C:2023:373 – UZ v Federal Republic of Germany.

do not make processing unlawful within the meaning of Art. 17 and 18 GDPR, as lawfulness of processing is governed exhaustively by Art. 5(2) read in conjunction with Art. 5(1)(a) and 6(1) GDPR, and that such organisational infringements of data protection must instead be addressed by the mechanisms available to the data protection supervisory authorities. It further found that the national court's use of the MARIS file in judicial proceedings is based on Art. 6(1)(e) GDPR and therefore does not depend on the data subject's consent, even if the *FOMR* in submitting the personal data to the national court failed to comply with Art. 26 or 30 GDPR.

II. Key legal findings

Whilst the ECJ recalled that Art. 17(1)(d) GDPR does confer a right to erasure of personal data where that data has been 'unlawfully processed' and Art. 18(1)(b) similarly confers a right to restriction of the processing of the data where the 'processing is unlawful', it repeated its long-standing view that not only the wording, but also the context and objectives of the legislation is necessary when interpreting provisions of EU law. Applying this principle, the Court considered that the provisions must be read in conjunction with Art. 5(1) GDPR and Art. 5(1)(a) GDPR in particular, so that the controller is required to ensure that its processing of personal data is lawful. In this context, the ECJ reiterated his prior case law that pursuant to Art. 5(2) GDPR, the controller is responsible for compliance with Art. 5(1) GDPR and bears the burden of such proof. Moreover, and unsurprisingly, the ECJ also noted that Art. 6(1) GDPR is the basis for determining the lawfulness of any processing of personal data itself – noting in particular that the title of Art. 6 GDPR itself indicates as such. The Court also stressed that the conditions for determining lawfulness of processing as set out in the first subparagraph of Art. 6(1) GDPR are exhaustive and restrictive, meaning that the sole determinant of whether the processing is lawful within the meaning of Art. 5(1)(a) is whether it falls into one of the bases for processing set out in Art. 6(1) GDPR (notably, as the case did not involve special categories of personal data, the ECJ did not mention Art. 9(2) GDPR).

Extrapolating from those initial conclusions, the ECJ held that infringement of Art. 26 and 30 GDPR, thereby also constituting an infringement of Art. 5(2) GDPR, does not result in the processing being unlawful, provided there is a legal basis for the processing under Art. 6(1) GDPR. The ECJ based its conclusion primarily on the structure of the GDPR itself: Art. 5 and 6 GDPR are part of Chapter II of the GDPR, relating to 'Principles', whereas Art. 26 and 30 GDPR are located in Chapter IV of the GDPR, relating to 'General Obligations'. This indicates that, whilst compliance with the provisions of Art. 26 and 30 GDPR is an obligation, it is not a prerequisite for the legality of the processing itself. This conclusion was also based in part on the penalties for infringements of each provision in the form of administrative fines, which, pursuant to Art. 83(4) and (5) GDPR sanction infringements of Art. 26 and 30 GDPR at a different level to those of Art. 5 and 6 GDPR, as the gravity of infringing Art. 26 and 30 GDPR is less than infringing Art. 5 and 6 GDPR. The ECJ also noted that the purpose of a joint controller agreement within the meaning of Art. 26 GDPR or a record of processing activities within the meaning of Art. 30 GDPR is as a means to ensure that the controllers comply with the guarantees laid down by the GDPR. However, the lack of a joint controller agreement or a record of processing activities does not, according to the Court, demonstrate by itself that the rights and freedoms of a data subject have, in fact, been infringed.

Finally, the ECJ dealt briefly with the remaining question referred by the Administrative Court of Wiesbaden, holding that the consent of the applicant was not required in order for the Administrative Court of Wiesbaden to decide upon the case relying on the MARIS file compiled about the applicant, as the legal basis for processing contained in Art. 6(1)(e) GDPR (the performance of a task carried out in the public interest or in the exercise of official authority) applied in the present interest, such that consent within the meaning of Art. 6(1)(a) GDPR was not required for processing to take place.

III. Systematic context and legal classification

Infringements of Art. 5(2) GDPR and the related burden of proof for compliance with the principles of Art. 5(1) GDPR play an increasingly important role in the enforcement practice of supervisory authorities.

The supervisory authorities seem more frequently minded to 'tack on' an infringement of Art. 5(2) GDPR alongside other GDPR violations when making decisions about enforcement action. The fundamental accountability principle is occasionally overlooked by controllers who are so concerned with their obligations under Chapters IV and V of the GDPR that they cannot see the wood for the trees. However, regulators have frequently found breaches of the accountability principle in Art. 5(2) GDPR when investigating other infringements of the GDPR, such as when the Polish data protection authority in 2025 fined a children's hospital not merely on the basis of its failures to implement appropriate technical and organisational measures pursuant to Art. 32 GDPR, which led to a ransomware attack effecting its employees, but also found an additional breach of Art. 5(2) GDPR because the hospital was unable to demonstrate that it had carried out regular tests, measurements and evaluations of the effectiveness of its technical and organisational measures, resulting in an additional, separate breach of the GDPR.[2] This is not an isolated practice – other data protection supervisory authorities across Europe have adopted the same approach and have tacked on additional infringements of Art. 5(2) GDPR to their enforcement actions, such as in Italy (for failure to conduct assessments on the risk of re-identification of data subjects from pseudonymised data sets),[3] in France (for failure to assess the compatibility of an employee surveillance technology with the GDPR)[4] and in Spain (for failure of a controller to conduct a risk assessment into its processor's activities),[5] amongst many other examples.

Occasionally, enforcement action has even been taken for an isolated (or almost entirely isolated) infringement of Art. 5(2) GDPR. It is a useful tool in the arsenal of the supervisory authorities in cases where a controller's record-keeping is questionable, the facts are unclear and the supervisory authority may not be able to conclusively determine whether or to what exact extent a breach of the controller's substantive obligations under the GDPR has occurred. They may, however, be able to definitively determine that the controller has at the very least not been unable to prove that it has complied with the provisions of the GDPR and is therefore subject

2 Urzad Ochrony Danych Osobowych, 'Ochrona danych osobowych osób fizycznych powinna być podstawą analizy ryzyka' (30.6.2025) <https://uodo.gov.pl/pl/138/3803>.

3 Garante per la Protezione dei Dati Personali, 'Provvedimento del 21 maggio 2025 [10149917]' (21.5.2025) <https://www.gpdp.it/web/guest/home/docweb/-/docweb-display/docweb/10149917>.

4 Commission Nationale de l'Informatique et des Libertés, 'Délibération SAN-2025-008 du 18 septembre 2025' (23.9.2025) <https://www.legifrance.gouv.fr/cnil/id/CNILTEXT000052266505>.

5 Agencia Espanola de Protección de Datos, 'Expediente N.º: EXP202304117' <https://www.aepd.es/documento/ps-00216-2023.pdf>, in particular p. 194 et seq.

to a fine for its breach of Art. 5(2) GDPR. For example, the Irish Data Protection Commission fined Meta € 17,000,000 in 2022, primarily for a violation of Art. 5(2) GDPR because Meta was unable to demonstrate that it implemented technical and organisational measures in practice that would adequately protect data subjects' personal data.[6]

Sanctioning solely using Art. 5(2) GDPR has also been employed where data protection measures are lacking in their entirety and the breaches of the GDPR would be too numerous to count, such as in 2025 when the Polish data protection authority fined a funeral home which lost 10 boxes of personal data off the back of a truck and failed to even notice doing so.[7]

As a result, Art. 5(2) GDPR is becoming ever more important and frequently serves to increase the severity of fines, if not to serve as the main basis of a fine.

IV. Author's analysis and commentary

With its judgement, the ECJ affirmed plainly that the sole basis for determining the lawfulness of processing under the GDPR remains Art. 5(1)(a) and 6(1) GDPR and drew a clear distinction between mere obligations as set out in Section 1 of Chapter IV GDPR (i.e., Art. 24 to 31 GDPR) which are imposed on the controller on the one hand and the principles of processing set out in Art. 5(1) GDPR and their further specifications in Art. 7 to 11 GDPR on the other hand. In this context, the case underscores the practical importance of Art. 5(2) GDPR and of the accountability duty enshrined therein. According to the ECJ, the controller is always required by Art. 5(2) GDPR, read in conjunction with Art. 5(1)(a) and 6(1) GDPR as the basis for determining lawfulness of the processing, to ensure the lawfulness of the processing AND be able to demonstrate the latter. However, the ECJ indicated that only infringements of the accountability principle in conjunction with violations of Art. 5(1) or Art. 6(1) GDPR will give rise to unlawfulness of processing within the meaning of Art. 17 and 18 GDPR – whereas infringements of Art. 5(2) GDPR in conjunction with violations

6 Data Protection Commission, 'Data Protection Commission announces decision in Meta (Facebook) inquiry' (15.3.2022) <https://dataprotection.ie/en/news-media/press-releases/data-protection-commission-announces-decision-meta-facebook-inquiry>.

7 Urzad Ochrony Danych Osobowych, 'Dobrze przeprowadzona analiza ryzyka mogłaby pozwolić uniknąć utraty danych' (15.4.2025) <https://uodo.gov.pl/pl/138/3639>.

of a controller's responsibilities under Chapter IV GDPR would not per se render the processing of personal data unlawful.

Most importantly, the case demonstrates the duality of the obligations contained in Art. 5(2) GDPR: The responsibility for ensuring compliance with the GDPR is a separate obligation from evidencing such compliance. As a result, while the failure of the controller to demonstrate compliance with the GDPR will not lead to the unlawfulness of the processing, it can (and likely will) be pursued by supervisory authorities with the enforcement measures available to them, such as warnings and fines. Therefore, companies should put a particular emphasis on their documentation evidencing their compliance with the GDPR. Without such robust documentation, companies are running the risk of GDPR sanctions even if a supervisory authority would be unable to prove violations of GDPR duties.

That said, this judgement of the ECJ does not reshape data protection law, as it largely merely clarifies that which was already clear to the vast majority of practitioners: Minor (or even major) breaches of a controller's obligations under the GDPR do not give rise to the unlawfulness of the processing *per se* and entitle the data subject to demand the deletion of their data – only breaches of Art. 6(1) GDPR give rise to such a right.

An interesting aside from the ECJ is that the absence of a joint controller agreement or a complete record of processing activities does not by itself indicate a violation of the rights and freedoms of a data subject. It confirms that these tools are a means to an end: They aim to ensure and boost protection of the fundamental right to data protection, but their existence is not an end in itself. However, just as the presence of a joint controller agreement or a complete record of processing activities does not conclusively indicate that processing is lawful, their non-existence (like any other GDPR violation) bears a considerable risk of sanctions imposed by supervisory authorities on the basis of Art. 5(2) GDPR.

V. Recommended further reading

Information Commissioner's Office, 'Guide to accountability and governance' <https://ico.org.uk/for-organisations/uk-gdpr-guidance-and-resources/accountability-and-governance/guide-to-accountability-and-governance/>.

Bavarian State Office of Data Protection Supervision, 'Prüfkatalog Rechenschaftspflicht' [Checklist on Accountability Principle] <https://www.lda.bayern.de/media/pruefungen/201810_rechenschaftspflicht_fragebogen.pdf>.

Chapter 4:
Lawfulness of Data Processing

An analysis of the Evolution of Consent under overlapping regulatory regimes since the ECJ's ruling in Meta Platforms Inc. v Bundeskartellamt (Case C-252/21)

Jonathan Dunne[*]

ECJ 4.7.2023 – case C-252/21, ECLI:EU:C:2023:537 – Meta Platforms Inc and Others v Bundeskartellamt

I. Introduction

The concept of consent is no longer intrepreted via the single criteria under GDPR but is now assessed in the context of overlapping regulatory requirements contained in an omnibus of laws where consent is not just about privacy but also about fair competition under the DMA, platform safety under the DSA, and algorithmic accountability under the AI Act.

We will consider how the ECJ's landmark decision in *Meta* vs *Bundeskartellamt* expanded the criteria for consent, has led to non-privacy regulatory authorities to issue decisions in 2025 that appropriate GDPR consent standards, and analyze the practical implications for consent.

II. Case summary

Meta's business model relies on profiling users for targeted online advertising. To create user profiles, *Meta* collects data not only from the user's activities on Facebook but also 'off-Facebook data.' This includes data from visits to third-party websites and apps and data from other Meta services such as Instagram and WhatsApp. In 2019, the *Bundeskartellamt* (German competition authority) prohibited *Meta* from conditioning Facebook use on processing this off-Facebook data without user consent, arguing that the extensive collection and linking of personal data violated the GDPR and constituted an abuse of a dominant position.

* All comments are personal and not representative of Google.

Meta appealed this decision on numerous grounds, including jurisidictional overreach by the *Bundeskartellamt*, to the Higher Regional Court in Düsseldorf, which referred questions regarding the interpretation of the GDPR to the ECJ. For the purposes of this analysis, we will focus solely on those aspects of the ruling relating to interpretation of Art. 6(1)(a) GDPR.

III. Key legal findings

The ECJ ruled as follows:

1) A national competition authority may find a GDPR breach when necessary to establish abuse of dominance. This is on the basis that 'access to personal data and the fact that it is possible to process such data have become a significant parameter of competition between undertakings in the digital economy". Importantly, the court emphasised competition authorities must consult and cooperate with data protection authorities to ensure a consistent application of the GDPR.
2) The Court effectively left consent as the only viable basis for the extensive data processing operations carried out by Meta (collecting and linking data from off-Facebook sources to create user profiles for advertising), rejecting Meta's purported reliance on Art. 6(1)(b) GDPR ('necessary for performance of a contract') on the basis that such processing is not indispensable for the provision of a socal network, and eliminated other primary bases.
3) Market dominance does not automatically invalidate consent under Art. 4 no. 11 GDPR, but it can create a 'clear imbalance' between the user and controller affecting the user's freedom of choice, and the court emphasised conditions for freely given consent:
   - Users must be free to refuse consent for data processing, (like the collection of off-Facebook data) not strictly necessary for the contract without detriment (as per Rec. 42 GDPR).
   - If consent is a condition to access a service, but the processing is not strictly necessary, consent is presumed not freely given (citing Art. 7(4) GDPR).
   - Users should be able to give 'separate consent' for different processing operations (e.g., separating core social network data from off-Facebook data).

4) Equivalent alternatives: The Court suggested that offering an 'equivalent alternative' service without extensive data processing, possibly for an 'appropriate fee,' may be necessary to ensure freedom of choice.

IV. Systematic context and legal classification

Meta Platforms Inc. v *Bundeskartellamt* fundamentally reshaped the intersection between competition law and data privacy, and introduced a new bar for 'freely given' choice.

While the GDPR focuses on individual rights, the DMA focuses on market fairness, and introduced a new consent requirement for 'Gatekeepers' (like Google, Meta, or Apple). Under Art. 5(2) DMA, 'Gatekeepers', are required to obtain consent to combine personal data from different 'core platform' services (e.g., combining Facebook data with WhatsApp data) or to use, for the purposes on online advertising, personal data of end users using services of third parties that make use of core platform services of the gatekeeper. The consent must be obtained in line with the GDPR standard for consent (i.e., it must be 'freely given, specific, informed, and unambiguous').

In the landscape of European data protection, the most seminal case regarding the interpretation of 'consent' is undoubtedly Planet49 decided by ECJ in 2019.[1] Before this ruling, many companies operated on a 'passive consent' or an 'opt-out' model. Planet49, a German online gaming company, hosted a lottery where one of the consent checkboxes for cookies was pre-ticked. The ECJ ruled that for consent to be valid under the GDPR and the ePrivacy Directive, users must make an active, unambiguous choice and consent cannot be obtained via a pre-ticked box.

The ECJ's ruling in *Meta Platforms Inc.* v *Bundeskartellamt*, has provided further guidance on how to ensure that the consent is 'freely given'.

To address the requirements set by the ECJ, in 2023, *Meta* introduced a subscription model in the EU, relying on the ECJ's obiter allowing charging an appropriate fee for an equivalent alternative service free of unnecessary data processing. This requires users to choose between paying a monthly fee (initially ~€10–€13) for an ad-free version of Facebook/Instagram or consenting to personalized advertising to use the free version.

1 ECJ 1.10.2019 – case C-673/17, ECLI:EU:C:2019:801 – Bundesverband der Verbraucherzentralen und Verbraucherverbände – Verbraucherzentrale Bundesverband e.V. v Planet49 GmbH.

This new consent model sparked a new debate across Europe regarding whether a paid alternative constitutes a 'freely given' choice or if the price acts as a penalty, resulting in regulatory rebuttal by data protection authorities and the EC under GDPR and DMA, respectively:

In April 2024, the *European Data Protection Board* (EDPB) issued an opinion stating that large online platforms ('gatekeepers') should not default to a binary choice between 'paying' and 'consenting'.[2] They argued that to ensure consent isn't coercised, a third option of a free version with 'less data-intensive' ads (i.e. contextual ads) should be provided. Consent is rarely 'freely given' when users must pay to protect a fundamental right.

In April 2025, the *European Commission* found *Meta* in non-compliance with Art. 5(2) DMA issuing a €200 million, the first under DMA. It ruled the binary choice 'coerced' users and failed to provide an 'equivalent' alternative and insisted *Meta* must offer a free version that uses less data.

Meta is appealing both decisions before the EU's GC.

V. Author's analysis and commentary

Even though enforcement on Pay or Ok consent models todate has focused on those with 'gatekeeper" status under DMA, the implications ripple far beyond Big Tech to everyone seeking to rely on consent under the GDPR.

While binary choice between paying or receiving targeted ads is not unlawful per se, each implementation will involve a case by case analysis. In determining whether consent is 'freely given", regulators will examine not just the form of the consent but also broader context, and consider key factors like market dominance, user dependence (e.g. is a service socially, professionally or practically necessary? Are there realistic alternatives?) and whether the price levels are punitive or exclusionary.

Others across industry, not just Big Tech players, including other publishers and developpers may now find that simply offering a 'premium ad-free' option is insufficient to justify tracking on the 'free' alternative. In its Opinion, the EDPB essentially 'upgraded' the requirements for consent to be considered 'freely given' by concluding that simply offering a choice between 'Paying' and 'Consenting' is often insufficient, and recommended

2 EDPB, 'Opinion 08/2024 on Valid Consent in the Context of Consent or Pay Models Implemented by Large Online Platforms' (17.4.2024) <https://www.edpb.europa.eu/system/files/2024-04/edpb_opinion_202408_consentorpay_en.pdf>.

a third option of a free alternative with less intrusive advertising – contextual ads that don't track your behavior.[3]

Unlike personalised advertising, which the EDPB has stated can only be performed with valid consent, contextual advertising is often viewed as the 'privacy-first' alternative. As such, contextual advertising can open the door to reliance on legitimate interests grounds (Art. 6(1)(f) GDPR), thereby allowing companies to bypass GDPR 'consent banners' and associated user fatigue while still providing a free service. For this to pass muster, the processing of personal data must be minimal and non-instrusive (e.g. not based on user's browsing history, and coarse location like city or borough rather than more granular location), and aligns with what a user would reasonably expect.

However, 'legimate interests' may not be a blank check for context ads. Of course, to the extent that advertising relies on cookies and similar technologies that involve any 'accessing or storing of information' on a user's device – consent will be required under the ePrivacy Directive even for a contextual ad.

In late 2025, the European Commission introduced the 'Digital Omnibus' package, a horizontal intervention aimed at harmonizing the GDPR, ePrivacy, and the DA to reduce administrative burdens. A central aspect of this package are proposals to amend cookie consent provisions. As the draft currently stands, consent remains a requirement for cookies used to deliver and support contextual advertising – this is an unfortunate missed opportunity to address concerns of user consent fatigue and to incentivise a transition towards less privacy intrusive advertising practices. Indeed, the EDPB has taken a more constructive approach in Opinion on the legislative proposal signalling willingness to support for an exemption from the consent requirement for contextual ads.

3 EDPB, 'Opinion 08/2024 on Valid Consent in the Context of Consent or Pay Models Implemented by Large Online Platforms' (fn. 2).

Contractual Necessity

Lilly Taranto

ECJ 12.9.2024 – Joined cases C-17/22 and C-18/22 – HTB Neunte Immobilien Portfolio and Ökorenta Neue Energien Ökostabil IV

I. Case summary

In the joined cases C-17/22 and C-18/22 the applicants in the main proceedings were investment companies holding shares indirectly in investment funds through trust companies. The applicants asked the defendants to share the personal data of all partners with indirect shareholdings in the investment funds through trust companies. The defendants refused to share such personal data based on the confidentiality clauses in the investment and trust agreements.

The applicants wanted to access the personal data to contact other partners for purposes such as negotiating the purchase of shares and coordinating to reach consensus on partnership resolutions. The defendants were concerned that the data might be used to harm partners' interests, such as advertising the applicants' investment products or purchasing shares below their value and making a profit by reselling them. The applicants in the main proceedings denied having such intentions.

The applicants' legal argument was that the disclosure of personal data of partners with indirect shareholdings is necessary for the performance of the partnership contract.

In both cases the local court of Munich noted that German case law generally supports the right of partners in a partnership to access the personal data of other partners, provided it is not abused. However, the local court questioned whether such disclosure is compatible with the GDPR as German case law on the matter in part predated the GDPR. The cases were, therefore, referred to the ECJ to determine whether the disclosure of personal data in this context is lawful under Art. 6(1)(b) and (f)[1]. For this analysis, we will focus on Art. 6(1)(b) GDPR, namely disclosure of personal data based on contractual necessity.[2]

II. Key legal findings

The ECJ citing other ECJ jurisprudence stated that the lawful ground of contractual necessity in Art. 6(1)(b) GDPR must be interpreted restrictively as it is a justification that allows the processing of personal data in the absence of the data subject's consent[3]. In the joined cases the ECJ noted that the partners had not provided consent to the disclosure of their personal data and therefore it was necessary to check whether Art. 6(1)(b) GDPR could be relied on to share the partners' personal information. The ECJ held that for Art. 6(1)(b) GDPR to apply:

- the processing of personal data must be objectively indispensable for a purpose integral to the contractual obligation intended for the data subject
- the processing of personal data by the controller must be essential for the proper performance of the contract concluded between the controller and the data subject
- there must be no workable, less intrusive alternatives.

The ECJ concluded that the disclosure of the partners' personal data to the defendants is not necessary for the performance of the contract if the contract expressly prohibits the disclosure of such data to other shareholders. The ECJ noted that the essential feature of acquiring an indirect shareholding through a trust company is the anonymity of the partners, which is a fundamental aspect of the contract.

The court went on to suggest alternative, less intrusive ways to achieve the same purpose without disclosing the partners' personal data unnecessarily (e.g., allowing the trust company to forward the request to the partners concerned).

---

1 The ECJ considered also Art. 6(1)(c) GDPR in its decision, but Art.6(1)(c) and Art. 6(1)(f) GDPR are not discussed in this analysis.

2 This case summary was generated with the support of a generative AI tool and subsequently reviewed
and revised by the author.

3 The ECJ cited judgment of 4 July 2023, Meta Platforms and Others (General terms of use of a social network), C 252/21, EU:C:2023:537, paragraphs 93, 98 and 99.

III. Systematic context and legal classification

The principle of contractual necessity in the GDPR is one of the six lawful bases for processing personal data outlined in Art. 6(1)(b) GDPR. It allows organisations to process an individual's personal data when it is necessary for the performance of a contract with that individual, or to take specific steps at their request before entering into a contract.

Keeping faithful to a consistent line of interpretation adopted by the European Data Protection Board (EDPB) and EU Member States' Data Protection Authorities including the UK ICO, the ECJ in the joined cases reinforced a narrow and stringent test for 'contractual necessity' under the GDPR.

The key criteria for the principle of contractual necessity to apply are:

- The processing must be strictly necessary and not merely useful or economically beneficial.
- Necessity is key: The processing must be a targeted and proportionate way of achieving a specific purpose that is integral to the contract. The service cannot, as a matter of fact, be performed without this data processing.
- No less intrusive alternative: It must not be possible to reasonably achieve the purpose by processing less data or using data in a less intrusive way. As mentioned above, the ECJ suggested alternative, less intrusive ways to achieve the same purpose without disclosing the partners' personal data unnecessarily (e.g., allowing the trust company to forward the request to the partners concerned).
- Processing must be expected: The individual must reasonably expect this processing to take place within the context of the contract. This means that organisations cannot use the contractual necessity basis to override specific confidentiality clauses within the same contract or process personal data in ways that individuals would not reasonably expect under the agreement.
- Specific to the individual's contract: The necessity applies to the contract with that person, not for other business purposes or contracts with third parties.
- Cannot be a condition of service if not necessary: If the processing is not actually necessary for the service, it is not possible to force the individual to agree to it as a precondition of the contract and rely on this basis.

A different legal basis, such as consent or legitimate interests, would be required for the additional processing.
- Excludes special category data: This lawful basis cannot be used for processing special category data. A separate condition under Art. 9 GDPR is required for that type of information.

IV. Author's analysis and commentary

The joined cases of C-17/22 and C-18/22 have significant doctrinal and practical implications for how personal data can be processed lawfully based on a contract.

From a doctrinal point of view, the ECJ has given a strict, binding interpretation of contractual necessity, which means that processing personal data under this lawful basis must be objectively essential for the core purpose of that specific contract and cannot be achieved by other less intrusive means. As a result, the controller's subjective assessment or business models do not determine contractual necessity and any ancillary, or merely useful or customary processing are excluded.

In practice, further to the judgment, businesses should re-evaluate their data processing activities and ensure that the correct legal basis is used. Where contractual necessity is broadly interpreted, other legal bases should instead be relied on. Businesses should consider reviewing customer-facing documentation such as privacy notices (these should contain the right lawful bases) and terms and conditions (these should cover essential not optional personal data). Other actions that businesses may want to consider are designing databases to separate personal data processed based on contractual necessity from personal data processed under other lawful bases. Such separation would also assist with data retention and data deletion – personal data based on contractual necessity should be kept for as long as contractual obligations are in force with automatic deletion or anonymisation afterwards, bearing in mind the statute of limitations and pending/threatened litigation.

Finally, businesses should consider putting in place technical controls (e.g., access controls) to enforce purpose limitation by default, ensuring data collected for one purpose isn't automatically used for another without the appropriate legal basis and technical safeguards. These actions would avoid relying on contractual necessity where the test of 'strictly necessary' isn't met.

Whilst these efforts represent an additional compliance burden for businesses, data subjects will enjoy greater protection and control over their personal data as the ruling prevents additional data subjects' personal data from being processed based on contractual necessity where the processing of that data is just useful and not strictly necessary for the performance of the contract.

With regard to data protection officers (DPOs) they should take note of the judgment and consider reviewing all instances where contractual necessity is the legal basis with a particular focus on processing activities like general service improvement, research and development, analytics, or unsolicited marketing as these are unlikely to be able to be based on contractual necessity (consent or legitimate interests may work better in these cases). Other actions that DPOs could consider include ensuring that DPIAs reflect the stricter interpretation of necessity, and providing training to internal stakeholders, especially those in product development, marketing, and legal, about the strict limits of contractual necessity.

On a positive note, for organisations working across the EU the ruling may boost uniformity in interpretation of contractual necessity at Member State level making it easier to operate in the single market. At the same time, contractual necessity may become a residual lawful ground for processing as many organisations may prefer to shift to legitimate interest or consent as lawful bases for processing personal data.

Outside the European Union, the ECJ judgment might affect the interpretation of GDPR-inspired laws internationally and GDPR-centric corporate policies of multinationals, who will need to adhere to a stricter meaning of contractual necessity and, as a result, where needed, adjust their data processing practices globally.

V. Recommended further reading

EDPB, 'Guidelines 2/2019 on the processing of personal data under Art. 6(1)(b) GDPR' version 2.0 (8.10.2019) <https://www.edpb.europa.eu/sites/default/files/files/file1/edpb_guidelines-art_6-1-b-adopted_after_public_consultation_en.pdf>.

Data Protection Commission, 'Decision of the Data Protection Commission made pursuant to Section 113 of the Data Protection Act, 2018 and Articles 60 and 65 of the General Data Protection Regulation, Meta Platforms Ireland Limited (formerly Facebook Ireland Limited) in respect of the Facebook Service' (IN-18-5-5, 31.12.2022) <https://www.dataprotection.ie/sites/default/files/uploads/2023-04/Meta%20FINAL%20DECISION%20%28ADOPTED%29%2031-12-22%20-%20IN-18-5-5%20%28Redacted%29.pdf>.

Data Protection Commission, 'Decision of the Data Protection Commission made pursuant to Section 113 of the Data Protection Act, 2018 and Articles 60 and 65 of the General Data Protection Regulation, Meta Platforms Ireland Limited (formerly Facebook Ireland Limited) in respect of the Instagram Service' (IN-18–5–7, 31.12.2022) <https://www.dataprotection.ie/sites/default/files/uploads/2023-04/Meta%20FINAL%20Decision%20%28ADOPTED%29%20-%20IN-18-5-7%20-%2031-12-22%20%28Redacted%29.pdf>.

Information Commissioner's Office, 'Contract' <https://ico.org.uk/for-organisations/uk-gdpr-guidance-and-resources/lawful-basis/a-guide-to-lawful-basis/contract/>.

The broad notion of 'legitimate interests' in Art. 6(1)(f) GDPR

Natascha Gerlach

ECJ 4.10.2024 – C-621/22, ECLI:EU:C:2024:858 – Koninklijke Nederlandse Lawn Tennisbond v Autoriteit Persoonsgegevens

I. Introduction

The rise of the digital economy has necessitated a regulatory framework capable of protecting fundamental human rights while simultaneously allowing for the dynamic flow of data to drive technological and commercial progress. Consequently, the GDPR sets out processing principles and requires a lawful basis for the processing of personal data.[1] Among the six grounds enumerated in Art. 6(1) GDPR, the reliance upon 'legitimate interests' pursuant to point (f) has proven to be at the same time the most adaptable as well as the most contentious foundation for the processing of personal data. Art. 6(1) (f) GDPR allows processing of personal data where it is 'necessary for the purposes of the legitimate interests pursued by the controller or by a third party', provided the principles of Art. 5 GDPR are satisfied and that the identified legitimate interests are not overridden by the data subject's fundamental rights and freedoms.[2] This legal concept of allowing for processing based on organisational necessity, subject to a stringent balancing test, is not novel to the GDPR. The GDPR itself represents a modernised and unified framework,[3] repealing the DPD and Art. 7(f) GDPR which already established the notion of a legitimate interest.[4]

1 Art. 5(1)(a) GDPR.

2 ECJ 6.10.2020 – joined cases C-511/18, C-512/18 and C-520/18, ECLI:EU:C:2020:791 para. 208 – La Quadrature du Net and Others, and ECJ 11.7.2024 – case C-757/22, ECLI:EU:C:2024:598 para 49- Meta Platforms Ireland (Representative action), Art. 6(1) (f) GDPR.

3 Rec. 7 and 9 GDPR confirming that the 'objectives and principles of the DPD remain sound', but new technical developments require an updated framework.

4 Art. 7(f) DPD provided that 'Member States shall provide that personal data may be processed only if [...] processing is necessary for the purposes of the legitimate

The ECJ has consistently established that the legitimate interest ground is subject to a stringent three-part cumulative test[5]:

1. Establishment of a legitimate interest.
2. The necessity of processing the personal data for that interest.
3. A balancing test to ensure the data subject's fundamental rights and freedoms do not take precedence.

However, the question of what can qualify as a legitimate interest in first step of the triparted test has been a point of contention to date; more specifically the question whether commercial or economic interests can qualify as such a legitimate interest.[6]

To that end, the GDPR itself provides some indication of the legislative intent in Rec. 47 GDPR. The GDPR's recitals function as interpretive guidance that frames the Regulation's substantive rules by articulating the normative ambitions, contextual justifications, and teleological considerations of the regulation itself. Rec. 47 GDPR provides that, for example, 'direct marketing purposes', which are generally a commercial activity, could qualify as a legitimate interest.[7]

However, some have argued that a legitimate interest must be provided in law.[8]

---

interests pursued by the controller or by the third party or parties to whom the data are disclosed, except where such interests are overridden by the interests for fundamental rights and freedoms of the data subject which require protection under Article 1 d)'. Contrary to Art. 7(f) DPD, the GDPR Legitimate Interest legal basis is no longer available to public authorities in the context of performing their tasks. Rec. 47 GDPR clarifies that it is for the legislator to set out legal basis for public authorities.

5 ECJ 4.7.2023 – case C-252/21, ECLI:EU:C:2023:537 para. 106 – Meta Platforms and Others v Bundeskartellamt.

6 The Dutch Data Protection Authority (AP) in a version of their explanatory note on Legitimate Interest from November 2019: 'What are not considered legitimate interest either, would be the following examples: processing personal data for purely commercial interests, profit maximisation, monitoring employee conduct without legitimate interest or tracking the (purchasing) behaviour of (potential) customers, etc.' (The explanatory note has been revised since); see reference in the Letter from the European Commission to AP: European Commission, 'Letter to Mr Aleid Wolfsen, Autoriteit Persoonsgegevens, on the Dutch DPA's interpretation of legitimate interests under Article 6(1)(f) GDPR' (6.3.2020), <https://static.nrc.nl/2022/pdf/letter-dutch-dpa-legitimate-interest.pdf>.

7 Rec. 47 GDPR also mentions fraud prevention which would often be deployed in the context of commercial activities.

8 Most notably the Dutch Data Protection Authority (AP) in their explanatory note (now revised); see also Kuner/Bygrave/Docksey The EU General Data Protection Regulation

This is not convincing and the scope of this first limb of the legitimate interests test—what can qualify as 'legitimate interest'—was subject of the recent Case C-621/22, Koninklijke Nederlandse Lawn Tennisbond (KNLTB) v Autoriteit Persoonsgegevens (AP).[9]

II. Case summary[10]

The *Royal Dutch Lawn Tennis Association (KNLTB)* is a sports federation; its members consist of tennis associations and their individual members. *KNLTB* engaged with different sponsors to, inter alia, increase their membership. In this context *KLNTB* disclosed the personal data of its members—including names, addresses, dates of birth, and contact information—to two external sponsors, a sports products company SportshopsDirect BV (TennisDirect) and Nederlandse Loterij Organisatie BV, the largest provider of games of chance in the Netherlands (NLO). This disclosure was performed for payment and intended for advertising and marketing activities. Member consent was not sought.

After individual complaints, the *Dutch Data Protection Authority (AP)* found *KNLTB* in violation of the GDPR for disclosing the data without consent or a legitimate interest and ultimately imposed a fine. *KNLTB* brought an action arguing claiming legitimate interests under Art. 6(1)(f) GDPR; *AP* argued that such legitimate interest must be 'enshrined in and determined by law' and 'worthy of protection' by EU or national law, which it found not to be the case. Conversely, the *KNLTB* argued that any interest may be legitimate unless it is contrary to law, which could include purely commercial interests.[11]

A core legal question referred to the ECJ was whether purely commercial interest, such as the sale of personal data for direct marketing purposes

(GDPR)/Kotschy 2018, GDPR Art. 6, 337, 1.2.6 'Mere Commercial interest will not suffice to establish a 'legitimate interest' with reference to fn. 60.

9 ECJ 4.10.2024 – case C-621/22, ECLI:EU:C:2024:858 – Koninklijke Nederlandse Lawn Tennisbond (KNLTB) v Autoriteit Persoonsgegevens (AP).

10 This case summary was generated with the support of a generative AI tool and subsequently reviewed and revised by the author.

11 ECJ 4.10.2024 – case C-621/22, ECLI:EU:C:2024:858 para. 16 et seq. – Koninklijke Nederlandse Lawn Tennisbond (KNLTB) v Autoriteit Persoonsgegevens (AP).

without consent, could ever qualify as a 'legitimate interest' within the meaning of Art. 6(1)(f) GDPR.[12]

III. Key legal findings

The KNLTB landmark judgment has now confirmed that the concept of 'legitimate interest' is indeed to be understood broadly, and capable of covering a '*wide range of interests*'. Crucially, the Court rejected the AP's strict interpretation, holding that the EU legislature did not require that the interest pursued by a controller be provided for by law.[13]

1. Commercial interests can be legitimate interests

The Court concluded that *commercial interest* of the controller, such as the disclosure of members' personal data for consideration to third parties for advertising or marketing purposes, could constitute a legitimate interest within the meaning of Art. 6(1)(f) GDPR.[14]

The Court clarified however, that a statutory prerequisite for the interest itself is that the alleged legitimate interest *must be lawful*.[15]

By confirming that a lawful commercial interest is not excluded from qualifying as a legitimate interest, the ECJ's KNLTB judgment explicitly also confirms previous case law,[16] in which the Court accepted economic interest to proceed to the next step of analysis required for the legitimate interest legal basis.

---

12 ECJ 4.10.2024 – case C-621/22, ECLI:EU:C:2024:858 para. 19 – Koninklijke Nederlandse Lawn Tennisbond (KNLTB) v Autoriteit Persoonsgegevens (AP).

13 ECJ 4.10.2024 – case C-621/22, ECLI:EU:C:2024:858 para. 38 et seq. – Koninklijke Nederlandse Lawn Tennisbond (KNLTB) v Autoriteit Persoonsgegevens (AP).

14 ECJ 4.10.2024 – case C-621/22, ECLI:EU:C:2024:858 para. 49 – Koninklijke Nederlandse Lawn Tennisbond (KNLTB) v Autoriteit Persoonsgegevens (AP).

15 ECJ 4.10.2024 – case C-621/22, ECLI:EU:C:2024:858 para. 40 – Koninklijke Nederlandse Lawn Tennisbond (KNLTB) v Autoriteit Persoonsgegevens (AP).

16 ECJ 4.5.2017 – case C-13/16, ECLI:EU:C:2017:336 para. 29 – Valsts policijas Rīgas reģiona pārvaldes Kārtības policijas pārvalde v Rīgas pašvaldības SIA 'Rīgas satiksme'; ECJ 1.5.2014 – case C-131/12, ECLI:EU:C:2014:317 para. 73 – Google Spain SL and Google Inc. v Agencia Española de Protección de Datos (AEPD) and Mario Costeja González.

This also aligns with the position of the European Commission (EC) and the predecessor of the European Data Protection Board (EDPB), the Article 29 Working Party, as well as the present day EDPB. The Article 29 Working Party was clear in their Opinion 06/2014 in the context of Art. 7 (f) of the DPD that a broad range of interest can be considered legitimate.[17] The EDPB has since confirmed this in their Guidelines 1/2024 that 'In the absence of a definition of that concept in the GDPR, a wide range of interests is, in principle, capable of being regarded as legitimate'.[18] The EC has emphasised that 'the freedom to conduct a business, including pursuing pure commercial interests such a profit maximization, is a human right enshrined in Art. 16 of the Charter of Fundamental Rights of the European Union',[19] which makes it difficult to reconcile as not legitimate or worthy of protection.

It is important to understand, however, that accepting economic or commercial interest as legitimate under Art. 6 (1)(f) GDPR is not equal to allowing the processing to proceed under the GDPR. KNLTB only clarifies, that controllers with economic interest are not instantly deprived of the possibility of carrying out the balancing test required by the tripartite analysis of Art. 6(1)(f) GDPR, by requiring statutory enshrining.

KNLTB also rigorously reinforces existing case law by confirming the cumulative necessity and balancing requirements; controllers must not only pursue a lawful interest but also actively prove that no less intrusive means are available and that the processing aligns with the data subject's reasonable expectations in that specific relational context.[20]

---

17 Article 29 Data Protection Working Party, 'Overview of results of public consultation on Opinion on legitimate interests of the data controller (Opinion 06/2014)' (14.11.2014) <https://ec.europa.eu/justice/article-29/press-material/public-consultation/notion-legitimate-interests/files/20141126_overview_relating_to_consultation_on_opinion_legitimate_interest_.pdf>, 24.

18 European Data Protection Board, 'Guidelines 1/2024 on processing of personal data based on Article 6(1)(f) GDPR' (08.10.2024) <https://www.edpb.europa.eu/our-work-tools/documents/public-consultations/2024/guidelines-12024-processing-personal-data-based_en>, 7, with reference to ECJ 7.12.2023 – joined cases C-26/22 and C-64/22, ECLI:EU:C:2023:958 para. 76 – SCHUFA Holding (Libération de reliquat de dette).

19 European Commission, 'Letter to Mr Aleid Wolfsen, Autoriteit Persoonsgegevens, on the Dutch DPA's interpretation of legitimate interests under Article 6(1)(f) GDPR' (6.3.2020) <https://static.nrc.nl/2022/pdf/letter-dutch-dpa-legitimate-interest.pdf>.

20 ECJ 4.10.2024 – case C-621/22, ECLI:EU:C:2024:858 para. 37,42, 44 – Koninklijke Nederlandse Lawn Tennisbond (KNLTB) v Autoriteit Persoonsgegevens (AP).

2. Necessity

The second leg of the tri-part test therefore demands that the processing be strictly necessary for the purposes of the legitimate interests pursued. This necessity requirement compels the controller to ascertain that the interest cannot reasonably be achieved just as effectively by other means less restrictive to the fundamental rights and freedoms of data subjects.[21]

This analysis must be performed in conjunction with the data minimisation principle (Art. 5(1)(c) GDPR), which dictates that personal data must be limited to what is necessary in relation to the purposes for which they are processed.[22] In the KNLTB context, the ECJ indicated that the referring court would have to consider whether a less intrusive measure might have been to inform members beforehand and asking them whether they wished their data to be transmitted to third parties for advertising purposes. The Court proposed that this might have given members control over the amount of data disclosed.[23]

3. Balancing of Interests

The third condition requires a balancing of the opposing rights and interests. This assessment is fact-specific and depends on the specific circumstances of the case.

The GDPR in Rec. 47 GDPR places particular emphasis on the reasonable expectations of the data subject for the balancing test. The controller must assess whether individuals can reasonably expect, at the time of data collection, that their personal data would be, for example disclosed for consideration to sponsors for marketing as in the KNLTB context.[24] Where data subjects do not reasonably expect further processing, their fundamental rights are more likely to override the controller's interest.

21 ECJ 4.10.2024 – case C-621/22, ECLI:EU:C:2024:858 para. 42 – Koninklijke Nederlandse Lawn Tennisbond (KNLTB) v Autoriteit Persoonsgegevens (AP).

22 ECJ 4.7.2023 – case C252/21, ECLI:EU:C:2023:537 para. 109 – Meta Platforms and Others (Conditions générales d'utilisation d'un réseau social).

23 ECJ 4.10.2024 – case C-621/22, ECLI:EU:C:2024:858 para. 51 et seq. – Koninklijke Nederlandse Lawn Tennisbond (KNLTB) v Autoriteit Persoonsgegevens (AP).

24 ECJ 4.10.2024 – case C-621/22, ECLI:EU:C:2024:858 para. 55 – Koninklijke Nederlandse Lawn Tennisbond (KNLTB) v Autoriteit Persoonsgegevens (AP).

Furthermore, the Court in KNLTB highlighted the need to consider the specific context of the processing, noting that the disclosure of data to a provider of games of chance and casino games did

a) not appear to be characterised by a 'relevant and appropriate relationship' between the data subjects and the controller;[25] and
b) the processing could result in *harmful effects* such as exposure to gambling addiction risks.[26]

The Court's instruction to consider all the relevant circumstances underscores that this balancing test must be context-specific, dynamic, and genuinely protective of individual rights. If the balance tips in favor of the data subject's rights and freedoms—even when the interest is lawful and the processing is strictly necessary— without further mitigating measures, the reliance on Art. 6(1)(f) GDPR may fail.

IV. Author's analysis and commentary

The legal basis of Legitimate Interest is dynamic but demanding. Its historical grounding, surviving the regulatory transition to the GDPR, affirms the legislator's understanding of its importance for *the digital economy to develop across the internal market*[27] in instances where consent is unsuitable or unobtainable.[28]

In a society increasingly reliant on data for everything from security and organisational funding to service delivery, *legitimate interest* provides the assurance that beneficial activities can flourish, while fundamental rights

25 ECJ 4.10.2024 – case C-621/22, ECLI:EU:C:2024:858 para. 56 – Koninklijke Nederlandse Lawn Tennisbond (KNLTB) v Autoriteit Persoonsgegevens (AP).

26 ECJ 4.10.2024 – case C-621/22, ECLI:EU:C:2024:858 para. 56 – Koninklijke Nederlandse Lawn Tennisbond (KNLTB) v Autoriteit Persoonsgegevens (AP).

27 Rec. 7 GDPR.

28 Centre for Information Policy Leadership (CIPL), 'Limiting Legal Basis for Data Processing Under the DMA: Considerations on Scope and Practical Consequences' (May 2023) <https://www.informationpolicycentre.com/uploads/5/7/1/0/57104281/cipl_dma_limiting_legal_basis_may2023.pdf> p. 20; Centre for Information Policy Leadership (CIPL), 'The Limitations of Consent as a Legal Basis for Data Processing in the Digital Society', (December 2024) <https://www.informationpolicycentre.com/uploads/5/7/1/0/57104281/cipl_bkl_limitations_of_consent_legal_basis_data_processing_dec24.pdf>, p. 9.

remain protected to a high standard.[29] It ensures that adaptability and the GDPR's inherent accountability principle are permanently linked.

The aims of the GDPR are not achieved through the most restrictively conceivable or nationally idiosyncratic interpretation of its provisions. An unnecessarily restrictive understanding of core concepts such as *legitimate interests* under Art. 6(1)(f) GDPR —create legal uncertainty and risks undermining the Regulation's dual objective of protecting fundamental rights while enabling lawful data processing.[30] The GDPR does not exclude economic or commercial interests from qualifying as legitimate interests; rather, the GDPR subjects all such interests to a contextual balancing against the rights and freedoms of data subjects. The GDPR is clear that it must be interpreted uniformly to preserve both the high level of protection it guarantees and the proper functioning of the internal market.[31]

In this spirit, the GDPR does not compel a de facto reduction of available legal bases to a single option – consent; rather, it supports innovation and the free flow of data by permitting controllers to rely on the most appropriate legal basis in each context, *provided that all applicable principles and safeguards are rigorously observed.* The KNLTB decision has cemented this adaptability of the GDPR framework further.

V. Recommended further reading

CIPL, The Limitations of Consent as a Legal Basis for Data Processing in the Digital Society (December 2024) <https://www.informationpolicycentre.com/uploads/5/7/1/0/57104281/cipl_bkl_limitations_of_consent_legal_basis_data_processing_dec24.pdf>.

CIPL, Legitimate Interests for Data in AI Training – The DPO Perspective (December 2025) <https://www.informationpolicycentre.com/uploads/5/7/1/0/57104281/cipl_legitimate_interests_for_data_ai_training_dpo_perspective_dec25.pdf>.

---

29 Centre for Information Policy Leadership (CIPL), 'The Limitations of Consent as a Legal Basis for Data Processing in the Digital Society' (fn. 27).

30 ECJ 9.3.2010 – case C-518/07, ECLI:EU:C:2010:125 para. 24 – Commission v Germany recalling the 'fair balance between, on the one hand, observance of the fundamental right to private life and, on the other hand, the interests requiring free movement of personal data'.

31 Rec. 9 GDPR; in ECJ 4.5.2023 – case C300/21, ECLI:EU:C:2023:317 – UI v Österreichische Post AG, the Court rejected national 'seriousness thresholds' for non-material damage on the basis that such divergence would erode the GDPR's coherence and uniformity across the Union.

Nettesheim, Data Protection in Contractual Relationships (Art. 6 (1) (b) GDPR) <https://papers.ssrn.com/sol3/papers.cfm?abstract_id=4427134>.

Data processing to protect vital interests

Dimitrios Linardatos

EDPB, 'Guidelines 02/2024 on Article 48 GDPR', version 2.1 (4.6.2025) <https://www.edpb.europa.eu/system/files/2025-06/edpb_guidelines_2024 02_article48_v2_en.pdf>

I. Case summary

The location of a person in mortal danger may require the processing of personal data of the data subject or another natural person who, due to absence, unavailability, unconsciousness, etc., is unable to give consent themselves in order to avert the mortal danger. The EDPB Guidelines[1] cite as another possible use case of Art. 6(1)(d) of the GDPR the exceptional situation in which a third country requests access to personal data on abducted minors, provided that the conditions for fulfilling the request as laid down in international law are met and that the transfer of the data is in the vital interest of the data subject themselves.

II. Key legal findings

With reference to Rec. 46 GDPR, the Guidelines confirm that the processing of personal data may be considered lawful even without any other legal basis if it is necessary to protect the vital interests of the data subject or another natural person from imminent threats.[2] Among other things, the provision is an expression of a humanitarian idea. The guidelines emphasize the narrow exceptional nature of Art. 6(1)(d) GDPR; the provision is strictly subsidiary to other legal bases, even in situations of imminent danger. Hence, the provision should only be applicable in urgent 'life-or-death'

1 EDPB, 'Guidelines 02/2024 on Article 48 GDPR', version 2.1 (4.6.2025) <https://www.edpb.europa.eu/system/files/2025-06/edpb_guidelines_202402_article48_v2_en.pdf>, mn. 28 in conjunction with fn. 12.

2 See again EDPB, 'Guidelines 02/2024 on Article 48 GDPR' (fn. 1), mn. 28.

scenarios where no other legal basis guarantees the legally compliant processing of personal data in order to avert the immediate threat. According to Rec. 46, sent. 3 of the GDPR, there may be an overlap between the circumstances addressed by Art. 6(1)(d) of the GDPR and data processing prompted by important reasons of public interest (e.g., natural disasters such as earthquakes, floods, epidemics, etc.) as well as the vital interests of the data subject (e.g., location of a person in difficult-to-access terrain).

III. Systematic context and legal classification

1. The subsidiary nature of Art. 6(1)(d) GDPR means that the primacy of consent is not entirely dispensed with.[3] However, the provision creates a justification for data processing if consent cannot be obtained in time in view of the immediate threat or if obtaining consent would unduly prejudice the vital interests of the data subject or a third party. It must therefore be clarified that, in situations of acute emergency or imminent danger, the rights to data protection and privacy (Arts. 7 et seq. CFR) may justifiably yield to the fundamental rights to life and physical integrity (Art. 2(1), 3(1) CFR).[4]

2. The provision in Art. 6(1)(d) GDPR corresponds to Art. 7(d) DPD, but with the distinction that processing is now permissible not only to protect the vital interests of the data subject, but also for the benefit of third parties.[5]

3. There may be instances in which the circumstances described in Art. 6(1)(d) GDPR overlap with those falling under Art. 6(1)(e) GDPR – particularly where the processing of personal data is necessary for the performance of a task carried out in the public interest or in the exercise of official authority vested in the controller. According to Rec. 46, sent. 3 GDPR, this may be relevant in the context of monitoring epidemics (apps for tracking personal contacts). Accordingly, lit. d is particularly relevant

3 Simitis/Hornung/Spiecker gen. Döhmann Datenschutzrecht/Schantz, 2nd edn. 2025, DSGVO Art. 6 mn. 64.

4 Simitis/Hornung/Spiecker gen. Döhmann Datenschutzrecht/Schantz DSGVO Art. 6 mn. 62; stricter Köllmann NZA 2020, 831 (833).

5 Kuner/Bygrave/Docksey The EU General Data Protection Regulation (GDPR)/Kotschy, 2020, GDPR Art. 6 p. 333; Simitis/Hornung/Spiecker gen. Döhmann Datenschutzrecht/Schantz DSGVO Art. 6 mn. 62.

for private controllers because they do not perform public tasks.[6] In such private domains, Art. 6(1)(f) GDPR may also be relevant, for example when employers collect personal data in connection with the COVID-19 pandemic in order to protect the health of all their employees, based on their duty of care under labor law.[7]

4. Parallel provisions to Art. 6(1)(d) GDPR can be found in Art. 9(2)(c) GDPR with regard to the processing of special categories of personal data; this was relevant during the COVID-19 pandemic, among other things, and is sometimes considered to take precedence for corresponding warning apps.[8] On the other hand, a similar provision is laid down in Art. 49(1)(f) GDPR with regard to the transfer of data to third countries.

IV. Author's analysis and commentary

1. In terms of its humanitarian dimension, the provision essentially articulates – in a standardized manner – a fundamental value judgement[9] that data protection and the associated interest in privacy cannot, self-evidently, take precedence over higher-ranking legal interests such as life or physical integrity, particularly in light of the irreversible nature of the harm that may occur.[10] In the situations envisaged by the legislator, data processing will typically be in the presumed interest of the data subject. Accordingly, the provision has a special regulatory effect insofar as it extends beyond the data subject to the vital interests of 'other natural persons,' i.e., it also enables the protection of third parties.[11]

---

6 See Hornung/Stroscher GSZ 2021, 185 (186).

7 For example, BayLfD, 'Datenschutzrechtliche Informationen zur Verarbeitung von personenbezogenen Daten durch Arbeitgeber und Dienstherren im Zusammenhang mit der Corona-Pandemie' <https://www.datenschutz-bayern.de/corona/arbeitgeber.html>.

8 Köllmann NZA 2020, 831 (833).

9 See also BeckOK DatenschutzR/Albers/Veit, 53rd edn. 1.8.2025, DS-GVO Art. 6 mn. 51.

10 See Kuner/Bygrave/Docksey/Kotschy GDPR Art. 6 p. 333; see also Paal/Pauly DS-GVO BDSG/Frenzel, 3rd edn. 2021, DS-GVO Art. 6 mn. 20.

11 For the corresponding proposal in the legislative process, see Council of the EU, 'Vorschlag für eine Verordnung des Europäischen Parlaments und des Rates zum Schutz natürlicher Personen bei der Verarbeitung personenbezogener Daten und zum freien Datenverkehr (Datenschutz-Grundverordnung) – Vorbereitung einer allgemeinen Ausrichtung' (Doc. 9565/15, 11.6.2015) <https://data.consilium.europa.eu/doc/document/ST-9565-2015-INIT/de/pdf>.

2. According to Rec. 46 sent. 2 GDPR, the circumstances set out in Art. 6(1)(d) GDPR are to be subsidiary in nature. In order to give effect to this legislative intent, the provision must, as a matter of principle, be applied in a restrictive manner. A situation of concrete and imminent danger for the data subject or a third (natural) person is a prerequisite.[12] Nevertheless, the question remains open of how the requirement of 'vital interests' is to be interpreted. Rec. 46 GDPR describes a 'vital interest' as one which is 'essential for the life' of an individual without clarifying whether this is to be determined objectively or subjectively.

An objective determination of the characteristic for the protection of highly personal legal interests is advocated,[13] but this interpretation would probably mean that no investigative measures could be based on Art. 6(1)(d) GDPR if the threat situation does not appear conclusively certain from a subjective point of view. Whether such a narrow interpretation is necessary in view of the potentially affected legal interests is open to criticism.[14] Ultimately, however, the problem is unlikely to become virulent because other grounds for permission already apply in this respect and justify data processing.[15] For example, circumstances relating to serious medical cases will be covered by Art. 9(2)(c) GDPR – and possibly also by Art. 9(2)(i) GDPR – the performance of a task in the public interest is addressed by Art. 6(1)(e) GDPR, and Art. 6(1)(c) GDPR may also often be relevant.[16] It is also notable that some authors assume that Art. 6(1)(f) of the GDPR will often be fulfilled regarding the data processing for the 'vital interests of another natural person'.[17]

3. With regard to the relationship between Art. 9(2) GDPR and Art. 6(1) GDPR, the ECJ clarified in Case C-667/21[18] that an exception under Art. 9(2) GDPR is in principle not sufficient to justify the lawfulness of data

12 Kuner/Bygrave/Docksey/Kotschy GDPR Art. 6 p. 333.

13 BeckOK DatenschutzR/Albers/Veit DS-GVO Art. 6 mn. 51; Plath GDPR/BDSG/TTDSG/Plath/Struck, 4th edn. 2023, DS-GVO Art. 6 mn. 47 et seq.; Paal/Pauly/Frenzel DS-GVO Art. 6 mn. 20.

14 This must be distinguished from abstract preventive measures without acute danger (e.g., general pandemic precautions); see Simitis/Hornung/Spiecker gen. Döhmann/Schantz DSGVO Art. 6 mn. 64.

15 See also Simitis/Hornung/Spiecker gen. Döhmann/Schantz DSGVO Art. 6 mn. 63.

16 Kühling/Buchner DS-GVO BDSG/Buchner/Petri, 4th edn. 2024, DS-GVO Art. 6 mn. 106, 108.

17 Kuner/Bygrave/Docksey/Kotschy GDPR Art. 6 p. 334.

18 ECJ 21.12.2023 – case C-667/21, ECLI:EU:C:2023:1022 – Krankenversicherung Nordrhein.

processing. However, Art. 6(1)(d) GDPR does not contribute any essential criteria to the requirements of Art. 9(2)(c) and (i) GDPR and does not provide any additional standard of protection in this respect.

4. The relationship between Art. 6(1)(d) GDPR and the data subject's right to self-determination appears unclear.[19] With reference to the previous provision (Art. 7(d) of the DPD), some legal literature argues that the permissibility of Art. 6(1)(d) of the GDPR should only be invoked if the data subject is unable to act on their own behalf and, moreover, it cannot be (hypothetically) assumed that they would consent to the data processing if they were capable of giving such consent.[20] This is countered by the argument that alternative grounds for permissibility are only provided for in order to protect the vital interests of *another* natural person, but not in situations involving the corresponding legal interests and interests of the data subject themselves.[21] Although this objection cannot be dismissed out of hand, it does not alter the fact that the control question raised by the restrictive interpretation, namely whether the data subject would consent if they were capable of doing so (presumed consent),[22] takes due account of the legislator's intention to create a subsidiary ground for permission.

5. In light of the neighbouring provisions and the numerous open questions of interpretation, the practical significance of Art. 6(1)(d) GDPR appears comparatively limited; at first glance, one might even conclude that its deletion would not materially affect the overall operation of the legal framework. However, the provision fulfils a symbolic and normative function by explicitly affirming that humanitarian principles – particularly the protection of life and physical integrity – are not to be subordinated to privacy interests. From a legal-policy perspective, this signalling effect represents a meaningful and welcome development, even if the provision's practical application remains modest. In addition, the provision is significant for private controllers who are not entrusted with public authority.[23]

---

19 Cf. Kuner/Bygrave/Docksey/Kotschy GDPR Art. 6 p. 334.

20 Gola/Heckmann DS-GVO BDSG/Schulz, 3rd ed. 2022, DS-GVO Art. 6 mn. 49; critical Paal/Pauly/Frenzel DS-GVO Art. 6 mn. 21.

21 Kühling/Buchner/Buchner/Petri DS-GVO Art. 6 mn. 109 f.

22 Gola/Heckmann/Schulz DS-GVO Art. 6 mn. 49 with further references.

23 Paal/Pauly/Frenzel DS-GVO Art. 6 mn. 20.

V. Recommended further reading

With regard to data-driven solutions for the general management of situations in which the vital interests of a natural person are affected, the Guidelines 04/2020 on the use of location data and contact tracing tools in the context of the COVID-19 outbreak (Adopted on 21 April 2020) serve as a further model.[24] Moreover, the EDPB-EDPS Joint Response to the LIBE Committee on the impact of the US Cloud Act on the European legal framework for personal data protection should be given due consideration in relation to direct foreign requests.[25]

24 EDPB, 'Guidelines 04/2020 on the use of location data and contact tracing tools in the context of the COVID-19 outbreak' (21.4.2020) <https://www.edpb.europa.eu/our-work-tools/our-documents/guidelines/guidelines-042020-use-location-data-and-contact-tracing_en>.

25 EDPB/EDPS, 'EDPB-EDPS Joint Response to the LIBE Committee on the impact of the US Cloud Act on the European legal framework for personal data protection' (12.7.2019) <https://www.edps.europa.eu/data-protection/our-work/publications/opinions/edpb-edps-joint-response-us-cloud-act_en>, Annex p. 4.

Personal data of representatives of legal persons, interpretation of Art. 6(2) and (3) GDPR, public access

Gero Ziegenhorn

ECJ 3.4.2025 – case C-710/23, ECLI:EU:C:2025:231 – L. H. v Ministerstvo zdravotnictví

I. Case summary

This preliminary ruling has been made in proceedings regarding a Czech citizen's request for information lodged with the Czech Ministry of Health. The citizen had, in particular, requested the first and last names, the signatures, and further contact details of natural persons who had, as representatives of a company (i.e. a legal person), entered into contractual obligations with the Czech state on behalf of that company and had signed certain certificates.

The Ministry partially granted the request and sent the certificates, redacting the information relating to the natural persons who had signed the certificates on behalf of the companies concerned, including the forename, surname, signature and position held by those natural persons. The Ministry justified this by stating that, under national law, it would have had to inform and consult these individuals and that this was not possible in the case at hand because the individuals operated in China and the UK and their place of residence was unknown.

II. Key legal findings

The judgment *Ministerstvo zdravotnictví II* addresses the relationship between public access to information and data protection, while particularly elaborating the interpretation of Art. 4 no. 1, 2 GDPR on the one hand, and of Art. 6(3) GDPR on the other.

Regarding the data of natural persons representing a legal person, the ECJ ruled that Art. 4 no. 1, 2 GDPR must be interpreted as meaning that the disclosure of the first name, surname, signature and further contact details of a natural person representing a legal entity constitutes processing of personal data. According to the ECJ, the fact that that information was provided for the sole purpose of enabling the identification of the natural person authorised to act on behalf of that legal person does not mean that it cannot be characterised as personal data.

On the other hand, the ECJ considered the redacting of certain information to be compatible with the GDPR. The Court concluded that Art. 6(1) (c) and (e) GDPR, read in conjunction with Art. 86 GDPR, must be interpreted as not precluding national case-law which requires a controller, being a public authority responsible for reconciling public access to official documents with the right to the protection of personal data, to inform and consult the natural person concerned prior to the disclosure of official documents containing such data. This interpretation is, however, subject to the proviso that such an obligation is not impossible to implement and that it does not require disproportionate effort and, therefore, does not result in a disproportionate restriction on public access to those documents.

III. Systematic context and legal classification

The ECJ's findings on Art. 4 no. 1, 2 GDPR are in line with its previous case-law. The Court traditionally applies a broad interpretation of Art. 4 no. 1 GDPR: Information relates to an identified or identifiable natural person where, by reason of its content, purpose or effect, it is linked to an identifiable person.[1] This case-law is continued in the judgment *Ministerstvo zdravotnictví II*. The data in question here were the first and last names, the signatures, and further contact details of persons who, as representatives of a legal person, had entered into contractual obligations with the Czech state on behalf of that legal person and had signed certain certificates. The ECJ classified the first and last names as well as the signatures as personal data. However, the Court leaves it to the referring court to decide whether, in the case at hand, the further contact details of the natural persons are also to be classified as personal data.

Furthermore, the Court considers the disclosure of personal data by a public authority when granting a legal request for information as 'process-

1 ECJ 4.10.2024 – case C-200/23, ECLI: EU:C:2024:827 para 131 – Agentsia po vpisvaniyata; cf. ECJ 23.7.2015 – case C-398/15, ECLI:EU:C:2017:197 para. 32, 34 – Manni.

ing' within the meaning of Art. 4 no. 2 GDPR. This, too, is consistent with the existing case-law. In prior judgments, the ECJ had already emphasised that it is apparent in particular from the expression 'any operation' that the EU legislature intended to give the concept of 'processing' a broad scope, which is corroborated by the non-exhaustive nature, expressed by the phrase 'such as', of the operations listed in that provision.[2]

The assessment of the redaction of certain information ultimately depends on the balancing of public access to information and data protection. Public access to documents is regulated by Art. 86 GDPR. The Court points out that this provision is linked to Art. 10 TFEU and Art. 15 TFEU. This is balanced against the protection of the data of those natural persons whose data would be disclosed in the course of providing access.

In this regard, the ECJ bases its ruling on a broad interpretation of the opening clause in Art. 6(3) GDPR. In this vein, the Court also considers case-law as 'Member State law' within the meaning of Art. 6(3)(b) GDPR. Data processing in the context of providing public access to information generally may be lawful in accordance with Art. 6(1)(c) and (e) GDPR. However, the case-law of the referring court additionally requires the public authority to inform and consult the data subject before proceeding with any disclosure of his or her data. The ECJ considers this to be compatible with Art. 6(3) GDPR (and Art. 86 GDPR), provided that such an obligation is not impossible to implement and that it does not require disproportionate effort and, therefore, does not result in a disproportionate restriction on public access to those documents.

IV. Author's analysis and commentary

It is hardly surprising that data relating to a representative of a legal person constitutes personal data given that the representative itself is a natural person. The referring court had, in a nutshell, questioned the classification as personal data because the only reason why the data related to a natural person was that very representation which was, of course, necessary for the legal person to conclude the contract. A multiple-reference of data, however, cannot deprive this data of its personal reference.

What is remarkable, however, is how the ECJ handles Art. 6(3) GDPR. The GDPR provides scope for Member State law in various areas through

2 ECJ 7.3.2024 – case C-740/22, ECLI:EU:C:2024:216 para. 29 – Endemol Shine Finland.

so-called 'opening clauses'. These allow for deviations or specifications by the Member States. Opening clauses aimed at specification are also contained in Art. 6(2) GDPR and in Art. 6(3) GDPR. Both relate to the legal bases of Art. 6(1)(c) and (e) of the GDPR, which apply to processing for compliance with a legal obligation or for the performance of a task carried out in public interest or in the exercise of official authority.

Based on the wording of Art. 6(2) GDPR and Art. 6(3) GDPR, it should be noted that they do not contain any explicit rule governing their relationship to one another. As a starting point, it can be said that the provisions overlap considerably. Both paragraphs require more specific (national) provisions to adapt the application of the rules of the GDPR. The subjects of regulation for such national law listed as examples in the two paragraphs are also largely identical, although paragraph 3 contains additional indication of what Member State law may refer to. In addition, paragraph 3 states further requirements for Member State law, specifically with regard to the aims and objectives on the one hand and proportionality on the other. These requirements are particularly important because, unlike the indication of what the national law may refer to, they must be complied with in all cases. In the end, it can be noted that paragraph 3 reflects all the regulatory content of paragraph 2, but goes further than paragraph 2 in terms of both the legal consequences and the requirements for Member State law. This suggests that paragraph 2 ultimately lacks an independent regulatory scope.

This is also reflected in the case-law of the ECJ to date. Although the Court has not yet expressly commented on the relationship between paragraph 2 and paragraph 3, it is striking that the case-law of the Court has so far only referred to paragraph 3, with paragraph 2 remaining largely ignored. The ECJ has emphasised that Art. 6(1)(e) of the GDPR must be read in conjunction with Art. 6(3) thereof.[3] The combined provisions of Art. 6(1)(e) of the GDPR and Art. 6(3) GDPR thereof require there to be a legal basis – national in particular – which serves as a basis for the processing of personal data by the relevant controllers acting in the performance of a task carried out in the public interest or in the exercise of official authority.[4]

3 ECJ 20.10.2022 – case C-306/21, ECLI:EU:C:2022:813 para. 49 – Koalitsia 'Demokratichna Bulgaria – Obedinenie'.

4 ECJ 15.4.2021 – case C-268/21, ECLI:EU:C:2023:145 para. 32 – Norra Stockholm Bygg; cf. ECJ 30.3.2023 – case C-34/21, ECLI:EU:C:2023:270 para. 85 et seqq. – Hauptpersonalrat der Lehrerinnen und Lehrer.

In the *Ministerstvo zdravotnictví II* judgment this case-law is continued. Here, the Court does mention both paragraph 2 and paragraph 3. In essence, however, the ECJ bases its assessment solely on paragraph 3. This is particularly reflected in the ECJ's findings: National case-law may form part of the legal basis for the processing, within the meaning of Art. 6(3) GDPR. The Court does not address paragraph 2 in this regard. And at large it appears correct to say: Art. 6(2) GDPR does not have an independent scope of application.

V. Recommended further reading

ECJ 23.7.2015 – case C-398/15, ECLI:EU:C:2017:197 – Manni.

ECJ 15.4.2021 – case C-268/21, ECLI:EU:C:2023:145 – Norra Stockholm Bygg.

Ziegenhorn/Krüger ZD 2024, 610.

Processing of special categories of personal data, and compensation for non-material damage

Arne Nordmeyer

ECJ 21.12.2023 – case C-667/21, ECLI:EU:C:2023:1022 – ZQ v Medizinischer Dienst der Krankenversicherung Nordrhein, Körperschaft des öffentlichen Rechts

I. Case summary

An employee of a German *Medizinischer Dienst* (medical service) is seeking damage compensation from his employer. This employer prepared a medical expert report on this employee on behalf of the statutory health fond to which the employee was affiliated and which paid sickness benefits after the employee became unable to work and the continued payment of remuneration ended. Since this medical service kept the related personal data in a special department ('special case organisational unit') but did not have another medical service carry out the medical report, the employee believes that his rights have been violated and is demanding compensation of 20,000 EUR for non-material damage from his employer. Due to its 'dual function' as employer and medical service, the employer should not have processed this medical report and the related data itself and should have taken precautions to ensure that none of the employee's colleagues could access his data regarding the mentioned medical report.

A medical service is a special public-law institution at the state level which, according to the German *Sozialgesetzbuch* (German Social Code – SGB), is inter alia set up to deal with questions of incapacity for work.

The ECJ had to rule on this matter based on five requests for a preliminary ruling by the German *Bundesarbeitsgericht* (German Federal Labour Court – BAG)[1]. The Labour Court and Higher Labour Court had previous-

1 BAG 26.08.2021 – 8 AZR 253/20 (A), ZD 2022, 56, with commentary by Leibold ZD 2022, 60. For previous proceedings, see also ECJ 21.12.2023 – case C-667/21, ECLI:

ly dismissed the claim, but the BAG seemed to be leaning towards the employee.[2]

II. Key legal findings

The ECJ ruled on questions of the lawfulness of processing in connection with Art. 9(2)(h), (3), (4), Art. 6(1) GDPR, and on questions of damage compensation under Art. 82(1) GDPR. It did not delve into the abysmal depths of the German SGB. In the end, the ECJ followed the medical service, whereby the specific organisational measures played no role. However, for further legal disputes, the ECJ ruled partly in favour of parties claiming damage compensation. Specifically, the ECJ held, based on the referring court's questions, that:

- Data processing pursuant to Art. 9(2)(h) GDPR is only lawful if the requirements of lawfulness stated in Art. 6(1) GDPR is also met.
- Compensation under Art. 82(1) GDPR does not have a deterrent or punitive function, but is intended to fully compensate for the (non-material) damage suffered. A claim for damage compensation does not require that the degree of fault be taken into account in assessing the damage.[3] It is also rebuttable to assume that the actions of the controller led to the damage; the burden of proof rests on the controller.

III. Systematic context and legal classification

1. Regarding Art. 9 GDPR

Germany has implemented extensive special data protection rules in the SGB. To this end, the German legislature has defined *Sozidaldaten* ('social data') in § 67(2) SGB X as personal data that is processed by an entity specified in § 35 SGB I with regard to the SGB. These *Sozialdaten* does

EU:C:2023:1022 – ZQ v Medizinischer Dienst der Krankenversicherung Nordrhein, Körperschaft des öffentlichen Rechts, with commentary by Bieresborn GuP 2024, 110.

2 BAG 26.08.2021 – 8 AZR 253/20 (A), ZD 2022, 56 mn. 29 et seqq.

3 ECJ 21.12.2023 – case C-667/21, ECLI:EU:C:2023:1022 – ZQ v Medizinischer Dienst der Krankenversicherung Nordrhein, Körperschaft des öffentlichen Rechts, with commentary by Schumacher/Stegemann EuZW 2024, 277.

not necessarily have to be sensitive data pursuant to Art. 9(1) GDPR.[4] The German legislator also equates *Sozialdaten* with trade and business secrets (§ 35(4) SGB I), which do not have to be personal data (cf. § 67(2) sent. 2 SGB X).

If an entity with a corresponding obligation processes *Sozialdaten*, it must observe the (known) 'need to know' principle in accordance with § 35(1) sent. 2 SGB I and, in accordance with sent. 3, ensure that *Sozialdaten* relating to its own employees is only accessible internally to a limited extent so that it cannot be used in internal personnel decisions.

There are currently 15 medical services in Germany, two of which are in North Rhine-Westphalia. These are public-law institutions. According to § 275(1) no. 3 (b) SGB V, statutory health insurance funds are obliged to obtain a medical expert report from the medical service if there are doubts about the incapacity to work of insured persons.

In general, the German legislature has created complex, fragmentary regulations in the SGB that are in need of (hardly expected) reform.[5] The ECJ did not deal with these details and instead focused on the sheer GDPR.[6]

Art. 9(3) GDPR only stipulates that the processing of health data pursuant to Art. 9(2)(h) GDPR requires professional subjects bound to professional secrecy. According to Art. 9(4) GDPR, Member States may impose further requirements.[7] Notwithstanding Art. 9(4) GDPR – according to the ECJ – could be additional organisational requirements may arise in individual cases – what was to be decided in individual cases by the trial court[8] – on the basis of Art. 5(1)(f) or Art. 32(1)(a) and (b) GDPR.[9]

---

4 On the question of whether and to what extent social data was affected in this case, see: ECJ 21.12.2023 – case C-667/21, ECLI:EU:C:2023:1022 – ZQ v Medizinischer Dienst der Krankenversicherung Nordrhein, Körperschaft des öffentlichen Rechts, with commentary by Bieresborn GuP 2024, p. 112.

5 Cf. Thüsing NZS 2025, 321.

6 ECJ 21.12.2023 – case C-667/21, ECLI:EU:C:2023:1022 – ZQ v Medizinischer Dienst der Krankenversicherung Nordrhein, Körperschaft des öffentlichen Rechts, with commentary by Bieresborn GuP 2024, 110.

7 ECJ 21.12.2023 – case C-667/21, ECLI:EU:C:2023:1022 para. 67 – ZQ v Medizinischer Dienst der Krankenversicherung Nordrhein, Körperschaft des öffentlichen Rechts: if these regulations 'are not excessive…'.

8 However, the court ultimately denied this: BAG 20.6.2024 – 8 AZR 253/20, ZD 2025, 298.

9 ECJ 21.12.2023 – case C-667/21, ECLI:EU:C:2023:1022 para. 65 et seqq. – ZQ v Medizinischer Dienst der Krankenversicherung Nordrhein, Körperschaft des öffentlichen Rechts.

Art. 9(2) GDPR does not 'override' the requirements of Art. 6(1) GDPR, but is only to be understood as an additional requirement regarding special categories of data, which does not in itself conclusively cover all requirements for lawfulness, but must be supplemented by a condition of lawfulness of Art. 6(1) GDPR.

This decision on Art. 9 GDPR is not surprising, especially since it does not turn the SGB 'upside down' but (rightly) rather ignores it. However, a look at the GDPR does not reveal why the BAG could have had doubts in these questions (set out with relative clarity by the GDPR in these matters)[10].

2. Regarding Art. 82 GDPR

The significance of the decision is therefore likely to lie more in the area of compensation law. The plaintiff himself is unlikely to benefit from this, as the GDPR has probably not been violated in his case. However, together with other rulings, this ruling has further defined the requirements of compensation law with regard to Art. 82(1) GDPR and in distinction to the sanctions, and penalties under Art. 83 and Art. 84 GDPR, particularly with regard to the nature compensation claim stated in Art. 82(1) GDPR and the burden of proof on the controller. This decision must be viewed in conjunction with other decisions of the ECJ.

IV. Author's analysis and commentary

For companies and other institutions subject to the GDPR, the ruling initially means that when reviewing and documenting concrete fulfilment of one of the conditions of lawfulness (e.g. in the register pursuant to Art. 30(1) GDPR or transparency documents fulfilling Art. 13 or Art. 14

10 ECJ 21.12.2023 – case C-667/21, ECLI:EU:C:2023:1022 para. 45 – ZQ v Medizinischer Dienst der Krankenversicherung Nordrhein, Körperschaft des öffentlichen Rechts: '... neither the wording... nor the legislative history... provides any evidence to suggest that the application...'; and ECJ 21.12.2023 – case C-667/21, ECLI:EU:C:2023:1022 para. 51 – ZQ v Medizinischer Dienst der Krankenversicherung Nordrhein, Körperschaft des öffentlichen Rechts: '... not at all apparent from the clear wording of the... provision.'.

GDPR[11]), it remains to be examined whether additional assessments are necessary for processing based on Art. 9 GDPR. Since for many companies, processing data in accordance with Art. 9(1) GDPR is likely to be the exception rather than the rule. Furthermore, the ruling expressly refers only to Art. 9(2)(h) GDPR, which means that the ruling is only relevant for a limited number of entities anyway. Apart from medical services, the ruling is also likely to be relevant for assessments in the context of civil service allowances or the investigation of occupational accidents involving employees of accident insurance providers.[12]

For positions under § 35 of the SGB I, it is not certain that the obligation to separate data or stricter requirements under the SGB are not required under German law; they are only presumably irrelevant under the GDPR or permitted under it (cf. Art. 9(3) GDPR). This may affect the prioritisation of entities subject to the SGB when assessing the risk of non-compliance.

In conjunction with other rulings,[13] the ECJ has given greater contour to the concept of damage compensation: on the one hand, not only must there be a violation of the GDPR, but also damage[14] although the requirements for this are not too high; this damage is compensated, but not overcompensated; unlike the damage, the fault does not have to be proven by the plaintiff, as the burden of proof lies with the controller. This has created a right to damages that is unlikely to fuel an unlimited litigation industry, but will certainly keep lawyers and courts busy in the coming years.[15]

V. Recommended further reading

Daum RDV 2025, 10.
Heinze/Steinrötter Tagungsband Herbstakademie 2024/Horn/Stegemann, 2024, 143.

---

11 ECJ 21.12.2023 – case C-667/21, ECLI:EU:C:2023:1022 – ZQ v Medizinischer Dienst der Krankenversicherung Nordrhein, Körperschaft des öffentlichen Rechts, with commentary by Halder/Maluszczak jurisPR-ITR 3/2024 mn. 4 D.

12 ECJ 21.12.2023 – case C-667/21, ECLI:EU:C:2023:1022 – ZQ v Medizinischer Dienst der Krankenversicherung Nordrhein, Körperschaft des öffentlichen Rechts, with commentary by Bieresborn GuP 2024, p. 114.

13 Wybitul/Jürgens EuDIR 2025, 148; Daum RDV 2025, 10.

14 ECJ 21.12.2023 – case C-667/21, ECLI:EU:C:2023:1022 – ZQ v Medizinischer Dienst der Krankenversicherung Nordrhein, Körperschaft des öffentlichen Rechts, with commentary by Schumacher/Stegemann EuZW 2024, p. 278; cf. Heinze/Steinrötter Tagungsband Herbstakademie 2024/Horn/Stegemann, 2024, p. 161.

15 Cf. Wybitul/Jürgens EuDIR 2025, 153.

Stegemann, Der immaterielle Schadensersatz bei Datenschutzverstößen, 2023.

Schwartmann/Jaspers/Thüsing/Kugelmann Heidelberger Kommentar DS-GVO/BDSG/Schwartmann/Keppeler/Jacquemain, 3rd edn Heidelberg 2024, DS-GVOArt. 82 mn. 18 et seqq.

Special categories of personal data

Christiane Wendehorst

ECJ 1.8.2022 – case C-184/20, ECLI:EU:C:2022:601 – OT v Vyriausioji tarnybinės etikos komisija

I. Case summary

OT is the director of an establishment under Lithuanian law that is active in the field of environmental protection and receives public funding. In this capacity, he may be subject to Law No VIII-371 of the Republic of Lithuania on the reconciliation of public and private interests in the public service, which requires the disclosure of various private circumstances, including information about spouses, partners or cohabiting partners. The Vyriausioji tarnybinės etikos komisija (Chief Ethics Commission) is an authority responsible, among other things, for enforcing Law No VIII-371 and publishing large parts of the disclosures on its website.

As OT refused to disclose the information, the authority found that OT had violated its obligations under the law. OT challenged the decision before the Vilnius Regional Administrative Court. As the court had doubts as to whether the disclosure rule was compatible with the GDPR, it referred two questions to the ECJ for a preliminary ruling: if firstly, Art. 6(1)(e) and (3) and, secondly, Art. 9(1) and Art. 9(2)(g) GDPR, both with regard to Art. 7 and 8 of the CFR, preclude such a publication obligation.

II. Key legal findings

The ECJ (Grand Chamber) examines the compatibility of Law No. VIII-371 of the Republic of Lithuania and any resulting publication obligation with EU law on the basis of both the GDPR and the DPD.

On the first question, the ECJ ultimately rejects the proportionality of the measure. It affirms the existence of a legal basis in Member State law that serves the protection of a legitimate public interest within the meaning of

Art. 6(1)(e) and (3) of the GDPR (or Art. 7(c) and (e) DPD) and Article 52(1) of the CFR, as well as the suitability of the measure, but not its necessity and proportionality. First, the ECJ rejected the argument of the Chief Ethics Commission that the necessary resources for an internal review by the authorities were lacking and that the measure was therefore necessary. The ECJ then explains that, in view of the only diminished public interest in the heads of non-governmental institutions that merely receive public funds, as well as in view of the gravity of the measure and, in particular, the sensitivity of the information published, the principle of proportionality can no longer be considered to have been upheld.

On the second question, the ECJ concluded that the publication of personal data that could indirectly reveal the sexual orientation of a natural person – such as the name of the spouse, cohabitee or partner – constitutes the processing of special categories of personal data within the meaning of Art. 9 GDPR ('sensitive data'). The publication was therefore to be assessed against Article 9(1) and (2)(g) GDPR, the requirements of which were not met in this case due to a lack of necessity, appropriateness and specific protective measures.

III. Systematic context and legal classification

1. Relationship between the questions referred

Although there are clear cross-connections between the two questions referred for a preliminary ruling, in that a rejection of the proportionality of the measure at the level of Art. 6 GDPR would almost inevitably lead to a rejection of proportionality within the meaning of Art. 9(2)(g) GDPR, the examination of proportionality on the one hand and the classification of the data as 'special categories of personal data' on the other had to be considered separately.

2. Assessment of proportionality

According to Art. 6(1)(e) and (3) GDPR, a legal basis under national law must pursue an objective in the public interest and be proportionate to the legitimate purpose pursued. Since these requirements are derived from the provisions of Art. 52(1) of the CFR, they must also be interpreted in the light of the latter provision, according to which restrictions must be provided for by law and must respect the essence of the fundamental rights set out in Articles 7 and 8 of the CFR and the principle of proportionality.

The ECJ ultimately bases its assessment on a four-step proportionality test, first examining the existence of a legitimate aim in the public interest,[1] then the appropriateness of the planned publication for achieving the objective[2] and finally the necessity[3] and appropriateness, weighing up all the interests to be taken into account.[4] Although these four stages are not always clearly recognisable in the case law of the ECJ and in some cases a three-stage or even only two-stage assessment can be observed, the four-stage structure is nevertheless in line with the usual practice.

3. Classification as 'special categories of personal data'

The question of whether data from which conclusions about sensitive characteristics can only be drawn indirectly by means of an intellectual operation involving comparison or deduction should be classified as 'special categories of personal data' was a question of interpretation of Art. 9 GDPR. The ECJ made this interpretation on the basis of the wording, context and objectives pursued by the GDPR. This triad of interpretation methods, in which the methods of historical and systematic interpretation distinguished in German methodology merge into a single context-related interpretation, is in line with the established case law of the ECJ.

The question was of fundamental importance not only for the application of the GDPR itself, but for almost all modern digital legislation, as the term 'special categories of personal data' is referred to in a wide variety of regulations.

1 ECJ 1.8.2022 – case C-184/20, ECLI:EU:C:2022:601 para. 74–81- OT v Vyriausioji tarnybinės etikos komisija.

2 ECJ 1.8.2022 – case C-184/20, ECLI:EU:C:2022:601 para. 82–84 – OT v Vyriausioji tarnybinės etikos komisija.

3 ECJ 1.8.2022 – case C-184/20, ECLI:EU:C:2022:601 para. 85–97 – OT v Vyriausioji tarnybinės etikos komisija.

4 ECJ 1.8.2022 – case C-184/20, ECLI:EU:C:2022:601 para. 98–113 – OT v Vyriausioji tarnybinės etikos komisija.

IV. Author's analysis and commentary

The ECJ's decision is remarkable in several respects and, at the same time, extremely unfortunate.

1. Misplaced emphasis and allocation of argumentative resources

Firstly, it is noteworthy that the detail with which the ECJ examines the various legal issues appears to be inversely proportional to the extent of their ambiguity and general significance.

It seemed more or less obvious that it would be disproportionate to require the head of an NGO that receives some public funding to disclose detailed information about his private life on the internet, where it could be viewed by anyone at any time. In this respect, it was surprising that the ECJ dealt with this issue in no less than 57 paragraphs.[5] and, for example, explained at length, citing Commission reports and international agreements, why the fight against corruption is an important public interest. The redundancy of the explanations is also disturbing.

In contrast, there are only 12, in some cases very brief, paragraphs[6] devoted to answering the second question, namely whether Art. 9 GDPR covers only processing that relates to sensitive data by its nature (e.g. a direct indication of sexual orientation) or also data from which sensitive information can be indirectly derived or compared by means of a thought process. However, this question was the only major legal issue in the entire case and also the only question that would have justified the involvement of the Grand Chamber of the ECJ. As mentioned above (III. 3.), it is also a question that is of considerable importance beyond the GDPR for all recent digital legislation.

5 ECJ 1.8.2022 – case C-184/20, ECLI:EU:C:2022:601 para. 60–116 – OT v Vyriausioji tarnybinės etikos komisija.

6 ECJ 1.8.2022 – case C-184/20, ECLI:EU:C:2022:601 para. 117–128 – OT v Vyriausioji tarnybinės etikos komisija.

2. Weakness of the decisive argumentation

What is astonishing is not only the brevity with which the ECJ deals with this central legal issue, but also the weakness of its reasoning. As already mentioned (III. 3. above), the ECJ interpreted Art. 9(1) GDPR on the basis of its wording, context and the objectives pursued by the provision.[7]

The wording is ambiguous:[8] the use of the verb 'reveal' suggests that it is not only data that is sensitive by its nature that is covered, but also data from which sensitive information can be indirectly derived or compared by means of a thought process. On the other hand, the preposition 'concerning' seems to signify the existence of a more direct and immediate link.

However, the ECJ then states that a contextual analysis points to a broad interpretation because, according to Art. 4 no. 15 GDPR, 'health data' is defined as personal data from which 'reveal' information about a person's health status.[9] However, this is hardly convincing, as the argument ultimately boils down to a repetition of the literal interpretation: if the verb 'reveal' is already used in Art. 9(1) GDPR, it does not contribute to clarification to point to the fact that it is also used in Art. 4 no. 15 GDPR.

The interpretation based on the rationale of the regulation and the effet utile is also unconvincing. Ultimately, it boils down to the standard argument that the broad interpretation of Art. 9(1) GDPR is supported by the objective of the GDPR to ensure a high level of protection of the fundamental rights and freedoms of natural persons[10] and to have enhanced protection for sensitive data.[11] This is unconvincing, if only because, according to its Art. 1 GDPR, the GDPR serves not only to protect personal data but also to ensure the free movement of personal data. In paragraph 70 of the same decision, the ECJ itself pointed out that the fundamental rights to respect for private life and to the protection of personal data, guaranteed in Art. 7 and 8 of the CFR, are not absolute rights, but must be considered in relation to their function in society and be weighed against other funda-

7 ECJ 1.8.2022 – case C-184/20, ECLI:EU:C:2022:601 para. 121 – OT v Vyriausioji tarnybinės etikos komisija.

8 ECJ 1.8.2022 – case C-184/20, ECLI:EU:C:2022:601 para. 123 – OT v Vyriausioji tarnybinės etikos komisija.

9 ECJ 1.8.2022 – case C-184/20, ECLI:EU:C:2022:601 para. 124 – OT v Vyriausioji tarnybinės etikos komisija.

10 ECJ 1.8.2022 – case C-184/20, ECLI:EU:C:2022:601 para. 125 – OT v Vyriausioji tarnybinės etikos komisija.

11 ECJ 1.8.2022 – case C-184/20, ECLI:EU:C:2022:601 para. 126 – OT v Vyriausioji tarnybinės etikos komisija.

mental rights. If the only consideration were to ensure the maximum level of data protection, any weighing against other fundamental rights would be undermined from the outset.

3. Consequence: Catastrophic legal uncertainty in Europe

The implications of the ruling are potentially enormous. If the ECJ's reasoning is taken seriously, a large proportion of all personal data could potentially be classified as 'special categories of personal data' – all the more so since the ECJ ruled in Meta Platforms et al. (C-252/21) that in the case of mixed data sets that also contain special categories of personal data, the requirements for special categories of personal data must be complied with overall. However, it is sometimes easy to draw conclusions about a person's health from supermarket shopping lists, for example, if certain hygiene products (e.g. incontinence products, cleaning tablets for dentures) or foods (e.g. gluten-free food) are purchased. Book orders can often be used to deduce political opinions or philosophical beliefs relatively easily, and mobility data can be used to deduce religious beliefs (e.g. going to church) or details of a person's sex life (e.g. visiting prostitutes).

The whole situation is all the more serious the more bans are imposed on making certain decisions involving the processing of special categories of personal data. For example, Art. 18(3) of the new Consumer Credit Directive prohibits the processing of information that qualifies as special categories of personal data when assessing a consumer's creditworthiness. Similarly, under Art. 26(3) DSA, operators of online platforms are not allowed to show users advertisements based on profiling using special categories of personal data. In Russmedia Digital (C-492/23), the ECJ also ruled that operators of an online marketplace are obliged, before publishing third-party advertisements, to identify advertisements that contain data within the meaning of Art. 9(1) GDPR and verify whether the advertising user is the data subject, or otherwise refuse publication or request proof that the conditions of Art. 9(2) GDPR are met.

Taken to its logical conclusion, this means that the processing of most personal data is only legally permissible on the basis of 'explicit' consent within the meaning of Art. 9(2)(a) GDPR, because it can never be ruled out that sensitive information can also be indirectly derived from individual pieces of information in a mixed data set. Of course, in theory, another reason for processing under Art. 9(2) GDPR could also apply, but this is only conceivable in very few situations.

This certainly does not serve the cause of data protection. Rather, such extreme positions are likely to further discredit data protection in the general consciousness or to create a situation in which data protection law is simply ignored by those subject to it because it cannot be complied with anyway.

V. Recommended further reading

ECJ 4.7.2023 – case C-252/21, ECLI:EU:C:2023:537 – Meta Platforms Inc and Others v Bundeskartellamt.

ECJ 4.10.2024 – case C-21/23, ECLI:EU:C:2024:846 – ND v DR, Lindenapotheke.

ECJ 2.12.2025 – case C-492/23, ECLI:EU:C:2025:935 – X v Russmedia Digital SRL and Inform Media Press SRL.

Children's Data Protection

Wioletta Kulińska

Data Protection Commission, ‚Inquiry concerning the processing of personal data relating to child users of the Instagram social networking service [IN-20–7–4]' (2.9.2022) <https://www.dataprotection.ie/en/resources/law/decisions/Meta-Platforms-Ireland-Limited-formerly-Facebook-Ireland-Limited-and-the-Instagram-social-media-network-September-2022>

I. Case summary

In its Decision of 2.9.2022, the Irish Data Protection Commission (DPC) found that Meta Platforms Ireland Limited (Meta), had infringed multiple provisions of the GDPR in relation to the processing of children's personal data. The inquiry concerned Instagram users aged 13 to 17 and focused on two processing operations: (i) processing and public disclosure of contact information of child users when using the business accounts, and (ii) the public-by-default configuration of child users' accounts.

The decision constitutes a landmark interpretation of children's data protection law and has generated practical consequences for minor users of social platforms, strengthening the safeguards afforded to them.

II. Key legal findings

On 2.9.2022, the Irish Data Protection Commission (DPC)[1]concluded that Meta Platforms Ireland Limited had infringed several provisions of the GDPR in relation to its processing of children's personal data on the Instagram social networking service. The decision resulted from an *own-volition*

1 Data Protection Commission, , Inquiry concerning the processing of personal data relating to child users of the Instagram social networking service [IN-20–7–4]' (2.9.2022) <https://www.dataprotection.ie/en/resources/law/decisions/Meta-Platforms-Ireland-Limited-formerly-Facebook-Ireland-Limited-and-the-Instagram-social-media-network-September-2022>.

inquiry into the processing of personal data of Instagram users aged 13 to 17, referred to by Meta as 'teens'.

The inquiry examined two principal processing operations. First, Instagram processed and publicly disclosed contact information for business accounts created by child users. This included the automatic population of email addresses and/or telephone numbers previously provided for personal accounts and the publication of such contact details in the HTML source code of profile webpages, making them accessible to an indeterminate audience on and off Instagram platform. Although Meta removed the obligation to provide contact information for business accounts in September 2019, the DPC found that the prior processing constituted an unlawful public disclosure of children's personal data. Second, Instagram accounts of child users were configured as public by default, allowing profiles and content to be viewed by anyone, including non-users off the platform via Instagram web version.

The DPC identified infringements of Art. 5(1)(a) and (c), 6(1), 12, 13, 24, 25(1) and (2), and 35 GDPR, read in light of Rec. 38, 39, 75 and 78 GDPR.

In the course of the dispute resolution procedure under Art. 65 GDPR, due to the objections of several national supervisors concerned, the EDPB required the DPC to add an explicit infringement of Art. 6(1) GDPR and to increase the administrative fine in order to ensure effectiveness and deterrence.[2] The final decision imposed a total fine of 405 million EUR, accompanied by a reprimand and an order to bring the processing operations into compliance within three months.

III. Systematic context and legal classification

The DPC Decision represents a landmark in the development of children's data protection under EU law.[3]

2 European Data Protection Board (EDPB), 'Binding Decision 2/2022 on the dispute arisen on the draft decision of the Irish Supervisory Authority regarding Meta Platforms Ireland Limited (Instagram) under Art. 65(1)(a) GDPR' (28.7.2022) <https://www.edpb.europa.eu/our-work-tools/our-documents/binding-decision-board-art-65/binding-decision-22022-dispute-arisen_en>.

3 Further review Data Protection Commission, 'Decision of the Irish Data Protection Commission made pursuant to Section 111 of the Data Protection Act, 2018 and Articles 60 and 65 of the General Data Protection Regulation, TikTok Technology Limited'

1. Children's data protection content

The GDPR does not establish a separate, standalone legal regime for children's personal data, nor does it classify 'minors' data' as a *special category* under Art. 9 GDPR. Instead, it adopts a cross-cutting protective paradigm, which is rooted in Rec. 38 GDPR, which states: 'Children merit specific protection with regard to their personal data, as they may be less aware of the risks, consequences and safeguards concerned and their rights in relation to the processing of personal data.(...)'.

Further, Art. 8 GDPR is the only provision that refers specifically to children and sets rules for consent for information society services offered directly to minors: processing is lawful if the child is at least 16 and Member States may lower the age to no less than 13, otherwise it requires parental verifiable consent.

Children, due to their immaturity, require reinforced protection to strengthen their right to the development of their personality. The DPC Decision confirms that the heightened level of protection for children permeates the application of all relevant GDPR provisions. The special considerations that must be taken into account are as follows:

- tailored communication: moving beyond formal transparency toward a 'child-friendly' format; this necessitates communication that is adjusted to the specific age and cognitive development of the target audience,[4]
- risk perception and capacity: considering the limited ability of children to fully grasp the long-term risks, consequences, and safeguards associated with data processing, particularly in new technologies and algorithmic environments,
- mitigation of child-specific harms: addressing unique vulnerabilities that may not necessarily apply to the general population,
- children's rights and freedoms: right to express themselves and participate in the digital public square, access information and communicate freely, express their views on aspects of the service that affect them.

The DPC Decision also reflects broader international standards, notably the United Nations Convention on the Rights of the Child, which recognis-

(IN-21-9-1, 1.9.2023) <https://www.edpb.europa.eu/system/files/2023-09/final_decision_tiktok_in-21-9-1_-_redacted_8_september_2023.pdf>.

4 Art. 12(1) GDPR.

es children's right to privacy and requires that the best interests of the child be a primary consideration in all actions concerning children.[5]

2. Key considerations

When assessing the circumstances of the case, notably, the DPC seems to emphasize that the vulnerability of child users is a mandatory factor when assessing the nature, scope, context, and purpose of processing.

a) Transparency and fairness

For infringements of Art. 12(1) and 5(1)(a) GDPR—concerning transparency and fairness, including the provision of information to data subjects where such information is addressed to children—the DPC imposed a fine of 196 million EUR, representing almost half of the total sanction. The DPC found that Instagram's privacy notices were not specifically tailored to children, were not drafted in a genuinely child-friendly manner and required multiple navigation steps to access relevant information.

Moreover, the notices failed to adequately explain the purposes of processing and the categories of recipients of children's personal data, in particular the fact that personal data could be shared with an unlimited audience by being made publicly available. In light of Rec. 38 and 39 GDPR, the DPC emphasised that a higher standard of transparency applies where children are concerned. Controllers are required not only to inform, but also to explain in clear and accessible terms the risks associated with public disclosure of children's personal data.

The DPC rejected Meta's arguments that the absence of child-specific notices was mitigated by the allegedly simple and accessible language of its general privacy notices as well as that public-by-default account settings merely reflected user expectations inherent in a social media service.

5 Convention on the Rights of the Child, United Nations, adopted and opened for signature, ratification and accession by General Assembly resolution 44/25 of 20.11.1989, as well as the CFR.

b) Data Protection Impact Assessments (DPIA)

Meta argued that DPIAs were not required because the processing operations at issue were not likely to result in a high risk to the rights and freedoms of data subjects and if any, not actual risk. The DPC rejected this reasoning. Following a detailed assessment of the nature, scope, context, and purposes of the processing, and taking into account the criteria set out in the Article 29 Working Party Guidelines[6], the DPC concluded that both processing operations were likely to result in a high risk to the rights and freedoms of child users. In particular, the authority emphasised the large-scale nature of the processing, the global reach resulting from public accessibility on and off the platform, the processing of data relating to vulnerable data subjects as young as 13 years old, and the sensitive or highly personal nature of certain data, i.e. telephone numbers. The DPC further noted that making contact information available in the HTML source code of profile pages rendered such data particularly susceptible to automated scraping.

The risks for minor users identified included unwanted communication, grooming, sexual exploitation, fraud, and identity theft and should have been dully addressed and mitigated through DPIAs.

c) Data minimisation and privacy by default

The DPC rejected Meta's contention that Instagram's primary purpose as an open social networking service justified public-by-default account settings. Relying *inter alia* on surveys and behavioural evidence relating to young users, the DPC observed that children's expectations regarding content visibility are not uniform. While some users may actively seek public exposure, others expect to share content only within a limited circle of approved followers.[7]

In this context, the DPC concluded that private account settings as well as optionality of contact information visibility should have constituted the

6 Article 29 Data Protection Working Party, 'Guidelines on Data Protection Impact Assessment (DPIA) and determining whether processing is "likely to result in a high risk" for the purposes of Regulation 2016/679' (wp248rev.01, 4.4.2017) <https://ec.europa.eu/newsroom/article29/items/611236/en>.

7 Data Protection Commission, , Inquiry concerning the processing of personal data relating to child users of the Instagram social networking service [IN-20-7-4]' (fn. 1), para. 456.

default configuration for child users. The design implemented by Meta was found to be incompatible with the final sentence of Art. 25(2) GDPR, as it enabled access to personal data by an indefinite number of persons by default and without user intervention.

d) Data protection by design

Meta's arguments that child users voluntarily elected to publish their contact information by switching to business accounts, joined the social media platform allowing the public nature of their posts, as well as its reliance on in-app safety tools and reporting mechanisms, were rejected. The DPC concluded that these measures were predominantly reactive and did not prevent the initial exposure of children's personal data.[8] In particular, the publication of contact information in HTML source code was found to significantly increase risks of misuse.

The authority emphasised that the design of the service facilitated increased visibility of child users and exposed them to foreseeable risks, including grooming, sexual exploitation, trafficking, impersonation, and fraud. Measures that only address harm after it has occurred were deemed insufficient to satisfy the requirements of data protection by design, and as such infringed Art. 25(1) GDPR.

e) Risk-based measures and accountability

For both processing operations, the DPC found that Meta failed to adopt measures proportionate to the risks faced by child users in contradiction to Art. 24(1) GDPR.

Available safety tools and informational resources were not considered adequate in light of the severity of potential harms. The absence of DPIAs further prevented Meta from demonstrating compliance, reinforcing the DPC's conclusion that the infringements reflected a systemic failure in governance and risk management relating to children's data[9].

8 Data Protection Commission, ‚ Inquiry concerning the processing of personal data relating to child users of the Instagram social networking service [IN-20-7-4]' (fn. 1), para. 462.

9 Data Protection Commission, ‚ Inquiry concerning the processing of personal data relating to child users of the Instagram social networking service [IN-20-7-4]' (fn. 1), para. 464.

f) Lawfulness of the processing

The infringement of Art. 6 GDPR was confirmed following the EDPB's binding decision under Art. 65 GDPR. Meta had relied primarily on Art. 6(1)(b) GDPR, arguing that the processing was necessary for the performance of a contract, and alternatively on Art. 6(1)(f) GDPR, invoking its legitimate interests.

The DPC rejected both legal bases. It held that necessity for contractual performance must be interpreted restrictively and in conjunction with the principle of data minimisation. Processing that is unilaterally imposed by the controller or that exceeds what is genuinely required to provide the core service cannot be regarded as necessary. The collection and public disclosure of children's contact information were not integral to the provision of Instagram's services, including business account functionality, and less intrusive means were available.

With regard to legitimate interest, the DPC acknowledged Meta's stated interests in enabling expression, communication, and community building. However, it concluded that the processing was neither necessary to achieve those interests nor proportionate in light of the high risks posed to children. The balancing test therefore failed, particularly given the lack of adequate transparency and the foreseeable harms associated with public disclosure of contact information[10].

IV. Author's analysis and commentary

1. Significance of the DPC Decision

The DPC Decision constitutes a cornerstone in the enforcement of GDPR obligations relating to children's personal data, particularly for large-scale online platforms. Its significance lies not only in the unprecedented level of the administrative fine (as of 2022), but primarily in the substantive interpretation of core GDPR principles when applied to child users. The case sets a compliance benchmark for child-centred platform design, transparency, and lawful-basis assessment.

10 EDPB, 'Binding Decision 2/2022 on the dispute arisen on the draft decision of the Irish Supervisory Authority regarding Meta Platforms Ireland Limited (Instagram) under Art. 65(1)(a) GDPR' (fn. 2), para. 131.

First, the DPC Decision clarifies that data protection by design and by default is not limited to abstract design considerations, but extends to concrete architectural choices, including default account settings, registration flows, and feature availability. By finding that public-by-default profiles for child users violated Art. 25(2) GDPR, the DPC confirmed that default configurations must actively minimise exposure to risks. This interpretation moves beyond formal compliance and anchors Art. 25 GDPR in user experience design and behavioural realities.

Second, the decision reinforces the principle that transparency obligations under Art. 12 and 13 GDPR require a higher standard where processing concerns children. The DPC's reasoning confirms that transparency is not satisfied by general or adult-oriented privacy notices, even if drafted in relatively simple language. Instead, information must be genuinely accessible and comprehensible to the specific audience concerned, taking into account children's cognitive development and their limited ability to assess complex data processing risks. The ruling therefore elevates transparency from a formal disclosure obligation to a substantive safeguard adjusted to the maturity level of the recipient (e.g. a good example of a privacy notice could be a short video explainer or an easy-to-understand notice with examples).

Third, the case significantly narrows the scope for relying on contractual necessity or legitimate interests under Art. 6(1)(b) and (f) GDPR in relation to children. The DPC, following the EDPB's binding decision, made clear that personal data processing in certain way cannot be justified merely because it is linked to a platform feature or business model. Where children are concerned, necessity must be interpreted strictly, and commercial objectives will not override the heightened protection afforded to vulnerable data subjects.

2. Compliance implications

The decision operationalises a duty of 'child-centred design' under the GDPR. Platforms that are accessible to minors must integrate age-appropriate interfaces, ensure privacy-by-default configurations, and communicate processing terms in a manner that is genuinely understandable for younger users. Importantly, the DPC's approach confirms that child protection considerations must be embedded at the earliest stages of product development and cannot be delegated solely to subsequent user controls or safety tools.

A central compliance lesson concerns the role of Data Protection Impact Assessments, which absence is a symptom of a broader governance failure, rather than as a purely procedural omission. For processing operations involving children, DPIAs must explicitly identify child-specific risks, including unwanted contact, possible grooming, abuse, data scraping, and secondary misuse of contact information. They should also document how design choices mitigate such risks and why less intrusive alternatives were not adopted. In practice, this requires interdisciplinary collaboration involving legal, technical, UX, and child-safety expertise.

For data protection officers and compliance counsel, the DPC Decision signals a shift in regulatory focus from policies to architecture. Regulators increasingly assess how systems function in practice, how defaults shape user behaviour, and whether protective measures are preventive rather than reactive. Documentation must therefore extend beyond legal assessments to include evidence of design decisions, default settings, and iterative risk reviews.

The DPC Decision highlights the importance of audience determination as a foundational compliance step. Where services are likely to attract or be used by children, controllers must explicitly recognise this audience and adapt their services accordingly. This entails, in particular:

- identifying and assessing risks that are specific to minors and the online environment, and implementing effective mitigation measures;
- designing child-adapted versions of services, including appropriate safety features and technical and organisational measures, as well as reliable and proportionate age-assurance mechanisms;
- maintaining comprehensive documentation demonstrating compliance with GDPR requirements in relation to children's data ('demonstrable compliance'); and
- ensuring ongoing monitoring and periodic reassessment of practices in light of technological developments, user behaviour, and evolving regulatory expectations.

What needs to be emphasised, the DPC interests in child users safety at that time and the inquiry in question produced tangible impact for Instagram's child users even before it was completed, such as allowing minors to select public or private profiles, removing the obligation to provide the contact details for business accounts, more account type options adjusted to youth expectations such as 'creator account', changes in design settings and more.

3. Further developments on children's privacy

The DPC Decision should be viewed in the context of a broader regulatory and societal shift towards strengthening children's privacy and safety online. Around and following its issuance, supervisory authorities across the EU intensified their focus on children's data protection, issuing dedicated guidance and enforcement priorities. Notably, data protection authorities in Ireland[11], France[12], and the United Kingdom[13] have published child-specific frameworks emphasising risk-based design, age-appropriate transparency, and preventive safeguards.

At the EU level, the adoption of the DSA further reinforces this trajectory by introducing explicit obligations on online platforms to protect minors, including through risk assessments and mitigation measures addressing systemic risks. While the DSA operates alongside the GDPR, the two regimes are increasingly interlinked, particularly where platform design choices affect children's rights and freedoms.

Internationally, similar developments can be observed. In the United States, state-level initiatives such as the California Age-Appropriate Design Code reflect a growing convergence with European child-centred design principles. Australia's Online Safety Act[14] and associated Online Safety Codes and Standards[15] including restrictions on minors' under 16 access to certain online services, further illustrate the global momentum towards stricter protection of children in digital environments.

---

11 Data Protection Commission, 'The Fundamentals for a Child-Oriented Approach to Data Processing' (December 2021) <https://www.dataprotection.ie/en/dpc-guidance/fundamentals-child-oriented-approach-data-processing>.

12 CNIL, 'CNIL publishes 8 recommendations to enhance the protection of children online' (9.8.2021) <https://www.cnil.fr/en/cnil-publishes-8-recommendations-enhance-protection-children-online>.

13 Information Commissioner's Office, 'Age appropriate design: a code of practice for online services' (2021) <https://ico.org.uk/for-organisations/uk-gdpr-guidance-and-resources/childrens-information/childrens-code-guidance-and-resources/age-appropriate-design-a-code-of-practice-for-online-services/>.

14 Online Safety Act 2021 (Cth), No. 76, 2021, as amended as amended and in force on 11.12.2024.

15 Australian Government, 'Online Safety Codes and Standards' (December 2025) <https://www.esafety.gov.au/industry/codes>.

V. Recommended further readings

OECD, How's Life for Children in the Digital Age? (15.5.2025) < https://www.oecd.org/content/dam/oecd/en/publications/reports/2025/05/how-s-life-for-children-in-the-digital-age_c4a22655/0854b900-en.pdf>.

European Commission, Communication from the Commission – Guidelines on measures to ensure a high level of privacy, safety and security for minors online, pursuant to Art. 28(4) of Regulation (EU) 2022/2065 (C/2025/6826, 7.10.2025) <https://eur-lex.europa.eu/legal-content/EN/TXT/?uri=CELEX:52025XC05519>.

Law Library of Congress (U.S.), Children's online privacy and data protection in selected European countries' (2021) <https://tile.loc.gov/storage-services/service/ll/llglrd/2021680641/2021680641.pdf>.

Chapter 5:
Data Subject Rights

Transparency obligations and dark patterns

Carolin Loy

ECJ 27.2.2025 – case C-203/22, ECLI:EU:C:2025:117 – CK v Magistrate of the City of Vienna, Dun & Bradstreet Austria GmbH

I. Case summary

The applicant (CK) was refused the renewal of a mobile telephone contract on the ground that, according to an automated credit assessment, carried out by Dun & Bradstreet Austria GmbH (D&B), she did not have sufficient financial creditworthiness. CK then requested, on the basis of Art. 15(1)(h) GDPR, information on the 'logic involved' of profiling. The Austrian data protection authority required D&B to provide meaningful information. D&B refused to provide further information, citing the protection of business secrets, and lodged an appeal against the authority's decision before the Austrian Bundesverwaltungsgericht (Federal Administrative Court). That court found an infringement of Art. 15 of the GDPR and the decision became final. CK then applied to the Magistrat der Stadt Wien (Magistrate of the City of Vienna, Austria) for enforcement of the judicial decision. That request was rejected on the ground that D&B had already complied sufficiently with its obligation to provide information. The Verwaltungsgericht Wien (Administrative Court, Vienna) then had to clarify what minimum information D&B had to comply with. In that regard, it referred a number of questions of interpretation to the ECJ concerning the scope of Art. 15(1)(h) GDPR, the relationship with Art. 22 GDPR and the balance with the rights of third parties and the protection of trade secrets.

II. Key legal findings

The court answered the questions referred, in particular with regard to the requirement of transparency and comprehensibility in the context of automated decision-making, thereby specifying the requirements for the right of access under Art. 15(1)(h) GDPR.

The key point of the judgement is that 'meaningful information about the logic involved' in automated decision-making, within the meaning of this provision includes, all relevant information about the procedure and principles of automated processing of personal data to obtain a specific result, and that this information must also be communicated in a precise, transparent, understandable, and easily accessible form due to the requirement for transparency.

The ECJ stresses that neither the mere transmission of a complex mathematical formula (such as an algorithm) nor the detailed description of each step of automated decision-making are sufficient in this regard, as neither would constitute a sufficiently precise and intelligible explanation. Rather, the decisive factor is a transparent explanation that enables the data subject to understand which personal data were included in the result of the assessment, to what extent and according to what criteria, and how deviations from individual elements hypothetically affected the result. The information must therefore contain a comprehensible description of the weighted factors and their significance for specific profiling.

With regard to conflicting rights of third parties or trade secrets, the Court emphasises the need for a case-by-case balancing exercise. The controller should not blanketly withhold information; instead, potentially protected content should be submitted to the competent supervisory authority or to the court, which must decide on the scope of disclosure. Blanket national exclusions – such as § 4(6) of the Austrian Data Protection Act[1] – are incompatible with EU law, as they would replace the necessary balancing exercise.

III. Systematic context and legal classification

These judicial findings demonstrate far-reaching requirements for the requirement of transparency and comprehensibility in the context of automated decision-making. They clarify how the requirement for transparent information under Art. 12(1) GDPR affects the right of access under Art. 15(1)(h) GDPR in the case of automated decision-making.

In that regard, the ECJ emphasises the bridging function of Art. 15(1)(h) GDPR with regard to the data subject's rights under Art. 22(3) GDPR,

1 Bundesgesetz zum Schutz natürlicher Personen bei der Verarbeitung personenbezogener Daten vom 17. August 1999 (BGBl. I 165/1999), hereinafter ‚DSG'.

according to which the right of access is an assisting right intended to enable the effective exercise of the rights to express one's point of view and to challenge automated decisions. Without the understanding how the decision-making mechanism works, these rights would be meaningless.

The court thus confirms its previous case-law,[2] which considers the right of access to be the starting point for the review of the lawfulness of data processing and thus for the exercise of other data subjects' rights.

The link with the principle of transparency, which is expressly enshrined in Art. 12(1) GDPR, has also already been established in the previous case-law of the ECJ in relation to Art. 15 GDPR, in order to ensure that the data subject is put in a position to fully understand the information addressed to him or her.

Specifically transposed to Art. 15(1)(h) GDPR, the ECJ therefore logically finds that mere technical or abstract descriptions are not sufficient.

Overall, the ruling systematically supplements the decision of the ECJ in SCHUFA Holding[3]: While the 'SCHUFA'-Decision determines the scope of Art. 22 GDPR and qualifies scoring as an automated decision, the decision 'D&B' clarifies the requirements for its explainability and comprehensibility and answers the question of how to resolve the tension between the data subjects' interests in access and the controllers' interests in the protection of trade secrets. Both decisions together form the legal framework for the processing of personal data in algorithmic decision-making systems.

IV. Author's analysis and comment

With this decision, the ECJ also indirectly creates a judgment on dark patterns, as the requirements for transparent information set out in the judgment are intended to prevent non-transparent, manipulative and incomprehensible structures in automated decision-making processes.

Dark patterns refer, in essence, to digital decision-making environments that are intended to incite users to act contrary to their presumed interests or that users would presumably not have done without being influenced.

2 Inter alia ECJ 4.5.2023 – case C-487/21, ECLI:EU:C:2023:369 – F.F. v Österreichische Datenschutzbehörde and CRIF GmbH.

3 ECJ 7.12.2023 – case C-634/21, ECLI:EU:C:2023:957 – OQ v Land Hessen, SCHUFA.

A concise definition describes *dark patterns* as *'dirty tricks designers use to make people do stuff'.*[4]

Dark patterns therefore regularly conflict with the overarching principle of fairness, according to which personal data must not be processed in a way that is detrimental, discriminatory, unexpected or misleading to the data subject. In its decision on the scope of the right of access, the ECJ sets a further significant limit to these practices by interpreting the principle of transparency in the light of Art. 15(1)(h) GDPR.

One of the structural problems of many data-driven systems is, that they are based on complex models where static weightings and algorithmic dependencies create a degree of opacity that tends to leave data subjects 'in the dark', thus depriving them of the ability to challenge decisions or bring about alternative outcomes.

Dark patterns are intended to encourage individuals to take decisions that run counter to their interests, to exclude rational decisions and thus to avoid autonomous decisions by behavioural control. The case concerns above all the risk of losing the capacity to react back in accordance with Art. 22(3) GDPR due to a lack of transparency and thus of accepting results as 'unchallengeable'.

In this respect, the judgment introduces a dogmatic shift in the EU law understanding of transparency: Transparency is no longer merely a requirement for the obligation to provide information but becomes a condition for the possibility for data subjects to exercise their autonomous decision-making and defensive rights at all.

As a result of the fact that the ECJ closely links Art. 15(1)(h) GDPR to Art. 22(3) GDPR, the right of access does not, according to judicial interpretation, serve an abstract interest in information, but directly serves to enable effective defence. Transparency thus becomes the central guarantor of the data subject's understanding of the factors that led to the specific result of profiling and ensures the necessary understanding of what changes would be needed to reach a positive result in future automated decision-making. The Court thus rejects both 'overloading' with technical documentation and a strategic shortage of information: Neither algorithmic formulae nor blanket statements on 'equivalent weighting' are sufficient because they do not provide an actual explanation of the decision-making

4 Brignull, 'Dark Patterns: Dirty tricks designers use to make people do stuff' (July 2010) <https://90percentofeverything.com/2010/07/08/dark-patterns-dirty-tricks-designers-use-to-make-people-do-stuff/index.html>.

mechanism. The ECJ thus moves away from the mere formal provision of information and takes as a benchmark the comprehensibility appropriate to the person to whom the information is addressed.

The ECJ's interpretation of the scope of the obligation to provide information makes an important contribution to the enforcement of the European digital law, which for example limits the use of dark patterns and non-transparent recommending systems under the Digital Services Act or requires gatekeepers to be fair and traceable under the Digital Markets Act.

The decision also supports the explainability-by-design approach, as enshrined in the AI Act (Art. 13 and 14 AI Act) for high-risk systems. The ECJ ultimately transposes this principle to the scope of the GDPR by implicitly requiring that scoring and profiling systems be designed in such a way that they can be intrinsically explained. This excludes the use of 'black box' models, if their results can no longer be clearly explained.

In the view of the court, the fact that, in practice, this is currently not possible, or only possible to a limited extent, in a large number of systems used and also in the case of the use of artificial intelligence, due to the complexity and understanding as 'black boxes', does not limit the requirements. In the view of the ECJ, complexity does not release the controller from its obligation to provide explanations.

In that regard, the judgment nevertheless also shows that, at least within the scope of the GDPR, there is no need for an unrealistic interpretation of the obligation of transparency, but that the spirit and purpose of Art. 15(1)(h) GDPR is to enable data subjects to understand the information transmitted to them, even without technical expertise. This strengthens the actual meaning of the standard and not only creates formalistic requirements with no practical added value.

As a result, the judgment leads to a better balance between data processors and data subjects by setting clear limits to algorithmic opacity.

V. Recommended further reading

See too:

ECJ 7.12.2023 – case C-634/21, ECLI:EU:C:2023:957 – OQ v Land Hessen, SCHUFA.

Article 29 Working Party, 'Guidelines on Automated individual decision-making and Profiling for the purposes of Regulation 2016/679' (WP251rev.01, 22.8.2018) <https://ec.europa.eu/newsroom/article29/items/612053>.

EDPB, 'Guidelines 3/2025 on the interplay between the DSA and the GDPR', version 1.1 (11.9.2025) <https://www.edpb.europa.eu/our-work-tools/documents/public-consultations/2025/guidelines-32025-interplay-between-dsa-and-gdpr_en>.

EDPB, 'Guidelines 03/2022 on deceptive design patterns in social media platform interfaces: how to recognise and avoid them', version 2.0 (14.2.2023) <https://www.edpb.europa.eu/our-work-tools/our-documents/guidelines/guidelines-032022-deceptive-design-patterns-social-media_en>.

Credit Rating Score and Right to an Explanation

Rebekka Weiß

ECJ 27.2.2025 – case C-203/22, ECLI:EU:C:2025:117 – CK v Magistrate of the City of Vienna, Dun & Bradstreet Austria GmbH

I. Case summary

Key message: The Court clarifies that Art. 15(1)(h) GDPR grants the data subject a genuine right to an explanation of the functioning of an automated decision, including profiling. This includes a comprehensible explanation of *the procedures and principles* by which their personal data is incorporated into a specific result (in this case: a credit rating 'score'). This explanation must be relevant, concise, transparent, and understandable. Simply communicating a complex mathematical formula is not sufficient.[1]

Delimitation: The obligation to provide an explanation does not require the complete disclosure of the algorithms or the transmission of all input data. Rather, the controller must explain how and which personal data influenced the result.[2] The right to verify the accuracy of the data used does not arise from Art. 15(1)(h) GDPR, but from the general right of access under Art. 15(1) sent. 1 GDPR.[3]

Trade secrets/third-party data: Art. 15(1)(h) GDPR does not allow controllers to generally refuse access on the basis of trade secrets or the protection of third-party personal data.[4] If the information contains protected information, the controller must submit it to the competent supervisory authority or the court. The competent state authority then weighs up the

1 ECJ 27.2.2025 – case C-203/22, ECLI:EU:C:2025:117 para. 59–61, 65–66 – CK v. Magistrate of the City of Vienna, Dun & Bradstreet Austria GmbH.

2 ECJ 27.2.2025 – case C-203/22, ECLI:EU:C:2025:117 para. 59–62 – CK v. Magistrate of the City of Vienna, Dun & Bradstreet Austria GmbH.

3 ECJ 27.2.2025 – case C-203/22, ECLI:EU:C:2025:117 para. 63 – CK v. Magistrate of the City of Vienna, Dun & Bradstreet Austria GmbH.

4 ECJ 27.2.2025 – case C-203/22, ECLI:EU:C:2025:117 para. 68–71 – CK v. Magistrate of the City of Vienna, Dun & Bradstreet Austria GmbH.

conflicting interests.[5] A national law that generally excludes information on trade secrets is contrary to EU law and therefore inapplicable.[6]

Compliance implications: Companies that use automated credit decisions must document their internal procedures so that they can explain the data and criteria used. In the case of trade secrets or third-party data, graduated disclosure solutions (e.g., to authorities) must be provided for. National regulations may not generally restrict rights of access.

II. Key legal finding and previous decisions on credit scoring

The discussion about transparency in credit scoring is not new. Both German courts and the ECJ had already dealt with the disclosure obligations of credit agencies such as SCHUFA prior to the present ruling. These preliminary rulings form the basis on which the present ruling is based.

1. BGH 28.1.2014 – VI ZR 156/13, ZD 2014, 306

In 2014, the Federal Court of Justice had to rule on a data protection claim for information against SCHUFA. It ruled that data subjects have the right to know what personal data is stored by SCHUFA and has been used to calculate their credit score (headnote lit. a). In addition to the specific credit scores, this also includes information on which data categories are classified as credit-relevant or credit-irrelevant, the numerical score, and the associated rating and risk category (headnote lit. a). However, the Federal Court of Justice clarified that the specific mathematical calculation method (known as the score formula) constitutes a trade secret and does not have to be disclosed (headnote lit. b). At the time, the decision was still based on the BDSG and did not include any consideration of EU law under the GDPR.

5 ECJ 27.2.2025 – case C-203/22, ECLI:EU:C:2025:117 para. 73–76 – CK v. Magistrate of the City of Vienna, Dun & Bradstreet Austria GmbH.

6 ECJ 27.2.2025 – case C-203/22, ECLI:EU:C:2025:117 para. 75 – CK v. Magistrate of the City of Vienna, Dun & Bradstreet Austria GmbH.

2. ECJ 7.12.2023 – case C-634/21, ECLI:EU:C:2023:957 – OQ v Land Hessen, SCHUFA

In December 2023, the ECJ had to answer for the first time whether the automated determination of a credit rating by a credit agency constitutes an 'automated individual decision' within the meaning of Art. 22(1) GDPR. The Court answered in the affirmative: if a third party (such as a bank) relies significantly on the score when deciding whether to establish, perform, or terminate a contract, the creation of this score must be classified as a decision with significant effects.[7] The ECJ emphasized that the term 'decision' must be understood broadly and also includes the determination of a probability value for creditworthiness.[8] The relevant specific obligations of Art. 22 GDPR (e.g., prohibition of purely automated decisions, exceptions under Art. 22(2) GDPR, and safeguards such as human intervention and the right to appeal) therefore already apply to the creation of the score.[9] Furthermore, the ECJ clarified that a national legal basis permitting automated decisions must fully comply with the requirements of Art. 22(2) GDPR and the general principles and conditions of lawfulness set out in Art. 5 and 6 GDPR.[10] The operative part of the judgment summarizes that the automated creation of a score by a credit agency is an automated individual decision if the score is used decisively by a third party.[11]

3. Facts of the ECJ ruling

The Austrian plaintiff CK applied for a mobile phone contract (€10 per month) with a mobile phone provider. The application was rejected on the basis of an automated credit rating by the private credit agency *Dun & Bradstreet Austria GmbH (D&B)*, as CK was not considered sufficiently

7 ECJ 27.2.2025 – case C-203/22, ECLI:EU:C:2025:117 para. 41–50 – CK v. Magistrate of the City of Vienna, Dun & Bradstreet Austria GmbH.

8 ECJ 27.2.2025 – case C-203/22, ECLI:EU:C:2025:117 para. 50 – CK v. Magistrate of the City of Vienna, Dun & Bradstreet Austria GmbH.

9 ECJ 27.2.2025 – case C-203/22, ECLI:EU:C:2025:117 para. 51–55 – CK v. Magistrate of the City of Vienna, Dun & Bradstreet Austria GmbH.

10 ECJ 27.2.2025 – case C-203/22, ECLI:EU:C:2025:117 para. 68–70 – CK v. Magistrate of the City of Vienna, Dun & Bradstreet Austria GmbH.

11 ECJ 27.2.2025 – case C-203/22, ECLI:EU:C:2025:117 para. 73 – CK v. Magistrate of the City of Vienna, Dun & Bradstreet Austria GmbH.

creditworthy.[12] CK contacted the data protection authority, which obliged D & B to disclose 'meaningful information about the logic involved' in the automated decision (para. 17).

D & B filed a lawsuit, citing trade secrets. The Federal Administrative Court ruled in favor of CK and found that D & B had violated Art. 15(1)(h) GDPR because it had not provided sufficient explanations.[13] The decision became final, but the Vienna Magistrate's Court refused to enforce it because D & B had already provided sufficient information.[14] CK brought an action for enforcement; the Vienna Administrative Court stayed the proceedings and referred several questions to the Court for a preliminary ruling.[15]

The questions referred essentially concerned:

1. **The content and scope of 'meaningful information'** within the meaning of Art. 15(1)(h) GDPR: Must the input data, parameters, mathematical formulas, and their influence on the result also be disclosed in order to be able to understand the score?[16]
2. **Reference to Art. 22(3) GDPR**: Is the information only 'meaningful' if it allows the data subject to effectively exercise their right to human intervention and to challenge the automated decision?[17]
3. **Verification of accuracy**: Does Art. 15(1)(h) GDPR grant a right to verify the accuracy of the data communicated by the controller, even if this would require the disclosure of third-party data?[18]
4. **Handling of trade secrets**: Is disclosure to authorities/courts permissible in order to verify the existence of a secret and check the accuracy of

12 ECJ 27.2.2025 – case C-203/22, ECLI:EU:C:2025:117 para. 16 – CK v. Magistrate of the City of Vienna, Dun & Bradstreet Austria GmbH.
13 ECJ 27.2.2025 – case C-203/22, ECLI:EU:C:2025:117 para. 18–20 – CK v. Magistrate of the City of Vienna, Dun & Bradstreet Austria GmbH.
14 ECJ 27.2.2025 – case C-203/22, ECLI:EU:C:2025:117 para. 21 – CK v. Magistrate of the City of Vienna, Dun & Bradstreet Austria GmbH.
15 ECJ 27.2.2025 – case C-203/22, ECLI:EU:C:2025:117 para. 22 et seq. – CK v. Magistrate of the City of Vienna, Dun & Bradstreet Austria GmbH.
16 ECJ 27.2.2025 – case C-203/22, ECLI:EU:C:2025:117 para. 24–27, 33 – CK v. Magistrate of the City of Vienna, Dun & Bradstreet Austria GmbH.
17 ECJ 27.2.2025 – case C-203/22, ECLI:EU:C:2025:117 para. 27–30, 33- CK v. Magistrate of the City of Vienna, Dun & Bradstreet Austria GmbH.
18 ECJ 27.2.2025 – case C-203/22, ECLI:EU:C:2025:117 para. 26–31, 33 – CK v. Magistrate of the City of Vienna, Dun & Bradstreet Austria GmbH.

the information?. Is § 4(6) DSG (AT), which generally excludes the right to information, in conformity with EU law?[19]

4. Decision and reasoning

a) Content of the right to information under Art. 15(1)(h) GDPR

The ECJ clarifies that Art. 15(1)(h) GDPR gives the data subject the right to an explanation of how the automated decision works. This right is motivated by the principle of transparency (Rec. 58 GDPR) and the right not to be subject to a decision based solely on automated processing (Art. 22 GDPR).

- The term 'meaningful information' is to be understood broadly. According to the wording in the various language versions, it covers both the 'procedure' and the 'principles' of data processing. It is not a question of the complete algorithm, but of the essential rules so that the data subject can understand the decision.[20]
- The Court emphasizes that the data subject has a genuine right to an explanation of the automated mechanism, including an explanation of how it works and the result. The explanation must be relevant, transparent, understandable, and easily accessible.[21]
- Simply providing complex mathematical formulas or a detailed list of all processing steps is not sufficient.[22] Instead, the controller must explain in an understandable way which data is weighted and how a change in certain data would affect the result.[23]
- The possibility of verifying the accuracy of the underlying data arises from the general right of access under Art. 15(1) sent. 1 GDPR and the right to rectification; it is not part of Art. 15(1)(h) GDPR. However,

19 ECJ 27.2.2025 – case C-203/22, ECLI:EU:C:2025:117 para. 30–33 – CK v. Magistrate of the City of Vienna, Dun & Bradstreet Austria GmbH.

20 ECJ 27.2.2025 – case C-203/22, ECLI:EU:C:2025:117 para. 59–61 – CK v. Magistrate of the City of Vienna, Dun & Bradstreet Austria GmbH.

21 ECJ 27.2.2025 – case C-203/22, ECLI:EU:C:2025:117 para. 65 et seq. – CK v. Magistrate of the City of Vienna, Dun & Bradstreet Austria GmbH.

22 ECJ 27.2.2025 – case C-203/22, ECLI:EU:C:2025:117 para. 59 – CK v. Magistrate of the City of Vienna, Dun & Bradstreet Austria GmbH.

23 ECJ 27.2.2025 – case C-203/22, ECLI:EU:C:2025:117 para. 60–62 – CK v. Magistrate of the City of Vienna, Dun & Bradstreet Austria GmbH.

the data subject may request access to their data and have it corrected pursuant to Art. 15(1) GDPR.[24]

b) Handling of trade secrets and third-party data

The Court recognizes that the protection of personal data and business and trade secrets is protected by fundamental rights and therefore requires a balancing of interests. Art. 23 GDPR allows restrictions on the right of access in order to protect the rights and freedoms of others, but these must be proportionate and must not lead to complete exclusion.[25]

- If the disclosure of 'meaningful information' concerns third-party data or trade secrets, the controller may not simply refuse to provide the information. Instead, it must submit the information to the competent supervisory authority or court so that they can weigh up the interests in each individual case and decide which information may be made available to the data subject.[26]
- The Court emphasizes that national regulations such as § 4 (6) DSG, which exclude the right of access to business secrets across the board, violate EU law because such a general predetermination prevents the weighing of interests in individual cases required by EU law.[27]

c) Result

The Court summarizes its answers in the operative part:

1. **Right to explanation** – Art. 15(1) 1(h) GDPR must be interpreted as meaning that, in the case of automated decision-making (including profiling), data subjects may request the controller to provide them with the procedures and principles used to process their personal data in an

24 ECJ 27.2.2025 – case C-203/22, ECLI:EU:C:2025:117 para. 63 – CK v. Magistrate of the City of Vienna, Dun & Bradstreet Austria GmbH.

25 ECJ 27.2.2025 – case C-203/22, ECLI:EU:C:2025:117 para. 68–70 – CK v. Magistrate of the City of Vienna, Dun & Bradstreet Austria GmbH.

26 ECJ 27.2.2025 – case C-203/22, ECLI:EU:C:2025:117 para. 70–73 – CK v. Magistrate of the City of Vienna, Dun & Bradstreet Austria GmbH.

27 ECJ 27.2.2025 – case C-203/22, ECLI:EU:C:2025:117 para. 75 – CK v. Magistrate of the City of Vienna, Dun & Bradstreet Austria GmbH.

automated manner in order to produce a result such as a credit profile in a relevant, concise, transparent, and understandable form.[28] (para. 66).

2. **Trade secrets/third-party data** – Art. 15(1)(h) GDPR must be interpreted as meaning that, in the case of protected third-party data or trade secrets, the controller is obliged to submit the relevant information to the supervisory authority or the court. They must weigh up the conflicting interests and determine the scope of the data subject's right to information.[29] (paras. 73–75).

5. Assessment and practical implications

The Schufa decision from 2023 defined the scope of application of Art. 22 GDPR and clarifies when the creation of a credit score is considered an automated decision and thus triggers the extended transparency and protection obligations. Building on this, the judgment in Case C-203/22 – CK v Magistrat Wien now clarifies the scope of the information obligation under Art. 15(1)(h) GDPR. While the Federal Court of Justice (BGH) in 2014 merely recognized a right to information about the data used, the ECJ in 2025 requires a comprehensible explanation of the procedures and principles of automated processing – i.e., the types of data, their weighting, and their significance for the result. At the same time, it confirms that trade secrets and third-party data can be protected, but only after a case-by-case assessment by supervisory authorities or courts. The new ruling thus closes the protection gap identified by the Schufa decision and sets the bar for transparency in scoring systems significantly higher.

a) Increased documentation and transparency requirements

For companies that use scoring and profiling procedures (especially in the credit and telecommunications sectors), the decision means a significant tightening of transparency requirements. They must be able to explain plausibly to the data subject:

---

28 ECJ 27.2.2025 – case C-203/22, ECLI:EU:C:2025:117 para. 66 – CK v. Magistrate of the City of Vienna, Dun & Bradstreet Austria GmbH.

29 ECJ 27.2.2025 – case C-203/22, ECLI:EU:C:2025:117 para. 73–75 – CK v. Magistrate of the City of Vienna, Dun & Bradstreet Austria GmbH.

- what personal data (e.g., age, address, payment data) was used,
- what weighing or other evaluation criteria were applied and how these criteria influence the result,
- how changes in the input data affect the result.

Full disclosure of the algorithm is not required; rather, an easily understandable presentation of the logic and criteria is sufficient. In order to meet these requirements, controllers should provide an explainability layer when designing their scoring models and make the relevant documentation (data catalogs, decision trees, example scenarios) available.

b) Relationship to Art. 22 GDPR and rights of control

'Meaningful information' is closely related to the right not to be subject to a decision based solely on automated processing (Art. 22(1) GDPR) and the right to human intervention, to express one's own point of view, and to contest the decision (Art. 22(3) GDPR). The explanation of the logic should enable the data subject to effectively exercise these rights. Companies should therefore establish procedures to promptly review objections to automated decisions and, if necessary, allow for human reassessment.

c) Handling of trade secrets and third-party data

The decision clarifies that trade secrets and the protection of third-party personal data may not serve as a blanket reason for excluding requests for information. Controllers must examine:

- Whether the request can be satisfied by partial anonymization or aggregation.
- Whether disclosure to the supervisory authority or the court is necessary so that a balancing of interests can be carried out there.
- Whether alternative forms of presentation (e.g., references to categories, weightings without specific numerical values) are sufficient.

Companies should define internal processes for dealing with conflicts between transparency obligations and confidentiality interests. Cooperation with supervisory authorities and the creation of non-confidential versions (so-called black box models) will become increasingly important.

d) Impact on national regulations

The Court has ruled that national laws such as the Austrian § 4(6) DSG, which generally exclude the right to information in the case of trade secrets, are not compatible with the GDPR. Member States may impose restrictions, but must ensure that each case is examined individually and may not undermine the essence of the right to information. Comparable regulations in other Member States must be reviewed and, if necessary, adapted.

e) Outlook and recommendations

- **Companies** should review their data protection and compliance programs and ensure that they can provide 'meaningful information' in the case of automated decisions. This includes documenting the data sources, weightings, and models used, as well as preparing comprehensible explanations for data subjects.
- **Supervisory authorities and courts** will play a central role in reviewing trade secrets and protecting third parties. They must develop criteria for weighing up interests and establish a practicable procedure (e.g., escrow solutions).
- **Legislators** are called upon to reform national provisions that generally exclude rights to information in the case of trade secrets and to bring them into line with the GDPR.

6. Conclusion

The ruling provides more detail regarding the rights of individuals who are subject to automated decisions and scoring procedures. It obliges companies to provide transparent and comprehensible explanations and limits the possibility of invoking trade secrets. At the same time, it emphasizes that the right to information is not absolute, but that a balancing of interests is necessary. In practice, this means increased data protection compliance requirements and greater involvement of supervisory authorities in conflicts between transparency and confidentiality.

III. Systematic context of the EDPB Guidelines and commentary

1. Starting point: Categories and basic principles of the EDPB guidelines

The EDPB Guidelines 03/2022 on Deceptive design patterns in social media platform interfaces[30] are aimed at social media providers, but are considered best practice for other digital services. They define *deceptive design patterns* as user interfaces that mislead users into making unintended or unwilling decisions about the processing of their personal data, thereby limiting their fair and informed decision-making. The guidelines distinguish between categories such as *overloading, skipping, stirring, obstructing, fickle, and left in the dark.*[31] The relevant legal basis for assessing such designs are the principles of fairness and transparency, as well as the obligations of data minimization, accountability, and data protection by design (Art. 5(1)(a), (c), and (2), Art. 25 GDPR).

2. Interfaces with the ruling

Judgment C-203/22 details the transparency requirement for automated decisions: Data subjects have a right to 'relevant, concise, transparent, and understandable' information about the logic involved. This right to explanation can only be effectively exercised if the information is easily accessible and not obscured by misleading design. This has the following consequences for the application of the dark pattern guidelines:

- The Court requires 'meaningful information' to include a comprehensible description of the procedures and principles: which data categories were included, how they were weighted, and how a change in certain data would affect the result; simply communicating complex formulas is not sufficient. The guidelines do not explicitly specify this level of detail

30 EDPB, 'Guidelines 03/2022 on Deceptive design patterns in social media platform interfaces: how to recognise and avoid them', version 2.0 (14.2.2023) <https://www.edpb.europa.eu/system/files/2023-02/edpb_03-2022_guidelines_on_deceptive_design_patterns_in_social_media_platform_interfaces_v2_en_0.pdf>.

31 Explanations of terms: EDPB, 'Guidelines 03/2022 on Deceptive design patterns in social media platform interfaces: how to recognise and avoid them' (fn. 30), p. 3 et seq.

for ADM, but rather formulate transparency in terms of interface and language (clarity, structure, no misleading information)[32]

- The Court prohibits a blanket refusal to provide an explanation on the grounds of trade secrets or the protection of third-party data and instead requires a case-by-case assessment by supervisory authorities or courts by means of graduated disclosure. The Guidelines primarily address design transparency (e.g., no 'dead ends,' clear language, linguistic continuity), but not the substantive weighing regime for trade secrets, so that the ruling provides independent, additional clarification in this regard.[33]
- The Court links the stated logic with the goal of actually enabling intervention and challenge (Art. 22(3) GDPR); the declaration therefore has a functional, legally enforceable quality, not merely an informative one. The Guidelines indirectly ensure this objective by prohibiting barriers in the rights journey (privacy maze, language barriers), but do not go so far as to standardize the ADM declaration content itself for legal enforcement.[34]

IV. Recommended further reading

EDPB, 'Guidelines 03/2022 on Deceptive design patterns in social media platform interfaces: how to recognise and avoid them', version 2.0 (14.2.2023) <https://www.edpb.europa.eu/system/files/2023-02/edpb_03-2022_guidelines_on_deceptive_design_patterns_in_social_media_platform_interfaces_v2_en_0.pdf>.

ECJ 7.12.2023 – case C-634/21, ECLI:EU:C:2023:957 – OQ v Land Hessen, SCHUFA.

BGH 28.1.2014 – VI ZR 156/13, ZD 2014, 306.

---

32 EDPB, 'Guidelines 03/2022 on Deceptive design patterns in social media platform interfaces: how to recognise and avoid them' (fn. 30), p. 13–15, 28–29.

33 EDPB, 'Guidelines 03/2022 on Deceptive design patterns in social media platform interfaces: how to recognise and avoid them' (fn. 30), p. 24–25, 53.

34 EDPB, 'Guidelines 03/2022 on Deceptive design patterns in social media platform interfaces: how to recognise and avoid them' (fn. 30), p. 53 et seq.

Rectification of Gender Data in Public Registers and Means of Proof

Yvette Reif

ECJ 13.3.2025 – case C-247/23, ECLI:EU:C:2025:172 – Deldits

I. Case summary[1]

In 2014, VP, an Iranian national, obtained refugee status in Hungary by relying on their transgender identity and producing medical certificates drawn up by specialists in psychiatry and gynecology. According to those certificates, although VP was born female, their gender identity was male. Following the recognition of their refugee status on that basis, VP was nevertheless registered as female in the asylum register, which is kept by the Hungarian asylum authority and contains identification data, including gender, of the persons who have obtained that status in Hungary.

In 2022, based on the abovementioned medical certificates, VP requested, inter alia, that the asylum authority rectify the entry concerning their gender in that register, pursuant to the GDPR. However, that request was rejected on the ground that VP had not proved that they had undergone gender reassignment surgery.

VP brought an action against that rejection before the Budapest High Court (Hungary). Whilst explaining that Hungarian law does not provide for a procedure for the legal recognition of transgender identity, that court asked the ECJ, first, whether the GDPR requires a national authority responsible for keeping a public register to rectify the personal data relating to the gender identity of a natural person where those data are inaccurate and, second, whether a Member State may, by way of an administrative practice, make the exercise of the right to rectification of those data conditional upon the production of evidence, in particular gender reassignment surgery.

1 This summary is based on the press release issued by the Court of Justice of the European Union concerning case C-247/23 (Deldits), judgment of 13.3.2025, ECLI:EU:C:2025:172.

II. Key legal findings

The ECJ ruled as follows:[2]

- Art. 16 GDPR must be interpreted as requiring a national authority responsible for keeping a public register to rectify the personal data relating to the gender identity of a natural person where those data are inaccurate, within the meaning of Art. 5(1)(d) of that regulation.
- Art. 16 GDPR must be interpreted as meaning that, for the purposes of exercising the right to rectification of the personal data relating to the gender identity of a natural person that are contained in a public register, that person may be required to provide relevant and sufficient evidence that may reasonably be required of that person in order to establish that those data are inaccurate. However, a Member State may not, under any circumstances, by way of an administrative practice, make the exercise of that right conditional upon the production of evidence of gender reassignment surgery.

According to the ECJ, the Hungarian court must verify the accuracy of the data at issue considering the purpose for which they were collected. If the purpose of collecting these data was to identify the data subject, the data would appear to refer to the person's lived gender identity, rather than the gender assigned at birth. Also, the right to rectification under Art. 16 GDPR is not affected by the absence of a procedure for the legal recognition of transgender identity under the applicable national law.

Furthermore, the Court concluded that a requirement to provide evidence of gender reassignment surgery undermines the fundamental rights and freedoms of the data subject, specifically the right to the integrity of the person and the right to respect for private life, as set out in Art. 3 and 7 CFR. The ECJ held that a medical certificate, including a psychiatric diagnosis, may constitute relevant and sufficient evidence in this regard.

2 The following two paragraphs reproduce the first and second operative parts of the judgment of ECJ 13.3.2025 – case C-247/23, ECLI:EU:C:2025:172 – Deldits.

III. Systematic context and legal classification

With regard to the GDPR, the ECJ identified the following recitals and articles as relevant to its decision:

- Rec. 1, 10, 59 and 73 GDPR
- Art. 1(2) GDPR
- Art. 2(1) GDPR
- the definitions of 'personal data' and 'processing' in Art. 4 GDPR
- Art. 5(1)(d) GDPR
- Art. 6(1)(c) and (e), (2) and (3) GDPR
- Art. 16 GDPR
- Art. 23(1)(a)-(e) and (h) GDPR

Art. 5 GDPR lays down general principles for the processing of personal data, including the principle that personal data shall be 'accurate and, where necessary, kept up to date; every reasonable step must be taken to ensure that personal data that are inaccurate, having regard to the purposes for which they are processed, are erased or rectified without delay ('accuracy')' (Art. 5(1)(d)).

IV. Author's analysis and commentary

1. General requirements of the right to rectification

According to the first sentence of Art. 16 GDPR, the data subject shall have the right to obtain from the controller, without undue delay, the rectification of inaccurate personal data concerning them. The second sentence of Art. 16 GDPR relates to the completion of incomplete personal data, which constitutes a specific form of rectification.

The right to rectification under Art. 16 GDPR is a fundamental element of the data subject's rights, as it provides the data subject with the opportunity to intervene in the processing of their personal data. This right can be invoked both against public and private bodies, including private-sector companies.

It is important to note, however, that, although this is not apparent from the wording of the regulation, the right to rectification applies only to personal information that concerns incorrect facts.[3] This is because, although value judgements about the personal or factual circumstances of the data subject constitute personal data, they cannot be assessed as being right or wrong. The very concept of a value judgement already implies that the circumstances in question allow for differing opinions. The decisive criterion for the existence of a fact is whether the information in question is amenable to objective clarification, that is, to verification by means of evidence.[4]

Data are considered correct only if they correspond to the factual circumstances.

2. The Duty to Substantiate Inaccuracy and the Means of Proof

In line with the principle of accountability and the requirement that personal data be accurate and kept up to date, the data controller generally bears the burden of demonstrating the accuracy of the processed information (see Art. 5(2) GDPR).

However, the data subject bears the burden of demonstrating and substantiating the inaccuracy of the data; they must therefore show, in a detailed and coherent manner, that the data being processed are incorrect.[5] The applicant must indicate precisely which data are inaccurate and explain in what respect.[6] An unsubstantiated claim of inaccuracy by the data subject does not, by itself, give rise to a right under Art. 16 GDPR.

As the ECJ held in the present case, the applicant may, moreover, be required to provide relevant and sufficient evidence demonstrating the inaccuracy of the contested data, if this can reasonably be expected in light

3 ECJ 20.12.2017 – case C-434/16, ECLI:EU:C:2017:994 – Nowak; see also, for example, Kühling/Buchner DS-GVO BDSG/Herbst, 4th edn. 2024, DS-GVO Art. 16 mn. 8; Paal/Pauly DS-GVO BDSG/Paal, 4th edn. 2026, DS-GVO Art. 16 mn. 15; Simitis/Hornung/Spiecker gen. Döhmann Datenschutzrecht/Dix, 2nd edn. 2025, DS-GVO Art. 16 mn. 7; Sydow/Marsch DS-GVO BDSG/Peuker, 3rd edn. 2022, DS-GVO Art. 16 mn. 7; for a 'functional interpretation' of Art. 16, particularly in cases where a value judgment can be traced back to factual circumstances Ehmann/Selmayr Datenschutz-Grundverordnung/Kamann/Braun, 3rd edn. 2024, DS-GVO Art. 16 mn. 19 et seqq.

4 ECJ 8.12.2022 – case C-460/20, ECLI:EU:C:2022:962 – Google (Dereferencing of allegedly inaccurate content).

5 ÖBVwG 19.4.2024 – W287 2276988-1, ECLI:AT:BVWG:2024:W287.2276988.1.00; Ehmann/Selmayr/Kamann/Braun DS-GVO Art. 16 mn. 22.

6 ÖBVwG 19.4.2024 – W287 2276988-1, ECLI:AT:BVWG:2024:W287.2276988.1.00.

of the circumstances of the individual case. This is one of the key findings of the ECJ in the *Deldits* case.

Although, in the case at hand, the ECJ held that the data subject was not required to provide the evidence requested by the authority concerning their gender identity—specifically, proof of gender-affirming surgery—the decision nevertheless confirms, beyond that specific instance, that data subjects will often be required to provide substantiating evidence when exercising their right to rectification.

Where a data subject requests the rectification of personal data relating to them, or indicates that information stored about them is inaccurate, their intention is that only accurate personal data concerning them be processed. The controller's knowledge of the correct information therefore directly serves the data subject's interests. Accordingly, as a rule, any corresponding obligation to provide evidence should not—apart from the resulting administrative burden—constitute a significant interference with the data subject's fundamental rights and freedoms.

The reason this was different in the *Deldits* case lay in the specific circumstances, namely that the authority had requested information that was unnecessary yet highly sensitive to determine the data subject's gender identity, having failed to recognize that the identification of a person depends solely on their lived gender identity.

Irrespective of the specific factual circumstances of the *Deldits* case, the following conclusions may be drawn from the ECJ judgment:

In particular, where personal data form part of official registers or administrative records, data subjects will generally be required to substantiate the alleged inaccuracy of the processed data.[7] A mere denial will not suffice; instead, reliable official documentation will be necessary.[8]

However, the ECJ's findings are not limited to processing activities carried out by public authorities. From a corporate perspective, it may also be appropriate to rectify personal data only after the applicant has provided adequate evidence. By way of example, a debtor may claim that their surname has changed due to marriage. If such a change were accepted without verification, the company could, in the event of abusive rectification requests, risk being unable to enforce its claims.

7 Diesendorf/Kramer DSB 2025, 93 (96).
8 Diesendorf/Kramer DSB 2025, 93 (96).

In practice, proof that data are incorrect is usually provided by demonstrating the correct information instead. If a person requests that their information be corrected in a specific way, they must show evidence that the replacement data is accurate.[9] In the case of public registers, the person may also be legally required to supply the correct information.

3. The Controller's Independent Duty of Rectification

While the right under Art. 16 GDPR depends on a request by the data subject, the obligations under Art. 5 GDPR are addressed to the controller. Consequently, an obligation to rectify inaccurate data may also arise independently of a request by the data subject under Art. 16 GDPR.[10] This, however, requires that the controller is aware of the inaccuracy of the processed data.[11] Such knowledge may, for example, arise from information provided by a person other than the data subject.

If the inaccuracy of the data is not established but there are reasonable doubts as to its correctness, the controller has a duty to verify the data, irrespective of whether a request has been submitted by the data subject (cf. Rec. 39 sent. 11 GDPR).[12]

Finally, it should be noted that, irrespective of any legal obligation, it is generally in the controller's own interest to process only accurate information.

4. The Relationship between the GDPR and the European Convention on Human Rights (ECHR)

The *Deldits* judgment is also noteworthy regarding the relationship between the GDPR and the ECHR, as the ECJ makes it clear that restrictions under the GDPR must not only comply with the CFR but also must not fall below the level of protection guaranteed by the Convention.[13] In this regard, the ECJ relies on Article 52(3) CFR, according to which the

9 BVerwG 2.3.2022 – 6 C 7.20, NVwZ 2022, 1205 (1210).

10 ÖBVwG 19.4.2024 – W287 2276988-1, ECLI:AT:BVWG:2024:W287.2276988.1.00.

11 ÖBVwG 19.4.2024 – W287 2276988-1, ECLI:AT:BVWG:2024:W287.2276988.1.00.

12 See also Ehmann/Selmayr/Heberlein DS-GVO Art. 5 mn. 32.

13 Callewaert, 'The GDPR and the Convention, no strangers to each other – Judgment of the CJEU in the case of Deldits' (15.4.2025) <https://johan-callewaert.eu/de/the-gd

rights guaranteed by the Charter have the same meaning and scope as the corresponding rights guaranteed by the ECHR, the latter constituting a minimum threshold of protection.[14] This is particularly interesting insofar as the GDPR itself makes no reference to the Convention, except in Rec. 73 GDPR.

V. Recommended further reading

Apart from *Deldits*, further relevant ECJ judgments with respect to the right to rectification under Art. 16 GDPR include:

ECJ 20.12.2017 – case C-434/16, ECLI:EU:C:2017:994 – Nowak: Scope of the right to rectification under EU data protection law and the protection of freedom of expression

ECJ 8.12.2022 – case C-460/20, ECLI:EU:C:2022:962 – Google (Dereferencing of allegedly inaccurate content) and ECJ 27.10.2022 – case C-129/21, ECLI:EU:C:2022:833 – Proximus NV: Relationship between the right to rectification (Art. 16 GDPR) and the right to erasure (Art. 17 GDPR)

ECJ 7.5.2009 – case C-553/07, ECLI:EU:C:2009:293 – Rijkeboer: Right to access and rectification under EU data protection law with respect to personal data held by public authorities

ECJ 12.1.2023 – case C-154/21, ECLI:EU:C:2023:3 – RW v Österreichische Post: Operational obligations of data controllers regarding data accuracy

The processing of personal data relating to gender identity has also been addressed by the ECJ in the *Mousse* case (C-394/23),[15] which concerned whether a data controller may lawfully require customers to provide a title/gender identity ('Monsieur' or 'Madame') when purchasing a train ticket online. The Court emphasized that such data collection must be objectively necessary for the service and comply with GDPR principles, including data minimisation.

---

pr-and-the-convention-no-strangers-to-each-other-judgment-of-the-cjeu-in-the-case-of-deldits/>.

14 ECJ 13.3.2025 – case C-247/23, ECLI:EU:C:2025:172 para. 46 – Deldits; Callewaert, 'The GDPR and the Convention, no strangers to each other – Judgment of the CJEU in the case of Deldits' (15.4.2025) <https://johan-callewaert.eu/de/the-gdpr-and-the-convention-no-strangers-to-each-other-judgment-of-the-cjeu-in-the-case-of-deldits/>.

15 ECJ 9.1.2025 – case C-394/23, ECLI:EU:C:2025:2 – Mousse.

Principle of accuracy – Right to rectification

Frederick Richter

ECJ 13.3.2025 – case C-247/23, ECLI:EU:C:2025:172 – Deldits

I. Case summary

In C-247/23 'Deldits'[1], a transgender refugee in Hungary, who later became Hungarian citizen, sought to have the gender marker in the national asylum register changed to reflect his lived male gender. The request was framed as rectification of inaccurate personal data under Art. 16 GDPR, not as a stand-alone fundamental rights claim. Hungarian authorities refused it, relying on an administrative practice that allowed changes only after gender-affirming surgery and in the absence of a specific legislative procedure for legal gender recognition. The referring court asked whether gender identity data fall under GDPR and when such data are accurate, and whether a Member State may, under Art. 23 GDPR, limit rectification through non-legislative practices and surgery requirements.

The Court held that gender identity is personal data; accuracy depends on reflecting the person's lived gender identity, and Member States cannot rely on mere administrative practice or surgery conditions to restrict rectification rights.[2]

II. Key legal findings

1. The decision clarifies that Art. 16 GDPR grants a comprehensive right that cannot be subject to severe obstacles. National law must not impede the exercise of the right to rectification. At the same time, the GDPR may take precedence over national regulations that may impose high require-

1 This unmeaning expression was created by the court to give the anonymized case some designation.

2 This case summary was generated with the support of a generative AI tool and subsequently reviewed and revised by the author.

ments for the amendment of official registers. Above all, the requirements for proof of accuracy must not be disproportionately high.

Art. 5(1)(d) and Art. 16 GDPR specify the right under Art. 8(2) of the Charter of Fundamental Rights. Member States therefore continue to have legislative autonomy in the area of civil status law and in establishing procedures for the legal recognition of gender identities. However, when exercising this discretion, they must comply with the GDPR in light of the Charter.

2. Correctness must be assessed solely on the basis of current criteria and not historical ones. This means that any previous correctness of the data that was later lost is irrelevant. At the same time, it means that the assessment must be based on the time of processing or the time of its commencement. In the present case, therefore, it was not important what gender was assigned to the entitled person at birth, but rather what gender identity was recorded in the asylum register.

The time at which the inaccuracy occurred or became inaccurate is irrelevant. The decisive trigger for a correction obligation in chronological terms is solely the data subject's request for correction. As soon as the data subject requests the correction, the controller must take action – regardless of the fact that, objectively speaking, the controller should have proactively rectified the data earlier in order to comply with the principle of accuracy under Art. 5 of the GDPR. In any case, it cannot make a difference whether the register entry in dispute was already incorrect when the data subject's data was collected or whether it only became incorrect subsequently, for example as a result of a change in circumstances regarding gender identity.

3. If a Member State wishes to restrict the exercise of data subjects' rights, it must enact provisions in national law. In doing so, it must comply with the requirements must respect the restrcitions of Art. 23 GDPR. A mere instruction to the state administration or order to a certain authority to directly or indirectly restrict the rights of data subjects, as in this case, does not comply with the requirement of the GDPR. A requirement for persons seeking to exercise their right to rectification to provide evidence of a medical change constitutes such an indirect restriction of rights. However, it does not stem from a law that complies with fundamental rights and is therefore not in line with EU law.

4. According to the ruling, a person may still be required to provide relevant evidence that can reasonably be demanded in order to establish the inaccuracy of data. However, proof of surgery cannot be required, as such a requirement would violate the essence of the right to integrity (Art. 3

GrCh) and the right to respect for private life (Art. 7 GrCh). Furthermore, such a requirement is neither necessary nor proportionate to ensure the reliability and consistency of public registers. A simple medical certificate, i.e. a psychiatric diagnosis, constitutes relevant and sufficient evidence in this respect.

The Court held that the only required evidence standard for rectifying the gender marker under the GDPR is that the data accurately reflect the person's lived gender identity, as expressed by that person. Gender identity has to be deemed as personal data and its accuracy is assessed against the individual's self-identified gender, not against medical, biological, or surgical criteria. Member States may not impose additional proof requirements such as gender-affirming surgery to restrict rectification, nor may they rely on mere administrative practice to demand such evidence.

III. Systematic context and legal classification

1. Art. 16 GDPR is not a provision that is particularly in the public eye or in the focus of experts. This is surprising, given that it is one of the stronger rights of data subjects. It offers a real opportunity for intervention rather than merely for achieving transparency, as provided by the right of access. Potentially, Art. 16 GDPR gives data subjects a certain power of practical influence as it contains up to three rights of data subjects, namely the primary right to rectification, the right to completion and a right to updating that is not explicitly mentioned.

With regard to inaccurate data, the subjective right to rectification supplements the objective obligation to ensure data accuracy under Art. 5(1)(d). With regard to outdated data, the subjective right to completion supplements the objective obligation to adapt data under Art. 5(1)(d), according to which controllers must keep the data stored on a data subject up to date 'where necessary'.

In view of this multi-layered nature of the right under Art. 16 GDPR, data subjects may well have a wide range of options for exercising rights. In addition to this personal options and the indirect expression of the idea of 'self-data protection', the rights under Art. 16 GDPR also require complementary areas of responsibility, namely with regard to data accuracy, a requirement for cooperation: In many constellations only the data subject itself can advance data accuracy for only they can deliver currents facts for the correct level of information. With the aim of ensuring data accuracy, they can be seen as having a certain obligation to 'help' the controller to achieve this. This can be done by exercising rights of rectification. A controller who is committed to the principles of Art. 5 GDPR should therefore actually welcome any legitimate exercise of the rights under Art. 16 GDPR. Or, as Advocate General Collins put it, 'the right of rectification and its enforcement at the initiative of private individuals assist in effecting compliance with the principle of accuracy laid down in Art. 5(1)(d) of the GDPR'.[3]

The importance of the right to rectification becomes clear when one considers that, in addition to the right of access, it is expressly guaranteed in Article 8(2) sentence 2 of the Charter of Fundamental Rights of the European Union – unlike the right to erasure, which is much more of a practical focus.

2. It remains a mystery to the Hungarian administration why the applicant was granted refugee status precisely because of his transgender status, but this status was then ignored or incorrectly recorded when he was entered in the refugee register. These inconsistent assessments can probably only be explained by the involvement of different competent authorities and individuals. This is because the transphobic tightening of Hungarian state policy and legislation only began half a decade after the refugee was incorrectly registered.[4]

IV. Author's analysis and commentary

1. The judgment in Case C-247/23 is brief. This is hardly surprising, since also parts of its content are rather unspectacular – at least from a purely data protection perspective. Rather, readers may feel that their sense of justice regarding the case has been confirmed.

It is unsurprising that the ECJ – with participation of rapporteur von Danwitz in this procedure – emphasises in the judgment that the objective of the GDPR is to ensure a high level of protection for the fundamental rights and freedoms of natural persons. Under this objective and the resulting obligation to comply without exception with the processing principles

3 AG Collins 12.9.2024 – case C- 247/23, ECLI:EU:C:2024:747- VP v Országos Idegenrendészeti Főigazgatóság, mn. 39.

4 See Roßbach EuZW 2025, 521 (524).

set out in Article 5 GDPR, it is an essential aspect of data protection to keep personal data records up to date.

Nonetheless the decision is deemed important as it concretises the obligation for public authorities to conduct registers regarding gender data based on lived reality but on the basis of possibly outdated records or medical-biological attributions.

At the same time, the judgement strengthens the scope of application of the GDPR in connection with the right to identity pursuant to the European Convention on Human Rights. Also with view to the German Self-Determination Act which has been in force since November 2024, the ECJ ruling has a reinforcing effect when it states that the recognition of gender identity must not be made dependent on medical procedures.

In practice, the ruling may pose challenges for registry-keeping institutions due to changing gender identities. According to the German Self-Determination Act, these identities could change within a few years, meaning that corrections may be required several times, at least in accordance with Art. 5 of the GDPR[5].

2. EU Member States should bring their regulations on civil status and gender identity issues and existing or planned procedures for changing gender entries in registers into line with the GDPR. This is because it has now been clarified by the ECJ that individuals can exercise their right to rectification under data protection law without any restriction by national regulations that are discriminatory or inadequate.

The only point of reference is the accuracy of the data, regardless of the personal status. Therefore, not only citizens of the data-processing state, but also refugees can invoke Art. 16 GDPR to request corrections in civil status registers in the EU. Nevertheless, conflicting national legal situations may make practical enforcement difficult for persons affected.

For persons in Germany who can make use of the German Self-Determination Act (SBGG), there is no additional need for action, as the German procedure already complies with the ECJ requirements. However, persons without a right of residence who are excluded from the SBGG can rely on Art. 16 GDPR to request a correction of their entry.[6]

5 Oldenburger NZFam 2025, 515.

6 See Roßbach EuZW 2025, 521 (525).

V. Recommended further reading

Marcia, ‚Trans*Rights Beyond Medicalisation? The CJEU in Case Deldits (C-247/23)' (European Law Blog, 3.4.2025) <https://doi.org/10.21428/9885764c.350f4fde>.

Sümer, ‚Let me be me – Rectification of gender-related Personal Data does not require Evidence of having undergone Gender Reassignment Surgery (C-247/23, Deldits)' (EU Law Live, 15.4.2025) <www.law.kuleuven.be/citip/blog/let-me-be-me-rectification-of-gender-related-personal-data-does-not-require-evidence-of-having-undergone-gender-reassignment-surgery-c-247-23-deldits-case>.

ECJ 20.12.2017 – case C-434/16, ECLI:EU:C:2017:994 – Nowak.

Concerning the Scope of the Data Subject's Right of Access

Daniel Pauly

ECJ 12.1.2023 – case C-154/21, ECLI:EU:C:2023:3 – RW v Österreichische Post AG

I. Case summary

The underlying case concerned a legal dispute between a natural person (RW) and Österreichische Post AG (Austrian Post). According to media reports, Österreichische Post AG used address data and socio-demographic information to calculate the so-called party affinity of several million customers by means of statistical analyses. The results obtained were then sold to third parties for advertising purposes. Against this background, RW, one of the data subjects, requested information from Austrian Post in accordance with Art. 15 GDPR about the data stored about him. Österreichische Post AG responded only to a limited extent. In the subsequent court proceedings, it stated that it had passed on the data to business customers for advertising purposes, but did not name any specific recipients, merely indicating categories of recipients. The lower courts considered this form of information to be sufficient and rejected any further obligation to name specific recipients. They justified this on the grounds that Art. 15(1)(c) GDPR gives the controller the option of naming either recipients or categories of recipients and granted the controllers discretion in this respect.

The plaintiff appealed against this decision to the Supreme Court of Austria. The Supreme Court had doubts about the interpretation of Art. 15(1)(c) GDPR, as the wording left open whether controllers could choose between disclosing specific recipients and naming categories of recipients. The proceedings were therefore suspended and referred to the ECJ for a preliminary ruling.[1]

1 OGH Österreich 18.2.2021 – 6 Ob 159/20f, BeckRS 2021, 19505.

In its judgment of 12.1.2023 – Case C-154/21 (RW v Österreichische Post AG), the ECJ dealt for the first time with the scope of the right of access of data subjects under Art. 15(1)(c) GDPR.

II. Key legal findings

Specifically, the ECJ clarified whether controllers must name the recipients of personal data only in general categories or by name and whether they have discretion in this regard. In its decision, the ECJ explains the principles of interpreting EU law in a law textbook manner. According to this, interpretation must take into account not only the wording of a provision, but also its systematic context and its purposes and objectives.[2] Priority is always given to the interpretation that best ensures the practical effectiveness of the provision in question.[3]

1. Wording

First, the ECJ notes that the terms 'recipient' and 'categories of recipients' are mentioned side by side in the wording of Art. 15(1)(c) GDPR.[4] This does not imply that one of the two elements takes precedence over the other. The wording alone therefore does not clearly indicate whether the data subject's right of access includes the naming of recipients in every case or whether the mere indication of categories is sufficient. An isolated interpretation based on the wording therefore cannot conclusively clarify the issue in dispute.

2. Systematic approach

From a systematic point of view, the ECJ first refers to Rec. 63 GDPR. According to this, the data subject must have the right to know who the

2 ECJ 12.1.2023 – case C-154/21, ECLI:EU:C:2023:3 para. 29 – RW v Österreichische Post AG.

3 ECJ 12.1.2023 – case C-154/21, ECLI:EU:C:2023:3 para. 29 – RW v Österreichische Post AG.

4 On this and the following: ECJ 12.1.2023 – case C-154/21, ECLI:EU:C:2023:3 para. 30 et seqq. – RW v Österreichische Post AG.

recipients of their personal data are. There is no provision for limiting this right to categories of recipients alone.[5]

The ECJ then emphasises the importance of the principle of transparency. According to Art. 5(1)(a) GDPR and Rec. 39 GDPR, the data subject must be informed in an easily accessible and understandable manner about how their data is processed.[6]

The ECJ further clarifies that, in the context of information rights, the GDPR distinguishes between the information obligations when collecting data (Art. 13 and 14 GDPR) and the right of access in Art. 15 GDPR. In contrast to the former provisions, which grant the controller a right to choose whether to specify the categories or specific recipients, Art. 15 GDPR expressly grants the data subject an individual right of access. It follows that it is up to the data subject to determine the scope and content of their request, i.e. to demand the names of specific recipients if necessary.[7]

The ECJ also emphasises that the practical effectiveness of the rights of data subjects under the GDPR requires that, where necessary, the identity of the specific recipients of personal data be disclosed. Only in this way can rights such as rectification, erasure, restriction of processing or objection be exercised meaningfully and effectively.[8] This interpretation is confirmed by Art. 19 sent. 2 GDPR, according to which the data subject has a right to information about the specific recipients within the framework of the notification obligations.

In summary, the ECJ clarifies that, according to the system of the GDPR, the decision-making power regarding the scope and content of the right of access lies with the data subject, not with the controller.

---

5 ECJ 12.1.2023 – case C-154/21, ECLI:EU:C:2023:3 para. 33 – RW v Österreichische Post AG.

6 ECJ 12.1.2023 – case C-154/21, ECLI:EU:C:2023:3 para. 35 et seq. – RW v Österreichische Post AG.

7 ECJ 12.1.2023 – case C-154/21, ECLI:EU:C:2023:3 para. 36 – RW v Österreichische Post AG.

8 ECJ 12.1.2023 – case C-154/21, ECLI:EU:C:2023:3 para. 38 et seq. – RW v Österreichische Post AG.

3. Telos

The purpose of the GDPR is to ensure a high level of protection for personal data and the greatest possible transparency for data subjects.[9] The right of access under Art. 15(1)(c) GDPR thus serves not only the general interest in information, but in particular the purpose of enabling effective enforcement of rights by the data subject. Only with knowledge of the specific recipients is it possible for the data subject to assert their rights specifically against these processors and to address potential data protection violations.

At the same time, the ECJ acknowledges, with reference to Rec. 4 GDPR, that the right to protection of personal data is not unlimited:[10] The disclosure of the identities of the recipients may be withheld in exceptional cases, either if their identity is unknown or cannot be determined, or if the request for information is manifestly unfounded or excessive within the meaning of Art. 12(5) GDPR.

III. Systematic context and legal classification

The ECJ concludes that Art. 15(1)(c) GDPR must be interpreted as meaning that the right of access of the data subject enshrined therein requires, in principle, that the identity of the recipients of personal data be disclosed to the data subject if disclosure to recipients has taken place or is planned.[11] Only in exceptional cases – for example, if the recipients cannot be identified or if the controller demonstrates that requests for information are manifestly unfounded or excessive within the meaning of Art. 12(5) GDPR – may the information be limited to categories of recipients.

In doing so, the ECJ largely follows the opinion of Advocate General Pitruzzella[12] and the legal opinion of the referring court[13], both in terms of content and reasoning. The European Data Protection Board's guidelines

9 Rec. 10 GDPR.

10 ECJ 12.1.2023 – case C-154/21, ECLI:EU:C:2023:3 para. 47 – RW v Österreichische Post AG.

11 ECJ 12.1.2023 – case C-154/21, ECLI:EU:C:2023:3 para. 51 – RW v Österreichische Post AG.

12 AG Pitruzzella 9.6.2022 – case C-154/21, ECLI:EU:C:2022:452 – RW v Österreichische Post AG.

13 OGH Österreich 18.2.2021 – 6 Ob 159/20f, BeckRS 2021, 19505 mn. 29 ff.

on the right under Art. 15 GDPR already pointed out that the information provided must be as specific and accurate as possible.[14]

With its decision, the ECJ has settled a long-standing dispute in data protection literature regarding the interpretation of Art. 15(1)(c) GDPR. Until now, there has been disagreement as to whether the controller has the right to choose between naming specific recipients and merely indicating categories of recipients when providing information in the context of the right of access.[15] Some voices affirmed such a right of choice, which was also the opinion of the lower courts in the original proceedings.[16] In contrast, another part of the literature called for a fundamental obligation to name the specific recipients.[17]

The ECJ concurred with the latter view, thereby significantly strengthening the position of data subjects in European data protection law. According to the interpretation of the highest court, there is now a right to be informed of the names of all recipients of personal data, insofar as this is actually possible and there is no excessive request of access. In the context of Art. 15(1)(c) GDPR, controllers can no longer limit themselves to providing general information about categories of recipients but must comply fully with above obligations.

IV. Author's analysis and commentary

1. Remaining unresolved questions

It remains unclear for the time being how information on the indeterminability of recipients or cases of excessive requests of access will be handled in future.[18] The ECJ recognises that such exceptions are possible but emphasises that they must be carefully justified and comprehensively

14 EDPB, ‚Guidelines 01/2022 on data subject rights – Right of access' version 2.1 (28.3.2023) <https://www.edpb.europa.eu/system/files/2023-04/edpb_guidelines_202201_data_subject_rights_access_v2_en.pdf>, mn. 115.

15 Evaluation of the state of the legal opinions: OGH Österreich 18.2.2021 – 6 Ob 159/20f, BeckRS 2021, 19505, mn. 17 ff.

16 See Paal/Pauly DS-GVO BDSG/Paal, DS-GVO, 3rd edn. 2021, DS-GVO Art. 15 mn. 26 with further references.

17 See in Kühling/Buchner DS-GVO BDSG/Bäcker, 3rd edn. 2020, DS-GVO Art. 15 mn. 16 et seq. with further references.

18 A preliminary ruling procedure is pending before the ECJ on the question of when a request of access is excessive (Case C-526/24).

documented in each individual case. The decision leaves open whether and how the guidelines on this will be further specified.

2. Transferability to other disputed GDPR topics

It also remains unclear to what extent the case law of the ECJ can be applied to the dispute regarding Art. 13(1)(e) and Art. 14(1)(e) GDPR. The wording of these provisions is identical to that of Art. 15(1)(c) GDPR ('recipients or categories of recipients'). Therefore, there is also disagreement here as to whether the controller has a right to choose or whether the specific recipients must always be named.[19]

The identical wording initially suggests that the decision is transferable. However, the ECJ expressly emphasises that the wording is not clear in itself and bases its decision largely on systematic and teleological arguments. In para. 36 of the decision, the ECJ refers to the structural differences between Art. 15 GDPR – as a subjective right of access – and the objective information obligations in Art. 13 and 14 GDPR. In particular, the ECJ deduces from this differentiation that the data subject's right of choice is mandatory for the exercise of the rights under Art. 15 GDPR. Conversely, there is a certain tendency for the ECJ to grant the controller the right to choose in relation to the information obligations under Art. 13(1)(e) and Art. 14(1)(e) GDPR.

3. Practical relevance

It is to be expected that both the supervisory authorities and the courts of the Member States will consistently take into account the principles of interpretation laid down by the ECJ in future.[20] The ECJ's decision has effect throughout the EU and is therefore of immediate practical relevance to all companies with processing activities in the European Union. Companies are advised to carefully review the scope of their documented recipient groups and adapt their internal processes to the requirements. This is

19 See the current state of legal opinions: Paal/Pauly DS-GVO BDSG/Hennemann, 4th edn. 2026, DS-GVO Art. 13 mn. 18.

20 The EDPB has incorporated the ECJ's opinion into its guidelines: EDPB, ‚Guidelines 01/2022 on data subject rights – Right of access' (fn. 14), para. 117.

because the ECJ has now clarified at the highest level that data controllers are generally obliged to disclose the specific recipients of personal data.

If a controller invokes one of the exceptions specified by the ECJ, it must explain in detail and, if necessary, prove that the request of access is manifestly unfounded or excessive, or that the specific recipients are not (yet) known to it. Violations of the obligation to disclose the specific recipients may result in regulatory fines. In addition, data subjects may, pursuant to Art. 82(1) GDPR, claim compensation for non-material damage caused by insufficient compliance with the right of access.[21]

The ECJ ruling thus clarifies that controllers must, in principle, name the specific recipients of personal data. Only in exceptional cases is it permissible to limit the information to categories of recipients if the recipients are not known or if the request for information is manifestly unfounded or excessive within the meaning of the GDPR. The decision leads to greater transparency for data subjects, strengthens the data subject's rights across Europe[22] and at the same time places increased demands on documentation and the provision of information in companies.

V. Recommended further reading

Petri NJW 2023, 975.

EDPB, ‚Guidelines 01/2022 on data subject rights – Right of access', version 2.1 (28.3.2023) <https://www.edpb.europa.eu/system/files/2023-04/edpb_guidelines_202201_data_subject_rights_access_v2_en.pdf>.

On the right to explanation under Art. 15(1)(h) GDPR: ECJ 27.2.2025 – case C-203/22, ECLI:EU:C:2025:117 – D&B v Magistrat der Stadt Wien = NJW 2025, 1471.

On the scope of the right to information under Art. 15(3) sent. 1 GDPR: ECJ 4.5.2023 – case C-487/21, ECLI:EU:C:2023:369 – F. F. v Österreichische Datenschutzbehörde = NJW 2023, 2253.

21 On the conditions for the entitlement: ECJ 4.5.2023 – case C-300/21, ECLI:EU:C:2023:370, – UI v Österreichische Post AG = NJW 2023, 1930.

22 Regarding the before mentioned in general: Paal/Pauly/Paal DS-GVO Art. 15 mn. 3.

Limits of the right of access

Christoph Werkmeister/Katharina-Isabelle Prenzel

ECJ 26.10.2023 – case C-307/22, ECLI:EU:C:2023:811 – FT (copy of the patient file)

I. Case summary

Due to suspected malpractice, and for the purpose of examining potential liability claims, a patient requested from his dentist, based on Art. 15 GDPR, to provide him with a free copy of his complete patient file. The dentist refused the provision of the file for free, referencing § 630g(2) sent. 2 BGB, which grants the treating party the right to seek reimbursement for incurred costs. Following the initial success of the patient, the Federal Court of Justice (BGH), which was overseeing the appeal, referred questions to the ECJ for a preliminary ruling, including those on the interpretation of Art. 15(1) and (3) GDPR. The main issue was whether the dentist had to give a full, free copy of the patient file, even if it was for legitimate reasons not related to data protection.

II. Key legal findings

The ECJ ruled that data subjects generally have the right to receive a free copy of their processed personal data in the form of an authentic and comprehensible reproduction, regardless of the purpose of the request for access.

The ECJ ruled that the GDPR generally only allows charging data subjects for a copy of their data when they request additional copies beyond the first. Member States may have the possibility to restrict the right of access. However, such restrictions under national law must not disproportionately undermine the right to receive a free copy. Hence, imposing a flat fee for responding to an initial access request, as foreseen in the provision of § 630g(2) sent. 2 BGB, would not be in line with primary Union law.

Moreover, the ECJ held that the right of access exists irrespective of the motives of data subjects, who are not required to justify their request for access. Data subjects are therefore free to pursue other legitimate purposes unrelated to data protection (e.g., obtaining information to facilitate liability claims). That being said, data controllers have no obligation to respond to abusive requests, and they may withhold certain information, for example if the data is of a confidential nature.

Further, the ECJ held that since the initial copy must be an authentic and comprehensible reproduction of all processed personal data, data subjects ultimately have the right to a complete copy of (excerpts from) documents in a medical file, insofar as this is necessary for understanding and verifying the accuracy of the data. In the context of the case at hand, a summary provided by the controller was not considered sufficient, as the ECJ held that there was a risk that relevant information may be omitted or reproduced incorrectly.

III. Systematic context and legal classification

The right of access under Art. 15 GDPR is a key provision of the GDPR, which strengthens data subjects' rights and promotes transparency. The ECJ put emphasis on the requirement that a copy must be provided free of charge.

The ECJ also clarified that data subjects have the right to receive a free initial copy, regardless of individual motives. Although this does not open the floor for abusive requests[1], it allows data subjects to use this provision to obtain information from the controller, for example, for the purpose of asserting liability claims. The ECJ explicitly rejected the requirement that data subject access requests must serve data protection purposes, even though Rec. 63 sent. 1 GDPR allowed for such a more restrictive interpretation. The ECJ concluded though that the main text of the Regulation is ultimately binding so that the notion of a Recital cannot impose a more restrictive concept.

At the same time, the ECJ made clear that the right of access is not without limits. In particular, this right must be weighed against other fundamental rights in accordance with the principle of proportionality. The controller is therefore permitted to impose a reasonable fee under certain

1 Ligocki/Sosna/Meyer ZD 2025, 137 (140).

circumstances, for example, where the data subjects already possess a copy of the data, or where the request for access is manifestly unfounded or excessive. As a counter-exception, the ECJ clarified though that the economic interests of the controller alone are not sufficient to limit the right of access.

The decision aligns with both earlier (and later) ECJ case law, that similarly adopted a broad interpretation of the right of access and consistently reinforced the rights of data subjects, and the view of various data protection authorities across Europe.[2] Previously, in particular some German courts[3] precluded the right to receive a free initial copy in instances where requests did not pursue data protection related purposes. The ECJ decision moves the focus from whether a controller can refuse or charge for a data subject access request to how such requests should be handled, including what information must be provided or excluded.

IV. Author's analysis and commentary

This decision highlights that data protection extends beyond regulatory compliance, granting individuals greater control over their personal data as part of strengthened access rights.

From a policy perspective, the ECJ emphasises the goal of a uniformly high level of data protection across the EU, criticises national standards that contradict or unduly restrict the GDPR, strengthens the autonomy of data subjects, and signals a trend towards stricter enforcement.

In particular, the ECJ seeks to protect data subjects from financial hurdles by invalidating national fee requirements that limit the provision of a free initial copy of personal data, at least in cases where such national requirements only or predominantly serve the economic interests of the controller. In doing so, the ECJ generally denies the controller the right to refuse an access request on the grounds of individual motives. Instead, the

2 ECJ 27.5.2024 – C-312/23, ECLI:EU:C:2024:458 – Addiko Bank; ECJ 22.6.2023 – C-579/21, ECLI:EU:C:2023:501 – Pankki S; ECJ 4.5.2023 – C-487/21, ECLI:EU:C:2023:369 – CRIF; ECJ 12.1.2023 – C-154/21, ECLI:EU:C:2023:3 – Österreichische Post; EDPB, ‚Guidelines 01/2022 on data subject rights – Right of access' (28.3.2023) <https://www.edpb.europa.eu/system/files/2023-04/edpb_guidelines_202201_data_subject_rights_access_v2_en.pdf>; DSK, ‚Auskunftsrecht der betroffenen Person, Art. 15 DS-GVO' (Kurzpapier Nr. 6, 17.12.2018) <https://www.datenschutzkonferenz-online.de/media/kp/dsk_kpnr_6.pdf>.

3 OLG Nürnberg 14.3.2022 – 8 U 2907/21, ZD 2022, 463; LG Wuppertal 29.7.2021 – 4 O 409/20, r+s 2021, 696.

ECJ allows that requests can be made for (legitimate) purposes unrelated to data protection, which may include the collection/securing of evidence. Consequently, Art. 15 GDPR emerges as a significant instrument for the preparation of legal proceedings. That being said, controllers do not have to disclose all information that they hold about a data subject as there are various exemptions which prevent the production of all information that a data subject might seek to prepare a legal claim.

From a practical perspective, companies of all sizes and sectors must be prepared to deal with data subject access requests. Ideally, internal processes proactively facilitate the provision of a (to the extent required) complete, free initial copy in an efficient, secure and cost-efficient manner. State of the art data governance and data privacy compliance management systems may support that personal data can be more easily produced in a structured and extractable electronic format. Finally, the training of employees plays an essential role in ensuring the secure handling of requests for access and, where necessary, to identify and adequately document exceptional cases where a controller has no obligation to respond or can withhold certain information from production.

From a technical perspective, data controllers are well advised to consider workflows and tools to automatically extract personal data and make it available in a usable form without disclosing, for example, internal confidential information. Nevertheless, responding to complex access requests still poses challenges, especially in cases where very large amounts of data are affected and potentially subject to review before production. Also considering the rulings of the ECJ it seems reasonable that certain restrictions of the right of access must still be possible, in particular in such circumstances. This is because in instances where potentially large amounts of data may have to be reviewed it is not just the economic interest of the controller, but also fundamental rights of third parties that are often affected, for example, if the review of large amounts of data requires that the controller also reviews personal data of unaffected third parties. In this regard it is likely only a question of time when the ECJ has to decide about the utilisation of AI-assisted processes to identify personal data relating to an individual if otherwise large amounts of personal data would have to be reviewed manually. The use of AI in such cases may help reduce the privacy impact for otherwise affected third parties and could therefore strike a reasonable balance between data subject rights on the one hand and competing interests of the controller and of other third parties on the other hand in the future.

V. Recommended further reading

ECJ 27.5.2024 – C-312/23, ECLI:EU:C:2024:458 – Addiko Bank.

ECJ 22.6.2023 – C-579/21, ECLI:EU:C:2023:501 – Pankki S.

ECJ 4.5.2023 – C-487/21, ECLI:EU:C:2023:369 – CRIF.

EDPB, ‚Guidelines 01/2022 on data subject rights – Right of access' (28.3.2023) <https://www.edpb.europa.eu/system/files/2023-04/edpb_guidelines_202201_data_subject_rights_access_v2_en.pdf>.

Ligocki/Sosna/Meyer ZD 2025, 137–144 (only available in German).

Right to Erasure and Right to Object

Desara Dushi[*]

ECJ 13.5.2014 – case C-131/12, ECLI:EU:C:2014:317 – Google Spain

I. Case summary

The seminal Google Spain judgement by the ECJ affirmed the existence in the EU of a right to have personal data deleted from search engines on request, also known as the right to be forgotten or the right to erasure. The case concerns a reference for a preliminary ruling made by the Spanish High Court to the ECJ, arising out of a dispute between *Google Spain* and *Google Inc.* and the Spanish citizen *Mr. Costeja Gonzalez*, together with the *Spanish Data Protection Agency*.[1]

Mr. Costeja Gonzalez has lodged a complaint with the *Spanish Data Protection Agency* against the daily newspaper *La Vanguardia* and *Google Spain* and *Google Inc* for failure to remove the links to the newspaper article published about him in 1998. The article revealed that at the time in question, he was unable to pay his social security debts and that his property had to be sold by real estate auction to pay off the money owed. Whenever a Google search of his name was carried out, the top results listed linked the Internet user to two property auction notices for the recovery of social security debts that *Mr Costeja González* had owed 16 years earlier, which still appeared on *La Vanguardia's* website. *Mr. Costeja Gonzalez* argued that such an over a decade old information was no longer of any relevance to readers and it infringed his right to privacy, hence it should be deleted by the newspaper and that *Google* should either delete or conceal links to those pages.

The Data Protection Agency dismissed his complaint against the newspaper based on legitimate interest but found that *Google* as a search engine

* This chapter was written in the author's personal capacity. All views, interpretations, and conclusions expressed herein are solely those of the author and do not represent the views of the author's employer or any affiliated institution.

1 ECJ 13.5.2014 – case C-131/12, ECLI:EU:C:2014:317 – Google Spain.

operator, was responsible for the dissemination of data and had a direct obligation to erase upon request of the individual the data concerning them when such information 'was liable to compromise the fundamental right to data protection and the dignity of persons in the broad sense'. *Google* appealed the decision to the Spanish High Court, which considered the question a matter of EU law and referred it to the ECJ.

II. Key legal findings

One of the key legal findings of this judgment is that an internet search engine operator is responsible for the processing it carries out of personal data that appears on web pages published by third parties. Thus, if, following a search made based on a person's name, the list of results displays a link to a web page which contains information on the person in question, that data subject may approach the operator directly and, where the operator does not grant his request, bring the matter before the competent authorities in order to obtain, under certain conditions, the removal of that link from the list of results.

Accordingly, the ECJ found that the operator of a search engine is considered to be collecting data under the DPD whenever it searches automatically, constantly, and systematically for information published on the internet. The later storage of that information on its servers, and the disclosure or making available to its users in the form of lists of results, amounts to 'processing' within the meaning of the Directive. The court also held that the latter is valid even when such information concerns material that has already been published by a third party.

The ECJ further holds that the operator of the search engine is the 'controller' in respect to that processing, within the meaning of the Directive, given that the operator determines the purposes and means of processing.[2] Hence, when the activity of a search engine can significantly affect the fundamental rights to privacy and the protection of personal data, the operator of that search engine should meet the requirements of the DPD, including data subject rights such as the right to erasure. The Court held that the operator of a search engine was, in certain circumstances, obliged to remove links to web pages that are published by third parties and

2 ECJ 13.5.2014 – case C-131/12, ECLI:EU:C:2014:317 – Google Spain.

contain information relating to a person from the list of results displayed following a search made based on that person's name, even if that information is not erased from the third-party web pages.[3] The Court observed that even initially lawful processing of accurate data may, in the course of time, become incompatible with the Directive where, having regard to all the circumstances of the case, the data appear to be *inadequate, irrelevant or no longer relevant, or excessive* in relation to the purposes for which they were processed and in the light of the time that has elapsed.[4] The request for erasure of such data may be refused under public interest reasons, such as if the data subject is a public figure.

III. Systematic context and legal classification

Art. 7 and 8 CFR, which form part of EU primary law, protect privacy and personal data, respectively. On the other hand, Art. 11 CFR protects the freedom of expression and information, and Art. 16 CFR protects the freedom to conduct business. The ECJ recognized that when balancing the different fundamental rights at stake, it is necessary to reach a fair balance between the rights to privacy and the right to the protection of personal data, on the one hand, and the freedom of expression and right to information of search engine users on the other.[5] That means that information is not automatically removed just because someone does not like it; a legal balancing test must be held. The ECJ further established that, as a general rule, the right to privacy and to protection of personal data prevail over freedom of information, except when there is public relevance in the information, depending on the role played by the data subject in public life.[6]

The Google Spain judgment pre-dates the GDPR, which was adopted in 2016. Personal data protection law in the EU consisted of the DPD of 1995. The Directive required Member States to enact legislation ensuring that personal data are processed fairly and lawfully.[7] It further imposes obligations on data controllers to collect personal data solely for specified,

3 ECJ 13.5.2014 – case C-131/12, ECLI:EU:C:2014:317 – Google Spain.
4 ECJ 13.5.2014 – case C-131/12, ECLI:EU:C:2014:317 – Google Spain.
5 ECJ 13.5.2014 – case C-131/12, ECLI:EU:C:2014:317 para. 81 – Google Spain.
6 ECJ 13.5.2014 – case C-131/12, ECLI:EU:C:2014:317 – Google Spain.
7 Art. 6(1)(a) DPD.

explicit, and legitimate purposes;[8] to limit collection to what is necessary for those purposes;[9] to ensure that data are accurate and kept up to date, taking every reasonable step to secure their rectification or erasure where they are inaccurate;[10] and to retain personal data only for so long as is necessary for the purposes for which they are processed.[11]

Erasure of data was one of the elements of the data subject's right of access to data.[12] As such, Art. 12(b) of the DPD enshrined the obligation of the controller to rectify, erase or block the data the processing of which did not comply with the Directive, in particular due to the incompleteness or inaccuracy of data. The Directive also granted data subjects the right to object to the processing of data relating to them.[13] Member States can make an exception to these rules where such measures are necessary in order to reconcile the right to privacy with freedom of expression, in particular in relation to processing undertaken for journalistic, artistic, or literary purposes.[14]

The ECJ affirmed the existence of a right to erasure in the EU, but clearly stated that such a right does not amount to the obligation of controllers to remove data immediately. The controller is obliged to first conduct a balancing test between the public interest of internet users and the data subject's fundamental rights to privacy and data protection.

IV. Author's analysis and commentary

The Google Spain judgment is particularly significant as it laid the foundation for an explicit right to erasure, commonly referred to as the right to be forgotten, which was subsequently enshrined in Art. 17 of the GDPR, the regulation that replaced the DPD. The Court established that search engine results containing outdated or irrelevant personal data may be delisted following a balancing exercise between privacy and public interest. The right to erasure, first recognized in this case and later set out in the GDPR, illustrates how EU legislation reacts to case law that reveals gaps in older legislation.

8 Art. 6(1)(b) DPD.
9 Art. 6(1)(c) DPD.
10 Art. 6(1)(d) DPD.
11 Art. 6(1)(e) DPD.
12 Art. 12(b) DPD.
13 Art. 14 DPD.
14 Art. 9 DPD.

ECJ bases its decision concerning the erasure of personal data on the fundamental rights to privacy and data protection as enshrined in the Charter. However, the Court does not go further into its assessment of these fundamental rights in its reasoning.[15] The Court establishes the need to perform a balancing test before complying with an erasure request, but it falls short of providing any particular specifications regarding the factors and circumstances that lead to such a balance. Additionally, the ECJ expresses a general presumption on the prevalence of the right to privacy, without any further elaboration. This statement seems to undermine the importance of the balancing test,[16] and the equal footing of fundamental rights. Despite these shortcomings, this case is of significant importance in that it establishes the responsibility of private corporations for the fundamental rights implications of their actions.[17]

While this case is famous for its relevance regarding the establishment of a right to erasure, elements of the right to object under Art. 14 of the DPD (subsequently Art. 21 GDPR) can be identified. The right to object in this judgment plays a complementary procedural role, allowing data subjects to challenge processing based on legitimate interests; in practice, successful objections in search engine contexts can lead to erasure or delisting. This interrelationship between the right to object and the right to erasure is expressly reflected in Art. 17(1)(c) GDPR. Art. 17(1)(c) GDPR recognises the right of the data subject to object to processing pursuant to Art. 21(1) GDPR when there are no overriding legitimate grounds for data processing, or when the data subject objects to data processing performed for direct marketing purposes as enshrined in Art. 21(2) GDPR.

V. Recommended further reading

Mantelero, 'One-Stop-Shop thematic case digest Right to Object and Right to Erasure' (9.12.2022) <https://www.edpb.europa.eu/system/files/2023-02/one-stop-shop_case_digest_on_the_right_to_object_and_right_to_erasure_en.pdf>.

15 Frantziou Human Rights Law Review, Volume 14, Issue 4, p. 761 et seqq.
16 Frantziou Human Rights Law Review, Volume 14, Issue 4, p. 761 et seqq.
17 Frantziou Human Rights Law Review, Volume 14, Issue 4, p. 761 et seqq.

Fomperosa Rivero, 'Right to Be Forgotten in the European Court of Justice Google Spain Case: The Right Balance of Privacy Rights, Procedure, and Extraterritoriality, European Union Law Working Papers, No. 19, Stanford-Vienna Transatlantic Technology Law Forum (2017)' (13.2.2017) <https://law.stanford.edu/publications/right-to-be-forgotten-in-the-european-court-of-justice-google-spain-case-the-right-balance-of-privacy-rights-procedure-and-extraterritoriality/>.

Frantziou Human Rights Law Review, Volume 14, Issue 4, p. 761 et seqq.

The Right to Erasure/The 'Right to be Forgotten'

Katelyn Ringrose

ECJ 13.5.2014 - case C-131/12, ECLI:EU:C:2014:317 - Google Spain SL and Google Inc. v Agencia Española de Protección de Datos (AEPD) and Mario Costeja González

I. Case summary

The 2014 ECJ judgment in *Google Spain* laid the groundwork for the GDPR's Art. 17 Right to Erasure (commonly known as the 'right to be forgotten'), fostering tension between new individual privacy rights and freedom of information.[1] The proceedings began in 2010 when Mario Costeja González lodged a complaint with the AEPD against Google, Google's Spanish subsidiary, and a Spanish newspaper, *La Vanguardia*, arguing that publicly accessible 1990s newspaper links detailing a property sale linked to past debt collection efforts which had concluded years prior was outdated, irrelevant, and infringed his right to privacy.

The AEPD dismissed the complaint against the publisher but upheld it against Google, instructing the company to withdraw the data from its search index. Google appealed to the Spanish National High Court and then to the ECJ, posing critical questions regarding the interpretation of the DPD. Google argued that it, and its subsidiary Google Spain, merely facilitated access to *La Vanguardia*. The ECJ ruled for Costeja González, holding that individuals may request that search engine operators—as controllers—remove links 'inadequate, irrelevant or no longer relevant, or excessive in relation to the purposes of the processing and in the light of the time that has elapsed.'[2] The balancing test used by the ECJ weighs

1 ECJ 13.5.2014 - case C-131/12, ECLI:EU:C:2014:317 - Google Spain SL and Google Inc. v Agencia Española de Protección de Datos (AEPD) and Mario Costeja González.

2 ECJ 13.5.2014 - case C-131/12, ECLI:EU:C:2014:317 para. 81, 97 - Google Spain SL and Google Inc. v Agencia Española de Protección de Datos (AEPD) and Mario Costeja González.

fundamental rights to privacy and data protection[3] against economic and public interests, concluding that the data subject's right to be forgotten generally take precedence.

II. Key legal findings

The *Google Spain* judgment introduced several groundbreaking interpretations of the DPD, setting the stage for modern EU data protection law as established by the GDPR. First, as described below, it laid the groundwork for extraterritorial application of EU law when it comes to 'establishing' activities within the EU. Second, it established the criteria for when a search engine operator is acting as a processor versus as a controller. Third, and finally, it established the importance of 'dereferencing,' also known as delisting, as an alternative to deleting data even when original content on a third-party website remains lawful and unaltered.

1. Establishment in the EU

The ECJ adopted an expansive, functional interpretation of the DPD's territorial scope. Google Inc. argued that the data processing for searches pertaining to Costeja González occurred outside the EU and that its Spanish subsidiary, Google Spain, was only involved in selling advertising. The AEDP and the ECJ found that Google's subsidiary were 'inextricably linked..'[4] Since advertising sales in Spain made the search engine economically viable, the Court held the entire data processing operation was carried out 'in the context of the activities of an establishment of the controller on the territory of a Member State,' subjecting Google Inc. to Spanish—and therefore EU—data protection law as applied by Spain's supervisory authority, the AEPD. This scope is carried through in Art. 3 of the GDPR, where the Regulation has extraterritorial application over controllers or processors processing the personal data of EU persons.

3 Art. 7 and 8 CFR.

4 ECJ 13.5.2014 – case C-131/12, ECLI:EU:C:2014:317 para. 55 – Google Spain SL and Google Inc. v Agencia Española de Protección de Datos (AEPD) and Mario Costeja González.

2. Search Engine Operators as Processors v. Controllers

The Court addressed the nature of a search engine's operations, differentiating between the operator's activities as a processor and controller:[5]

a) Processor

The activities of automatically, constantly, and systematically exploring, indexing, retrieving, and making online information available were classified as 'processing of personal data.' Such activities qualify as more than mere temporary storage. This classification was deemed valid regardless of the search engine's, or in this case the Spanish subsidiary of Google's (available at www.google.es), failure to distinguish between personal and non-personal data.[6]

b) Controller

A search engine operator was held to be the controller' when it 'determines the purposes and means' of the data processing. The Court explicitly dismissed the Advocate General's opinion, which had required operators to have knowledge or intention to achieve controller status. The court's interpretation instead focused on the significant *impact* of the search engine's activities on the data subject's fundamental rights, necessitating its classification as a controller to ensure effective data protection. After all, in the court's view, there is no larger changemaker than the search engine indexing the world's information and, amongst other controller-like behav-

5 See Article 29 Data Protection Working Party, ‚Guidelines on the implementation of the court of justice of the European Union Judgement on "Google Spain"' (WP225, 26.11.2014) <https://ec.europa.eu/newsroom/article29/items/667236/en>; see also EDPB, ‚Guidelines 07/2020 on the Concepts of Controller and Processor in the GDPR', version 2.1 (7.7.2021) <https://www.edpb.europa.eu/system/files_en?file=2023-10/EDPB_guidelines_202007_controllerprocessor_final_en.pdf>.

6 ECJ 13.5.2014 – case C-131/12, ECLI:EU:C:2014:317 para. 28 – Google Spain SL and Google Inc. v Agencia Española de Protección de Datos (AEPD) and Mario Costeja González.

iors, Google Spain had held itself out as a controller in its negotiations over previous advertising contracts with Google Inc.[7]

3. Dereferencing as an Alternative to Deletion

The ECJ affirmed that the aggregation of scattered information by a search engine—compiling a 'vast number of aspects' concerning an individual's digital life—creates an especially comprehensive set of sensitive information such that the information is of a heightened impact when searchable. Consequently, the Court found the right to erasure. The right, under *Google Spain's* logic, mandates dereferencing where the information is outdated or irrelevant, effectively introducing the *Google Spain* balancing test: the individual's rights will, as a general rule, override the economic interest of the operator and the general public's interest, unless the latter is critical, especially when the person plays a prominent role in public life.

III. Systematic context and legal classification

The *Google Spain* judgment is the judicial precursor and foundational reference point for the modern Right to Erasure, codified in Art. 17 of the GDPR.

While the DPD provided a right to have data erased if its processing was unlawful or incompatible with the Directive; *Google Spain* expanded this right by recognizing that even lawful original data could become unlawful for a company's continued publication due to the passage of time or loss of relevance. The concept of *unnecessary information* forms the philosophical bedrock of Art. 17 of the GDPR. The decision of when data is no longer necessary is, of course, complicated in the age of AI—when models are fueled by the ingestion of large amounts of data, much of it perhaps unnecessary for alternative uses.[8]

The *Google Spain* decision is fundamentally an affirmation of the data subject's right to informational self-determination. By focusing on the

7 ECJ 13.5.2014 – case C-131/12, ECLI:EU:C:2014:317 para. 33 – Google Spain SL and Google Inc. v Agencia Española de Protección de Datos (AEPD) and Mario Costeja González.

8 Christakis, AI Hallucinations and Data Subject Rights under the GDPR, 2024 (discussing how data subject rights function in light of the rise of AI adoption).

uniquely detrimental effects a search engine results page can have on a person's life, the ECJ embraced a data subject's ability to control their digital identity. The ECJ's interpretation provided a specific mechanism to allow for practical obscurity. Information that was once difficult to find (e.g., an archived newspaper notice available on microfiche) is rendered almost instantly accessible by a name search. The judgment countered this perceived digital permanence by establishing a right to erase that digital record. Importantly, the case did not outline a stringent retention guideline for exactly when information available over a search engine becomes outdated, rather that over time information may become no longer necessary—a standard that will vary upon the circumstances of each data subject request.

The core innovation offered by *Google Spain* was the explicit systematic integration of the CFR into the DPD's application. The Court's analysis anchored data protection in Art. 7 and 8 of the CFR and clarified that while the public interest in freedom of information (Art. 11 CFR) is protected, the rights to privacy and data protection are generally paramount. The act of enshrining data protection into a rights-centric model is a key feature of EU law. The decision also drew a clear boundary: the right to erasure applies to the search engine index, not the source publication, attempting to protect journalistic freedom and the public's right to access public information while addressing the issues posed by search engine results. This nuance often prevents the ruling from being interpreted as a generalized form of censorship.

IV. Author's analysis and commentary

Google Spain significance lies in its successful, yet controversial, extension of pre-digital data protection principles to the structure of internet intermediaries, particularly those operating across borders. It firmly established that an organization's role in aggregating and indexing information is sufficient to incur the highest data protection obligations (and the highest penalties when those obligations are violated). The judicial version of the 'right to be forgotten' based on the principle of information being 'no longer relevant' for processing was adopted as a tool to individual privacy the internet's so-called perfect memory, while attempting to preserve public knowledge.

Despite the balancing test adopted by the ECJ, the ruling created a massive compliance burden for search engine operators, requiring them to transition from being purely technical facilitators of information to being adjudicators of fundamental rights in each individual dereferencing request. This forced companies like Google to devise a detailed, case-by-case assessment model, which considers: the nature and sensitivity of the data (e.g., health information, sexual orientation or gender identity data, criminal records); how long ago the event occurred; the public role of the data subject (e.g., is the person a public figure where the public interest in access is heightened?); and whether the data is critical to journalistic, artistic, or academic purposes.

For data protection officers and compliance professionals responding to Data Subject Requests, the outcome of *Google Spain* mandates not only a robust, auditable system for managing requests but also a comprehensive internal policy on how to weigh competing fundamental rights. The default position of those decisions should be to favor the data subject unless an overriding public interest can be clearly demonstrated.

Google Spain also provided the model for the EU's asserted extra-territorial reach. By tying the search engine's non-EU data processing to its EU-based, revenue-generating establishment, the ECJ created a nexus that has since been expanded in subsequent EU regulations. This set the global standard for how multinational companies structure their compliance programs, further differentiating between EU and non-EU data processing activities, although a number of global laws (e.g., US state legislation like the California Consumer Privacy Act (CCPA), Canada's[9] Personal Information Protection and Electronic Documents Act (PIPEDA), South Korea's Personal Information Privacy Law, and more) have adopted the ideas outlined in *Google Spain.*[10]

The critical policy debate of global enforcement was addressed later in the 2019 *Google v CNIL* case. The French Data Protection Authority

9 See the CCPA's right to deletion, codified at California Civil Code Section 1798.105; Canada's Personal Information Protection and Electronic Documents Act is S.C. 2000, c. 5. (the right to dereferencing); South Korea's PIPC (right to request deletion).

10 Cofone, I. (ed.), The Right to be Forgotten: A Canadian and Comparative Perspective, 2020 (discussing various global perspectives).

(CNIL) sought to impose dereferencing globally.[11] The ECJ chose not to require global dereferencing, ruling that EU law does not currently impose an obligation to apply the right to be forgotten on all global versions of a search engine. However, the Court mandated that search operators must implement 'sufficiently effective measures,' such as geo-blocking from within all EU Member States, to prevent EU users from accessing the dereferenced links.[12] The case prioritized the effective protection of EU data subjects *within the Union* while attempting to avoid an aggressive assertion of regulatory authority over the entire global internet, a move that would have provoked greater international legal conflict, particularly with US-based organizations and free-speech advocates. This decision attempts to balance the goals of robust EU data protection with the reality of international sovereignty and cross-border data governance. Of course, dereferencing in one region over another poses its own technical challenges for global operators.

The *Google Spain* framework is now embodied by Art. 17 of the GDPR, but its principles remain essential for interpretation. Art. 17(1)(a) GDPR mandates erasure when data is 'no longer necessary' for the purposes for which it was collected or otherwise processed, a direct reference to the 'no longer relevant' standard set by the ECJ. The exceptions, especially those outlined in Art. 17(3) GDPR as 'overriding legitimate grounds,' reflect the ECJ's balancing test, where processing necessary for exercising the right of freedom of expression and information or public interest archiving is taken into account. The ongoing challenge for policymakers and courts is the application of this balance to new forms of data processing, such as AI-driven content generation which is often reliant on personal information. The fundamental right to control one's digital narrative, embodied by *Google Spain*, will continue to serve as the benchmark for balancing individual rights against freedom of information and technological advancement.

V. Recommended further reading

Bartolini/Siry CLSR Vol. 32 (2016), 218–237.

11 Fleischer, 'Implementing a European, not global, right to be forgotten' (Google Europe Blog, 30.7.2015) <https://europe.googleblog.com/2015/07/implementing-european-not-global-right.html>.

12 ECJ 24.9.2019 – case C-507/17, ECLI:EU:C:2019:772 para. 64–73 – Google.

Cofone (ed.), The Right to be Forgotten: A Canadian and Comparative Perspective, 2020.

Christakis, AI Hallucinations and Data Subject Rights under the GDPR: Regulatory Perspectives and Industry Responses, 2024.

On the deletion of personal data from government registers

Stefan Brink

BGH 23.1.2024 – II ZB 7/23, NJW 2024, 1577

I. Case summary

The managing director of a limited liability company (GmbH) is entered in the commercial register with his date of birth and place of residence. His request to have this data removed from the commercial register on the grounds that his professional activity involves handling explosives, meaning that he could become the victim of kidnapping or robbery in order to obtain the substances he handles, was rejected by the registry court, as was the appeal to the Higher Regional Court of Celle, in which he had alternatively requested that his date of birth and place of residence be disclosed to third parties from the commercial register only after a balancing of interests. The appeal was also unsuccessful.

II. Key legal findings

In the opinion of the Federal Court of Justice, the appellant's claim for the removal of his date of birth and place of residence from his entry as managing director of a limited liability company in the commercial register does not arise from the GDPR or from national law. A claim for the removal of the data pursuant to Art. 17(1) and (2) GDPR is excluded under Art. 17(3)(b) alt. 1 GDPR, according to which the entry, storage, and disclosure of the date of birth and place of residence of a GmbH managing director in the commercial register is necessary to fulfill a legal obligation of the registry court.

The date of birth and place of residence of the Ast. are personal data within the meaning of Art. 2(1), Art. 4(1) GDPR. Their entry and storage in the electronically maintained commercial register (§§ 8(1) and 8a(1) HGB) and their disclosure by allowing unrestricted access to the commercial register (§§ 9 and 10(2) HGB) constitute processing within the meaning of Art. 2(1)(1) and (2) and Art. 4 no. 2 GDPR. The registry court entrusted with maintaining the electronic commercial register pursuant to § 8(1) HGB at is the controller for this data processing within the meaning of Art. 4 no. 7 GDPR, including for its disclosure via the central register portal (www.handelsregister.de) set up on the Internet pursuant to § 9(1) sent. 4 HGB.

According to Art. 17(1) GDPR, the data subject may, on one of the grounds specified therein, request the controller to erase data concerning him or her in accordance with Art. 17(2) GDPR; however, this right is excluded in the present case because the data processing in the commercial register is necessary for the fulfillment of a legal obligation of the registry court. As follows from Rec. 41 sent. 1 of the GDPR, this legal obligation does not necessarily have to be standardized in a parliamentary law; in the present case, it arises from pre-constitutional law and customary law pursuant to Art. 123 (1) GG. According to § 7(1) and § 8(1)(1) and (2) GmbHG, the registration of the company must be accompanied by the identification of the managing directors and the date of birth of the managing director must be stated (§ 24(1) Commercial Register Order of August 10, 1937). Although there is no express legal obligation to state the place of residence of the managing director when registering the company, this is nevertheless justified under customary law. These legal obligations of the registry court pursue an objective in the public interest within the meaning of Art. 6(3) sent. 2 and 4 GDPR; they ensure the protection of the security, fairness, and ease of legal transactions in the commercial and corporate sector. The principle of proportionality is upheld in this regard, as the disclosure of the date of birth and place of residence is suitable for enabling the reliable individualization and identification of the managing director. The necessity of disclosing this data through its unrestricted availability on the internet must also be affirmed. The goal of giving any interested person the opportunity to obtain essential information about the formation of commercial companies and the persons entrusted with their representation as easily as possible, regardless of their location and without delay, from a reliable source of information can only be achieved by granting unrestricted access to this data on the internet without any particular effort or obstacles. The disadvantages caused by this data processing are not disproportionate to the objectives pursued, since the processing is limited to a small amount of personal data which is neither particularly sensitive within the meaning of Rec. 51 sent. 1 of the GDPR nor particularly intrusive in terms of privacy;

this also applies to the disclosure of the place of residence, as this does not reveal the full private address, but merely provides a local restriction. By limiting the personal details of a GmbH managing director that must be entered and disclosed to a few basic pieces of personal data, the legislator has, in accordance with the principle of data minimization (Art. 5(1)(c) GDPR) and the guarantee of data security, the legislator has found an appropriate compromise between the interest in information for legal transactions on the one hand and the interest in confidentiality of the persons concerned on the other.

This also applies if, due to the nature of the company's business, there is a generally increased risk to the managing director. If exceptions to the processing of basic data of a GmbH managing director were to be allowed on the basis of a general risk, the publicity and information function of the commercial register, which is in the public interest, would no longer be sufficiently guaranteed.

The Federal Court of Justice left open the question of whether, in special exceptional cases, such as evidence of concrete danger to life and limb, a different assessment or possibly a restrictive interpretation of the legal requirements might be appropriate.

The court also ruled that the manager could not demand a restriction of processing under Art. 18(1)(d) or Art. 21(1) sent. 2 GDPR on the basis of the objection raised by him, because the conditions for a right of objection pursuant to Art. 21(1) sent. 1 GDPR are not met if the data processing is carried out on the basis of Art. 6(1)(c) GDPR to fulfill a legal obligation of the controller. This also applies if the processing is permitted at the same time under Art. 6(1)(e) GDPR. In any case, the data subject must present specific facts relating to their particular situation which could exceptionally justify refraining from collection, which is not the case here.

III. Systematic context and legal classification

The right to erasure under Art. 17 GDPR, similar to the right to restriction of processing under Art. 18 GDPR, is at the heart of the rights of data subjects under the GDPR. Information obtained from the controller about its data stocks via the right of access under Art. 15 GDPR can be effectively restricted in practice via the right to erasure or blocking, as well as via the right to rectification (Art. 16 GDPR).

In return, Art. 17(3) GDPR provides the controller with arguments in its favor with which it can defend its data against requests for erasure by the data subject. An important aspect here, according to Art. 17(3)(b) GDPR, is that the controller processes the data to fulfill a legal obligation – in this case, to fulfill the purposes of the commercial register – and in doing so complies with the principle of data minimization under Art. 5(1)(c) GDPR. The law of the Union or of the Member State is decisive for this legal obligation of the controller. In addition to formal and substantive laws, this law also includes customary law, insofar as the EU or the Member State recognizes this as a source of law. This also establishes a link to the processing conditions of Art. 6 GDPR: According to Art. 6(1)(c) GDPR, processing is lawful if it is necessary for compliance with a legal obligation to which the controller is subject. According to Art. 6(3) sent. 2 GDPR, this legal basis must specify the purpose of the processing and, according to Art. 6(3) sent. 4 GDPR, pursue an objective in the public interest and be proportionate to the legitimate purpose pursued.

IV. Author's analysis and commentary

The thoroughly reasoned decision is convincing in many respects, as it accurately sets out the relevant national and European law and presents it in a systematically correct manner.

However, doubts arise on one crucial point: the assumption that a customary legal obligation to register—in this case, to provide the place of residence of the managing director—could constitute a sufficient legal basis for data processing by the registry court is not convincing. It is true that both Art. 17(3)(b) GDPR and Art. 6(1)(c), (3) sent 1 GDPR refer only to a 'legal' and not a statutory processing obligation and thus seem to open the field for unwritten legal bases for processing. However, this is flanked at the European level by Art. 6(3) sent. 2 GDPR, according to which this legal basis must determine the purpose of the processing, and at the national constitutional level by the reservation of law. According to this, a restriction of fundamental rights (Art. 7 and 8 CFR, Art. 2(1) in conjunction with Art. 1(1) GG) can only be considered through written law.

Although the Federal Court of Justice endeavors to derive the binding nature of the obligation to register the place of residence of the managing director under national law from a historical perspective,[1] doubts as to its scope already arise from the Commercial Law Reform Act of June 22, 1998,[2] which for the first time created an obligation to state the date of birth and replaced the previous requirement to state the profession or status, but did not expressly include a registration requirement for the place of residence in the law. Thus, the Federal Court of Justice's argumentation becomes problematic at the latest when it comes to the mandatory determination of the purpose of processing 'in this legal basis' (Art. 6(3) sent. 2 GDPR), which is hardly possible in the case of a customary legal basis. The Federal Court of Justice's comments on this processing purpose[3] therefore remain deficient. The Federal Court of Justice also recognizes that the purpose of data processing is not expressly named as such in the above-mentioned legal bases, but it follows from the provision in § 9(1) sent. 1 HGB, according to which 'anyone is permitted to inspect the commercial register ... for information purposes by means of individual retrievals'. This satisfies the legal requirement for the purpose to be specified in Art. 6(3) sent. 2 GDPR.

Although this is a bold argument, it is not at all convincing.[4] This is particularly true since § 9 HGB clearly defines the group of persons authorized to inspect the register and does not specify any specific purposes for inspection. The objections are also clear under constitutional law, as the reservation of law is intended to safeguard the parliamentary purpose of the legislature – and this is obviously lacking in customary law.

The further supporting argumentation of the Federal Court of Justice is also unconvincing: Insofar as it states[5] that the managing director, 'by taking up his office and applying for entry in the commercial register, himself gives rise to the data processing or is responsible for it', 'whereby he is aware at that moment of the associated disclosure of the data in question in the commercial register', this is clearly a petitio principii. The Federal Court of Justice is attempting to use the provision, the effectiveness of which is currently under review, to justify the lawfulness of the data processing. This is already systematically flawed; moreover, the consent of the managing director pursuant to Art. 6(1)(a) GDPR is not at issue here, which is why his 'state of mind' is precisely irrelevant.

1 BGH 23.1.2024 – II ZB 7/23, NJW 2024, 1577 mn. 20 et seq.
2 BGBl 1998 I 1474.
3 BGH 23.1.2024 – II ZB 7/23, NJW 2024, 1577 mn. 32.
4 As was already the case in BFH 5.9.2023 – IX R 32/21, NJW 2023, 3668 mn. 43.
5 BGH 23.1.2024 – II ZB 7/23, NJW 2024, 1577 mn. 52.

However, we agree with the Federal Court of Justice insofar as it rejects an extension of the right to object under Art. 21(1) GDPR to the cases covered by Art. 6(1)(c) GDPR. The grounds for permission under Art. 6(1) GDPR are fundamentally independent and of equal rank, meaning that each ground for permission under Art. 6 GDPR justifies the processing independently and completely. This independent legitimizing effect of the other grounds for permission would be devalued if the right to object under Art. 21 GDPR were to be extended arbitrarily and applied to grounds not mentioned.[6]

V. Recommended further reading

Further relevant decisions can be found in ECJ 9.3.2017 – case C-398/15, ECLI:EU:C:2017:197 para. 57, 60 – Camera di Commercio, Industria, Artigianato e Agricoltura di Lecce v Salvatore Manni, according to which, when weighing up the conflicting interests in the case of disclosure of personal data of the representative body of a corporation, both the need to protect the interests of third parties vis-à-vis these companies and to ensure legal certainty, as well as the fairness of commercial transactions and thus the smooth functioning of the internal market, take precedence over the fundamental rights of the data subject under Art. 7 and 8 CFR.

Also instructive is ECJ 22.11.2022 – joined cases C-37/20 and C-601/20, ECLI:EU:C:2022:912 para. 87 – Luxembourg Business Registers on public access to information about the beneficial owners of registered companies or legal entities.

Reference is made to the parallel decision BGH 23.1.2024 – II ZB 8/23, FGPrax 2024, 109 on the limited partner's application for deletion of his date of birth and place of residence from the commercial register.

6 See also Paal/Pauly DS-GVO BDSG/Martini, 4th edn. 2026, DS-GVO Art. 21 mn. 45a, end of sentence.

Strongly Drawing on Automated Decision-Making Preparations

Moritz Köhler

ECJ 7.12.2023 – case C-634/21, ECLI:EU:C:2023:957 – OQ v Land Hessen, SCHUFA

I. Case summary

The judgment to be discussed here is based on a reference for a preliminary ruling referred by the Administrative Court of Wiesbaden. The latter had to deal with the question of whether the business practices of the German credit agency SCHUFA are compatible with the prohibition of automated individual decision-making laid down in Art. 22(1) GDPR.[1] SCHUFA collects information on individuals and uses mathematical and statistical methods to predict the solvency and willingness to pay of the person concerned. SCHUFA's contractual partners can request the calculated score. They use it, for example, when preparing a decision on granting credit to the data subject. The final decision on whether to conclude a contract therefore lies with the credit institutions. In practice, however, SCHUFA's score has a strong influence on the decision-making.[2]

While the Administrative Court of Wiesbaden already considered the applicability of Art. 22(1) GDPR to be justified in the initial proceedings due to the calculation of the score by SCHUFA,[3] the credit agency argued that its contribution to the decision-making process was limited to a mere supporting role, so that the prohibition of automated individual decision-

1 VG Wiesbaden 1.10.2021 – 6 K 788/20, ZD 2022, 121.

2 In this regard VG Wiesbaden 1.10.2021 – 6 K 788/20, ZD 2022, 121 mn. 25; Commissioner for Data Protection and Freedom of Information Baden-Württemberg, ‚Scoring – solide Prognose oder miese Nummer?' (Juni 2021) <https://www.baden-wuerttemberg.datenschutz.de/wp-content/uploads/2021/06/20210629_Scoring_web.pdf>, p. 5.

3 VG Wiesbaden 1.10.2021 – 6 K 788/20, ZD 2022, 121 mn. 21.

making only came into play when the contractual partners made the actual contractual decision.[4]

II. Key legal findings

In its ruling, the ECJ has decided ‚that the automated establishment, by a credit information agency, of a probability value based on personal data relating to a person and concerning his or her ability to meet payment commitments in the future constitutes "automated individual decision-making" within the meaning of that provision, where a third party, to which that probability value is transmitted, draws strongly on that probability value to establish, implement or terminate a contractual relationship with that person'[5].

The ECJ thus expressly interprets the term 'decision' within the meaning of Art. 22(1) GDPR broadly.[6] It does not merely encompass the final choice between two alternative courses of action, such as accepting or rejecting a contract offer. Rather, the term 'decision' within the meaning of the prohibition of automated individual decision-making may also include measures that, according to conventional understanding, are attributable to decision preparation.[7] The decisive factor for the applicability of Art. 22(1) GDPR is whether someone's actions draw strongly on a solely automated measure of decision preparation and whether these actions have legal effects on the data subject or similarly significantly affect them.[8] In this case, the automated measure of decision preparation is already to be regarded as a decision within the meaning of Art. 22(1) GDPR.

4 ECJ 7.12.2023 – case C-634/21, ECLI:EU:C:2023:957 para. 16 – OQ v Land Hessen, SCHUFA.

5 ECJ 7.12.2023 – case C-634/21, ECLI:EU:C:2023:957 para. 73 – OQ v Land Hessen, SCHUFA.

6 ECJ 7.12.2023 – case C-634/21, ECLI:EU:C:2023:957 para. 45 – OQ v Land Hessen, SCHUFA.

7 Cf. ECJ 7.12.2023 – case C-634/21, ECLI:EU:C:2023:957 para. 46 – OQ v Land Hessen, SCHUFA.

8 ECJ 7.12.2023 – case C-634/21, ECLI:EU:C:2023:957 para. 48 – OQ v Land Hessen, SCHUFA.

III. Systematic context and legal classification

The ECJ did not follow the prevailing opinion in German-language literature with this interpretation. The latter had interpreted the term 'decision' narrowly and defined it as an act of choice between at least two alternative courses of action.[9] The undisputed influence of decision-preparation measures on decision-making was then discussed on the basis of the criterion ‚solely' within the meaning of Art. 22(1) GDPR.[10] Based on etymological considerations alone, the majority of German-language literature had to conclude on this dogmatic basis that the establishment of score values by SCHUFA does not constitute a decision and that the decision of the contracting parties is not made solely on automated processing.[11]

From a German perspective, the ECJ's decision represents a dogmatic upheaval. Numerous reactions to the ruling were correspondingly critical. *Paal*, for example, considered the Advocate General's opinion to be 'in need of further justification' and deemed his reasoning insufficient.[12] However, in the opinion of some commentators, the ECJ also failed to provide a satisfactory justification.[13]

Nevertheless, the final word rests with the ECJ: the term 'decision' within the meaning of Art. 22(1) GDPR must be interpreted broadly and does not *a priori* exclude measures taken in preparation for a decision. Since a measure taken in preparation for a decision does not in itself have a qualifying effect within the meaning of Art. 22(1) GDPR, the criterion of drawing strongly on preparatory measures, which the ECJ has taken over from the question referred by the Administrative Court of Wiesbaden, will play a central role in the further debate. The Advocate General had already pointed out the need for national courts to define this criterion more

9 Schwartmann/Jaspers/Thüsing/Kugelmann Heidelberger Kommentar DS-GVO/BDSG/Atzert, 3rd edn. 2024, DSGVO Art. 22 mn. 46; Ehmann/Selmayr Datenschutz-Grundverordnung/Hladjk, 3rd edn. 2024, DSGVO Art. 22 mn. 5; BeckOK Datenschutzrecht/v. Lewinski, 54th edn. 2025, DSGVO Art. 22 mn. 14; Paal/Pauly DS-GVO BDSG/Martini, 4th edn. 2026, Art. 22 mn. 15a.

10 Schwartmann/Jaspers/Thüsing/Kugelmann/Atzert DSGVO Art. 22 mn. 46; Ehmann/Selmayr/Hladjk DSGVO Art. 22 mn. 5; BeckOK Datenschutzrecht/v. Lewinski DSGVO Art. 22 mn. 14; Paal/Pauly/Martini Art. 22 mn. 15a.

11 Krämer NJW 2020, 497 (498); Paal ZfDR 2023, 114 (138); Taeger RDV 2017, 3 (6).

12 Paal ZfDR 2023, 114 (138).

13 Dubovitskaya/Bosold ZIP 2024, 1805 (1807); Söbbing/Schwarz ZD 2024, 157 (163 f.); Thüsing RDV 2026, 5 (6 f.); Ziegenhorn CR 2024, 586 (589).

precisely.[14] Subsequently, the Regional Court of Bamberg first had to deal with the interpretation of Art. 22(1) GDPR in civil proceedings. It took the view that even the consideration of other factors outside the score value, such as income and assets, was not sufficient to exclude the applicability of Art. 22(1) GDPR. According to the interpretation of the Regional Court of Bamberg, a strong drawing on the preparatory measure can only be rejected if the probability values 'play no role' in the decision-making process.[15]

IV. Author's analysis and commentary

The ECJ's broad interpretation of the term 'decision' within the meaning of Art. 22(1) GDPR is to be welcomed. A decision consists of several phases or actions.[16] A behavioural science model distinguishes, for example, between problem formulation, information gathering, searching for alternatives, comparative evaluation, selection between the formulated alternatives and their implementation.[17] Contrary to what was assumed in German-language legal literature prior to the ECJ ruling, the act of selection alone cannot be decisive for the application of Art. 22(1) GDPR, as it is usually only the implementation of the selection made that has a qualifying effect within the meaning of the provision.

Furthermore, the narrow interpretation of the term 'decision' fails to recognise the substantive determination of the selection act, which results from the various preceding decision-making measures. Ignoring this substantive predetermination of the selection act would render the prohibition of automated individual decisions ineffective in numerous cases. In the GDPR, this circumstance is also taken into account in a similar manner in the broad formulation of the requirement of a significant impairment.[18] Furthermore, it follows from Rec. 71 sent. 1 GDPR that a decision may

14 AG Pikamäe 16.3.2023 – case C-634/21, ECLI:EU:C:2023:220 para. 45 – OQ v Land Hessen, SCHUFA.

15 LG Bamberg 26.3.2025 – 41 O 749/24 KOIN, GRUR-RS 2025, 7269 mn. 28. Critical of this judgement Köhler RDV 2025, 188 f.

16 In detail SWK-Legal Tech/Nink, 6th edn. 2024, Entscheidungsfindung, automatisierte mn. 7.

17 Haun, Cognitive Organisation, 2016, p. 49.

18 ECJ 7.12.2023 – case C-634/21, ECLI:EU:C:2023:957 para. 44 – OQ v Land Hessen, SCHUFA.

comprise various measures and, accordingly, also actions prior to the final selection act.[19]

The ECJ's broad interpretation of the term 'decision' is not limited to SCHUFA's specific business practice, but can be applied to other cases, in particular two-person constellations. The ECJ justifies the applicability of Art. 22(1) GDPR, among other things, on the grounds that otherwise there would be a risk of a gap in legal protection in three-person constellations.[20] However, this is only part of the argumentative basis on which the ECJ bases its broad interpretation of the term 'decision'. From an overall perspective, the gap that the ECJ identifies in the case of a narrow interpretation, which would leave the data subject unprotected in the case of preliminary measures that clearly determine the content of the decision, appears to be more important: The calculation of a score would then not have to meet the requirements of Art. 22(2) to (4) GDPR, 'even though that procedure is based on automated processing and that it produces effects significantly affecting the data subject to the extent that the action of the third party to whom that probability value is transmitted draws strongly on it'.[21] Against this background, the broad interpretation of the term 'decision' must also apply to other forms of decision preparation and is not limited to the calculation of scores.[22]

With its ruling, the ECJ has placed the discussion about the sufficient influence of humans on decision-making on a new dogmatic footing. From now on, the legal debate will have to address the question of whether the entire decision-making process comprises a solely automated measure on which the final selection and its implementation with qualified effect draws strongly. The decisive guidance of the final selection act must be

19 ECJ 7.12.2023 – case C-634/21, ECLI:EU:C:2023:957 para. 45 – OQ v Land Hessen, SCHUFA.

20 ECJ 7.12.2023 – case C-634/21, ECLI:EU:C:2023:957 para. 61 – OQ v Land Hessen, SCHUFA.

21 ECJ 7.12.2023 – case C-634/21, ECLI:EU:C:2023:957 para. 62 – OQ v Land Hessen, SCHUFA.

22 Schwartmann/Keber/Zenner KI-VO/Schwartmann/Benedikt/Köhler, 3rd edn. 2024, mn. 781; Bronner jurisPR-ITR 5/2024 Anm. 4; Juszczyk DSB 2024, 19 (21); Paal/Schulz ZfDR 2025, 89 (97); Richter DuD 2024, 503 (506); Schild ZD 2024, 157 (165); Voudoulaki EuZW 2024, 75 (80); The Hamburg Commissioner for Data Protection and Freedom of Information, ‚Effects of the Schufa judgement on AI applications – automated decisions must not play a decisive role', (7.12.2023), <https://datenschutz-hamburg.de/fileadmin/user_upload/HmbBfDI/Datenschutz/Informationen/20231207_PM_EuGH_Judgement_Schufa_Effects_on_AI.pdf>.

determined by examining the intended decision-making process *ex ante*.[23] The scope of application of Art. 22(1) GDPR is opened up if there is no substantive discussion of the automated decision proposal by a human being.[24] When using systems that, based on the model of Art. 6(3) AI Act, do not have a material influence on decision-making due to their design, this requirement is automatically met.[25] However, since Art. 22(1) GDPR recognises the possibility of automated individual decisions in principle, no unreasonably high requirements may be imposed on human influence beyond this. In principle, therefore, a plausibility check of the individual case will be sufficient.[26] Nevertheless, a comprehensive assessment of the content, taking into account additional factors outside the automated decision proposal, is necessary in light of the ECJ's case law on the PNR Directive if a system developed using machine learning methods is used in the decision-making process and, at the same time, the right to an effective remedy pursuant to Art. 47 subpara. 2 CFR must be guaranteed at a high level of protection.[27]

V. Recommended further reading

LG Bamberg 26.3.2025 – 41 O 749/24 KOIN, RDV 2025, 206.
LG Bayreuth 29.4.2025 – 31 O 593/24, ZD 2025, 651.
Heine NZA 2024, 1384.
Thüsing RDV 2026, 5.

---

23 Langenbucher FS Gounalakis, 2025, 711 (722–726); Heine NZA 2024, 1384 (1388); Langenbucher BKR 2024, 66 (67); Radtke MMR 2024, 153 (157).

24 Already Köhler EuDIR 2025, 16 mn. 13. Likewise Kühling/Buchner DS-GVO BDSG/Buchner, 4th edn. 2024, DSGVO Art. 22 mn. 15; Paal/Pauly/Martini DSGVO Art. 22 mn. 19a; Article 29 Data Protection Working Party, ‚Guidelines on Automated individual decision-making and Profiling for the purposes of Regulation 2016/679' (wp251rev.01, 22.8.2018) <https://ec.europa.eu/newsroom/article29/items/612053/en>, p. 21; Hessel/Dillschneider RDi 2023, 458 (464); Hoeren/Niehoff RW 2018, 47 (53); Kätscher/Pesch KIR 2024, 46 (51); Kremer CR 2024, 50 (58); Lang/Schwaab LTZ 2025, 28 (35); Malorny RdA 2022, 170 (176 f.); Richter DuD 2024, 503 (504).

25 In this regard Köhler EuDIR 2025, 16 mn. 15.

26 Köhler EuDIR 2025, 16 mn. 16. In agreement and in detail Thüsing RDV 2026, 5 (11).

27 ECJ 21.6.2022 – case C-817/19, ECLI:EU:C:2022:491 para. 194 et seq. – Ligue des droits humains. In this regard Köhler EuDIR 2025, 16 mn. 18–21.

Chapter 6:
Governance, Compliance and Accountability

Record of Processing Activities

*Dieter Kugelmann**

ECJ 4.5.2023 – case C-60/22, ECLI:EU:C:2023:373 – UZ v Bundesrepublik Deutschland

I. Significance and content

1. Significance

The record of processing activities according to Art. 30 GDPR is a topic of ongoing political debate. The issue of discussion is which companies and institutions are subject to the obligation to maintain a record. This puts the rather boring provision of maintaining a record in the spotlight of legal and political debates concerning simplification for small and medium-sized enterprises (SMEs), which are particularly affected by the more formal requirements of the GDPR. However, Art. 30 GDPR shares this fate with Art. 37 GDPR regarding the appointment of a data protection officer by the controller and the processor. This appointment, which is specified in the provisions of §§ 5 and 38 BDSG, is also considered a formal requirement, the fulfillment of which, from the political point of view, should not be imposed on all controllers. Both provisions share a characteristic: they name a specific number. Thus, they are an understandable target in political discourse and they are a simple reference point for public proposals and public debate.

In academic discourse, Art. 30 GDPR, on the other hand, is not an issue of interest. Also the case law of the courts rarely deals with the record of processing activities. The reason is the specific legal character of Art. 30 GDPR, which was subject to the ECJ's decision presented here.

* This text was translated from the German text into English by an AI tool developped by the State Commissioner for Data Protection and the Freedom of Information Rhineland-Palatinate.

2. Obligations under Art. 30 GDPR

According to Art. 30(1) sent. 1 GDPR, each controller and, where applicable, their representative shall maintain a record of all processing activities falling within their responsibility. This obligation extends to processors under Art. 30(2) GDPR. The contents of the record include, among others, the names of the controllers, the purposes of the processing, the categories of data subjects and recipients, and information on transfers to third countries and technical and organizational measures. According to Art. 30(5) GDPR, this obligation does not apply to companies or organizations employing fewer than 250 employees, unless the processing involves a risk to the rights and freedoms of data subjects.

Maintaining the record can provide important support in fulfilling a number of further requirements of the GDPR.[1] Essentially, it is about demonstrating compliance with the obligations of the GDPR (Rec. 82). This particularly concerns the accountability required by Art. 5(2) GDPR. Against the background of further documentation requirements, the record can be understood and structured as a flexible instrument.[2] A violation of the proper fulfillment of the obligation to maintain a processing record can lead to a fine under Art. 83(4)(a) GDPR.

II. Case summary

The ECJ issued a statement on maintaining a record of processing activities in the context of legal proceedings between a third-country national and the Federal Republic of Germany regarding the processing of the third-country national's application for international protection.[3] The decision was issued in a preliminary ruling proceeding under Art. 267 TFEU following a referal from the Wiesbaden Administrative Court.

The plaintiff filed an application for international protection. The Federal Office for Migration and Refugees rejected the application, based on

1 Datenschutzkonferenz, ‚Hinweise zum Verzeichnis von Verarbeitungstätigkeiten' (February 2018) <https://www.datenschutzkonferenz-online.de/media/ah/201802_ah_verzeichnis_verarbeitungstaetigkeiten.pdf>.

2 Schwartmann/Jaspers/Thüsing/Kugelmann Heidelberger Kommentar DS-GVO/BDSG/Müthlein, 3rd edn. 2024, DS-GVO Art. 30 mn. 16.

3 ECJ 4.5.2023 – case C-60/22, ECLI:EU:C:2023:373 – UZ v Bundesrepublik Deutschland.

the electronic file 'MARIS' it had created, which contained the plaintiff's personal data. The referring court had doubts as to whether maintaining this electronic file was in compliance with the requirements of the GDPR. It was not proven that the Federal Office complied with Art. 5(1) GDPR in conjunction with Art. 30 GDPR, because the Federal Office had not presented a complete record of processing activities in relation to this file.[4] An agreement under Art. 26 GDPR legitimizing data transfer between administration and courts was also not apparent. Therefore, the Administrative Court submitted the following question to the ECJ: whether a violation of the accountability of a controller under Art. 5(2) GDPR, e.g. through a missing or incomplete record of processing activities under Art. 30 GDPR or a missing agreement on a joint controllership under Art. 26 GDPR, would lead to unlawful data processing within the meaning of Art. 17(1)(d) GDPR and Art. 18(1)(b) GDPR, such that a right of erasure or restriction of processing would exist for the data subject.

III. Key legal findings

The ECJ first clarifies that the controller bears the burden of proof to fulfil its accountability obligation under Art. 5(2) GDPR.[5] The legality of processing requires compliance with the principles of Art. 5 and 6 GDPR.[6] The ECJ then states that compliance with the obligation under Art. 26 GDPR to conclude an agreement to establish joint controllership and the obligation under Art. 30 GDPR to maintain a record of processing activities do not constitute grounds for the legality of processing as defined in Art. 6

4 ECJ 4.5.2023 – case C-60/22, ECLI:EU:C:2023:373 para. 32 – UZ v Bundesrepublik Deutschland.

5 ECJ 4.5.2023 – case C-60/22, ECLI:EU:C:2023:373 para. 53 – UZ v Bundesrepublik Deutschland; ECJ 24.2.2022 – case C-175/20, ECLI:EU:C:2022:124 para. 77 et seq., 81 – Valsts ieņēmumu dienests.

6 ECJ 4.5.2023 – case C-60/22, ECLI:EU:C:2023:373 para. 57 – UZ v Bundesrepublik Deutschland; ECJ 6.10.2020 – Joined Cases C-511/18, C-512/18 and C-520/18, ECLI: EU:C:2020:791 para. 208 – La Quadrature du Net and Others v Premier ministre and Others; ECJ 22.6.2021 – case C-439/19, ECLI:EU:C:2021:504 para. 96 – Latvijas Republikas Saeima; ECJ 201.0.2022 – case C-77/21, ECLI:EU:C:2022:805 para. 49, 56 – Digi Távközlési és Szolgáltató Kft. gegen Nemzeti Adatvédelmi és Információszabadság Hatóság.

(1) GDPR.[7] The objective of Art. 26, 30 GDPR is not to determine the scope of legality. A violation of Art. 26 or Art. 30 GDPR does not lead to a violation of the accountability obligation under Art. 5(2) GDPR and therefore does not constitute unlawful processing.[8]

The ECJ relies on the distinction between the principles of Chapter II and the general obligations of Chapter IV in its Section 1, which is also reflected in their inclusion in different paragraphs of Art. 83 GDPR.[9]

The fundamental objective of the GDPR is to ensure a high level of protection for the fundamental rights and freedoms of natural persons in the processing of their personal data against the background of Art. 8 CFR, Art. 16(1) TFEU.[10] However, the absence of an agreement establishing joint controllership pursuant to Art. 26 GDPR or a record of processing activities as defined in Art. 30 GDPR alone cannot contitute a violation of the fundamental right to the protection of personal data. Rather, they are means of ensuring that controllers comply with the guarantees for fundamental rights protection.[11] A violation of Art. 26, 30 GDPR could also be remedied, in particular by appropriate orders of the supervisory authorities pursuant to Art. 58(2) GDPR or by lodging a complaint according to Art. 77 GDPR.[12]

IV. Systematic context and legal classification

The legal obligation of Art. 30 GDPR is to be seen in the context of the entirety of the obligations stipulated by the GDPR. As part of the general obligations under Section 1 of Chapter IV of the GDPR, the record is one of the measures that controllers and processors must take to ensure lawful data processing. A violation only of Art. 30 GDPR does not, therefore, yet justify the assumption that the lawfulness of the processing according to

7 ECJ 4.5.2023 – case C-60/22, ECLI:EU:C:2023:373 para. 59 – UZ v Bundesrepublik Deutschland.

8 ECJ 4.5.2023 – case C-60/22, ECLI:EU:C:2023:373 para. 61 – UZ v Bundesrepublik Deutschland.

9 ECJ 4.5.2023 – case C-60/22, ECLI:EU:C:2023:373 para. 62 et seq. – UZ v Bundesrepublik Deutschland.

10 ECJ 27.2.2025 – case c-203/22, ECLI:EU:C:2025:117 para. 51 – CK v Magistrat der Stadt Wien; ECJ 4.10.2024 – case C-446/21, ECLI:EU:C:2024:834 para. 45 – Maximilian Schrems v Meta Platforms Ireland Limited; cf. Kugelmann EuR 2023, 336.

11 ECJ 4.5.2023 – case C-60/22, ECLI:EU:C:2023:373 para. 65 – UZ v Bundesrepublik Deutschland.

12 ECJ 4.5.2023 – case C-60/22, ECLI:EU:C:2023:373 para. 67 – UZ v Bundesrepublik Deutschland.

Art. 5, 6 GDPR does not exist. This is because there is no direct and immediate relevance to fundamental rights in this respect. The violation can be remedied in order to re-examine the lawfulness. However, a violation of general obligations such as Art. 30 GDPR can be linked to Art. 5 GDPR, thus rendering the lawfulness of the data processing invalid.

An administrative fine under Art. 83(4)(a) GDPR can be imposed for a violation of Art. 30 GDPR. However, resulting from the proportionality test, a fine is likely to be considered only if further violations exist. This is because the nature, gravity and duration of the violation within the meaning of Art. 83(2)(a) GDPR often prove to be of minor importance in the case of violations of Art. 30 GDPR, particularly if only limited information is missing, incomplete or not up-to-date. However, if the record is completely missing, maybe even for a long period of time, this may be lead to a different assessment in an individual case. As a rule, however, violations of Art. 30 GDPR do not occur only in their own respect, but are part of inadequate data management, so that further provisions of the GDPR are violated.

V. Author's analysis and commentary

The ECJ limits the scope of Art. 30 GDPR. Maintaining a record of processing activities is an obligation of the controller and processor. The purpose of this obligation is to facilitate and support the fulfilment of other requirements of the GDPR. However, it does not have an independent character, so it must always be seen in the context of other obligations. The data subject is not violated in their subjective rights acccording to § 42(2) of the VwVfG solely because Art. 30 GDPR is affected. They can assert a violation of objective law, but must submit further violated legal provisions which justify a subjective right, such as in particular the indvidual rights of the data subject of Art. 12 to 22 GDPR.

The provision of Art. 30 GDPR establishes an objective legal obligation. A violation of this obligation alone does not lead to the unlawfulness of the data processing. Thus, the ECJ limits the consequences of a violation of Art. 30 GDPR. However, as there is a close connection with the need to prove the lawfulness of processing within the meaning of Art. 5, 6 GDPR, Art. 30 GDPR still retains its importance. Because the record of processing activities facilitates not only the proof of lawfulness, but also requires a constant self-assurance of the controller and processor about the concrete data processing. The supporting function of the record promotes the lawfulness of data processing and active and appropriate data management.

A complaint by a data subject under Art. 77 GDPR alleging a violation of Art. 30 GDPR triggers a review by the supervisory authority. It has discretion in its decision-making and selection, so there is no entitlement of a person to claim specific action.[13] In practice, however, the review often reveals further violations of the GDPR, so the contextual approach of the ECJ is then also reflected in the activities of the supervisory authorities.

The ECJ's judgment also clarifies that maintaining the record of processing activities is a processing activity in the sense of Art. 4 no. 2 GDPR. The ECJ explicitly mentions the order under Art. 58(2)(d) GDPR as a means to remedy a violation of Art. 30 GDPR. Accordingly, the supervisory authorities can instruct the controller or processor to bring processing operations into compliance with the GDPR by issuing orders to maintain the record of processing activities.

VI. Recommended further reading

The CNIL's decision of 15 September 2021 is based on an understanding of Art. 30 GDPR as a legal obligation within the context of general responsibilities.[14] In a simple case, the operator of a website violated some basic rules of the GDPR. The CNIL imposed a fine of EUR 3000 on him due to the cumulative violations of Art. 16, 17, 30, 31 GDPR.

The CNIL first analysed the individual violations. A record of processing activities did not exist and this was not accidental, even if the company was operated by a single person.[15] It justified the fine with the totality of the violations.[16] This can be reconciled with the later decision of the ECJ, as the determination of the violation of Art. 30 GDPR is examined separately, but then only leads to a sanction in combination with other violations.

---

13 Schwartmann/Jaspers/Thüsing/Kugelmann/Schwartmann/Keppeler DS-GVO Art. 77 mn. 13.

14 CNIL, 'Déliberation SAN 2021-014' (15.9.2021) <https://www.legifrance.gouv.fr/cnil/id/CNILTEXT000044043045>.

15 CNIL, 'Déliberation SAN 2021-014' (fn. 14), mn. 57.

16 CNIL, 'Déliberation SAN 2021-014' (fn. 14), mn. 77.

Data protection management system (DPMS) in accordance with the GDPR in connection with the implementation of the AI Act

Christian Jaksch/Klaus Alpmann

CNIL, ‚Délibération SAN-2025–014 of December 11, 2025' (11.12.2025), <https://www.legifrance.gouv.fr/cnil/id/CNILTEXT000053048614>

I. Initial situation: Authority decision and practical example regarding Art. 30 GDPR

1. Introduction

On 15.12.2025, the French data protection supervisory authority CNIL imposed a fine of €1 million because a company had failed to comply with numerous requirements of the GDPR (including Art. 28, 29, and 30 GDPR). In particular, the company did not keep any records of its processing activities, thereby violating Art. 30 GDPR, which is the central documentation standard for ensuring internal transparency regarding purpose-specific data processing activities.[1] At the same time, two data protection authorities (HmbBfDI and ULD Schleswig-Holstein) drafted a supervisory authority paper dealing with the interrelated requirements of the GDPR and the AI Act.[2] The key message from the two supervisory authorities is: 'The abstract, principle-based requirements of the GDPR are fleshed out and made applicable by the specific technical requirements of the AI Act. Anyone who implements the requirements of the AI Act correctly should, in principle,

1 See CNIL, 'Délibération SAN-2025–014' (11.12.2025) <https://www.legifrance.gouv.fr/cnil/id/CNILTEXT000053048614> and <https://www.cnil.fr/en/data-breach-mobius-solutions-ltd-fined-eu1-million>.

2 Fuchs/Wünschelbaum/Hansen/Walczack, 'The Bridge Blueprint – Theses on the uniform application of data protection and AI regulation in the use of AI' <https://datenschutz-hamburg.de/fileadmin/user_upload/HmbBfDI/Datenschutz/Informationen/DE-Bridge-Blueprint-v.0.9.pdf>.

also be on the safe side in terms of data protection law'.[3] This raises the question of whether this official elaboration provides an opportunity to implement the AI Act and GDPR as interlocking EU regulations together via a central data protection management system (DPMS) and to ensure compliance with both EU regulations with a combined documentation.

2. Starting point: GDPR

According to Art. 5(2) GDPR, the controller (Art. 4 no. 7 GDPR) is responsible for ensuring compliance with the data protection principles (Art. 5(1) GDPR) and must be able to demonstrate this ('demonstrate compliance'). Art. 5(2) GDPR is clarified by Art. 24 GDPR, which requires that appropriate technical and organizational measures be taken to ensure that the processing of personal data is carried out in accordance with the GDPR.[4] A core component of the implementation of the GDPR is transparency through a clear overview of the processing activities taking place within the company. Rec. 82 sent. 1 of the GDPR explains: 'In order to demonstrate compliance with this Regulation, the controller or processor should maintain records of processing activities under its responsibility'.[5] Consequently, Art. 30(1) GDPR obliges a controller to maintain a record of processing activities with the minimum content specified therein, while Art. 30(2) obliges processors to maintain a record of processing activities with the minimum content specified therein. The transparency created by a properly and neatly maintained and up-to-date record of processing activities is the starting point for ensuring the rights of data subjects (Art. 12 et seq. GDPR – information, access), the performance of a data protection impact assessment (Art. 35 GDPR), the evaluation of the necessary data security measures (Art. 32 GDPR), and the risk assessment of suspected cases of personal data breaches (Art. 4 no. 12, Art. 33, Art. 34 GDPR).[6] The German data protection authorities have issued two documents for the implementa-

3 Fuchs, 'Bridge Blueprint – Building bridges with explosive force' (anwaltsblatt.de, 1.12.2025) <https://doi.org/10.70919/anwbl10151>.

4 Gola/Heckmann DS-GVO – BDSG/Pötters, 3rd edn. 2022, DSGVO Art. 5 mn. 25 et seqq.

5 Rec. 82 GDPR.

6 Data Protection Conference (DSK), 'Notes on the record of processing activities, Art. 30 GDPR' (2018), <https://www.datenschutzkonferenz-online.de/media/ah/201802_ah_verzeichnis_verarbeitungstaetigkeiten.pdf>, p. 2.

tion of the requirement for a record of processing activities.[7] The key points are as follows:

- 'The record of processing activities covers all fully or partially automated processing as well as non-automated processing of personal data';
- 'A description must be prepared for each individual processing activity in accordance with Art. 30 GDPR. A processing activity is generally understood to be a business process at a suitable level of abstraction. A strict standard must be applied so that each new purpose of the processing constitutes a separate processing activity. In the event of only a minor change in purpose, it must be examined whether an existing description of a processing activity needs to be adapted or whether a completely new description needs to be prepared. The sum of the individual contributions results in the record of processing activities.'
- 'In order to avoid redundancies and reduce the effort required to create and maintain the directory, references to existing documents can be included in the individual descriptions. (...) For example, a company-wide (...) information security framework concept will only be created once'.[8]

The German Data Protection Conference has the opinion, that a properly maintained record of processing activities can be used as a basis for fulfilling further data protection obligations. Consequently, the record of processing activities can also be usefully employed or utilized as follows:

- 'for determining the purposes of processing in accordance with Art. 5(1)(b) GDPR';
- 'for the purposes of accountability and documentation obligations, Art. 5(2), Art. 24 GDPR:
- as proof of the lawfulness of processing pursuant to Art. 5(1)(a) GDPR [in conjunction with Art. 6(1) and Art. 9(2) GDPR],
- as evidence of data minimization pursuant to Art. 5(1)(c) GDPR [in conjunction with Art. 17 GDPR],
- as evidence of the accuracy and timeliness of the data pursuant to Art. 5(1)(d) GDPR [in conjunction with Art. 16 GDPR]';

7 Data Protection Conference (DSK), 'Notes on the record of processing activities, Art. 30 GDPR (fn. 6); Data Protection Conference (DSK), 'Brief Paper No. 1 – Record of processing activities – Art. 30 GDPR' (2018) <https://www.datenschutzkonferenz-online.de/media/kp/dsk_kpnr_1.pdf.

8 Data Protection Conference (DSK), 'Notes on the record of processing activities, Art. 30 GDPR' (fn. 6), p. 1 et seq.

- 'as an appropriate measure to fulfill the rights of data subjects pursuant to Art. 12(1) GDPR [Art. 13 – Art. 15 GDPR]';
- 'for the creation and as proof of appropriate technical and organizational measures pursuant to [Art. 5(1) lit. f in conjunction with] Art. 24(1) and Art. 32 GDPR';
- 'to check whether a data protection impact assessment pursuant to Art. 35 GDPR must be carried out [or, if applicable, an IT-supported integrated data protection impact assessment]';
- 'as a basis for the data protection officer to perform their duties in accordance with Art. 39 GDPR'[9]

Consequently, this documentation can be usefully consulted or supplemented for the performance of other tasks, up to and including a comprehensive IT-supported DPMS system. Due to the significant time savings in terms of unnecessary working hours for operational employees and departments, authors *Grob/Wergen* assume that investing in a comprehensive IT-supported data protection management tool can ultimately be worthwhile from a business perspective as a form of 'return on investment'.[10]

II. Authorities' opinion on the interaction between the GDPR and the AI Act

According to the clear wording of the AI Act (see Rec. 10 in conjunction with Art. 2(7) of the AI Act), European data protection law – i.e., the GDPR, the LED for police and criminal justice, the EUDPR, and also the ePrivacy Directive as amended by the Citizens' Rights Directive – remain completely 'untouched' by the AI Act. However, it is completely unclear what this means for operational implementation, because the AI Act does synchronize with European data protection in several places, e.g.:

- Art. 26(9) of the AI Act, addressed to operators of an AI system (Art. 3 no. 4 AI Act), stipulates that the operating instructions and other information to be provided by the provider of an AI system (Art. 3 no. 3 AI Act) in accordance with Art. 13 AI Act are to be used for the purpose of

9 Data Protection Conference (DSK), 'Notes on the record of processing activities, Art. 30 GDPR' (fn. 6), p. 2.
10 Grob/Wergen DSB 2025, 225.

conducting a data protection impact assessment by the operator of the AI system (Art. 3 no. 4 AI Act) as the data controller (Art. 4 no. 7 GDPR).[11]
- Certain provisions of the AI Act are based on the EU's legislative competence in the field of data protection pursuant to Art. 16 TFEU (see Rec. 3 AI Act).
- The European Data Protection Supervisor is the supervisory authority responsible for enforcing the AI Act in the European institutions (e.g., EU Commission, ECB, etc.). The European Data Protection Supervisor thus enforces both the EUDPR and the AI Act synchronously.[12]
- The national data protection authority (enforcement of the GDPR and/or LED is, in accordance with Art. 74(8) AI Act, the supervisory authority (market surveillance authority) responsible under the AI Act for the high-risk AI systems specified therein (including those used for law enforcement, border management, justice, and democracy).[13]

In addition to these connections between data protection law and the AI Act, the two German supervisory authorities HmbBfDI and ULD Schleswig-Holstein consider the view that the GDPR and the AI Act are completely independent specialist laws to be a hindrance to the practice and future of AI in Europe. Both authorities are of the opinion that there are numerous overlaps between the two EU regulations. Specifically, the clear overlap between the GDPR and the AI Act is evident in the regulation of high-risk AI systems.[14] The risk to the security and fundamental rights of people in Europe identified by the EU legislator as posed by such high-risk AI systems is usually directly related to the processing of personal data by these AI systems (e.g., biometrics; vocational training and employment; law enforcement, migration; administration of justice; etc.). This raises the question for the two authorities: 'How exactly do AI regulations and data protection interact—do they result in useful synergies?'[15] The authorities have identified the following direct interactions, which can subsequently be mapped in an IT-supported data protection management system:

11 Art. 26(9) AI Act.

12 See Art. 70(9), Art. 100, and Art. 57(3) AI Act; EDPS, 'Artificial Intelligence Act' <https://www.edps.europa.eu/artificial-intelligence/artificial-intelligence-act_en>.

13 Art. 74(8) AI Act.

14 See Art. 6 in conjunction with Annex III AI Act.

15 Fuchs/Wünschelbaum, 'AI and data protection – New paper builds bridges for practical application' (tagespiegel.de, 18.9.2025) <https://background.tagesspiegel.de/digitalisierung-und-ki/briefing/neues-papier-ist-brueckenschlag-fuer-die-praxis.

- The data protection principle of 'data minimization' (Art. 5 (1) (c) GDPR) has been criticized in Germany due to a previous national interpretation in the sense of 'data avoidance and data thrift ('Datenvermeidung und Datensparsamkeit'). German politicians would like to see the term 'data thrift ('Datensparsamkeit') replaced by the term 'data sovereignty' in Germany.[16] However, the GDPR does not recognize the concept of data thrift at all, but only recognizes the concept of data minimization in the sense of an objective necessity test (proportionality test). The concept of data minimization originates from the old § 3a BDSG (old version) ('data avoidance and data thrift), which represented the excessive ('gold plating') German implementation of Art. 6(1) (c) of the DPD (data minimization), with the result that Art. 5(1) (c) GDPR is still interpreted in part today in the light of the old § 3a BDSG (old version).[17] The two supervisory authorities therefore propose interpreting the principle of data minimization (Art. 5(1) (c) GDPR) as an objective necessity test for the achievement of the purpose, with the result that even the storage of very extensive data sets can be GDPR-compliant, because it is based on objective necessity. If the processing of even extensive data sets is necessary, e.g., for the mitigation of harmful or discriminatory results by AI systems, because the data is actually necessary for the legitimate purpose of avoiding harmful or discriminatory AI results, there can be no GDPR violation because only the data necessary for the pre-definied purpose is processed (data minimization).[18]
- The two authorities are of the opinion that the abstract requirements for 'privacy by design and privacy by default' pursuant to Art. 25 GDPR[19] are becoming increasingly important due to the specific design requirements for high-risk AI systems pursuant to Art. 6 ff AI Act and certain AI

16 Krempl, 'Digital offensive: CDU wants to finally do away with the principle of data minimization' (heise.de, 30.9.2019) <https://www.heise.de/news/Digitaloffensive-CDU-will-das-Prinzip-Datensparsamkeit-endgueltig-entsorgen-4543180.html>.

17 See the old German law on 'data minimization': Eßer in Eßer/Kramer/von Lewinski BDSG/Eßer, 2014, BDSG § 3a mn. 1 et seq.; In Austria, for example, the old DPD was never implemented with 'data avoidance and data thrift' – cf. § 6 (1) No. 3 Austrian DSG 2000 old version: 'Data may only be used (...) insofar as they are essential for the purpose of data use and do not go beyond this purpose' = objective necessity.

18 Fuchs/Wünschelbaum/Hansen/Walczack, 'The Bridge Blueprint – Theses on the uniform application of data protection and AI regulation in the use of AI' (fn. 2).

19 EDPB, 'Guidelines 4/2019 on Article 25 Data protection by design and by default' (20.10.2020) < https://www.edpb.europa.eu/our-work-tools/our-documents/guidelines/guidelines-42019-article-25-data-protection-design-and_en>.

systems pursuant to Art. 50 AI Act. The joint 'by design' approach, which is specified in great detail by the AI Act, ensures that protective measures are already embedded during the development phase (by design) and also during use (by default).[20]

- In many cases, the legal basis of 'legitimate interest' (Art. 6(1) (f) GDPR) will be the central permission standard for the use of personal data in AI systems. However, it is precisely this legal basis that offers the greatest possible legal uncertainty, because there is generally no case law yet for the intended use of the new technology, and the weighing up and individual weighting of legitimate interests may well differ across Europe due to different perspectives. As *Fuchs* notes, 'Individual weighing is difficult to implement'.[21] In order to reduce this significant legal uncertainty with the legal basis of 'legitimate interests', the two authorities propose an interpretation of the legal basis of 'legitimate interests' with regard to AI systems based on the reasonable expectations of a citizen, i.e., the expectation of a data subject that an AI product on the European market complies with applicable law and that the associated AI practices are legally compliant with the AI Act. This would shift the balancing of interests from a purely context-related assessment or singular evaluation to a benchmark anchored in a specific legal obligation as a general system-related standard. If an AI system is operated in compliance with the AI Act or developed in compliance with the AI Act (= legal compliant AI practices defined by the AI Act as legitimate purposes to process personal data), there is also a legal basis of 'legitimate interest' because data subjects in Europe have a legitimate expectation that an AI product complies with applicable law and that the associated AI practices are legally compliant (Art. 5, Art. 6 in conjunction with Annex I and Annex III; Art. 50; Art. 51 ff AI Act).[22] *Fuchs* clarifies: 'If a company processes personal data to fulfill obligations under the AI Act (e.g., risk management), it is acting within the scope of this expectation'.[23] An additional problem exists with regard to 'special categories of personal data' within the meaning of Art. 9 (1) GDPR, because according to Art. 9 (2) GDPR, there is no legal basis

20 Fuchs/Wünschelbaum/Hansen/Walczack, 'The Bridge Blueprint – Theses on the uniform application of data protection and AI regulation in the use of AI' (fn. 2).

21 Fuchs, 'Bridge Blueprint – Building bridges with explosive force' (fn. 3).

22 Fuchs/Wünschelbaum/Hansen/Walczack, 'The Bridge Blueprint – Theses on the uniform application of data protection and AI regulation in the use of AI' (fn. 3).

23 Fuchs, 'Bridge Blueprint – Building bridges with explosive force' (fn. 3).

for weighing up interests. It is precisely the unavailability of such 'special categories of personal data' that can have the effect in AI systems that the purpose of protection against discrimination and disadvantage intended by the EU legislator is achieved precisely because the AI system is not allowed to process any or too little of this highly sensitive data from which it would learn. This increases the risk of discrimination by AI systems. Consequently, Art. 10(5) AI Act in conjunction with Art. 9(2)(g) GDPR provides a legal basis for the processing of 'special categories of personal data' as a purpose consistent with a 'substantial public interest' in preventing discrimination.[24]

- Despite of a possible AI Act compliance, the GDPR only allows computer-only decisions about people that have legal effects or could otherwise lead to significant impairment under the conditions of Art. 22 GDPR, including appropriate technical and organizational measures for the effective exercise of data subjects' rights. However, there is currently a lack of clear, legally certain standards regarding decisions on the protective measures to be taken in the case of sole computer decisions based on Art 22(2)(b) GDPR. In the opinion of the two authorities, the AI Act now provides a remedy for this. Through the implementation of the binding measures in the AI Act (transparency, human oversight, robust verifiability through logging), there are now binding legal requirements in the AI Act for secure and verifiable AI systems as automated systems within the meaning of Art. 22 GDPR. Consequently, in the opinion of the two supervisory authorities, the AI Act is Union law within the meaning of Art. 22(2)(b) GDPR, and an AI system that fully complies with the AI Act could be used in a legally secure manner for sole computer decisions about people within the framework defined therein, in accordance with Art. 22(2)(b) GDPR.[25]

In general, a data protection impact assessment (DPIA) must be carried out when using AI systems that process personal data.[26] Here, too, close integration with the documentation required under the AI Act is advisable.

---

24 Fuchs/Wünschelbaum/Hansen/Walczack, 'The Bridge Blueprint – Theses on the uniform application of data protection and AI regulation in the use of AI' (fn. 2).

25 Fuchs/Wünschelbaum/Hansen/Walczack, 'The Bridge Blueprint – Theses on the uniform application of data protection and AI regulation in the use of AI' (fn. 2); Fuchs, 'Bridge Blueprint – Building Bridges with Explosive Power' (fn. 3).

26 See, inter alia, Data Protection Conference (DSK), List of processing activities for which a DPIA must be carried out (2018) No. 11.

This is recognized in particular by Art. 26(9) of the AI Act, which is addressed to the operators of an AI system (Art. 3 no. 4 AI Act) and stipulates that the operating instructions and other information to be provided by the supplier of an AI system (Art. 3 no. 3 AI Act) in accordance with Art. 13 AI Act should be used for the purpose of conducting a data protection impact assessment by the operator of the AI system (Art. 3 no. 4 AI Act) as the data controller (Art. 4 no. 7 GDPR).[27] The data protection impact assessment must document the effective management of the risks to data subjects, but not abstract dangers. A key data protection risk in AI systems is – in addition to misinformation, misrepresentation, manipulation, violation of data protection principles, etc. – the unintentional disclosure of personal data. In general, the challenge is that the assessment of the impact on fundamental rights in the context of the data protection impact assessment cannot be standardized, but is always context-specific. If a controller (Art. 4 no. 7 GDPR) must also carry out a fundamental rights impact assessment in accordance with Art. 27 AI Act as the operator of an AI system (Art. 3 no. 4 AI Act), synergies arise here as well. Even though the level of consideration between the data protection impact assessment (Art. 35 GDPR) and the fundamental rights impact assessment (Art. 27 AI Act) is quite different, both are part of the evidence of a comprehensive risk assessment.[28]

According to *Fuchs*, the abstract, principle-based requirements of the GDPR are fleshed out by the specific technical requirements of the AI Act and made applicable in concrete terms.[29]

If we follow this opinion quoted from *Fuchs* (and thus also the 'blueprint' of the two supervisory authorities HmbBfDI and ULD Schleswig-Holstein), the operational consequence – in our opinion – is that a joint and coherent review and documentation of the requirements of the GDPR and AI Act is necessary from a business perspective and makes sense in an IT-supported DPMS. This is also in line with the *Grob/Wergen* analysis regarding the return on investment of data protection tools.[30] If the assurance of data protection requirements (privacy by design; legitimate interests, automated individual decision-making, etc.) is justified and explained with

27 Art. 26(9) AI Act.

28 Art. 29 Working Party, 'Guidelines on Data Protection Impact Assessment (DPIA)' (wp248rev.01, 2017) <https://ec.europa.eu/newsroom/article29/items/611236>; Fuchs/Wünschelbaum/Hansen/Walczack, 'The Bridge Blueprint – Theses on the uniform application of data protection and AI regulation in the use of AI' (fn. 2).

29 Fuchs, 'Bridge Blueprint – Building bridges with explosive force' (fn. 3).

30 Grob/Wergen DSB 2025, 225.

concrete technical and organizational measures for the implementation of the AI Act, the implementation of the AI Act is immediately available in the same DPMS in an interlinked and referenced form. This ensures that the accountability requirement under Art. 5(2) GDPR is met in a very comprehensive manner.

III. Architecture for an IT-supported DPMS in accordance with the GDPR with integrated data protection-related testing in accordance with the AI Act

Operationally, the described interlocking of the GDPR and AI Act can be illustrated as follows:

The audit of a processing activity is carried out with the help of a web-based expert system that 'takes the user by the hand' and, similar to software for recording, evaluating, and submitting a private income tax return, guides them step by step through the fulfillment of their accountability obligations. The system itself uses AI components to describe data protection processing procedures in accordance with Art. 30 GDPR, to compare similar processing procedures, or to generate risk reduction measures. The following describes the logical structure (this is an abridged excerpt from the overall concept)[31] of the expert system and highlights the components integrated in accordance with AI Act.

1) Process description
    a) Process name/ID
    b) Targeted use of AI for the intended processing purpose within the process
    c) Company covering the process, business unit if applicable
    d) Process description and objectives, **taking AI into account**
2) Process environment
    a) Process participants with a role in data protection law (controller, processor, recipient/recipient categories)
    b) Process-specific IT systems (applications, platforms)
        aa) Use of an IT system with AI capabilities
        bb) In-house development of an AI system
        cc) Is the AI system being developed solely for a third party as a pure development activity

31 See <https://viaspro.eu>.

    - **dd) In-house development of an AI model for general use (GPAI)**
    - **ee) Systemic risk**
  - c) Related processes
- 3) Collect data on the process
  - a) Data types, form of data (unchanged, anonymous, pseudonymous, public), with pre-classification for confidentiality
  - b) Affected groups of persons, direct collection, necessity, minors
  - c) Processing criticality and threshold analysis for PIA
    - **aa) AI-driven data processing**
    - bb) (List of additional criteria for increased processing criticality)
  - d) Purpose of processing and change of purpose
  - e) Legal basis for processing
  - f) CIA risk assessment (confidentiality, integrity, availability)
  - **g) Determine AI risk class**
    - **aa) Prohibited AI**
    - **bb) High-risk AI**
    - **cc) Exemptions/exceptions from high-risk provisions**
    - **dd) Additional transparency requirements Emotions, biometrics, or manipulation**
    - **ee) Provider fiction for operators of high-risk AI**
    - **ff) AI systems with limited risk**
    - **gg) AI systems with minimal risk**
  - h) Data deletion concept
- 4) Perform assessment (privacy impact assessment, **fundamental rights impact assessment**)
  - a) Risk identification (high risk to the rights and freedoms of natural persons)
  - **b) Risk events for AI-controlled data processing**
    - **aa) Incorrect processing results**
    - **bb) Monitoring/evaluation/control of employees/applicants**
    - **cc) Unintended information generation or de-pseudonymization/de-anonymization**
    - **dd) Lack of transparency/traceability**
    - **ee) Unintended/non-compliant input**
    - **ff) Unintended processing of training data**
  - c) Result of the impact assessment

   d) Risk level for the processing activity
   e) Remedial measures
5) Legal, technical, and organizational measures implemented (critically specific, **AI risk class specific**)
   a) Test object Processing activity/process
      aa) Basic legal controls (e.g., legal basis)
      bb) Basic controls for compliance with data protection principles (e.g., data minimization)
      cc) Special controls according to AI Act
   b) Test object: Process participants
   c) Test object: Process-specific IT systems
6) Vulnerability management/risk management
7) Follow-up management (PDCA)
8) Documentation – automated generation of, among other things, the description of processing activities, data protection impact assessment and fundamental rights impact assessment, transparency statements

IV. Conclusion

The concept of a systemic interaction between the GDPR and the AI Act developed in the 'Bridge Blueprint' of the data protection supervisory authorities makes it clear that data protection accountability in the context of AI is no longer to be understood as a selective case-by-case assessment, but as an architecturally anchored system requirement. This shift towards a process- and system-related 'by design' approach corresponds with practical findings on the use of data protection tools, according to which manual and fragmented data protection processes are structurally inefficient and risky. An integrated, IT-supported data protection management system such as Vias Pro enables to combine the requirements of the GDPR and the AI Act in a uniform governance framework, to review them on an ongoing basis, and to document them in a traceable manner. This not only makes the system logic required by both regulations practicable, but also opens up a viable path to legally compliant, scalable, and future-proof data protection and AI compliance.

Technical and organisational measures

Marit Hansen

ECJ 14.12.2023 – case C-340/21, ECLI:EU:C:2023:986 – Natsionalna agentsia za prihodite

I. Case summary

The ECJ judgment in case C-340/21 (VB v Natsionalna agentsia za prihodite) from 14.12.2023 concerned a cyberattack on the Bulgarian National Revenue Agency (NAP). NAP is an authority attached to the Bulgarian Minister for Finance and responsible for identifying, securing and recovering public debts. Following the cyberattack that led to unauthorised access to the NAP IT system, personal data from more than 6 million data subjects were published on the internet.

The appellant in the main proceedings is one of several hundred data subjects who sought compensation from NAP for non-material damage allegedly resulting from the disclosure of their personal data. She brought an action before the Administrative Court, Sofia (Administrativen sad Sofia-grad) seeking a compensation of 1,000 leva (BGN) (approx. € 510) on the basis of Art. 82 GDPR for having suffered fear that her personal data might be misused in the future as a result of the personal data breach. After the Administrative Court dismissed the action, the appellant brought an appeal against that decision before the Supreme Administrative Court, Bulgaria (Varhoven administrativen sad) which referred five questions to the Court of Justice for a preliminary ruling.

II. Key legal findings

In its ruling, the Court clarifies important aspects regarding the right to compensation in the event of data breaches. In particular, the roles and responsibilities of the controller concerning the security of personal data, the data subject seeking for compensation and the competent national courts are being elaborated. The key findings are summarised along the lines of the answers to the questions referred for a preliminary ruling:

1. Need for assessment of security measures on a case-by-case basis

The fact that a controller has fallen victim to a successful cyberattack resulting in a personal data breach does not automatically mean that the technical and organisational measures for security required by Art. 24 and 32 GDPR were inadequate.[1] In the event of a claim for compensation, the competent national courts must assess the appropriateness of the implemented security measures on a case-by-case basis, taking into account the risks associated with the processing.[2] An expert's report cannot constitute a systematically necessary and sufficient means of proof of the appropriateness of the security measures.[3]

2. The controller's burden of proof

Following the GDPR's general principle of accountability set out in Art. 5(2) and 24 GDPR, the controller is responsible for demonstrating that the implemented security measures were appropriate.[4]

3. Liability of the controller for actions by a third party

In the case of unauthorised disclosure of personal data by a third party (here: the cybercriminals), the controller is not exempt of the obligation to pay compensation to affected data subjects unless the controller can prove that it is in no way responsible for the damage.[5]

1 ECJ 14.12.2023 – case C-340/21, ECLI:EU:C:2023:986 para. 39 – Natsionalna agentsia za prihodite.
2 ECJ 14.12.2023 – case C-340/21, ECLI:EU:C:2023:986 para. 47 – Natsionalna agentsia za prihodite.
3 ECJ 14.12.2023 – case C-340/21, ECLI:EU:C:2023:986 para. 64 – Natsionalna agentsia za prihodite.
4 ECJ 14.12.2023 – case C-340/21, ECLI:EU:C:2023:986 para. 57 – Natsionalna agentsia za prihodite.
5 ECJ 14.12.2023 – case C-340/21, ECLI:EU:C:2023:986 para. 74 – Natsionalna agentsia za prihodite.

4. Fear as non-material damage

The fear experienced by a data subject with regard to a possible misuse of his or her personal data by third parties as a result of an infringement of the GDPR can itself constitute non-material damage within the meaning of Art. 82(1) GDPR.[6]

III. Systematic context and legal classification

Four categories can be distinguished for the classification of the judgment: (1) the duties of the controller in the sense of accountability, (2) a loss of control as potential damage to the data subject, (3) responsibility in the event of damage caused by third parties, and (4) the burden of proof in court proceedings.

1. Accountability

Regarding the controller's accountability, the ECJ does not provide specific guidelines on how the controller should select and implement the technical and organisational measures to comply with the requirements, particularly those of Art. 32 GDPR, and how they can demonstrate their appropriateness. The ECJ merely answers the specific questions posed by the referring court: Not every breach of personal data protection constitutes proof of a GDPR violation; and an expert opinion is neither generally necessary nor sufficient to demonstrate GDPR compliance. In this respect, the ECJ assigns the task of selecting the appropriate evidence for each individual case to the competent court.

2. Loss of control and non-material damage

In paragraph 82, the ECJ, referring to Rec. 85 of the GDPR, states that the EU legislator intended the term 'damage' to encompass, in particular, the mere 'loss of control' of data subjects over their own data as a result of a GDPR breach, even if the data had not been misused. However, in

6 ECJ 14.12.2023 – case C-340/21, ECLI:EU:C:2023:986 para. 86 – Natsionalna agentsia za prihodite.

paragraph 84, the Court, referring to ECJ Case C-300/21, paragraph 50, points out that the plaintiff must prove that these consequences constitute non-material damage within the meaning of Art. 82 GDPR. Thus, the ECJ does not automatically consider every loss of control to be non-material damage, but rather a loss of control can cause non-material damage. If the plaintiff alleges such damage, e.g., the fear of abuse, the court must examine whether this fear can be considered justified in the individual case.[7]

Regarding the claim of loss of control as non-material damage, the decisions of the courts in the Member States diverged, so this ECJ case law should contribute to greater clarity and uniformity.

3. Liability for damage caused by third parties

The ECJ holds that a controller cannot be exempted from liability for damages simply because the damage resulted from the unauthorized disclosure of personal data by third parties (in this case, cybercriminals).[8] The controller would have to prove that it is 'in no way' responsible for the event that caused the damage.[9] Especially in the case of a breach of the protection of personal data with unauthorized access, there is a high risk that third parties will misuse the data, so that damage is only then realized for which the responsible party becomes liable for damages.

4. Burden of proof

According to the ruling, the burden of proof for the appropriateness of the technical and organizational measures implemented under Art. 32 GDPR lies with the controller.[10] If the burden of proof were to lie with the data subject, the right to compensation provided for in Art. 82(1) GDPR would be deprived of much of its effectiveness[11] – contrary to the intention of

7 ECJ 14.12.2023 – case C-340/21, ECLI:EU:C:2023:986 para. 85 – Natsionalna agentsia za prihodite.

8 ECJ 14.12.2023 – case C-340/21, ECLI:EU:C:2023:986 para. 74 – Natsionalna agentsia za prihodite.

9 ECJ 14.12.2023 – case C-340/21, ECLI:EU:C:2023:986 para. 74 – Natsionalna agentsia za prihodite.

10 ECJ 14.12.2023 – case C-340/21, ECLI:EU:C:2023:986 para. 57 – Natsionalna agentsia za prihodite.

11 ECJ 14.12.2023 – case C-340/21, ECLI:EU:C:2023:986 para. 56 – Natsionalna agentsia za prihodite.

the EU legislator. This is also appropriate because the plaintiff, as the data subject, does not have knowledge of the specific processing activities and the measures taken.

With regard to the plaintiff, the ECJ explains in para. 84, referring to ECJ Case C-300/21, para. 50, that the plaintiff must prove that the consequences of the loss of control constitute non-material damage within the meaning of Art. 82 GDPR.

IV. Author's analysis and commentary

The judgment of the ECJ C-340/21 is highly relevant, although its statements are hardly surprising:[12] The ECJ derives most of its answers to the preliminary ruling questions directly from the text of the GDPR. It should be emphasized that the court answers questions of responsibility, jurisdiction, and the tasks of national courts when examining individual cases. While the answers to the questions regarding risk management and technical and organisational aspects are obvious from an information technology perspective, they have caused some surprise in legal scholarship. One of the most important findings in the area of security is that the occurrence of a data breach does not necessarily mean that the technical and organisational measures taken by the controller are inadequate to address the risks.

It is therefore possible that a risk will materialise despite the controller's implementation of appropriate security measures, and that data subjects will suffer damages. The controller would thus be complying with the GDPR requirements, and despite the occurrence of the incident, there would be no GDPR violation. Consequently, the controller could not be held liable for the damage.

Indeed, the GDPR does not require the controller to guarantee absolute security – such a thing is impossible in the world of information technology. Instead, the GDPR requires the implementation of appropriate technical and organisational measures to ensure a level of security appropriate to the risk.[13]

---

12 Nusselder Intersect Policy Brief 4, p. 5.

13 Bygrave refers to this provision of Art. 32 GDPR as an 'obligation of means, rather than result' and further explains: 'in the sense, that a security breach as such will not necessarily amount to an infringement of the legislation; rather an infringement will

This is consistent with the statement that security is a process, not a product.[14]

At its core, data protection law is about maintaining an appropriate level of protection on an ongoing basis and, to this end, regularly testing, assessing and evaluating the effectiveness of the technical and organisational measures and adapting them accordingly, cf. Art. 32(1)(d) GDPR. The remaining residual risk must be sufficiently low – but not zero. One example of a particularly difficult-to-defend cyberattack is zero-day exploits. Here, cybercriminals exploit vulnerabilities for which manufacturers have not yet released a patch and whose existence is usually unknown to the controller.[15]

However, a breach of personal data protection is often an indication that the controller has not taken sufficient measures and has therefore violated the GDPR. In the present case, the cybercriminals are alleged to have gained access to the data via an SQL injection attack.[16] This attack vector and the possible countermeasures have been known for a long time.[17] The impression arises that the measures taken were inadequate and that security audits, as required by Art. 32(1)(d) of the GDPR, were lacking.

The ruling provides the following recommendation for controllers: Anyone who takes appropriate protective measures and can prove this in accordance with the accountability principle is not liable for damages that may nevertheless occur.

V. Recommended further reading

ECJ 4.5.2023 – case C-300/21, ECLI:EU:C:2023:370 – Österreichische Post.

ECJ 14.12.2023 – case C-456/22, ECLI:EU:C:2023:988 – Gemeinde Ummendorf.

---

only arise if the controller or processor has failed to take the measures required by Article 32.', Bygrave Oslo Law Review, Volume 8, No. 3, 126 (167).

14 'Security is a process, not a product.' Schneier, 'The Process of Security' (Blog, April 2000) <https://www.schneier.com/essays/archives/2000/04/the_process_of_secur.html>.

15 Ablon/Bogart, Zero Days, Thousands of Nights: The Life and Times of Zero-Day Vulnerabilities and Their Exploits, 2017, p. 2 et seq.

16 Siebelt, Hacking the government: a comparative case study in Europe – To what extent do the national cybersecurity strategies of France, Germany, and Bulgaria address hack-and-leak operations?, p. 40 et seq.

17 This was also true during the operation of the IT system underlying the case; see OWASP, OWASP Foundation: OWASP Top 10 – 2017: The Ten Most Critical Web Application Security Risks, 2017, p. 7.

ECJ 21.12.2023 – case C-667/21, ECLI:EU:C:2023:1022 – Krankenversicherung Nordrhein.

ECJ 25.1.2024 – case C-687/21, ECLI:EU:C:2024:72 – MediaMarktSaturn.

ECJ 11.4.2024 – case C-741/21, ECLI:EU:C:2024:288 – juris GmbH.

ECJ 20.6.2024 – case C-590/22, ECLI:EU:C:2024:536 – PS (Adresse erronée).

ECJ 4.10.2024 – case C-200/23, ECLI:EU:C:2024:827 – Varhovna administrativna prokuratura.

ECJ 4.9.2025 – case C-655/23, ECLI:EU:C:2025:655 – Quirin Privatbank AG.

BGH 13.5.2025 – VI ZR 186/22, NJW 2025, 2927.

Navigating between GDPR and AI Act: FRIA and DPIA – Two Interplay Use Cases

Tobias Keber/Peter Nägele

EDPB/EDPS, ‚EDPB-EDPS Joint Opinion 5/2021 on the proposal for a Regulation of the European Parliament and of the Council laying down harmonised rules on artificial intelligence (Artificial Intelligence Act)' (18.6.2021) <https://www.edpb.europa.eu/system/files/2021-06/edpb-edps_joint_opinion_ai_regulation_en.pdf>

I. Introduction

The AI Act is based on a risk regime that is specific to products and partly differentiated by sectors, whereas the GDPR addresses the processing of personal data and the associated risks and impacts on data subjects. This article examines the implications of typical use cases (1. Retrieval Augmented Generation and 2. Automated Administrative Decisions), considering the benefits for data subjects and society as a whole. As we will show, even if the regulatory perspectives of AI- and Data-Protection-Law are different, synergies e.g. concerning the Fundamental Rights Impact Assessment (FRIA) and the Data Protection Impact Assessment (DPIA) exist and must be made fruitful.[1]

II. Art. 27 AI Act, FRIA

1. Scope and Addressees

The obligation to conduct a FRIA does not apply to all actors, but rather to specific deployers of high-risk AI systems as defined in Art. 6(2) AI

1 Cf. Fuchs/Wünschelbaum/Hansen/Walczack, 'The Bridge Blueprint – Theses on the uniform application of data protection and AI regulation in the use of AI' <https://datenschutz-hamburg.de/fileadmin/user_upload/HmbBfDI/Datenschutz/Informationen/DE-Bridge-Blueprint-v.0.9.pdf>.

Act. These addressees include public sector bodies and private entities providing public services, such as in education or critical infrastructure. They also include those using AI systems for creditworthiness assessments or risk assessments in life and health insurance.

2. Systematic Integration within the AI Act

Despite the lack of direct sanctions in Art. 99 AI Act, the FRIA is far from being a 'paper tiger'. It is closely linked to other substantive requirements: data governance requires an investigation into the negative impact on fundamental rights;[2] human oversight must be designed to minimise the risk to fundamental rights;[3] and provider obligations effectively require a risk analysis, which would be impossible to perform without assessing the interference with fundamental rights.[4]

3. Relationship with the Data Protection Impact Assessment (DPIA)

Pursuant to Art. 2(7) AI Act, Union law on the protection of personal data remains unaffected. As soon as an AI system is likely to pose a high risk to the rights and freedoms of natural persons, a presumption of high risk is triggered under the GDPR and a DPIA under Art. 35 GDPR will often be mandatory.[5]

Although the FRIA and the DPIA may overlap in some areas (e.g. the right to privacy and the protection of personal data), the FRIA has a broader scope, covering non-discrimination, freedom of expression and freedom of assembly, for example.[6] In practice, an integrated process is recommended to avoid redundancies and ensure a coherent risk assessment.

---

2 Art. 10(2)(f) AI Act.

3 Art. 14(2) AI Act.

4 Art. 16 AI Act.

5 EDPB/EDPS, 'EDPB-EDPS Joint Opinion 5/2021 on the proposal for a Regulation of the European Parliament and of the Council laying down harmonised rules on artificial intelligence (Artificial Intelligence Act)' (18.6.2021) <https://www.edpb.europa.eu/our-work-tools/our-documents/edpbedps-joint-opinion/edpb-edps-joint-opinion-52021-proposal_en>.

6 Cf. Rec. 48 AI Act.

III. Art. 35 GDPR, DPIA

In the context of high-risk AI systems, the non-exhaustive list of examples in Art. 35(3) GDPR that require a DPIA is very important because AI systems can provide the technical means to carry out such processing. For example, Art. 35(3)(a) GDPR may apply to education, employment, access to essential public services, law enforcement, migration, asylum and border control management in Annex III AI Act. Art. 35(3)(b) GDPR 'only' requires processing on a large scale of special categories of personal data or personal data relating to criminal convictions and offences. If the processing is not found in Art. 35(3) GDPR, the controller should conduct a threshold analysis as described in the Article 29 Data Protection Working Party's guidelines on data protection impact assessments.[7]

IV. Common Core Principles between FRIA and DPIA

Both impact assessments are based on the same core principles.[8] These are, inter alias, (1) Risk Orientation: both regulatory systems require the identification, assessment and minimisation of risks before deployment; (2) Accountability: there are obligations for documentation, demonstrable proof of measures taken and impact assessments; (3) Interdisciplinarity: the assessment processes must integrate law, information security, ethics and sociology; and (4) Proportionality and effectiveness: protective measures must be scaled according to the severity and likelihood of the risks. And additionally, (5) Risk-Benefit Analysis: The benefits to data subjects and groups or even society as a whole can be taken into account when balancing interests. This point is often disregarded in risk and impact assessments, which tend to focus exclusively on potential harm to data subjects. The European Parliament clarified in 2020 that AI also has advantages for Europe, including for businesses and public services, and that underutilising AI constitutes a 'major threat', as 'missed opportunities for the EU could mean poor implementation of major programmes, such as

7 Article 29 Data Protection Working Party, 'Guidelines on Data Protection Impact Assessment (DPIA) and determining whether processing is "likely to result in a high risk" for the purposes of Regulation 2016/679' (wp248rev.01, 4.4.2017) < https://ec.europa.eu/newsroom/article29/items/611236>.

8 Thomaidou/Limniotis Journal of Cybersecurity and Privacy 2025, 5, 7; Mantalero Computer Law & Security Review 54 (2024) 106020.

the EU Green Deal, losing competitive advantage towards other parts of the world, economic stagnation and poorer possibilities for people'.[9] Similarly, in the field of medicine: 'The underuse of AI can be grasped as a waste of time, money, resources, and quality of life. This is a human tragedy. No country can afford it'.[10] The legislators and courts do not consider a perspective focused solely on the data subject to be effective. For example, in the Kalkar decision of the German administrative high court from 1978, the benefits to society were weighed against the risks to data subjects in order to avoid the blanket prohibition of technology.[11] The principle that infringements of fundamental rights must be prevented at all costs is without significance in the context of society as a whole. A utilitarian approach may also be sensible if justified by a consideration of risks and benefits. However, the threshold for public interests to override the fundamental right to the protection of personal data is high. Indeed, any interference with fundamental rights must be (strictly) necessary and a proper balance must be achieved between public interest and personal data protection.[12]

Both impact assessments reveal some overlap. Art. 27(1)(a) AI Act requires a description of the deployer's processes in which the high-risk AI system will be used, in line with its intended purpose. Similarly, Art. 35(7) GDPR requires a systematic description of the envisaged processing operations and their purposes. Further overlaps result from Art. 27(1)(b, c, d) AI Act and Art. 35(7)(c) of the GDPR. While the GDPR obliges data controllers to assess the risks to the rights and freedoms of data subjects, the

9 European Parliament, 'Artificial intelligence: threats and opportunities' (23.9.2020., last updated: 24.4.2025) <https://www.europarl.europa.eu/topics/en/article/20200918STO87404/artificial-intelligence-threats-and-opportunities>.

10 Pagallo et al. Health and Technology (2024), 1.

11 BVerfG 8.8.1978 – 2BvL 8/77, NJW 1979, 359: 'To demand from the legislator, in fulfillment of its duty to protect, a regulation that precludes with absolute certainty any threats to fundamental rights potentially arising from the licensing and operation of technical installations, would be to misjudge the limits of human cognition and would largely ban any state licensing of technology. For the structuring of the social order, one must rely on assessments based on practical reason. Uncertainties beyond this threshold of practical reason are inescapable and must therefore be borne by all citizens as socially adequate burdens' (free translation of guiding principle 6 of the decision).

12 ECJ 9.11.2010 – Joined cases C-92/09 and C-93/09, ECLI:EU:C:2010:662 para. 77, 86 – Volker und Markus Schecke GbR (C-92/09) and Hartmut Eifert (C-93/09) v Land Hessen; ECJ 16.12.2008 – case C-73/07, ECLI:EU:C:2008:727 para. 56 – Tietosuojavaltuutettu v Satakunnan Markkinapörssi Oy and Satamedia Oy; Art. 52 CFR.

AIA also requires them to consider also the time periods and frequencies with which each high-risk AI system is intended to be used. Additionally, the AIA expressly distinguishes between natural persons and groups. However, as mentioned above, the DPIA should also evaluate the risks for groups, and there is little difference in practice. Finally, the requirement from Art. 27(1)(e, f) of the AI Act and Art. 35(7)(d) GDPR are similar to some extent. The AIA explicitly mentions human oversight, which is an obligation under Art. 14 AI Act, whereas the GDPR only expressly requires the right to obtain human intervention in certain cases of automated decision-making, Art. 22 GDPR. Further measures must be taken if risks materialise. Art. 35(7)(d) GDPR requires measures to address risks and ensure the protection of personal data, not only in the event that those risks materialise.

There are no direct overlaps with the requirement in Art. 35(7)(b) GDPR. This is logical, given that the assessment of necessity and proportionality ultimately corresponds to the assessment of the legal basis for processing under data protection law. This is part of the GDPR and not the AI Act.

The main difference is that the AI Act's FRIA assesses the impact on fundamental rights, while the GDPR's DPIA main objective is the assessment of risks to the rights and freedoms of data subjects.[13] It is only in this sense that the latter is a subset of the former. Otherwise, they can be combined very well because they are very similar.

V. Art. 22 GDPR, Automated Decision Making

Art. 22(1) GDPR establishes the right of data subjects to not be subject to a decision based solely on automated processing, including profiling, that has legal effects or similarly significantly affects them. This does not apply if one of the exceptions of Art. 22(2) GDPR applies; for example, if the automated decision-making is necessary for a contract; if it is authorised by Union or Member State law; or if the decision is based on the data subject's explicit consent.

13 The GDPR's objective is to protect all fundamental rights and freedoms of natural persons and in particular their right to the protection of personal data, Art. 1(2) GDPR.

High-risk AI systems require the provider to fulfil transparency requirements, among other things. Art. 13 AI Act obliges providers of high-risk AI systems to design systems in such a way that they are sufficiently transparent to the deployer. This serves as a necessary condition for the deployer (i.e. the controller) to fulfil their duty of transparency to the data subject under Art. 13 GDPR.[14] Art. 14 AI Act corresponds directly to the requirement for human intervention under Art. 22(3) GDPR. In order to ensure effective human oversight, the interfaces must be designed in such a way that the overseer can understand the system's functionality, limitations and anomalies.

VI. Use Cases

The following use cases illustrate the requirements for conduction a FRIA or DPIA, respectively, on the basis of the characteristics of the processing.

1. Use Case Retrieval Augmented Generation

1) A public authority provides a RAG[15] system for citizens. The RAG is only used for publicly accessible documents. The function is employed as a knowledge base/research tool. Text generation is not possible; only search results are output. No input or usage data etc. are stored permanently.
   a) **GDPR**: Only processing of personal data which is public, as the system only accesses publicly available documents and functions merely as a knowledge database/research tool without storing or

14 In particular, Art. 13(2)(f) GDPR.

15 A RAG (Retrieval Augmented Generation) system is an architecture that enhances a generative Artificial Intelligence (AI) model, typically a Large Language Model (LLM), by augmenting the user input with relevant information from dedicated data sources before generating the output. This is intended to ensure that the generative AI system focuses on the relevant information when creating its response. Cf. Konferenz der unabhängigen Datenschutzaufsichtsbehörden des Bundes und der Länder (DSK), ‚Orientierungshilfe zu datenschutzrechtlichen Besonderheiten generativer KI-Systeme mit RAG-Methode', version 1.0 (October 2025) <https://www.datenschutzkonferenz-online.de/media/oh/DSK_OH_RAG.pdf>. Cf. Meier/Möstl/Starl, 'Digitalising Justice: A Fundamental Rights-based Approach' (May 2025) <https://fra.europa.eu/sites/default/files/fra_uploads/digitalising_justice_-_country_research_-_austria.pdf>, box 'AI-based justice chatbots in Austria and Portugal' on p. 65.

processing personal data. The system is low risk from a GDPR perspective, e.g., in the case of a data breach only information already public is affected. Nevertheless, it should be noted that additional information may make data personal. For example, IP addresses may be considered personal data and will be stored, at least temporarily, and could be relevant in the event of a data breach.[16]

b) **AI Act**: The function shown here does generally not constitute a high-risk AI system according to Art. 6 in conjunction with Annex III AI Act. The system typically falls under the category of a low-risk AI system or might be exempted according to, for example, Art. 6(3)(a) AI Act (a purely simple research tool without complex model interaction). Transparency obligations under Art. 50 AI Act still apply.

2) As in (1), but additionally, (output) texts are generated for a specific topic/query, etc., where the information in the output is typically based on that in the reference documents.
   a) **GDPR**: Since texts are generated, it must be, inter alia, determined whether these generated texts or the underlying reference documents and the input prompts contain and process personal data (e.g., names, contact details from the documents). Information obligations (Art. 13/14 GDPR) and transparency must be observed.
   b) **AI Act**: The generative function must be evaluated concerning its intended purpose. Whether all derived obligations can be fulfilled if a GPAI model becomes a high-risk AI system must be taken into account under Art. 25(1)(c) of the AI Act.
3) As in (2), but only information regarding a public authority, opening hours, contact persons, etc. is stored in the reference documents.
   a) **GDPR**: low risk as is (1). Provided the information (contact persons) is strictly public (e.g., on a website) and the use adheres to the purpose limitation principle, the processing is generally permissible (e.g., Art. 6(1)(e) GDPR in conjunction with § 3 BDSG). Information obligations (Art. 13/14 GDPR) and transparency must be observed.
   b) **AI Act**: Low risk AI system. The generation of general information is typically not a high-risk AI system. It will likely fall under the transparency obligations for AI systems that generate content (Art. 50 AI Act).

16 ECJ 19.10.2016 – case C-582/14, ECLI:EU:C:2016:779 – Breyer.

4) As in (2), but generated outputs are used as a basis for administrative acts.
   a) **GDPR**: High-risk processing: The creation of administrative acts, especially if they lead to legal effects or similarly significantly affects data subjects (Art. 22 GDPR), may constitute highly sensitive processing. A DPIA according to Art. 35 GDPR is likely mandatory.
   b) **AI Act**: High-risk AI system. The use of an AI system to support or replace administrative decision-making by public authorities concerning fundamental rights or administrative actions is highly likely to fall under Annex III No. 8 of the AIA. This necessitates strict requirements for data quality, technical robustness, human oversight, and transparency (Chapter III AI Act).

2. Use Case Automated Administrative Decisions

1) Pre-Processing: A citizen completes an application with the required but non-sensitive personal data. The system subsequently provides the citizen with information on the completeness of the application and an estimation of the chances of success for the application, along with a justification of which points are usually relevant for the result of the estimation. The citizen then decides independently whether to pursue the application further or not, and whether the application is to be submitted for human processing. The risk, of course, may depend on further parameters of the application. The mere estimation of the chances of success may, under certain circumstances, already constitute profiling (Art. 4 no. 4 GDPR), which entails a high risk for the rights of the data subjects (e.g., stigmatization, implicit refusal).
   a) **GDPR**: Since no (final) decision is made, the scope of application according to Art. 22 GDPR is not open. However, whether a DPIA is required depends on the system's influence on the citizen's decision. In any case, as 'personal data' is defined as any information relating to an identified or identifiable natural person (Art. 4 no. 1 GDPR), including 'opinions and assessments' that are linked to a particular person by 'reason of its content, purpose or effect',[17] the pre-processing and the result of the pre-processing constitute personal data.

17 ECJ 20.12.2017 – case c-434/16, ECLI:EU:C:2017:994 para. 34 et seq. – Nowak. in Case C-434/16 (Nowak).

This means that all the data subject's rights (Chapter 3 GDPR) must be implemented. Even in the absence of automated decision-making referred to in Art. 22(1) and (4) GDPR, public bodies should, as a best practice, provide 'meaningful information about the logic involved, as well as the significance and the envisaged consequences of such processing for the data subject'[18].

b) **AI Act**: The application may constitute an assessment of the eligibility for a fundamental public assistance or service pursuant to Annex III No. 5 lit. a AIA, which likely necessitates a FRIA.

2) Final Decision-Making: The citizen now submits their application, and the same application is used by the public authority for an automated decision, without a human decision being made.
   a) **GDPR**: This corresponds to an automated decision under Art. 22 GDPR with legal effects or which similarly significantly affects the citizen, and a DPIA is required. A DPIA may also be necessary if the result only serves as a basis for a human decision. In the latter case, however, it depends on a human decision that draws strongly on an automated one.[19] In such cases, it is essential that the controller can demonstrate the logic involved and provide the necessary transparency to the data subject. Otherwise, data subjects may even be denied their right to an effective judicial remedy, as set out in Art. 47 CFR.[20] Such an automated decision making may be less problematic if, for example, Union or Member State law allows such processing. For example, German law sometimes allows automated decisions for administrative acts ('Verwaltungsakt'), if no discretion is possible ('Ermessensspielraum') and where the derogation of Art. 22(2)(b) GDPR applies.[21]
   b) **AI Act**: A FRIA is likely required, as already described above. This necessitates strict requirements for data quality, technical robustness, human oversight, and transparency (Chapter III AI Act).
3) Post-Decision-Making: The application is used by the public authority after a human decision has been made and in order to detect deviations from previous decisions. In this context, the prior human decision is

18 Art. 13(2)(f), 14(2)(g) and 15(1)(h) GDPR.

19 ECJ 7.12.2023 – case C-634/21, ECLI:EU:C:2023:957 – SCHUFA.

20 ECJ judgement 21.6.2022 – case 817/19, ECLI:EU:C:2022:491 para. 195 – Ligue des droits humains.

21 § 35a VwVfG.

not replaced, but the results are used to adapt processes and train employees.

a) **GDPR**: No DPIA required, as the system is not used for individual case decision-making (similar to Scenario A). The use must adhere to the purpose limitation principle and be proportionate. To adhere to data minimisation and purpose limitation, personal data must be anonymised or pseudonymised insofar as possible.
b) **AI Act**: According to Art. 6(3)(c) AI Act, an exception applies, and it is therefore not a high-risk AI system, as the system is used after a human decision and for the detection of deviations without replacing or influencing the previous human decision. Consequently, no FRIA is required because the AI system is a low-risk AI system.

VII. Conclusion

Implementing AI systems that process personal data requires a dual risk assessment that considers both product safety under the AIA and the protection of personal data under the GDPR. While the AIA focuses on ensuring products are safe for the European market, the GDPR addresses the risks associated with processing personal data. The FRIA and DPIA impact assessment frameworks share core principles such as risk orientation, accountability and proportionality. However, the FRIA has a broader scope, covering rights such as non-discrimination and freedom of expression, whereas the DPIA primarily focuses on data protection. As the use cases demonstrate, the necessity for a DPIA and a FRIA can be concurrent or divergent, depending strongly on the specifics of the use case (e.g. whether processing takes place before or after a human decision is made). Ultimately, a case-by-case assessment is required. Nevertheless, as the FRIA and the DPIA are based on the same principles and overlap, knowledge and resources relating to DPIAs can be utilised.

Stricter national rules on the dismissal of data protection officers are compatible with the GDPR

Andreas Jaspers

ECJ 9.2.2023 – case C-453/21, ECLI:EU:C:2023:79 – X-FAB Dresden GmbH & Co. KG v FC

I. Case summary

The subject of the proceedings was the dismissal of employee FC from his position as data protection officer by X-FAB Dresden GmbH & Co. KG.

FC had been employed by X-FAB since 1993 and was also chairman of the works council and deputy chairman of the general works council.[1] In 2015, he was appointed data protection officer at X-FAB, its parent company and several German subsidiaries of the group in order to ensure a uniform group-wide data protection standard.[2]

In 2017, at the request of the Thuringian State Commissioner for Data Protection and Freedom of Information, X-FAB and the other group companies dismissed FC as data protection officer with immediate effect. Following the applicability of the GDPR, this dismissal was repeated in 2018 as a precautionary measure, now expressly based on Art. 38(3) sent. 2 GDPR and with reference to internal operational reasons within the group.[3] The reason given was that his work as data protection officer conflicted with his professional duties. In particular, the processing of citizens' financial data and his work as an application consultant led to a conflict of interest with his duties as data protection officer.[4]

1 ECJ 9.2.2023 – case C-453/21, ECLI:EU:C:2023:79 para. 10 et seq. – X-FAB Dresden GmbH & Co. KG v FC.

2 ECJ 9.2.2023 – case C-453/21, ECLI:EU:C:2023:79 para. 12 – X-FAB Dresden GmbH & Co. KG v FC.

3 ECJ 9.2.2023 – case C-453/21, ECLI:EU:C:2023:79 para. 13 – X-FAB Dresden GmbH & Co. KG v FC.

4 BAG 27.4.2021 – 9 AZR 621/19 (A), NJW 2023, 1045.

FC then filed a lawsuit before the labour court with the request to declare that he was still effectively appointed as data protection officer. The labour court in Dresden and, in the appeal instance, the Saxony Regional Labour Court upheld the lawsuit.[5]

X-FAB then lodged an appeal with the Federal Labour Court. The latter had doubts as to whether the strict national regulations on the dismissal of a data protection officer (§ 38(1) and (2) in conjunction with § 6(4) sent. 1 BDSG (previous version) in conjunction with § 626 BGB), which only allow dismissal for good cause, were compatible with Art. 38(3) GDPR.[6] It also asked the Court of Justice to clarify the conditions under which a conflict of interest within the meaning of Art. 38(6) GDPR exists, in particular when the office of data protection officer and works council chairperson are held simultaneously. The proceedings were therefore suspended and the following questions were referred to the ECJ for a preliminary ruling:[7]

1. Does Art. 38(3) sent. 2 GDPR preclude stricter national rules, such as those in § 38(1) and (2) in conjunction with § 6(4) sent. 1 BDSG, on the dismissal of data protection officers?
2. If so, does this also apply if the appointment of the data protection officer is required under national law but not mandatory under Art. 37 GDPR?
3. If so: Is Art. 38(3) sent. 2 GDPR based on a sufficient legal basis, in particular for employees as data protection officers?
4. If not: Is there a conflict of interest if the same employee is both the chair of the works council and the data protection officer, and does this require a special distribution of tasks within the works council?

II. Key legal findings

With regard to the first question referred, the ECJ clarified in its judgment of 9.2.2023 that Art. 38(3) sent. 2 GDPR does not preclude a national provision under which a DPO can only be dismissed for good cause, even if

5 ECJ 9.2.2023 – case C-453/21, ECLI:EU:C:2023:79 para. 15 – X-FAB Dresden GmbH & Co. KG v FC.

6 ECJ 9.2.2023 – case C-453/21, ECLI:EU:C:2023:79 para. 16 – X-FAB Dresden GmbH & Co. KG v FC.

7 ECJ 9.2.2023 – case C-453/21, ECLI:EU:C:2023:79 para. 17 – X-FAB Dresden GmbH & Co. KG v FC.

the dismissal is not related to the performance of his or her tasks, as long as this does not undermine the objectives of the GDPR.[8]

The subject matter of protection under Art. 38(3) sent. 2 GDPR is the functional independence of the DPO so that he or she can effectively perform his or her tasks under Art. 39 GDPR, in particular monitoring compliance with data protection regulations.[9] This applies regardless of whether the DPO is employed by the controller or works on the basis of a service contract.[10] Only overly strict national protection that prevents the dismissal of a DPO who no longer performs his or her tasks properly or independently would be incompatible with the GDPR.[11]

Because the answer to the first question clarified the central legal issues, there was no need to answer the second and third questions referred.[12]

With regard to the fourth question referred on the subject of 'conflict of interest' under Art. 38(6) of the GDPR, the ECJ clarified that a DPO may also perform other tasks, provided that these do not interfere with the independent performance of the DPO's activities.[13] A conflict of interest exists in particular where tasks or duties would enable the DPO to determine the purposes or means of the processing of personal data, which would compromise its monitoring function.[14] Whether a conflict of this nature exists must be examined on a case-by-case basis by the national court, taking into account the organisational structure of the controller, internal rules and other circumstances.[15]

---

8 ECJ 9.2.2023 – case C-453/21, ECLI:EU:C:2023:79 para. 36 – X-FAB Dresden GmbH & Co. KG v FC.

9 ECJ 9.2.2023 – case C-453/21, ECLI:EU:C:2023:79 para. 24 et seqq. – X-FAB Dresden GmbH & Co. KG v FC.

10 ECJ 9.2.2023 – case C-453/21, ECLI:EU:C:2023:79 para. 23 – X-FAB Dresden GmbH & Co. KG v FC.

11 ECJ 9.2.2023 – case C-453/21, ECLI:EU:C:2023:79 para. 32 et seqq. – X-FAB Dresden GmbH & Co. KG v FC.

12 ECJ 9.2.2023 – case C-453/21, ECLI:EU:C:2023:79 para. 37 – X-FAB Dresden GmbH & Co. KG v FC.

13 ECJ 9.2.2023 – case C-453/21, ECLI:EU:C:2023:79 para. 39 et seqq. – X-FAB Dresden GmbH & Co. KG v FC.

14 ECJ 9.2.2023 – case C-453/21, ECLI:EU:C:2023:79 para. 44 – X-FAB Dresden GmbH & Co. KG v FC.

15 ECJ 9.2.2023 – case C-453/21, ECLI:EU:C:2023:79 para. 45 et seq. – X-FAB Dresden GmbH & Co. KG v FC.

III. Systematic context and legal classification

1. Relevant legal provisions

With regard to the GDPR, the ECJ identified the following recitals and articles as relevant to its decision:

- Rec. 10 and 97
- Art. 38(3), (5) and (6)
- Art. 37(5), (6)
- Art. 39(1)(b)

In addition, the following provisions were cited with regard to national implementation:

- § 6(4) BDSG
- § 38(1), (2) BDSG
- § 626 BGB

Art. 38(3) sent. 2 GDPR stipulates that the data protection officer 'shall not be dismissed or penalised by the controller or processor for performing his or her tasks'. This is intended in particular to ensure the functional independence of the data protection officer.

Art. 38(6) GDPR stipulates that the data protection officer may perform other tasks as long as these do not lead to a conflict of interest.

Art. 39(1)(b) GDPR describes the supervisory duties of the data protection officer, including compliance with the GDPR and other data protection regulations, as well as the implementation of strategies for the protection of personal data.

§ 6(4) and § 38(1–2) BDSG specify the national regulations on the dismissal and appointment of data protection officers in non-public bodies, while § 626 BGB determines the conditions for termination without notice for good cause.

2. In the context of the Court's existing case law

In an earlier decision, the ECJ already dealt with the dismissal of data protection officers and the compatibility of national dismissal protection regulations with Art. 38 GDPR, namely in its judgment of 22 June 2022 –

C-534/20 (Leistritz).[16] In the underlying legal dispute, a company intended to dismiss its internal data protection officer for operational reasons and to have the function performed by an external person in future. The employee brought an action for unfair dismissal, invoking in particular the special protection against dismissal pursuant to § 38(2) in conjunction with § 6(4) BDSG.[17]

In this decision, the ECJ already clarified that Member States are free to provide for stricter rules for the protection of data protection officers than those contained in the GDPR itself. However, the question of under what conditions a conflict of interest within the meaning of Art. 38(6) GDPR is to be assumed did not play a role in the proceedings.

IV. Author's analysis and commentary

1. Stricter national regulations

With its X-FAB decision, the ECJ confirms that stricter national rules on the dismissal of data protection officers for company DPOs are permissible, provided that they remain within the scope of the Member States' reserved competence.

The German regulation on protection against dismissal for internal DPOs (§ 6(4) BDSG in conjunction with § 626 BGB) does indeed tighten protection by limiting dismissal to 'important reasons', but it still allows dismissal if the data protection officer can no longer perform his or her duties independently, professionally or in compliance with the GDPR. The German regulation thus supplements Art. 38(3) sent. 2 GDPR in terms of labour law without counteracting its protective purpose. From the perspective of German labour law, Art. 38(3) sent. 2 GDPR does not constitute a conclusive provision under EU law.

At the same time, this protection does not constitute absolute irremovability, as dismissal must still be possible, for example in the event of a lack of professional competence, performance of duties in breach of the GDPR or a lack of independence as a result of a conflict of interest.[18]

---

16 ECJ 22.6.2022 – case C-534/20, ECLI:EU:C:2022:495 – Leistritz AG gegen LH.

17 ECJ 22.6.2022 – case C-534/20, ECLI:EU:C:2022:495 – Leistritz AG gegen LH.

18 Benkert NJW-Spezial 2023, 180.

For external data protection officers, doubts remain as to the conformity with European law of the stricter protection against dismissal based on labour law, as the reasoning in the judgment focuses only on internal constellations.[19]

In practical terms, *Klasen* sees the problem that the ruling could motivate cross-border companies to appoint DPOs outside Germany.[20]

Greiner/Winkel correctly point out that the ECJ leaves key dogmatic questions open – such as the basis for authorisation and application to data protection officers who are only required to be appointed at national level – which means that considerable legal uncertainty remains in practice.[21]

2. Members of a works council as data protection officers

According to the ECJ ruling, a conflict of interest between the role of works council chairperson and that of company data protection officer must be examined by the national court on a case-by-case basis, taking into account the organisational structure of the controller, internal regulations and other circumstances.

Based on the ECJ's guidelines, the Federal Labour Court[22] has ruled that the duties of works council chairperson and data protection officer cannot typically be performed by the same person without a conflict of interest. This conflict of interest arises from the fact that the works council decides by resolution under which specific circumstances it requests which personal data from the employer in the performance of its statutory duties and how it processes this data. In this context, it determines the purposes and means of processing personal data.

The Federal Labour Court left open the question of whether other works council members can monitor compliance with data protection obligations sufficiently independently as data protection officers. In any case, the Federal Labour Court believes that the prominent role of the works council chairperson, who represents the works council in the context of the resolutions passed, negates the reliability required to fulfil the duties of a data protection officer.

---

19 Schwartmann/Jaspers/Thüsing/Kugelmann DS-GVO BDSG/Jaspers/Reif, 3. Aufl. 2024, DS-GVO Art. 38 mn. 20.

20 Klasen NJW 2023, 1045 (1048).

21 Greiner/Winkel EuZA 2023, 433.

22 BAG 6.6.2023 – 9 AZR 383/19, ZD 2023, 761.

The literature has assessed the ECJ's decision in a more differentiated manner in some cases.

According to *Haußmann*, the ECJ ruling makes it clear that the question of a conflict of interest in the case of a data protection officer does not depend solely on his role as a works council member, but on the powers he exercises in the performance of other tasks or duties within the company.[23] In particular, a conflict of interest could arise if the DPO, as a works council member, were involved in determining the purposes and means of data processing within the works council. Since the internal organisation and data processing of the works council is shielded from access by the employer in accordance with § 79a BetrVG, the employer cannot monitor the activities of the works council and its compliance with data protection regulations. This makes it difficult to actually identify a conflict of interest, as the DPO, as a member of the works council, also performs control functions. Even internal regulations on data processing in the works council office cannot completely resolve the conflict.

According to *Greiner/Winkel*, the ECJ demonstrates in practice that the dual role of a DPO and works council member can regularly lead to a conflict of interest, which the employer has limited ability to identify and manage.[24]

In their practical assessment, *Moos/Dirkers*, like the Federal Labour Court, conclude that the dual role of a works council chairperson is always prone to conflict because the chairperson can hardly act without defining the purposes and means of personal data processing, so that companies should refrain from such a combination of functions for reasons of caution.[25]

Klasen points out that the ruling does not provide any practical clarity on the specific dismissal. The determination of conflicts of interest remains the responsibility of the national courts, and the ECJ transfers this competence to national law. For Germany, this means that the strict protection of the DPO against dismissal remains in place, but dismissals are only conceivable in exceptional cases (e.g. in the event of failure to perform duties or conflicts of interest).[26]

23 Haußmann ArbRAktuell 2023, 153.
24 See also Greiner/Winkel EuZA 2023, 433.
25 Moos/Dirkers ZD 2023, 334; similarly Brinkmann GWR 2023, 217.
26 Klasen NJW 2023, 1045 (1048).

However, the ECJ ruling leaves important practical questions unanswered and delegates further potential conflicts to the national courts for clarification.

V. Recommended Further Reading

Schröder, Datenschutzrecht für die Praxis, 6th ed. 2026, 3. Chap. XVI. 7.

Weth/Herberger/Wächter/Sorge, Praxishandbuch zum Arbeitnehmerdatenschutz/Breyer, 3rd ed. 2026, Chapter 31, mn. 27.

Koreng/Lachenmann, Formularhandbuch Datenschutzrecht/Sander/Diekmann, 4th ed. 2025, Form. B. I. 2. Note 1.-5. mn. 1.

Data breach notification requirements and supervisory discretion under Art. 33 and 34 of the GDPR

Isabelle Stroot

ECJ 26.9.2024 – case C-768/21, ECLI:EU:C:2024:785 – TR v Land Hessen

I. Case summary

An employee of a bank had accessed customer data without authorisation. The bank reported this incident to the Hessian Data Protection and Information Authority (HBDI) on 15.11.2019, in accordance with Art. 33 of the GDPR.[1] However, it refrained from notifying the data subject under Art. 34 GDPR, as it considered that there was no high risk to the rights and freedoms of the data subjects. Subsequently, the data subject became aware of the incident and lodged a complaint with the HBDI (Art. 77 GDPR), requesting regulatory action, particularly the imposition of an administrative fine.[2]

The HBDI found that a personal data breach hat occured but did not consider the bank's risk assessment to be manifestly erroneous.[3]. Therefore, it refrained from taking corrective measures under Art. 58(2) GDPR.[4] Consequently, the data subject brought an action before the Administrative Court of Wiesbaden (VG), seeking an order requiring the HBDI to take action. According to the claimant, while the supervisory authority had discretion over the choice of measures, it did not have discretion over whether to act at all.[5]

The Administrative Court of Wiesbaden ruled that the claimant's interpretation, which is supported to some extent in the literature, was too

1 ECJ 26.9.2024 – case C-768/21, ECLI:EU:C:2024:785 para. 14-17 – TR v Land Hessen.

2 ECJ 26.9.2024 – case C-768/21, ECLI:EU:C:2024:785 para. 15 and 19 – TR v Land Hessen.

3 ECJ 26.9.2024 – case C-768/21, ECLI:EU:C:2024:785 para. 17 – TR v Land Hessen.

4 ECJ 26.9.2024 – case C-768/21, ECLI:EU:C:2024:785 para. 17 and 36 – TR v Land Hessen.

5 ECJ 26.9.2024 – case C-768/21, ECLI:EU:C:2024:785 para. 19-21 – TR v Land Hessen.

broad. The court granted the supervisory authority a margin of discretion, allowing it to refrain from adopting corrective measures in certain cases where an infringement has been established.[6]

The Administrative Court therefore referred to the question of whether supervisory authorities are always required to take measures under Art. 58(2) of the GDPR once an infringement has been identified, or whether they have the discretion to refrain from such measures in specific cases.[7]

II. Key legal findings

In its judgment, the ECJ clarifies the scope of supervisory authorities' discretion in cases of established infringements of data protection law. The central issue concerns the interpretation of Art. 57(1) and 58(2) GDPR. A supervisory authority is not automatically obliged to impose corrective measures, particularly an administrative fine, whenever an infringement of personal data protection is established.[8] The Court emphasises that all supervisory action is subject to the principle of proportionality.[9] There is no 'automatic sanctioning' in the sense of a strict legality principle that requires sanctions to be issued in every case.[10] Instead the chosen measure must be appropriate, necessary and proportionate in order to ensure effective compliance with the Regulation and remedy the specific shortcomings of the case in question.[11]

Regarding notification obligations, the judgment reaffirms the graduated protection concept underlying Art. 33 and 34 of the GDPR. Notification to the supervisory authority under Art. 33 GDPR is required where a breach is likely to result in a risk to the rights and freedoms of natural persons. Conversely, notification of the data subject under Art. 34 GDPR

6 ECJ 26.9.2024 – case C-768/21, ECLI:EU:C:2024:785 para. 22 and 36 et seq. – TR v Land Hessen.

7 ECJ 26.9.2024 – case C-768/21, ECLI:EU:C:2024:785 para. 20-23 – TR v Land Hessen.

8 ECJ 26.9.2024 – case C-768/21, ECLI:EU:C:2024:785 para. 41 et seq., 50 – TR v Land Hessen.

9 ECJ 26.9.2024 – case C-768/21, ECLI:EU:C:2024:785 para. 37 – TR v Land Hessen, Rec. 129 GDPR.

10 ECJ 26.9.2024 – case C-768/21, ECLI:EU:C:2024:785 para. 35 and 38 – TR v Land Hessen, Rec. 129 and 148 GDPR.

11 ECJ 26.9.2024 – case C-768/21, ECLI:EU:C:2024:785 para. 37, 42- TR v Land Hessen.

presupposes a higher threshold, namely a high risk. This differentiation reflects the GDPR's risk-based approach, which the EDPB further specifies in its Guidelines 01/2021 through detailed practical scenarios such as ransomware attacks or the accidental disclosure of highly sensitive data.[12]

Further key statements relate to the operational level. The 72-hour notification period begins when the controller becomes aware of the incident, provided that this has been established sufficiently reliably.[13] Incomplete information may justify so-called staged notifications pursuant to Art. 33(4) GDPR. Additionally, the judgment clarifies that the internal documentation obligation under Art. 33 (5) GDPR is independent of the notification obligation, and infringements may be sanctioned separately. This is illustrated by supervisory practice, notably in the Twitter/DPC case, where deficiencies in documentation and timeliness were sanctioned independently of the underlying breach.[14] From a doctrinal perspective, therefore, the ECJ prioritises the effectiveness of remedial action over the imposition of a purely formal obligation to sanction.[15]

III. Systematic context and legal classification

The judgment should be considered in the context of the accountability principle (Art. 5(2) GDPR) and the procedural enforcement of the GDPR. Art. 33 and 34 of the GDPR form the basis of incident response management. Judgment C-768/21 recalibrates the tension between controllers and public supervision. While, in earlier decisions such as Schrems II,[16] the ECJ emphasised an obligation on supervisory authorities to act in cases involving data transfers to third countries, the Court now clarifies that

12 EDPB, 'Guidelines 01/2021 on Examples regarding Personal Data Breach Notification', version 2.0 (14.12.2021) <https://www.edpb.europa.eu/system/files/2022-01/edpb_guidelines_012021_pdbnotification_adopted_en.pdf>, para. 13–18, 76 et seqq.

13 Paal/Pauly DS-GVO BDSG/Martini, 4th edn. 2026, DS-GVO Art. 33 mn. 33; Kühling/Buchner DS-GVO BDSG/Jandt, 4th edn. 2024, Art. 33 mn. 15.

14 Data Protection Commission, 'Decision of the Data Protection Commission made pursuant to Section 111 of the Data Protection Act 2018, Twitter International Company' (IN-18-5-1., 9.12.2020) < https://www.edpb.europa.eu/sites/default/files/decisions/final_decision_-_in-19-1-1_9.12.2020.pdf>.

15 ECJ 26.9.2024 – case C-768/21, ECLI:EU:C:2024:785 para. 44 – TR v Land Hessen; see also Rec. 129 GDPR.

16 ECJ 16.7.2020 – case C-311/18, ECLI:EU:C:2020:559 paras 112 et seqq. – Data Protection Commissioner v Facebook Ireland and Schrems ('Schrems II').

such 'action' does not necessarily have to take the form of a sanction.[17] However, the Court clarifies that this duty to act relates to the effectiveness of supervision rather than the imposition of punitive measures.

The judgment is consistent with Art. 83 GDPR, which requires various criteria to be balanced when imposing administrative fines, such as the gravity and duration of the infringement and the degree of cooperation. The ECJ clarifies that the supervisory authority is a regulatory body, not a 'criminal court', whose primary objective is to restore lawful conditions. This strengthens the institutional architecture of European data protection law by granting authorities the flexibility needed to respond to controllers who cooperate.

Another important contextual factor is the role of the European Data Protection Board (EDPB).[18] The Guidelines 01/2021 on the notification of personal data breaches provide practical examples that give concrete meaning to the legal concepts of Art. 33 and 34 GDPR, such as 'awareness' and 'high risk'. Judgment C-768/21 supports this interpretative framework by validating the supervisory authority's assessment of these criteria as a core element of supervision.

Tis classification is particularly significant in cross-border cases. Although the one-stop-shop (OSS) mechanism is intended to promote consistency within the EU, the EDPB Guidelines 9/2022 clarify that this privilege does not extend to controllers without an establishment in the EU (Art. 3(2) GDPR). Such controllers may be required to notify multiple national supervisory authorities simultaneously, which significantly increases the procedural burden of breach notification. The EU representative under Art. 27 GDPR does not establish a 'lead supervisory authority'.[19] Judgment C-768/21 indirectly highlights that, despite the absence of OSS competence, the substantive standards governing supervisory discretion must be applied uniformly throughout the EU in accordance with the principle of proportionality.

---

17 ECJ 26.9.2024 – case C-768/21, ECLI:EU:C:2024:785 para. 33 et seq. – TR v Land Hessen.

18 EDPB, 'Guidelines 9/2022 on Personal Data Breach Notification under the GDPR', version 2.0 (28.3.2023) < https://www.edpb.europa.eu/system/files/2023-04/edpb_guidelines_202209_personal_data_breach_notification_v2.0_en.pdf>.

19 EDPB, 'Guidelines 9/2022 on Personal Data Breach Notification under the GDPR' (fn. 18), para. 73.

Alongside the case law on damages (Saturn[20] and NAP[21]), this judgment establishes a consistent framework where prevention, remediation and proportionality take precedence over mere formalism.

IV. Author's analysis and commentary

Judgment C-768/21 sends a clear signal against the 'automatic sanctioning' approach, strengthening the position of data protection officers within organisations.[22] The doctrinal significance of the judgement lies in the ECJ's explicit recognition of the cooperative behaviour of data controllers.[23] Where a controller reports an incident in accordance with Art. 33 GDPR and conducts a plausible risk assessment and promptly implements appropriate countermeasures, the supervisory authority may refrain from imposing further sanctions.[24] This creates a strong incentive for transparency and proactive organisational 'self-remediation'.

1. Operational implications for organisations

From a compliance management perspective, the judgment means that the quality of internal documentation under Art. 33(5) of the GDPR may become the decisive line of defence in cases of doubt. Simply reporting an incident is not sufficient. Rather, the notification must form part of a comprehensible risk analysis. Ideally, organisations should rely on a standardised process or framework[25] that objectively considers factors such as the sensitivity of the data, the number of data subjects affected, and the effectiveness of technical safeguards, such as encryption. The judgment demonstrates that a well-reasoned decision not to notify data subjects under Art. 34 GDPR, on the basis that no high risk exists, may be respected

20 ECJ 11.4.2024 – case C-687/21, ECLI:EU:C:2024:72 – MediaMarktSaturn v ZQ.
21 ECJ 14.12.2023 – case C-340/21, ECLI:EU:C:2023:986 – VB v Natsionalna agentsia za prihodite.
22 See also ECJ 14.12.2023 – case C-340/21, ECLI:EU:C:2023:986 – VB v Natsionalna agentsia za prihodite.
23 ECJ 26.9.2024 – case C-768/21, ECLI:EU:C:2024:785 para. 48 – TR v Land Hessen.
24 See Art. 83(2) GDPR.
25 ECJ 26.9.2024 – case C-768/21, ECLI:EU:C:2024:785 para. 41-48 – TR v Land Hessen; EDPB, 'Guidelines 01/2021 on Examples regarding Personal Data Breach Notification' (fn. 12), para. 36-40.

by the supervisory authority provided that the reasoning is professionally sound.

2. Practical recommendations

Organisations must be 'incident-ready'. This requires predefined escalation paths to ensure compliance with the 72-hour deadline. As the ECJ emphasises proportionality, communication with the supervisory authority should take the form of a dialogue. Early-stage notifications to the relevant authority demonstrate cooperation and professionalism. From a technical and organisational perspective, controllers should prioritise their technical and organisational measures. In the event of an infringement of data subjects' rights, such measures may influence the risk assessment in favour of the controller or at least mitigate the outcome.

3. Regulatory policy and global perspective

From a regulatory policy standpoint, the judgment eases companies' concerns about viewing notification as an admission of guilt. A carefully considered risk assessment prevents supervisory authorities from being overwhelmed with trivial cases, enabling them to focus their resources on serious infringements. In this respect, the GDPR emerges as a system that recognises and rewards individual efforts and compliance initiatives.[26]

4. Concluding remarks on legal development

The judgment establishes a link between strict notification obligations and the goal of effective regulation. It emphasises that data protection law and the GDPR are not ends in themselves but rather serve to protect data subjects. From a practical perspective, the judgment may also help supervisory authorities prioritise their enforcement resources, encouraging them to focus on systemic or high-risk infringements rather than isolated incidents that are well managed. Imposing an 'enforced' fine in cases where infringements have already been remedied and are minor would undermine acceptance of the GDPR. By anchoring discretion in the princi-

26 See generally regarding the discussion Petri NJW 2024, 3427; Theusner DSB 2024, 246.

ple of proportionality, the ECJ strengthens risk-based compliance within organisations. Consequently, the focus of supervisory reporting shifts from determining whether to report to ensure that incidents are reported in the most appropriate manner. This development will help reconcile the protective purpose of the GDPR with practical feasibility and the realities faced by organisations.

By embedding discretion within the framework of proportionality, the ECJ is promoting a risk-based compliance culture. Looking into the future, it is likely that the focus will shift from whether a notification is made to how incidents are handled. This strengthens the position of European data protection law as a standard that combines high levels of protection with practical workability.

V. Recommended further reading

EDPB, 'Guidelines 01/2021 on Examples regarding Personal Data Breach Notification', version 2.0 (14.12.2021) <https://www.edpb.europa.eu/system/files/2022-01/edpb_guidelines_012021_pdbnotification_adopted_en.pdf>.

EDPB, 'Guidelines 9/2022 on Personal Data Breach Notification under the GDPR', version 2.0 (28.3.2023) < https://www.edpb.europa.eu/system/files/2023-04/edpb_guidelines_202209_personal_data_breach_notification_v2.0_en.pdf>.

Data Protection Commission, 'Decision of the Data Protection Commission made pursuant to Section 111 of the Data Protection Act 2018, Twitter International Company' (IN-18-5-1., 9.12.2020) < https://www.edpb.europa.eu/sites/default/files/decisions/final_decision_-_in-19-1-1_9.12.2020.pdf>.

Kühling/Buchner DS-GVO/BDSG/Jandt, 4th edn. 2024, Art. 33 et seq.

Federmann/Ringel/Schorer/Bernheim CCZ 2024, 121.

Codes of Conduct under the GDPR

Gabriela Mercuri

EDPB, ‚Opinion 16/2021 on the draft decision of the Belgian Supervisory Authority regarding the "EU Data Protection Code of Conduct for Cloud Service Providers" submitted by Scope Europe' (19.5.2021) <https://www.edpb.europa.eu/our-work-tools/our-documents/opinion-board-art-64/opinion-162021-draft-decision-belgian-supervisory_sk>

EDPB, ‚Opinion 17/2021 on the draft decision of the French Supervisory Authority regarding the European code of conduct submitted by the Cloud Infrastructure Service Providers (CISPE)' (19.5.2021) <https://www.edpb.europa.eu/our-work-tools/our-documents/opinion-board-art-64/opinion-172021-draft-decision-french-supervisory_en>

I. Opinions' summary

EDPB Opinion 16/2021 assessed the draft decision of the Belgian Supervisory Authority on the *EU Data Protection Code of Conduct for Cloud Service Providers* ('EU Cloud Code'), submitted by SCOPE Europe under Article 40 GDPR. The Board confirmed that the draft code aligns with the GDPR's requirements for codes of conduct and contributes to the proper application of the Regulation in the cloud computing sector (XaaS).

EDPB Opinion 17/2021 assessed the draft decision of the French Supervisory Authority regarding the European Code of Conduct submitted by Cloud Infrastructure Service Providers in Europe (CISPE) under Article 40 GDPR. The Board confirmed that the draft code aligns with GDPR's requirements for codes of conduct and contributes to the proper application of the Regulation by cloud Infrastructure service providers (IaaS).

Opinion 16/2021 and Opinion 17/2021 ('the Opinions') acknowledged that the respective codes reflect the specific features of cloud services and provide practical guidance on key GDPR obligations, particularly those related to processors under Article 28 GDPR. The Opinions also emphasised that although adherence to the codes can help demonstrate sufficient guarantees of compliance with Article 28, adherence to the codes do not replace supervisory enforcement powers nor automatically validate overall compliance. The Opinions also noted that the codes' scope (applicable to processors, not B2C or controller activities) and clarified that the codes do not serve as standalone transfer mechanisms under Chapter V GDPR. The Board concluded that the drafts meet GDPR requirements and recommended submission of any future amendments for review.[1]

II. Key legal findings

In the absence of case law, supervisory authorities' decisions and opinions are pivotal for legal interpretation development and operationalisation. In the EU data protection space, opinions by the European Data Protection Board ('EDPB' or 'The Board') are therefore fundamental, providing a degree of normative harmonisation and consequent legal certainty that is hardly achievable in other *fora*. As of 2025, only three GDPR ('The Regulation') transnational codes of conduct have received a positive opinion from the EDPB[2], which makes the latter – alongside EDPB Guidelines[3] – crucial references in the field.

A common and notable aspect across the Opinions issued in 2021, concerning both the EU Cloud Code of Conduct and the CISPE Code of Conduct (hereinafter the 'EU Cloud CoC' and 'CISPE CoC') is the recurrent referencing to the EDPB Guidelines on Codes of Conduct and Monitoring Bodies ('The Guidelines')[4]. In spite of their non-binding character, such consistent allusion reinforces the critical role of the Guidelines as a complementary source for legal interpretation within GDPR's regulatory regime.

1 This summary was generated with the support of a generative AI tool and subsequently reviewed and revised by the author.

2 All EDBP opinions on transnational GDPR codes of conduct can be found at < https://www.edpb.europa.eu/our-work-tools/consistency-findings/opinions_en>.

3 In this case particularly the following Guidelines: EDPB, ‚Guidelines 1/2019 on Codes of Conduct and Monitoring Bodies under Regulation 2016/679', version 2.0 (4.6.2019) < https://www.edpb.europa.eu/our-work-tools/our-documents/guidelines/guidelines-12019-codes-conduct-and-monitoring-bodies-0_en>; EDPB, ‚Guidelines 04/2021 on Codes of Conduct as Tools for Transfers under Regulation (EU) 2016/679', version 2.0, (22.2.2022) <https://www.edpb.europa.eu/our-work-tools/our-documents/guidelines/guidelines-042021-codes-conduct-tools-transfers_en>.

4 EDPB, Guidelines 1/2019 on Codes of Conduct and Monitoring Bodies under Regulation (EU) 2016/679 (fn. 3).

Another prominent consideration raised by the EDPB is the practical dimension of Codes. In both Opinions, the Board expressly welcomed the inclusion of specific and concrete implementation mechanisms (namely the Controls Catalogue for the EU Cloud CoC[5] and the Compliance Checklist for the CISPE Code[6]). The Board's commendations of the efforts present in both Codes with regards to the developing of structures that assist compliance assessments in a measurable way illustrates the relevance of operational meaning and transparency.

The Opinions have also solidified the notion of ongoing compliance, which is depicted by adherence processes that encompass three phases: 1 – eligibility assessment of signatory companies; 2 – monitoring mechanism on an ongoing basis and 3 – *ad hoc* monitoring. This appraisal illustrates how a monitoring framework under Art. 41 GDPR embodies and concretises GDPRs risk-based approach as well as its accountability principle as a continuous due diligence exercise.

A last point that must be highlighted as one of the main legal findings under the Opinions is the positive chain effects that can be triggered by the adherence to an approved code. The Board emphasizes that 'additional guarantees of compliance'[7] apply also to consumers that choose to entrust their personal data to controllers that have picked cloud services that adhere to an approved code.

III. Systematic context and legal classification

Since the very conception of GDPR, its principle-oriented and sector-agnostic approach has been broadly recognized as a significant challenge for regulatory implementation. Rightfully anticipating such challenges, and grasping the importance of specifying these provisions for practical enactment, legislators have incorporated into the GDPR soft-law instruments such as codes of conduct ('codes'), pursuant to Art. 40 and 41 GDPR.

5 See ‚EU Cloud Code of Conduct' (December 2020) <https://www.edpb.europa.eu/system/files/2024-02/eucloudcoc.pdf>, Annex A – Controls Catalogue.

6 See ‚CISPE' (9.2.2021) <https://www.edpb.europa.eu/system/files/2023-03/2021_cispe_cloud_iaas_data_protection_code_of_conduct_-_gdpr_compliance_0.pdf>, Annex B – Compliance Checklist.

7 EDPB, ‚Opinion 17/2021 on the draft decision of the French Supervisory Authority regarding the European code of conduct submitted by the Cloud Infrastructure Service Providers (CISPE)' (19.5.2021) <https://www.edpb.europa.eu/our-work-tools/our-documents/opinion-board-art-64/opinion-172021-draft-decision-french-supervisory_en>.

Considering the diversity of economic activities circumscribed by the Regulation, and the subsequent asymmetries in terms of the risks to the freedom and rights of individuals, creating methods to specify GDPR provisions within different contexts became an effort of the utmost importance. Against this background, codes are mechanisms that enable categories of controllers[8] or processors[9] to demonstrate compliance with the GDPR.

Increasing consistency across a given sector or processing activity[10], as well as fostering regulatory congruency among different Member States are some of the core objectives of codes. These tools must, therefore, capture particular industry needs and create tailored technical and organizational measures that can be uniformly implemented, in a practical and cost-effective manner[11]. In other words, codes are meant to translate open-ended provisions into actionable steps that can be adopted by all-size companies, and ultimately promote transparency and accountability while facilitating risk-assessments throughout data processing chains.

The incorporation of these soft-law mechanisms appears within a broader trend of involving a variety of stakeholders in policy making processes – which is often referred to as the Better Regulation Agenda[12]. This movement was not limited to the data protection sphere and has been consolidated by several EU documents discussing the notion of simplifying regulatory frameworks and increasing effectiveness.

Amidst other instruments, such as certifications and technical standards, codes were clearly a part of this tendency, being progressively introduced across different policy developments. Recurring to soft-law as complementary tools became especially relevant within efforts to regulate areas subject to rapid technological change – besides the GDPR, other recent examples are the AI Act and the DSA. Nonetheless, the particular application of these tools diverge significantly, notably in terms of: 1 – the level of institutional involvement (ranging from 'pure self-regulation' to 'legislation led co-regu-

8 Art. 24 GDPR.

9 Art. 28 GDPR.

10 According to EDPB, ‚Guidelines 1/2019 on Codes of Conduct and Monitoring Bodies under Regulation (EU) 2016/679‘ (fn. 3): 'Codes do not necessarily need to be confined or limited to an specific sector'.

11 EDPB, ‚Guidelines 1/2019 on Codes of Conduct and Monitoring Bodies under Regulation (EU) 2016/679‘ (fn. 3).

12 Vander Maelen European Law Review 2022, 752 (760).

lation'[13]), 2 – the degree of legal incentive, and 3 – the role and strictness of overseeing/monitoring mechanisms.

Although the DPD (Art. 27 GDPR) already integrated codes of conduct as contributing factors to its proper implementation, the GDPR went beyond and created a more comprehensive and robust framework for codes, notably by the inclusion of Art. 41 GDPR, which introduces a mechanism to enable effective compliance oversight by an accredited independent third-party. One of the foundational features of the monitoring of GDPR codes of conduct is its continuous character. This continuity aspect solidifies the notion of ongoing compliance, which has been the most clearly expressed in the obligation of setting up complaints handling procedures.

IV. Author's analysis and commentary

In order to analyse the current state of play of GDPR codes, it is helpful to look back at the experience with soft-law under the Directive – which solely generated one adopted code at the EU level[14]. Besides the lack of an oversight apparatus, the Directive also failed to provide sufficient detailing, appropriate incentive, and established procedures – particularly for codes at the transnational level, which are instrumental to reduce fragmentation across Member States. Other considerable issues identified in the implementation of codes of conduct under the Directive were the difficulties in the exchanges between supervisory authorities and the industry. The combination of these factors have led private stakeholders to express dissatisfaction with the tool[15].

The accumulated experience under the Directive, alongside the growing pressure to enhance the protection of individuals amidst the swift development of data-driven technologies, were some of the contributing factors for the revamping of the recipe for codes. It is also vital to situate these legal developments in a broader context where economic and political dynamics played a fundamental role and cannot be underestimated.

13 European Commission, ,'Better Regulation' Toolbox' (July 2023), <https://commission.europa.eu/document/download/9c8d2189-8abd-4f29-84e9-abc843cc68e0_en?filename=BR%20toolbox%20-%20Jul%202023%20-%20FINAL.pdf>.

14 Article 29 Working Party, ,Opinion 3/2003 on the European Code of Conduct of FEDMA for the Use of Personal Data in Direct Marketing' (WP 77, 13.6.2003) <https://ec.europa.eu/justice/article-29/documentation/opinion-recommendation/files/2003/wp77_en.pdf>.

15 Vander Maelen European Data Protection Law Review 2021, 228 (230).

All things considered, once compared to its predecessor, GDPR has clearly developed a more sturdy and sophisticated infrastructure for complementary soft-law instruments – this time around, putting forward a more accurate and vigorous example of co-regulation[16].

With GDPR, the legislator has deliberately addressed several conceptual and practical shortcomings of the Directive's architecture for these tools. In addition to the introduction of a well-rounded approach combining Art. 40 and 41 GDPR as inextricable components of the same whole, this core legal skeleton has been largely supported by accompanying EDPB guidelines as well as the Opinions here discussed. The abovementioned compilation provides a considerable degree of clarity for the interested parties and, ultimately, of legal certainty.

Another key variable that generated positive expectations in regards to GDPRs formula for codes was its reward system. Within this new model, the legislator did provide important incentives for the industry to voluntarily contribute to the development and adhere to approved codes, especially at the EU level. This incentive package comprises the recognition of codes as tools to legally demonstrate compliance and give them the possibility of mitigating fines. Moreover, the benefits of code adherence can cascade through, positively impacting several stakeholders throughout processing chains, particularly small and medium-sized business whose protection is a priority of the Regulation.

Besides the primary and direct advantages codes can generate, secondary – but yet, highly valuable – benefits can appear as a product of the approval and accreditation processes under Art. 40 and 41 GDPR. The latter and the former create structured platforms of cooperation between industry stakeholders and supervisory authorities, enabling meaningful exchange and mutual understanding. These processes are especially helpful when complex technologies are involved. Knowing such technologies are regulatory targets, given the volume and nature of personal data being processed and the respective risks entailed, it is likely not a coincidence that the first two EU-wide codes covered the cloud industry.

It is also critical to highlight the potential of codes to generate positive spillover effects beyond EU borders. The widespread adoption of these instruments can promote bottom-up harmonisation, notably in the context of the digital industry, where companies often operate at a global scale and

16 See definitions of self-regulation and co-regulation at European Commission, ,'Better Regulation' Toolbox' (fn. 13), p. 3.1.

implement a common compliance framework across jurisdictions based on the highest benchmark to be met. This process can spontaneously influence the establishment of comparable levels of protection and significantly support extensive implementation of European data protection standards, favouring data subjects and businesses across the Union.

Once observing the benefits that codes can yield, which have been summarized here in a non-exhaustive manner, next to the low adoption rates of this tool, particularly at the EU level[17], one cannot help but wonder about what we are missing in this equation. Why has the strong and unique potential of codes has not yet been fulfilled after nearly ten years of GDPR?

Before attempting to answer this question, it is worth noting that insufficient research alongside a lack of targeted and systematic impact assessments on the topic significantly challenge this analysis. The absence of ample and diverse evaluation sources also hinders the possibility of improving existing procedures, extending dissemination avenues, as well as enhancing incentives for the development of codes.

With the Directive, the main reasons given by the industry for the low uptake of codes were the slowness and overly detailed reviewing process by competent authorities[18]. Fast-forwarding to the second and latest European Commission's report on the application of the GDPR[19], the diagnosis remains quite similar. According to the latter, businesses have stressed that although recognizing the major potential of codes as tailored and cost-effective instruments, approval and accreditation requirements are burdensome, and data protection authorities are not sufficiently engaged. In a nutshell, and despite of some successful experiences with the approval and operationalisation of a few codes, their added value seems to be persistently outweighed by their procedural path to approval.

For those working in the field, there are several technical and procedural considerations that can be decisive for boosting the uptake and optimising the deployment of codes. Nevertheless, for this exercise, looking at a wider context seems more valuable for the comprehension and tackling of these

17 As of December 2025, only few codes of conduct under Art. 40 GDPR have been approved at Member State level, while only three transnational codes have received a positive EDPB opinion.

18 Korff/Douwe, ‚Comparative study on different approaches to new privacy challenges, in particular in the light of technological developments' (2010) <https://repository.londonmet.ac.uk/8985/>.

19 European Commission, ‚Second Report on the Application of the General Data Protection Regulation', COM(2024) 357 final (25.7.2024).

recurrent and perhaps now chronic issues. In this spirit of searching for the bigger picture, a couple of elements stand out as structural challenges: 1 – systematic misunderstandings around the role of codes by both public and private stakeholders and 2 – the lack of clear and uniform communication around these tools, specifically in terms of their potential benefits.

Although the GDPR itself, accompanying guidelines, and the Opinions discussed here are coherent and far more developed than other provisions under the Regulation, misconceptions around codes appear as a repeated concern. Information asymmetry between different stakeholders and discrepancies across national data protection authorities impose a serious challenge to widespread uptake.

An uneven understanding around the codes' normative role portrays a symptomatic example of such misconceptions. Despite the clear and assiduous references to the complementary character of compliance tools, which aim at specifying GDPR prescriptions within a given processing context, supervisory authorities still perceive these tools differently. These divergencies can be deemed as a product of conflicting legal tradition, lack of familiarity with the tool, or fear that they can undermine their own authority and enforcement powers.

Considering the issues in terms of the proper communication around these tools and their benefits, it is crucial to note that Art. 40 GDPR clearly states in its opening provision the encouraging role of the Commission, the Board, and Supervisory Authorities for the development of these instruments. Notwithstanding this straight-forward obligation, there seems to be a shortage of (coordinated) institutional efforts to support the harmonisation of legal interpretation regarding codes, as well as their overall dissemination.

The irony of the case of codes of conduct is that they pose workable solutions to several of the most pressing implementation challenges of the GDPR. The consistent and effective implementation of these tools can provide the necessary degree of flexibility to accommodate rapid technical advancements as well as the legal guidance and certainty sought by all stakeholders involved. As a matter of fact, codes, as an existing and attainable compliance mechanism, could address some of the core concerns raised in the context of the GDPR simplification[20] discussions, minimising the need for major and potentially harmful legislative reforms.

In light of these features, although severely underutilised, codes can be instrumental for an increase in transparency, accountability, and to cover interpretative gaps and promote harmonisation not only within, but beyond the EU. Properly exploring these existing tools will certainly have a significant impact on regulatory effectiveness in the next ten years to come.

V. Recommended further reading

Vander Maelen European Data Protection Law Review 2021, vol. 7, no. 2, p. 228–231.
Vander Maelen European Law Review 2022, vol. 47, no. 6, p. 752–772.
Vander Maelen European Data Protection Law Review 2020, vol. 6, no. 2, p. 231–242.
Wittmann/Haidenthaler MMR 2022, 8.

20 European Commission, ‚Proposal for a Regulation of the European Parliament and of the Council Amending Regulations (EU) 2016/679, (EU) 2018/1724, (EU) 2018/1725, (EU) 2023/2854 and Directives 2002/58/EC, (EU) 2022/2555 and (EU) 2022/2557 as Regards the Simplification of the Digital Legislative Framework, and Repealing Regulations (EU) 2018/1807, (EU) 2019/1150, (EU) 2022/868, and Directive (EU) 2019/1024 (Digital Omnibus)', COM/2025/837 final (19.11.2025).

Chapter 7: International Data Transfers, Enforcement and Institutional Architecture

Transfers of Personal Data (to the US)

Helen Dixon

ECJ 16.7.2020 – case C-311/18, ECLI EU:C:2020:559 – Data Protection Commissioner v Facebook Ireland Limited and Maximillian Schrems

GC 3.9.2025 – case T-553/23, ECLI:EU:T:2025:831 – Philippe Latombe v European Commission

I. Case Summaries

There have been a series of EU cases and decisions, spanning over a decade, that deal with the issue of transfers of personal data from the EEA, specifically transfers to the US. EU data protection legislation seeks to ensure that the level of protection guaranteed in the EU is not undermined when personal data is transferred outside of the EU and provides for mechanisms to enable the transfer of personal data. Mechanisms include adequacy decisions, where the European Commission finds that a country ensures an adequate level of protection or Standard Contractual Clauses (SCCs), which require data importers to commit to contractual provisions guaranteeing a certain level of protection. The cases sought to clarify the foundational concepts of 'adequate' and 'essentially equivalent' protection of personal data. Data flows between the US and Europe were said in 2022 to enable a 7.1 trillion USD economic and social relationship.[1]

1 'FACT SHEET: United States and European Commission Announce Trans-Atlantic Data Privacy Framework' (The White House, 25.3.2022) <https://bidenwhitehouse.archives.gov/briefing-room/statements-releases/2022/03/25/fact-sheet-united-states-and-european-commission-announce-trans-atlantic-data-privacy-framework/>.

1. C-311/18 – Data Protection Commissioner v Facebook Ireland Limited and Maximillian Schrems ('Schrems II')

In April 2018, following proceedings commenced by the Irish Data Protection Commission (DPC) in 2016,[2] the Irish High Court made a preliminary reference to the ECJ regarding the validity of the SCCs for transfers of personal data from the EU to the US. The preliminary reference was made in the context of on-going complaints issued by Maximillian Schrems regarding Facebook Ireland Limited's transfers of personal data from the EU to Facebook, Inc. in the US[3] and claims that US law required Facebook, Inc. to make personal data available to US authorities such as the National Security Agency (NSA). The DPC considered that there were well-founded concerns raised in the complaints in respect of the transfer mechanism (SCCs) and initiated plenary proceedings before the Irish High Court[4] which resulted in the preliminary reference by the ECJ posing a series of detailed questions aimed at getting 'consistency and clarity' across the EU in relation to Chapter V transfers and in particular the SCCs.

In July 2020, the ECJ issued its decision (*Schrems II*).[5] The ECJ upheld the validity of SCCs as a valid transfer mechanism and found that data transferred pursuant to SCCs must be afforded an essentially equivalent level of protection to that guaranteed in the EU. The ECJ also found that the EU-US Privacy Shield adequacy decision was invalid.[6]

---

2 The proceedings were issued by the DPC specifically to seek a preliminary reference by the High Court to the ECJ. Facebook and M Schrems were invited to take up the option of being joined as parties to the DPC's application in order to facilitate their participation if they so wished. As a technicality relating to the use of plenary proceedings in this novel application by the DPC, the latter parties would be joined as 'defendants'. It was clear, however, at all times that the DPC sought no remedies as against Facebook Ireland or Schrems in these proceedings. Both parties chose to participate and the Court also agreed to join several other *amicus curiae*, including the United States Government.

3 'Data Protection Authorities in Ireland, Belgium and Germany requested to review and suspend Facebook's data transfers over US spy programs' (europe-v-facebook.org, 2.12.2015) <http://www.europe-v-facebook.org/prism2_en.pdf>.

4 This was in accordance with ECJ 6.10.2015 – case C-362/14, ECLI:EU:C:2015:650 para. 65 – Maximillian Schrems v Data Protection Commissioner.

5 ECJ 16.7.2020 – case C-311/18, ECLI EU:C:2020:559 – Data Protection Commissioner v Facebook Ireland Limited and Maximillian Schrems.

6 This decision followed the ECJ's decision in 2015, in C-311/18 Schrems V Data Protection Commissioner (‚Schrems I'), finding that the 'EU-US Safe Harbour' agreement was invalid and therefore could not be relied on as a framework for transfers of personal data. The 'EU-US Privacy Shield' decision was adopted by the European

2. T- 553/23 – Philippe Latombe v European Commission

Following regulatory uncertainty after the *Schrems II* decision, the European Commission and the US Government engaged in detailed negotiations in respect of a new adequacy decision that would align with the standards set by the ECJ. The EU-US Data Privacy Framework was adopted by the European Commission as an adequacy decision under Art. 45 GDPR in July 2023 following the invalidation of Privacy Shield.[7] The Data Privacy Framework provides a mechanism for transfers from the EU to the US for organisations that participate in the framework. Philippe Latombe, an MP and commissioner at the CNIL (French Data Protection Authority) brought direct annulment proceedings against the Data Privacy Framework adequacy decision before the GC.[8] He argued that the Data Privacy Framework did not uphold EU data protection standards.[9] Latombe brought his case by reference to being a user of various internet platforms rather than by reference to one specific company.

The GC dismissed his challenge finding that the Data Privacy Framework satisfied the EU's 'essential equivalence' standards on the basis of the analysis conducted by the European Commission at the time it concluded its adequacy assessment.[10] Latombe has since lodged an appeal against this ruling to the Grand Chamber ECJ.

II. Key Legal Findings

These cases have produced a broad range of significant legal findings.

In *Schrems II*, the ECJ provided important clarifications on the requirements for transfers under Chapter V GDPR. While the judgment was issued in the context of transfers of personal data to the US, the key legal findings

Commission following this decision to provide a new legal framework for transfers of personal data from the EU to the US.

7 European Commission, 'Commission Implementing Decision EU 2023/1795 of 10 July 2023 pursuant to Regulation (EU) 2016/679 of the European Parliament and of the Council on the adequate level of protection of personal data under the EU-US Data Privacy Framework (notified under document C(2023)4745)', (20.9.2023), OJ 2023 L 231.

8 Under Art. 263 TFEU.

9 Art. 7, 8 and 47 CFR.

10 GC 3.9.2025 – case T-553/23, ECLI:EU:T:2025:831 – Philippe Latombe v European Commission.

are relevant for the European Commission for any adequacy decisions that they adopt and for organisations who are transferring personal data to a third country. On the level of protection that is required under EU law when data is transferred to a third country, the ECJ confirmed that, where relying on appropriate safeguards, such as SCCs, under Art. 46 GDPR, the guarantees given under those safeguards must be capable of ensuring that data subjects are afforded a level of protection which is essentially equivalent to that guaranteed in the EU. The level of protection must be determined on the basis of the provisions of the GDPR read in light of the fundamental rights enshrined in the CFR. This requires an assessment of the transfers, which must be carried out before the transfers take place and must take into account the clauses between the exporter and importer (e.g. SCCs) and, regarding any access by public authorities of the third country, the relevant aspects of the legal system of that third country taking into account the factors set out in Art. 45(2) GDPR. To ensure that the level of protection is not undermined, the ECJ found that it may also prove necessary to adopt supplementary measures and additional safeguards to those offered by the SCCs. The ECJ, in finding that the Privacy Shield decision was invalid, also re-emphasised the importance of the right to an effective legal remedy before an independent tribunal.

In *Latombe*, the GC heavily cited European Court of Human Rights ('ECHR') jurisprudence and afforded a significant margin of appreciation to the European Commission in terms of its analysis of adequacy at the time of conclusion of the Data Privacy Framework. The two most important issues which the General Court upheld included (i) the status of the US Data Protection Review Court, finding that it provided sufficient guarantees of independence and impartiality to address the issues identified in *Schrems II* regarding Art. 47 CFR[11] and (ii) that US laws regarding bulk collection by intelligence agencies contain appropriate limitations and *Schrems II* does not require prior authorisation provided there is *ex post facto* judicial review[12] (which is provided by the Data Protection Review Court) and so dismissed the arguments that US laws infringed Art. 7 and 8 CFR.

11 GC 3.9.2025 – case T-553/23, ECLI:EU:T:2025:831 para. 81 – Philippe Latombe v European Commission.

12 GC 3.9.2025 – case T-553/23, ECLI:EU:T:2025:831 para. 106 – Philippe Latombe v European Commission.

In relation to the other arguments considered in the *Latombe* judgment, namely, that there are insufficient rules on Art. 22 GDPR (automated decision making) and Art. 32 GDPR (technical and organisational security measures), the GC rejected Latombe's arguments essentially explaining that the protection to be afforded by a third country must be substantivally equivalent, not identical.

There was almost no standing or admissibility analysis in the GC's decision. Instead, it decided to rule on the substance of the issues in the interests of the proper administration of justice.

III. Systematic Context and Legal Classification

The *Schrems II* and *Latombe* decisions followed the *Schrems I* decision which introduced a somewhat novel obligation on national authorities to initiate proceedings before national courts to seek a preliminary reference on the validity of any EU instrument about which the authority may have well-founded concerns.[13] The ECJ's jurisprudence, while introducing regulatory instability for organisations in the context of commercial transfers, has served to ensure that the fundamental rights of EU individuals remain robustly centre of focus.

The ECJ's analysis on necessity and proportionality remains consistent with its previous rulings[14] and with *Schrems I*. It, additionally, provided important clarity on the entitlement of an individual to access a remedy before an independent tribunal when it considered the Ombudsperson mechanism in Privacy Shield insufficient, given that it was not independent from the executive branch and its decisions were not binding on the intelligence agencies. The Court's decision to uphold the validity of SCCs and to instead essentially impose a requirement for 'ad hoc small-scale adequacy' assessments[15] in respect of transfers to third countries under SCCs was based on the court's finding that Art. 45 and 46 GDPR had to be read in a complementary manner on the basis of Art. 44 GDPR. This has now provided a framework for data transfer impact assessments for transfers on the basis of SCCs to third countries.

13 ECJ 6.10.2015 – case C-362/14, ECLI:EU:C:2015:650 para. 65 – Maximillian Schrems v Data Protection Commissioner.

14 ECJ 8.4.2014 – joined cases C-293/12 and C-594/12, ECLI:EU:C:2014:238 – Digital Rights Ireland and Seitlinger and Others.

15 Costello European Papers 2020, 1024.

In *Latombe*, the GC approach appears to be consistent with its typical manner of handling of a direct annulment action in that it reviewed the 2023 Data Privacy Framework as at the time of the conclusion of the agreement between the EU and US.

IV. Author's Analysis and Commentary

The series of cases on data transfers to the US as a third country spans more than ten years (and ongoing) of legal uncertainty in an area that underpins widescale economic activity but one of equally high stakes for fundamental rights. The *Latombe* judgement marks the first time in a decade that an EU court has signalled any form of approval for a European Commission adequacy agreement with the US. This decision of the General Court, as of the 10-year anniversary of application of GDPR, is under appeal to the ECJ so the matter remains unsettled. The impact of the actions of the national authorities and the ECJ's decision in *Schrems II* can be seen in the intense efforts of both the European Commission and the US to implement a framework that meets EU law standards.[16]

Despite repeated acknowledgements that the issue of data transfers to the US from the EU is essentially a political issue that requires resolution in practice,[17] the matter has continued to trundle to and fro between national courts and EU courts as a set of legal disputes over this 10-year period.

For the majority of that time, the case law has focussed on one organisation (Facebook/Meta) although now we are starting to see the issues move beyond transfers to the US to other jurisdictions, with China for example, coming under the spotlight. The decisions of national authorities and EU courts in the context of US transfers have in the meantime set a path and baseline for assessments of transfers to other third countries. While the European Commission is required to conduct a detailed and onerous assessment of the legal regime of third countries for the purposes of adopting an adequacy decision, the ECJ has also now applied that requirement to organisations which are transferring data using appropriate safeguards such as SCCs. Transfer impact assessments are now regularly conducted

16 The negotiations between the European Commission and US administration on new adequacy agreements are taking longer and longer to conclude and also evolving to more reciprocity over time: Safe Harbour took two years of negotiation; Privacy Shield two and half years; and the Data Privacy Framework three years.

17 Kuner German Law Journal 2017, 881.

(and expected by regulators) where data is being transferred outside the EU which shows the practical day to day impact of the ECJ's decision in *Schrems II*.

While the ECJ also noted the possibility to rely on Art. 49 GDPR derogations 'for specific situations' for data transfers following the invalidity of the Privacy Shield decision in Schrems II, in practice, regulators continue to interpret these provisions narrowly and they consider that they cannot become the rule in practice. In addition, beyond the issue of Chapter V compliance, the cases relating to data transfers surface repeatedly some key questions in the context of challenges brought against European Commission decisions that are not yet fully resolved. While the preliminary reference procedure has long been regarded as an EU 'crown jewel' as it promotes important dialogue between national and EU courts and ensures consistency of application of law across the EU, there still remain challenges with the process. In particular:

1. Standing

The DPC in 2014 challenged the standing of M Schrems to bring judicial review proceedings in the absence of evidence his data had been accessed by the NSA. In rejecting the DPC's standing arguments, the Irish High Court essentially pointed out that anyone and everyone had reason to be apprehensive post -Snowden that their data could be accessed. That the Court regarded the complaint as being much broader than just relating to Facebook, much broader than one Member State and broader than any one individual is explicit.[18] What is then the best approach to addressing

18 'While the complaint was formerly directed at the major social network, Facebook (Ireland) Ltd., the gist of the objection does not really concern Facebook at all. The complaint was rather that in the light of the revelations made from May, 2013 onwards by Edward Snowden concerning the activities of the US National Security Agency (NSA), there was no meaningful protection in US law and practice in respect of data so transferred to the US so far as State surveillance was concerned.
Here the real objection is not to the conduct of Facebook as such, but rather to the fact that the Commission has already determined that the US law and practice provides adequate data protection in circumstances where it is clear from the Snowden disclosures that personal data of EU citizens so transferred to the US can be accessed by the US authorities on a mass and undifferentiated basis, thus permitting the physical transfer of such data from Ireland and elsewhere in the European Union to the United States.' Justice Gerard Hogan – Schrems v Data Protection Commissioner [2014] IEHC 351.

legal cases of this nature? Does it make sense to keep repeating on a loop through the Irish High Court by reference to one company, one complainant to the ECJ?

Mr Latombe broke the cycle by taking a direct annulment action to the GC. Many EU law observers speculated about whether his case would be admissible (on grounds of whether he was directly and individually affected)[19] but ultimately the GC side-stepped the standing /admissibility question on the basis that the issues were of considerable importance and for reasons of judicial economy. Because the appeal now lodged with the ECJ by *Latombe* can review only based on points of law and the GC ruling contained little by way of findings on admissibility, it is not clear at this point whether or how it would be open to the ECJ to rule on the question of admissibility/standing.

2. Facts

The question of how facts are found in these cases is also an interesting thread. The ECJ is not a court of facts but relies on the national referring court.

In invalidating Privacy Shield, the ECJ considered that it had a more detailed set of facts and law, as established by the Irish High Court on foot of a hearing in Dublin over many weeks involving multiple qualified expert witnesses for all participating parties, available to it and on which it relied.[20] In the *Latombe* case, it is clear the only facts that the GC sought to rely on were those established by the European Commission at the time of concluding the Data Privacy Framework. A further distinction between the *Latombe* case and the previous preliminary reference cases also relates to the fact that his challenge was by reference to his being a user of multiple internet platforms and no specific evidence or analysis about the application of the law to any particular platform and its features was considered.

19 The Plaumann Test, ECJ 15.7.1963 – case C-25/62, ECLI:EU:C:1963:17 – Plaumann & Co. v Commission.

20 The ECJ does not establish facts in its preliminary rulings. Accordingly, the ECJ did not make any findings in Schrems II regarding Facebook Ireland Limited's data transfers to the US.

3. Temporal scope

This brings us to the issue of temporal scope. In Privacy Shield, the ECJ relied on findings of facts and law as found by the Irish High Court to strike down Privacy Shield but also brought its own analysis right up-to-date by recognising that the GDPR had come into application and Privacy Shield had been adopted since the time the proceedings in the case had been lodged by the DPC in the Irish High Court. In contrast, the GC looked only at the status of matters at the point where the Data Privacy Framework was concluded, which appears to be consistent with the approach generally in annulment actions. It found that it was for the EU Commission to ensure ongoing monitoring of the Data Privacy Framework with an obligation to take appropriate action if US practices began to fall short of EU Standards. Given the ECJ can only review, in the *Latombe* appeal, points of law, it is not yet clear how the Court would be in a position to consider new facts on the ground in the US today that may bear on the adequacy of US practices. While at first glance, the direct annulment procedure looked like it may have speed advantages over the preliminary reference procedure via the national courts, it may ultimately prove to be a case of the tortoise and the hare.

At this juncture of the 10-year anniversary of the application of the GDPR, we again await a ruling of the Grand Chamber ECJ and insights into how it will approach the issues of EU to US transfers – this time through the framework of an appeal to an annulment action judgement from the GC.

Re-reading Justice Gerard Hogan's (Irish High Court) ruling of June 2014, it is striking what a clear-eyed view he had of the question of EU to US data transfers:

> While it is true that the Snowden disclosures caused – and are still causing – a sensation, only the naïve or the credulous could really have been greatly surprised. The question of transnational data protection and state surveillance is admittedly difficult and sensitive and, subject to fundamental legal protections, a satisfactory via media can in many respects be resolved only at the level of international diplomacy and realpolitik. While a court must naturally be aware of these underlying realities, in resolving issues such as arise in the present case it must nonetheless endeavour to apply neutrally the applicable legal materials.

How do we measure any progress made in the intervening decade both in terms of protecting rights while also ensuring appropriate data flows? As third countries beyond the US are considered by the Courts, how do the issues evolve?

This important story is still being written.

V. Recommended Further Reading

Costello European Papers 2020, 1045.

Cristakis 'The 'Zero Risk' Fallacy: International Data Transfers, Foreign Governments' Access to Data and the Need for a Risk-Based Approach', (Center for Information Policy Leadership, February 2024) <https://www.informationpolicycentre.com/uploads/5/7/1/0/57104281/the_zero_risk_fallacy_-_t.christakis_feb24.pdf>

Kuner German Law Journal 2017, 881.

No *'Strict Liability'*: The ECJ on Corporate Liability under Fines and the Principle of Fault in Data Sanction Law

Tim Wybitul

ECJ 5.12.2023 – case C-807/21, ECLI:EU:C:2023:950 – Deutsche Wohnen SE v Staatsanwaltschaft Berlin

I. Case summary

In October 2019, the Berlin Commissioner for Data Protection and Freedom of Information ('BlnBDI') imposed an administrative fine of EUR 14.5 million against *Deutsche Wohnen* company (*'Deutsche Wohnen'*). The fine concerned the storage of tenants' personal data in an electronic filing system which the BlnBDI argued had not ensured the erasure of data that were no longer necessary for the purposes for which they were processed. The BlnBDI alleged that the company had failed to implement appropriate and effective technical and organisational measures according to Art. 25(1) GDPR to ensure regular erasure of such data.

Deutsche Wohnen challenged the fining decision. The Berlin Regional Court set it aside and discontinued the proceedings. In the court's view, imposing a fine on a legal person requires establishing culpable conduct by an identified person with a representative or managerial role (§ 30 OWiG). As the decision did not identify a specific natural person, the Berlin Regional Court found the conditions for an administrative fine were not met.

The Berlin Public Prosecutor's Office lodged a so-called 'immediate appeal' (*'Sofortige Beschwerde'*). The Berlin Court of Appeal ('Kammergericht') stayed the proceedings and referred questions to the ECJ for a preliminary ruling on whether a legal person may be fined under Art. 83 GDPR without identifying the natural person who committed the infringement.

II. Key legal findings

The ECJ's judgment in C-807/21 (*Deutsche Wohnen*) turns on the interpretation of Art. 83 GDPR. The ECJ clarifies whether the identification of a natural person is a necessary precondition for the imposition of an administrative fine and, in part, what is required regarding fault.

The ECJ holds that legal persons may be fined directly, in their capacity as controllers, for infringements referred to in Art. 83(4) to (6) GDPR. It is not a condition precedent that the infringement be attributed to an identified natural person. What matters is that the data protection authority must prove that the infringement was committed in the course of the business of the legal person by a legal representative and on its behalf and is therefore attributable to it. Acts performed outside that scope are not attributable.

The Court rejects any form of strict (corporate) liability without proof of culpable actions. An administrative fine may be imposed only where it is established that an infringement was committed intentionally or negligently. An objective breach alone is insufficient. Administrative fines must be effective, proportionate and dissuasive, and the system adheres to the requirement of fault; the judgment does not, however, reclassify the nature of the fines within national criminal or administrative systems.

For determining the maximum amount of the fine only, the ECJ refers to the concept of an undertaking under EU competition law (Art. 101 and 102 TFEU). The worldwide turnover of the undertaking (i.e., the relevant economic unit as established under the case law of the ECJ on EU competition law) sets the ceiling.

The assessment of the fine must have due regard to the criteria listed in Art. 83(2) GDPR, e.g. nature, gravity and duration of the infringement, the number of data subjects affected, the level of damage and the intentional or negligent character. Turnover or revenue are not listed as relevant criteria in Art. 83(2) GDPR. Regarding other relevant aspects, Member State procedural rules remain applicable insofar as they do not add substantive conditions such as a requirement to attribute the infringement to an identified natural person.

III. Systematic context and legal classification

The ruling is of lasting significance for EU data protection sanctions. It affirms that fault requires intentional or negligent acts. The decision shields companies from purely strict liability and reinforces the constitutional safeguards attaching to sanctions. It resolves a longstanding debate on the lawfulness of a strict liability concept under the GDPR. While supervisory authorities and some authors in legal literature supported direct corporate liability modelled on competition law, courts had insisted on attribution to a natural person.

The ECJ states that, under EU law, it is not necessary to identify a specific natural person who has committed a GDPR violation to fine a legal person acting as controller. The judgment strengthens the effectiveness of the GDPR while preserving appropriate procedural safeguards under EU and national law. It is consistent with the ECJ's prior case law, emphasising fault and specifying that supervisory authorities and courts must establish that violations have been committed within a corporate organization. National law continues to apply provided it does not undermine the effectiveness and uniform application of EU law.

Under German law, the interaction with § 30 and § 130 OWiG in future fining practice yet remains to be clarified. § 30 OWiG allows a corporate fine, particularly where a manager or representative commits a criminal or administrative offence that breaches the entity's duties. § 30(4) OWiG permits an independent corporate fine even if the individual case is not pursued. § 130 OWiG creates a separate offence of organizational fault, enabling or not preventing an offence in the business. § 9 OWiG provides attribution, treating acts of organs or authorized agents as acts of the undertaking. Read together, these rules align with the Court's requirements under Art. 83 GDPR.

The precise formulation of the reference by the Kammergericht limited the ECJ's review of § 130 OWiG. However, the Federal Government had already indicated that, for an effective approach to corporate sanctions, the triad of §§ 9, 30 and 130 OWiG must be considered together. An 'anonymous' fine under § 30(4) OWiG does not require identifying the individual perpetrator of the predicate offence. A correct interpretation of national law does not diverge from the substantive requirements established by the ECJ.

The Berlin Regional Court will also have to address, again, the applicability of the legal-entity principle in data protection sanctioning. The choice between a legal-entity-related principle (*Rechtsträgerprinzip*) and a functionary principle had long been controversial. The ECJ confines the undertaking concept to the calculation of the fine. That approach excludes a functionary principle for attribution. The legal-entity principle embedded in § 30 OWiG therefore speaks in favour of the conformity of the national framework with the sanction requirements identified by the Court.

IV. Author's analysis and commentary

The ECJ has set a new, but vague, standard for administrative fines under the GDPR. However, it dispels uncertainty about strict liability by committing to the requirement that the controller acted intentionally or negligently. The judgment does not resolve all classification issues in national systems, but Art. 83 GDPR has an undeniably punitive and deterrent function. The fines available are significant and designed to be effective, proportionate and dissuasive.

In practice, supervisory authorities cannot rely solely on structural alleged shortcomings within an undertaking. They must demonstrate culpably committed GDPR violations in a clear, concrete and comprehensible manner. This supports the rule of law, though it still remains unclear how far competition-law concepts can be transposed to the definition and attribution of the controller; beyond setting the turnover-based ceiling via the undertaking concept, their role is limited. Authorities can be expected to intensify investigations and to document decisional bases more thoroughly.

The consequences for fine calculation are not certain either. Competition-law practice cannot be directly transplanted, given the potentially higher fines and different protective aims. Competition law protects undistorted competition, whereas the GDPR aims at a consistent and high level of protection of fundamental rights across the EU. This compels a nuanced, case-by-case evaluation of the circumstances of the infringement and the intentional or negligent character.

With increased enforcement, corporate GDPR compliance will assume even greater importance. In the absence of a requirement to identify a specific natural person within a corporate organisation, controllers should document GDPR compliance measures in a manner that will withstand judicial scrutiny.

The European Data Protection Board's fining guidelines require adjustment insofar as the ECJ accepts the undertaking concept only for setting the maximum fine amount and not as the universal starting point for assessment. Given the ECJ's clear differentiation from competition law, industry-specific compliance models from antitrust are not directly transferable. Companies should nevertheless align with familiar 'Prevent, Detect,

Respond' pillars, regularly reviewing processes, responsibilities, and controls and adjusting them to current legal requirements. Defense strategies will pivot towards careful fact development, procedural objections, and robust review of the calculation of fines. The judgment also elevates the role of the data protection officer, who must both ensure compliance and substantiate the measures taken.

Overall, the ruling somewhat increases legal certainty for undertakings and supervisory authorities alike. It provides guidance for sanctioning practice and defense. Some key questions remain open, including how the separation between the fine framework and the concrete determination of amount will translate to other digital regulatory regimes such as the AI Act or the DMA. Companies would be well advised to further professionalize GDPR compliance and related documentation, and to strengthen internal organization and communication. Practice will show how authorities and courts implement these requirements and whether defense prospects for companies improve.

V. Recommended further reading

Wybitul/Brink ZD 2024, 137.

Brink NJW 2023, 2548.

EDPB, 'Guidelines 04/2022 on the calculation of administrative fines under the GDPR', version 2.1 (24.5.2023) <https://www.edpb.europa.eu/system/files/2023-06/edpb_guidelines_042022_calculationofadministrativefines_en.pdf>.

Hoeren/Mayer/Schenke NZWiSt 2024, 434.

Klaas/Schäfer NZWiSt 2024, 293.

Moosmayer/Lösler, Corporate Compliance, 4th edn. 2024.

Compensation for non-material damage under Art. 82(1) GDPR

Boris P. Paal

ECJ 4.5.2023 – case C-300/21, ECLI:EU:C:2023:370 – UI v Österreichische Post AG

I. Case summary

The judgment discussed here concerns a claim for compensation under Art. 82(1) GDPR. The defendant, Österreichische Post AG, had processed personal data relating to individuals' party-political affinities without consent.[1] Although these data had not been disclosed or sold to third parties, the claimant sought compensation for non-material damage, invoking negative feelings associated with the now-established party affinity.[2]

The Supreme Court of the Republic of Austria (Oberste Gerichtshof der Republik Österreich – OÖGH), acting under Art. 267 TFEU, referred three questions to the ECJ for a preliminary ruling.[3] As regards the constituent elements of liability, the Court asked whether compensation under Art. 82 GDPR, in addition to the existence of an infringement of the GDPR, presupposes that the claimant has actually sustained damage (Question 1),[4] and whether it is compatible with EU law to make recognition of legally relevant non-material damage dependent on a threshold of seriousness derived from national case-law (Question 3).[5] On the level of legal consequences, the ÖOGH asked whether, when assessing the amount of

1 ECJ 4.5.2023 – case C-300/21, ECLI:EU:C:2023:370 para. 11 et seqq. – UI v Österreichische Post AG.

2 ECJ 4.5.2023 – case C-300/21, ECLI:EU:C:2023:370 para. 12 – UI v Österreichische Post AG.

3 ECJ 4.5.2023 – case C-300/21, ECLI:EU:C:2023:370 para. 20 – UI v Österreichische Post AG.

4 ECJ 4.5.2023 – case C-300/21, ECLI:EU:C:2023:370 para. 20 – UI v Österreichische Post AG.

5 ECJ 4.5.2023 – case C-300/21, ECLI:EU:C:2023:370 para. 20 – UI v Österreichische Post AG.

compensation, there are, alongside the generally recognized principles of equivalence and effectiveness, any further requirements laid down by EU law (Question 2).[6]

II. Key legal findings

1. Causal damage as a condition for liability under Art. 82 GDPR

On Question 1, the Court held that a mere infringement of the GDPR as such does not, in itself, amount to the occurrence of damage relevant as an element of the claim.[7] In its reasoning, the Court emphasized that the wording of Art. 82(1) GDPR requires both an infringement of the GDPR and the occurrence of material or non-material damage on the part of the person entitled to compensation, and that these two elements must moreover be linked by a causal connection.[8]

These cumulative[9] conditions are also consistent with the structure of the GDPR; Art. 82(2) GDPR reproduces these three requirements. Reference to Rec. 75, 78 and 146 GDPR further confirms the distinction between the concepts of 'infringement' and 'damage' and the requirement of a causal link.[10] With regard to the other sanctioning mechanisms in Art. 77 and 78, and in Art. 83 and 84 GDPR, it also becomes apparent that Art. 82(1) GDPR does not use the terms 'damage' and 'infringement' synonymously.[11]

2. No threshold of seriousness for non-material damage

In answering the third question referred, the ECJ clarified that the right to compensation established in Art. 82(1) GDPR is not subject to any

6 ECJ 4.5.2023 – case C-300/21, ECLI:EU:C:2023:370 para. 20 – UI v Österreichische Post AG.

7 ECJ 4.5.2023 – case C-300/21, ECLI:EU:C:2023:370 para. 42 – UI v Österreichische Post AG.

8 ECJ 4.5.2023 – case C-300/21, ECLI:EU:C:2023:370 para. 30 et seqq. – UI v Österreichische Post AG.

9 ECJ 4.5.2023 – case C-300/21, ECLI:EU:C:2023:370 para. 32 – UI v Österreichische Post AG.

10 ECJ 4.5.2023 – case C-300/21, ECLI:EU:C:2023:370 para. 35 et seqq. – UI v Österreichische Post AG.

11 ECJ 4.5.2023 – case C-300/21, ECLI:EU:C:2023:370 para. 39 et seqq. – UI v Österreichische Post AG.

threshold of seriousness.[12] No such threshold can be inferred from the wording of the provision and applying a national practice requiring a certain degree of seriousness would be incompatible with the autonomous concept of damage in EU law.[13]

Moreover, Rec. 10 and 146 GDPR argue in favor of a broad notion of damage, consistent with the objectives of the GDPR, in particular the aim of ensuring effective data protection.[14] That said, these objectives do not relieve the claimant of the burden of proving that they have actually suffered damage as a result of the GDPR infringement.[15]

3. Assessment of the amount of compensation under national law subject to EU-law constraints

On the level of legal consequences, the ECJ answered Question 2 to the effect that, in the absence of a specific provision in the GDPR on the quantification of damages, the amount of compensation under Art. 82(1) GDPR is determined, by virtue of the principle of procedural autonomy, under national law.[16] At the same time, the EU-law principles of effectiveness and equivalence must be respected.[17]

In addition, reference must be made to the sixth sentence of Rec. 146 GDPR, according to which Member States are to ensure full and effective compensation for the damage suffered.[18] This requires full reparation of

12 ECJ 4.5.2023 – case C-300/21, ECLI:EU:C:2023:370 para. 5 – UI v Österreichische Post AG.

13 ECJ 4.5.2023 – case C-300/21, ECLI:EU:C:2023:370 para. 44 et seqq. – UI v Österreichische Post AG.

14 ECJ 4.5.2023 – case C-300/21, ECLI:EU:C:2023:370 para. 47 et seqq. – UI v Österreichische Post AG.

15 ECJ 4.5.2023 – case C-300/21, ECLI:EU:C:2023:370 para. 50 – UI v Österreichische Post AG.

16 ECJ 4.5.2023 – case C-300/21, ECLI:EU:C:2023:370 para. 53 et seqq. – UI v Österreichische Post AG.

17 ECJ 4.5.2023 – case C-300/21, ECLI:EU:C:2023:370 para. 53 et seqq. – UI v Österreichische Post AG.

18 ECJ 4.5.2023 – case C-300/21, ECLI:EU:C:2023:370 para. 57 – UI v Österreichische Post AG.

the damage actually incurred – but without the compensation serving the purpose of punitive damages.[19]

III. Systematic context and legal classification

1. Three cumulative conditions: infringement – damage – causation

Even before this judgment, case-law and academic literature – rightly – largely agreed that, under Art. 82(1) GDPR, a claimant must show, in addition to an infringement of provisions of the GDPR, material or non-material damage that is causally linked to that infringement.[20]

By contrast, following the opposing view, the German Federal Labor Court (Bundesarbeitsgericht, BAG) held in an order for reference in 2021 that Art. 82(1) GDPR did not require the claimant to additionally bring proof of actual damage suffered, but that the violation of the GDPR as such already gives rise to non-material damage that must be compensated.[21]

As regards to this aspect, the ECJ has now – in line with the prevailing view – formulated clear guidance for the application of Art. 82(1) GDPR. The provision therefore requires the existence of a legally relevant infringement of the GDPR, specific (material or non-material) damage based on that infringement, and a causal link between the two. Only when all of these conditions are cumulatively met does a right to compensation arise.[22]

2. No threshold of seriousness for non-material damage

The view that non-material damage caused by a GDPR infringement must reach a certain level of seriousness in order to be compensable under

---

19 ECJ 4.5.2023 – case C-300/21, ECLI:EU:C:2023:370 para. 58 – UI v Österreichische Post AG; opinion of AG Sánchez-Bordona 6.10.2022 – C-300/21, ECLI:EU:C:2022:756 para. 34 et seqq – UI v Österreichische Post AG.

20 See OLG Bremen 16.7.2021 – 1 W 18/21, BeckRS 2021, 19934 mn. 6; OLG Frankfurt a.M. 2.3.2022 – 13 U 206/20, GRUR 2022, 1252 mn. 61 et seqq.; OLG Düsseldorf 16.2.2021 – 16 U 269/20, ZD 2022, 47 mn. 6; Eichelberger WRP 2021, 159 (164); Paal NJW 2022, 3673 (3673); Spittka GRUR-Prax 2021, 417.

21 BAG 26.8.2021 – 8 AZR 253/20 (A), ZD 2022, 56 mn. 33.

22 ECJ 4.5.2023 – case C-300/21, ECLI:EU:C:2023:370 para. 32 et seqq. – UI v Österreichische Post AG.

Art. 82(1) GDPR[23] had already been rejected by the ÖOGH in its order for reference, relying on the wording of Art. 82(1) GDPR and the broadly framed concept of damage chosen by the EU legislature.[24]

In academic literature and case-law, however, there were conflicting positions on how to assess merely minor non-material impairments in the context of Art. 82(1) GDPR and on whether there exists an unwritten threshold of seriousness. Following the judgment in Österreichische Post, the issue of the seriousness of non-material damage has now been settled, for the purposes of awarding compensation under Art. 82(1) GDPR, in that the ECJ has clearly rejected such a threshold of seriousness.

3. Burden of proof

For the practical application of Art. 82(1) GDPR, the ECJ's statement is of particular importance that its interpretation of the provision does not release the claimant from the obligation to prove that they have in fact suffered damage as a result of a GDPR infringement. Since the ECJ has not laid down specific requirements for such proof, it is up to the national courts to develop robust criteria for non-material damage and its proof in the context of Art. 82(1) GDPR.

4. Quantification of damage under national law

According to the ECJ, it is for the national law of the Member States, at the stage of legal consequences, to determine the type and extent of compensation under Art. 82(1) GDPR.

IV. Author's analysis and commentary

Compensation for non-material damage under Art. 82 GDPR has been, and remains, the subject of numerous legally and practically significant questions. This first landmark judgment of the ECJ on Art. 82 GDPR was therefore awaited with considerable interest. While in Österreichische Post the Court has provided important clarification on several issues, it has not

23 See Knyrim Der DatKomm/Schweiger DSGVO Art 82 mn. 2; following this view OLG Innsbruck 13.2.2020 – 1 R 182/19b.

24 ÖOGH 15.4.2021 – 6 Ob 35/21x para. 23.

– as was foreseeable in light of the specific questions referred and the nature of proceedings under Art. 267 TFEU – (yet) achieved a fully uniform and legally certain application of the law.

It is certainly welcome that the ECJ has taken a clear position on the cumulative conditions laid down in Art. 82(1) GDPR and has convincingly advocated a precise differentiation between the various prerequisites of the provision. By contrast, the requirements for non-material damage within the meaning of Art. 82(1) GDPR remain largely open. Although a threshold of seriousness is no longer tenable, there is still a lack of clear standards, sufficiently suitable for legal practice in assessing non-material damage.

The Court's interpretation, based on a methodologically sound analysis of the relevant sections of the GDPR, provides important indications for the systematic and doctrinal application of the provisions in Chapter VIII and for their relationship to the general objectives of the GDPR, pointing towards a broad notion of damage. At the same time, however, the Court's ruling falls short of what would have been possible in terms of a sufficiently reliable basis for the application of Art. 82 GDPR. It would have been desirable if the ECJ had devoted more attention to the conditions for compensation for material damage as well.

In practice, compensation under Art. 82(1) GDPR will in most cases take the form of a financial compensation, the amount of which is determined having regard to all the circumstances of the case, with national courts enjoying a considerable margin of assessment.[25] Prior to the Court's ruling, there has been a lack of uniform and reliable criteria in judicial practice. It was therefore clear after Österreichische Post that further clarification of the quantification of damages under Art. 82 GDPR would depend crucially on future judgments of the ECJ and national courts on this subject – in particular on the question whether, and to what extent, the criteria set out in Art. 83(2), second sentence, GDPR could serve as guidance in assessing compensation for non-material damage under Art. 82(1) GDPR.[26]

It also remained to be seen whether the ECJ would in future, alongside its – particularly coherent in systematic terms – reference to the compensatory function of Art. 82 GDPR and its rejection of punitive damages, provide further clarification on the functions of Art. 82 GDPR and their

25 Comp. Eichelberger WRP 2021, 159 (165 et seqq.); Paal NJW 2022, 3673 (3675, 3679).

26 LG Saarbrücken, 22.11.2021 – 5 O 151/19, ZD 2022, 162 (referred question no. 3), ECJ 11.4.2024 – case C-741/21, ECLI:EU:C:2024:288 – GP v juris GmbH; AG Wesel court notice from the ECJ 9.9.2022 – case C-590/22, ECLI:EU:C:2024:536 – AT and BT v PS GbR and Others (referred question no. 4).

relevance for determining the amount of compensation for non-material damage.

Taken as a whole, the ECJ's reasoning in Case C-300/21 on the liability regime under Art. 82 GDPR represents an important step towards a uniform and legally certain application of the law throughout the Union. The key requirements are to be further developed by subsequent judgments of the ECJ on the numerous requests for preliminary rulings already pending under Art. 82 GDPR, in order to arrive at sufficiently concrete and reliable guidelines on liability under Art. 82 GDPR.

V. Recommended further reading

The parameters for the interpretation and application of Art. 82 GDPR have been refined and consolidated by subsequent judgments.[27]

1. ECJ 20.6.2024 – Joined Cases C-182/22 and C-189/22, ECLI:EU:C:2024:531 – JU and SO v Scalable Capital GmbH

In this judgment, the ECJ once again underlined the exclusively compensatory function of damages under Art. 82 GDPR and rejected any punitive-oriented function.[28] Considering this, the Court rejected the consideration of the degree of intent on the part of the data processor with regard to the GDPR violation in the context of assessing damages.[29] Compensation must serve solely to compensate in full the damage actually sustained and, depending on the extent of that damage, may also be set at a relatively low amount[30]

27 A list of judgments on GDPR damages are provided by Matthiesen/Heinzke/Glocker/Dreyer, ‚DSGVO-Schadensersatz: Aktuelle Urteile und Entwicklungen im Überblick und laufend aktualisiert' (9.2.2026) <https://www.cmshs-bloggt.de/tmc/datenschutzrecht/dsgvo-schadensersatz-uebersicht-ueber-aktuelle-urteile-und-entwicklungen-laufend-aktualisiert/>.

28 ECJ 20.6.2024 – Joined Cases C-182/22 and C-189/22, ECLI:EU:C:2024:531 para. 22 et seqq. – JU and SO v Scalable Capital GmbH.

29 ECJ 20.6.2024 – Joined Cases C-182/22 and C-189/22, ECLI:EU:C:2024:531 para. 29 – JU and SO v Scalable Capital GmbH.

30 ECJ 20.6.2024 – Joined Cases C-182/22 and C-189/22, ECLI:EU:C:2024:531 para. 45 – JU and SO v Scalable Capital GmbH.

The Court also addressed the nature of non-material damage resulting from a breach of data protection rules, clarifying that such damage – as reflected in the evaluation in Rec. 75 and 85 GDPR – should, in principle, not to be regarded as less serious than physical injury.[31]

2. BGH 18.11.2024 – VI ZR 10/24, GRUR 2024, 1910

In this leading-case decision, which is of particular interest for German national legal practice, the German Civil Federal Court of Justice (Bundesgerichtshof – BGH) dealt, inter alia, with compensation for non-material damage arising from loss of control over personal data. According to the BGH, the relevant ECJ rulings are to be understood as meaning that the mere loss of control over personal data already constitutes non-material damage within the meaning of Art. 82(1) GDPR; accordingly, the claimant need not adduce further proof that he or she has suffered any additional specific damage.[32]

In doing so, the BGH – on the basis of an argument that is subject of dogmatic criticism – interprets the ECJ's case-law differently from the other high courts.[33] While the BGH correctly reiterates that the claimant must prove the loss of control over his personal data (i.e. the infringement of the GDPR), it then concludes that this loss of control as such already constitutes compensable non-material damage within the meaning of Art. 82(1) GDPR.[34] This approach unduly blurs the necessary clear distinction between infringement and damage laid down by the ECJ (and by the wording and structure of the provision).[35]

Furthermore, the BGH set out considerations regarding the amount and assessment of compensation for non-material damage under Art. 82 GDPR. The deciding XI. Civil Senate of the BGH suggested an indicative amount of EUR 100 in cases involving loss of control over personal data

---

31 ECJ 20.6.2024 – Joined Cases C-182/22 and C-189/22, ECLI:EU:C:2024:531 para. 37 et seqq. – JU and SO v Scalable Capital GmbH.

32 BGH 18.11.2024 – VI ZR 10/24, GRUR 2024, 1910 mn. 30 ff.; discussion of the judgement in Paal NJW 2025, 261.

33 Comp. VerfGH NRW 10.9.2024 – VerfGH 24/24.VB-1, ZD 2025, 97 mn. 16; BAG 20.6.2024 – 8 AZR 124/23, NJW 2025, 319 mn. 13; BSG 24.9.2024 – B 7 AS 15/23 R, ZD 2025, 110 mn. 31.

34 BGH 18.11.2024 – VI ZR 10/24, GRUR 2024, 1910 para. 31.

35 For a more detailed analysis see Paal NJW 2025, 261 para. 9 et seqq.

and listed additional criteria to be applied when determining the amount in individual cases.[36]

3. ECJ 4.9.2025 – case C-655/23, ECLI:EU:C:2025:655 – IP v Quirin Privatbank AG

This ECJ judgment provides a clear overview of the relevant elements of Art. 82(1) GDPR[37] and the key EU-law requirements on the level of legal consequences,[38] with reference to its prior rulings regarding the matter. In particular, the ECJ again addressed the assessment of negative feelings as non-material damage for the purposes of Art. 82 GDPR and the conditions under which such damage is compensable.[39]

For national legal practice, it is especially important that the ECJ held that the compensability of non-material damage arising from negative feelings may be accepted under Art. 82 GDPR irrespective of whether that damage can, in terms of adequate causation, be attributed to the general risks of life.[40]

36 BGH, 18.11.2024 – VI ZR 10/24, GRUR 2024, 1910 mn. 92 et seqq.; An overview of court decisions that award or reject damages under Art. 82 of the GDPR is presented by Leibold ZD-Aktuell 2025, 01150.

37 ECJ 4.9.2025 – case C 655/23, ECLI:EU:C:2025:655 para. 55 et seqq. – IP v Quirin Privatbank AG.

38 ECJ 4.9.2025 – case C 655/23, ECLI:EU:C:2025:655 para. 66 et seqq. – IP v Quirin Privatbank AG.

39 ECJ 4.9.2025 – case C 655/23, ECLI:EU:C:2025:655 para. 58 et seqq. – IP v Quirin Privatbank AG.

40 ECJ 4.9.2025 – case C 655/23, ECLI:EU:C:2025:655 para. 62 – IP v Quirin Privatbank AG.

Compensation for non-material damages

Ruben Plum-Schneider

ECJ 4.9.2025 – case C-655/23, ECLI:EU:C:2025:655 – Quirin Privatbank

I. Case summary

This ruling is the interim conclusion of European case law on compensation for non-material damages resulting from data protection violations according to Art. 82(1) GDPR. The plaintiff applied for a job at a bank and was supposed to receive a message from the bank via an online career network rejecting his salary expectations and making him a new offer. This message was accidentally sent to a person not involved in the application process who knew the plaintiff and forwarded it to him. The plaintiff sought (i) injunctive relief ordering the defendant to refrain from processing personal data relating to the plaintiff in connection with his application to the defendant and (ii) compensation for the non-material damage caused by the disclosure of his data. The court of first instance granted the injunction and awarded compensation of €1,000. The court of second instance dismissed the claim for compensation as the plaintiff was unable to prove any specific damage. Both parties appealed. The German Federal Court of Justice (*Bundesgerichtshof* – BGH) referred the case to the ECJ requesting a preliminary ruling, particularly on the questions of (i) when non-material damages within the meaning of the GDPR exist and (ii) whether the degree of fault and a parallel claim for injunctive relief must be taken into account when assessing it.

II. Key legal findings

In addition to establishing that the GDPR does not provide for a singular right for data subjects to obtain a preventive order that the controller refrain from carrying out further unlawful processing in the future, if they do not also request the erasure of their personal data,[1] the ECJ issued three key findings regarding claims for compensation under data protection law pursuant to Art. 82(1) GDPR.

First, the ECJ ruled that Art. 82(1) GDPR must be interpreted as meaning that the concept of non-material damage in that provision encompasses negative feelings experienced by the data subject as a result of an unauthorised transmission of its personal data to a third party, such as fear or annoyance, which are caused by a loss of control over those data, by a potential misuse of those data or by harm to its reputation, provided that the data subject demonstrates that it has such feelings, with their negative consequences, on account of the infringement of the GDPR.[2] The ECJ insofar refers to Rec. 1, 10, 75, 85, and 146 of the GDPR. It notes that, although Art. 82(1) GDPR does not require a 'de minimis threshold' due to the intended high level of protection for data subjects, damage exceeding a GDPR violation must nevertheless be proven by the data subject.

Second, the ECJ ruled that Art. 82(1) GDPR must be interpreted as precluding the degree of the controllers fault from being taken into account for assessing the compensation for non-material damage payable under that article.[3] According to the ECJ, this results from the compensatory function of Art. 82(1) GDPR, in contrast to fines under Art. 83 GDPR, which have a deterrent or punitive function.

Third, the ECJ ruled that Art. 82(1) GDPR must be interpreted as precluding the fact that the data subject has obtained, under the applicable national law, an injunction to prohibit the reiteration of an infringement of the GDPR, enforceable against the controller, from being taken into account in order to reduce the extent of the financial compensation for non-material damage payable under that article or, a fortiori, to replace that compensation.[4] The ECJ bases this finding on the compensatory function of Art. 82(1) GDPR as well, in contrast to the preventive function of injunctive relief.

---

1 ECJ 4.9.2025 – case C-655/23, ECLI:EU:C:2025:655 para. 36 et seqq. – Quirin Privatbank.

2 ECJ 4.9.2025 – case C-655/23, ECLI:EU:C:2025:655 para. 53 et seqq. – Quirin Privatbank.

3 ECJ 4.9.2025 – case C-655/23, ECLI:EU:C:2025:655 para. 65 et seqq. – Quirin Privatbank.

4 ECJ 4.9.2025 – case C-655/23, ECLI:EU:C:2025:655 para. 74 et seqq. – Quirin Privatbank.

III. Systematic context and legal classification

With this decision, the ECJ remains consistent with its case law on Art. 82(1) GDPR. It laid the groundwork for this in the Österreichische Post case, where the ECJ dealt with Art. 82(1) GDPR for the first time and identified three central cumulative requirements for a corresponding claim for compensation: (1) the existence of a damage, (2) a GDPR violation, and (3) a causal link between damage and violation.[5]

An important finding of this initial ruling was that a GDPR violation does not automatically constitute damage. The ECJ convincingly pointed out in the PS GbR,[6] MediaMarktSaturn,[7] juris,[8] Österreichische Post[9] and Gemeinde Ummendorf[10] cases that otherwise there would be no need to distinguish between a 'violation' and a 'damage' in Art. 82 GDPR and that Chapter VIII of the GDPR specifically provides instruments whose application does not require damage, but a violation.

In its cases Österreichische Post,[11] MediaMarktSaturn,[12] juris,[13] Krankenversicherung Nordrhein,[14] PS GbR[15] and Scalable Capital[16] the ECJ has already pointed that the claim for damages pursuant to Art. 82(1) GDPR has a purely compensatory function rather than a deterrent function. Therefore, the ECJ's current ruling consistently continues its case law in this regard.

---

5 ECJ 4.5.2023 – case C-300/21, ECLI:EU:C:2023:370 para. 32 et seqq. – Österreichische Post.

6 ECJ 20.6.2024 – case C-590/22, ECLI:EU:C:2024:536 para. 20 et seqq. – PS GbR.

7 ECJ 25.1.2024 – case C-687/21, ECLI:EU:C:2024:72 para 56 et seqq. – MediaMarktSaturn.

8 ECJ 11.4.2024 – case C-741/21, ECLI:EU:C:2024:288 para. 32 et seqq. – juris.

9 ECJ 4.5.2023 – case C-300/21, ECLI:EU:C:2023:370 para 28 et seqq. – Österreichische Post.

10 ECJ 14.12.2023 – case C-456/22, ECLI:EU:C:2023:988 para. 21 et seqq. – Gemeinde Ummendorf.

11 ECJ 4.5.2023 – case C-300/21, ECLI:EU:C:2023:370 para 38 et seqq. – Österreichische Post.

12 ECJ 25.1.2024 – case C-687/21, ECLI:EU:C:2024:72 para 46 et seqq. – MediaMarktSaturn.

13 ECJ 11.4.2024 – case C-741/21, ECLI:EU:C:2024:288 para 59 et seqq. – juris.

14 ECJ 21.12.2023 – case C-667/21, ECLI:EU:C:2023:1022 para. 80 et seqq. – Krankenversicherung Nordrhein.

15 ECJ 20.6.2024 – case C-590/22, ECLI:EU:C:2024:536 para. 41 et seqq. – PS GbR.

16 ECJ 20.6.2024 – joined cases C-182/22 and C-189/22, ECLI:EU:C:2024:531 para. 21 et seqq. – Scalable Capital.

In the Natsionalna agentsia za prihodite case the ECJ stated for the first time that the even mere fear of damage occurring can constitute non-material damage.[17] According to the MediaMarktSaturn case, this necessarily presupposes that there is a possibility that another person may have gained knowledge of the data. Otherwise, damage cannot be considered due to the lack of realisable fears.[18]

Further case law of the ECJ on Art. 82(1) GDPR underlines its broad understanding of the article: It ruled in the Scalable Capital case that data protection violations are not per se less serious than physical injuries in the context of assessing non-material damages and that – despite the lack of serious damage – symbolic damages can also be compensated.[19] Consequently, the ECJ has also already ruled in the MediaMarktSaturn,[20] Krankenversicherung Nordrhein[21] and Scalable Capital[22] cases that the intent of a GDPR violation has no influence on the assessment of a claim for damages.

Exculpation for controllers pursuant to Art. 82(3) GDPR is not easily feasible. The controller must prove that it is in no way responsible for the circumstances that caused the damage in question. According to the Natsionalna agentsia za prihodite case,[23] proof of unauthorized access to data by third parties is not sufficient for this purpose. Hacker attacks or data leaks resulting from criminal activities therefore only exonerate controllers if they have taken the usual care to protect personal data, i.e., sufficient technical and organizational measures in accordance with Art. 24 and 32 GDPR. According to the juris case,[24] it is not sufficient for exculpation if a controller claims that damage was caused by the misconduct of a person under his authority. The ECJ concludes this from the fact that data is

17 ECJ 14.12.2023 – case C-240/21, ECLI:EU:C:2023:986 para. 75 et seqq. – Natsionalna agentsia za prihodite.

18 ECJ 25.1.2024 – case C-687/21, ECLI:EU:C:2024:72 para 68 et seqq. – MediaMarktSaturn.

19 ECJ 20.6.2024 – joined cases C-182/22 and C-189/22, ECLI:EU:C:2024:531 para. 31 et seqq. – Scalable Capital.

20 ECJ 25.1.2024 – case C-687/21, ECLI:EU:C:2024:72 para 52 et seqq. – MediaMarktSaturn.

21 ECJ 21.12.2023 – case C-667/21, ECLI:EU:C:2023:1022 para. 102 et seqq. – Krankenversicherung Nordrhein.

22 ECJ 20.6.2024 – joined cases C-182/22 and C-189/22, ECLI:EU:C:2024:531 para. 26 et seqq. – Scalable Capital.

23 ECJ 14.12.2023 – case C-240/21, ECLI:EU:C:2023:986 para. 65 et seqq. – Natsionalna agentsia za prihodite.

24 ECJ 11.4.2024 – case C-741/21, ECLI:EU:C:2024:288 para. 44 et seqq. – juris.

generally only processed on the controllers' instructions and that, pursuant to Art. 32(4) GDPR, the controllers have to ensure that persons under their authority only process the data on their instructions.

Finally, the ECJ has also pointed to an interesting alternative to monetary damages: in the Patērētāju tiesību aizsardzības centrs case, it introduced the concept of excuse. The ECJ insofar stated that Art. 82(1) GDPR must be interpreted as meaning that the making of an apology may constitute sufficient compensation for non-material damage, inter alia where it is impossible to restore the situation that existed prior to the occurrence of that damage, provided that that form of redress is such as to compensate in full the damage suffered by the data subject.[25]

IV. Author's analysis and commentary

Overall, the ECJ's decision is to be welcomed. The decision is consistent with the ECJ's case law on Art. 82(1) GDPR and provides further clarification. The ECJ receives continuous referrals for preliminary rulings from the EU member states requesting further differentiation of Art. 82(1) GDPR. These referrals are correct and important as claims for damages, in addition to requests for information, constitute a significant part of data protection practice.

The ruling is to be approved insofar as it establishes that negative feelings such as fear or annoyance are also covered as damages within the meaning of Art. 82(1) GDPR. Such emotional states are classic intangible losses, which ultimately constitute a form of psychological pain. In particular, Rec. 75 and 85 of the GDPR are worded broadly in this respect and do not provide for any exceptions regarding non-compensable non-material damages. It must be admitted, however, that this opens the floodgates for claims for damages under data protection law. Nevertheless, it remains unchanged that data subjects must present and prove damages in court, even if this consists of negative feelings such as fear or annoyance. This hurdle is sufficient to ensure that compensation is only awarded in cases where data subjects have actually suffered non-pecuniary damage that is considered compensable under legal policy. It remains to be seen to what extent the national courts will yield. Contrary to the case law of the ECJ,

25 ECJ 4.10.2024 – case C-507/23, ECLI:EU:C:2024:854 para. 30 et seqq.– Patērētāju tiesību aizsardzības centrs.

the German Federal Court of Justice (*Bundesgerichtshof* – BGH) ruled in 2024 in the context of scraping that the mere loss of control is sufficient as damage within the meaning of Art. 82(1) GDPR and that no other additional tangible consequences are required,[26] although the ECJ ruled in the Agentsia po vpisvaniyata case one month before that additional damage is required.[27]

The ECJ's overarching finding that Art. 82(1) GDPR's function is merely a compensatory one also deserves approval. Granting compensation exceeding the damage suffered is only necessary if no other sanction mechanisms or comparable deterrent instruments are available. However, Art. 83 and 84 GDPR contain inherent sanction mechanisms which, not least because of their significant potential amount, have a sufficiently deterrent effect. Art. 82 GDPR serves the purpose of private enforcement, in which compensation based on the principle of full reparation is always at the forefront under EU law,[28] rather than sanctioning, which is attributable to public enforcement. This is in line with the legal systems of most EU member states, which do not provide for punitive damages.[29]

In this respect, it is consistent and deserves approval that neither the severity of a GDPR violation and the degree of fault of a controller nor a parallel claim for injunctive relief have any influence on the assessment of damages pursuant to Art. 82(1) GDPR: On the one hand, no upward adjustment of damages may be made due to the compensatory function of Art. 82(1) GDPR. On the other hand, no downward adjustment of damages may be made due to Art. 82(3) GDPR, as this provision stipulates that a controller shall not be liable only if 'it proves that it is not in any way responsible for the event giving rise to the damage'. There is insofar no legal provision for deviating from the actual damage.

Ultimately, the problem of quantifying non-material damages remains. The ECJ made it clear to legal practitioners that not every GDPR violation constitutes damage, but that any damage, even minor damage, can give rise to a claim for compensation. For data subjects, the hurdle remains of presenting and proving damage in court proceedings – in particular negative feelings such as fear or anger. If non-material damage is proven,

---

26 BGH 18.11.2024 – case VI ZR 10/24, GRUR 2024, 1910 mn. 15 ff. – Scraping.

27 ECJ 4.10.2024 – case C-200/23, ECLI:EU:C:2024:827 para. 137 et seqq. – Agentsia po vpisvaniyata.

28 ECJ 17.12.2015 – case C-407/14, ECLI:EU:C:2015:831 para. 33 – Camacho.

29 Schneider, Gemeinsame Verantwortlichkeit, 2021, p. 281, with further evidence.

compensation tables can be used to facilitate assessment in future, as is the case with physical injuries.

V. Recommended further reading

ECJ 4.5.2023 – case C-300/21, ECLI:EU:C:2023:370 – Österreichische Post.

ECJ 14.12.2023 – case C-240/21, ECLI:EU:C:2023:986 – Natsionalna agentsia za prihodite.

ECJ 14.12.2023 – case C-456/22, ECLI:EU:C:2023:988 – Gemeinde Ummendorf.

ECJ 21.12.2023 – case C-667/21, ECLI:EU:C:2023:1022 – Krankenversicherung Nordrhein.

ECJ 25.1.2024 – case C-687/21, ECLI:EU:C:2024:72 – MediaMarktSaturn.

ECJ 11.4.2024 – case C-741/21, ECLI:EU:C:2024:288 – juris.

ECJ 20.6.2024 – case C-590/22, ECLI:EU:C:2024:536 – PS GbR.

ECJ 20.6.2024 – joined cases C-182/22 and C-189/22, ECLI:EU:C:2024:531 – Scalable Capital.

ECJ 4.10.2024 – case C-200/23, ECLI:EU:C:2024:827 – Agentsia po vpisvaniyata.

ECJ 4.10.2024 – case C-507/23, ECLI:EU:C:2024:854 – Patērētāju tiesību aizsardzības centrs.

Representative action for transparency breaches under Art. 80(2) GDPR

Carolin Gäthke

ECJ 11.7.2024 – case C-757/22, ECLI:EU:C:2024:598 – Meta Platforms Ireland v vzbv II

I. Case summary

Meta's App Centre promoted free third-party games. Users were informed of the third-party game providers' permission to collect certain personal data and publish it on the users' behalf.[1] Users granted consent for this processing by using the game. The *Verbraucherzentrale Bundesverband e.V.* (Federation of German Consumer Organisations – *vzbv*) sought an injunction on grounds of unfair data protection notices, invalid consents, and unreasonable disadvantage created for users. Following successful rulings in the lower courts, the *Bundesgerichtshof* (German Federal Court of Justice – *BGH*) stayed the proceedings to await a separate ECJ ruling.[2] The *BGH* then submitted two references of its own for a preliminary ruling. The first concerned the general standing of consumer associations under Art. 80(2)

1 This case summary was generated with the support of a generative AI tool and subsequently reviewed and revised by the author; regarding the case summary see BGH 28.5.2020 – I ZR 186/17, GRUR 2020, 896 (896 et seqq.) – App-Zentrum I; ECJ 28.4.2022 – case C-319/20, ECLI:EU:C:2022:322 para. 34 et seqq. – Meta Platforms Ireland v vzbv I; Gurkmann, 'Data protection violations by Meta and Co: ECJ confirms extensive right of consumer organisations to take legal action to enforce GDPR' (website vzbv, 28.4.2022) <www.vzbv.de/en/data-protection-violations-meta-and-co-ecj-confirms-extensive-right-consumer-organisations-take>; BGH 10.11.2022 – I ZR 186/17, GRUR 2023,193 (193) – App-Zentrum II; AG de la Tour 25.1.2024 – case C-757/22, ECLI:EU:C:2024:88 para. 5 et seqq. – Meta Platforms Ireland v vzbv II; ECJ 11.7.2024 – case C-757/22 ECLI:EU:C:2024:598 para. 25 et seqq. – Meta Platforms Ireland v vzbv II.

2 See BGH 11.4.2019 – I ZR 186/17, BeckRS 2019, 6990 (6990); OLG Düsseldorf 19.1.2017 – I-20 U 40/16, GRUR Int. 2017, 466 mn. 11 et seqq.

GDPR.[3] The second addressed whether an infringement is asserted 'as a result of the processing' within the meaning of that provision in cases involving a breach of information duties – typically occurring prior to the processing.[4]

II. Key legal findings

The ECJ first reaffirms its earlier jurisprudence regarding standing: Consumer protection associations may be regarded as qualified entities within the meaning of Art. 80(1) GDPR (personal scope).[5] In terms of material scope, neither the identification of a specific data subject nor a concrete violation is required.[6]

However, the ECJ clarifies its previous findings, stating that the processing must not be purely hypothetical.[7] In line with Rec. 142 of the GDPR, it is sufficient if the claimant entity has reasons to consider that a violation of the rights of identifiable persons has occurred as a result of the data processing.[8]

The ECJ then finds that a breach of the information rights under Art. 12(1), Art. 13(1)(c) and (e) GDPR constitutes a violation of data subject rights 'as a result of the processing' and is therefore actionable.[9] The fact that the breach of information obligations precedes the actual data

3 See BGH 28.5.2020 – I ZR 186/17, GRUR 2020, 896 (896 et seqq.) – App-Zentrum I.

4 BGH 10.11.2022 – I ZR 186/17, GRUR 2023,193 mn. 12, 20 – App-Zentrum II.

5 ECJ 28.4.2022 – case C-319/20, ECLI:EU:C:2022:322, para. 64 et seq. – Meta Platforms Ireland v vzbv I; ECJ 11.7.2024 – case C-757/22, ECLI:EU:C:2024:598 para. 41 – Meta Platforms Ireland v vzbv II.

6 ECJ 28.4.2022 – case C-319/20, ECLI:EU:C:2022:322, para. 70, 72 – Meta Platforms Ireland v vzbv I; ECJ 11.7.2024 – case C-757/22, ECLI:EU:C:2024:598 para. 43 – Meta Platforms Ireland v vzbv II.

7 See already AG de la Tour 25.1.2024 – case C-757/22, ECLI:EU:C:2024:88 para. 48 – Meta Platforms Ireland v vzbv II; ECJ 11.7.2024 – case C-757/22, ECLI:EU:C:2024:598 para. 44 – Meta Platforms Ireland v vzbv II.

8 ECJ 11.7.2024 – case C-757/22, ECLI:EU:C:2024:598 para. 44, 46 – Meta Platforms Ireland v vzbv II.

9 ECJ 11.7.2024 – case C-757/22, ECLI:EU:C:2024:598 para. 61 – Meta Platforms Ireland v vzbv II.

processing is immaterial; it must merely occur in the course of the data processing.[10]

As a justification, the ECJ states that ensuring a high level of protection for the fundamental rights and freedoms of natural persons is the primary objective of the GDPR.[11] The information obligations are closely linked to the principles of lawfulness, fairness, transparency, and purpose limitation under Art. 5(1)(a) and (b) GDPR.[12] According to Rec. 60 of the GDPR, transparent and fair processing requires the provision of sufficiently comprehensive information.[13] In particular, a valid consent can only be given in full knowledge of the facts.[14] A controller's obligation to provide information about the processing operations is understood as a corollary of the individual's right to information.[15] The breach of information rights therefore constitutes a simultaneous violation of the fundamental principles of Art. 5 GDPR and is regarded by the ECJ as a violation 'as a result of the processing'.[16]

III. Systematic context and legal classification

The judgment contours the scope of Art. 80(2) GDPR consistent with previous case law.[17] Representative action is confirmed as an instrument for

---

10 See already AG de la Tour 25.1.2024 – case C-757/22, ECLI:EU:C:2024:88 para. 57 – Meta Platforms Ireland v vzbv II; ECJ 11.7.2024 – case C-757/22, ECLI:EU:C:2024:598 para. 45, 65 – Meta Platforms Ireland v vzbv II.

11 See already AG de la Tour 25.1.2024 – case C-757/22, ECLI:EU:C:2024:88 para. 54 – Meta Platforms Ireland v vzbv II; ECJ 11.7.2024 – case C-757/22, ECLI:EU:C:2024:598 para. 48, 63 – Meta Platforms Ireland v vzbv II.

12 ECJ 11.7.2024 – case C-757/22, ECLI:EU:C:2024:598 para. 50 – Meta Platforms Ireland v vzbv II.

13 ECJ 11.7.2024 – case C-757/22, ECLI:EU:C:2024:598 para. 57 – Meta Platforms Ireland v vzbv II.

14 ECJ 11.7.2024 – case C-757/22, ECLI:EU:C:2024:598 para. 59 et seq. – Meta Platforms Ireland v vzbv II.

15 ECJ 11.7.2024 – case C-757/22, ECLI:EU:C:2024:598 para. 58 – Meta Platforms Ireland v vzbv II.

16 ECJ 11.7.2024 – case C-757/22, ECLI:EU:C:2024:598 para. 61 et seq. – Meta Platforms Ireland v vzbv II.

17 See already AG Bobek 19.12.2018 – case C-40/17, ECLI:EU:C:2018:1039 para. 24 et seqq. – Fashion ID v Verbraucherzentrale NRW; ECJ 29.7.2019 – case C-40/17, ECLI:EU:C:2019:629 para. 43 et seqq. – Fashion ID v Verbraucherzentrale NRW; ECJ 28.4.2022 – case C-319/20, ECLI:EU:C:2022:322 para. 48 et seqq, with case note by Rieländer NVwZ 2022, 945 (949) – Meta Platforms Ireland v vzbv I; ECJ 11.7.2024 –

objective enforcement of data protection law, albeit subject to certain limitations.[18] While no specific violation of a data subject's rights is required,[19] a breach of provisions intended to protect data subjects must be contended.[20] The claiming entity must at least assert that the infringement of data subject rights occurs in the course of the (not merely hypothetical) processing of personal data.[21] In short: Art. 80(2) GDPR enables the objective enforcement of subjective rights.

Breaches of information rights fall within the scope of representative actions.[22] The text 'as a result of the processing' in Art. 80(2) GDPR requires a causal link between the processing and the breach, which is difficult to reconcile with pre-processing information duties. The ECJ bypasses this temporal divergence by pointing to the central importance of the principles of transparency and fairness, framing information provision as a mandatory prerequisite for the lawfulness of subsequent processing.[23] As early

---

case C-757/22, ECLI:EU:C:2024:598 para. 41 et seqq., with case note by Petri EuZW 2024, 963 (966) – Meta Platforms Ireland v vzbv II; see Rieländer RDi 2025, 42 (45).

18 See generally regarding the discussion Lühmann/Stegemann NJW 2022, 1715 (mn. 15 et seqq.); Halder, Private Enforcement und Datenschutzrecht Rechtsdurchsetzungsmöglichkeiten nach UWG und UKlaG, 2nd edn. 2022, p. 367 mn. 3; Spiecker gen. Döhmann/Papakonstantinou/Hornung/De Hert GDPR/Tambou, 2023, GDPR Art. 80 mn. 10 et seqq.; Kühling/Buchner DS-GVO BDSG/Bergt, 4th edn. 2024, DSGVO Art. 80 mn. 14; Halder/Maluszczak NJOZ 2024, 417 (422 et seq.); Schumacher/Stegemann NJW 2024, 2506 mn. 16 et seqq.; BeckOK Datenschutzrecht/Karg, 54th edn, 1.2.2024, DSGVO Art. 80 mn. 17, 18c; Simitis/Hornung/Spiecker gen. Döhmann Datenschutzrecht/Boehm, 2nd edn. 2025, DSGVO Art. 80 mn. 15, 20; Rieländer RDi 2025, 42 (44).

19 Kühling/Buchner/Bergt DS-GVO Art. 80 mn. 14; Ehmann/Selmayr Datenschutz-Grundverordnung/Nemitz, 3rd edn. 2024, DS-GVO Art. 80 mn. 16; Schumacher/Stegemann NJW 2024, 2506 mn. 16; Schmidt/Kämpfe NVwZ 2025, 1313 (1320); Taeger/Gabel DSGVO–BDSG–TDDDG/Moos/Schefzig, 5th edn. 2026, DSGVO Art. 80 mn. 24.

20 Kühling/Buchner/Bergt DSGVO Art. 80 mn. 14; Ehmann/Selmayr/Nemitz DS-GVO Art. 80 mn. 14; Halder/Maluszczak NJOZ 2024, 417 (422 et seq.); Schumacher/Stegemann NJW 2024, 2506 mn. 20; BeckOK Datenschutzrecht/Karg DSGVO Art. 80 mn. 17; Simitis/Hornung/Spiecker gen. Döhmann/Boehm DS-GVO Art. 80 mn. 15; Taeger/Gabel/Moos/Schefzig DSGVO Art. 80 mn. 25.

21 See ECJ 11.7.2024 – case C-757/22, ECLI:EU:C:2024:598 para. 44 et seq. – Meta Platforms Ireland v vzbv II; Schumacher/Stegemann NJW 2024, 2506 mn. 18; Rieländer RDi 2025, 42 (44).

22 ECJ 11.7.2024 – case C-757/22, ECLI:EU:C:2024:598 para. 47 et seqq. – Meta Platforms Ireland v vzbv II.

23 See already AG de la Tour 25.1.2024 – case C-757/22, ECLI:EU:C:2024:88 para. 50 et seqq. – Meta Platforms Ireland v vzbv II; similar Rieländer RDi 2025, 42 (45 et seq.).

as under the DPD, fair processing required providing data subjects with comprehensive information regarding the conditions of data processing (Rec. 38 DPD).[24] Only clear, intelligible, and easily accessible information enables an informed decision and the effective exercise of data subject rights.[25] The duty to give notice is thus classified as an integral part of lawful processing and a key mechanism for guaranteeing the right to privacy enshrined in Art. 8(1) CFR and Art. 16(1) TFEU.[26]

Overall, the ECJ's approach reinforces the role of consumer protection associations as a vital pillar of the GDPR's multi-level enforcement system, complementing public oversight.[27] The Court aligns itself with the legislative intent of the Representative Actions Directive.[28] While not directly applicable to the dispute in the main proceedings, the Court noted that 'it contains several elements confirming that Art. 80 GDPR does not preclude [...] representative actions in the field of consumer protection'.[29] Indeed, the Directive aims to protect collective consumer interests across the sectors listed in Annex I, including the GDPR.[30]

As an opening clause, Art. 80(2) GDPR has seen limited uptake by the EU Member States.[31] Its practical significance is now further reduced by

24 See ECJ 11.7.2024 – case C-757/22, ECLI:EU:C:2024:598, with case note by Petri EuZW 2024, 963 (967) – Meta Platforms Ireland v vzbv II.

25 See also Rieländer RDi 2025, 42 (45 et seq.).

26 See ECJ 11.7.2024 – case C-757/22, ECLI:EU:C:2024:598 para. 48 et seqq., with case note by Hense ZD 2024, 510 (513 et seq.) – Meta Platforms Ireland v vzbv II; with reference to ECJ 7.3.2024 – case C-604/22, ECLI:EU:C:2024:214 para. 53 – IAB Europe; also Rieländer RDi 2025, 42 (46).

27 See generally ECJ 28.4.2022 – case C-319/20, ECLI:EU:C:2022:322 para. 80 et seq., with case note by Meyer ZVertriebsR 2022, 311 (316); Rieländer NVwZ 2022, 945 (948 et seqq.); Rentsch/Vogel EuZW 2022, 522 (526 et seqq.) – Meta Platforms Ireland v vzbv I; see Payandeh, JuS 2022, 890 (892); Dereje/Fuhrmann GRUR-Prax 2025, 335 (335); Rieländer RDi 2025, 42 (45).

28 ECJ 28.4.2022 – case C-319/20, ECLI:EU:C:2022:322 para. 80 et seq., with case note by Meyer ZVertriebsR 2022, 311 (316); Rentsch/Vogel EuZW 2022, 522 (527), – Meta Platforms Ireland v vzbv I; see Fervers RDi 2022, 363 (364).

29 ECJ 28.4.2022 – case C-319/20, ECLI:EU:C:2022:322 para. 81 – Meta Platforms Ireland v vzbv I.

30 European Commission, 'Representative Actions Directive' (Website of the European Commission) <commission.europa.eu/law/law-topic/consumer-protection-law/representative-actions-directive_en>; see ECJ 28.4.2022 – case C-319/20, ECLI:EU:C:2022:322 para. 80, with case note by Ohly GRUR 2022, 920 (925) – Meta Platforms Ireland v vzbv I.

31 See Halder/Maluszczak NJOZ 2024, 417 (424); see European Commission, 'Second Report on the application of the General Data Protection Regulation' (25.7.2024)

the Directive, applicable since 25.6.2023.[32] For instance, the Representative Actions Directive expands protection via remedial measures.[33] Yet, it limits the circle of representative bodies compared to Art. 80 GDPR and does not grant associations the right to lodge complaints, unlike Art. 80(2) read with Art. 77 GDPR.[34] This shows that Art. 80(2) GDPR and the Directive (including national implementation)[35] differ in scope and hence function in parallel.[36]

IV. Author's analysis and commentary

From the perspective of consumer associations, the decision represents a positive signal.[37] The ECJ's emphasis on the preventive function of representative actions is reflected in resumed stays and rising claims by national and cross-border associations, including collective redress under the Direc-

---

COM(2024) 357 final, 12 <https://eur-lex.europa.eu/legal-content/EN/TXT/PDF/?uri=CELEX:52024DC0357>.

32 See BEUC, 'EU court confirms consumer groups can take representative enforcement action when companies break GDPR' (press release BEUC, 28.4.2022) <www.beuc.eu/press-releases/eu-court-confirms-consumer-groups-can-take-representative-enforcement-action-when>; see Halder/Maluszczak NJOZ 2024, 417 (423 et. seq.); see Geminn in Jandt/Steidle Datenschutz-HdB/Geminn, 2nd edn 2025, VIII. mn. 106 et seqq.; see Schubert/Halder GRUR 2024, 1862 (1862).

33 See European Commission, 'Representative Actions Directive' (fn. 30).

34 Halder/Maluszczak NJOZ 2024, 417 (424); Jandt/Steidle Datenschutz-HdB/Geminn VIII. mn. 107.

35 Regarding the implementation of the Representative Actions Directive see <https://eur-lex.europa.eu/legal-content/EN/NIM/?uri=CELEX:32020L1828>.

36 See Cadiet/Hess/Isidro Privatizing Dispute Resolution/Pato, 2019, p. 129 (145 et seq., pre adoption of the Representative Actions Directive); see Halder/Maluszczak NJOZ 2024, 417 (423 et. seq.); see Jandt/Steidle Datenschutz-HdB/Geminn VIII. mn. 106 et seqq.

37 See BEUC, 'EU court confirms consumer groups can take representative enforcement action when companies break GDPR' (fn. 32) (regarding the BGH's first preliminary reference); Pop, 'EU-Generalanwalt: Verbraucherverbände dürfen bei DSGVO Verstößen klagen' (press release vzbv, 25.1.2024) <https://www.vzbv.de/pressemitteilungen/eu-generalanwalt-verbraucherverbaende-duerfen-bei-dsgvo-verstoessen-klagen> (regarding the AG's Opinion); see Pop, 'European Court of Justice: consumer organisations can take legal action in cases of GDPR violations' (press release vzbv, 11.7.2024) <https://www.vzbv.de/en/european-court-justice-consumer-organisations-can-take-legal-action-cases-gdpr-violations>.

tive.[38] This may benefit data subjects who lack the resources or expertise to pursue individual actions.[39] Conversely, the operational and legal risks for businesses are significantly increased,[40] particularly as several detailed questions remain:

The judgment specifically addresses information duties under Art. 12(1) and 13(1)(c) and (e) GDPR[41] – namely, the modality of information and details on purposes and recipients. It remains unclear whether representative actions encompass all GDPR information duties and data subject rights, such as notice under Art. 14 GDPR, access, or erasure.[42] However, the ECJ confirmed that processing must comply with the principles of Art. 5 and 6 GDPR and respect the data subject rights set out in Art. 12 to 22 GDPR.[43]

Furthermore, the Court caused consternation by finding that a representative action under Art. 80(2) GDPR 'implies' an infringement of rights in the course of data processing.[44] Some view this as an intentional reversal of the burden of proof in favour of associations (*praesumptio iuris tantum*).[45] Others argue that the ECJ tightened the conditions for standing by requiring the claiming entity to consider that an infringement of data subject rights arose from a not purely hypothetical processing of personal data.[46] Consequently, entities must demonstrate an existing processing operation

38 See ECJ 28.4.2022 – case C-319/20, ECLI:EU:C:2022:322, with case note by Rieländer NVwZ 2022, 945 (950); Meyer ZVertriebsR 2022, 311 (317) – Meta Platforms Ireland v vzbv I; see Nemitz in Ehmann/Selmayr DSG-VO Art. 80 mn. 15; list of vzbv's representative actions <www.sammelklagen.de/verbandsklagen>; list of BEUC's representative actions <https://www.beuc.eu/enforcement?page=1>.

39 See Jandt/Steidle Datenschutz-HdB/Geminn VIII. mn. 105; see Dereje/Fuhrmann GRUR-Prax 2025, 335 (335).

40 See Gernhardt GRUR-Prax 2024, 584 (584); see Dereje/Fuhrmann GRUR-Prax 2025, 335 (335).

41 ECJ 11.7.2024 – case C-757/22, ECLI:EU:C:2024:598 para. 65 – Meta Platforms Ireland v vzbv II.

42 Supporting: Gernhardt GRUR-Prax 2024, 584 (584); see ECJ 11.7.2024 – case C-757/22, ECLI:EU:C:2024:598, with case note by Petri EuZW 2024, 963 (967) – Meta Platforms Ireland v vzbv II; Assion NJW 2024, 2590 (mn. 10).

43 ECJ 11.7.2024 – case C-757/22, ECLI:EU:C:2024:598 para. 49 – Meta Platforms Ireland v vzbv II.

44 ECJ 11.7.2024 – case C-757/22, ECLI:EU:C:2024:598 para. 45 – Meta Platforms Ireland v vzbv II.

45 See ECJ 11.7.2024 – case C-757/22, ECLI:EU:C:2024:598 para. 49, with case note by Hense ZD 2024, 510 (513) – Meta Platforms Ireland v vzbv II.

46 See Lühmann/Stegemann NJW 2022, 1715 (mn. 27); Schumacher/Stegemann NJW 2024, 2506 (mn. 18, 27); Rieländer RDi 2025, 42 (45).

that could affect identifiable individuals.[47] This is convincing, especially as associations may otherwise initiate, by means of a representative action, an abstract review of a presumed infringement of rights of (any) data subject,[48] including information rights.

Since every breach of notice requirements can affect a large number of individuals, representative action aggregates collective interests.[49] Whilst collective redress is a common instrument in the US,[50] the UK's decision not to implement Art. 80(2) UK GDPR highlights that collective enforcement remains contested terrain. In the EU, and particularly in Germany, case law consistency is debated.[51] On the one hand, it is assumed that collective enforcement reduces the risk of conflicting individual decisions.[52] On the other hand, numerous actors across Europe can bring representative actions based on alleged breaches of information duties – irrespective of any specific data subject being affected, a mandate, or damage, and even in proceedings not designed for the enforcement of data protection law.[53] Although cooperation and mutual assistance procedures or the obtaining of opinions can promote the consistent application of law,[54] they usually lead to lengthy proceedings, and the final resolution of legal fragmentation remains reserved for the ECJ.

---

47 See Lühmann/Stegemann NJW 2022, 1715 (mn. 27); Schumacher/Stegemann NJW 2024, 2506 (mn. 18, 27); Rieländer RDi 2025, 42 (45).

48 See Fervers RDi 2022, 363 (364); see Simitis/Hornung/Spiecker gen. Döhmann/Boehm DS-GVO Art. 80 mn 15.

49 See Simitis/Hornung/Spiecker gen. Döhmann/Boehm DS-GVO Art. 80 mn. 15.

50 Ehmann/Selmayr/Nemitz DS-GVO Art. 80 mn. 15.

51 See Cadiet/Hess/Isidro Privatizing Dispute Resolution/Pato, p. 129 (145 et seqq.); see BGH 28.5.2020 -I ZR 186/17, GRUR 2020, 896 mn. 47 et seqq. – App-Zentrum I; see ECJ 28.4.2022 – case C-319/20, ECLI:EU:C:2022:322, with case note by Rieländer NVwZ 2022, 945 (949) – Meta Platforms Ireland v vzbv I; see Fervers RDi 2022, 363 (364); see Spittka GRUR-Prax 2022, 19; Spittka GRUR-Prax 2022, 323; see in Gola/Heckmann DS-GVO–BDSG/Werkmeister DS-GVO Art. 80 mn. 18.

52 See Fervers RDi 2022, 363 (364).

53 See ECJ 29.7.2019 – case C-40/17, ECLI:EU:C:2019:629 para. 63 – Fashion ID v Verbraucherzentrale NRW; see Paun EuCML 2020, 35 (36); ECJ 28.4.2022 – case C-319/20, ECLI:EU:C:2022:322 para. 83, with case note by Ohly GRUR 2022, 920 (924 et seq.) – Meta Platforms Ireland v vzbv I; Payandeh, JuS 2022, 890 (892); ECJ 11.7.2024 – case C-757/22 ECLI:EU:C:2024:598 para. 43 et seqq. – Meta Platforms Ireland v vzbv II.

54 See Halder p. 114, mn. 272 et seqq.; regarding national competition authorities see ECJ 4.7.2023 – case C-252/21, ECLI:EU:C:2023:537 para. 52 et seqq. – Meta Platforms Inc. and others v BKartA.

In light of the ECJ's constant endeavour to ensure the principle of effectiveness (*effet utile*) of European norms, the Court's broad interpretation of Art. 80(2) GDPR is unsurprising.[55] As almost every instance of data processing contains a transparency dimension, the practical risk should not be underestimated.[56] Businesses face a dilemma: they must provide maximum detail to fully satisfy transparency obligations, yet at the same time maintain sufficiently broad formulations to ensure operational flexibility. Moreover, 'information overload' must be avoided, as a formalistic focus on privacy notices may not substantially improve the data subject's position.

The multifaceted requirements arising from the convergence of data protection, competition, and consumer laws[57] impose an almost unmanageable regulatory burden, rendering rigorous auditing and continuous monitoring of transparency and consent mechanisms[58] not merely advisable, but indispensable for any organisation processing personal data subject to the GDPR.

V. Recommended further reading

Initial preliminary ruling regarding the standing of associations to bring collective actions: ECJ 28.4.2022 – case C-319/20, ECLI:EU:C:2022:322 – Meta Platforms Ireland v vzbv I.

Subsequent national judgment: BGH (German Federal Court of Justice) 27.3.2025 – I ZR 186/17, ECLI:DE:BGH:2025:270325UIZR186.17.0, NJW 2025, 1958 – App-Zentrum III.

On the standing of competitors (among other things): ECJ 4.10.2024 – case C-21/23, ECLI:EU:C:2024:846 – Lindenapotheke (Arzneimittelbestelldaten).

---

55 See ECJ 28.4.2022 – case C-319/20, ECLI:EU:C:2022:322, with case note by Kentsch/Vogel EuZW 2022, 522 (526 et seq.); Ruttmann/Rott VuR 2022, 392 (397) – Meta Platforms Ireland v vzbv I; ECJ 11.7.2024 – case C-757/22, ECLI:EU:C:2024:598, with case note by Hense ZD 2024, 510 (513 et seq.) – Meta Platforms Ireland v vzbv II.

56 See ECJ 28.4.2022 – case C-319/20, ECLI:EU:C:2022:322, with case note by Rieländer NVwZ 2022, 945 (950) – Meta Platforms Ireland v vzbv I; see ECJ 11.7.2024 – case C-757/22 ECLI:EU:C:2024:598 with case note by Hense ZD 2024, 510 (514 et seq.) – Meta Platforms Ireland v vzbv II.

57 See generally regarding consumer and data protection law Helberger/Borgesius/Reyna CMLR 2017, 1427 (1427 et seqq.); see ECJ 28.4.2022 – case C-319/20, ECLI:EU:C:2022:322 para. 81, with case note by Hense ZD 2022, 384 (386 et seqq.); Rieländer NVwZ 2022, 945 (949 et seq.) – Meta Platforms Ireland v vzbv I.

58 Similar Gernhardt GRUR-Prax 2024, 584 (584).

On the competence of national competition authorities to review data protection violations (among other things): ECJ 4.7.2023 – case C-252/21, ECLI:EU:C:2023:537 – Meta Platforms Inc. and others v BKartA.

One-Stop-Shop

Henry Ogunrinde

ECJ 15.6.2021 – case C-645/19, ECLI:EU:C:2021:483 – Facebook Ireland Ltd and Others v Gegevensbeschermingsautoriteit

I. Case summary

In its ruling of 15 June 2021 (Case C-645/19), the European Court of Justice (ECJ) decided on the competence of national data protection authorities in cross-border data processing. The legal proceedings under consideration were initiated by a Belgian data protection supervisory authority against Facebook. The authority claimed that the company had unlawfully processed personal data of data subjects in Belgium with the help of cookies and social plugins without obtaining effective consent. The court of first instance followed this argumentation. Facebook then appealed against this decision. Since Facebook Ireland was found to be responsible for the alleged unlawful data processing under data protection law, the court of appeals had doubts about the Belgian data protection authority's competence to bring an independent lawsuit against Facebook Ltd., which is based in Ireland.

II. Key legal findings

Subsequently, the court of appeal referred a number of questions to the ECJ for a preliminary ruling concerning the procedural and jurisdictional rules applicable to cases that have an element of cross-border involvement.

1. Responsibility under the one-stop shop procedure

Initially, the ECJ focused on the question of how the competences of the supervisory authorities relate to each other and how they should be distinguished from each other. In this context, the ECJ underlined the principle of the one-stop-shop (OSS)[1] enshrined in Art. 56 GDPR. According to the OSS, the data protection supervisory authority at the location of the controller's main establishment, the so-called lead supervisory authority, is generally responsible for initiating sanctions for data protection violations.[2]

Although it is possible to make derogations from the OSS, these are exceptional and must be limited to the cases specified in the GDPR. An exception to this is purely local cases within the meaning of Art. 56(2) GDPR, according to which a non-lead supervisory authority is responsible for handling complaints that either exclusively concern an establishment in its Member State or significantly affect the rights of individuals in that Member State. The ECJ mentions the urgency procedure regulated in Art. 66(1) GDPR as a second exception. This exception authorizes the non-lead supervisory authority to immediately adopt provisional measures in cases of urgent need for action to protect the rights and freedoms of data subjects.[3]

2. Main establishment and addressee of the lawsuit

The ruling also addressed the question of whether the initiation of legal proceedings requires that the data controller operates a main or other establishment in the territory of the supervisory authority that is not responsible for the case. The ECJ ruled that the only decisive factor is whether the cross-border data processing is carried out by the controller in the European Union, thereby making the GDPR applicable. However, this requires that the action is directed against data processing activities carried out in the context of the operations of the defendant establishment, for which the non-lead supervisory authority is competent.[4]

---

1 Löffler RuP 2021, 391 (392); Spittka/Brunnenberg K&R 2021, 560 (562).

2 Taeger/Gabel DSGVO – BDSG – TDDDG/Grittmann/Böhm, 5. Aufl. 2026, DSGVO Art. 56 mn. 10; Kühling/Buchner DS-GVO BDSG/Dix, 4. Aufl. 2024, DS-GVO Art 56 mn. 17; Ambrock DSB 2021, 235.

3 ECJ 15.6.2021 – case C-645/19, ECLI:EU:C:2021:483 para. 75 – Facebook v Gegevensbeschermingsautoriteit.

4 ECJ 15.6.2021 – case C-645/19, ECLI:EU:C:2021:483 para. 96 – Facebook v Gegevensbeschermingsautoriteit; Löffler RuP 2021, 391 (392); Spittka/Brunnenberg K& R 2021, 560 (562), Datenschutzbehörde Republik Österreich, Datenschutzbericht 2021, S. 65.

3. Direct Right of Action under Art. 58 (5) GDPR

The ECJ has also provided its perspective on the specification clause in Art. 58(5) GDPR. This clause is intended to be implemented by national legislators in all member states in a manner that enables the respective supervisory authorities to initiate legal proceedings. The ECJ has opined that the provision has direct effect. It can therefore be concluded that a national supervisory authority is empowered to invoke it directly in order to initiate legal proceedings against private companies, even in instances where the specific provision has not been implemented in its member state.[5]

III. Systematic context and legal classification

The ECJ decision of 15.6.2021 (Case C-645/19), addresses the important question of the allocation of competences in cross-border constellations. In essence, the Court confirms the existing regulatory framework of European data protection law and leaves the distribution of powers between supervisory authorities unchanged.[6] In line with the structure set out in Art. 56 GDPR, the Court confirms that the lead supervisory authority has primary competence for data protection measures in the context of cross-border data processing. The OSS mechanism thus remains the central instrument for regulating cross-border processing activities. The judgment does not entail an extension of the substantive powers of non-lead supervisory authorities.[7]

The ECJ has explicitly stated that Art. 58(5) GDPR does not represent a standalone exception to the principle of lead supervisory authority as established in Art. 56 GDPR. The court posits that the prospect of legal action by a non-lead authority remains constrained to the exceptional cases already delineated in the GDPR (in particular, so-called 'local cases' within the meaning of Art. 56(2) GDPR and the urgent procedure under Art. 66

---

5 ECJ 15.6.2021 – case C-645/19, ECLI :EU :C :2021 :483 paras. 109–113 – Facebook v Gegevensbeschermingsautoriteit; Spittka/Brunnenberg K& R 2021, 560 (562); Datenschutzbehörde Republik Österreich, Datenschutzbericht 2021, S. 65.

6 Ambrock DSB 2021, 235 (236); Spittka/Brunnenberg K& R 2021, 560 (563); Die Landesbeauftragte für den Datenschutz Niedersachsen, 27. Tätigkeitsbericht, 2021, S. 59.

7 Ambrock DSB 2021, 235 (236); Datenschutzkonferenz (DSK), 2. Zwischenkonferenz (Top 17d), AK Grundsatz, 100514/2021, S. 1.

GDPR).[8] The prospect of autonomous legal action by a non-lead authority in accordance with Article 58(5) GDPR should not be interpreted as an expansion of substantive powers.[9]

In effect, this means that, provided the cooperation and consistency mechanism set out in the GDPR has been properly followed, but the lead supervisory authority fails to act or refrains from participating, other supervisory authorities may also be entitled to take legal action under Art. 58(5) GDPR against unlawful cross-border data processing.

Overall, the decision reinforces the existing procedural and competence framework of the European data protection system. However, it does not entail a structural shift in the allocation of competences in favour of individual national authorities. The ruling is consistent with the ECJ's previous case law on the competence of non-lead supervisory authorities, as reflected in particular in the judgments in Google Spain[10] and Wirtschaftsakademie Schleswig-Holstein.[11]

IV. Author's analysis and commentary

1. Practical Relevance

The ECJ's ruling holds particular relevance in practice, especially in light of the long-standing criticism of the reserved enforcement practices of certain supervisory authorities. This applies in particular to the Irish data protection authority, which, due to the establishment of numerous international technology companies, regularly acts as the lead supervisory authority in the OSS procedure, as was the case in this instance. Historically, this phenomenon has led companies to strategically select Member States characterized by less stringent enforcement practices as the location for their headquarters in order to avoid stricter regulatory measures.[12] This de facto

8 ECJ 15.6.2021 – case C-645/19, ECLI:EU:C:2021:483 para. 65 – Facebook v Gegevensbeschermingsautoriteit; Datenschutzkonferenz (DSK), 2. Zwischenkonferenz (Top 17d), AK Grundsatz, 100514/2021, S. 1.

9 Die Landesbeauftragte für den Datenschutz Niedersachsen, 27. Tätigkeitsbericht, 2021, S. 59.

10 ECJ 13.5.2014 – case C-131/12, ECLI:EU:C:2014:317 – Google Spain v Agencia Española de Protección de Datos (AEPD) and Mario Costeja González.

11 ECJ 5.6.2018 – case C-210/16, ECLI:EU:C:2018:388 – Landeszentrum für Datenschutz Schleswig-Holstein v Wirtschaftsakademie Schleswig-Holstein GmbH.

12 Farrell/Hardiman The Oxford Handbook of Irish Politics/McIntyre, 2020, p. 13.

'forum shopping' was facilitated by the fact that other national supervisory authorities had limited options for action due to a lack of jurisdiction.

The ECJ has explicitly addressed this issue in its ruling, clarifying that controllers cannot escape their data protection responsibilities by invoking the sole jurisdiction of an inactive supervisory authority that is not in charge.[13] The Court made it clear that data protection obligations continue to apply regardless of the effectiveness of enforcement by the authorities. In this context, the ECJ position against such evasion behind structural or institutional deficits of individual supervisory authorities is expressly welcome and strengthens the effectiveness and enforceability of the EU data protection regime.

Despite this clarification, which is fundamentally welcome, the ruling falls short of expectations on one key point. The ECJ has demonstrated a marked reluctance to establish explicit criteria that would delineate the circumstances under which actions by national supervisory authorities, undertaken outside the parameters of the OSS procedure, might be deemed permissible. Instead, the Court has confined its role to a mere reference to the exceptions that have already been codified within the provisions of Art. 60 GDPR and subsequent articles of the GDPR.[14] However, the Court has conspicuously abstained from delineating the practical scope of these exceptions, thereby leaving a significant gap in the regulatory framework. The decision of the ECJ to abstain from determining the fulfillment of the conditions for an exception to the OSS procedure in the case under review, thereby delegating this assessment to the national court, lends credence to the criticism that has been voiced. The court, therefore, limits itself to the elaboration of abstract standards without applying them to the specific facts of the case, thereby further relativizing the practical significance of the decision.

2. Legal Implications

From a legal perspective, the interpretation of Art. 58(5) GDPR by the ECJ deserves special attention. An examination of the provision's wording ('Each member state shall provide by law...') suggests that this is an

13 ECJ 15.6.2021 – case C-645/19, ECLI:EU:C:2021:483 para. 68 – Facebook v Gegevensbeschermingsautoriteit; Spittka/Brunnenberg K& R 2021, 560 (563).

14 Ambrock DSB 2021, 235 (236); Datenschutzkonferenz (DSK), 2. Zwischenkonferenz (Top 17d), AK Grundsatz, 100514/2021, S. 1.

implementation requirement for member states.[15] Nevertheless, the Court expands upon this interpretation and recognizes the provision as having direct effect. Therefore, supervisory authorities can rely directly on Art. 58 (5) GDPR, even in the absence of a national implementing provision, to initiate legal proceedings against private controllers.[16] This interpretation gives rise to a number of questions of a systematic nature. The ECJ does not understand the text of the provision as a mere implementation mandate, but rather as a sufficiently specific basis with direct effect. In doing so, the ECJ clearly opposes an interpretation that sees the wording of the provision as a clear regulatory mandate to the member states.[17] At the same time, the ECJ qualifies a provision that apparently opens up scope for national implementation as directly applicable. It is particularly worth noting that the Court also affirms this direct effect in vertical relationships—i.e., for lawsuits brought by public authorities against private individuals—which is not a matter of course in the context of EU law.

It may be assumed that, based on this decision, supervisory authorities that are not in charge will also increasingly take legal action against data protection violations in the future. For data-processing companies, this means that they can no longer rely exclusively on the jurisdiction of the authority in charge of them. This decision can be regarded as a step in the right direction toward more effective enforcement of data protection law at the European level.

Nevertheless, the efficacy of this measure in addressing the practice of forum shopping remains to be observed.

V. Recommended further reading

Ambrock DSB 2021, p. 235. For a detailed and critical analysis of the judgment.

Farrell/Hardiman The Oxford Handbook of Irish Politics/McIntyre, 2020, p. 13. On the topic of effective enforcement within the framework of European data protection law.

Spittka/Brunnenberg K&R 2021, p. 560. Especially on the applicability of Art. 58(5) GDPR and the question of direct legal standing for supervisory authorities.

15 Spittka/Brunnenberg K& R 2021, 560 (563).

16 ECJ 15.6.2021 – case C-645/19, ECLI:EU:C:2021:483 para. 80 – Facebook v Gegevensbeschermingsautoriteit; Kühling/Buchner/Boehm DS-GVO Art 58, mn. 47; Ambrock DSB 2021, 235 (236).

17 Spittka/Brunnenberg K& R, Heft 7/8, 2021, 560 (563).

Cooperation between Data Protection Authorities and Competition Authorities

Thomas Fuchs

ECJ 4.7.2023 – case C-252/21, ECLI:EU:C:2023:537 – Meta Platforms Inc and Others v Bundeskartellamt

I. Case summary

The proceedings before the ECJ concerned a competition and data protection dispute between the *Federal Cartel Office (Bundeskartellamt (BKartA)* and *Meta Platforms Ireland Limited* (formerly Facebook). The starting point was a decision by the *BKartA* in 2019 prohibiting Meta from combining personal data from various sources without the express consent of users. Meta lodged an appeal against this decision with the Higher Regional Court of Düsseldorf and initially successfully applied for interim relief and suspensive effect. After the Federal Court of Justice (BGH) lifted the suspensive effect, the Higher Regional Court suspended the main proceedings and referred several questions to the ECJ for a preliminary ruling in accordance with Art. 267 TFEU. The decisive issue in the dispute was whether the *BKartA* was entitled to investigate data protection violations in the context of antitrust abuse proceedings and to issue a cease-and-desist order on the basis of the GDPR, even though the GDPR in Art. 51 ff. generally provides for the competence of the data protection supervisory authorities. In addition, it had to be clarified when consent given to a market-dominating company is to be regarded as effective.

II. Key legal findings

The ECJ upheld the decision of the *BKartA* against *Meta Platforms Ireland. Meta* was prohibited from collecting personal data across multiple devices and combining it into a profile without the express consent of users. Among other things, the ECJ clarified that personal data from different sources may only be processed for the purpose of fulfilling contractual obligations, but not for personalised advertising or content, even in the case of free services such as Facebook. However, the voluntary nature of the consent required for this data processing means that market-dominating companies must offer an alternative without data processing, which may be subject to a fee.

For the first time, the ECJ dealt with the relationship between data protection supervisory authorities and competition authorities in a specific supervisory procedure. According to the ECJ ruling, national competition authorities are obliged to coordinate and cooperate loyally with the relevant national or lead supervisory authorities. To this end, they must first check whether there are already relevant decisions by the competent national supervisory authority or the lead supervisory authority, or even by the Court of Justice. If this is the case, the national competition authority may not deviate from it, but is free to draw its own conclusions from it from the point of view of the application of competition law.[1] In case of doubt, the competition authority must consult the competent data protection supervisory authority and request its cooperation in order to dispel its doubts or clarify whether it must await a decision by the supervisory authority concerned before commencing its own assessment.[2]

The primary responsibility for monitoring compliance with data protection law therefore lies with the data protection supervisory authorities. Competition authorities are obliged to coordinate in advance and maintain a loyal and cooperative relationship with the competent data protection authorities. Such cooperation ensures legal certainty in the regulation of data-driven business models operated by companies with a dominant market position. The Court expressly confirms that the application of data protection rules does not preclude the enforcement of competition law, but rather requires harmonious interaction between the two regulatory systems.

1 ECJ 4.7.2023 – case C-252/21, ECLI:EU:C:2023:537 para. 56 – Meta Platforms Inc and Others v Bundeskartellamt.

2 ECJ 4.7.2023 – case C-252/21, ECLI:EU:C:2023:537 para. 57 – Meta Platforms Inc and Others v Bundeskartellamt.

III. Systematic context and legal classification

1. Interaction between data protection supervision and competition supervision

At the beginning of the proceedings in 2016, the responsibilities and cooperation between the *BKartA* and the data protection authorities in the field of digital markets were not yet legally defined. In the absence of a statutory framework, cooperation initially followed general administrative principles, particularly with the Federal Commissioner for Data Protection (BfDI) and the Hamburg Commissioner for Data Protection (HmbBfDI) as the authority responsible for Facebook. With the entry into force of the GDPR in May 2018, lead responsibility for data protection matters shifted to the Irish Data Protection Commission (IDPC); however, a normative framework for intersectoral information exchange was still lacking. The DMA and the Second Amendment to the GWB of 2021 restructured the supervision of digital markets. § 50f(1) GWB now allows coordinated information exchange between competition, data protection, and regulatory authorities, though limited to the national level. At the EU level, the ECJ emphasizes the principle of sincere cooperation under Art. 4(3) TFEU and the cooperation duties under Art. 60 et seq. GDPR. The Court clarified that, despite the proactive role of the lead authority—the IDPC—national data protection authorities remain equal counterparts, thereby strengthening the coherent and effective enforcement of competition and data protection law.

2. 'for an appropriate fee'

The ECJ addresses in detail the question referred for a preliminary ruling as to the extent to which consent within the meaning of the GDPR can be assumed to be voluntary in the case of market-dominating online platforms such as Facebook. In the case of quasi-monopolies in particular, users have virtually no possibility of rejecting certain terms of use if they wish to use the service offered and, due to pronounced network effects, effective use is essentially only possible via a specific provider. Nevertheless, the ECJ does not rule out the possibility that voluntary consent within the meaning of data protection law may exist even in the case of a dominant market position, provided that users have a tracking-free alternative available to them. To date, the question of whether this alternative may be subject to a fee has been particularly controversial.

Back in 2023, the German Data Protection Conference (DSK) had already passed a resolution on the evaluation of pure subscription models on websites at the suggestion of the HmbBfDI, according to which 'the tracking of user behaviour must be based on consent if a tracking-free model is offered as an alternative, even if this is subject to a fee'. The fee must then be 'in line with market conditions'. The ECJ is now arguing similarly for the first time:[3]

> Thus, those users must be free to refuse individually, in the context of the contractual process, to give their consent to particular data processing operations not necessary for the performance of the contract, without being obliged to refrain entirely from using the service offered by the online social network operator, which means that those users are to be offered, if necessary for an appropriate fee, an equivalent alternative not accompanied by such data processing operations.

IV. Author's analysis and commentary

1. Coordination between supervisory authorities

The close cooperation between the *BKartA* and the nationally competent data protection supervisory authorities (*BfDI* and *HmbBfDI*) in the proceedings against *Meta* has, against the backdrop of the progressive consolidation of legal requirements over the years, led to a comprehensive further development and consolidation of the formalisation of intersectoral supervisory practice, which is unprecedented in this form. It is not without reason that this case is widely regarded in literature and practice as a decisive starting point for multi-level, intersectoral cooperation and is explicitly referred to as a reference in numerous publications.[4]

At the beginning of the proceedings, the *BKartA's* actions were characterised by a rather one-sided, questioning approach towards data protection, which required a cautious approach to the proceedings due to a lack of experience and unclear normative guidelines. However, the authorities involved soon realised that close involvement of the data protection super-

3 ECJ 4.7.2023 – case C-252/21, ECLI:EU:C:2023:537 para. 150 – Meta Platforms Inc and Others v Bundeskartellamt.

4 E.g. EDPB, 'Position paper on Interplay between data protection and competition law' (16.1.2025) <https://www.edpb.europa.eu/system/files/2025-01/edpb_position-paper_20250116_interplay-between-data-protection-and-competition-law_en.pdf>.

visory authority and consumer protection would be crucial for the successful conclusion of the proceedings – especially as it became apparent that the matter would go through all court instances. The successful conclusion of the proceedings can only be understood in the context of the parallel dispute before the European Data Protection Board (EDPB). The starting point was complaints made in 2018 against Facebook and Instagram for lack of consent for personalised advertising. The Irish Data Protection Commission (IDPC) initially saw a contractual legal basis for *Meta's* data processing, which was disputed by numerous supervisory authorities, including the HmbBfDI. The EDPB then ruled against the IDPC's opinion in a binding manner under Art. 65 GDPR with Decisions 3/2022 and 4/2022. These decisions ensured uniform application of the GDPR and formed the basis for the subsequent ECJ ruling in favour of the Federal Cartel Office.

2. Cooperation between authorities

In its position paper the EDPB rightly calls on decision-makers to ensure that the authorities responsible for the digital sector systematically expand their cooperation. In addition to legislative activities, cooperation in cross-sectoral cases could be further developed through so-called soft law instruments such as the establishment of best practices, guidelines or model agreements, thereby making the procedures more legally secure. In particular, cooperation agreements (memoranda of understanding) could be concluded between the authorities involved, which would regulate the individual process steps, responsibilities and exchange of information in a binding manner. Ultimately, effective cooperation requires that the authorities understand each other's legal frameworks (in particular data protection and competition law) and integrate them into their practices. Numerous examples already exist, such as in France between the CNIL and the *Autorité de la concurrence*.[5]

An important body that deals with questions concerning the interaction of sector-specific legislation and cooperation among the respective supervisory authorities is the High Level Group (HLG) established under Art. 40 DMA. The main task of the HLG under the DMA is to advise the European Commission on the implementation and enforcement of the DMA in order

5 CNIL, 'Data protection and competition: the CNIL and the Autorité de la concurrence sign a joint declaration' (12.12.2023) <https://www.cnil.fr/en/data-protection-and-competition-cnil-and-autorite-de-la-concurrence-sign-joint-declaration>.

to ensure coherent regulation and safeguard the future viability of the legislation by contributing expertise on emerging markets and practices, for example in the field of artificial intelligence.

3. Case study: 'for an appropriate fee'

The key difference between antitrust and data protection law lies in their objectives: antitrust law protects competition and regulates markets, while data protection law safeguards the fundamental rights of individuals, in particular their right to informational self-determination. Data protection assessments should therefore be carried out independently of market structures and should be based on the rights of the individuals concerned. At the same time, the assessment of the appropriateness of a fee within the framework of data protection supervisory powers requires objective standards that ensure verifiability by data protection supervisory authorities.

When assessing the voluntary nature of consent – particularly in 'pay or consent' models – the perspective of an average, reasonable user should be decisive. Individual economic differences should take a back seat to objective standards based on consumer law.

The appropriateness of a data protection-friendly subscription price could be determined according to the compensation principle, according to which only lost advertising revenue as a result of the failure to use data may be taken into account, but not general operating or development costs. The economic risk of the business model remains with the company.

Under Art. 5(2) and Art. 58(1)(a) GDPR, controllers would be obliged to disclose their pricing in order to enable a full review of its legality by data protection supervisory authorities, involving competition authorities where appropriate.

Chapter 8:
The GDPR in the Context of Emerging Technologies

The Challenge of Defining Artificial Intelligence in EU Law

Kai Zenner[*]

European Commission, ‚Commission Guidelines on the definition of an artificial intelligence system established by Regulation (EU) 2024/1689 (AI Act)', C(2025) 5053 final

I. Case summary

On 29.7.2025, the European Commission presented its 'Guidelines on the definition of an artificial intelligence system' to provide the much-needed legal clarity on the scope of the AI Act.[1] With that publication, it also fulfilled one of its many implementation duties; in this case one that is laid down by Art. 96(1)(f) AI Act. While guidelines are legally not binding and authoritative interpretation remains fully with the ECJ[2], they still represent the Commission's official interpretation and heavily influence enforcement practice across the European Union. As the law's regulatory obligations – including the requirements for high-risk systems under Art. 8 to 15 AI Act – apply only to those technologies that meet the legal definition of an 'AI system', this guidance document can in fact be seen as one of the gatekeepers for the entire AI regulatory framework of the EU.

II. Key legal findings

In paragraph 9, the guidelines identify seven cumulative elements that constitute the definition of an AI system under Art. 3 no. 1 AI Act: (1) a machine-based system; (2) designed to operate with varying levels of

* All expressed views are personal and do represent neither the position of the European Parliament nor of the EPP Group.

1 European Commission, ‚Commission Guidelines on the definition of an artificial intelligence system established by Regulation (EU) 2024/1689 (AI Act)', C(2025) 5053 final.

2 European Union, 'Types of Legislation – Recommendations' <https://european-union.europa.eu/institutions-law-budget/law/types-legislation_en>.

autonomy; (3) that may exhibit adaptiveness after deployment; (4) that is operating for explicit or implicit objectives; (5) that infers how to generate outputs from received inputs; (6) that is producing outputs such as predictions, content, recommendations, or decisions; (7) which can influence physical or virtual environments.

The key conceptual contribution of the guidelines is the introduction of a lifecycle-based perspective. The Commission acknowledges that AI systems evolve through the pre-deployment ('development') phase as well as through the post-deployment ('use') phase, and that the seven criteria do not necessarily need to be present simultaneously across both phases.[3] For instance, the 'inference' capability may be established during the development phase, even if it remains static during use. The Commission also strongly emphasises that the capability to infer is the key characteristic distinguishing AI systems from traditional software.[4] Consequently, the guidelines clarify that certain categories of technologies fall outside of the AI definition.

The legal classification of a system as 'AI' is only the first step in the AI Act's overall risk-based approach. The guidelines emphasize that the qualification as an AI system does not automatically lead to regulatory burdens. The vast majority of AI systems will not be subject to any requirements under the EU law.[5] Obligations will only arise for three specific categories of AI systems: those that qualify under prohibited practices (Art. 5 AI Act), high-risk systems (Art. 6 AI Act) or systems subject to specific transparency requirements (Art. 50 AI Act).

III. Systematic context and legal classification

The definition in Art. 3 no. 1 AI Act is systematically designed to be technologically neutral while providing the flexibility to accommodate the rapid

3 European Commission, ‚Commission Guidelines on the definition of an artificial intelligence system established by Regulation (EU) 2024/1689 (AI Act)', C(2025) 5053 final, para. 10.

4 Cf. Rec. 12 AI Act and European Commission, ‚Commission Guidelines on the definition of an artificial intelligence system established by Regulation (EU) 2024/1689 (AI Act)', C(2025) 5053 final, para. 26.

5 European Commission, ‚Commission Guidelines on the definition of an artificial intelligence system established by Regulation (EU) 2024/1689 (AI Act)', C(2025) 5053 final, para. 63.

innovation in the field of AI. By aligning closely with the OECD AI definition[6], the EU ensures international consistency for global developers and deployers.

1. The key definitional elements

a) Machine-based system

The term 'machine-based' encompasses both hardware components (i.e. processing units, memory, storage) and software components (i.e. code, programs, operating systems). This understanding is largely uncontroversial, as all AI systems require computational infrastructure. Notably, the guidelines confirm that emerging technologies such as quantum computing systems and biological computing systems might qualify as machine-based, provided they offer computational capacity.[7]

b) Autonomy

The autonomy requirement refers to the system being designed to operate with 'some degree of independence of actions from human involvement'. This excludes systems designed to operate solely with full manual human control.[8] The guidelines clarify that human involvement may be direct (i.e. manual controls) or indirect (i.e. automated systems-based controls enabling delegation or supervision). Crucially, a system requiring manually provided inputs but generating outputs autonomously would satisfy the 'autonomy' criterion.

---

6 OECD, 'Explanatory memorandum on the updated OECD definition of an AI system', (OECD Artificial Intelligence Papers, No. 8, 2024) <https://www.oecd.org/content/dam/oecd/en/publications/reports/2024/03/explanatory-memorandum-on-the-updated-oecd-definition-of-an-ai-system_3c815e51/623da898-en.pdf>.

7 European Commission, ‚Commission Guidelines on the definition of an artificial intelligence system established by Regulation (EU) 2024/1689 (AI Act)', C(2025) 5053 final, paras. 11–13.

8 Rec. 12 AI Act and European Commission, ‚Commission Guidelines on the definition of an artificial intelligence system established by Regulation (EU) 2024/1689 (AI Act)', C(2025) 5053 final, para. 14.

c) Adaptiveness

Unlike autonomy, adaptiveness is only facultative. The use of 'may' in Art. 3 no. 1 AI Act indicates that self-learning capabilities after deployment are not required for a system to qualify as an AI system. This means systems that do not learn or adapt post-deployment can still fall under the definition of AI.[9]

d) Objectives

AI systems operate according to explicit objectives (i.e. directly encoded goals, such as optimisation functions) or implicit objectives (i.e. goals deduced from behaviour, training data, or environmental interaction). The guidelines thereby distinguish system objectives from the 'intended purpose' under Art. 3 no. 12 AI Act: objectives are internal task-oriented goals, while intended purpose concerns the external context of deployment.[10]

e) Output and Environmental Influence

The guidelines also clarify how one must understand that AI systems generate predictions, content, recommendations, or decisions. Accordingly, these outputs are not passive but must be capable of influencing the environments in which they are deployed, whether physical (e.g. a robot arm) or virtual (e.g. software ecosystems).[11]

2. The inferencing requirement

The inferencing capability constitutes the definitional core. The guidelines interpret 'infers, from the input it receives, how to generate outputs' broad-

9 European Commission, ‚Commission Guidelines on the definition of an artificial intelligence system established by Regulation (EU) 2024/1689 (AI Act)', C(2025) 5053 final, para. 23.

10 European Commission, ‚Commission Guidelines on the definition of an artificial intelligence system established by Regulation (EU) 2024/1689 (AI Act)', C(2025) 5053 final, para. 24.

11 European Commission, ‚Commission Guidelines on the definition of an artificial intelligence system established by Regulation (EU) 2024/1689 (AI Act)', C(2025) 5053 final, para. 60.

ly, encompassing both the use phase (i.e. generating outputs from inputs) and the building phase (i.e. deriving models or algorithms from data).[12] The Commission explains that two categories of AI techniques enable inference: machine learning approaches (i.e. supervised, unsupervised, self-supervised, and reinforcement learning, including deep learning) and logic- and knowledge-based approaches (i.e. expert systems, knowledge bases, inference engines, symbolic reasoning).[13]

3. Exclusions from the definition

Some technologies fall outside the AI system definition. Systems that improve mathematical optimisation but do not transcend 'basic data processing' are excluded, including machine learning models that merely accelerate traditional methods.[14] Basic data processing systems following predefined rules without learning, reasoning, or modelling (such as database management systems or standard spreadsheet applications) are similarly excluded.[15] Classical heuristics relying on experience-based problem-solving without data-driven learning, and simple prediction systems achieving only baseline performance (such as mean estimators), also fall outside the scope.[16]

---

12 European Commission, ‚Commission Guidelines on the definition of an artificial intelligence system established by Regulation (EU) 2024/1689 (AI Act)', C(2025) 5053 final, para. 30–31.

13 European Commission, ‚Commission Guidelines on the definition of an artificial intelligence system established by Regulation (EU) 2024/1689 (AI Act)', C(2025) 5053 final, para. 32–39.

14 European Commission, ‚Commission Guidelines on the definition of an artificial intelligence system established by Regulation (EU) 2024/1689 (AI Act)', C(2025) 5053 final, para. 42 – 45.

15 European Commission, ‚Commission Guidelines on the definition of an artificial intelligence system established by Regulation (EU) 2024/1689 (AI Act)', C(2025) 5053 final, para. 46 – 47.

16 European Commission, ‚Commission Guidelines on the definition of an artificial intelligence system established by Regulation (EU) 2024/1689 (AI Act)', C(2025) 5053 final, para. 48 – 51.

IV. Author's analysis and commentary

1. Strengths of the Guidelines

The guidelines stand for an important contribution to legal certainty, especially after recently more than 50 % of all German companies pointed to unclear AI rules as their biggest obstacle to use AI.[17] By systematically analysing each definitional element and providing concrete examples, the Commission has created a practical reference document for compliance departments, legal practitioners, and enforcement authorities alike. The lifecycle-based approach, acknowledging that all elements of the definition need not persist across both development and use phases, reflects the technical reality of modern AI development. Last but not least, the explicit exclusion of basic data processing systems helps to address legitimate industry concerns about the potential over-regulation of conventional software applications.

Particularly valuable is the clarification that adaptiveness is facultative. This prevents an overly narrow interpretation that would exclude most rule-based expert systems, meaning AI systems that, despite lacking learning during use, can pose similar risks to machine learning systems in high-risk contexts. The alignment with the OECD's updated AI definition also promotes international regulatory coherence.

2. Remaining ambiguities

Despite their considerable utility, the guidelines leave significant interpretive questions unresolved. The boundary between systems that 'transcend basic data processing' and those that do not remains very much unclear. The document acknowledges that systems used in a 'consolidated manner for many years' may indicate basic processing, but this temporal criterion lacks the precision required for confident compliance determinations. When does an established technique become sufficiently novel or sophisticated to qualify as AI? The answer remains unclear.

Another problem is the treatment of hybrid systems (i.e. combination of traditional software with AI components). Many contemporary applications embed AI functionality within larger software ecosystems, raising

17 Bitkom, 'Breakthrough in Artificial Intelligence' (2025), <https://www.privacy-conference.com/en/news/breakthrough-artificial-intelligence>.

difficult questions about the AI Act's regulatory scope. The guidelines do not adequately address whether the entire integrated system or only the specific AI component falls within the definition's scope, nor how to assess systems where AI functionality plays a complementary rather than central role in the overall system architecture.

Ultimately, the autonomy threshold might also require further adjustments. While the guidelines exclude systems that require 'full manual human involvement', the boundary between minimal autonomy (sufficient for qualification) and de minimis autonomy (insufficient) remains undefined. This ambiguity may generate divergent enforcement practices across Member States.

3. Practical implications

The Commission's AI definition guidelines focus on a case-by-case assessment based on 'specific characteristics'[18] places considerable interpretive burden on developers, deployers, and national authorities. The absence of exhaustive lists, while preserving flexibility, may create compliance uncertainty, especially for all borderline systems. Providers of AI systems should document their classification rationale thoroughly, particularly for systems that come close to definitional boundaries.

The grandfathering provision in Art. 111(2) AI Act is a positive step. It will provide transitional relief for systems placed on the market before 2.8.2026. Yet new deployments in a very dynamic field will require careful definitional analysis on a constant basis. Companies or organisations deploying technologies that incorporate machine learning or knowledge-based reasoning should presumptively treat them as AI systems unless clear exclusion criteria apply.

The risk-based architecture of the AI Act means qualification as an AI system does not automatically trigger regulatory obligations.[19] Only systems falling within prohibited practices (Art. 5 AI Act), high-risk categories (Art. 6, Annexes I and III AI Act), or transparency obligations (Art. 50 AI Act) face substantive requirements. Nevertheless, the definitional AI system

18 European Commission, ‚Commission Guidelines on the definition of an artificial intelligence system established by Regulation (EU) 2024/1689 (AI Act)', C(2025) 5053 final, para. 6.

19 European Commission, ‚Commission Guidelines on the definition of an artificial intelligence system established by Regulation (EU) 2024/1689 (AI Act)', C(2025) 5053 final, para. 63.

threshold remains the gateway to the entire regulatory framework, making its interpretation foundational to AI Act compliance.

V. Recommended further reading

AI Act, in particular Art. 3 and Rec. 12.

European Commission, 'Guidelines on the definition of an artificial intelligence system established by Regulation (EU) 2024/1689 (AI Act)', C(2025) 5053 final.

European Commission, 'Guidelines on prohibited artificial intelligence practices', C(2025) 925 final.

OECD, 'Explanatory memorandum on the updated OECD definition of an AI system', (OECD Artificial Intelligence Papers, No. 8, 2024) <https://www.oecd.org/content/dam/oecd/en/publications/reports/2024/03/explanatory-memorandum-on-the-updated-oecd-definition-of-an-ai-system_3c815e51/623da898-en.pdf>.

ISO/IEC 22989:2022, 'Information technology — Artificial intelligence — Concepts and terminology', Edition 1 (2022).

Personal Data in AI Development and Use

Eduardo Ustaran

EDPB, ‚Opinion 28/2024 on certain data protection aspects related to the processing of personal data in the context of AI models' (17.12.2024) <https://www.edpb.europa.eu/our-work-tools/our-documents/opinion-board-art-64/opinion-282024-certain-data-protection-aspects_en>

I. Introduction and context

The development and deployment of artificial intelligence (AI) systems rely on processing vast amounts of data, much of which is personal data. This reality brings AI squarely within the scope of European data protection law. Art. 5, 6 and 9 GDPR establish fundamental principles for processing personal data and set out the conditions for lawful processing. Art. 12 to 22 GDPR confer rights on individuals whose data is processed. Crucially, these provisions apply to any form of personal data processing, including when such processing takes place in the context of AI.

The legal challenge that arises in this context is how to apply data protection principles and rights to AI's unique characteristics: its huge technical complexity, its need for extremely large datasets, the fact that it is very early days in the evolution of mainstream AI, and its unprecedented potential for automated decision-making. Over the past years, European data protection authorities have issued guidance and taken enforcement action to clarify how these rules apply in practice.

This chapter examines how European regulators and courts are interpreting data protection principles and rights in the context of AI. It focuses on six key areas where regulatory attention has been most relevant: lawfulness, transparency, data minimisation, accuracy, individual rights and automated decision-making. The analysis draws on guidance from the European Data Protection Board and national authorities, as well as enforcement actions that have tested these principles in real cases. The chapter's aim is to consider these regulatory positions in order to identify practical approaches for reconciling AI development and use with European data protection law.

II. Legitimacy in the use of data: lawfulness and transparency

1. Lawfulness – Legitimate interests for AI training

The first AI-related data protection compliance question is whether processing personal data for AI development or use is lawful. Art. 6 GDPR requires meeting one of six legal bases, but in practice the choice for AI training will invariably come down to either consent under Art. 6(1)(a) GDPR or legitimate interests under Art. 6(1)(f) GDPR. In reality, consent is unworkable for training large language models on data scraped from the internet, where it is impossible to obtain consent from millions of individuals. This makes legitimate interests the primary and only realistic candidate for AI training.

a) Regulatory guidance and interpretation

The European Data Protection Board (EDPB) has confirmed that legitimate interests can be a valid legal basis for AI training, but only after a rigorous three-part assessment which follows a well-established doctrine. Controllers must first demonstrate a legitimate interest in developing the AI system, then show that processing personal data is necessary for that purpose, and finally balance their interests against the rights and freedoms of data subjects. The EDPB's Opinion 28/2024 emphasises that this balance depends heavily on context. Key aspects that need to be taken into account include: the nature of the data processed, the risks for the data subjects, the reasonable expectations of the data subjects, and the mitigating measures.[1]

National authorities have taken a similar line. The CNIL has stated that creating a training database can often be legitimate where the AI system's intended use is itself lawful, but that each case requires individual assess-

1 EDPB, ‚Opinion 28/2024 on certain data protection aspects related to the processing of personal data in the context of AI models' (17.12.2024) <https://www.edpb.europa.eu/our-work-tools/our-documents/opinion-board-art-64/opinion-282024-certain-data-protection-aspects_en>.

ment to ensure processing is not disproportionate.[2] The Irish Data Protection Commission's engagement with Meta and LinkedIn demonstrates this proportionality focus in practice. Both companies were required to implement enhanced transparency notices, improved measures to protect users and detailed risk assessments before proceeding with AI training using user data.[3]

Enforcement action has shown the limits of legitimate interests. Italian authorities fined both OpenAI[4] and Luka[5] for processing personal data without an adequate legal basis. The multiple enforcement actions against Clearview AI across Europe all concluded that large-scale facial recognition data scraping could not be justified under legitimate interests given the scale, intrusiveness and lack of proportionality.[6] The Dutch authority's decision against Clearview in 2024 emphasised that the freedom to perform economic or commercial activities does not extend so far as to cover activities that almost fully coincide with infringing the fundamental rights of others.[7]

One complication is special category data under Art. 9 GDPR. Current guidance from the EDPB explicitly excludes this from its analysis, leaving uncertainty about what specific condition applies to the processing of spe-

2 CNIL, ‚Recommendations on the development of artificial intelligence systems' (2025) <https://www.cnil.fr/en/ai-cnil-finalises-its-recommendations-development-artificial-intelligence-systems>.

3 Data Protection Commission, ‚Statement on engagement with Meta regarding AI training' (21.5.2025) <https://www.dataprotection.ie/en/news-media/latest-news/dpc-statement-meta-ai>; Data Protection Commission, ‚Statement on engagement with LinkedIn regarding AI training' (7.11.2025) <https://www.dataprotection.ie/en/news-media/latest-news/dpc-statement-linkedin-ai-training>.

4 Garante per la protezione dei dati personali, ‚Decision against OpenAI' (December 2024), <https://www.garanteprivacy.it/web/guest/home/docweb/-/docweb-display/docweb/10085432>, fine of €15 million.

5 Garante per la protezione dei dati personali, ‚Decision against Luka Inc.' (Replika) (April 2025), <https://gpdp.it/home/docweb/-/docweb-display/docweb/10132048>, fine of €5 million.

6 See enforcement actions by Italian, French, Greek, UK and Austrian authorities against Clearview AI (2021–2024).

7 Autoriteit Persoonsgegevens, ‚Decision against Clearview AI' (16.5.2024) <https://www.autoriteitpersoonsgegevens.nl/en/current/dutch-dpa-imposes-a-fine-on-clearview-because-of-illegal-data-collection-for-facial-recognition>, fine of €30.5 million, para. 91.

cial category data in this context, given that Art. 9 GDPR does not include legitimate interests as a possible option.[8]

A further complexity is that different stages of the AI lifecycle may require different legal bases. Training a model, deploying it and using it to make decisions about individuals involve distinct purposes and risks. The EDPB, ICO and others have emphasised that controllers should assess each stage separately rather than assume a single legal basis covers the entire lifecycle.[9]

b) Practical analysis

The regulatory position is now reasonably clear: legitimate interests can work for AI training and use, but only with serious attention to proportionality. Controllers should focus on three practical steps. First, be realistic about necessity. Can the AI system achieve its purpose with aggregated data or with synthetic data? If personal data is genuinely necessary, document why. Second, implement meaningful safeguards aimed at eliminating or minimising any potential privacy intrusions. Relying on technical measures like differential privacy, organisational measures like access controls, and contractual restrictions on downstream use will significantly strengthen the proportionality case. Third, be transparent from the outset about the use of personal data for AI training and use. The Irish DPC's approach with Meta and LinkedIn shows that proactive transparency and engagement can contribute to legitimacy and allow development to proceed.

For organisations scraping data from the internet, the message from regulators is clear: this processing activity will face intense scrutiny and may not satisfy lawfulness requirements without certain limitations on scope and use. Respecting robots.txt files, excluding sensitive categories of websites and implementing time-based restrictions are now baseline expectations, not optional extras.

---

8 EDPB, ‚Opinion 28/2024 on certain data protection aspects related to the processing of personal data in the context of AI models‘ (fn. 1), para. 17 (noting that special category data is excluded from the scope of analysis).

9 EDPB, ‚Opinion 28/2024 on certain data protection aspects related to the processing of personal data in the context of AI models‘ (fn. 1); Information Commissioner's Office, ‚Guidance on AI and data protection‘ <https://ico.org.uk/for-organisations/uk-gdpr-guidance-and-resources/artificial-intelligence/guidance-on-ai-and-data-protection/>.

2. Transparency – Expectations and creativity

Transparency about the use of personal data in AI raises particular challenges. Training datasets may include data from millions of individuals who have no relationship with the controller and no expectation their data would be used for AI. The complexity of AI systems makes it extremely difficult to explain the use of data involved in simple terms. Yet data protection law requires clear information about such use, and regulators have consistently identified transparency as a key compliance requirement.

a) Regulatory guidance and interpretation

The EDPB has called for transparency that arguably goes beyond the specific requirements of Art. 13 and 14 GDPR. Its guidance recommends that controllers provide public, easily accessible communications about their AI systems, including details about collection criteria and the datasets used. Alternative forms of communication are encouraged, including media campaigns with different media outlets, information campaigns by e-mail, use of graphic visualisation, FAQs, transparency labels, model cards and annual transparency reports.[10]

This enhanced approach reflects the reality that traditional privacy notices cannot reach everyone whose data is used in AI training. The Irish DPC's work with Meta and LinkedIn illustrates what regulators expect in practice. Both companies were required to update their privacy notices to explain more clearly how user data would be used for AI training and to implement user-friendly opt-out mechanisms. The key was not just providing information but making it accessible and actionable for users.

Enforcement has focused on transparency failures alongside other violations. The Italian authority's fines against OpenAI (€15 million) and Luka (€5 million) both cited insufficient transparency about data use and inadequate information for users.[11]

The intersection with automated decision-making has also clarified transparency obligations. The ECJ's judgment in Dun & Bradstreet, while

10 EDPB, ‚Opinion 28/2024 on certain data protection aspects related to the processing of personal data in the context of AI models‘ (fn. 1), para. 103.

11 Garante per la protezione dei dati personali, ‚Decision against OpenAI‘ (fn. 4); Garante per la protezione dei dati personali, ‚Decision against Luka Inc.‘ (fn. 5).

concerning credit scoring rather than AI specifically, established that individuals subject to automated decisions are entitled to meaningful information about the logic involved.[12] German authorities have confirmed this applies equally to AI systems.[13] The required information must explain the procedure and principles actually applied, such as how variations in input data would affect the outcome, rather than simply describing the algorithm in abstract terms. The ICO and Alan Turing Institute have developed detailed joint guidance on explaining AI decisions to individuals in accessible ways.[14]

b) Practical analysis

Transparency in AI requires creativity, not just compliance with formal notice requirements. Organisations should think about transparency as an ongoing communication exercise rather than a one-time disclosure. Layered and multi-channel approaches are particularly suitable because they combine the type of information prescribed by law with other information tailored to different audiences. For example, model cards that document training data, performance characteristics and known limitations serve a technical purpose but can be part of good transparency practices.

In web scraping scenarios, transparency is demonstrated by showing a willingness to be open and accountable. Advance publicity about data collection practices, clear information about exclusion mechanisms and responsive handling of objection requests can demonstrate good faith even where individual notice is impractical. The key lesson from enforcement is that regulators distinguish between organisations that make genuine efforts at transparency and those that obscure or downplay their data use.

---

12 ECJ 27.2.2025 – case C-203/22, ECLI:EU:C:2025:117 – Dun & Bradstreet Austria GmbH.

13 See statement by Der Hamburgische Beauftragte für Daten Schutz und Informationsfreiheit, ‚Auswirkungen des Schufa-Urteils auf KI-Anwendungen – automatisierte Entscheidungen dürfen keine maßgebliche Rolle spielen' (7.12.2023) <https://datenschutz-hamburg.de/fileadmin/user_upload/HmbBfDI/Pressemitteilungen/2023/2023-12-07-PM_EuGH_Urteil_Schufa_Auswirkungen_auf_KI.pdf> in relation to a similar credit scoring decision available at.

14 Information Commissioner's Office/Alan Turing Institute, ‚Explaining decisions made with AI' <https://ico.org.uk/for-organisations/uk-gdpr-guidance-and-resources/artificial-intelligence/explaining-decisions-made-with-artificial-intelligence/>.

Where AI systems make significant decisions about individuals, transparency obligations become even more relevant. The Dun & Bradstreet doctrine requires explaining the actual logic applied in specific cases, not just the general approach. This means organisations need systems in place to reconstruct how particular decisions were reached, which has implications for model design, logging and documentation practices.

III. Technical tensions: data minimisation and accuracy

1. Data minimisation – The volume conflict

Data minimisation is a core principle of European data protection law, particularly in today's data-rich world. Art. 5(1)(c) GDPR requires that personal data be adequate, relevant and limited to what is necessary in relation to the purposes for which it is processed. This principle sits uncomfortably with AI development, which typically depends on processing vast quantities of data for training purposes. This is an intrinsic conflict to resolve because AI models necessarily rely on large-scale datasets to be trained and function, while data minimisation pushes toward collecting and processing as little personal data as possible.

a) Regulatory guidance and interpretation

Regulators have not resolved this tension by relaxing data minimisation requirements. Instead, they have insisted that controllers demonstrate genuine necessity and implement mitigation measures. The EDPB's Opinion 28/2024 emphasises that data minimisation must be considered as part of the necessity assessment when relying on legitimate interests for AI training, and recommends mitigating measures including pseudonymisation and the use of technical measures to mask personal data or to substitute it with fake personal data where appropriate.[15] The ICO's guidance provides

15 EDPB, ‚Opinion 28/2024 on certain data protection aspects related to the processing of personal data in the context of AI models‘ (fn. 1), para. 101.

more detailed technical recommendations such as perturbation or adding 'noise', synthetic data and federated learning.[16]

The web scraping context has received particular attention in EDPB Opinion 28/2024. The EDPB recommends that controllers consider excluding content from websites that present particularly high risks, such as those containing personal data about vulnerable individuals who might face abuse or prejudice if their information were publicly released. Controllers should also avoid collecting from websites dealing with particularly sensitive or intrusive subject matter. The EDPB further recommends respecting technical signals like robots.txt or ai.txt files that indicate objection to automated collection.[17]

The CNIL's guidance has taken a holistic approach to data minimisation in this context and provided wide ranging recommendations, including carefully considering in advance what data is actually necessary, conducting pilots with fictitious, synthetic and anonymised data, consulting with an ethics committee, and taking detailed practical steps to keep control of the data used for AI-related purposes.[18]

Enforcement has shown the consequences of ignoring data minimisation. The Austrian authority's deletion order against Clearview AI cited the company's permanent storage of facial recognition data as constituting a breach of the data minimisation principle.[19]

b) Practical analysis

Data minimisation in AI requires accepting certain constraints on data collection rather than treating every data source as readily available. The practical question is not whether to apply data minimisation but how to demonstrate compliance in a context where large datasets are technically beneficial. Controllers should start by documenting why the volume and variety of data they intend to process is genuinely necessary for their AI

16 Information Commissioner's Office, ‚Guidance on AI and data protection' (fn. 9), section on data minimisation.

17 EDPB, ‚Opinion 28/2024 on certain data protection aspects related to the processing of personal data in the context of AI models' (fn. 1), para. 105.

18 CNIL, ‚Développement des systèmes d'IA : les recommandations de la CNIL pour respecter le RGPD' (22.7.2025) <https://www.cnil.fr/fr/developpement-des-systemes-dia-les-recommandations-de-la-cnil-pour-respecter-le-rgpd>, section on data minimisation.

19 Österreichische Datenschutzbehörde, Decision against Clearview AI (10.5.2023).

system's legitimate purpose. The documentation should explain what the AI system does, why that purpose requires personal data rather than synthetic or aggregated alternatives, and what steps have been taken to limit collection to what is really needed.

Technical mitigation measures considerably strengthen the compliance position. Using synthetic data for AI development, even if real personal data is needed for fine-tuning purposes, is likely to become an expected common practice in the same way encryption is seen as a given in a data security context. Differential privacy, federated learning and data perturbation techniques can reduce privacy risks while maintaining model performance. For web scraping, implementing exclusion mechanisms and respecting opt-out signals is now a baseline expectation. Controllers that ignore robots.txt files or scrape from obviously sensitive websites face significant enforcement risk. The emerging regulatory message is clear: AI's need for data does not override data minimisation. Controllers must justify their data collection practices and implement meaningful limitations.

2. Accuracy – Hallucinations and inferences

Art. 5(1)(d) GDPR requires that personal data be accurate and, where necessary, kept up to date. This principle becomes complex when applied to AI systems that generate outputs through statistical inference rather than factual retrieval, as many everyday examples show. AI systems, particularly large language models, can produce outputs that are plausible but woefully incorrect, a phenomenon commonly known as AI hallucinations. The question is how the data accuracy principle applies to these AI-generated outputs.

a) Regulatory guidance and interpretation

The ICO has drawn an important distinction between data protection accuracy and statistical accuracy. The data accuracy principle applies to all personal data processed by an AI system, whether as input or output, but this does not mean an AI system must be 100 % statistically accurate to comply with this principle. However, an AI system must be sufficiently statistically accurate to ensure that any personal data generated by it is processed lawfully and fairly.[20]

In practice, the ICO recommends several steps: ensure staff understand statistical accuracy requirements and their limitations, clearly label AI outputs as inferences or predictions rather than facts, manage expectations about system performance, and adopt common terminology for discussing accuracy measures within the organisation. The overall message is that transparency about the nature of AI outputs, and about the system's known limitations, forms part of accuracy compliance.

The CNIL has focused on the data annotation phase of AI development as critical for accuracy. Annotation involves assigning labels or descriptions to training data that the model learns to recognise and reproduce. If this ground truth data is inaccurate or inconsistent, the resulting model will perpetuate those inaccuracies. The CNIL recommends implementing continuous verification procedures to check annotation quality through discussion panels, sample analysis, audits and user feedback.[21]

Enforcement attention to accuracy is also palpable. The EDPB's ChatGPT Taskforce stated that while the purpose of the data processing was to train ChatGPT and not necessarily to

provide factually accurate information, the outputs provided by ChatGPT are likely to be taken as factually accurate by end users and the principle of data accuracy must be complied with. The EDPB went on to say that it is of importance that proper information on the probabilistic output creation mechanisms and on their limited level of reliability is provided by the controller. However, although the measures taken in order to comply with the transparency principle are beneficial to avoid misinterpretation of the output of ChatGPT, they are not regarded as sufficient to comply with the data accuracy principle.[22]

---

20 Information Commissioner's Office, ‚Guidance on AI and data protection' (fn. 9), section on accuracy.

21 CNIL, ‚IA : Annoter les données' (22.7.2025) <https://www.cnil.fr/fr/ia-annoter-les-donnees>.

22 EDPB, ‚Report of the work undertaken by the ChatGPT Taskforce' (23.5.2024) <https://www.edpb.europa.eu/system/files/2024-05/edpb_20240523_report_chatgpt_taskforce_en.pdf>, paras. 29–31.

b) Practical analysis

Over time and as AI becomes nearly infallible, this issue may resolve itself, but today's AI limitations present an accuracy compliance challenge. Clear labelling of outputs as AI-generated, as predictions or inferences goes a long way towards meeting accuracy requirements. But regulatory guidance indicates that where AI systems may generate false information about individuals, controllers need to implement mechanisms to identify and correct inaccurate outputs.

Documentation and testing should be part of the process to avoid, or at least mitigate, inaccuracies. Controllers should maintain records of their AI system's accuracy performance across different use cases and demographics. Where accuracy varies significantly for different groups, this has both accuracy and fairness implications. Regular testing with diverse datasets will help identify when models are generating systematically inaccurate outputs for particular populations.

For training data, quality control during the annotation phase prevents accuracy problems from being baked into the model. The CNIL's recommendation for continuous verification is particularly sound. Using multiple annotators and different verification practices can identify problematic data before it affects model training.

Where AI systems have generated inaccurate personal data, controllers must be prepared to correct or delete it. This may require adjusting outputs or even retraining models. Controllers who cannot correct inaccurate outputs generated by their AI systems face a fundamental compliance problem, which is also easy to spot by regulators and third parties. This reality should inform model design choices from the outset. Ultimately, systems should be built with the capability to identify and address accuracy issues when they arise.

IV. Individual agency: rights and automated decision-making

1. Individual rights – Putting people in control

Data protection law gives individuals the ability to control how their personal data is used by others through certain rights: access, rectification, erasure, restriction, portability and objection. AI systems create particular difficulties for exercising these rights, especially where personal data has been incorporated into training datasets or where individuals have no direct relationship with the controller. This challenge is both technical and practical, but data protection rights are at the essence of what compliance with data protection law requires.

a) Regulatory guidance and interpretation

While the EDPB has recognised the difficulty of exercising data protection rights in an AI context, its Opinion 28/2024 points out that regulators must ensure that all data subject rights are respected when AI models are developed and deployed by controllers.[23] The EDPB's technical report on effective implementation of data subjects' rights examines the practical challenges of rectification and erasure in relation to AI. The report acknowledges that complying with these rights may require retraining models with corrected data or without the data to be erased. While this is technically demanding and potentially costly, the report's position is that technical difficulty does not excuse non-compliance. The report explores various technical approaches including machine unlearning methods, though it acknowledges these are still developing technologies.[24]

The ICO's guidance emphasises that personal data processed at the pre-processing stage of AI development, and de-identified data, remains personal data for GDPR purposes. Individuals therefore retain data subject rights even where identifying them is difficult in practice. Crucially, the ICO states that data subjects' rights requests should not be regarded as unfounded or excessive just because they may be harder to fulfil in the context of AI or the motivation for requesting them may be unclear in comparison to other access requests. On rectification and erasure specifically, the ICO confirms that controllers must address requests even where inaccuracies seem minor. The ICO acknowledges that rectification or erasure may not be possible without retraining the model or deleting it altogether. While

23 EDPB, ‚Opinion 28/2024 on certain data protection aspects related to the processing of personal data in the context of AI models‘ (fn. 1), para. 65.

24 Shrishak, ‚Effective implementation of data subjects' rights‘ (2024), <https://www.edpb.europa.eu/system/files/2025-01/d2-ai-effective-implementation-of-data-subjects-rights_en.pdf>.

not legally required, having well-organised model management systems and deployment pipelines makes accommodating these requests less costly.[25]

The Irish DPC's engagement with Meta and LinkedIn puts this regulatory thinking into practice. In both cases, the DPC has recommended concrete measures to facilitate the exercise of individual data protection rights. These include notifications advising users on how they can assert their right to object under the GDPR by opting out of their personal data being used for the purpose of AI training as well as the availability of objection forms.

b) Practical analysis

Individual rights compliance in AI starts with accepting that these rights apply fully, regardless of technical difficulty. The practical question is how to design AI systems that can accommodate rights requests without requiring complete rebuilding every time.

Regulatory guidance and action show that data management becomes critical. AI developers should maintain clear records of what data is used for AI model training and what data sources are employed. This documentation enables controllers to respond to data subject rights requests and to assess the appropriate mechanism to enable rectification and erasure.

In terms of pre-emptive practical measures, providing extended notice periods before using data for AI training, as recommended by the DPC, gives individuals time to object before their data becomes embedded in models. Designing opt-out mechanisms from the outset, rather than adding them after complaints arise, is also aligned with the data protection by design principle. For web-scraped data, where individual notice is impossible, controllers should consider implementing mechanisms that allow individuals to discover whether their data was collected and to request removal.

The clear message for anyone involved in the use of personal data for AI development purposes is that data protection rights must not only be honoured, but they must be actively facilitated.

25 Information Commissioner's Office, ‚Guidance on AI and data protection' (fn. 9), section on individual rights.

2. Automated decision-making – Calling the shots

Art. 22 GDPR gives individuals the right not to be subject to decisions based solely on automated processing, including profiling, which produce legal effects or similarly significantly affect them. This right has particular importance for AI systems, which will be increasingly designed precisely to make or support crucial decisions about individuals.

a) Regulatory guidance and interpretation

Art. 22 GDPR applies only to decisions that are both solely automated and produce legal or similarly significant effects. The ICO's guidance clarifies that AI systems fall within the scope of Art. 22 GDPR only where they meet both criteria. Many AI systems assist human decision-making rather than replacing it entirely, and many AI outputs do not produce legal or similarly significant effects. Where Art. 22 GDPR does apply, the processing can proceed only if it is necessary for entering into or performing a contract, authorised by law, or based on the individual's explicit consent.

The interpretation of 'solely automated' has been clarified through regulatory guidance and case law. The ICO emphasises that the human input needs to be meaningful. As the ICO puts it, a decision does not fall outside the scope of Art. 22 GDPR just because a human has 'rubber-stamped' it. The degree and quality of human review and intervention before a final decision is made about an individual are key factors in determining whether a decision is solely automated and fully reliant on an AI system or simply assisted by AI.[26]

The meaning of 'legal or similarly significant effects' is more difficult to define, as also indicated by the ICO, but it refers to a decision that has some sort of impact on someone's circumstances or choices. For example, a computer decision to offer someone a job, or a decision to agree or decline a person's mortgage application fit that categorisation, and these effects can be positive or negative.

At a practical level, the ICO makes the following concrete recommendations: consider the system requirements necessary to support a meaningful human review from the design phase, design and deliver appropriate train-

26 Information Commissioner's Office, ‚Guidance on AI and data protection' (fn. 9), section on automated decision-making.

ing and support for human reviewers, and give staff the appropriate authority, incentives and support to address or escalate individuals' concerns and, if necessary, override the AI system's decision.

b) Practical analysis

Art. 22 GDPR compliance requires controllers to first determine whether their AI system falls within the scope of application. This means properly assessing whether humans exercise meaningful judgment or simply rubber-stamp AI outputs. Controllers should document the decision-making process, including at what stage and how humans are involved, what information they consider beyond the AI's output, and what authority they have to deviate from AI recommendations.

Where Art. 22 GDPR applies, controllers must establish one of the three legal grounds: contractual necessity, legal authorisation or explicit consent. Contractual necessity is often the most workable, but controllers must show the automated decision-making is actually necessary for the contract, not merely convenient. Legal authorisation requires specific legislation permitting the processing. Explicit consent is difficult in practice as it requires clear affirmative action and must be freely given, which is challenging where individuals need the service.

For AI systems that support rather than make decisions, controllers should carefully document how human judgment is deployed. Training decision-makers on how to critically evaluate AI recommendations, maintaining records of when AI recommendations are overridden and why, and ensuring sufficient time and information for humans to exercise real judgment all demonstrate that decisions are not solely automated. The goal is genuine human agency in the decision-making process, not simply inserting a human step to avoid Art. 22 GDPR.

V. Recommended further reading

EDPB, ‚Opinion 28/2024 on certain data protection aspects related to the processing of personal data in the context of AI models' (17.12.2024) <https://www.edpb.europa.eu/our-work-tools/our-documents/opinion-board-art-64/opinion-282024-certain-data-protection-aspects_en>.

EDPB, ‚Report of the work undertaken by the ChatGPT Taskforce' (23.5.2024) <https://www.edpb.europa.eu/system/files/2024-05/edpb_20240523_report_chatgpt_taskforce_en.pdf>.

CNIL, ‚Recommendations on the development of artificial intelligence systems' (2025) <https://www.cnil.fr/en/ai-cnil-finalises-its-recommendations-development-artificial-intelligence-systems>.

Data Protection Commission, ‚Statement on engagement with Meta regarding AI training' (21.5.2025) <https://www.dataprotection.ie/en/news-media/latest-news/dpc-statement-meta-ai>.

Data Protection Commission, ‚Statement on engagement with LinkedIn regarding AI training' (7.11.2025) <https://www.dataprotection.ie/en/news-media/latest-news/dpc-statement-linkedin-ai-training>.

Information Commissioner's Office, ‚Guidance on AI and data protection' <https://ico.org.uk/for-organisations/uk-gdpr-guidance-and-resources/artificial-intelligence/guidance-on-ai-and-data-protection/>.

Information Commissioner's Office/Alan Turing Institute, ‚Explaining decisions made with AI' <https://ico.org.uk/for-organisations/uk-gdpr-guidance-and-resources/artificial-intelligence/explaining-decisions-made-with-artificial-intelligence/>.

ECJ 27.2.2025 – case C-203/22, ECLI:EU:C:2025:117 – Dun & Bradstreet Austria GmbH.

Sensitive data in AI development

Rolf Schwartmann

OLG Köln 23.5.25 – 15 UKI 2/25, NJW 2025, 3156

I. Case summary

In the proceedings before the Higher Regional Court of Cologne discussed here, the *Consumer Advice Centre of North Rhine-Westphalia* filed a motion for a preliminary injunction prohibiting Meta from processing public personal data of its users on Facebook and Instagram for the purpose of developing and improving artificial intelligence (AI) systems.

On 10.6.2024, Meta announced in an amendment to its privacy policy that it intended to process publicly available user data for the purpose of training its large language model. After doubts were raised by both regulatory authorities[1] and civil society organisations[2] about the admissibility of this approach under data protection law, the company initially distanced itself from its plans.[3]

Based on an opinion from the European Data Protection Board (EDPB)[4] and in consultation with the competent Irish Data Protection Commission (DPC)[5], Meta revised its data processing concept and announced

---

1 Cf. Data Protection Commission, ‚The DPC's Engagement with Meta on AI' (14.6.2024) <https://www.dataprotection.ie/en/news-media/latest-news/dpcs-engagement-meta-ai>.

2 Noyb, ‚noyb urges 11 DPAs to immediately stop Meta's abuse of personal data for AI' (6.6.2024), <https://noyb.eu/en/noyb-urges-11-dpas-immediately-stop-metas-abuse-personal-data-ai>.

3 Cf. Steiner, ‚Meta cancels AI training with data under GDPR for the time being' (heise online, 15.6.2024) <https://www.heise.de/en/news/Meta-cancels-AI-training-with-data-under-GDPR-for-the-time-being-9764716.html>.

4 EDPB, ‚Opinion 28/2024 on certain data protection aspects related to the processing of personal data in the context of AI models' (17.12.2024) <https://www.edpb.europa.eu/system/files/2024-12/edpb_opinion_202428_ai-models_en.pdf>.

5 DPC, ‚DPC statement on Meta AI' (21.5.2025) <https://www.dataprotection.ie/en/news-media/latest-news/dpc-statement-meta-ai>.

on 14.4.2025 that it intended to use certain data from its users on the Facebook and Instagram platforms to train the AI model from 27.5.2025 onwards.[6] The processing was to include data publicly posted by adult users (first-party data) and these users' interactions with the AI model (flywheel data).

II. Key legal findings

In summary proceedings, the Higher Regional Court of Cologne ruled that Meta may train its large language model using data from public profiles on its Facebook and Instagram platforms without first obtaining the consent of the data subjects.

Firstly, the prohibition on combining personal data from different core platform services set out in Art. 5(2) subpara. 1(b) DMA does not preclude the processing of data intended by Meta. The inclusion of partially de-identified and disaggregated data from two core platform services in an unstructured training data set for AI does not constitute a combination within the meaning of Art. 5(2) subpara. 1(b) DMA, as there is ‚no targeted linking of a user's personal data from one core platform service with the same user's personal data from another core platform service'.[7]

From the perspective of the GDPR as well, no consent from the data subjects is required, as the data processing is based on Meta's legitimate interests and is therefore justified in accordance with Art. 6(1) subpara. 1(f) GDPR. The summary examination in the context of the urgent proceedings revealed that the data processing was necessary to safeguard Meta's legitimate interests and that the interests or fundamental rights and freedoms of the users concerned did not outweigh Meta's legitimate interests.[8]

Finally, the prohibition on processing special categories of personal data pursuant to Art. 9(1) GDPR does not preclude the training of an AI model with user data. Given the broad scope of the provision, it can certainly be assumed that the intended training data set also contains special categories

6 Meta, ‚Making AI Work Harder for Europeans' (14.4.2025) <https://about.fb.com/news/2025/04/making-ai-work-harder-for-europeans/>.

7 OLG Köln 23.5.2025 – 15 UKI 2/25, NJW 2025, 3156 mn. 32 (translated by the author).

8 OLG Köln 23.5.2025 – 15 UKI 2/25, NJW 2025, 3156 mn. 43.

of personal data.[9] Furthermore, the exception in Art. 9(2)(e) GDPR does not apply to the processing of third-party data shared by users.[10] However, taking into account the case law of the ECJ on search engine operators, an activity-related interpretation of the scope of application must be made, which means that the processing prohibition in the specific case requires 'activation' by a request from the third parties concerned to remove their data from the published post or from the training data set.[11]

III. Systematic context and legal classification

The ruling by the Higher Regional Court of Cologne was the first ruling by a national court on the admissibility of processing personal data for AI training. The question of the compatibility of AI training with the GDPR has been preoccupying authorities[12] and academics[13] for some time, but particularly since the advent of the modern generation of generative AI. However, official statements in particular initially lacked detailed discussions of the processing of special categories of personal data. While it is generally assumed that there is a possibility of justifying data processing in accordance with Art. 6(1) subpara. 1(f) GDPR,[14] the processing prohibition

9 OLG Köln 23.5.2025 – 15 UKI 2/25, NJW 2025, 3156 mn. 93.

10 OLG Köln 23.5.2025 – 15 UKI 2/25, NJW 2025, 3156 mn. 99.

11 OLG Köln 23.5.2025 – 15 UKI 2/25, NJW 2025, 3156 mn. 100, 105.

12 Datenschutzkonferenz, ‚Orientierungshilfe der Konferenz der unabhängigen Datenschutzaufsichtsbehörden des Bundes und der Länder vom 6. Mai 2024, Künstliche Intelligenz und Datenschutz‘ (6.5.2024) <https://www.datenschutzkonferenz-online.de/media/oh/20240506_DSK_Orientierungshilfe_KI_und_Datenschutz.pdf>; Der Landesbeauftragte für Datenschutz und Informationsfreiheit Baden-Württemberg, ‚Diskussionspapier: Rechtsgrundlagen im Datenschutz beim Einsatz von Künstlicher Intelligenz‘, version 2.0 (17.10.2024) <https://www.baden-wuerttemberg.datenschutz.de/rechtsgrundlagen-datenschutz-ki/>. For the English version of the first draft of the second paper, see <https://www.baden-wuerttemberg.datenschutz.de/legal-bases-in-data-protection-for-ai/>.

13 Before the ruling of the Higher Regional Court of Cologne Paal ZfDR 2024, 129; Hüger ZfDR 2024, 263.

14 In detail Paal ZfDR 2024, 129 (149–154). See also Franke RDi 2023, 565 (566–568); Hüger ZfDR 2024, 263 (271–275); Piltz/Weiss EuDIR 2025, 90 (92 f.); Werry MMR 2023, 911 (912 f.).

in Art. 9(1) GDPR is widely seen as a difficult hurdle for AI developers to overcome.[15]

Unlike simple data processing, there is no exception for the processing of special categories of personal data based on the legitimate interests of the controller. Therefore, only in rare individual cases is an exception under Art. 9(2) GDPR applicable to AI training. For the processing of sensitive user data, Art. 9(2)(e) GDPR may be considered, but this does not apply to third-party data that users have published.[16] The situation for AI developers is complicated by the ECJ's broad interpretation of the scope of Art. 9(1) GDPR.[17]

In this ruling, the Higher Regional Court of Cologne offers a solution to the difficulties faced by those responsible: Since the responsibility of AI developers only arises secondarily, after a user has first published sensitive data belonging to third parties, the processing prohibition is only applicable after an examination based on a request by the data subject to have their data record removed, in accordance with the case law of the ECJ on the responsibility of search engine operators.[18]

In the literature, the approach taken by the Higher Regional Court of Cologne has been largely criticised. Commentators have pointed out, above all, the lack of practical feasibility of the request requirement. According to critics, third parties are often unaware that their sensitive data is being published on users' social media profiles and thus also being processed for AI training. This precludes an effective possibility of objection.[19] In addition, systematic concerns have been expressed: Art. 9(1) GDPR establishes an objective prohibition, not a right of the data subject.[20] Exceptions to this prohibition are reserved for the legislator under the exception in Art. 9(2)(g) GDPR and cannot be established by the courts.[21] The Higher

15 Hüger ZfDR 2024, 263 (275); Piltz/Weiss EuDIR 2025, 90 (93–95); Werry MMR 2023, 911 (913).

16 Likewise OLG Köln 23.5.2025 – 15 UKI 2/25, NJW 2025, 3156 mn. 99.

17 See, for example, ECJ 1.8.2022 – case C-184/20, ECLI:EU:C:2022:601 para. 123 – OT v Vyriausioji tarnybinės etikos komisija.

18 OLG Köln 23.5.2025 – 15 UKI 2/25, NJW 2025, 3156 mn. 105.

19 Hornung KIR 2025, 407 (411); Paal RDV 2025, 230 (234 f.); Wasilewski CR 2025, 461 (463). Also critical Glocker RDi 2025, 427 (431).

20 Paal RDV 2025, 230 (234).

21 Hornung KIR 2025, 407 (412).

Regional Court of Schleswig also did not follow the approach of the Higher Regional Court of Cologne in an *obiter dictum*.[22]

IV. Author's analysis and commentary

Although the solution offered by the Higher Regional Court of Cologne is rightly subject to dogmatic doubts, it has, as a kind of icebreaker, made an important contribution to the necessary debate on the compatibility of the GDPR with the practical needs of AI development.[23] The challenges arising from Art. 9(1) GDPR and its broad interpretation by the ECJ were largely ignored in public discourse until the Higher Regional Court of Cologne's decision.[24] This is likely due in particular to the fact that no one had developed a satisfactory solution until then. The Higher Regional Court of Cologne therefore deserves credit for addressing the crucial question in such depth in its reasoning.

Fundamentally, the approach taken by the Higher Regional Court of Cologne is also dogmatically comprehensible. After all, the ECJ has expressly ruled that activity-related particularities may affect the scope of responsibility and the specific obligations of a controller with regard to Art. 9(1) GDPR.[25] Just as the search engine operator is not responsible for the presence of special categories of personal data on a third party's website, Meta is not responsible for a user of its platforms publishing sensitive data of third parties on their profile.[26] The search engine operator's responsibility begins with the listing of this website and, in particular, with the display of the link leading to it in the results list, while Meta's responsibility begins with the automated inclusion of the user contribution in the training data set.

22 OLG Schleswig 12.8.2025 – 6 UKI 3/25, GRUR-RS 2025, 19976 mn. 30 f.

23 Similar Wybitul/Kramer/Maturana/Ziegler NZKart 2025, 423 (429).

24 Particularly clear EDPB, ‚Opinion 28/2024 on certain data protection aspects related to the processing of personal data in the context of AI models' (fn. 4), mn. 17, after which the problem was identified but not taken into account in the opinion.

25 ECJ 24.9.2019 – case C-136/17, ECLI:EU:C:2019:773 para. 45 – GC and Others v Commission nationale de l'informatique et des libertés (CNIL).

26 Different viewpoint Glocker RDi 2025, 427 (431), who refers to the lack of responsibility on the part of users for entering data into the AI model. With ECJ 2.12.2025 – case C-492/23, ECLI:EU:C:2025:935 para. 106 – X v Russmedia Digital SRL and Inform Media Press SRL, the assessment of responsibilities may have shifted to the detriment of the platform operator.

In any case, it is not entirely without foundation when the Higher Regional Court of Cologne states that the processing prohibition in Art. 9(1) GDPR cannot apply to the AI developer as if he had made the sensitive user data visible himself: 'Logically, the activities [...] intervene only after (sensitive) data have been placed online and are secondary in nature.'[27] The decisive factor is therefore that no *ex ante* control can be required for an *ex post* activity in which publicly available personal data is processed without regard to the specific category.[28] The objection that AI developers cannot delete sensitive data after a corresponding request has been made is also unfounded: the risk that a data subject's request cannot be complied with by deleting individual data points from the AI model lies within the responsibility of the AI providers and is rightly not taken away from them.[29]

Nevertheless, critics of the ruling are right to complain that the requirement to activate the processing prohibition is hardly feasible in practice and therefore results in a significant impairment of the fundamental rights of the persons concerned.[30] Unlike listings in search engine results, sensitive data from third parties that has been processed for the training of an AI model cannot be reliably reproduced by the persons concerned. However, this does not mean that it is not contained in the trained AI model.[31]

It would have far-reaching consequences if the approach taken by the Higher Regional Court of Cologne were to prevail. In any case, a decision by the ECJ would be desirable in this context. The deciding senate itself regrets that it was not possible to refer the matter to the ECJ in summary proceedings.[32] However, in view of some judgments in recent years, it is doubtful whether the ECJ would have found a practical solution to the problem. Rather, it should be the task of the legislature to enable AI development while maintaining an appropriate level of data protection.

Despite all the (justified) criticism, the ruling of the Higher Regional Court of Cologne at least triggered a solution-oriented debate, which most

---

27 AG Szpunar 10.1.2019 – case C-136/17, ECLI:EU:C:2019:14 para. 55 – GC and Others v Commission nationale de l'informatique et des libertés (CNIL).

28 Cf. AG Szpunar 10.1.2019 – case C-136/17, ECLI:EU:C:2019:14 para. 54, 56 – GC and Others v Commission nationale de l'informatique et des libertés (CNIL).

29 See already Schwartmann/Köhler EuDIR 2025, 287 (292).

30 Cf. Hornung KIR 2025, 407 (411); Paal RDV 2025, 230 (234 f.); Wasilewski CR 2025, 461 (463).

31 On this matter Schwartmann/Köhler RDV 2024, 317; Hansen/Walczak KIR 2024, 82.

32 Cf. OLG Köln 23.5.2025 – 15 UKI 2/25, NJW 2025, 3156 para. 10.

recently culminated in a legislative proposal by the European Commission as part of the Digital Omnibus Package[33]: According to this proposal, the training of AI systems using special categories of personal data shall in future be permitted, provided that strict technical and organizational measures are applied.

V. Recommended further reading

EDPB, ‚Opinion 28/2024 on certain data protection aspects related to the processing of personal data in the context of AI models' (17.12.2024) <https://www.edpb.europa.eu/system/files/2024-12/edpb_opinion_202428_ai-models_en.pdf>.

Schwartmann/Köhler EuDIR 2025, 287.

Schwartmann EuDIR 2026, 3.

Die „Meta-KI-Entscheidung des OLG Köln" – Ein Urteil und fünf Meinungen, RDV 2025, 221.

Paal ZfDR 2024, 129.

33 Proposal for a REGULATION OF THE EUROPEAN PARLIAMENT AND OF THE COUNCIL amending Regulations (EU) 2024/1689 and (EU) 2018/1139 as regards the simplification of the implementation of harmonised rules on artificial intelligence (Digital Omnibus on AI), COM/2025/836 final.

Licensing Datasets for Generative AI Training

Stepanka Havlikova

Garante per la protezione dei dati personali, 'Provvedimento del 27 novembre 2024 [10077129]' (27.11.2024) <https://www.garanteprivacy.it/home/docweb/-/docweb-display/docweb/10076913>

I. Case summary

In November 2024, the *Italian Data Protection Authority (Garante)* issued a formal warning to publisher *GEDI Gruppo Editoriale S.p.A.* (and its affiliated companies – together referred to as '*Gedi*') concerning its planned data-sharing agreement with *OpenAI*.[1] Shortly before the order, on 26.9.2024, *Gedi*, and *OpenAI*, announced a strategic partnership which would enable *OpenAI* using Italian-language content from *Gedi's* publications, including La Repubblica and La Stampa (including attributed quotes, content and links).[2] The order followed after an investigation into *Gedi* which explained that

> all editorial content will be used by *OpenAI* to allow users [of the ChatGPT service, ed.] to search for current news in real time, with the simultaneous provision of a summary (generated by *OpenAI's* artificial intelligence systems) and a direct link to the news itself' and that 'all editorial content will also be used by *OpenAI* to improve its services and train its algorithms of artificial intelligence.[3]

1 Garante per la protezione dei dati personali, 'Provvedimento del 27 novembre 2024 [10077129]' (27.11.2024) <https://www.garanteprivacy.it/home/docweb/-/docweb-display/docweb/10076913>.

2 ‚OpenAI and GEDI announce strategic partnership to bring Italian-language news content to ChatGPT' (press release published by GEDI, 26.9.2024) <https://www.gedi.it/en/media/news/openai-and-gedi-announce-strategic-partnership-bring-italian-language-news-content>; ‚OpenAI and GEDI partner for Italian news content' (press release published by OpenAI, 26.9.2024) <https://openai.com/index/gedi/>.

3 Garante per la protezione dei dati personali, 'Provvedimento del 27 novembre 2024 [10077129]' (fn. 1).

The Garante noted that *GEDI's* digital newspaper archives contain personal data on millions of individuals, including sensitive data and extremely delicate information that cannot be licensed for use by third parties to train artificial intelligence, without due precautions.[4] The *Garante* expressed concern that *GEDI's* processing of personal data and their disclosure to *OpenAI* could violate the GDPR and noted that the chosen legal basis – the publisher's legitimate interest in innovative journalism – was not suitable for this processing. In particular, the authority found that *GEDI's* Data Protection Impact Assessment (DPIA) did not adequately analyse the legal basis for licensing or communicating personal data to a third party (*OpenAI*) for AI training. It pointed out gaps in transparency (the required privacy notices had not been updated or published) and observed that data subjects could not effectively exercise their rights (for example, any objection would have to be made directly to *OpenAI*, not *GEDI*).

II. Key legal findings

The Garante concluded that sharing *GEDI's* archives could likely violate Art. 9 and 10 GDPR (processing of special category and judicial data), Art. 13 and 14 GDPR (transparency), and Chapter III (data subject rights) GDPR. It issued a formal warning under GDPR Art. 58(2)(a), alerting Gedi that non-compliance could lead to enforcement action. The Authority did not sanction Gedi at this stage but made clear that moving forward with the data transfers all or part would trigger enforcement. *GEDI* responded that the project was under review, no data had been transferred yet, and it was open to dialogue with the Authority.[5]

1. Legal basis and special category data

The Garante highlighted that *Gedi's* news archives may contain special category data and judicial data under Art. 9 and 10 GDPR. Under the GDPR,

4 Garante per la protezione dei dati personali, ‚Garante privacy a Gedi: attenzione a vendere i dati personali contenuti nell'archivio del giornale a OpenAI perché li usi per addestrare gli algoritmi' (29.11.2024) <https://www.garanteprivacy.it/home/docweb/-/docweb-display/docweb/10076913>.

5 Garante per la protezione dei dati personali, ‚Garante privacy a Gedi: attenzione a vendere i dati personali contenuti nell'archivio del giornale a OpenAI perché li usi per addestrare gli algoritmi' (fn. 4).

processing special category personal data (e.g. health, political opinions, religion, sexual orientation, criminal history) is generally prohibited except under narrow exceptions set forth by Art. 9 GDPR (e.g. explicit consent, vital interests, manifestly public data). Importantly, legitimate interests is not one of the exceptions in Art. 9 GDPR for processing such data. The Authority found that invoking legitimate interest to transfer such data to OpenAI for AI training was unlawful and infringing mainly based on Art. 9 GDPR. *GEDI* claimed a journalism-related legal basis under Italy's data protection Code (arts. 136–137) and Art. 85 GDPR. The Garante questioned whether this could extend to training *OpenAI's* AI – especially since the publication will take place entirely outside *GEDI's* participation and control – while noting that licensing an entire archive for AI training goes beyond traditional reporting and thus, cannot be justified by a journalistic exception.

2. Transparency and reasonable expectations

The Garante found the transparency obligations of Art. 13 et seq. GDPR were not satisfied. *Gedi* indicated its intention to publish a supplemental privacy information on its websites. As the Garante noted, informing all data subjects in the archives is effectively impossible, and the draft notice *GEDI* provided was only aimed at registered users. This falls short of the GDPR's requirements to give timely, clear information to individuals when their data are processed for new purposes. The Garante also noted lack of data subject reasonable expectations as individuals whose data could be contained in Gedi's archives and Art. could not reasonably expect disclosure of such data to *OpenAI* (whereas supplemental notices were not considered sufficient).

3. Data subject rights

The ruling stressed that data subjects could not exercise their rights through *Gedi*. Under the proposed scheme, *Gedi's* role as controller ends once content is transferred, and *OpenAI* becomes independent controller. In practice, an individual wishing to object to or control the use of their personal data would have to contact *OpenAI*, not *Gedi*. The Garante observed that *Gedi* is not able to guarantee the rights of data subjects. This undermines the effectiveness of data subject rights under Chapter III GDPR (rights of access, erasure, objection, etc.).

III. Systematic context and legal classification

This decision sits at the intersection of GDPR principles, dissemination of journalistic content, intellectual property and licensing content for secondary reuse. Licensing journalistic content to third parties is a structural feature of the press sector and has been considered compatible with EU data protection law, provided that appropriate safeguards are in place.

Garante's order aptly reminded the importance of personal data appearing in licensed content but applied a very restrictive interpretation of the GDPR. If Garante's reasoning were taken to its conclusion, it could imply that licensing journalistic content containing personal data could rarely be allowed for secondary uses. Such an outcome would be difficult to reconcile with decades of established practices, including licensing to archives, databases, syndicators, re-publishers or aggregators, and would not follow the existing ECJ case law on search engines.

From a systematic EU law perspective, the Garante's warning regarding content license arrangements represents a rather standalone supervisory authority position, not widely echoed – at least publicly – by other EU data protection authorities.

The warning also predates the EDPB Opinion 28/2024 on data protection aspects of AI models.[6] Although the EDPB Opinion does not address the issue of licensing content for generative AI training, it does address the questions of legitimate interests, data subject reasonable expectations, proportionality, transparency, as well as additional measures which may be adopted by model developers to balance protection of personal data. This case also foreshadows the AI Act, which imposes additional safeguards on developers of general-purpose AI models and reinforces copyright protections through regulatory landscape.

IV. Author's analysis and commentary

First, it is essential to distinguish between the two processing purposes identified in the Garante's order: (i) enabling users to search for current news in real time, accompanied by an AI-generated summary and a direct link to the original Art. – a use functionally comparable to search engines

6 EDPB, ‚Opinion 28/2024 on data protection aspects related to the processing of personal data in the context of AI models' (17.12.2024) <https://www.edpb.europa.eu/system/files/2024-12/edpb_opinion_202428_ai-models_en.pdf>.

and news aggregation; and (ii) training AI models – a novel processing involving converting large volumes of input data into numerical representations, learning statistical patterns and relationships from the training data and using the resulting mathematical structure to generate new outputs in response to user prompts rather than storing or retrieving the original data – thus, process is conceptually and functionally distinct from real-time information retrieval.

1. Training AI models and compliance approach to special category data

The Garante highlighted that Gedi's news archives may contain special category data and judicial data and invoked Art. 9 and 10 GDPR. However, the decisive issue is whether the AI training in question actually involves processing aimed at inferring or otherwise handling special-category data. Art. 9 GDPR is not triggered merely because sensitive data may be incidentally present in large-scale datasets. Rather, it applies only where data are processed to deduce special categories of personal data. As the EDPB noted in its analysis on video surveillance systems, Art. 9 GDPR applies if the data is 'is processed to deduce special categories of data'.[7] Accordingly, the relevant assessment is not whether such data could theoretically appear in the dataset, but whether the training process is designed or used to extract, infer, or operationalise sensitive attributes and whether appropriate measures are in place to prevent such processing. For example, passively including a photo in a training set does not in itself trigger Art. 9 GDPR unless the model is designed to extract sensitive traits from it.[8] This interpretation is consistent with EDPB guidance. In its guidelines on the targeting of social media users the EDPB explained that:

---

7 EDPB, ‚Guidelines 3/2019 on processing of personal data through video devices', version 2.0 (29.1.2020) <https://www.edpb.europa.eu/sites/default/files/files/file1/edpb_guidelines_201903_video_devices_en_0.pdf>, p. 17.

8 Similarly, the EDPB concluded re processing of special categories of data by video surveillance systems: 'Video surveillance systems usually collect massive amounts of personal data which may reveal data of a highly personal nature and even special categories of data. Indeed, apparently non-significant data originally collected through video can be used to infer other information to achieve a different purpose (e.g. to map an individual's habits). However, video surveillance is not always considered to be processing of special categories of personal data.'. See EDPB, ‚Guidelines 3/2019 on processing of personal data through video devices' (fn. 7).

the mere fact that a social media provider processes large amounts of data which potentially could be used to infer special categories of data does not automatically mean that the processing falls under Art. 9 GDPR. Art. 9 GDPR will not be triggered if the social media provider's processing does not result in inference of special categories of data and the social media provider has taken measures to prevent that such data can be inferred.

Accordingly, where appropriate safeguards – such as dataset cleansing, anonymisation or pseudonymisation, and filtering[9] – are implemented, and where training is not intended to profile or categorise individuals by sensitive attributes, the mere inclusion of personal data should not be treated as processing under Art. 9 GDPR.

This does not, however, exempt the controller from compliance with other GDPR obligations, including privacy by design and by default, lawfulness, transparency, and data security.

2. Analogy to search engines

As regards the search features enabling users to search for current news in real time (as per purpose (i), such processing is by its nature closely comparable to processing of personal data by search engines. Accordingly, existing ECJ case law and WP29 guidance on search engine indexing and delisting provide a relevant and instructive analogy. In *GC* (Case C-136/17) the ECJ ruled that 'having regard to the responsibilities, powers and capabilities of the operator of a search engine', Art. 9 GDPR obligations require search engines dereferencing of specific search results *ex post* on the basis of a request by the data subject. The Advocate General noted that 'ex ante systematic control is neither possible nor desirable' and reminded fundamental protection of the right of the public to receive and impart information made available on the internet. AG Szpunar noted that literal application of prohibition to process special category data[10] would 'require a search engine to ascertain that a list of results displayed following a search carried out on the basis of the name of a natural person does not contain

9 For more details about privacy safeguards across all stages of AI model development, see: EDPB, ‚Opinion 28/2024 on data protection aspects related to the processing of personal data in the context of AI models' (fn. 6).

10 Decision refers to Art. 8(1) DPD but its conclusions are similarly applicable to Art. 9(1) GDPR.

any link to internet pages comprising data covered by that provision, and to do so ex ante and systematically'.

Reports suggest that users increasingly rely on AI tools as substitutes for traditional search engines; accordingly, the same data protection principles developed for search engine services should, in principle, apply to AI-powered search functionalities.[11] Requiring systematic ex ante review and removal of all potential special category data from journalistic content would not only be technically impracticable and disproportionately costly, but could also unduly interfere with the public's right of access to information albeit in different form than 10 years ago.

3. Transparency and data subject rights

Art. 13 and 14 GDPR require controllers to inform data subjects when their personal data are collected or when they are further processed for a new purpose. The Garante found that Gedi had failed to update its privacy notices to reflect the envisaged data-sharing arrangement for AI model training. While Gedi reportedly considered publishing a supplemental notice online, the authority observed that merely informing registered users would be insufficient, and that reaching all individuals mentioned in historical journalistic content would in practice be extremely difficult. The GDPR mandates timely and clear information to data subjects when their data are processed for new purposes but also recognises these practical constraints. Art. 14(5)(b) GDPR allows data controllers to make information publicly available instead of providing the information directly to data subjects if the provision of such information proves impossible or would involve a disproportionate effort. As noted by the EDPB, this exception may be relevant in the context of AI model training involving large-scale datasets, provided that the controller can demonstrate that the conditions of Art. 14(5) GDPR are met and that appropriate safeguards are in place.[12] Considering factors referred to Rec. 62 GDPR which contribute to disproportionate effort to notify – number of data subjects, the age of the

11 See for example McKinsey & Company, ‚New front door to the internet: Winning in the age of AI search' (16.10.2025) <https://www.mckinsey.com/capabilities/growth-marketing-and-sales/our-insights/new-front-door-to-the-internet-winning-in-the-age-of-ai-search>.

12 EDPB, ‚Opinion 28/2024 on data protection aspects related to the processing of personal data in the context of AI models' (fn. 6);EDPB, ‚Report of the work undertaken

data and appropriate safeguards adopted[13] – these factors may support the applicability on processing of journalistic content for generative AI training if additional transparency safeguards are adopted (such as transparency campaigns described in the EDPB AI Opinion).[14]

However, transparency is also closely connected to the assessment of data subjects' reasonable expectations, which form a key element of the legitimate interests balancing test under Art. 6(1)(f) GDPR. Data subjects must '*reasonably expect*' the processing at issue (although, as the EDPB noted, fulfilling transparency obligations does not automatically establish data subjects' reasonable expectations). In the context of licensing journalistic content for AI training, relevant factors include the nature of the data source, in particular whether the content is publicly accessible online or confined to non-public archives, as well as model's specific capabilities and means of use of the licensed content.

Thus, requiring licensors or model developers to provide individual privacy notices to all persons mentioned in journalistic content would constitute an unduly expansive reading of Art. 14 GDPR.

This does not, however, diminish the importance of transparency. Rather, transparency remains a core element of the legitimate interests balancing test and meaningfully shapes the scope and composition of content that may be included in training datasets. Viewed in this light, the approach achieves a proportionate balance between safeguarding data subjects' rights and ensuring a workable framework that supports innovation and the reuse of high-quality data. This assessment may be complemented by additional measures that facilitate or expedite the exercise of individuals' rights, thereby helping to balance the protection of fundamental rights and the privacy of persons referenced by AI outputs (for example, in a manner analogous to the ECJ's conclusion that ex post dereferencing mechanisms can constitute an effective means of protecting individuals' rights in the context of search engine results – as described above).

---

by the ChatGPT Taskforce' (23.5.2024) <https://www.edpb.europa.eu/system/files/2024-05/edpb_20240523_report_chatgpt_taskforce_en.pdf>.

13 Article 29 Working Party, ‚Guidelines on transparency under Regulation 2016/679', (WP260 rev.01, 11.4.2018) <https://www.edpb.europa.eu/system/files/2023-09/wp260rev01_en.pdf>, para 63.

14 EDPB, ‚Opinion 28/2024 on data protection aspects related to the processing of personal data in the context of AI models (fn. 6).

4. Conclusion

While concerns about large-scale AI training on personal data are legitimate, the decision implicitly advances a position that is not grounded in settled EU law and, if generalized, would have far-reaching and likely unintended consequences for the media sector. If followed strictly, the Garante's reasoning would imply that publisher could hardly lawfully license archives containing personal data. Thus, a more practicable risk-based approach could focus on risk mitigation and additional measures which can be applied across all stages of model development, design and deployment. Such an approach is not novel. It closely mirrors the logic applied by the ECJ to search engines, which are permitted to index and process journalistic content containing personal data, provided that safeguards exist and individual rights can be exercised ex post.

V. Recommended further reading

1. Position papers from supervisory authorities

EDPB, 'Opinion 28/2024 on data protection aspects related to the processing of personal data in the context of AI models' (17.12.2024) <https://www.edpb.europa.eu/system/files/2024-12/edpb_opinion_202428_ai-models_en.pdf>.

Art. 29 Data Protection Working Party, 'Guidelines on the Implementation of the Court of Justice of the European Union Judgment on 'Google Spain and Google Inc. v. Agencia Española de Protección de Datos (AEPD) and Mario Costeja González' C-131/12' (WP225, 26.11.2014).

EDPB, 'Report of the work undertaken by the ChatGPT Taskforce' (23.5.2024) <https://www.edpb.europa.eu/system/files/2024-05/edpb_20240523_report_chatgpt_taskforce_en.pdf>.

CNIL, 'AI. The CNIL finalises its recommendations on the development of artificial intelligence systems and announces its upcoming work' (22.7.2025) <https://www.cnil.fr/en/ai-cnil-finalises-its-recommendations-development-artificial-intelligence-systems>.

The Hamburg Commissioner for Data protection and freedom of information, 'Discussion Paper: Large Language Models and Personal Data' <https://datenschutz-hamburg.de/fileadmin/user_upload/HmbBfDI/Datenschutz/Informationen/240715_Discussion_Paper_Hamburg_DPA_KI_Models.pdf>.

2. Academic Art. or book chapters

European Union Intellectual Property Office (EUIPO), 'The Development of Generative Artificial Intelligence from a Copyright Perspective – Full Report' (May 2025) <https://www.euipo.europa.eu/en/publications/genai-from-a-copyright-perspective-2025>.

Hamann, 'Artificial Intelligence and the Law of Machine-Readability: A Review of Human-to-Machine Communication Protocols and Their (In)compatibility with Art. 4(3) of the Copyright DSM Directive' (2024) 15(2) JIPITEC, 105 – 106. <https://www.jipitec.eu/jipitec/article/view/407>.

Havlikova, 'Technical Challenges of Rightsholders' Opt-out From Gen AI Training after Robert Kneschke v. LAION' (2025) 16(1) JIPITEC, 88 – 106 <https://www.jipitec.eu/jipitec/article/view/422?articlesBySimilarityPage=2>

Lucchi, 'Study Generative AI and Copyright: Training, Creation, Regulation, Study requested by the JURI Committee. European Union, Policy Department for Justice, Civil Liberties and Institutional Affairs Directorate-General for Citizens' Rights, Justice and Institutional Affairs. PE 774.095. July 2025 <https://www.europarl.europa.eu/thinktank/en/document/IUST_STU(2025)774095>.

Gema ruling on AI training – transferability of copyright limitations to data law?

Christian-Henner Hentsch

LG München 11.11.2025 – 42 O 14139/24, MMR 2026 74 (under appeal)

I. Case summary

The Munich Regional Court has handed down a landmark ruling in the case brought by GEMA against the US AI provider OpenAI, which has attracted worldwide attention.[1] According to the ruling, OpenAI is violating applicable copyright law with the training and operation of ChatGPT. For the first time, the use of copyright-protected works by generative AI systems has been legally assessed on the basis of EU law, and in particular, the limitation provisions on text and data mining (TDM)[2] have been interpreted and applied.

Although the ruling focuses on a copyright case, generative AI systems always process data in addition to copyrighted material. In principle, every copyright-protected work is also personal data. This raises the question of the extent to which copyright assessments and standards can also be applied to data processing. If the use of copyright-protected works is permitted by law, does this not also mean that the use of personal data from these works must also be permitted?

This article discusses the similarities and differences between fully harmonized European data protection law and partially harmonized copyright law, drawing on the GEMA ruling. In order to make these comparable, the permissions in data law for the processing of personal data and the permissions in copyright law for the use of copyright-protected works are first presented and classified against the background of the GEMA case. On this basis, the relationship between data protection and copyright law will

---

1 LG München 11.11.2025 – 42 O 14139/24, MMR 2026 74; see also OLG Hamburg 10.12.2025 – 5 U 104/24, MMR 2026, 140.

2 § 44b UrhG came into force on June 7, 2021, and implements Art. 4 of the DSM Directive.

be discussed in order to finally clarify, taking into account the case law on the primacy of the KUG over the GDPR, whether the TDM exception or at least the assessments of copyright law can be transferred to data law.

II. Permissions in data law for the processing of personal data

The right to use personal data for AI purposes has so far been derived primarily from the GDPR and is thus fully harmonized at the European level. With the Digital Omnibus[3] published on 19.11.2025, the European Commission aims to harmonize existing regulations, reduce duplicate structures, and standardize terms, procedures, and responsibilities across various legal acts. This includes, in particular, the proposed reform of the AI Act, which aims to clarify the interfaces with data law.

1. GDPR, in particular Art. 6(1)(f) GDPR

The GDPR is the fundamental regulatory framework for all data use and, in the absence of more specific existing regulations in data law on AI training, it therefore applies without restriction. This applies to principles such as data minimization, data accuracy, purpose limitation, and the principle of transparency, as well as to the permissions under Art. 6 GDPR.[4]

Although consent pursuant to Art. 6(1 (a) GDPR is conceivable in principle, it will be virtually impossible in practice and legally in connection with AI training and the large amounts of data required for this purpose. In addition, there is always the risk that consent will be invalid because the characteristic of 'informed consent' is difficult to achieve. Furthermore, consent can always be freely revoked. In this respect, consent plays only a minor role in AI training.

Lawful processing based on a legitimate interest pursuant to Art. 6(1)(f) GDPR may be considered, provided that the interests or fundamental rights

3 European Commission, 'Proposal for a REGULATION OF THE EUROPEAN PARLIAMENT AND OF THE COUNCIL amending Regulations (EU) 2016/679, (EU) 2018/1724, (EU) 2018/1725, (EU) 2023/2854 and Directives 2002/58/EC, (EU) 2022/2555 and (EU) 2022/2557 as regards the simplification of the digital legislative framework, and repealing Regulations (EU) 2018/1807, (EU) 2019/1150, (EU) 2022/868, and Directive (EU) 2019/1024 (Digital Omnibus)', COM/2025/837 final.

4 On AI training with publicly available data in light of the GDPR requirements Paal ZfDR 2024, 129, 140ff.

of the data subject do not override this.[5] Although this requires a case-by-case assessment, it is currently the only relevant basis for permission for AI training with publicly available data. As a rule, the weighing of interests takes place in three steps. First, the legitimate interest of the controller must be determined, then the necessity of the specific processing to safeguard this interest, and finally, a comprehensive weighing of interests with the conflicting interests or fundamental rights of the data subject.

In the GEMA case decided by the Munich Regional Court, song lyrics were reproducible in the defendant's language models. These were also memorized, meaning they could be extracted as outputs. It was thus determined that the song lyrics were used as training data and were copied in their entirety. In a data protection assessment, it can initially be noted that the AI developer had an economic interest in processing data for training purposes in order to be able to offer the system on the market. Public interest considerations such as social added value, freedom of information, or even artistic freedom (to create new musical works) may also play a role in this regard). The collection and gathering of training data is also indispensable and absolutely necessary, because without training data, an AI system would not be possible. Quality improvements may also justify the need for extensive data collection. Other equally effective means, such as synthetic data sets, are currently unknown or insufficient. However, the complete transfer and storage of song lyrics may not be necessary.[6] The final balancing of interests is ultimately a balancing of fundamental rights between the general right of personality and other fundamental rights. Due to the lower intensity of the intervention, effective anonymization and pseudonymization in particular argue in favor of admissibility, as do technical and organizational measures to protect the data subject. According to Art. 47 GDPR, the balancing of interests should take into account, among other things, the reasonable expectations of the data subject with regard to the specific processing. This raises the fundamental question of whether data subjects must expect their data to be used by AI. In this context, it must be taken into account whether the data subject has published their data on the internet themselves and is therefore less deserving of protection. This can certainly be assumed in the case of authors of well-known music. As a result, the training of musical works by AI would probably

5 See in detail Schwartmann EuDIR 2026, 3 mn. 7–24.
6 Bernzen K&R Supplement 1 to Issue 10/2023, 6, 9.

be permissible under data protection law, but not permanent storage and memorization.

2. Digital Omnibus

The amendments to the GDPR proposed by the EU Commission in the Digital Omnibus with regard to AI training are also unlikely to bring about any significant changes in this area.

This is because the draft first states in Art. 9(2) GDPR that AI training is generally subject to the provisions of the GDPR and that the above-described requirements for data processing therefore also apply and the threshold for legitimate interests remains unchanged. However, the term 'personal data' in Art. 4 GDPR is clarified to mean that information in a specific facility is not considered personal data if it cannot reasonably be used to identify the natural person to whom it relates. Consequently, such a facility would not fall within the scope of the aforementioned regulation. In addition, Art. 9(5) of the draft provides for special requirements for the processing of special categories of personal data for the development and operation of an AI system or AI model under certain conditions, including appropriate organizational and technical measures to avoid the collection of special categories of personal data and the removal of such data. Furthermore, Article 5(1)(b) of the draft on purpose limitation specifies when the use of existing data for training is compatible with the original purpose. This is based on existing criteria such as context, relationship to data subjects, type of data, and protective measures. A third focus addresses transparency and data subject rights so that the training is recognizable in the information. In the case of high risks, additional protective mechanisms are to be added, such as technical and organizational measures against the unintentional reconstruction of personal content.

This draft primarily aims to standardize existing data law and the AI Act and, in doing so, to update the GDPR to reflect the new possibilities offered by AI. It does not include blanket permissions or even a general carte blanche for AI training, meaning that, in accordance with data protection law, AI training will continue to be possible only in cases of anonymization and pseudonymization, as well as under specific – now, at least, concrete – requirements.

III. Copyright limitations

In terms of copyright law, there are two possible permissions for training works: text and data mining for scientific research purposes (§ 60d UrhG) – not relevant in the GEMA case – and the general text and data mining limitation (§ 44b UrhG). In addition to these two specific AI limitations, other cross-cutting copyright permissions such as the incidental works limitation (§ 57 UrhG) could also apply. In any case, unlike in data law, copyright law provides for specific permissions that replace the weighing of interests in individual cases. However, since the limitations are generally interpreted narrowly, further permissions – for example, as a weighing of fundamental rights – are generally excluded. This means that solutions such as the fair use doctrine in the US are not possible in Germany.

The TDM limitation was introduced throughout Europe with the DSM Directive and was originally intended to enable data analysis and big data applications. In this respect, it is somewhat controversial whether this limitation can also be applied to AI systems.[7] At least the Munich Regional Court applies both § 44b UrhG and § 57 UrhG to AI training in principle. However, in the court's view, these only cover the acts of reproduction involved in compiling the data corpus for AI training. However, because not only information is extracted from training data here, but entire works are reproduced, the chamber considers that this no longer constitutes text and data mining. The incidental works limitation also does not apply because the song lyrics cannot be regarded as incidental and dispensable alongside the entire training data set.

Furthermore, consent is also ruled out because the training of models cannot be considered a normal and expected type of use that the rights holder must anticipate.

IV. Provisions in copyright law as lex specialis to Art. 6(2), (3) GDPR

Based on the findings above, it can be concluded that the GEMA case probably comes to similar conclusions under data law and copyright law. AI training is generally possible, but storing and memorizing data is not. However, there are also differences, because data processing for AI training is linked to a balancing of interests and measures to minimize the intensity

7 See Schwartmann/Köhler NJW 2026, III. 1. (forthcoming).

of the intervention. Under copyright law there are no requirements, but § 44b(3) UrhG provides for the possibility of declaring a reservation of use (opt-out). In this respect, the legality of AI training under data law or copyright law may therefore differ in individual cases.

Copyright protection is also a form of qualified data protection, at least with regard to moral rights.[8] This raises the question of whether copyright or data law takes precedence in a specific case. The GDPR resolves this conflict in Art. 85 GDPR, which allows for opening clauses to reconcile data law with other rights and data processing purposes. In this regard, the Federal Court of Justice ruled on 7.7.2020[9] that §§ 22 and 23 KUG are applicable due to the opening clause in Art. 85 of the GDPR and therefore take precedence. In this case, no strict standards need to be applied to the data protection regulations. In principle, this case law should also be transferable to copyright law, so that the UrhG would be lex specialis to the GDPR for copyright-protected works.

With regard to the EU regulations on AI, it can be noted that the AI Act merely sets out a liability framework and certain obligations. Data protection requirements for AI training will now only be added in the Digital Omnibus and even then will merely refer to the principles and general permissions. In copyright law, the more specific regulations can be found in the DSM Directive, while the provisions relating to copyright in the AI Act are limited to documentation obligations. Thus, the TDM exceptions (§§ 44b and 60d UrhG and Art. 4 and 3 DSM Directive) are currently the most specific regulations on the permissibility of AI training.

V. Conclusion: What is permitted under copyright law cannot be prohibited under data protection law, can it?

With regard to the GEMA case, it can therefore be concluded that the European legislator has created clear conditions for the permissibility of AI training in copyright law. This was also confirmed by the Munich Regional Court in a first ruling on GEMA's lawsuit against OpenAI. Since these provisions are more specific than the basic data protection standards, they also take precedence in principle. Therefore, at least AI training with copyright that is permissible under copyright law cannot be inadmissible under data protection law.

---

8 See Schwartmann/Hentsch RDV 2015, 221, (223 et seq.).

9 BGH 7.7.2020 – VI ZR 246/19, GRUR 2021, 100.

However, since all copyright-protected works always have a personal reference as an expression of the author's personality, the considerations of copyright restrictions could also have an impact on all data protection considerations in AI training. Precisely because works are specific personal data that are also protected by property rights under Art. 14 GG, these assessments should apply all the more to comparatively trivial data such as IP addresses. It cannot be the case that personal messages, creative melodies, and other original works should get less protection under copyright law than all other - less original - personal data, which, depending on the intensity of the interference, may or may not be used for AI training under Art. 6(1)(f) of the GDPR. In any assessment, care should at least be taken to ensure that there are no contradictions in the evaluation. The Munich Regional Court has provided clarity on copyright law with its GEMA ruling. This should now be respected by the data protection supervisory authorities and taken into account in all data protection assessments on AI training.

VI. Recommended further reading

Schwartmann EuDIR 2026, 3.
Schwartmann/Köhler NJW 2026 (forthcoming).
Wendehorst EuDIR 2026, 81.

The Emergence of Literacy Expectations in GDPR Enforcement

Isabel Hahn[*]

Commission for Personal Data Protection (Bulgaria), 'Final Decision Ref. № ПАИКД-13-28/2022' (26.10.2022), <https://www.edpb.europa.eu/system/files/2023-08/bg_2023-01_decisionpublic.pdf>

I. Introduction

AI literacy can be defined as 'a set of competencies that enables individuals to critically evaluate AI technologies; communicate and collaborate effectively with AI; and use AI as a tool online, at home, and in the workplace.'[1] As AI systems increasingly become deployed in contexts involving the processing of personal data, questions of competence, understanding, and oversight become particularly salient for organisations that act as data controllers and processors.

The practical necessity of this competence is clear. AI literacy – as well as general data protection literacy – helps employees of data controllers and processors understand what data they may use, for what purposes, and under which legal bases, reducing the risk of unlawful or opaque processing. Well-trained employees are better able to recognize and avoid risky practices, such as unauthorized data sharing or inappropriate use of AI tools. This, in turn, supports compliance, protect individuals' rights, and prevents costly incidents or fines.

Yet the legal mandate for literacy in general, whether AI or data protection related, is not immediately obvious within the text of the GDPR. While the GDPR establishes a comprehensive framework for the lawful and accountable processing of personal data, it does not contain any explicit

* The information and views set out in this article are those of the author and do not reflect the official opinion of the European Commission or European External Action Service.

1 Long/Magerko, 'What is AI Literacy? Competencies and Design Considerations' (Proceedings of the 2020 CHI Conference on Human Factors in Computing Systems, 2020) <https://doi.org/10.1145/3313831.3376727>.

obligations requiring data controllers or processors to ensure technological literacy among their staff. The only direct reference to training staff can found in Art. 39(1)(b) GDPR, which places an obligation on the Data Protection Officer (DPO) to monitor the policies of a controller or processor regarding the 'training of staff involved in processing obligations.' Beyond this provision, the GDPR does not articulate a general duty to educate or train personnel, even where processing activities rely on complex or automated technologies.

This chapter will argue, however, that literacy expectations emerge implicitly but concretely from existing GDPR principles. In enforcement practice, Data Protection Authorities (DPAs) have begun to treat organisational failures of understanding, instruction, and internal awareness as legally relevant. There is a growing number of decisions referring to the competence of staff, adequacy of training measures, and ability of organisations to ensure that those acting under their authority understand both the tools they deploy and the data protection obligations that govern their use.

The central claim advanced here is not that the GDPR contains a hidden or fully articulated literacy mandate. Rather, it is that literacy operates as an enabling condition for compliance with core GDPR obligations, particularly those relating to accountability and security of processing. Through their interpretation of these obligations, DPAs are increasingly assessing not only whether policies and safeguards exist on paper, but whether they are meaningfully understood, internalised, and applied within organisations.

This chapter proceeds in three steps. First, it identifies the provisions of the GDPR from which implicit literacy expectations may be derived, with particular attention to Art. 5(2), 24, and 32 GDPR. Second, it analyses selected decisions and guidance issued by DPAs to illustrate how these expectations are articulated in practice. Finally, it reflects on the emerging literacy trend, considering also how data protection literacy provides a foundation for emerging discussions of AI literacy within the GDPR framework.

It is worth noting that in contrast to the GDPR, the AI Act does introduce an explicit and horizontal obligation to ensure AI literacy, commensurate with the role of personnel and the risks associated with the use of AI systems. This chapter, however, does not assess that provision or the AI Act. Beyond the fact that its practical meaning has yet to be clarified through case law or enforcement decisions, the analysis undertaken here is deliberately confined to the GDPR framework, where data protection authorities are beginning to articulate concrete expectations regarding employee instruction, training, and organisational responsibility.

II. The GDPR & literacy requirements

Several of the GDPR's core provisions presuppose a level of organisational competence that cannot be achieved without adequate understanding on the part of those involved in processing operations. In particular, Art. 5(2), 24, and 32 GDPR function as key anchors through which expectations relating to staff awareness, instruction, and comprehension can be derived. Together, these provisions frame compliance not merely as the adoption of formal policies or technical safeguards, but as an ongoing organisational capacity to ensure lawful and secure processing in practice.

1. Accountability and demonstrability under Art. 5(2) GDPR

Art. 5 GDPR sets out the foundational principles governing the processing of personal data. Art. 5(2) GDPR in particular, introduces an obligation known as the 'accountability principle'. Under this principle, controllers shall be 'responsible for, and be able to demonstrate compliance with'[2] all other data protection principles that are listed in Art. 5 GDPR.

This obligation to 'be able to demonstrate compliance' entails being able to show what has been done to operationalize certain compliance measures. One way of evidencing such compliance could be demonstrating the ability of staff to appropriately handle personal data. When considered from a practical perspective, if employees lack the ability to interpret and apply data protection principles in their daily work, the controller's capacity to demonstrate compliance is substantially weakened. Supervisory Authority guidance also reflects this reading. For instance, the United Kingdom's Data Protection Authority, the Information Commissioner's Office, has gone so far as to state that:

> Without an overarching training programme that is fully supported and overseen by senior management, there is a risk that staff are not trained in data protection and how it applies in the context of their role. There is also a risk that they will have access to personal information without

2 Art. 5(2) GDPR.

fully understanding their responsibilities in its protection and security. This may breach Art. 5(1) and 5(2) of the UK GDPR.[3]

Training thus functions as a mechanism through which accountability is rendered observable and verifiable, and as a direct means through which to demonstrate compliance with not only Art. 5(2) GDPR, but Art. 5 GDPR principles in general.

2. Organisational measures and internal understanding under Art. 24 GDPR

Art. 24 GDPR further operationalises the accountability principle by requiring controllers to implement appropriate 'technical and organisational measures'[4] to ensure, and to be able to demonstrate, that processing is performed in accordance with the GDPR. In some instances, this will include an 'implementation of appropriate data protection policies' by the controller, as specified in Art. 24(2) GDPR. This introduces a so-called 'demonstrability test', whereby controllers need to be able to demonstrate what measures have been taken to implement a policy. As emerging case law demonstrates, DPAs are starting to rule that a measures such as a policy is not 'implemented' if the staff of a controller do not know about it or how to use it. For instance, the Irish Data Protection Commission (DPC) found in one case that although a public authority had a policy for prohibiting the use of unencrypted portable devices, the policy was ineffective in practice because employees were unaware of it and did not comply, which led the DPC to conclude that the policy measure had not been implemented.[5]

This interpretation introduces an implicit expectation of internal literacy. Organisational measures presuppose that employees possess sufficient understanding of relevant rules, risks, and procedures to give those measures practical effect. Without such understanding, controllers may struggle to demonstrate that they have taken appropriate steps to embed data protection obligations within their organisational structures.

---

3 Information Commissioner's Office, 'Training and awareness' (ICO, n.d.) <https://ico.org.uk/for-organisations/advice-and-services/audits/data-protection-audit-framework/toolkits/accountability/training-and-awareness/>.

4 Art. 24(1) GDPR.

5 Data Protection Commission, 'Failure to implement data protection policies in place' (DPC, n.d.) <https://dataprotection.ie/en/dpc-guidance/case-studies/data-breach-notification/failure-implement-data-protection-policies-place>.

3. Security of processing and instruction under Art. 32 GDPR

Beyond general accountability and organisational responsibility, Art. 32 GDPR occupies a central role in linking security of processing with staff understanding and instruction. While Art. 32 GDPR does not spell out 'training' by name, it does require controllers and processors to implement appropriate technical and organisational measures to ensure security of processing. Specifically, Art. 32(1) GDPR states that:

> Taking into account the state of the art, the costs of implementation and the nature, scope, context and purposes of processing as well as the risk of varying likelihood and severity for the rights and freedoms of natural persons, the controller and the processor shall implement appropriate technical and organisational measures to ensure a level of security appropriate to the risk [...]

The reference to 'organisational measures' alongside technical ones indicates that security under the GDPR is not conceived solely as a matter of infrastructure or system design. Rather, it can also encompasses internal arrangements, procedures, and practices through which risks are identified, mitigated, and managed.[6] In practice, such organisational measures depend on the capacity of staff to understand the systems they use, the risks associated with processing activities, and the legal and procedural constraints governing their conduct. Without such understanding, organisational measures risk remaining formal or ineffective, particularly in technologically complex environments.

This human dimension of security is made more explicit in Art. 32(4) GDPR, which states that:

> The controller and processor shall take steps to ensure that any natural person acting under the authority of the controller or the processor who has access to personal data does not process them except on instructions from the controller, unless he or she is required to do so by Union or Member State law.

Art. 32(4) GDPR imposes an obligation not merely to issue instructions, but to *ensure* that processing occurs in accordance with them. This requirement presupposes that instructions are intelligible and that those receiving

6 Data Protection Commission, 'Failure to implement data protection policies in place' (fn. 5).

them possess the capacity to understand and apply them in practice. Logically, what follows from this is that where processing activities involve complex technical systems, such as large databases, automated decision-making tools, or AI systems, compliance with instructions may require a degree of technical and contextual understanding that goes beyond basic procedural awareness.

For example, an instruction to 'ensure data minimisation' or to 'restrict access to authorised purposes' may be straightforward in abstract terms, yet difficult to operationalise without sufficient literacy regarding the underlying technical architecture or processing logic. If staff lack the ability to translate such instructions into concrete actions within a given system, the controller's obligation under Art. 32(4) GDPR to ensure compliant processing may not be fulfilled, notwithstanding the formal existence of internal rules.

This reading is reinforced by the role assigned to the Data Protection Officer under Art. 39(1)(b) GDPR, which includes monitoring compliance with the Regulation 'including the assignment of responsibilities, awareness-raising and training of staff involved in processing operations'[7]. While Art. 39 GDPR also does not itself create a general training obligation, it signals that staff awareness and instruction are regarded as relevant mechanisms through which organisational compliance, including security of processing, is achieved.

Taken together, Art. 32(1) and 32(4) GDPR suggest that security of processing under the GDPR is inseparable from the ability of individuals within an organisation to understand and act upon data protection requirements. In this sense, literacy functions as an implicit enabling condition for the effectiveness of organisational security measures.

Moreover, the French Data Protection Authority, Commission Nationale de l'Informatique et des Libertés (CNIL), has also issued guidance under which it expressly recommends the 'implementation of periodic training and awareness programmes' for staff involved in processing operations.[8] The CNIL emphasises that technical measures alone are insufficient to ensure the protection of personal data, noting that security incidents frequently arise from how individuals interact with information systems,

7 Art. 39(1)(b) GDPR.

8 Commission nationale de l'informatique et des libertés, 'Consignes pour renforcer la sécurité des grandes bases de données' (CNIL, n.d.) <https://www.cnil.fr/fr/consignes-pour-renforcer-la-securite-des-grandes-bases-de-donnees>.

including through misconfiguration, misuse, or insufficient awareness of risks. For this reason, CNIL presents training and awareness programmes as integral components of organisational security, intended to enable users to identify risky situations, avoid common errors, and respond appropriately to incidents. The CNIL guidance reinforces an interpretation of Art. 32 GDPR that treats staff understanding as a core element of security of processing.

As the following section demonstrates, data protection authorities increasingly reflect this understanding in their enforcement practice, particularly in cases where security failures are linked to human error, insufficient instruction, or inadequate internal awareness.

III. From abstract obligations to enforcement practice: takeaways

The preceding analysis has shown that implicit literacy expectations can be derived from several core provisions of the GDPR. Art. 5(2) and 24 GDPR establish accountability as an organisational obligation that must be demonstrable in practice, while Art. 32 GDPR connects that obligation to the concrete management of risk through technical and organisational measures. Taken together, these provisions presuppose that those acting within a controller's organisation possess sufficient understanding to apply policies, instructions, and safeguards in real processing environments.

When these abstract obligations are tested in practice, however, it is Art. 32 GDPR that most frequently serves as the primary point of engagement for supervisory authorities. This is partly because questions of staff understanding and instruction tend to arise most visibly in the context of security incidents and personal data breaches, where the role of human action – or inaction – is increasingly visible. In such cases, supervisory authorities are required to assess whether controllers have implemented organisational measures capable of preventing, detecting, and responding to risks, and whether those measures functioned effectively in practice. It is therefore within the context of Art. 32 GDPR enforcement that expectations concerning staff understanding, instruction, and internal competence become most explicitly articulated.

1. Training is a relevant organisational measure following a data breach

In a number of cases[9], supervisory authorities have treated the provision of internal training to employees as a relevant organisational measure in the aftermath of a personal data breach. Lead supervisory authorities have considered the delivery of cybersecurity and data protection training aimed at raising staff awareness as a factor supporting compliance with Art. 32 GDPR, particularly where such measures were introduced to mitigate identified risks or prevent recurrence.

For example, in a case involving the accidental publication of login credentials for an in-house communication platform, in assessing how the data controller had responded to the breach, the Berlin Commissioner for Data Protection and Freedom of Information considered the introduction of additional data protection training for staff as an adequate remedial measure for the breach.[10] Similarly, in a case involving the unauthorised access to a Booking.com account, where an attacker impersonated a Booking.com employee, the Berlin Commissioner for Data Protection and Freedom of Information took into account the fact that staff had received additional training on the use of the platform as part of the controller's mitigation measures as well.[11]

In Estonia too, in a case regarding fraudulent calls[12], the Estonian Data Protection Inspectorate took into account the fact that the controller had a cybersecurity training plan in place when deciding to not penalize the controller for the occurrence of a data breach.

9 See for instance Commission for Personal Data Protection (Bulgaria), Final Decision Ref. № ПАИКД--13–28/2022 concerning LockTrip Ltd (26 October 2022) (GDPR Articles 32 & 33) EDPBI:SE:OSS:D:2023:652 and Andmekaitse Inspektsioon (Estonian Data Protection Inspectorate) 4.11.2021 nr 2.2.-2/20/3028, Reprimand for failure to comply with the requirements of the General Data Protection Regulation & notice of termination of the proceeding in regard to the protection of personal data, EDPBI:EE:OSS:D:2021:004.

10 Der Berliner Beauftragte für Datenschutz und Informationsfreiheit (Berlin Commissioner for Data Protection and Freedom of Information) 2020–04 personal data breach decision, EDPBI:DEBE:OSS:D:2020:103.

11 Der Berliner Beauftragte für Datenschutz und Informationsfreiheit (Berlin Commissioner for Data Protection and Freedom of Information) SA Berlin 2021–03, Personal data breach decision (2021), EDPBI:DEBE:OSS:D:2021:147.

12 Andmekaitse Inspektsioon (Estonian Data Protection Inspectorate) 4.11.2021 nr 2.2.-2/20/3028, Reprimand for failure to comply with the requirements of the General Data Protection Regulation & notice of termination of the proceeding in regard to the protection of personal data, EDPBI:EE:OSS:D:2021:004.

2. Literacy measures and staff training cannot just be superficial or reactive

However, it is important to point out that DPAs are considering staff training to be *inadequate* where it is reactive, superficial, or disconnected from the underlying cause of a breach. A particularly detailed illustration of this approach can be found in a decision of the Bulgarian Commission for Personal Data Protection (CPDP) concerning LockTrip Ltd., an IT services provider.[13] There, the controller submitted a personal data breach notification under Art. 33 GDPR after an employee's personal computer was compromised following use of public Wi-Fi. As a result of the breach, passwords providing access to shared internal spaces and partner platforms were leaked.

Among the measures adopted to prevent recurrence, the controller pointed to internal cybersecurity training delivered to all employees and noted that follow-up training sessions were held periodically to ensure familiarity with the regulatory framework, data security risks, and mitigation strategies. The CPDP requested evidence of these training activities, including the training materials themselves.

Upon review, however, the CPDP found that the submitted documents did not contain concrete rules governing the processing of personal data. Moreover, there was no evidence that employees had been familiarised with the training materials or had engaged with the self-study elements included in them. The CPDP expressly noted a lack of 'factual evidence' demonstrating that employees had undergone initial or periodic training in personal data protection, such as attendance records, examination tests, or declarations of participation.

On this basis, the CPDP concluded that the controller had infringed the accountability principle under Art. 5(2) in conjunction with Art. 33(5) GDPR. Importantly, the CPDP ordered the controller to draft internal rules regulating the delivery of both initial and periodic data protection training, including mechanisms to monitor compliance. It further required that such rules ensure the availability of evidence demonstrating that training had been conducted, specifying elements such as attendance forms, training materials, and records of employee participation.

---

13 Commission for Personal Data Protection (Bulgaria), Final Decision Ref. № ПАИКД--13–28/2022 concerning LockTrip Ltd (26 October 2022) (GDPR Articles 32 & 33) EDPBI:SE:OSS:D:2023:652.

Similarly in Poland, the Polish DPA (UODO) has emphasised the limits of minimal or infrequent training. In a case involving a ransomware attack where an employee had disabled an anti-virus programme, UODO ruled that having conducted only two data protection training sessions was insufficient in circumstances where the controller itself identified the 'human factor' as posing a significant risk to personal data within the organisation.[14] The decision reflects an expectation that training measures must be proportionate to identified risks and tailored to organisational realities.

In another Polish case, where patient documents containing health information were stolen from a doctor's car, the UODO pointed to the fact that implementing training measures only reactively following a breach is also insufficient to fulfill Art. 32 GDPR obligations.[15]

3. Literacy also encompasses proper processing instructions and correctly interpreting legal principles

While the aforementioned decisions focus on literacy and training as a risk-management measure under Art. 32 GDPR, another case exposes a more specific literacy failure: the absence of instructions given to staff on how to process personal data. This is best illustrated in a decision by the Romanian DPA (ANSPDCP), where Raiffeisen Bank S.A. was fined €150,000 for using WhatsApp and unauthorised workflows to process identity documents and conduct credit eligibility checks.[16] In this case, two employees of Raiffeisen Bank S.A. had used ID card photos received on WhatsApp from employees of Vreau Credit S.R.L. in order to perform queries on the Credit Bureau system to determine the credit eligibility of the respective individuals.[17] The data of 1,177 individuals had been used. When imposing the fine, the

14 Prezes Urzędu Ochrony Danych Osobowych, Decyzja nr DKN.5131.1.2021 nakładająca administracyjną karę pieniężną za naruszenie przepisów RODO oraz nakaz dostosowania operacji przetwarzania danych osobowych (09 października 2024).

15 Prezes Urzędu Ochrony Danych Osobowych, Decyzja nr DKN.5131.17.2022 w sprawie naruszenia przepisów RODO związanych z ransomware (Warszawa, 3 lipca 2025).

16 Autoritatea Națională de Supraveghere a Prelucrării Datelor cu Caracter Personal, 'Comunicat de presă – sancțiune aplicată și recomandări privind securitatea datelor cu caracter personal' (ANSPDCP, 9.10.2019).

17 Autoritatea Națională de Supraveghere a Prelucrării Datelor cu Caracter Personal, 'Comunicat de presă – sancțiune aplicată și recomandări privind securitatea datelor cu caracter personal' (ANSPDCP, 9.10.2019).

ANSPDCP specifically pointed to the fact that Raiffeisen Bank had not implemented 'appropriate technical measures' to ensure that those acting under its authority only used personal data following specific instructions.

A different, though related, manifestation of literacy failure emerges from a decision of the Hellenic Data Protection Authority (HDPA) concerning PricewaterhouseCoopers Business Solutions SA (PwC BS).[18] Here, the HDPA imposed a €150,000 fine on PwC BS for unlawfully processing the data of its own employees by relying on consent as the legal basis, where the processing should instead have been grounded in the performance of a contract. Unlike cases centered on technical misuse or security incidents, this infringement stemmed from a misunderstanding of core legal concepts. Read as a literacy case, the decision highlights a failure of legal, rather than technical, understanding within the organisation. The issue here was not the absence of formal documentation, but the inability to correctly interpret and operationalise fundamental data protection concepts in practice. The case thus illustrates how deficits in internal legal literacy can undermine accountability and lawfulness, even in the absence of a data breach or security incident.

IV. From data protection literacy to AI literacy

Although the cases and guidance discussed above concern data protection literacy rather than AI literacy as such, their underlying logic readily extends to AI-enabled processing environments. Contemporary data processing increasingly relies on algorithmic systems whose functioning, limitations, and risks may be opaque to non-specialist users. In such contexts, compliance with GDPR obligations, particularly those relating to security, accountability, and processing on instructions, depends on the ability of staff to understand how AI systems shape data flows, automate decisions, and generate risk. Where personnel lack the literacy necessary to interpret system outputs, recognise errors or biases, or translate legal requirements into technically meaningful actions, organisational control over processing is weakened. Read in this light, AI literacy can be understood as a specific instantiation of the broader literacy expectations already visible in GDPR enforcement practice: a means of ensuring that human oversight, instruc-

18 Hellenic Data Protection Authority, 'Summary of Decision 26/2019' (HDPA, 2019).

tion, and responsibility remain effective even as data processing becomes more complex and automated.

V. Conclusion

The analysis in this chapter shows that while the GDPR does not articulate a general obligation to ensure staff literacy and training, DPA decisions are increasingly giving concrete content to what organisational understanding is expected to include. Read together, the emerging case law does more than signal that 'training matters' in a general sense. Instead, it offers relatively clear guidance on how DPAs understand literacy, where they look for it within the GDPR framework, and what they expect controllers to do in practice.

First, enforcement practice consistently treats training as a relevant organisational measure, particularly in the context of personal data breaches and the application of Art. 32 GDPR. Decisions assessing post-breach measures demonstrate that training is expected to be risk-based, documented, and capable of influencing how staff actually handle systems and personal data. Where training is superficial, reactive, or poorly evidenced, supervisory authorities have been willing to find infringements of accountability and security obligations.

Second, DPA decisions show that literacy also encompasses the ability of staff to process personal data in accordance with appropriate instructions. Decisions involving unauthorised workflows or communication channels indicate that it is not sufficient for instructions to exist formally; controllers must ensure that those acting under their authority understand how such instructions apply in practice.

Third, supervisory authorities have treated misunderstandings of core legal concepts, such as the choice of an appropriate legal basis, as organisational failures rather than individual mistakes. This illustrates that literacy under the GDPR extends beyond technical awareness and includes legal understanding where this is necessary to ensure lawful processing.

Taken together, these strands of enforcement practice allow a clearer understanding of what literacy under the GDPR requires. Literacy emerges as a composite organisational expectation: that controllers ensure their personnel are able to recognise risks, follow and apply instructions, and correctly operationalise legal requirements within real processing environments.

As data processing practices increasingly become more complex and begin to incorporate AI-enabled systems, this trajectory will take on added significance. Although the cases examined here concern data protection literacy, the underlying enforcement logic presupposes a level of system intelligibility and human oversight that is directly relevant to AI-assisted processing. AI literacy, alongside data protection literacy, is also likely to be taken into account by DPAs in the future as a natural extension of the expectations already taking shape within the GDPR, particularly where organisational responsibility depends on the ability of staff to understand, supervise, and meaningfully control complex data-processing systems. Looking ahead, the emerging literacy expectations in GDPR enforcement provide a foundation from which broader discussions of organisational understanding, including AI literacy, can develop.

Data protection in connected vehicles

Simone Vogel

EDPB, 'Guidelines 01/2020 on processing personal data in the context of connected vehicles and mobility related applications', version 2.0 (9.3.2021) <https://www.edpb.europa.eu/system/files/2021-03/edpb_guidelines_2020 01_connected_vehicles_v2.0_adopted_en.pdf>

CNIL, 'Projet de recommendation. Use of location data from connected vehicles' (20.5.2025) <https://www.cnil.fr/sites/default/files/2025-03/projet _de_recommandation_relative_aux_traitements_de_donnees_de_localisati on.pdf>

I. The transformation of the connected vehicle

While motor vehicles have long embodied the possibility of self-determined mobility without external influence, in the age of digitalization, the focus is increasingly shifting to fully connected devices that offer a complete digital ecosystem via mobile communications, Bluetooth, and Wi-Fi, similar to a smartphone.[1] The so-called 'connected car' offers infotainment functions such as navigation with real-time traffic information, music and video streaming, weather services, voice assistants, voice control, online maps, telephone function, charging planning for electric cars, parking services, and much more.[2] Driver assistance systems such as parking, lane departure warning, and brake assist increase driving safety and comfort. Automatic emergency call systems help in the event of accidents, and continuous monitoring of vehicle components detects risks or repair needs at an early stage.

1 See also Wiebe/Helmschrot/Kreutz, ‚Studie zur Notwendigkeit und Ausrichtung von spezifischen Datenzugangsregelungen im Bereich des vernetzen Fahrzeugs in der Automobilwirtschaft' (28.2.2023) <https://data.bundesnetzagentur.de/Bundesnetzagentur/DE/Fachthemen/Digitalisierung/Daten/Datenoekonomie/ schlussbericht.pdf>, p. 11.

2 Weisser/Färber MMR 2015, 506 (506, 507).

To do this, the vehicle collects and transmits vast amounts of data about the driver, the vehicle, and the environment.[3] The significance of this data can be illustrated by the example of location data. Collected over a longer period of time, this data can be used to draw surprisingly reliable conclusions about the identity, movement profiles, lifestyle habits, or personal interests of the individuals concerned.[4]

Given the critical nature of vehicle data, implementing data protection in vehicles is becoming increasingly important. The European Data Protection Board (EDPB) has addressed data protection issues in its 'Guidelines 01/2020 on the processing of personal data in the context of connected vehicles and mobility related applications'[5]. In 2025, the French supervisory authority CNIL conducted a public consultation on a new recommendation project[6], in which it specifically covered location data from connected vehicles. This article examines the data protection solutions provided by the two guidelines to the various legal issues.

II. EDPB Guidelines 01/2020 on the processing of personal data in connection with connected vehicles and mobility related applications

In the Guidelines 01/2020, the EDPB highlights the data protection risks associated with connected vehicles and provides solutions for selected cases.[7]

---

3 Hansen, ‚Fahrzeugvernetzung: Datensammelwut moderner Fahrzeuge‘ (c't online, 24.12.2021) <https://www.heise.de/hintergrund/Fahrzeugvernetzung-Datensammelwut-moderner-Fahrzeuge-6296768.html>; detailed information in Wiebe/Helmschrot/Kreutz, ‚Studie zur Notwendigkeit und Ausrichtung von spezifischen Datenzugangsregelungen im Bereich des vernetzen Fahrzeugs in der Automobilwirtschaft‘ (fn. 1), p. 17.

4 See details in Beuth/Flüpke/Hppenstedt/Kreil/Rosenbach/Wilkin, ‚Wir wissen wo Dein Auto steht‘ (DER SPIEGEL, 27.12.2024) <https://www.spiegel.de/netzwelt/web/volkswagen-konzern-datenleck-wir-wissen-wo-dein-auto-steht-a-e12d33d0-97bc-493c-96d1-aa5892861027>.

5 EDPB, 'Guidelines 01/2020 on processing personal data in the context of connected vehicles and mobility related applications', version 2.0 (9.3.2021) <https://www.edpb.europa.eu/system/files/2021-03/edpb_guidelines_202001_connected_vehicles_v2.0_adopted_en.pdf>.

6 CNIL, 'Projet de recommendation. Use of location data from connected vehicles' (20.5.2025) <https://www.cnil.fr/sites/default/files/2025-03/projet_de_recommandation_relative_aux_traitements_de_donnees_de_localisation.pdf>.

7 Borges/Keil Rechtshandbuch Big Data/Duisberg, 2024, para. 334.

The scope of application is limited to the processing of personal data in connection with the non-commercial use of connected vehicles and excludes company cars, commercially used vehicles, or exterior images.[8]

In addition to the GDPR, the ePrivacy Directive also applies to data processing in vehicles. The EDPB considers the vehicle to be a terminal equipment within the meaning of Art. Art. 1(1)(a) of the Commission Directive on competition in the markets in telecommunications terminal equipment, just like a computer or smartphone.[9] According to Art. 5(3) of the ePrivacy Directive, consent is therefore generally required for the storage of and access to data collected in the vehicle. As an example of an exception to the consent requirement, the EDPB cites data processing that is necessary for the provision of navigation services requested by the data subject.[10]

All further processing of vehicle data, which is generally personal data, is then governed by the GDPR. Here too, the EDPB considers consent to be the most appropriate legal basis.[11]

The EDPB sees risks in the lack of control and information asymmetry that could arise in particular from a vehicle being used by several people without this being fully taken into account technically in the processing of data and the provision of data protection information in the vehicle. In the EDPB's opinion, the increasing automatic transmission of data to enable services and functions also increases data protection risks due to the increasingly poor control options available to individual vehicle users.[12] Added to this are the challenges of obtaining consent in the proper manner, in particular due to a lack of transparency for the diverse range of users about the data processing activities, as well as the risk of uncontrolled further processing of the data for other purposes.[13] According to the EDPB,

8 EDPB, 'Guidelines 01/2020 on processing personal data in the context of connected vehicles and mobility related applications' (fn. 5), para. 20–35.

9 EDPB, 'Guidelines 01/2020 on processing personal data in the context of connected vehicles and mobility related applications' (fn. 5), para. 13.

10 EDPB, 'Guidelines 01/2020 on processing personal data in the context of connected vehicles and mobility related applications' (fn. 5), para. 18.

11 EDPB, 'Guidelines 01/2020 on processing personal data in the context of connected vehicles and mobility related applications' (fn. 5), para. 15.

12 EDPB, 'Guidelines 01/2020 on processing personal data in the context of connected vehicles and mobility related applications' (fn. 5), para. 46 et seq.

13 EDPB, 'Guidelines 01/2020 on processing personal data in the context of connected vehicles and mobility related applications' (fn. 5), para. 48 et seq., para. 53 et seq.

the increasing number of sensors also increases the risk of excessive data processing in the vehicle and the criticality of security breaches.[14]

The EDPB provides recommendations for action for particularly critical data categories, location data, biometric data, special categories of data pursuant to Art. 9 GDPR, and data that could reveal criminal offenses or traffic violations.[15] It emphasizes the importance of complying with data protection principles such as data minimization, data protection by design, and privacy-friendly default settings. Local processing of data in the vehicle is preferable to processing outside the vehicle in order to ensure users' control options.[16] The EDPB considers transparency towards the data subjects to be crucial. Information must be provided in a clear, understandable, and easily accessible manner. To this end, the EDPB recommends simple profile management systems that allow users to view and change their privacy settings at any time.[17]

The EDPB also provides specific implementation recommendations on other data protection requirements, such as anonymization and pseudonymization, conducting data protection impact assessments, data subject rights, and taking appropriate security measures.[18]

III. CNIL recommendation project on location data in connected vehicles

The CNIL's recommendation project on the handling of location data from connected vehicles is currently being finalized by the CNIL and is intended to supplement the EDPB Guidelines.[19]

---

14 EDPB, 'Guidelines 01/2020 on processing personal data in the context of connected vehicles and mobility related applications' (fn. 5), para. 57 et seq.

15 EDPB, 'Guidelines 01/2020 on processing personal data in the context of connected vehicles and mobility related applications' (fn. 5), para. 62 et seq.

16 EDPB, 'Guidelines 01/2020 on processing personal data in the context of connected vehicles and mobility related applications' (fn. 5), para. 73, para. 76.

17 EDPB, 'Guidelines 01/2020 on processing personal data in the context of connected vehicles and mobility related applications' (fn. 5), para. 83 et seq., para. 91.

18 EDPB, 'Guidelines 01/2020 on processing personal data in the context of connected vehicles and mobility related applications' (fn. 5), para. 79 et seq.

19 CNIL, 'Véhicules connectés et localisation : la CNIL lance une consultation publique sur son projet de recommandation' (25.3.2025) <https://www.cnil.fr/fr/vehicules-connectes-et-localisation-consultation-publique-projet-de-recommandation#:~:text=Quel%20est%20le%20calendrier%20de,peut%20participer%20%C3%A0%20la%20consultation.#:~:text=Quel%20est%20le%20calendrier%20de,peut%20participer%20%C3%A0%20la%20consultation>.

Due to its particular relevance, the guideline focuses on location data of private individuals as owners or renters of a vehicle. The CNIL provides specific recommendations for various processing purposes, in particular theft protection, accident assistance, optimization of products and services, and fleet management.[20] It explains the associated data protection issues in detail using various case studies.[21]

Like the EDPB, the CNIL considers both the ePrivacy Directive and the GDPR to be applicable in principle and distinguishes between the collection and storage of data in the vehicle and the subsequent processing of data.[22]

In the case of data processing purely for the purposes of the users themselves, e.g., within the scope of the vehicle's own display options, without data transfer to the manufacturer or third parties, the GDPR does not apply in accordance with Art. 2(2) GDPR.[23] The CNIL provides extensive examples to determine the respective roles of the actors and discusses the various legal bases in detail.[24]

The CNIL attaches particular importance to the principles of data minimization and storage limitation and also recommends local processing of location data in the vehicle.[25]

In order to effectively exercise their rights under the GDPR, it is essential that data subjects are provided with comprehensive information about the use of their location data. The CNIL makes specific recommendations for implementing the information requirements, e.g., in purchase or rental agreements, through digital notices or pictograms. In addition to central options for data protection settings, sufficient deletion options must always

20 CNIL, 'Projet de recommendation. Use of location data from connected vehicles' (fn. 6), para. 11 et seq.

21 CNIL, 'Projet de recommendation. Use of location data from connected vehicles' (fn. 6), para. 140 et seq.

22 CNIL, 'Projet de recommendation. Use of location data from connected vehicles' (fn. 6), para. 17 et seq.

23 EDPB, 'Guidelines 01/2020 on processing personal data in the context of connected vehicles and mobility related applications' (fn. 5), para. 73 et seq.; CNIL, 'Projet de recommendation. Use of location data from connected vehicles' (fn. 6), para. 15.

24 CNIL, 'Projet de recommendation. Use of location data from connected vehicles' (fn. 6), para. 27 et seq., para. 39 et seq.

25 CNIL, 'Projet de recommendation. Use of location data from connected vehicles' (fn. 6), para. 50 et seq.

be ensured to prevent subsequent users from accessing the movement data of their predecessors.[26]

Given the high sensitivity of location data, the guideline calls for the implementation of robust security measures. These include data encryption, the implementation of strict authorization profiles, access restrictions, and systematic logging. The CNIL also refers to helpful technical standards for vehicle cybersecurity and the management of cybersecurity risks.[27]

As an example of the implementation of data protection by design, the CNIL devotes considerable attention to the anonymization of location data and notes that simple pseudonymization or removal of direct identifiers is not sufficient to ensure effective protection against re-identification. It therefore recommends combining various techniques such as generalization, aggregation, and randomization of data.[28]

IV. Evaluation based on specific data protection issues

The solutions proposed in the two papers will be examined in more detail below on the basis of three highly relevant practical issues.

1. Personal reference in the vehicle

It is highly relevant in practice to determine when vehicle data is personal information and to which person this data can be specifically assigned. When fulfilling the rights of data subjects, the controller must ensure that the request comes from the right person and that no risks to third parties can arise.[29] Location data in particular can be used to draw many conclusions about the very private lives of different drivers.[30]

---

26 CNIL, 'Projet de recommendation. Use of location data from connected vehicles' (fn. 6), para. 58 et seq.

27 CNIL, 'Projet de recommendation. Use of location data from connected vehicles' (fn. 6), para. 69 et seq.

28 CNIL, 'Projet de recommendation. Use of location data from connected vehicles' (fn. 6), para. 98 et seq., para. 119 et seq.

29 Taeger/Gabel DSGVO – BDSG – TDDDG/Spittka, 5th edition 2026, DS-VGO Art. 11 mn. 18.

30 linus, 'Wir wissen, wo dein Auto steht' (Chaos Computer Club, 27.12.2024) <https://www.ccc.de/de/updates/2024/wir-wissen-wo-dein-auto-steht>.

Both guidelines are based on the principle that data generated when a vehicle is used by a natural person is personal data.[31]

The vehicle identification number is assigned to the owner in the registration certificate and can be linked to the owner by the vehicle manufacturer and third parties.[32] Any related vehicle data can therefore generally be linked to the owner in conjunction with the identification number.[33] However, when a vehicle is used, other data is also generated that allows conclusions to be drawn about specific individuals, e.g., time, seat or steering wheel height, geo-position, user profiles created, etc.[34] These may well be persons other than the owner, e.g., other drivers or passengers of the vehicle, who may themselves have an interest in preventing the vehicle owner from accessing their data.

This raises the question of whether the personal reference should be assessed purely from the perspective of the controller or whether other characteristics in the sphere of the data recipient should also be taken into account. The case law of the ECJ is becoming more consistent in that it also takes into account means that can be used for identification, e.g., by the data recipient at their discretion. Objective factors, such as the costs and time required for identification, should be taken into account.[35] In many cases, it should be fairly easy for the vehicle owner to identify other users of the vehicle, e.g., based on the steering wheel position, a time stamp, or a location.

Although the CNIL has recognized this complexity in principle, it concludes only that controllers are not required to comply with data protection claims from third parties unknown to them.[36] This view is debatable in itself. It also remains unclear how to deal with claims from the owner if

31 EDPB, 'Guidelines 01/2020 on processing personal data in the context of connected vehicles and mobility related applications' (fn. 5), para. 3, para. 29.

32 ECJ 9.11.2023 – case C-319/22, ECLI:EU:C:2023:837 – Scania.

33 Deutsch/Eggendorfer DSRITB 2020, 1001 (1005).

34 Koch, ‚Datenschutz im Auto: Sorgfältig mit personenbezogenen Daten umgehen' (heise online, 24.12.2021) <https://www.heise.de/hintergrund/Datenschutz-im-Auto-Sorgfaeltig-mit-personenbezogenen-Daten-umgehen-6297222.html>.

35 See ECJ 4.9.2025 – case C-413/23, ECLI:EU:C:2025:645 – European Data Protection Supervisor v Single Resolution Board; ECJ 7.3.2024 – case C-604/22, ECLI:EU:C:2024:214 – IAB Europe v Gegevensbeschermingsautoriteit; ECJ 7.3.2024 – case C-479/22 P, ECLI:EU:C:2024:215 – OC v European Commission; ECJ 9.11.2023 – case C-319/22, ECLI:EU:C:2023:837 – Scania.

36 CNIL, 'Projet de recommendation. Use of location data from connected vehicles' (fn. 6), para. 38.

there is a risk that the vehicle data in question cannot be attributed to the owner himself but to third parties.

2. Consent as a legal basis

Consent as the legal basis for processing vehicle data raises numerous problems, especially the question of how consent can be obtained effectively and verifiably from each of the constantly changing drivers,[37] without massively disrupting the driving and user experience by repeatedly displaying information and consent windows or identity confirmations after each stop of the vehicle. Given the large amount of data processing in the vehicle, the required transparency is an issue, but the revocability of consent also poses technical challenges, which are exacerbated by the multi-user principle of the vehicle.[38]

Both the EDPB and the CNIL place high demands on consent under both the ePrivacy Directive and the GDPR[39], but consider it unavoidable, particularly due to the applicability of Art. 5(3) ePrivacy Directive, unless one of the exceptions provided for applies.[40] Any subsequent reuse of the data collected in this way must be based on a further legal basis. Here, the CNIL concurs with the opinion of the EDPB, which sees no scope for further processing in accordance with Art. 6(4) GDPR for data that requires consent under the ePrivacy Directive, as this would undermine the data protection standard required by the ePrivacy Directive.[41]

Although the EDPB recognizes the problem of different users of a vehicle,[42] it ultimately leaves the question open. The CNIL, on the other hand, attempts to find different solutions for some specific case constella-

37 Taeger/Gabel/Taeger DS-VGO Art. 6 mn. 40.

38 See also Leupold/Wiebe/Glossner, IT Recht, 4th edition 2021, Part 10.2, mn. 35.

39 EDPB, 'Guidelines 01/2020 on processing personal data in the context of connected vehicles and mobility related applications' (fn. 5), para. 48 et seq.; CNIL, 'Projet de recommendation. Use of location data from connected vehicles' (fn. 6), para. 41.

40 EDPB, 'Guidelines 01/2020 on processing personal data in the context of connected vehicles and mobility related applications' (fn. 5), para. 13; likewise CNIL, 'Projet de recommendation. Use of location data from connected vehicles' (fn. 6), para. 17 ff.

41 CNIL, 'Projet de recommendation. Use of location data from connected vehicles' (fn. 6), para. 41; referring to
EDPB, 'Guidelines 01/2020 on processing personal data in the context of connected vehicles and mobility related applications' (fn. 5), para. 53.

42 EDPB, 'Guidelines 01/2020 on processing personal data in the context of connected vehicles and mobility related applications' (fn. 5), para. 51.

tions.[43] In the example of theft prevention, the CNIL attempts to base the processing on the contract with the owner for the location service, without, however, considering whether this is actually suitable as a legal basis for processing the thief's location data.[44] It also disregards consent as the legal basis for storing location data in the vehicle, which, according to Art. 5(3) ePrivacy Directive, would also have to be obtained from the specific user, in this case the thief. The case scenarios addressed by the CNIL clearly show that the consent requirement under the ePrivacy Directive in particular does not meet many perfectly legitimate uses of vehicle data.

3. Technical requirements and competitiveness

There are many framework conditions in vehicle development that also influence the implementation of data protection. There are restrictions with regard to the implementation of technical solutions, such as limited storage and computing capacities in the vehicle or restrictions on the quantity of data transfers from the vehicle. Customers expect increasingly highly networked, intelligent, and, above all, AI-supported functions in vehicles,[45] while price pressure is increasing due to competition from China.[46] Networked functions are an important component in terms of competitiveness, and their added value lies precisely in the exchange of data with the manufacturer, other road users, or accompanying service providers.[47] For example, a navigation function with real-time traffic information cannot be implemented without transferring the necessary data to the service provider, including linking the individual pieces of information to form an overall picture of the current traffic conditions. While on-board processing is technically feasible for most driving functions, local data processing is not sufficient if the purpose of the processing requires processing by the

43 For example, CNIL, 'Projet de recommendation. Use of location data from connected vehicles' (fn. 6), discussion point in para. 146.

44 CNIL, 'Projet de recommendation. Use of location data from connected vehicles' (fn. 6), para. 161 et seq.

45 Baule et al., 'Car connectivity: What consumers want and are willing to pay' (McKinsey, 8.1.2024) <https://www.mckinsey.com/industries/automotive-and-assembly/our-insights/car-connectivity-what-consumers-want-and-are-willing-to-pay#/>.

46 Scheel, ‚Qualitativ gut und innovativ – wie gut sind die E-Autos aus China?' (WDR, 23.4.2025) <https://www1.wdr.de/nachrichten/automesse-shanghai-qualitaet-eautos-china-100.html>.

47 Federal Office for Information Security, 'Vernetztes Fahren – Chancen und Risiken' <https://www.bsi.bund.de/dok/12578020>.

manufacturer or a service provider as the responsible party, e.g., when performing product monitoring obligations with the help of fault data from the entire vehicle fleet.

In this context, both guidelines rightly emphasize the importance of protecting the increasing amount of vehicle data and attempt to demonstrate practical solutions through examples and case studies.

For example, the CNIL recommends separating location data from the vehicle identification number wherever possible or pseudonymizing the latter.[48] Like the EDPB, it calls for data processing to be carried out locally in the vehicle wherever possible.[49] It also makes specific proposals for the anonymization of location data, but points out that the specific possibilities for anonymization must be assessed on a case-by-case basis.[50] The EDPB emphasizes above all the need for vehicle users to have control over their data. To this end, it sets out various requirements, such as sufficient information in the appropriate language, options for deactivation for various processing purposes, options for deletion, and direct access to the data.[51]

It is essential to consider data protection at an early stage when designing the various functions. Nevertheless, both guidelines focus on data protection requirements and only take the practical challenges into account to a limited extent. It is left to vehicle manufacturers and service providers to implement these requirements in an economically viable manner. Implementing the best possible data protection requirements often incurs costs,[52] which must be taken into account in pricing. Resolving this tension in individual cases, will remain a challenge for which neither of the two guidelines offers suitable solutions.

48 CNIL, 'Projet de recommendation. Use of location data from connected vehicles' (fn. 6), para. 100 et seq.

49 EDPB, 'Guidelines 01/2020 on processing personal data in the context of connected vehicles and mobility related applications' (fn. 5), para. 73 et seq.

50 CNIL, 'Projet de recommendation. Use of location data from connected vehicles' (fn. 6), para. 124, para. 129 f.

51 EDPB, 'Guidelines 01/2020 on processing personal data in the context of connected vehicles and mobility related applications' (fn. 5), para. 77 f.

52 Bitkom, ‚Datenschutz als Herausforderung für die Digitalisierung' (May 2022) <https://www.bitkom.org/sites/main/files/2023-01/Studie-Datenschutz-als-Herausforderung-fur-die-Digitalisierung-final.pdf>, p. 12; Bitkom, ‚Datenschutz: Aufwand für Unternehmen nimmt zu' (1.10.2024) <https://www.bitkom.org/Presse/Presseinformation/Datenschutz-Aufwand-Unternehmen-nimmt-zu>.

V. Conclusion

The EDPB guidelines take a broad approach and cover all types of personal data in connection with connected vehicles. With regard to the legal focus and approaches to solutions, the CNIL largely builds on the EDPB guidelines. The stronger focus on location data enables the CNIL to address the specific challenges in much greater depth and detail. While the EDPB therefore formulates rather general principles, the CNIL identifies specific problem cases and offers actual solutions. Ultimately, however, neither document resolves the issues surrounding the data protection-compliant processing of vehicle data. Neither set of guidelines provides answers to the key legal questions and implementation problems.

VI. Recommended further reading

EDPB, 'Guidelines 01/2020 on processing personal data in the context of connected vehicles and mobility related applications', version 2.0 (9.3.2021) <https://www.edpb.europa.eu/system/files/2021-03/edpb_guidelines_202001_connected_vehicles_v2.0_adopted_en.pdf>

CNIL, 'Projet de recommendation. Use of location data from connected vehicles' (20.5.2025) <https://www.cnil.fr/sites/default/files/2025-03/projet_de_recommandation_relative_aux_traitements_de_donnees_de_localisation.pdf>

Chapter 9:
The GDPR within the EU Digital Regulatory Framework

The tension between data protection and data use in EU digital law

Michael Dose

EDPB/EDPS, 'EDPB-EDPS Joint Opinion 2/2022 on the Proposal of the European Parliament and of the Council on harmonised rules on fair access to and use of data' (4.5.2022) <https://www.edpb.europa.eu/system/files/2022-05/edpb-edps_joint_opinion_22022_on_data_act_proposal_en.pdf>

I. Position summary

Almost ten years after the GDPR came into force, the DA has been published, another piece of European data legislation that is likely to revolutionize the legal framework for the access and use of (non-)personal data for the digital economy. Although the scope of the DA explicitly extends to personal data, particularly concerning the proposed provisions on making IoT data available, the EU legislator has not made any clear legal distinction between the DA and the GDPR: According to Art. 1(5) DA, the DA applies 'without prejudice' to the GDPR, in the event of a conflict, data protection law should 'prevail'.

During the legislative process, EDPB and EDPS took a comprehensive position on this tension in a joint statement.[1] In addition to data protection issues relating to obligations on making data available in the B2C and B2B sectors, EDPB and EDPS also commented on the proposed obligations for companies on making data available in the B2G relationship.

1 EDPB/EDPS, 'EDPB-EDPS Joint Opinion 2/2022 on the Proposal of the European Parliament and of the Council on harmonised rules on fair access to and use of data (Data Act)' (1.5.2022) <https://www.edpb.europa.eu/our-work-tools/our-documents/edpbedps-joint-opinion/edpb-edps-joint-opinion-22022-proposal-european_en>.

II. Key statements

In their joint statement, EDPB and EDPS point out that the DA could fundamentally undermine data protection law.[2] In order to avoid any conflicts between the DA and the GDPR, legal specifications are required to ensure that any inconsistency or conflict with applicable data protection legislation is avoided.[3]

The problem is that the data access, use, and sharing rights not only apply on the data subject within the meaning of the GDPR, but also on third parties, whether natural or legal persons.[4] Considering this, it must be ensured that data access by third parties under Art. 5(3) DA is not interpreted to the detriment of the obligations under the GDPR and that any further processing must be carried out in accordance with the requirements of Art. 6(4) GDPR.[5] EDPB and EDPS further emphasize that the right to the protection of personal data is inalienable and cannot be waived, which is why any incentives to monetize the data must be eliminated.[6] At the same time, in order to promote data minimization, the possibility of using IoT products anonymously should be granted.[7] To ensure that data provision agreements between data holders and data recipients cannot be interpreted as a legal basis within the meaning of Art. 6(1)(c) GDPR, contractual terms that undermine the data subject's right to data protection to their detriment should not be binding.[8]

EDPB and EDPS also express clear criticism with regard to B2G data provisions pursuant to Art. 15 et seqq. DA, as there are serious concerns regarding the principle of proportionality.[9] In particular, the cases envisaged by the EU Commission outside of public emergencies, in which data sharing obligations are legitimized, for example, to fulfill a task in the public interest, constitute a problematic interference with the fundamental rights of the persons concerned.[10]

---

2 EDPB/EDPS, 'Joint Opinion 2/2022' (fn.1), mn. 15.
3 EDPB/EDPS, 'Joint Opinion 2/2022' (fn.1), mn. 8.
4 EDPB/EDPS, 'Joint Opinion 2/2022' (fn.1), mn. 14, 24.
5 EDPB/EDPS, 'Joint Opinion 2/2022' (fn.1), mn. 47 ff.
6 EDPB/EDPS, 'Joint Opinion 2/2022' (fn.1), mn. 59 ff.
7 EDPB/EDPS, 'Joint Opinion 2/2022' (fn.1), mn. 47.
8 EDPB/EDPS, 'Joint Opinion 2/2022' (fn.1), mn. 69.
9 EDPB/EDPS, 'Joint Opinion 2/2022' (fn.1), mn. 73.
10 EDPB/EDPS, 'Joint Opinion 2/2022' (fn.1), mn. 79.

III. Systematic context and legal classification

As the legislative core of the EU data strategy,[11] the DA is intended to ensure fair data access and fair data use in the genuine single market for data in B2B, B2C, and B2G relationships, thereby increasing competitiveness and innovation potential in the EU. Accordingly, the new regulations are intended to supplement and strengthen the right to data portability under Art. 15 and 20 GDPR.[12] The core element of the new legal framework is the granting of extensive data sharing rights to users of IoT devices and related services *vis-à-vis* the so-called data holders regarding the product data generated through their use. In its Inception Impact Assessment, the EU Commission already points out that the increasing use of IoT products in the private sphere is leading to an increase of personal data.[13]

1. Developments in data protection law in the DA during the legislative process

During the legislative process of the DA, the distinction from the provisions of the GDPR is made even clearer and, in this respect, parts of the EDPB/EDSB opinions were adopted. For example, Art. 1(5) DA additionally stipulates that in the event of a conflict with the DA, data protection law shall prevail. At the same time, Art. 15(1)(b) DA introduced the restriction that in the case of B2G data provision requests from public authorities outside of a public emergency, only non-personal data must be provided.

2. Current developments following completion of the legislative process

Shortly after the DA came into force, the European Commission provided legally non-binding guidance on implementing the new legal requirements in the form of FAQs.[14] These FAQs also address questions about the

---

11 European Commission, 'A European strategy for data' (19.2.2020), COM(2020) 66 final.

12 European Commission, 'Inception Impact Assessment', (28.5.2021), Ares(2021)3527151, <https://eur-lex.europa.eu/legal-content/EN/TXT/?uri=intcom:Ares(2021)3527151>, p. 6.

13 European Commission, 'Inception Impact Assessment' (fn. 12), p. 3.

14 European Commission, 'Frequently Asked Questions – Data Act', version 1.3 (12.9.2025) <https://ec.europa.eu/newsroom/dae/redirection/document/108144>.

relationship between the DA and the GDPR – however, key questions arising from the tension between data protection and data use requirements remain unanswered. On November 19, 2025, the EU Commission adopted the model contractual terms and standard contractual clauses provided for in Art. 41 DA, which are intended to support practical application as non-binding terms and clauses.[15] In advance of this, the EDPB had already critically examined the draft version of the clause texts in a statement, as they did not take sufficient account of the (additional) requirements of data protection law.[16]

The DA has come into force on September 12, 2025, but until now, no official decisions have yet been made that address the tension in its practical application.

IV. Author's analysis and commentary

In the legal text of the DA, the EU legislator decided against resolving its tensions with the GDPR. A possible solution in the form of a legal basis for the data holder in fulfilling the data provision claim pursuant to Art. 6 and 9 GDPR is expressly excluded in Rec. 7 DA. Instead, it is clarified that any processing of personal data must comply with data protection law and that the DA itself does not constitute a legal basis under data protection law pursuant to Art. 6 and 9 GDPR. The political intention was to protect data subjects in constellations with multiple users.[17] Even in its current legislative proposal on the so-called 'Digital Omnibus', the EU Commission does not make any corresponding legislative corrections regarding the DA.[18]

15 European Commission, 'Communication to the Commission – Approval of the draft Commission Recommendation on non-binding model contractual terms on data access and use and non-binding standard contractual clauses for cloud computing contracts (with Annexes), annexed hereto' (19.11.2025) C(2025) 7750 final.

16 EDPB/EDPS 'Statement 4/2025 on the European Commission's Recommendation on draft non-binding model contractual terms on data sharing under the Data Act (version of 22.5.2025)' (8.7.2025) <https://www.edpb.europa.eu/system/files/2025-07/edpb_statement_202504_commission-s_draftmcts_dataact_en.pdf>.

17 European Commission, 'Frequently Asked Questions – Data Act' (fn. 14), p. 23.

18 European Commission, 'Proposal for a Regulation of the European Parliament and of the Council amending Regulations (EU) 2016/679, (EU) 2018/1724, (EU) 2018/1725, (EU) 2023/2854 and Directives 2002/58/EC, (EU) 2022/2555 and (EU) 2022/2557 as regards the simplification of the digital legislative framework, and repealing Regula-

1. Challenges for those applying the law

In practice, companies face the challenge of individually deciding whether the provision of IoT data complies with the legal requirements of the DA and / or the GDPR. This will not be a problem in cases where the data subject pursuant to Art. 4 no. 1 GDPR is identical to the entitled user pursuant to Art. 2(12) DA and no other data subjects are involved.[19]

However, in practice it will be more likely for data holders to face a situation in which the IoT data contains not only the user's personal data but also that of other data subjects. In such cases, the data holder faces the challenge of having to decide, under threat of sanctions by competent authorities, whether all legal requirements are met. In the event of a misjudgement, the liability and sanction regime pursuant to Art. 82 et seq. GDPR applies, as well as the sanction regime to be determined by the member states in the event of a breach of the DA obligations of Chapters II, III, and V pursuant to Art. 40(1) DA.[20] It will be interesting to see to what extent the current concerns expressed regarding an 'escape from the Data Act'[21] will actually be used in practice to circumvent DA data sharing obligations.

2. Possible solutions

The legislator itself sees the anonymization of personal data as a solution to the challenges of practical application. Regarding IoT data sharing obligations in Chapter II/III DA, Rec. 7 sent. 12 DA explicitly stipulates that the data holder can comply with data access requests by anonymizing personal data. The same applies to B2G data provision obligations, where the legal text itself has corresponding provisions in Art. 17(1)(g) and Art. 18(4) DA.

The anonymization of personal data has great potential to bridge the gap between a high level of data protection and the simultaneous economic use of data. It is also explicitly recognized in Rec. 26 sent. 5 GDPR. Nevertheless, there is still legal uncertainty in the practical application of anonymization. In addition to the legal question of whether an 'absolute'

tions (EU) 2018/1807, (EU) 2019/1150, (EU) 2022/868, and Directive (EU) 2019/1024 (Digital Omnibus)' (19.11.2025) COM(2025) 837 final.

19 Baumann/Brunnbauer ZD 2025, 132.

20 Bomhard/Merkle RDi 2022, 168 (172); Krause/Maasjost ZD-Aktuell 2024, 01494.

21 Bomhard/Zdanowiecki RDi 2025, 419 (420).

or merely 'relative' understanding of anonymization is required,[22] there are also technical uncertainties as to the extent to which anonymization must be carried out to comply with the GDPR requirements.[23] The guidance provided by European data protection supervisory authorities is currently of little help in this regard, as the last statement dates back to 2014.[24]

With its SRB/Deloitte ruling,[25] the ECJ recently remedied this situation by ruling that pseudonymized data from third parties can be treated as anonymized data if there is no access to the pseudonymization key. The ruling is to be welcomed because it strengthens the relative understanding of anonymization and is also likely to ease the data provision obligations of data controllers / data holders. Further clarification is expected from the long-awaited EDPB guidelines on anonymization, which were announced for 2025.[26]

Overall, further clarification and guidance is needed from both the EU legislator and the EDPB in order to address the unresolved tensions between the requirements of the DA and the GDPR in terms of practical application. The EU Commission's latest initiatives on the so-called 'Digital Omnibus' and the 'Digital Fitness Check' must also be seriously considered, for example in the form of presumptions regarding the anonymization of personal data, so that data protection and data use in Europe can succeed simultaneously.

V. Recommended further reading

Steinrötter GRUR 2023, 216.
Baumann/Brunnbauer ZD 2025, 132.
Bomhard/Żdanowiecki RDi 2025, 419.
Brink/Eckhardt ZD 2015, 205.

22 Brink/Eckhardt ZD 2015, 205.

23 BDI Handbook, 'Anonymization of personal data' (2.11.2020), <https://english.bdi.eu/publication/news/anonymization-of-personal-data>.

24 Article 29 Data Protection Working Party, Opinion 5/2014 on Anonymisation Techniques‘ (WP216, 10.4.2014), <https://ec.europa.eu/justice/article-29/documentation/opinion-recommendation/files/2014/wp216_de.pdf>.

25 ECJ 4.9.2025 – case C-413/23 P, ECLI:EU:C:2025:645 – EDPS v SRB.

26 German Data Protection Conference, ‚Datenschutzkonferenz plant Hilfestellungen für die effektive Anonymisierung und Pseudonymisierung von personenbezogenen Daten‘ (30.1.2025) <https://datenschutzkonferenz-online.de/media/pm/20250130-DSK-PM-ZwiKo.pdf>.

The Google Android case: redefining the intersection of competition law and data governance

Boris Rigod

GC 14.9.2022 – case T-604/18, ECLI:EU:T:2022:541 – Google et al. vs. EU Commission (Android)

I. Introduction

The GC's judgment in *Google vs. Commission (Android)* is a landmark. It addresses heads on how courts and regulators legally assess dominant online platforms' architecture design decisions regarding user choice and data flows. At heart an antitrust case, concerning the abuse of a dominant market position, its implications extend into the domain of data governance and privacy law.

This paper analyzes the GC's decision, first by outlining the factual background and legal reasoning, second, by comparing the decision to the approach adopted by US courts with respect to similar factual patterns, and finally, by exploring its implications for data law and the broader principles of data governance. Given the global nature of both the services but also the legal questions at issue, it seems more than pertinent to not restrict the analysis to the EU only.

II. The EU General Court's ruling

In September 2022, the GC mostly upheld the European Commission's 2018 decision that Google had abused its dominant market position on the market for licensable smart mobile operating systems through practices related to its Android mobile operating system, in breach of Art. 102 TFEU.[1]

In particular, the GC confirmed that Google's unlawful restrictions imposed on mobile phone device manufacturers and mobile network opera-

1 GC 14.9.2022 – case T-604/18, ECLI:EU:T:2022:541 – Google et al. vs. EU Commission (Android).

tors aimed at protecting its general internet search service from competition. That is to say, while Google's behaviour primarily targeted the market for mobile operating systems, its ultimate goal was to protect its market position on the far more lucrative market for general internet search. The means to attain this end were restrictions imposed on mobile phone device manufacturers and mobile network operators that prevented them from collaborating with competing search services providers.

1. The EU Commission's 2018 Decision

In 2018 the European Commission imposed a fine of over EUR 4 billion and ordered Google to cease certain practices.[2] The practices at issue primarily affected the market for licensable smart mobile operating systems on which Google was considered dominant within the meaning of Art. 102 TFEU, i.e. in view of the EU Commission, Google faced no or little competitive constraints with respect to its market behaviour on this market.[3] A mobile operating system is a specialized software platform that controls the hardware and software of mobile devices, such as smartphones, tablets, and wearables. It is essential for, *inter alia*, the smooth functioning of apps on smartphones. The most prominent examples of such mobile operating systems are Google's Android operating system, an open-source system used by many mobile phone manufacturers (e.g. Samsung), and Apple's iOS, a closed system exclusive to Apple devices.

The European Commission identified three distinct types of illegal practices through which Google abused its dominance in the market for such licensable smart mobile operating systems.

First, the European Commission found that Google had engaged in illegal tying.[4] 'Tying' describes a business practice where a company sells one product (the 'tying' product) only on the condition that the buyer also purchases a second, different product (the 'tied' product). According to the European Commission, Google exploited the manufacturer's dependence on the Google Play Store application, a gateway for users to obtain apps for their mobile devices.[5] Because a smartphone is close to impossible to sell without access to the Play Store, Google used it to incentivize

2 EU Commission, ‚Decision of 18 July 2018', AT.40099 – Google Android.
3 EU Commission, ‚Decision of 18 July 2018', AT.40099 – Google Android, para. 439 et seq.
4 EU Commission, ‚Decision of 18 July 2018', AT.40099 – Google Android, para. 740 et seq.
5 EU Commission, ‚Decision of 18 July 2018', AT.40099 – Google Android, para. 754 et seq.

manufacturers into a bundle, consisting of various Google apps. To gain licensing for the Play Store, manufacturers were required to pre-install the Google Search app and the Chrome browser. By tying these services together, Google ensured its own products were the default for millions of mobile phone users, thereby rendering it less likely that consumers would download competing browsers or search engines.

Second, in an effort to obstruct the growth of rival operating systems, Google leveraged its control over essential apps to enforce so-called anti-fragmentation agreements.[6] These agreements addressed the following issue: while the basic code for Android is open source and thus free for anyone to modify, Google contractually prohibited manufacturers from using modified versions of Android.[7] To obtain a license for certain Google apps, manufacturers had to commit to not selling devices that ran unofficial or unauthorized versions of Android.[8] This strategy stifled potential competition before it could even start, as manufacturers were unwilling to risk losing access to Google apps only to experiment with rival operating systems.

Finally, the European Commission found that to secure its position in the mobile market, Google concluded so-called revenue sharing agreements. These agreements were, essentially, exclusivity payments to mobile phone manufacturers.[9] By offering phone manufacturers like Samsung and network operators like Verizon a share of the profit generated from search advertisements, Google aimed at incentivizing these partners to favor Google's apps over those of its competitors. Notably, the exclusivity payments were conditional on the other party's promise not to pre-install competing search engines, such as Bing or DuckDuckGo, on their devices.[10]

2. The GC's Findings

The General Court largely upheld the European Commission's findings. Central to the ruling was the Court's rejection of Google's argument that Apple's iOS would exert significant competitive pressure on its Android operating system. The EU General Court, however, rejected this line of

6 EU Commission, ,Decision of 18 July 2018', AT.40099 – Google Android, para. 1015 et seq.
7 EU Commission, ,Decision of 18 July 2018', AT.40099 – Google Android, para. 153 et seq.
8 EU Commission, ,Decision of 18 July 2018', AT.40099 – Google Android, para. 1032 et seq.
9 EU Commission, ,Decision of 18 July 2018', AT.40099 – Google Android, para. 1188 et seq.
10 EU Commission, ,Decision of 18 July 2018', AT.40099 – Google Android, para. 1195 et seq.

argumentation because Apple does not license its iOS to third parties.[11] Having confirmed Google's dominant position, the EU General Court also upheld the EU Commission's findings regarding the unlawful tying of Google Search and Chrome to the Play Store, based on the reasoning that such practices exploited users' status quo bias, and thereby created a barrier to entry for rival browsers and search engines.[12] Furthermore, it confirmed that Google's anti-fragmentation agreements constituted an abuse by effectively banning Android modifications, which stifled innovation and prevented competitors from entering the market.[13] However, the Court partially annulled the Commission's findings on exclusivity payments.[14] It ruled that the Commission did not meet the required standard of proof for market foreclosure.

III. Transatlantic Convergence? Comparing the EU and the US Approach

This section provides an overview of the approach taken by US courts regarding Google's mobile distribution strategy and compares this to the EU General Court's judgement.

1. The U.S. District Court's Decision

In August 2024 the U.S. District Court for the District of Columbia found that Google unlawfully monopolized the markets for general search services and general search text advertisements through exclusive contracts with browser developers, mobile device manufacturers, and wireless carriers.[15] The US District Court held that Google violated Section 2 of the Sherman Act by unlawfully maintaining monopolies in the markets for general search services and general search text advertising.[16] The court found that

11 GC 14.9.2022 – case T-604/18, ECLI:EU:T:2022:541 para. 154 – Google et al. vs. EU Commission (Android).

12 GC 14.9.2022 – case T-604/18, ECLI:EU:T:2022:541 para. 274 et seq., 320 et Seq., 619 – Google et al. vs. EU Commission (Android).

13 GC 14.9.2022 – case T-604/18, ECLI:EU:T:2022:541 para. 894 – Google et al. vs. EU Commission (Android).

14 GC 14.9.2022 – case T-604/18, ECLI:EU:T:2022:541 para. 802 – Google et al. vs. EU Commission (Android).

15 United States v. Google LLC, 747 F. Supp. 3d 1 (D.D.C. 2024).

16 United States v. Google LLC, 747 F. Supp. 3d 1 (D.D.C. 2024).

Google possessed monopoly power protected by significant entry barriers, including the high capital costs of web crawling, brand recognition, and a virtuous cycle of data scale that uniquely improves search quality as user volume increases.[17]

The liability finding rested on Google's exclusive distribution agreements, which secured its status as default search engine on browsers and mobile devices. Although the contracts did not explicitly prohibit the use of rivals, the court deemed them de facto exclusive because 'choice friction' effectively foreclosed nearly half of the search market to competitors.[18]

In September 2025, the U.S. District Court ordered a set of remedies against Google that echo the approach of the EU General Court's *Android* decision.[19] The remedies prescribed by the US Court are categorized into two categories. First, the US court prohibited Google from entering or maintaining exclusive distribution agreements for its key applications.[20] Moreover, Google shall be prohibited from tying any application license to the pre-installation or default placement of Google Search, Chrome, Google Assistant, or the Gemini app. Second, to foster competition, the court ordered measures that would force Google to share data with its competitors.[21] Specifically, Google would be required to make certain search index and user-interaction data available to certain competitors. By treating Google's data as an essential facility, i.e an infrastructure access to which is a precondition to be able to compete on the relevant market, the U.S. court has moved from simply cease and desist orders into the field of market design.

2. The EU's and the US' approach in comparison

The legal treatment of Google's practices on both sides of the Atlantic represents an illuminating case study into the diverging approaches of EU and US courts with respect to the legal treatment of the intersection of competition law and data governance. Both the European General Court's 2022 *Google Android* judgment and the United States District Court for the District of Columbia's 2024 ruling in *United States v. Google LLC* reached

17 United States v. Google LLC, 747 F. Supp. 3d 1 (D.D.C. 2024).
18 United States v. Google LLC, 747 F. Supp. 3d 1 (D.D.C. 2024).
19 United States v. Google LLC, No. 1:2020cv03010 – Document 1436 (D.D.C. 2025).
20 United States v. Google LLC, No. 1:2020cv03010 – Document 1436 (D.D.C. 2025).
21 United States v. Google LLC, No. 1:2020cv03010 – Document 1436 (D.D.C. 2025).

similar conclusions regarding the anti-competitive nature of default settings. However, due to differences in the institutional organization, it was only the US District Court that directly addressed the question of remedies.

Having said this, a significant point of convergence between the two jurisdictions is the recognition of default bias as a structural barrier to market entry. The European General Court affirmed the Commission's finding that the mandatory pre-installation of Google Search and Chrome created a status quo advantage that effectively foreclosed the market to rivals. This analysis was echoed by the US District Court, which characterized Google's payments for default status as exclusive dealing that prevented competitors from accessing users. Both courts rejected the 'competition is only a click away' narrative, used as a defense by Google, acknowledging that in a digital economy characterized by high user inertia, the control of defaults is pivotal for access to users.

Despite these shared observations, the legal paths taken by the two courts reflect differing jurisdictional priorities. The European General Court operated within the framework of Art. 102 TFEU, focusing on the abuse of dominance within the licensable mobile operating system market. By excluding Apple's iOS from the relevant market the EU General Court established a high degree of dominance for Google. This allowed the Court to also address the anti-fragmentation agreements as a specific harm to innovation, as these agreements prevented manufacturers from developing, for instance, privacy-centric modifications of the Android OS.

In contrast, the US case focused more narrowly on the general search services and search advertising markets under Section 2 of the Sherman Act. The US court's analysis was less concerned with the technical governance of the operating system and more focused on the effect of the exclusionary agreements at issue. While the EU General Court emphasized the loss of non-price competition — specifically privacy and innovation — the US court's initial focus remained closer to the traditional consumer welfare standard.

The most profound difference, however, concerns the remedies. The European Union has traditionally favored behavioral remedies, such as cease and desist orders, the imposition of fines and, most interventionist, the mandate of 'choice screens.' However, the perception of the limited effectiveness of these measures have led the EU to adopt *ex-ante* regulation via the DMA. The DMA seeks to prevent anti-competitive conduct by dominant online platforms before it even occurs by imposing obligations on so-called gatekeepers, thereby reducing the reliance on protracted *ex-*

post litigation. These obligations closely mirror behaviour that was found to be anticompetitive in past antitrust cases.

Notably in this context, however, is the remedy in the ECJ's *Android Auto* (C-233/23) ruling,[22] that moves beyond the classic cease-and-desist logic. The ECJ's 2025 judgment mandates an obligation for a dominant platform to develop software templates to allow interoperability for the benefit of rivals. While the wider implications are not clear yet, this marks a shift from a negative duty of abstaining from anticompetitive conduct seen in the 2022 mobile ecosystem case to a positive duty to accommodate third-party interoperability in the 2025 ruling.

The US District Court, similarly, has signaled a more aggressive and interventionist approach than the EU General Court in its Android ruling, and more along the lines of the ECJ's Android Auto judgement. The reasons for this are rooted in the respective legislative philosophies. The EU's market structure approach seeks to protect the competitive process and the autonomy of market participants as a social and political good. The US system, while historically more cautious of 'Type I' errors, i.e. over-regulation, has moved closer to the European view in light of the unique challenges posed by data-driven feedback loops. Ultimately, the *Google Android* and *US v. Google* decisions demonstrate that while the procedural mechanisms and remedies may differ, there is quite some consensus that the control of data flows through architectural and contractual defaults is a primary driver of market dominance and monopolization.

IV. The Android Judgements Implications for Data Law and Governance

The *Google Android* decision is an important milestone in the evolution of data law in general and digital competition law in particular. It confirms that data control and market power are closely linked within the digital economy. Moreover, it is a seminal case for data governance as it addresses the specific architectural and contractual mechanisms employed by dominant platforms to control data flows and user choice, which have the potential excluding competitors. At its core lies the question of how app pre-installations and other potentially exclusive practices by dominant platform providers may restrict manufacturer autonomy and consumer choice.

22 ECJ 25.2.2025 – case C-233/23, ECLI:EU:C:2025:110 – Android Auto.

Through its practices, Google essentially created a bi-directional lock-in effect where its supply-side advantages were fortified by users' default bias, i.e. the tendency of users to rarely deviate from pre-installed settings. By tying the Google Play Store to the mandatory pre-installation of the Google Search and Chrome applications, Google thus secured a permanent presence on users' mobile home screen. These defaults in turn function as means for the collection of granular user data, including, amongst others, search intent and real-time location. Through this effect, Google was able to collect even more and better user data, thereby cementing its market position and shielding its general search activities from competitors. This lock-in effect led to a data feedback loop. Dominant digital platforms in general and Google in particular benefit from a self-reinforcing cycle in which a larger user base generates more data, which is subsequently utilized to refine advertising targeting and service quality, thereby attracting a larger audience and so on.

The EU institutions' decisions directly address the practices that implement this cycle and as a logical consequence require the unbundling of Google's different services. These decisions make clear that control over data access is not merely a consequence of market dominance but a strategic instrument used to perpetuate and expand that dominance.

Furthermore, the decisions' condemnation of anti-fragmentation agreements is equally significant for questions of data governance. The anti-fragmentation agreements' effect was to, inter alia, prevent the development of privacy-friendly alternatives to the Android operating system. In a competitive market, a manufacturer might have developed a more privacy friendly Android fork designed to minimize data collection and provide users with more granular controls. However, the anti-fragmentation agreements rendered such innovation commercially unattractive by forcing mobile phone manufacturers to either accept them or forgo the benefits of the Android operating system in their entirety. This effectively prevented competition between different Android versions. By striking down these restrictions, the EU General Court fostered innovation in mobile operating system governance, permitting, for instance, the emergence of competitors who differentiate themselves through user-friendly data protection frameworks.

Furthermore, the business practices examined by the General Court demonstrate how the exploitation of consumer inertia can structurally undermine the validity of user consent under Art. 6 GDPR.[23] When a choice architecture is designed to lead users toward the path of least resistance, click-through consent can rarely be characterized as 'freely given.' This reflects a shift in the legal understanding of consumer harm. Historically, antitrust analysis focused rather on monetary metrics such as prices.

Finally, by treating data privacy as a crucial parameter of non-price competition, the ruling aligns with the logic observed in the *Bundeskartellamt* (BKartA) Facebook case.[24] It recognizes that a lower standard of data protection may constitute a reduction in product quality, thereby treating privacy as a quality differentiator. Thus, the *Google Android* decision acted as a predecessor and inspiration for some of the concepts now enshrined in the DMA.

V. Conclusion

The *Google Android* and *U.S. v. Google* decisions demonstrate a transatlantic consensus: the control of data flows through architectural defaults is a primary example of the exercise of market power in the digital world. While the EU is trying to tackle this issue primarily through *ex-ante* regulation via the DMA, and the U.S. explores more structural remedies, both jurisdictions now recognize that competition law must integrate questions of data governance to protect both in a digital economy: competition and privacy.

23 EDPB, ‚Guidelines 05/2020 on consent under Regulation 2016/679' (4.5.2020) <https://www.edpb.europa.eu/sites/default/files/files/file1/edpb_guidelines_202005_consent_en.pdf>.

24 Bundeskartellamt, ‚Decision of 6 February 2019', B6–22/16 – Facebook; ECJ 4.7.2023 – case C-252/21, ECLI:EU:C:2023:537 – Meta Platforms Inc and Others v Bundeskartellamt.

Chapter 10:
Opening Clauses

Artistic creativity and the GDPR: assessing the impact of Art. 85 GDPR in the European Union

Rafaela Nicolazzi Corrêa da Silva

ECJ 16.12.2008 – case 73/07, ECLI:EU:C:2008:727 – Tietosuojavaltuutettu v Satakunnan Markkinapörssi Oy and Satamedia Oy

I. Introduction

Artists are individuals who make it their vocation to create works that evoke meaning, emotion, or reflection through aesthetic or conceptual expression. Their practice often goes beyond any utilitarian or commercial function, engaging with inner emotions but also with social, political, or cultural realities, through countless forms — visual, audio, performative, or digital. In many cases, personal data and human stories serve as the raw material for such creations. Think about Sophie Calle's voyeuristic investigations (Suite Vénitienne, The Hotel) capture the tension between intimacy and surveillance; Gillian Wearing's confessional portraits invite voluntary exposure of private identities; and Ai Weiwei's memorial installations transform the personal data of others into collective reflection.

From left to right: Sophie Calle ‚Suite Vénitienne‘ (1985); Gillian Wearing ‚Signs that say what you want them to say and not Signs that say what someone else wants you to say‘ (1993); Ai Weiwei ‚Trace‘ (2014).

These works reveal that in art, data are not merely processed but embodied. The artist becomes both controller and subject of personal information, reframing personal data as a medium of expression rather than just a legal concept.

From the European Union (EU) data protection framework perspective, such practices fall within Art. 85 GDPR, which created exemptions for the usage of personal data for 'artistic or literary expression'. According to Art. 85 GDPR:

> Member States shall by law reconcile the right to the protection of personal data pursuant to this Regulation with the right to freedom of expression and information, including processing for journalistic purposes and the purposes of academic, artistic or literary expression.
>
> For processing carried out for journalistic purposes or the purpose of academic artistic or literary expression, Member States shall provide for exemptions or derogations from Chapter II (principles), Chapter III (rights of the data subject), Chapter IV (controller and processor), Chapter V (transfer of personal data to third countries or international organisations), Chapter VI (independent supervisory authorities), Chapter VII (cooperation and consistency) and Chapter IX (specific data processing situations) if they are necessary to reconcile the right to the protection of personal data with the freedom of expression and information.

> Each Member State shall notify to the Commission the provisions of its law which it has adopted pursuant to paragraph 2 and, without delay, any subsequent amendment law or amendment affecting them.

In other words, Art. 85 GDPR requires each EU Member State to find a fair balance between data protection and freedom of expression, especially when personal data are used for journalistic, academic, artistic, or literary purposes.[1] In practice, this means countries can create exceptions or relax certain GDPR rules—for example, limits on data subject rights or obligations for data controllers—when these rules would otherwise restrict free expression. Each Member State must then set out these exemptions in national law and inform the European Commission of any such measures[2]. The ambition was to ensure that protecting privacy does not silence journalism, research, or art, but the way this balance is achieved is left largely to national governments.

With this backdrop, this paper aims to examine whether Art. 85 GDPR functions as an effective legal safeguard for artistic creativity in practice, or whether it remains largely symbolic. Methodologically, the paper adopts a doctrinal analysis of the EU data protection framework, complemented by a qualitative review of national implementations across Member States and relevant archival material. Particular attention should be noted to the conditional nature of the Art. 85 GDPR exemption, which applies to artistic creation containing personal data only insofar as it is intended for publication—such as exhibition in an art gallery, inclusion in a library collection, or dissemination through a scientific journal. Conversely, data processing activities carried out by the artist, writer, or academic that are not aimed at public discussion—such as maintaining records of gallery visitors or other administrative datasets—fall outside the scope of the exemption.

In terms of structure, the discussion unfolds in three parts. The first section traces the legislative and historical background of Art. 85 GDPR, exploring how the artistic exemption emerged during the drafting process and identifying the institutional and political actors who shaped its final wording. The second section analyses the judicial and practical interpretation of the provision, assessing how the ECJ and national courts have applied the exemptions and whether artists have invoked them in practice. The final section evaluates the practical impact of Art. 85 GDPR on artistic creativity across the EU, considering whether the intended balance between

1 See also Rec. 153 GDPR.
2 Reventlow AJILU 2020, 31.

data protection and freedom of artistic expression has been achieved or merely theorized.

II. Legislative and historical background

The ambition to safeguard artistic creativity from the constraints of personal data regulation emerged well before the adoption of the GDPR. The roots of Art. 85 GDPR lie in Art. 9 DPD, which recognised that data protection must be balanced with freedom of expression, particularly for journalistic, artistic, and literary purposes. However, the Directive left broad discretion to Member States, resulting in fragmented and inconsistent safeguards for creative and media activities across Europe.[3]

Member States shall provide for exemptions or derogations from the provisions of this Chapter, Chapter IV and Chapter VI for the processing of personal data carried out solely for journalistic purposes or the purpose of artistic or literary expression only if they are necessary to reconcile the right to privacy with the rules governing freedom of expression.

More than two decades later, in 2012, when the European Commission proposed the GDPR, this tension re-emerged with greater intensity. Lawmakers, regulators, and civil-society groups clashed over how to preserve the right to free expression within a framework designed to strengthen individual control over personal data. Journalistic and academic associations warned that excessive uniformity could chill creative work, while privacy advocates—backed by several national delegations and data protection authorities—argued for narrow, case-by-case limitations. The legislative debates between 2012 and 2016 thus transformed an already delicate balance into a central political fault line of the GDPR.

During the negotiation of the GDPR between 2012 and 2016, most lobbying activities concerning the exemptions later codified in Art. 85 GDPR were driven by journalistic and academic organisations, rather than by artistic or cultural associations. The debate was dominated by the media sector, which feared that strict data protection obligations would restrict investigative journalism and press freedom. Groups such as the European Newspaper Publishers' Association (ENPA)[4], and the European Federation

3 Erdos ICLQ 2016, 139 (139 et seqq.). Also see Art. 13 CFR.

4 European Publishers Council, 'GDPR: Journalists and Publishers urge the Justice Council to maintain current safeguards for Press' (20.10.2014) <www.epceurope.eu/pos

of Journalists (EFJ)[5] submitted position papers and met with EU institutions to argue for broad derogations for journalistic work. Academic institutions[6] also mobilised to protect research and teaching activities from excessive compliance burdens: the European University Association (EUA) and the British Academy[7] published recommendations calling for explicit safeguards for academic expression and research data. In contrast, few artists or visual-arts organisations appear in the EU's transparency register or legislative archives as active participants in these negotiations.

Opposing proposals for broad and generous exemptions, several Member State delegations—most notably France—advocated for narrow, case-by-case limitations. This position was consistent with long-standing French constitutional and administrative traditions, in which the protection of privacy and human dignity is treated as a fundamental value requiring active oversight, even in contexts involving freedom of expression.[8] During the legislative negotiations, the French data-protection authority (CNIL) stressed that exemptions for journalistic, artistic, or literary expression should remain subject to proportionality and necessity assessments, in order to prevent abuses of personal data under the guise of expressive

---

t/gdpr-journalists-and-publishers-urge-the-justice-council-to-maintain-current-safeguards-for-press#:~:text=It%20therefore%20goes%20without%20saying,media%20freedom%20in%20the%20EU>.

5 ENPA, EMMA, EPC and EFJ, 'Statement on the need to preserve press freedom and journalism in the EU draft General Data Protection Regulation – Call by journalists and publishers across Europe to safeguard press freedom and journalism under Article 80' (2013) <https://www.bitsoffreedom.nl/static/lobby-tomie-documenten/EU/20140911-020-enpa-emma.pdf>.

6 British Society, ‚ASA, BSA, ESA and RGS-IBG statement on Anthropology, Sociology, Human Geography and the implementation of new data protection legislation in UK academic institutions' (2018) <https://www.britsoc.co.uk/media/24742/joint_asa_bsa_esa_rgs_statement_april2018.pdf>.

7 British Academy for Humanities and Social Sciences, ‚A British Academy and Economic & Social Research Council submission to the Department of Culture, Media and Sport (DCMS) call for views on the General Data Protection Regulation derogations' (2017) <https://www.thebritishacademy.ac.uk/documents/104/2017-05-10_DCMS_GDPR_Derogations_submission.pdf>.

8 On the constitutional centrality of privacy and human dignity in France, see e.g. Conseil constitutionnel, ‚Decision No 94–352 DC' (18.1.1995) <https://www.conseil-constitutionnel.fr/decision/1995/94352DC.htm>; see also Dreyer, Droit de la Vie Privée, 2nd edn. 2018, p. 45–52.

freedom.[9] Within the Council of the European Union, discussions on the GDPR reform repeatedly highlighted the risk that overly broad or open-ended derogations left to Member States could undermine the Regulation's overall coherence and consistent application, prompting calls for careful drafting of flexibility clauses.[10]

At the institutional level, Viviane Reding, then Vice-President of the European Commission and Commissioner for Justice, emphasised during parliamentary debates that freedom of expression could not operate as a 'blank cheque' exempting data processing from fundamental-rights safeguards, and that Member States would retain responsibility for striking the appropriate balance in their national legal orders.[11] Taken together, these interventions reflect a privacy-conscious and structurally cautious vision for the GDPR provision, in which expressive exemptions were accepted as necessary but deliberately constrained.

After many discussions and arguments, the final compromise was a text which allowed considerable discretion to Member States to determine how the right to freedom of expression should be reconciled with data protection. Rather than adopting a harmonised EU-wide rule, the Regulation simply required national legislatures to 'reconcile by law' the two rights and to define exemptions or derogations where necessary for journalistic, academic, artistic, or literary purposes. This decision reflected a political impasse during negotiations: while some legislators wanted a uniform framework, others insisted on preserving national constitutional traditions surrounding freedom of the press, academic research, and artistic expression. The result was a deliberately open clause that delegated the substance of protection to domestic law.

A closer look at how several Member States transposed Art. 85 GDPR reveals significant divergence in legislative technique and scope. In Germany, the freedom of expression exemption is implemented primarily through media and press law, notably the *Medienstaatsvertrag* and the press laws of

9 Commission nationale de l'informatique et des libertés (CNIL), ‚Position de la CNIL sur la réforme européenne de la protection des données' (12.9.2013), esp. sections on freedom of expression and journalistic exemptions.

10 Council of the European Union, 'Proposal for a Regulation on the Protection of Individuals with Regard to the Processing of Personal Data and on the Free Movement of such Data (General Data Protection Regulation) – Preparation of a General Approach', (11.6.2015) OJ EU Doc. 9369/15.

11 European Parliament/Committee on Civil Liberties, Justice and Home Affairs (LIBE), Hearing on the EU Data Protection Reform, statements by Viviane Reding, 2013; see also Reding SPEECH/12/26, European Commission 2012.

the Länder, rather than through a broad federal carve out in the BDSG. This framework limits the application of the GDPR to a defined set of provisions for journalistic processing while preserving structured oversight and safeguards. In France, the *Loi Informatique et Libertés* establishes enumerated derogations for processing carried out solely for journalistic or literary and artistic expression, linking the availability of those derogations to professional standards and a statutory balancing of rights, as reflected in the relevant provisions governing journalistic and artistic processing. The United Kingdom's Data Protection Act 2018, prior to Brexit, adopted a more expansive and detailed approach by introducing a dedicated 'special purposes' regime in Schedule 2, Part 5, which conditions exemptions for journalistic, academic, artistic, and literary processing on a reasonable belief that publication is in the public interest and that compliance with GDPR obligations would be incompatible with that purpose. Italy's Codice in materia di protezione dei dati personali, as amended by Legislative Decree No. 101/2018, expressly implements Art. 85 GDPR for journalistic and other expressive activities and subjects them to the long-standing standard of the essentiality of the information in relation to the public's right to be informed, as articulated in the applicable deontological rules. By contrast, Spain's *Ley Orgánica* 3/2018 does not establish a comprehensive 'special purposes' exemption equivalent to Art. 85 GDPR; instead, its most prominent provision in this area addresses the right of rectification in online contexts, with expressive activities continuing to be framed through constitutional guarantees of honour, privacy, and image.

Country	National Law / Provision	Scope of Exemption	Main Conditions / Limitations	Notable Features or Issues
France	Loi Informatique et Libertés (as amended in 2018), provisions on journalistic and literary/artistic expression (often cited in earlier versions as Art. 67; now structured within the section on journalism and artistic/literary expression)	Processing carried out solely for professional journalistic purposes or for literary and artistic expression	Enumerated derogations from GDPR apply only within the defined scope; remaining GDPR principles continue to apply where not expressly excluded; journalism is linked to professional standards/deontology	No blanket exemption; derogations are statutory and limited. CNIL remains competent for enforcement, but the law itself does not codify a general proportionality test beyond the structured derogations set out in statute
Italy	Codice in materia di protezione	Journalistic activity and other	Processing must pursue expressive	Long-standing "essentiality of

Country	National Law / Provision	Scope of Exemption	Main Conditions / Limitations	Notable Features or Issues
	dei dati personali (Legislative Decree 196/2003 as amended by Legislative Decree 101/2018), Arts. 136–139 and journalistic deontological rules	manifestations of thought (including artistic and literary expression) carried out pursuant to Article 85 GDPR	purposes; disclosure of personal data is permitted only where 'essential to the information' in relation to the public's right to be informed; safeguards are articulated in binding deontological rules	information" (essenzialità dell'informazione) standard; strong role for sector-specific deontological rules adopted under the supervision of the Garante
Germany	Media and press law, notably the Medienstaatsvertrag (§ 23) and the press laws of the Länder; not primarily the BDSG	Journalistic processing by media actors; artistic and literary expression addressed indirectly through constitutional law and sectoral regulation	GDPR applies only to a limited set of provisions specified in media law; DPAs retain competence but without prior content control; safeguards and accountability are maintained.	Decentralised implementation: Article 85 is realised mainly outside the BDSG. Practice varies by Land; reflects constitutional protection of freedom of expression and media (Art. 5 GG) rather than a single federal exemption.
United Kingdom	Data Protection Act 2018, Schedule 2, Part 5 ("special purposes")	Journalistic, academic, artistic, and literary purposes	Processing must be with a view to publication and based on a reasonable belief that publication is in the public interest; exemptions apply where GDPR compliance would be incompatible; regard must be had to relevant ethical codes	One of the most detailed and explicit Article 85 implementations; combines statutory tests with ethical-code reference rather than categorical immunity
Spain	Ley Orgánica 3/2018 (LOPDGDD), Art. 85 (online rectification) and constitutional framework	No comprehensive "special purposes" exemption equivalent to Article 85 GDPR	Expressive activities remain framed primarily through constitutional rights (honour, privacy, image) and sectoral rules; Art. 85 LOPDGDD concerns rectification in	Spain did not adopt a standalone Article 85-style exemption clause for journalism/art comparable to the UK or Italy; emphasis re-

Country	National Law / Provision	Scope of Exemption	Main Conditions / Limitations	Notable Features or Issues
			online media, not a general exemption	mains on constitutional balancing and post-publication remedies

Together, these five European countries illustrate how the GDPR's aspiration for coherence coexists with pronounced national variation—leaving artists, journalists, and cultural institutions to navigate a fragmented landscape of expressive freedoms and compliance obligations across the Union.[12]

In sum, the legislative and historical analysis of Art. 85 GDPR demonstrates that the tension between data protection and freedom of expression not only predates the Regulation but also remained unresolved during its adoption. Shaped by opposing political and institutional forces—some pressing for strong expressive exemptions, others for strict privacy safeguards—the final compromise delegated the reconciliation of these rights to Member States. This created a fragmented normative landscape rather than the harmonised 'single market'. Turning this analysis into a practical case: an artwork deemed lawful under one national implementation of Art. 85 GDPR may infringe privacy standards in another. A photographic installation, for example, might be exhibited in London under the United Kingdom's 'special purposes' regime for artistic expression, which allows exemptions where publication is reasonably believed to be in the public interest. The same work could be subject to stricter post-hoc scrutiny in Paris under the enumerated derogations of French data protection law, to constitutional balancing between artistic freedom and personality rights in Berlin, or to Italy's distinctive requirement that the disclosure of personal data be strictly essential to the public's right to be informed.

III. Judicial cases

Following the legislative and historical examination of Art. 85 GDPR, it becomes essential to analyse how the ECJ has interpreted the provision's underlying balance between data protection and freedom of expression,

12 Erdos, European Data Protection Regulation, Journalism, and Traditional Publishers: Balancing on a Tightrope?, 2019.

and to what extent artists or other creative actors have relied on this judicial framework to defend their art creations.

While the ECJ has not yet decided a case explicitly centred on artistic expression after the enactment of the Art. 85 GDPR, its broader jurisprudence on freedom of expression and data processing provides interpretative guidance.[13] Thus the analysis of three ECJ cases for comparison is imperative to assess the ECJ's balancing methodology—developed in journalistic and informational contexts—to artistic expression, even in the absence of explicit 'art cases'.

One of the earliest and most influential judgments, *Tietosuojavaltuutettu v. Satakunnan Markkinapörssi Oy and Satamedia Oy*[14] (2008), concerned the scope of the 'journalistic purpose' exemption under the DPD. In this case, the ECJ was asked to determine whether publishing individuals' income and tax data in a newspaper could qualify as processing 'for journalistic purposes' under Art. 9 DPD. The Court ruled that the journalistic exemption should be interpreted broadly, covering all activities whose object is to disclose information, opinions, or ideas to the public, irrespective of the medium or profit motive. The decisive factor, it held, is the purpose of disclosure to the public of information, opinions or ideas rather than the professional status of the actor. This reasoning, though developed in the journalistic context, can be analogised to artistic creation, where artworks similarly aim to communicate ideas or provoke reflection in the public sphere.

Another relevant case for this study is in *GC and Others v. CNIL*[15] (2019), where the ECJ addressed the conflict between data subjects' 'right to be forgotten' and the public's right to information. The case concerned requests to remove search engine results linking to sensitive personal data, such as religious beliefs or criminal proceedings. The Court held that while data subjects enjoy enhanced protection for special-category data, the right to erasure is not absolute and must be balanced against the public's legitimate interest in access to information. National authorities and courts, it ruled, must conduct a contextual and proportionality based assessment, weighing the sensitivity of the data, the public role of the person concerned, and the

13 GDPRhub, 'Article 85 GDPR' (15.12.2025) <https://gdprhub.eu/index.php?title=Article_85_GDPR>.

14 ECJ 16.12.2008 – case C-73/07, ECLI:EU:C:2008:727 – Tietosuojavaltuutettu v. Satakunnan Markkinapörssi Oy and Satamedia Oy.

15 ECJ 24.9.2019 – case C-136/17, ECLI:EU:C:2019:773 – GC and Others v Commission nationale de l'informatique et des libertés (CNIL).

contribution of disclosure to public debate. For the arts, arguably, this proportional logic is directly relevant: an artist who uses personal narratives or identifiable imagery could potentially rely on the expressive value and cultural significance of the work as justification for processing, provided the representation serves a broader social, historical, or critical function.

Last but not least, the landmark *Google Spain v. Costeja case*[16] (2014). In Google Spain, the Court articulated a structured balancing test needed between the fundamental rights to privacy and data protection (Art. 7 and 8 CFR) and the public's interest in access to information (Art. 11 CFR). Although the case concerned journalistic content indexed by a search engine, the Court made clear that freedom of expression is not absolute and must be weighed against the nature of the information, its sensitivity, its role in public debate, and the data subject's role in public life. Crucially, the Court rejected categorical outcomes, insisting on contextual, case-by-case assessment. This methodology—especially the emphasis on proportionality, relevance over time, and public interest—provides a helpful balancing logic to artistic expression under Art. 85 GDPR.

Taken together, *Satakunnan, GC and Others v. CNIL and Google Spain* articulate a coherent ECJ methodology for reconciling freedom of expression with data protection that, while developed in journalistic and informational contexts, is highly instructive for artistic expression by analogy. First, *Satakunnan* establishes a functional and purpose-based conception of expression, rejecting formal distinctions based on medium, profit motive, or professional status and instead focusing on whether the processing aims at the public disclosure of information, opinions, or ideas. Second, *Google Spain* confirms that expressive interests do not operate categorically, but must be balanced against privacy and data protection rights through a context sensitive and proportional assessment, attentive to the nature and sensitivity of the data, the role of the data subject in public life, and the contribution of the disclosure to public debate. Finally, *GC v. CNIL* refines this balancing logic by demonstrating that even where personal data fall within special categories, heightened protection does not entail automatic exclusion; rather, authorities must weigh competing rights in light of the specific expressive and societal value of the processing. Arguably and in the absence of court decisions directly related to artists, it may suggest that artistic

16 ECJ 13.5.2014 – case C-131/12. ECLI:EU:C:2014:317 – Google Spain SL and Google Inc. v. Agencia Española de Protección de Datos (AEPD) and Mario Costeja González.

creativity involving personal data should neither be presumed lawful nor categorically restricted, but assessed through a graduated proportionality analysis that considers the communicative purpose of the work, its cultural or critical contribution, the degree of interference with individual rights, and the availability of less intrusive means—thereby offering a principled framework for operationalising Art. 85 GDPR in the artistic domain despite the absence of explicit 'art cases' before the Court.

IV. Practical Observations on Artistic Creativity

Having examined the legislative history of Art. 85 GDPR and its interpretation by the ECJ, it is necessary to assess whether the derogations it provides meaningfully enable artistic freedom in practice. Given the absence of systematic empirical data on artists' legal practices, the following observations draw on policy reports, sectoral guidance, and documented artistic projects.

A notable first observation is the limited visibility of artists and artistic associations in the public debate surrounding the GDPR, both during its drafting and in its early years of application. Unlike journalistic organisations, academic bodies, and data protection authorities—whose positions are well documented in consultation responses, policy papers, and legislative records—there is little evidence of sustained, collective engagement by artists' organisations with the Regulation or with Art. 85 GDPR in particular. Scholarly and policy analyses of the GDPR's negotiation history similarly identify press, research, and civil liberties actors as the dominant contributors, with the cultural and artistic sectors largely absent from EU-level deliberations.[17]

Second: this limited engagement is best explained not as indifference, but as a structural feature of artistic labour markets. Most artists in Europe operate as self-employed individuals or within very small, project-based collectives, rather than through large institutions with legal or administra-

17 UNESCO's culture report from 2023 notes that artists often lack leverage to influence policy compared to corporate players, linking sector structure to weaker influence. UNESCO, ‚Empowering Creativity: Implementing the Unesco 1980 Recommendation Concerning the Status of the Artist' (2023) <https://unesdoc.unesco.org/ark:/48223/pf0000387452>.

tive capacity.[18] Unlike journalists—often represented by unions, publishers' associations, or press councils—or researchers embedded in universities and research organisations, artists typically lack stable intermediary bodies capable of coordinating legal expertise and sustained participation in EU policymaking processes. The marginal presence of artistic voices in debates on Art. 85 GDPR therefore reflects structural under representation, rather than a lack of normative stake in data-protection law.

When artists do appear in GDPR-related discussions, it is most often indirectly, through practical guidance and compliance-oriented materials aimed at galleries, museums, or small cultural organisations, rather than through rights-based claims advanced by artists themselves. It is usually focused on risk management, consent practices, and documentation obligations.[19] This framing positions the Regulation primarily as a compliance challenge rather than as a potential safeguard for artistic expression under Art. 85 GDPR.

Third: the limited available empirical evidence further suggests that the GDPR is commonly experienced by practitioners—particularly in photography, visual arts, and data-driven artistic practices—as a source of legal uncertainty that influences creative choices ex ante. Artists and cultural professionals report concerns about street photography, the reuse of archival images, the withdrawal of consent by identifiable subjects, and the handling of biometric or behavioural data.[20] In the context of EU-funded data-art and research-art collaborations, project documentation and evaluative reports indicate that artistic concepts involving personal data are sometimes adapted to mitigate perceived GDPR risks.[21]

The examination of practical impacts suggests that the promise of Art. 85 GDPR for the arts remains largely under-operationalised. Artists and artistic associations have had limited visibility in the legislative and post-legislative debates surrounding the GDPR, a pattern that reflects their structural distance from EU-level policymaking rather than a lack of interest in data protection issues. The available evidence indicates that the Regulation is often experienced less as a rights-enabling instrument and more as a source

18 Ginsburgh/Throsby Handbook of the Economics of Art and Culture/Menger, 2006, p. 765 et seqq.

19 Spero, 'A secretive art world grapples with data protection legislation'. (FT, 21.3.2018) <https://www.ft.com/content/f8fba768-2136-11e8-a895-1ba1f72c2c11>.

20 Levine/Philpot/Nightingale/Kordoni SAP 2024, 109.

21 Oliver/Hamilton/Ingram, Best Practices for Working Creatively with Personal Data, 2022.

of legal uncertainty or compliance pressure, particularly in image-based and data-intensive artistic practices.[22] The recommendation is risk-avoidant strategies—such as anonymisation, self-limitation of subject matter, blurring techniques—rather than invoking Art. 85 GDPR as a protective legal basis.[23] As an illustrative comment, Duhnkrack argues that bearing in mind the nature of street photography, the conditions for consent are fundamentally contradicting an 'authentic reflection of reality' – as to make art, they (usually) do not ask for permission.[24]

At the same time, artistic engagement with the GDPR is not exclusively defensive or distant. A growing body of data-art and critical media art – such as Julia Janssen and Adam Harvey – explicitly incorporates data protection rights (such as access, erasure, or transparency) into artistic practice, using the Regulation as both material and method to expose contemporary regimes. In such works, GDPR rights function as performative or critical tools that invite audience participation and reflection.

From left to right: Julia Janssen's 'book' (2024), which collects hundreds of privacy-policy texts challenges audiences to confront consent choices and data-collection practices; Adam Harvey in MegaPixels (2017) explores facial-recognition technologies through art, raising awareness of large training datasets and developing anonymisation tools. He invited participants to match their faces against a dataset, exposing how biometric systems identify individual.

Nevertheless, even in these cases, the Regulation operates primarily as a thematic and conceptual resource, rather than as a source of concrete legal

22 Oliver/Hamilton/Ingram, Best Practices for Working Creatively with Personal Data, 2022.

23 Oliver/Hamilton/Ingram, Best Practices for Working Creatively with Personal Data, 2022.

24 Duhnkrack Journal of Intellectual Property Law & Practice 15(1), 66.

certainty for personal data usage. Taken together, the available evidence suggests that Art. 85 GDPR's promise for artistic expression remains largely symbolic and under-operationalised: while it formally recognises artistic creativity as deserving protection, it offers limited guidance, visibility, or practical reassurance to artists navigating data protection law in everyday practice.

V. Conclusion

This paper set out to examine whether the exemptions provided under Art. 85 GDPR for journalistic, academic, artistic, and literary expression have had a tangible impact on artistic creativity within the European Union. The analysis of the provision's legislative history points that the tension between data protection and artistic expression long predates the GDPR and remained unresolved at the moment of its adoption. Art. 85 GDPR emerged as a political compromise between actors advocating for robust expressive exemptions and those insisting on strong and enforceable privacy safeguards. By delegating the reconciliation of these competing rights to Member States, the Regulation deliberately adopted an open-textured clause that recognises artistic expression in principle while leaving its concrete protection to national legal frameworks, institutional traditions, and regulatory cultures.

The comparative analysis of national implementations demonstrates that this delegation has resulted in a fragmented rather than harmonised legal landscape. Across the five jurisdictions examined—Germany, France, Italy, Spain, and the United Kingdom—, artistic processing of personal data is subject to markedly different conditions, variously framed in terms of necessity, proportionality, essentiality of information, public interest, or constitutional concepts such as dignity and honour. In some systems, artistic uses of personal data are approached cautiously and embedded in structured oversight mechanisms; in others, they are afforded comparatively broader space, at least at the level of statutory design. The practical consequence is legal variability: an artwork that may be lawfully exhibited in one Member State can become legally uncertain, or even contestable, in another—particularly in fields such as photography, audiovisual art, and data-driven installations involving identifiable individuals.

Although the Court of Justice of the European Union has not yet adjudicated a case explicitly centred on artistic expression under Art. 85

GDPR, its jurisprudence in cases such as *Tietosuojavaltuutettu v. Satakunnan Markkinapörssi Oy and Satamedia Oy*, *Google Spain*, and *GC and Others v. CNIL* provides important interpretative guidance. Across these decisions, the Court has consistently endorsed a contextual and proportional balancing of fundamental rights, rejecting both absolute privacy claims and categorical expressive exemptions. Privacy is treated as a non-absolute right, and expressive interests are recognised where processing contributes to public discourse, collective memory, or broader societal reflection. Nevertheless, in the absence of explicit judicial engagement with artistic expression, this remains a doctrinal extrapolation rather than a settled judicial guarantee.

At the same time, artistic engagement with the GDPR is not exclusively defensive. A growing body of data-driven and critical art appropriates data-protection rights—such as access, transparency, or erasure—as artistic material, using them to expose and interrogate contemporary data practices. These works demonstrate that the Regulation can function as a conceptual resource and object of critique. Yet even in these instances, the GDPR operates primarily as a thematic or methodological device rather than as a stable legal guarantee of artistic autonomy.

Taken together, the findings of this paper support the conclusion that Art. 85 GDPR has had, to date, only a modest and indirect impact on artistic creativity in the European Union. While it symbolically affirms artistic expression as deserving of protection and provides doctrinal tools that could, in principle, shield certain creative uses of personal data, it has not been operationalised in a manner that offers harmonized, predictable, or accessible safeguards for artists in practice. If the European Union seeks to ensure that data protection does not unduly chill artistic creativity, further steps are warranted. These may include:

- EU-level interpretative guidance on the application of Art. 85 GDPR to artistic practices;
- development of sector-specific codes of conduct in collaboration with artists and cultural institutions;
- and more explicit engagement by authorities with the realities of contemporary artistic production.

Future research should complement doctrinal analysis with empirical inquiry—through interviews, case studies, and surveys—to assess more systematically how artists navigate data-protection law in their daily work and whether Art. 85 GDPR can evolve from a largely declaratory safeguard into an effective instrument for protecting artistic freedom in Europe's data-protection era.

Art. 88 GDPR: National discretion or European constraint?

Lorenz Fander

ECJ 30.3.2023 – case C-34/21, ECLI:EU:C:2023:270 – Hauptpersonalrat der Lehrerinnen und Lehrer

ECJ 19.12.2024 – case C-65/23, ECLI:EU:C:2024:1051 – K-GmbH

I. Case summaries

The scope of regulatory powers in the field of employee data protection has been the subject of sustained debate for years. Especially in Germany the protection of employees' personal data has long been recognised as a regulatory challenge requiring distinct and autonomous solutions. This is why Germany sought to preserve national regulatory discretion during the legislative process that led to the adoption of the GDPR.[1] Against this background, it is hardly surprising that the two cases examined here were adjudicated before German courts.

1. C-34/21 – Hauptpersonalrat der Lehrerinnen und Lehrer

The first case dates back to the coronavirus pandemic. The *Minister of Education and Cultural Affairs of the State of Hessen* issued decrees regulating the framework conditions for school instruction during the pandemic. In particular, students were given the opportunity to participate in classes via video conferencing. Before participating in the video conference, students or their parents had to consent to the processing of their data. The decree did not provide for the consent of teachers to be obtained as well. The teachers' staff council therefore initiated legal proceedings at the Administrative Court of Wiesbaden. *The Minister of Education*, for his part, argued that the processing of personal data in the context of livestreamed

1 See Forgó/Helfrich/Schneider Betrieblicher Datenschutz/Hanloser, 3. Aufl. 2019, S. 411 et. seqq.

instruction via video conference was authorised under national legislation and could therefore be carried out without the consent of the teachers concerned. The referring court expressed doubts as to whether § 23(1) of the Hessian Data Protection and Freedom of Information Act (HDSIG) and § 86(4) of the Hessian Civil Service Act (HBG) — the provisions upon which the Minister had relied on — were compatible with European Union law. In particular, the court questioned whether these provisions could genuinely be regarded as 'more specific rules' within the meaning of Art. 88(1) of the General Data Protection Regulation, given that both rely on the criterion of necessity for data processing and thus effectively mirror the standard laid down in Art. 6(1)(b) GDPR.

2. C-65/23 – K-GmbH

In the second decision, the focus shifted to the rights of the collective parties. In the course of introducing the cloud-based personnel information management system 'Workday', the employer transferred employee data to a server in the United States. To this end, the employer and the works council concluded a works agreement permitting the upload of specified categories of employee data, including personnel numbers, names, telephone numbers and place of work, to the new software. An employee subsequently sought erasure of the data and compensation pursuant to Art. 82 GDPR. This raised questions about the regulatory powers of collective parties in the field of employee data protection and the extent to which courts can review their agreements.

The two cases are closely linked, as they jointly allowed the ECJ to provide a comprehensive interpretation of the regulatory powers granted under Art. 88(1) GDPR.

II. Key legal findings

The *Hauptpersonalrat* case provided the ECJ with its first opportunity to clarify the limits and scope of the regulatory powers granted under Art. 88 GDPR. The Court first addressed the material scope of the provision, ruling that the term 'employee' in its ordinary meaning refers to a person who performs work within the context of a subordinate relationship with an employer and is therefore under the employer's control. Similarly, the Court decided that the essential feature of an 'employment relationship' is that, for a certain period of time, a person performs services for and under the direction of another person in return for remuneration. Consequently, the ECJ ruled that persons employed in the public sector also qualify as 'employees' for the purposes of Art. 88 GDPR.

In addition to clarifying the scope, the decision provided guidance on the requirements for 'more specific rules' within the meaning of Art. 88(1) GDPR. The Court identified three conditions that such rules must meet:

- they must have normative content specific to the area regulated, distinct from the general rules of the GDPR;
- they must aim to protect employees' rights and freedoms in relation to the processing of personal data in the employment context;
- they must include appropriate and specific measures to safeguard the data subjects' human dignity, legitimate interests, and fundamental rights in accordance with Art. 88(2) GDPR.[2]

Building on that framework, the ECJ in the *K-GmbH* case further held that Art. 88(1) and (2) GDPR must be interpreted as meaning that, even when Member States rely on this provision to introduce such rules into their national legal systems - whether by law or through collective agreements - the requirements arising from other provisions, namely Art. 5, 6(1), and 9(1) and (2) GDPR, must also be satisfied. The Court had already signalled this approach in *Hauptpersonalrat*, noting that Chapters II and III of the GDPR contain the fundamental principles to be respected in any processing of personal data.[3]

Furthermore, the ECJ decided that these principles are likewise applicable to collective parties. Although the Court confirmed that collective parties are entitled to a margin of discretion comparable to that afforded to Member States, it emphasised that this does not prevent the national court from conducting a full judicial review of the rules in question.

III. Systematic context and legal classification

The ruling exemplifies the tensions that arise between national legal systems and EU law when areas of law are increasingly, but not fully, harmonised. According to Rec. 10 GDPR, the regulation seeks to establish

2 See Kätscher ZD 2025, 63 (64 et. seqq.).
3 See also Warter AuR 2025, 294 (295).

a uniform and high level of data protection across the European Union. However, this objective is not pursued without limitation: the GDPR contains numerous opening clauses that permit national deviations, resulting in a degree of regulatory diversity. The discretion afforded by these clauses has frequently been the subject of legal debate.

Before the ECJ's rulings, three main questions were at the centre of the debate regarding Art. 88 GDPR. First, there was uncertainty regarding the material and personal scope of Art. 88 GDPR, particularly how the term 'employee' should be understood. Second, it was disputed whether Member States and collective parties may legitimately deviate from the level of protection established by the GDPR. The discussion arose specifically in the context of interpreting the notion of 'more specific rules'.[4] This was hardly surprising, as the term was deliberately framed in neutral language, reflecting the difficulty of reaching a political compromise.[5] Third, there was disagreement over the extent to which collective parties enjoy a margin of discretion in exercising their regulatory powers that is subject only to limited judicial review. All these factors contributed to substantial uncertainty in the ongoing efforts to establish a national law on employee data protection in Germany. The ECJ's pronouncements were therefore awaited with particular interest. In its rulings, the Court addressed nearly all of the contentious issues, providing clear and detailed guidance on some points while offering only more limited or implicit clarification on others. In doing so, it outlined a narrow but viable path for national regulation in the field of employee data protection.

IV. Author's analysis and commentary

While some of the ECJ's statements are persuasive, the judgement remains vague in other respects. Nonetheless, it is clear that the Court interprets Art. 88(1) GDPR in a restrictive manner.

---

4 Detailed description in Meinecke, Data Protection and Data Science, 2022, p. 84 et seqq.; Morasch, Datenverarbeitung im Beschäftigungskontext, 2019, p. 60 et seqq.; Wünschelbaum, Kollektivautonomer Datenschutz, 2022, p. 44 et seqq.

5 Morasch, Datenverarbeitung im Beschäftigungskontext, 2019, p. 100.

1. Scope of application: The concept of 'employee' under Art. 88 GDPR

Firstly, the Court is correct in identifying the existence of a relationship of subordination as the decisive characteristic of the concept of 'employee'. The external control associated with subordination increases the risk of undermining the protections established under the GDPR. Accordingly, the Court correctly concluded that persons employed in the public sector fall within the definition of 'employee' under Art. 88 GDPR. The ECJ's attempt to limit the scope of Art. 88 GDPR by reference to the remunerated nature of the activity is less persuasive. While remuneration may be an indication of subordination, it is not a necessary condition for such a relationship to exist. Unpaid activity can have particular personal or even economic significance, which establishes a subordinate relationship. The employment relationship is distinguished from other forms of dependency by the degree of data exposure involved. Therefore, the scope of application should be determined by the interplay between subordination and data exposure, rather than by remuneration alone.

2. Defining 'more specific rules'

By clarifying that rules adopted on the basis of Art. 88 GDPR must have normative content distinct from the general provisions of the GDPR, the ECJ invokes the prohibition on mere repetition embedded in the *Effet-Utile*-principle.[6] However, the ECJ fails to seize the opportunity to provide clear guidance on the distinction between permissible reiterations with regard to Rec. 8 GDPR and forms of repetition that are impermissible.[7] This would have been valuable in providing legal certainty for national legislation enacted under Art. 88 GDPR. Nonetheless, the ECJ has clarified that any reiteration must always serve a subordinate function and must therefore follow from the decision to adopt 'more specific rules'.

---

6 See ECJ 10.10.1973 – case C-34/73, ECLI:EU:C:1973:101 para. 10 – Fratelli Variola S.p.A. v Amministrazione italiana delle Finanze. The fact that the ECJ not only rejected mere reiterations but also references to Art. 5 and 6 GDPR may have come as a surprise to the Finnish legislature, which had planned to include a reference to the GDPR provisions on data processing based on consent in the national Employee Data Act, see Government proposal to Parliament to amend Section 4 of the Act on Protection of Privacy in Working Life (unofficial translation), GP 35/2022.

7 See Meinecke NZA 2023, 492 (492).

Particularly noteworthy are the ECJ's statements regarding the binding nature of the GDPR's level of protection. When the Court holds that Chapters II and III – particularly Art. 5, 6, and 9 GDPR – contain requirements that must always be met,[8] it presumably means that a national provision adopted under Art. 88(1) GDPR must first be assessed in the abstract against the requirements of Chapters II and III, before it can be relied upon as the sole standard for specific data processing activities. Therefore, a national provision cannot reduce the level of protection afforded to the rights and freedoms of natural persons. To establish a permissible regulatory framework, the legislature may adopt measures that further specify the provisions of the GDPR. But as the interpretation of the GDPR falls within the remit of the ECJ rather than the Member States, legal certainty can only be partially secured through the adoption of 'more specific rules'. However, this does not mean that the Member States have no discretion at all, as the ECJ clarified.[9] In creating 'more specific rules', the legislature must balance conflicting interests, as required by Art. 6(1) GDPR. When balancing these conflicting interests, the national legislature enjoys a certain margin of discretion, as such assessments inevitably require weighing factors that cannot be quantified objectively.[10] Just as this task is typically assigned to national courts,[11] Member States must likewise be able to exercise it as an expression of the discretion recognised by the ECJ.[12] The limit of this discretion is set by Art. 6 GDPR. This competence also extends to collective parties, provided that it is always ensured that any compromise is not made solely on the basis of economic or practical considerations.[13] The Court has expressly accepted that such specifications can result in a lack of harmonisation.[14] Accordingly, some regulatory discretion remains, but it is clear that Art. 88

8 ECJ 19.12.2024 – case C-65/23, ECLI:EU:C:2024:1051 para. 45 et. seqq. – K-GmbH; ECJ 30.3.2023 – case C-34/21, ECLI:EU:C:2023:270 para. 68 et. seqq. – Hauptpersonalrat der Lehrerinnen und Lehrer.

9 ECJ 19.12.2024 – case C-65/23, ECLI:EU:C:2024:1051 para. 40 – K-GmbH.

10 The German Federal Court of Justice (BGH) has reached a similar conclusion with regard to Codes of Conduct under Art. 40 GDPR, BGH 18.12.2025 – I ZR 97/25, WM 2026, 113 mn. 50.

11 See ECJ 9.1.2025 – case C-394/23, ECLI:EU:C:2025:2 para. 51 –Mousse; ECJ 12.9.2024 – case C-17/22, ECLI:EU:C:2024:738 para. 55 – HTB Neunte Immobilien Portfolio; ECJ 4.7.2023 – case C-252/21, ECLI:EU:C:2023;537, para. 96 – Meta Platforms.

12 Taeger/Gabel DSGVO – BDSG – TDDDG/Zöll, 5. Aufl. 2026, Art. 88 DS-GVO mn. 21.

13 See ECJ 19.12.2024 – case C-65/23, ECLI:EU:C:2024:1051 para. 57 – K-GmbH.

14 ECJ 19.12.2024 – case C-65/23, ECLI:EU:C:2024:1051 para. 40 – K-GmbH.

GDPR is not intended to alter the balancing of interests already established by the GDPR in the employment context. Rather, the provision is intended to enable the adoption of legislation that clarifies the implications of the GDPR's general principles in the context of employment.

According to the prevailing view in Germany, stricter measures are permissible in light of the ECJ's judgments.[15] While this might be true, the scope for permissible and appropriate stricter measures will inevitably be limited. Prohibiting necessary data processing is not only questionable,[16] but may also infringe fundamental rights, in particular the freedom to conduct a business under Art. 16 CFR and the right to property under Art. 17 CFR.

3. Judicial review of collective agreements

The ECJ held that the margin of discretion granted to the parties to a collective agreement does not prevent the courts from conducting a full judicial review.[17] In doing so, the Court seeks to ensure that the high protection standards of the GDPR are not undermined by extraneous considerations. Accordingly, national courts are empowered to assess compliance with the requirements of Art. 5, 6, and 9 GDPR. However, the ECJ did not hold that the courts must replace the parties' balancing of interests with their own. It is sufficient to verify that the provisions of Chapters II and III GDPR are respected. How national courts will exercise this leeway in the future remains to be seen. In the *K-GmbH* case, the Federal Labour Court (BAG) no longer had to address this issue following the conclusion of the preliminary ruling proceedings, as the plaintiff chose to base his claims solely on data processing not covered by the collective agreement.[18]

15 Janko/Krüger/Bretz NZA 2025, 154 (157); Kätscher ZD 2025, 63 (64); Kort EuZA 2025, 303 (309); Kuß/Sura EuZW 2025, 290 (291); Linke ZIP 2025, 2424 (2425); Mangold EuZA 2025, 261 (273); Pionteck AuR 2025, 292 (293 et. seq.); Schild DuD 2025, 83 (85); Trabert BB 2025, 1780 (1781); Warter AuR 2025, 294 (296); Wedde CuA 2024, 22 (23); contrary view: Kaufmann FD-ArbR 2025, 803105; Monreal ZD 2025, 208 (209); Monreal DB 2025, 940 (943); Monreal RDV 2025, 301 (305).

16 Thüsing DB 2025, 2830 (2833).

17 ECJ 19.12.2024 – case C-65/23, ECLI:EU:C:2024:1051 para. 60 – K-GmbH.

18 BAG 8.5.2025 – 8 AZR 209/21, NJW 2025, 3250 mn. 13.

V. Recommended further reading

AG Sánchez-Bordona 22.9.2022 – case C-34/21, ECLI:EU:C:2022:710 – Hauptpersonalrat der Lehrerinnen und Lehrer.

ECJ 22.6.2021 – case C-439/19, ECLI:EU:C:2021:504 – Latvijas Republikas Saeima (Penalty points).

BGH 18.12.2025 – I ZR 97/25, WM 2026, 113.

BAG 22.9.2022– 8 AZR 209/21(A), NZA 2023, 363.

VG Wiesbaden 21.12.2020 – 23 K 1360/20.WI.PV, ZD 2021, 393.

Forgó/Helfrich/Schneider Betrieblicher Datenschutz/Hanloser, 3. Aufl. 2019, p. 407 et. seqq.

Overview

Case	Author(s)
Judgements	
ECJ 6.11.2003 – case C-101/01, ECLI:EU:C:2003:596 – Lindqvist	Marek Steffen Jansen
ECJ 16.12.2008 – case 73/07, ECLI:EU:C:2008:727 – Tietosuojavaltuutettu v Satakunnan Markkinapörssi Oy and Satamedia Oy	Rafaela Nicolazzi Corrêa da Silva
ECJ 13.5.2014 – case C-131/12, ECLI:EU:C:2014:317 – Google Spain	Desara Dushi
ECJ 8.4.2014 – Joined Cases C 293/12 and C 594/12, ECLI:EU:C:2014:238 – Digital Rights Ireland Ltd v Minister for Communications, Marine and Natural Resources and Others and Kärntner Landesregierung and Others	Robert Spano/Miles Lynn
ECJ 13.5.2014 – case C-131/12, ECLI:EU:C:2014:317 – Google Spain SL and Google Inc. v Agencia Española de Protección de Datos (AEPD) and Mario Costeja González	Katelyn Ringrose
ECJ 6.12.2016 – case C-582/14, ECLI:EU:C:2016:779 – Patrick Breyer v Bundesrepublik Deutschland	Per Meyerdierks
ECJ 5.6.2018 – case C-210/16, ECLI:EU:C:2018:388 – Wirtschaftsakademie; ECJ 10.7.2018 – case C-25/17, ECLI:EU:C:2018:551 – Jehovan todistajat; ECJ 29.7.2019 – case C-40/17, ECLI:EU:C:2019:629 – FashionID	Indra Spiecker gen. Döhmann/ Loïc Reissner
ECJ 24.9.2019 – case C-507/17, ECLI:EU:C:2019:772 – Google LLC, successor in law to Google Inc. v Commission nationale de l'informatique et des libertés (CNIL)	Axel Spies
ECJ 16.7.2020 – case C-311/18, ECLI EU:C:2020:559 – Data Protection Commissioner v Facebook Ireland Limited and Maximillian Schrems; GC 3.9.2025 – case T-553/23, ECLI:EU:T:2025:831 – Philippe Latombe v European Commission	Helen Dixon
ECJ 15.6.2021 – case C-645/19, ECLI:EU:C:2021:483 – Facebook Ireland Ltd and Others v Gegevensbeschermingsautoriteit	Henry Ogunrinde
ECJ 1.8.2022 – case C-184/20, ECLI:EU:C:2022:601 – OT v Vyriausioji tarnybinės etikos komisija	Christiane Wendehorst

Case	Author(s)
ECJ 20.10.2022 – case C-77/21, ECLI:EU:C:2022:805 – Digi Távközlési és Szolgáltató Kft. v Nemzeti Adatvédelmi és Információszabadság Hatóság	María González Gordon/Antonio Negueruela Maldonado
ECJ 12.1.2023 – case C-154/21, ECLI:EU:C:2023:3 – RW v Österreichische Post AG	Daniel Pauly
ECJ 9.2.2023 – case C-453/21, ECLI:EU:C:2023:79 – X-FAB Dresden GmbH & Co. KG v FC	Andreas Jaspers
ECJ 30.3.2023 – case C-34/21, ECLI:EU:C:2023:270 – Hauptpersonalrat der Lehrerinnen und Lehrer; ECJ 19.12.2024 – case C-65/23, ECLI:EU:C:2024:1051 – K-GmbH	Lorenz Fander
ECJ 4.5.2023 – case C-60/22, ECLI:EU:C:2023:373 – UZ v Federal Republic of Germany	Ulrich Baumgartner
ECJ 4.5.2023 – case C-60/22, ECLI:EU:C:2023:373 – UZ v Bundesrepublik Deutschland	Dieter Kugelmann
ECJ 4.5.2023 – case C 300/21, ECLI:EU:C:2023:370 – UI v Österreichische Post AG	Boris P. Paal
ECJ 4.7.2023 – case C-252/21, ECLI:EU:C:2023:537 – Meta Platforms Inc and Others v Bundeskartellamt	Jonathan Dunne
ECJ 4.7.2023 – case C-252/21, ECLI:EU:C:2023:537 – Meta Platforms Inc and Others v Bundeskartellamt	Thomas Fuchs
ECJ 26.10.2023 – case C-307/22, ECLI:EU:C:2023:811 – FT (copy of the patient file)	Christoph Werkmeister/Katharina-Isabelle Prenzel
ECJ 5.12.2023 – case C-683/21, ECLI:EU:C:2023:949 – Nacionalinis visuomenės sveikatos centras prie Sveikatos apsaugos ministerijos v Valstybinė duomenų apsaugos inspekcija	Florian Thoma
ECJ 5.12.2023 – case C-683/21, ECLI:EU:C:2023:949 – Nacionalinis visuomenės sveikatos centras prie Sveikatos apsaugos ministerijos v Valstybinė duomenų apsaugos inspekcija	Dominik Roderburg
ECJ 5.12.2023 – case C-807/21, ECLI:EU:C:2023:950 – Deutsche Wohnen SE v Staatsanwaltschaft Berlin	Tim Wybitul
ECJ 7.12.2023 – case C-634/21, ECLI:EU:C:2023:957 – OQ v Land Hessen, SCHUFA	Moritz Köhler
ECJ 14.12.2023 – case C-340/21, ECLI:EU:C:2023:986 – Natsionalna agentsia za prihodite	Marit Hansen
ECJ 14.12.2023 – case C-340/21, ECLI:EU:C:2023:986 – VB gegen Natsionalna agentsia za prihodite	Thoralf Knuth
ECJ 21.12.2023 – case C-667/21, ECLI:EU:C:2023:1022 – ZQ v Medizinischer Dienst der Krankenversicherung Nordrhein, Körperschaft des öffentlichen Rechts	Arne Nordmeyer

Case	Author(s)
ECJ 16.1.2024 – case C-33/22, ECLI:EU:C:2024:46 – Österreichische Datenschutzbehörde	Bernd Grzeszick
ECJ 7.3.2024 – case C-740/22, ECLI:EU:C:2024:216 – Endemol Shine Finland Oy	Sophie Sohm/Steffen Sundermann
ECJ 11.7.2024 – case C-757/22, ECLI:EU:C:2024:598 – Meta Platforms Ireland v vzbv II	Carolin Gäthke
ECJ 12.9.2024 – Joined cases C-17/22 and C-18/22 – HTB Neunte Immobilien Portfolio and Ökorenta Neue Energien Ökostabil IV	Lilly Taranto
ECJ 26.9.2024 – case C-768/21, ECLI:EU:C:2024:785 – TR v Land Hessen	Isabelle Stroot
ECJ 4.10.2024 – C-621/22, ECLI:EU:C:2024:858 – Koninklijke Nederlandse Lawn Tennisbond v Autoriteit Persoonsgegevens	Natascha Gerlach
ECJ 9.1.2025 – case C-394/23, ECLI:EU:C:2025:2 para. 64 – Mousse v Commission nationale de l'informatique et des libertés (CNIL), SNCF Connect	Natallia Karniyevich/Beyza Ermis
ECJ 27.2.2025 – case C–203/22 – ECLI:EU:C:2025:117 – CK v Magistrate of the City of Vienna, Dun & Bradstreet Austria GmbH	Rebekka Weiß
ECJ 13.3.2025 – case C-247/23, ECLI:EU:C:2025:172 – Deldits	Yvette Reif
ECJ 13.3.2025 – case C-247/23, ECLI:EU:C:2025:172 – Deldits	Frederick Richter
ECJ 3.4.2025 – case C-710/23, ECLI:EU:C:2025:231 – L. H. v Ministerstvo zdravotnictví	Gero Ziegenhorn
ECJ 4.9.2025 – case C-413/23 P, ECLI:EU:C:2025:645 – EDPS v SRB	Peter Craddock
ECJ 4.9.2025 – case C-655/23, ECLI:EU:C:2025:655 – Quirin Privatbank	Ruben Plum-Schneider
GC 14.9.2022 – case T-604/18, ECLI:EU:T:2022:541 – Google et al. vs. EU Commission (Android)	Boris Rigod
BGH 23.1.2024 – II ZB 7/23, NJW 2024, 1577	Stefan Brink
OLG Köln 23.5.25 – 15 UKI 2/25, NJW 2025, 3156	Rolf Schwartmann
LG München 11.11.2025 – 42 O 14139/24, MMR 2026 74 (under appeal)	Christian-Henner Hentsch

Case	Author(s)
Guidelines	
EDPB, ‘Guidelines 3/2019 on processing of personal data through video devices’ version 2.0 (29.1.2020) <https://www.edpb.europa.eu/sites/default/files/files/file1/edpb_guidelines_201903_video_devices_en_0.pdf>	Pilar Arzuaga
EDPB, ‘Guidelines 01/2020 on processing personal data in the context of connected vehicles and mobility related applications’, version 2.0 (9.3.2021) <https://www.edpb.europa.eu/system/files/2021-03/edpb_guidelines_202001_connected_vehicles_v2.0_adopted_en.pdf>; CNIL, ‘Projet de recommendation. Use of location data from connected vehicles’ (20.5.2025) <https://www.cnil.fr/sites/default/files/2025-03/projet_de_recommandation_relative_aux_traitements_de_donnees_de_localisation.pdf>	Simone Vogel
EDPB, ‘Guidelines 02/2024 on Article 48 GDPR’, version 2.1 (4.6.2025) <https://www.edpb.europa.eu/system/files/2025-06/edpb_guidelines_202402_article48_v2_en.pdf>	Dimitrios Linardatos
European Commission, ‚Commission Guidelines on the definition of an artificial intelligence system established by Regulation (EU) 2024/1689 (AI Act)‘, C(2025) 5053 final	Kai Zenner
Opinions	
EDPB, ‚Opinion 16/2021 on the draft decision of the Belgian Supervisory Authority regarding the “EU Data Protection Code of Conduct for Cloud Service Providers” submitted by Scope Europe‘ (19.5.2021) <https://www.edpb.europa.eu/our-work-tools/our-documents/opinion-board-art-64/opinion-162021-draft-decision-belgian-supervisory_sk>; EDPB, ‚Opinion 17/2021 on the draft decision of the French Supervisory Authority regarding the European code of conduct submitted by the Cloud Infrastructure Service Providers (CISPE)‘ (19.5.2021) <https://www.edpb.europa.eu/our-work-tools/our-documents/opinion-board-art-64/opinion-172021-draft-decision-french-supervisory_en>	Gabriela Mercuri
EDPB, ‚Opinion 28/2024 on certain data protection aspects related to the processing of personal data in the context of AI models‘ (17.12.2024) <https://www.edpb.europa.eu/our-work-tools/our-documents/opinion-board-art-64/opinion-282024-certain-data-protection-aspects_en>	Eduardo Ustaran

Case	Author(s)
EDPB/EDPS, ‚EDPB-EDPS Joint Opinion 5/2021 on the proposal for a Regulation of the European Parliament and of the Council laying down harmonised rules on artificial intelligence (Artificial Intelligence Act)‘ (18.6.2021) <https://www.edpb.europa.eu/system/files/2021-06/edpb-edps_joint_opinion_ai_regulation_en.pdf>	Tobias Keber/Peter Nägele
EDPB/EDPS, ‘EDPB-EDPS Joint Opinion 2/2022 on the Proposal of the European Parliament and of the Council on harmonised rules on fair access to and use of data’ (4.5.2022) <https://www.edpb.europa.eu/system/files/2022-05/edpb-edps_joint_opinion_22022_on_data_act_proposal_en.pdf>	Michael Dose
Documents from national supervisory authorities	
Data Protection Commission, ‘Inquiry concerning the processing of personal data relating to child users of the Instagram social networking service [IN-20-7-4] ‘ (2.9.2022) <https://www.dataprotection.ie/en/resources/law/decisions/Meta-Platforms-Ireland-Limited-formerly-Facebook-Ireland-Limited-and-the-Instagram-social-media-network-September-2022>	Wioletta Kulińska
Commission for Personal Data Protection (Bulgaria), ‘Final Decision Ref. № ПАИКД-13-28/2022’ (26.10.2022), <https://www.edpb.europa.eu/system/files/2023-08/bg_2023-01_decisionpublic.pdf>	Isabel Hahn
Garante per la protezione dei dati personali, ‘Provvedimento del 27 novembre 2024 [10077129]’ (27.11.2024) <https://www.garanteprivacy.it/home/docweb/-/docweb-display/docweb/10076913>	Stepanka Havlikova
CNIL, ‚Délibération SAN-2025-014 of December 11, 2025‘ (11.12.2025), <https://www.legifrance.gouv.fr/cnil/id/CNILTEXT000053048614>	Christian Jaksch/Klaus Alpmann

Author profiles

Alpmann, Klaus is a lawyer with extensive expertise in data protection and information security. As Global Head of Group Data Protection and Vice President at CARIAD SE, a Volkswagen Group company, he successfully leads global data protection strategies and implements innovative solutions for data protection management. During his career, he has developed groundbreaking data protection and compliance systems at MAN, Munich Re, and the WEKA Media publishing group, among others, which have received the highest ratings in audits. *Mr. Alpmann* combines legal expertise with technical competence and has led numerous international projects. He lives with his family in Wolfsburg.

Arzuaga, Pilar is a partner at McDermott, Will and Shulte in London specialising in EU and UK data protection, privacy, artificial intelligence, cybersecurity and digital regulation, with a focus on GDPR compliance, regulatory investigations and emerging technologies.

Baumgartner, Ulrich, Dr., LL.M. (King's College London), CIPP/E is a lawyer with more than two decades of practical experience in data and IT law. Ulrich assists international clients in complex legal matters with a focus on GDPR litigation, AI and the EU Data Act. He has authored numerous other publications and acts as the German Country Leader for the International Association of Privacy Professionals. After having worked in international law firms for almost two decades, Ulrich is a founding partner of the boutique law firm BAUMGARTNER BAUMANN based in Munich, Germany.

Brink, Stefan, Dr., Stefan Brink, born in 1966, studied law in Mainz, Heidelberg, Dijon, and Paris. After completing his doctorate under Prof. Dr. Hans Herbert von Arnim (DUV Speyer), he worked for the Scientific Service of the Rhineland-Palatinate State Parliament, then as a judge at the Administrative Court of Koblenz, and as a research assistant at the Federal Constitutional Court (1st Senate, Prof. Dr. Reinhard Gaier). From 2008 to 2016, he was Head of Private Data Protection at the State Commissioner for Data Protection in Rhineland-Palatinate, and since 2012 he has also been Deputy State Commissioner for Freedom of Information in Rhineland-Palatinate; from January 2017 to December 2022, Dr. Stefan Brink was State Commissioner for Data Protection and Freedom of Information in Baden-Württemberg. Since January 2023, Dr. Stefan Brink has headed the independent institute wida in Berlin (Scientific Institute for the Digitization of the Working World), which accompanies digital change with a view to our civil rights and promotes digital projects.

Craddock, Peter is a lawyer with a software development background, based in Brussels. Whether as a data litigator or as a global data strategy advisor, he helps clients with highly technical issues, notably on the scope of data protection rules, AdTech, AI training and ePrivacy.

Dienst, Sebastian is a lawyer and associated partner at Noerr. He is responsible for the European Data Legislation & Case Law Trackers at noerr.com/europeandatalaw. He regularly publishes updates on ECJ data case law in the German legal journals Recht der Datenverarbeitung (RDV) (starting 03/2026) and Zeitschrift für Europäisches Daten- und Informationsrecht (EuDIR) (starting 1/2027).

Dixon, Helen is former Data Protection Commissioner for Ireland (2014 to 2024).

Dose, Michael, Dr. is Senior Manager for Data Protection, Data Law, and Data Economy at the Federation of German Industries (BDI). He studied business law and earned his PHD at the University of Kassel and also works part-time as a lecturer at various universities.

Dunne, Jonathan is a Director in Regulatory Affairs at Google, adivising on GDPR, ePrivacy, and AI. He is a dual-qualified lawyer in Ireland and England & Wales.

Dushi, Desara, Dr. holds a double PhD in Law, Science, and Technology from the University of Bologna and the University of Luxembourg. She is an EU Policy Counsel at the Future of Privacy Forum, and an affiliated researcher at the Law, Science, Technology & Society Research Group (LSTS) of Vrije Universiteit Brussel (VUB), where she previously worked as a senior postdoctoral researcher. Dr. Dushi's career spans diverse roles, including in academia, government, and civil society. Her research and professional focus center on critical issues such as human rights in the digital age, privacy and data protection, cybercrime, online child safety, artificial intelligence, as well as broader topics related to Internet governance.

Ermis, Beyza is a research assistant at McDermott Will & Schulte in Düsseldorf focusing on privacy and cybersecurity. She supports clients on EU and German data protection law, cybersecurity regulatory frameworks, and compliance projects, including matters related to NIS2 and other emerging digital regulations.

Fander, Lorenz is a doctoral candidate at the Institute for Labour Law and Social Security Law, Chair of Prof. Dr. Thüsing LL.M. (Harvard).

Fuchs, Thomas, LL.M.EUR. has been the Hamburg Commissioner for Data Protection and Freedom of Information since 2021. He is a member of the High-Level Group for the DMA. From 2008 to 2021, he served as the Director of the State Media Regulatory Authority of Hamburg/Schleswig-Holstein and was a member of the federal Commission for Youth Media Protection. Thomas studied law in Hamburg and Brussels.

Gäthke, Carolin, German Attorney-at-law (*Syndikusrechtsanwältin*) and M.A. (*Magistra Artium*) in Philosophy and Ethnology, offers over 16 years of expertise in the tech sector. With a proven track record in IT law, she steers key strategic and complex data governance and privacy initiatives. Currently serving as Senior Legal Counsel (Regulatory Affairs) at Google, her professional foundation is built upon a versatile career spanning M&A, Private Equity, and the digital entertainment industry, encompassing both elite law firms and senior in-house roles.

Gerlach, Natascha holds the position of Director of Privacy and Data Policy at the Center for Information Policy Leadership (CIPL). Her work is focused on a range of privacy and data related topics including AI, Privacy Enhancing Technologies, children's privacy and safety, data governance, and cross-border data flows. Before joining CIPL, Natascha was a Senior Attorney with Cleary Gottlieb in their Brussels office, where she headed Cleary's European eDiscovery group, an early adopter of AI technology. Natascha is a member of the OpenAge Advisory Board; Chair Emerita of The Sedona Conference Working Group 6 on International Electronic Information Management, Discovery and Disclosure (WG6) Steering Committee. She is a member of the advisory board for the Georgetown Law AEDI, and a founding member of the IDLF.

González Gordon, María has more than 24 years of experience in intellectual property and leads the Industrial / Intellectual Property & Digital Business department at CMS Albiñana & Suárez de Lezo. She advises domestic and international clients on IP, copyright, and technology, with a strong focus on the full spectrum of IP litigation (trademarks, trade secrets, patents, designs, copyrights, and unfair competition), transactional work, and the design of IP and technology strategies. She also counsels international clients on cyber incidents, with a particular emphasis on the liabilities of boards of directors and corporate officers in crisis scenarios. Internationally, she serves as global co-head of the CMS Digital Business group, coordinating 250+ partners worldwide, and leads the CMS Digital Regulation Hub Initiative. She has represented sector-leading companies on high-impact matters, including Spain's largest media outlets in litigation against collective management organisations, culminating in a landmark preliminary ruling before the Court of Justice of the European Union that significantly influenced Europe's music and broadcasting industries. She has extensive experience litigating before the EU trade mark courts in Alicante in cases with pan-European effects. She is an authorised representative before the SPTO and EUIPO, has represented clients before the Spanish Supreme Court and the EU General Court, and is recognised by Chambers & Partners, Legal 500, Managing IP, World Trademark Review, IAM Patents, MLI, and Who's Who Legal.

Grzeszick, Bernd, Prof. Dr., LL.M. Professor for Public Law, first in Münster, then in Erlangen and Mainz, now in Heidelberg as Director of the institute for Constitutional Law, Constitutional Theory and Legal Philosophy. Director of the Heidelberg Center for American Studies, Member of the Heidelberg Academy of Sciences and Humanities and Fellow of the Marsilius-Kolleg. Since 2021 Judge at the Constitutional Court of the State North Rhine-Westphalia.

Hahn, Isabel works for the Delegation of the European Union to the United States and the European Commission's AI Office. She previously served as a Member of Cabinet at the European Data Protection Supervisor. She holds law degrees from Harvard Law School and the London School of Economics and is admitted to the New York Bar.

Hansen, Marit, Dr. h. c. has been the State Data Protection Commissioner of Land Schleswig-Holstein and Chief of Unabhängiges Landeszentrum für Datenschutz (ULD) since 2015. After graduating with a diploma degree in computer science in 1995, Marit has been working on data protection by design & by default from both the technical and the legal perspectives.

Havlikova, Stepanka is a seasoned data privacy & AI lawyer and a researcher. She advises on AI, data privacy, IP, software contracts and licensing. Her dissertation research focuses on web scraping and generative AI training. Stepanka is endorsed as a Leading Associate and Rising Star by Legal500.

Hentsch, Christian-Henner, Prof. Dr., a professor of copyright and media law at the Cologne Research Center for Media Law at TH Köln. He is also Director Legal & Regulatory Affairs at game – The German Games Industry and managing director of VHG – Verwertungsgesellschaft für die Hersteller von Games, the very first collecting society for games. Previously, he represented the interests of television and radio stations as well as newspaper and magazine publishers as Head of Policy for the collecting society VG Media and worked as a research assistant in the German Bundestag. He studied law and history in a double degree programme in Freiburg and Bonn and completed his legal clerkship in Düsseldorf, Washington DC, Frankfurt and Berlin.

Jaksch, Christian, Dr., LL.M. works as Compliance & Legal Lead at CARIAD SE in the department of Integrity, Compliance & Data Protection and currently advises the cross-brand bundling of the software development activities in the in the Volkswagen Group. He is particularly concerned with issues related to vehicle data processing and the implementation of data protection in the context of software development. Before joining CARIAD SE, Dr. *Christian Jaksch* worked for the Group Data Protection Officer of Volkswagen AG. Dr. *Christian Jaksch* studied law with a focus on International Law, followed by PhD studies (University of Vienna, Leibniz University Hannover) with a PhD at the University of Vienna. In addition, he completed a postgraduate master's degree (LL.M.) in information and media law. He regularly publishes on data protection law topics in German and Austrian journals.

Jansen, Marek Steffen, Dr., LL.M., AIGP, CIPP/E, Attorney-at-law, specializing in regulatory strategy and innovation governance. Held senior roles across Volkswagen Group, Google, the Federation of German Industries and the German Parliament, shaping digital and AI policy and advising at the intersection of industry, technology and regulation.

Jaspers, Andreas, Attorney-at-law, is Deputy Managing Director of the Society for Data Protection and Data Security (Gesellschaft für Datenschutz und Datensicherheit – GDD) e.V., Bonn. He is co-author of several legal commentaries on data protection law. Together with Yvette Reif, he heads the annual expert forum of the journal *Recht der Datenverarbeitung* (RDV). He also serves as a lecturer in the GDD training programme for certified data protection officers (GDDcert. EU).

Karniyevich, Natallia, Dr. is a lawyer and partner at McDermott Will & Schulte in Düsseldorf. Natallia focuses on global privacy and cybersecurity, advising multinational companies on regulatory compliance and the management of cybersecurity incidents. She has extensive experience supporting digital service providers, the electronic communications sector, healthcare and life sciences, financial institutions, and operators of critical and digital infrastructure. A key focus of her practice in the context of cybersecurity is advising on the implementation of NIS2, the CER Directive, the Cyber Resilience Act, and DORA.

Keber, Tobias, Prof. Dr. has been the Commissioner for Data Protection and Freedom of Information in Baden-Württemberg since July 2023. Tobias Keber was Professor of Media Law and Media Policy in the Digital Society at Stuttgart Media University (HdM), lecturer in internet law in the Master's program in Media Law at the Mainz Media Institute at Johannes Gutenberg University Mainz and a member of the steering committee of the Institute for Digital Ethics (IDE) at Stuttgart Media University. Before his academic career, he worked as a lawyer. He is chairman of the Scientific Advisory Board of the Society for Data Protection and Data Security (GDD), editorial board member of the journal Recht der Datenverarbeitung (RDV), member of the advisory board of Transparency Germany and the Institute for Consumer Research and Sustainable Consumption (vunk). He is co-editor and author of numerous specialist publications on national and international media, IT, and data protection law. He is the co-chair of the German Data Protection Authorities' AI working group, alongside Rhineland-Palatinate.

Knuth, Thoralf is Chief Data Protection Officer and Global Head of Information Security and Privacy for Bosch. He previously worked as the deputy head of compliance investigations. Before that, he was a senior lawyer at Freshfields Bruckhaus Deringer, advising multinational clients on complex technology, corporate governance, and compliance matters and providing strategic counsel to mitigate risk. A key focus of his work is on a holistic approach to Governance, Risk, and Compliance (GRC) that breaks down silos between legal, technology and security disciplines.

Köhler, Moritz, Dr. is a legal trainee at Mainz Regional Court. He has written his doctoral thesis on the distinction between the impermissible replacement of human judges and their permissible support by artificial intelligence.

Kugelmann, Dieter, Prof. Dr. has been the State Commissioner for Data Protection and Freedom of Information in Rhineland-Palatinate since October 1, 2015, and was re-elected in 2023 for a second term of office. He finished his habilitation in 2000 at Johannes Gutenberg University Mainz on the subject of the citizen's informational legal status. Most recently, he was a full university professor of Public Law, with a focus on Police Law including International Law and European Law, at the German Police University in Münster. He is the editor of a commentary on the Rhineland-Palatinate State Data Protection Act and co-editor of a commentary on the General Data Protection Regulation. He leads the working group DSK 2.0, which deals with the further development of the Data Protection Conference, and jointly with Baden-Württemberg is in the lead of the working group AI.

Kulińska, Wioletta, AIGP, CIPP/E, CIPP/US, CIPM is the founder and attorney-at-law at Kulinska Legal, specializing in privacy, digital law, AI governance, former Global Privacy & Compliance Lead and DPO at Huuuge Games and a guest lecturer in video-games law.

Linardatos, Dimitrios, Prof. Dr. holds the Chair of Civil Law, Digitalization Law, and Business Law at Saarland University since April 2023. His research focuses on the distribution of responsibility in the use of autonomous and networked systems as well as issues relating to the data economy.

Loy, Carolin, has been working at the Bavarian Data Protection Authority for the Private Sector since 2020, where she heads the 'Digital Economy and Legal Issues of Artificial Intelligence' department.

Lynn, Miles is an Associate at Gibson Dunn (London/New York), specializing in AI, privacy, and cybersecurity law. He brings a background in computer science to his technology-focused legal practice.

Mercuri, Gabriela is Managing Director of SCOPE Europe, a two-time accredited Monitoring Body pursuant to Art. 41 GDPR. In this capacity, she oversees the development, negotiation, and implementation of codes of conduct under the GDPR.

Meyerdierks, Per is an attorney and privacy legal expert with over 18 years of experience. As former Director, Privacy Legal at Google, he led teams on AI governance, privacy legal strategy, cloud computing, international data transfers and regulatory engagement. He is a frequent speaker and published author on privacy law.

Nägele, Peter, Dr. is an AI officer and technical expert in the German and European Cooperation Department at the Office of the Commissioner for Data Protection and Freedom of Information in Baden-Württemberg. He is rapporteur at the European Data Protection Board. Prior to joining the Office of the Commissioner for Data Protection, he earned a doctorate in physics and worked as a software engineer for many years.

Negueruela, Antonio is a senior associate in the Industrial / Intellectual Property & Digital Business department at CMS Albiñana & Suárez de Lezo. He specialises in advising on intellectual and industrial property, unfair competition, privacy, e-commerce, and digital business. He provides contentious and non-contentious advice related to information technology, audiovisual law, copyright, trademarks and unfair competition, including advising on disputes before the different industrial property title registration offices such as the SPTO, EUIPO and WIPO. He has a strong focus on advising clients with the negotiation of a wide range of contracts (from complex information technology agreements, such as software licenses or software development, to production of audiovisual content contracts or acquisition of audiovisual content contracts for media services). He works with clients across a wide range of sectors and industries, in particular, Tech and Media. He is a member of the Madrid Bar Association and the Spanish Entertainment Law Association (DENAE) and he has been recognized by Legal 500 as *key lawyer* for the CMS TMT industry practice.

Nicolazzi, Rafaela is a dual-qualified lawyer holding a Master's in Private International Law from the University of São Paulo. She is the author of a 2024 Thomson Reuters book about data protection and international cooperation in the BRICS countries and has over 15 years' experience across law firms and tech companies. She currently works on EMEA privacy and consumer protection for a leading AI lab.

Nordmeyer, Arne, Dr., LL.M. studied law and legal informatics in Göttingen, Hanover and Stockholm. Ph.D. in software and antitrust law from HU Berlin. He completed his legal clerkship at the German Consulate General in Guangzhou (China), among other places. Lawyer since 2013, in-house lawyer since 2015 (first in legal tech, then in the automotive industry). Since mid-2025, he has been head of data protection management at one of Germany's largest health insurances.

Ogunrinde, Henry, Dr., LL.M.: Law studies in Germany and Austria; legal work at a smart mobility provider; research assistant and data protection officer at the Institute for the Theory and Future of Law, University of Innsbruck; PhD awarded in 2024 in cooperation with Audi AG; legal advisor on data protection and data governance in Audi AG's technical development division; currently active in the area of data protection at Volkswagen Group Charging GmbH.

Paal, Boris P., Prof. Dr., M.Jur. (Oxford) holds the chair for Law and Regulation of the Digital Transformation at the Technical University of Munich (TUM). He serves as Of Counsel at BAUMGARTNER BAUMANN, a boutique law firm for data and digital regulation, and practices as a certified business mediator. From 2020 to 2023, he sat as a judge at the Hamburg District Court (chamber for IP and IT Law). Professor Paal has more than 25 years of experience in academia and legal advisory. He is the editor and author of leading commentaries and influential publications in data and digital regulation. Professor Paal has authored more than 250 publications, including standard works on privacy, information, media, and data (protection) law. He advises public and private institutions in various capacities and serves on several advisory boards. Among others, he acts as an expert to the European Commission, the German Bundestag, the Alexander von Humboldt Foundation, the Leibniz Institute for Media Research, and EUMETSAT. Research stays and guest lectureships have included stays and guest lectures at leading international universities, including Berkeley, Cambridge (UK), Harvard, New York (Columbia, Fordham, NYU), Oxford (UK), Peking (CUPL, Tsinghua), Seoul (SNU), Shanghai (ECUPL, Jiao Tong), Stanford, and Yale.

Pauly, Daniel A., Dr. is a lawyer and partner at the international law firm Linklaters LLP. He has been advising on data protection law for over two decades, is co-editor and co-author of Paal/Pauly – Commentary on the

GDPR and the BDSG, now in its 4th edition – and regularly speaks on the various facets of data protection law at conferences and seminars.

Plum-Schneider, Ruben, Dr. is the personal advisor to the German Federal Commissioner for Data Protection and Freedom of Information. Previously, he worked as a data law attorney at an international law firm and holds a doctorate in data protection law from the University of Bonn.

Prenzel, Katharina-Isabelle is a research assistant in the 'Data & Technology' practice at Freshfields. She is currently undertaking her doctorate in the field of digitalisation of administration with a focus on fully automated administrative acts.

Reif, Yvette, attorney-at-law, LL.M., is Deputy Managing Director of the Society for Data Protection and Data Security (Gesellschaft für Datenschutz und Datensicherheit – GDD) e.V., Bonn. She is a co-author of several legal commentaries on data protection law and a co-editor of a handbook on data protection on the Internet. Together with Attorney-at-law Andreas Jaspers, Managing Director of the GDD, she co-heads the annual specialist forum of the journal *Recht der Datenverarbeitung* (RDV). She also serves as a lecturer at the GDD training programme for certified data protection officers (GDDcert. EU).

Reissner, Loïc is Senior Researcher at Prof. Indra Spiecker genannt Döhmann's Chair for Public and Administrative Law, Information Law and Legal Theory and the Institute of Digitization at the University of Cologne, Germany, and at University of Frankfurt, Germany. He is presently completing the mandatory legal clerkship in Frankfurt, Germany.

Richter, Frederick, LL.M. has been Chairman of the German Data Protection Foundation since 2013. Prior to this, he was digital policy advisor in the German Bundestag and an industry association's DPO. He studied law at University of Hamburg and earned a master's degree at Universities of Vienna and Hanover.

Rigod, Boris, Dr. is a technology and competition lawyer with over a decade of experience in both private practice and in-house. He holds a Ph.D. and an LLM from the EUI and was, inter alia, a Fulbright-Schuman Scholar at Stanford Law School and NYU School of Law. He has published widely on competition, data protection and international trade law.

Ringrose, Katelyn, CIPP/EU, CIPP/US, CIPM, FIP manages data protection issues for multinational companies at McDermott Will & Schulte. As Google's former Global Policy Lead for Law Enforcement and Government Access, she handled cross-border data flows, access, and retention.

Roderburg, Dominik, Dr. judge at the Higher Regional Court of Cologne, currently seconded as head of department to the State Chancellery of North Rhine-Westphalia, research assistant at the Federal Constitutional Court under Federal Constitutional Court Judge Dr. Sibylle Kessal-Wulf from 2016 to 2018, lawyer, specialist lawyer for tax law and tax advisor until 2012.

Schwartmann, Rolf, Prof. Dr is head of the Cologne Research Centre for Media Law at the Technical University of Cologne and chairman of the board of the Gesellschaft für Datenschutz und Datensicherheit e.V. (Society for Data Protection and Data Security). In September 2025, he was appointed by German Federal Minister of Education Karin Prien to the expert commission 'Kinder- und Jugendschutz in der digitalen Welt' (Protection of Children and Young People in the Digital World).

Sohm, Sophie, MBA, FIP, is a fully qualified lawyer which currently works as a Privacy and Data Policy Manager at Meta. *She also serves as the WISP Chapter Lead for the DACH region.* She brings a strong academic and professional background, including experience as a policy expert at the European Parliament and as a legal professional at a major Spanish law firm. Her expertise spans privacy management, policy development, and stakeholderengagement across the tech, policy, and legal sectors

Spano, Robert is a Partner at Gibson Dunn (London/Paris) and Co-Chair of the AI Practice Group. He served as President of the European Court of Human Rights (2020–2022) and is an expert in EU law and fundamental rights.

Spiecker genannt Döhmann, Indra, Prof. Dr., LL.M. (Georgetown Univ.) holds the chair for Public and Administrative Law, Information Law and Legal Theory and heads the Institute of Digitization at the University of Cologne, Germany. She is co-editor of the leading commentary on the GDPR.

Spies, Axel Dr. is a partner at Potomac Law Group, also licensed as "Rechtsanwalt" in Germany as an attorney, holds a French degree and is CIPP/E certified. He is a trusted advisor for organizations navigating the evolving intersections of technology, privacy, and global regulation and a prolific author. With decades of international experience, he has handled complex cross-border matters ranging from licensing and competition to telecommunications, national and international data privacy, and AI. A recognized thought leader, Axel has co-authored books and published more than 100 articles on various legal topics. He co-publishes the German Journal of Data Protection (ZD) that he co-founded and the European telecoms journal MultiMedia & Law (MMR).

Stroot, Isabelle is a fully qualified lawyer. She studied law in Hamburg and Hanover, specializing in IT and intellectual property law. She is a certified data protection officer and data protection auditor. As Head of Data Protection Law and Policy at Bitkom, she is responsible for regulatory and data protection policy matters.

Sundermann, Steffen, Dr. is a lawyer and Senior Associate at Noerr. He advises companies on legal issues relatingto data protection, telecommunications, and artificial intelligence. Before joining Noerr, he held a position in the legal department of the Hamburg Commissioner for Data Protection, where he was responsible for enforcing the GDPR. He regularly publishes oncurrent topics in data protection law.

Taranto, Lilly is an experienced data privacy, AI and cybersecurity lawyer. Currently serving as Director of Global Privacy and AI at Sony, Lilly previously held the position of Global Digital and Privacy Counsel at GSK. Prior to going in-house, she was a Senior Associate at Hogan Lovells and had Associate positions at Field Fisher Waterhouse and Orrick, Herrington & Sutcliffe.

Thoma, Florian is a German attorney-at-law (Rechtsanwalt) and Senior Director, Data Privacy, Data & AI Compliance with Accenture where he oversees data privacy compliance globally. Prior to that role, he was Chief Privacy Officer of a large German electronics multinational. In addition, he has held various roles including in Bitkom e.V. and the International Association of Privacy Professionals.

Ustaran, Eduardo is global co-head of Hogan Lovells' Data, Privacy and Cybersecurity practice, author of *The Future of Privacy*, and co-founder and editor of *Data Protection Leader*. He advises multinationals and governments on privacy and AI compliance strategies.

Vogel, Simone has been a legal counsel in the automotive industry since 2013 and a freelance lawyer since 2016, focusing on IT and digitalization law. Her most recent areas of expertise have been AI and data law, telecommunications, IT security, and licensing law. Since 2024, she has been head of data protection law consulting at Dr. Ing. h.c. F. Porsche AG.

Weiß, Rebekka, LL.M. is Head of Regulatory Policy at Microsoft Germany. Rebekka is a fully qualified lawyer ad studied law in Germany, Switzerland, and the UK. She is co-editor of various legal journals and regularly publishes on the AI Act, data law, IT security law, and related legal fields.

Wendehorst, Christiane, Prof. Dr., LL.M. (Cambridge) is a professor at the University of Vienna and, among other things, Scientific Director of the European Law Institute (ELI) and a member of the Presidium of the Austrian Academy of Sciences. Her research focuses on the law of digitalisation, and she was, among other things, co-chair of the German Federal Government's Data Ethics Commission.

Werkmeister, Christoph, Dr., LL.M. (Cambridge) is a partner and global co-head of the 'Data & Technology' practice at the global law firm Freshfields. He has advised on some of the highest-profile GDPR (fine) proceedings and data-related (mass) litigation and he is a leading advisor on digital regulation and AI.

Wybitul, Tim is a partner at Latham & Watkins LLP in Frankfurt am Main (GER), certified specialist in employment law, CIPP/E. He defends companies in fine and court proceedings on data protection law and regularly publishes on European data law.

Zenner, Kai is a digital policy expert based in Brussels. He currently serves as Head of Office to Axel Voss MEP in the European Parliament. He was a central figure in the technical negotiations of the EU AI Act and focuses on the intersection of law, technology, and European digital sovereignty.

Ziegenhorn, Gero Dr. is partner at Redeker Sellner Dahs specialising in all aspects of data protection law. He has many years of experience in litigation before German courts of all instances and the CJEU and is a Lecturer for data protection law at the FernUniversität in Hagen.